Chasing
the Sun

Chasing the Sun

Dictionary

Makers and the

Dictionaries

They Made

JONATHON GREEN

Henry Holt and Company
New York

For Colin MacCabe

Henry Holt and Company, Inc.
Publishers since 1866
115 West 18th Street
New York, New York 10011

Henry Holt® is a registered
trademark of Henry Holt and Company, Inc.

Copyright © 1996 by Jonathon Green
All rights reserved.
First published in the United States in 1996 by
Henry Holt and Company, Inc.
Published in Canada by Fitzhenry & Whiteside Ltd.,
195 Allstate Parkway, Markham, Ontario L3R 4T8.
Originally published in Britain in 1996 by
Jonathan Cape

Library of Congress Cataloging-in-Publication Data

Green, Jonathon.
Chasing the sun: dictionary makers and the dictionaries they made /
Jonathon Green.—1st American ed.
p.   cm.
Includes bibliographical references and index.
1. Lexicography—History.   I. Title.
P327.G74   1996   96-25574
413'.028'09—dc20   CIP

ISBN 0-8050-3466-8

Henry Holt books are available for special promotions and
premiums. For details contact: Director, Special Markets.

First American Edition—1996

Designed by Michelle McMillian

Printed in the United States of America
All first editions are printed on acid-free paper.∞

1   3   5   7   9   10   8   6   4   2

"When I first engaged in this work, I resolved to leave neither words nor things unexamined, and pleased myself with a prospect of the hours which I should revel away in feasts of literature, the obscure recesses of northern learning, which I should enter and ransack, the treasures with which I expected every search . . . to reward my labour, and the triumph with which I should display my acquisitions to mankind . . . But these were the dreams of a poet doomed at last to wake a lexicographer . . . and that thus to pursue perfection was, like the first inhabitants of Arcadia, to chace the sun, which, when they had reached the hill where he seemed to rest, was still beheld at the same distance from them."

Samuel Johnson
Preface to *The Dictionary of English Language,* 1755

CONTENTS

ILLUSTRATIONS

PREFACE

What follows is a history of lexicography, the making of dictionaries, and of some of the people who made them—from the earliest such word books, 2,500 years before Christ, through to the present day. It is not an academic history, although it has drawn on the work of many academic metalexicographers, but an attempt to offer an accessible study of an area of writing—the nodal point, as it were of linguistics and literature—that has all too often been overlooked.

Dr. Johnson was wrong: the lexicographer is not a harmless drudge. Not that Johnson ever really believed he was, but many others, conveniently swayed by the Great Cham's authority, have been happy to assume that he did. If anything, especially in America, but in Britain as well, the reverse is true. The lexicographer, the interpreter and arbiter of the very language that underpins every aspect of communication, is far more deity than drudge. Or if not a deity, then certainly a priest, charged by society—whether consciously or not—with the revelation of the linguistic verities.

Of late those priests have become less individually visible but their church, "the dictionary," remains as authoritative as ever. The individual lexicographer has ceded power to the team, the computerized corpus has come to stand side by side with, if not actually to replace, the readers of earlier research, but what has been termed the "Unidentified Authorizing Dictionary" is still the court of last resort. "Is it in the dictionary?" remains a constant question. And if it is not . . .

What I have tried to do here is twofold. On the one hand I have attempted to put a little flesh on lexicographical bones. For many people, as Sir James

Murray noted in 1900, "the dictionary" meant Samuel Johnson's work of 1755. For America, he might have added, it meant Noah Webster's pioneering volume of 1828, and the successive works that appeared under Webster's name, if not from his pen. In time it would come to mean Murray's own project, the *Oxford English Dictionary,* which, in England at least, supplanted Johnson. But as Murray added, the roots of the dictionary lay many centuries, even millennia, in the past. There had been dictionaries, and thus lexicographers before Johnson, and indeed Johnson (and in time Murray) could not have created his lexicon without those predecessors. Webster too, for all that he strove to create a strictly "American" English, needed his transatlantic forebears. It is thus that this book begins in pre-Babylonian Sumeria and moves on to Greece, Rome, and Byzantium, before arriving at the relative modernity of English-language lexicography.

On the other hand I have tried to look behind the UAD and beyond its supposed authority. However pervasive and alluring the myth, dictionaries do not emerge from some lexicographical Sinai; they are the products of human beings. And human beings, try as they may, bring their prejudices and biases into the dictionaries they make. As will become clear, neither Webster nor Johnson, nor any other dictionary maker, has been able to restrain his own beliefs and personality. In some cases there was little effort to do so: neither of those two figures can be seen as even remotely self-effacing. Humility, supposedly central to the Christianity both men professed, was obviously one virtue they felt to be disposable. But the lexicographer does not need an overweening ego to confer his or her prejudices on the dictionary. The nature of dictionary making, whether in form or content, brings with it decisions, and with decisions, however disinterested, comes choice. As far as form is concerned, the perfect dictionary, the all-encompassing dictionary of every word in a given language, is of course an impossibility. The linguistic "big bang" has been expanding since the dawn of language. It will not stop, however much some lexicographers seek to delineate a "fixed" version of their particular tongue. But even were one to attempt the codification of the whole of a given language at one given moment in time, the sheer volume of vocabulary renders the attempt impossible. Thus any dictionary, however large, is but a subset of the greater ideal, and therein, since choices must be made, lies the first statement of individual intent. Once that major choice has been made, the lesser, but far wider-ranging choices that deal in definition, pronunciation, etymology, citation, usage, and the other essentials that go, all or in part, to make up each dictionary entry are all susceptible to individual, or for that matter team, prejudice. It is inescapable and, in the end, it is not especially reprehensible.

On the face of it, the dictionary has changed vastly since its pre-Babylonian origins. Yet for all that clay tablets have been replaced by CD-ROMs, its essential function, and the function of those who labor on its pages, remains in the end the same: the compilation and definition of a given linguistic word store. As Samuel Johnson declared, in the pragmatic if regretful lines that serve as my epigraph, the making of dictionaries is an endless task. But it is also a rewarding one, and this book, it is very much hoped, will serve as a tribute to the appeal of that reward.

My thanks must go, in the wider field, to the dictionary makers of three millennia, and to those rather more immediate individuals who have commented on, discussed, analyzed, and criticized them and their efforts. The names of all of these—makers and metalexicographers alike—are to be found in the Bibliography.

On a more personal level I must offer my thanks to Leigh Priest, who prepared the index, and Mark Thomas, who photographed the illustrations; to the staffs of the London Library, the Bodleian Library, the British Library, and the New York Public Library; to Karen Thomson, whose catalogs provided a number of the primary sources; to Andrew Hobson, who directed me toward the scribes of Greece, Rome, and Byzantium; to my agent Julian Alexander; to my dedicatee Colin MacCabe, to Dan Franklin, my publisher in London, and to Darcy Tromanhauser and Bill Strahan at Henry Holt in New York.

Chasing
the Sun

INTRODUCTION

What Is a Lexicographer?

The word *lexicographer* enters the English language in 1658. It is originally Greek, combining *lexicon:* a dictionary, and *graphos:* writing or a writer. It means, quite simply, the compiler of a dictionary.

Thus the word, for English purposes, is relatively modern, but the job description is not. By 1658, the year which saw the publication of a new lexicon, Edward Phillips' *New World of English Words,* the roll call of English dictionaries was already growing—the first, Robert Cawdrey's *Table Alphabeticall,* had appeared in 1604—and if one extended the list backward first through the Latin-English and English-Latin works of the previous century, and then to medieval Europe and even further back to Greece and Rome, the lexicographers could claim a long and distinguished pedigree. Indeed, the *Oxford English Dictionary*'s first citation refers to "Calepine and other Lexicographers of his gang," which reference, aside from providing an image not usually associated with the profession, immediately jumps back to the fifteenth-century monk Ambrogio Calepino, whose polyglot *Dictionarium* remained a dictionary-maker's staple for three centuries. Similarly, the chemist Robert Boyle invokes in his memorial of "Suidas, Stephanus [and] Hesychius" the dictionary makers of tenth-century Byzantium and of sixteenth-century France. If one wishes, and this book has opted for that path, it is possible to set the dawn of lexicography as early as 2500 B.C. in the pre-Babylonian world of Sumeria and its conquerors of neighboring Akkad. The act, then, stems from antiquity. What it entails has both remained the same and at the same time changed quite radically. The desire to codify information, whether merely for the purposes of easier access or, more portentously, thus to codify the world to which that information refers, is deeply rooted in the human psyche. The dictionary is, of course, merely one form of rendering that desire concrete. Those who have chosen to undertake such codification have all produced lists of words: so much is a constant; the attitude they have taken to their list, the methods of their compilation, the lists themselves and the audiences at which the list is targeted, have all varied.

The Sumerian-Akkadian scribes were essentially translators: they took the codes of a vanquished nation and rendered them accessible to the conquering one. It might seem paradoxical that the conquered culture was acknowledged as superior to that of the victors, history tends to the opposite conclusion, but in this case the conqueror could, it seems, only impose his own political and social superiority if he acknowledged and utilized the linguistic ascendancy of those he had invaded. The word collectors of Greece, working onward from the fourth-century B.C., in some ways echoed this earliest lexicography. The words they listed and translated were those of an earlier culture, and they undertook their task in recognition of the fact that that culture, once again, was a superior one. The difference was that the culture in question was already theirs and that their stimulus was not conquest but chronology: times were passing, people, even the greatest of scholars, were finding it increasingly hard to read the classics of antiquity. The works of Homer, created in the eighth century B.C. either by a single individual or, as generally believed today, by a number of authors, were becoming incomprehensible. What would become known to lexicographical jargon two thousand years later as "hard words," essentially those of an exclusively literary rather than generally popular usage, were gathered together to give greater access to the classics. The same process would dominate mainstream lexicography until midway through the seventeenth century. The Roman lexicographers offered access to their ancient writers, as well as to those of Greece, the scholars of Byzantium followed suit; those of the late Middle Ages did much the same, now drawing on the whole classical world, and the first monoglot English-English dictionaries of the seventeenth century held to the same course. The lexicographers were writing for their peers, fellow members of the world of scholarship. More general vocabularies existed, but they were aimed at children, teaching them the essentials of the Latin vocabulary so as to habituate them to the classical tongues that would be the basis of all their scholarly inquiry. Indeed, this casting back, while notably less central to the dictionaries of the eighteenth century and beyond, especially as regards those produced in the United States, can be seen as continuing on as the basis of the world's best-known academic English-language dictionary: the *Oxford English Dictionary*. Its first edition, at least, can be seen as much as a *vade mecum* to the scholarly appreciation of the previous millennium of English literature as it can as a reference work plain and simple.

In England at least, but equally so in any of the countries of Europe, the sixteenth century witnessed the first great shift in modern dictionary making. Once Latin, the language of scholarship, had been displaced, or at least paralleled by the national "vulgar" tongue, then the lexicographer was duty-bound to echo the shift. The Renaissance, which revolutionized European culture, extended to lexicography as much as it did to any discipline.

> Among the factors inducing the intellectual ferment were the rediscovery and study of the classical Greek and Latin authors, the revival of a pagan philosophy of life, the expansion of the physical world through voyage and discovery, and the invention of the printing press and cheap paper. These and other forces altered the physical and intellectual world and powerfully stimulated man to utterance. But the expression of new ideas requires new symbols—words—and the meaning of new symbols must be made clear to those who would learn as well as to those who would teach. Convenient means of making available the revived language of Cicero and Terence and novel terms of English and other current living languages were enlarged wordbooks, lexicons, and dictionaries.[1]

The scholars of continental Europe had been imbued with such impulses for nearly a century already. Men such as Laurentius Valla, Calepino, Erasmus, Gulielmus Budaeus, Estienne Dolet, and the French lexicographer Robert Stephanus were major proponents of the new attitudes. Many of these had made their own dictionaries. The intellectual movement arrived late in England but there too it found a home. Sir Thomas Elyot, preeminent among England's "Renaissance men," also produced a wordbook and he was perhaps the first English compiler to take on board the importance of the vulgar tongue and the needs of those who, however grand, now used it in place of Latin. As such he was not just reflecting the prevailing intellectual climate, he was promoting it too. In him the lexicographer was not simply recording, he was setting the pace. No longer merely the curator of the classical past, although the importance of the classics was central to Renaissance scholarship, he was becoming a major force in shaping the society in which he worked.

The Lexicographer as God

In his celebrated definition of the profession which provided him with the greatest of his own achievements, Samuel Johnson declared the lexicographer to be "a writer of dictionaries; a harmless drudge, that busies himself in tracing the original, and detailing the signification of words." It is a concept endlessly reiterated by those in search of a trite literary sound bite, but there is little in Johnson's persona or in his *Dictionary* to persuade one that his coinage was delivered with anything but a good deal of irony and his tongue thrust firmly into his cheek. Drudgery there might be, but he was no drudge. To see how he properly felt the reader need only move on one lemma, to *lexicon:* "a dictionary" and the citation from Milton that underpins it: "Though a linguist should pride himself to have all the tongues that Babel cleft the world into, yet if he had not studied . . . the lexicons, yet he were nothing so much to be esteemed a learned man as any yeoman competently wise in his mother dialect only." Aside, perhaps unconsciously, from noting the rivalry between linguists and lexicographers which remains unabated to this day, Johnson was making his position clear. Dictionaries mattered, and if he had taken on the compilation of his own great lexicon at the urging of booksellers, and with the vagaries of his own rollercoaster income to keep him hard at work, then the finished product reflected the extent to which he had committed himself to his labors. To take the self-deflating tropes of polite mid-eighteenth-century discourse at face value is a definite mistake. Johnson's preface may commence with a few paragraphs of statutory demurrers, but once he hits his stride such niceties fall away. This is a man who has met the work for which he is destined. In terms of pop standards Johnson may begin with a *piano* "Send in the Clowns" but he ends with an undilutedly *fortissimo* "My Way." Only America's Noah Webster, publishing three quarters of a century later, but consciously pitting himself against Johnson in every aspect of his own *American Dictionary,* would offer so literally self-conscious a declaration of intent.

More than any other lexicographers Johnson and Webster stand as the ultimate personifications of the solo artiste. Johnson had his amanuenses, and they if anyone were indeed the harmless drudges of his definition; Webster had a single proofreader, enlisted toward the end of the project. But these assistants were secondary figures. In neither case did the man whose name adorns the title page allow such helpers to influence his end product. The lexicographer, whether as an individual or as part of a team, has always, to a greater or lesser extent, stamped his (and more recently her) imprint upon the dictionary on which he works. The fact of defining a word, no matter how disinterested is the definer, must reflect some form of prejudice. Today it is more likely to be that of a given society at a given moment; for Johnson and Webster too there was the social background, but it is their own prejudices and beliefs that shine out of so many pages. Setting aside the "rights" and "wrongs" of their work—Johnson died too soon to assimilate the new philology that emerged at the very end of the eighteenth century, and Webster chose unequivocally to ignore its advances, substituting his own gloriously erroneous methods—what is most fascinating about their role as lexicographer is the way in which each sets himself up, quite unashamedly, as the arbiter of linguistic standards. This is not so much a matter of "fixing" the language—Johnson may have started out with such ideas, but practical researches soon disabused him of that fantasy, while the very nature of the fast-expanding population for which Webster promoted his "American English" defeated any attempt to set a boundary on its development—but of slanting it, and thereby promoting a specific moral or political agenda. Johnson gives his readers an Anglican, Tory world, Webster a low church, Republican one. They cheerfully bent the language to their own requirements. Webster deplores Johnson's unabashed truncation, even falsification of quotes to suit his own purpose, but he too was happy to squeeze the material into a straitjacket of his own contrivance.

What both men were doing, although neither articulated it as such, was playing God. Or if not God, then at least Moses, descending from Sinai with the tablets of the law. For them their role was not simply to select a word list, define it, and make it available to the reading public; in addition they took on the priestly task of revealing a truth, in this case a linguistic one, to those who, like lay parishioners, were less than perfectly versed in its subtleties. Viewed thus, lexicography becomes less of an educative force, best seen in the amelioration of learning that underpinned the "hard-word" volumes of the early- to mid-seventeenth century, and more of a theological-cum-social one. The task of lexicography might, viewed with the jaundiced eye, entail a good deal of drudgery, but like even the lowliest of parish priests, its practitioner remained the guardian of the sacred truths, the conduit that delivered them to the unversed masses. His might be a relatively lowly calling but even its detractors had to acknowledge "the nature and scope of the erudition involved."[2] The importance of the dictionary as a form of social diktat was a feature of late-seventeenth-century word collection onward. The sixteenth-century works of writers such as Thomas Elyot had certainly impinged on society, but their effect was primarily upon the élite of scholars and gentry. A courtier and a diplomat, as well as a leading Renaissance scholar, Elyot wrote for his peers and for those who aspired to join their number. His dictionary abounds in English neologisms, the "ink-horn terms" that so embellished the language for all that they irritated his critics, but the fact that in the end it is an English-Latin work ensures that its audience remains a restricted one. He believed, as did many contemporaries, that it was possible, not to mention necessary, to enhance the status of "vulgar" English, and by so doing replace Latin as the scholarly tongue, but one still had to know one's Latin. Mass literacy, which would mean English-language literacy, was still to come. The dictionaries of the seventeenth and even more so eighteenth century took on a very different character. By ordering the words one might order the world. As Rod Mengham puts it,

> The compiling of a dictionary . . . entailed an exercising of authority on an unprecedented scale. The lexicographer would determine what should be included in, and what should be excluded from, a body of knowledge that the pragmatic user of his work would learn to regard as the foundation of a national language and culture. The body of knowledge would be subject to stratification, thus helping to inculcate a sense of rank and respect for privilege identified by degrees of breadth of command over language-use. The dictionary could become an instrument of social control, dispensed indirectly and fostering assumptions that need not be insisted on too forcibly.[3]

The power and importance of definition is central to the political philosophy of Thomas Hobbes, who deals in 1651 with the "Necessity of Definitions" in Chapter 4—"Of Speech"—in Part I of *Leviathan.* Having established the importance of "names," essentially proper nouns, he notes that "Seeing then that *truth* consisteth in the right ordering of names in our affirmations, a man that seeketh precise *truth,* had need to remember what every name he uses stands for; and to place it accordingly or else he will find himselfe entangled in words, as a bird in lime-twiggs; the more he struggles, the more belimed."[4] Hobbes also acknowledges the need for critical borrowing, adding that it is "necessary for any man that aspires to true Knowledge, to examine the Definitions of former Authors; and either to correct them, where they are negligently set down; or to make them himselfe."[5]

Hobbes represents one strand of seventeenth-century thought; Ephraim Chambers, who is acknowledged as an important influence on Johnson, published his *Cyclopaedia or Universal Dictionary* nearly eighty years later, in 1728. He had no doubts as to the role of the lexicographer as a linguistic law giver, and envisages that the earliest dictionaries, which he equates with Egypt rather than Sumeria (the modern assumption), were compiled very much as an extension of the priestly role.

> Probably this was in the early days of the Egyptian sages, when words were more complex and obscure than now; and mystic symbols and hieroglyphics obtained; so that an explication of their marks or words might amount to a revelation of their whole inner philosophy: in which case, instead of a grammarian, we must put perhaps a priest or mystagogue at the head of Dictionaries.[6]

If Chambers is right, the lexicographer has moved far beyond his downgraded existence as a harmless drudge and as Mengham says, this theory "turns the lexicographer's guardianship of the cultural tradition into a sacred trust and thus sanctions the privileged position of those who control the flow of information to the uninitiated."[7] The lexicographer Rosamund Moon, one of those working on the vast COBUILD (Collins Birmingham University International Language Database) corpus of contemporary English texts, puts it quite simply: "Dictionaries only succeed because of an act of faith on the part of their users, and that act of faith is dependent on those users believing their dictionaries both authoritative and beyond subjectivity."[8] That the dictionary, however wide-ranging its team of compilers and editors, is essentially the record "of the beliefs about language of a very small subset of the users of that language"[9] is equally true. But as in any religion, the congregation is willing to make the necessary leap of faith without question. It is only when, as will be seen in the bitter controversy over *Webster's Third New International,* the priest abdicates what is seen as his or her responsibility, that blind faith can turn to outraged scrutiny. Two and a half centuries later, within the confines of a quite different technology, one could see the persistence of that theocratic role. Not for nothing were those who understood the mainframe computers of the 1950s and 1960s known, not wholly jocularly, as "the Priesthood." Like the lexicographers they held jobs that were, in many ways, mere drudgery—they pressed buttons, flipped switches, fed in and extracted punched cards—but, again like the lexicographers, their knowledge erected an indispensable gateway through which the uninitiated were forced to pass. Just as those who cannot read, and in Johnson's time this represented a far greater proportion of the population than it does today, may confer on literacy an almost mystical role, so too, in a world that predated the ubiquity of the personal computer (at least in the West), did the noncomputerate—virtually everyone but the "priests"—stand in awe of the million-dollar calculating machines, their all too fallible circuitry isolated in the Holy of Holies, the air-conditioned "clean room."

With the emergence of the lexicographer as a quasi priest, one can also witness his emergence as a professional. Few of those who concerned themselves with dictionary making in the sixteenth and even seventeenth century could be called full-time lexicographers. Schoolmasters, clergymen, dons, lawyers, diplomats, mathematicians—they all resisted any urge to give up the day job. The eighteenth century saw a new status for the dictionary compiler. DeWitt Starnes and Gertrude Noyes summed up the dictionary-maker's changing role:

> Early seventeenth-century lexicographers were dilettantes or specialists; they undertook their task in spare moments that their time might not be "worse employed," and they aimed to assist the ladies or the artisans or the foreigners. After the turn of the century . . . the function of the lexicographer comes to be regarded with increasing gravity. A scholar of depth and scope, the lexicographer now devotes his best years and abilities to his task and stands ready to serve alike Englishmen and foreigners, men and women, the educated and the would-be educated . . . By the mid-century not only are more able scholars feeling the call to dictionary-making; but modern methods of organization are taking shape, and the scholarly editor now deputes routine tasks to competent subordinates while he directs the whole.[10]

Dictionaries became best-sellers—especially in recently independent America, where a polyglot immigration demanded standards by which the newly arrived could assess and absorb their new common language—and, as they reached an increasingly wide public, the subject of informed debate. America's "dictionary wars" of the mid-nineteenth century would have been unthinkable a century earlier when such debates were a matter for scholars only. Now the dictionary was one more consumable, and subject like any other to public evaluation. At the same time, the public, the congregation as it were, was willing to give the lexicographers themselves a new appreciation. Writing in the *Gentleman's Magazine* in June 1799 under the headline "The Labours of Dictionary-makers inadequately appreciated," the otherwise anonymous "B." declared,

> The productions of fancy and genius have always excited more public notice, and procured to their authors more celebrity, than those useful

works which, though called *ladders of learning,* are yet the laboured efforts of learned men; as it is by their means that the most celebrated *Literati* have acquired those rudiments which led them on to eminence, yet the grammarian, the etymologist, and the lexicographer, are generally over-looked, and considered as mere plodders, who sow what others reap. But as in agriculture, a plentiful crop cannot be expected without a judicious dissemination of the seed, and as in military operations much depends on the pioneer . . . ought we not, in the department of literature, equally to distinguish those who smooth the rugged paths of learning, and trans-plant from Parnassus what ever may be either useful or ornamental in our academic groves?

To what extent the lexicographers whose stories make up this book saw themselves as linguistic priests, let alone gods, is debatable. Johnson seems to have had the self-confidence, and Webster the flinty rejection of beliefs con-trary to his own stern ideology, to qualify them for some such role, but neither man would surely have admitted to so blasphemous a conceit. The majority of their more recent predecessors saw themselves as educators; their successors have accepted a similar role. Perhaps the metalexicographer Henri Béjoint is broadly right when he agrees, irony or not, with Johnson's definition and cites the lumpen lexicographer's work as "a humble one . . . There is little inven-tiveness, let alone genius, at play." But that, Béjoint adds, is to focus only on the lowest common denominator, reducing the whole process to "culling words from texts and listing them in alphabetical order with some explanation of their meanings." As Henry Wheatley noted, in his preface to the Early English Text Society's edition of Peter Levins' *Manipulus Vocabulorum:*

> It would be a mistake to confuse such men as Levins, Huloet, Baret and Cotgrave with the 'harmless drudges' who, in later times, followed the trade of Dictionary making. Nothing is more remarkable in the older dic-tionaries than the originality displayed in them. Their authors wrote out of the fullness of their knowledge, and the consequence is that their works teem with instances of their geniality and good sense. Unfortunately we know nothing of these men; their works remain as their only monuments, but every year as they become more known, more honour is given to the compilers for their labours.[11]

Béjoint agrees. Obviously there is unavoidable drudgery in dictionary mak-ing. The Renaissance scholar J. J. Scaliger suggested that "the worst criminals should be neither executed nor sentenced to forced labour, but should be condemned to compile dictionaries, because all the tortures are included in the work."[12] And as the Norwegian lexicographer Einar Haugen has versified the profession: "At the dictionary's letter A | Mr Brandt is young and gay. | But when at last he reaches Zed, | He's in his wheelchair, nearly dead."[13] Yet there can be pleasure in the work. The lexicographer J. R. Hulbert spoke for many of his peers when he said, "I know of no more enjoyable intellectual activity than working on a dictionary." Unlike other research, the chasing of what the poet William Cowper, versifying on philology, called the "panting syllable"[14] does not on the whole lead to disappointment and the reduction of hours, let alone months or even years, of hypothesizing to ruins. Lexicography presents a succession of "small, but absorbingly interesting problems" which on the whole permit themselves to be solved. And "at the end of the day one feels healthily tired, but content in the thought that one has accomplished something and advanced the whole work towards its completion."[15] Nor are the lexicographers unexceptional figures in themselves. The novelist has a more glamorous image, but despite the fantasies of those who believe that "everyone has a novel in them," there's drudgery (and drudges) in "creative writing" too. And in both these branches of literature are those who transcend that drudgery. In the eighteenth to early twentieth centuries, the era that immediately predates the necessary turning over of mainstream lexicography from the individual to the team, "many dictionaries . . . were compiled by people with strong personalities, who produced highly idiosyncratic dictionaries . . . the idealists, the missionaries, those who used their dictionaries to scold, to preach, to mock, to fight not only ignorance but fatuity, with little respect for the ideal of objectivity as we understand it. The paradox is that their dictionaries are those that are best remembered. Dictionaries aim at being faithful, objective, exact, unimaginative records, and yet they are clearly better if they are produced by a powerful, independent mind . . ."[16] As the American lexicographer Stuart Berg Flexner has remarked, "Old dictionaries were named after their writers, whereas modern dictionaries are named after their publishers."[17] Many people, suggests Béjoint, "regret the old days, when dictionaries were much worse, and also much better." Thus lexicographers, especially these veterans, may perhaps join Shelley's poets as the "unacknowledged legislators of the world."[18]

What Is a Dictionary?

While *dictionary,* and occasionally *lexicon,* are the current words of choice when describing a wordbook arranged in alphabetical order, there have been a number of contenders for that role. Among the titles given to wordbooks have been an *abecedarium* (an alphabetical order), an *alveary* (a beehive), a *catholicon* (a cure-all), an *ortus* (a garden), a *medulla* (a marrow or pith), a *glossary,* a *manipulus* (a handful), a *sylva* (a wood), a *promptuarium* or a *thesaurus* (both a treasury or store-house), a *vocabulary* and a *vulgar* (a common thing). By 1700 dictionary, from the Latin *dictionarius:* "a repertory of dictiones, phrases or words,"[19] had won through, and ever since it has been the predominant term. As Tom McArthur has noted, the word *dictionary* "has tended to be a coverall term for all sorts of presentations about 'words' however conceived . . . The Latin term may well have been popular as a convenient title for anything remotely dealing with words."[20]

Restricting oneself simply to the field of monolingual lexicography, there are now a number of dictionary types. These can vary as to their content: typically general purpose, dialect, slang, or technical. They can vary as to size: unabridged (250,000+ words), semi-unabridged (130,000–250,000 words), or abridged (less than 130,000). Size can also be defined as "extensive": when the word list coincides more or less with the set of the lexical items that ideally exist in the language, or "intensive": the dictionary represents a subset of the overall lexis (the word stock of a language), based on clearly defined criteria. Then there are those which, on traditional lines, are produced by a compiler or more likely a team of compilers, or those, as modern lexicography increasingly prefers, which are drawn from a corpus (a widely ranging collection of written material, not necessarily literary, from which the word list can be selected). A further distinction can be made between academic and commercial dictionaries. The former tend to be large, unabridged, and possibly multivolumed; the latter are the "concise" or "college" dictionaries and their smaller derivatives. The function for which a dictionary is designed may also come into play. Those "learners' dictionaries" that are designed for use as primers of "English as a Foreign Language" (U.K.) or "English as a Second Language" (U.S.) are typical of this type. And there are more divisions: as lexicography becomes increasingly sophisticated, so has the fine-tuning become even more delicate. In the end the variety is overwhelming. As Henri Béjoint has said, somewhat despairingly, "The conclusion to be drawn . . . is that it is impossible to classify dictionaries in a way that would be both orderly and applicable to all societies. Dictionaries come in more varieties than can ever be classified in a simple taxonomy."[21]

Nor does the name "dictionary" guarantee that the reader will automatically receive what he or she might usually expect. "Dictionaries" of quotations certainly contain words, but they offer no definitions, and the words are arranged not in lemmas, but in sentences and paragraphs. The "headwords," as it were, are the names of those being quoted. If there is a "definition," it is the quotation. Nor need the dictionary, however much it may ostensibly resemble the "real thing," act as a legitimate work of reference. Ambrose Bierce's irresistibly cynical *Devil's Dictionary* (1906) is a collection of *mots,* albeit in "dictionary" format. One might gain greater amusement from referring to its definitions than from the drier pages of, say, the *OED,* but it would be foolish to use them as a basis of linguistic accuracy. Similarly Gustave Flaubert's ironic *Dictionary of Received Ideas* (1881), a masterpiece of deflation, pricking the safe banalities of nineteenth-century French bourgeois life, is to be appreciated, but not trusted for "truth." The "proper" dictionary ought not to be witless, but nor should it be overly witty.

Taxonomy aside, the general-purpose dictionary, which is the primary subject of this book, has various consistent characteristics. It is "a book dealing with the individual words of a language (or certain specified classes of them), so as to set forth their orthography, pronunciation, signification, and use, their synonyms, derivation, and history, or at least some of these facts: for convenience of reference, the words are arranged in some stated order, now, in most languages, alphabetical; and in larger dictionaries the information given is illustrated by quotations from literature; a word-book, vocabulary, or lexicon. Dictionaries proper are of two kinds: those in which the meanings of the words of one language or dialect are given in another (or, in a polyglot dictionary, in two or more languages), and those in which the words of a language are treated and illustrated in this language itself. The former were the earlier";[22] "a reference book containing words, usually alphabetically arranged along with information about their forms, pronunciations, functions, etymologies, meanings, and syntactical and idiomatic uses";[23] "1 a. a book that consists of an alphabetical list of words with their meanings, parts of speech, pronunciations, etymologies, etc. b. a similar book giving equivalent words in two or more languages. 2. a reference book listing words or terms and giving information about a particular subject or activity. 3. a collection of information or examples with the entries alphabetically arranged."[24] In brief, according to Samuel Johnson, it is "a book explaining the words of any language alphabetically"[25] and, taken as an abstract, it is "according to that idea of it which seems to be alone capable of being logically maintained . . . an inventory of the language."[26]

Thus the definitions. They are by no means universally accepted—the Oxford one has been particularly challenged—but if these essentially popular definitions, designed for general consumption, are by no means settled, then the lexicographical professionals, writing for their own, move the idea of a "dictionary" into an even more rarefied zone. Ladislav Zgusta, in his influential *Manual of Lexicography* (1971), quotes as "one of the best definitions" that of

C. C. Berg: "A dictionary is a systematically arranged list of socialized linguistic forms compiled from the speech-habits of a given speech-community and commented on by the author in such a way that the qualified reader understands the meaning . . . of each separate form, and is informed of the relevant facts concerning the functions of that form in its community."[27] The dictionary as a concept is a more complex, fluid thing than might initially appear. As Henri Béjoint puts it, "There is a wide range of lexicographical products that can be called dictionaries: *dictionary* is a term with a wide extension and a complex intension . . . The concept is a complex one that can only be defined by specialists."[28] In his own study, *Tradition and Innovation in Modern English Dictionaries* (1994), Béjoint quotes the French metalexicographer J. Rey-Debove,[29] who in her own work *Étude linguistique et sémiotique des dictionnaires français contemporains* (1971) suggests eight underlying characteristics which make a reference book a "dictionary."[30]

For her, it is necessary for the book to be 1. A list of separate graphic statements; 2. A book designed for consultation; 3. A book with two structures, sometimes one only (these are the "macrostructure": the rough equivalent of the word list; and the "microstructure": the actual contents entry by entry); 4. A book in which items are classed by form or content; 5. A repository of information that is linguistic in nature; 6. A repository of information that is explicitly didactic; 7. A source of information about signs; 8. A place where the word list corresponds to a predetermined set, and is structured if not exhaustive.

This is a complex and technical list. It is also subject to a number of provisos, which merely underline just how difficult it is to define so difficult a concept once one moves beyond the relative simplicities of the lay definition. For instance, as Béjoint points out, dictionaries are hardly the only lists of separate graphic statements: phone books and mail-order catalogs can also fit that bill. As far as consultation is concerned, a book need not be a dictionary to be consulted. Today's dictionaries all offer a relatively consistent microstructure; it was not always so. Johnson's entries vary enormously in length: *cat* for instance is brief, while *armadillo* and *opium* seem better fitted to an encyclopedia than to a dictionary. Even the *OED,* which is generally seen as a model of lexicographical style, has its extremes. Most modern dictionaries have abandoned classification by content, i.e., the encyclopedia model, for that of form, i.e., alphabetical order, yet the adoption of alphabetical order was by no means inevitable. There is a strong sense that the encyclopedic method, grouping words by themes, meets far more efficiently the human need to see links and method amid the chaos of existence. Life after all does not come in alphabetical order. But if one is dealing with a language, there is much to be said for the adoption of an A–Z listing: nothing works better for those who wish, however illusorily, thus to see the whole extent of a language. "The dictionary represents an illusion of totality, of an immobile order of things, of harmony. It seems to exhaust the universe and the lexicon."[31] It is a concept that seems to appeal especially to writers: Anatole France suggested that "the dictionary is the universe in alphabetical order," while Jean Cocteau reversed the image when he said that "the greatest masterpiece in the world is only a dictionary out of order."[32] All that accepted, American dictionaries in particular have never really given up on the encyclopedic aspects of lexicography, even if that information tends (as it often was in English dictionaries of the sixteenth and seventeenth centuries) to be set aside in its own addendum. A number of recent British dictionaries, usually of the "concise" variety, have followed suit. And while lexicographers might balk at the crossover, the public seems happy to accept these somewhat hybrid productions. Paradoxically, it might be noted, the latest editions of Roget's *Thesaurus*—the supreme exemplar, outside an actual encyclopedia, of the thematic method—are being recast as alphabetical wordbooks.

The dictionary is a reference book and reference books have a primary function: to pass on knowledge. To quote Béjoint once more,

A dictionary is primarily an instrument to be used when one needs a piece of information about a word in particular, about the language in general, or about the world. During the consultation process the users learn, or verify, something they did not know, or had momentarily forgotten. Dictionaries are intruments for self-teaching and they have all the characterstics of all didactic books: they contain definitions, they give information which is presented as the knowledge and opinions of the community in general—as opposed to the knowledge and opinions of the lexicographer.[33]

Thus the perfect work: factual, accurate, disinterested. The extent to which this must remain a myth has been suggested above. Neither Johnson nor Webster were paragons of selflessness, but nor were many of their peers, before or after. Even if the lexicographer can suppress his or her own prejudices, the society that provides the dictionary's background ensures that certain positions must, willy-nilly, be taken. "Obscenity" and "taboo language" illustrate the most obvious of such pressures, but there are others. Current attitudes to a variety of -isms cannot be discounted. The imperatives of political ideologies have always been influential, and those of today's "political correctness" (PC), all discussed in Chapter 15, have elbowed their way into any dictionary they can suborn. Nor is the substitution of a team for the individual lexicographer any guarantee of impartiality. Chambers' *Twentieth Century Dictionary* (1972) offers such definitions as "*jaywalker:* a careless pedestrian whom motorists are expected to avoid running down"; "*civil:* polite (in any degree short of discourtesy)"; "*middle-aged:* between youth and old age, variously reckoned to suit the reckoner"; "*noose:* a snare or bond generally, esp. hanging or marriage." This is nearer Bierce's *Devil's Dictionary* than any conventional idea of lexicography. Teams may also have class biases, or racial ones. Neither the individual lexicographer nor the team of which he or she may form a part, can escape their social background and the mindset that forms them. As Rey puts it: "All lexicographers . . . who are the mouthpieces of a social class, the instruments of an ideology, no doubt believe that they objectively represent a set of forms. But there is no objectivity, no picture so accurate as to eliminate the model."[34] Even the myth of education rests on sand: given the time that must elapse between the assembling and defining of the word list and the actual publication of the dictionary, any real educative value is inevitably diluted.

Finally, one is faced with the eternal problem of just what goes into the dictionary and why. Whatever publishers claim, one cannot ever list a *whole* language. The English language has been estimated at four million words, a figure based on adding together the largest current corpus to a variety of marginal vocabularies—slang, jargon, dialect—plus various neologisms yet to enter the dictionary and similar fringe terminology. But how accurate is this? There are, for instance, more than six million registered chemical compounds, and research throws up new additions every day. Medical terms, perhaps 200,000, would bulk the list even further. America's largest unabridged dictionary, *Webster's Third New International,* which takes its starting point as 1755, holds *c.* 450,000 words; the second edition of the *OED,* dating from *c.* 1100 and combining the *NED* and the modern *Supplements,* runs to approximately 475,000. On the basis of the estimated lexis, neither can be seen as truly "unabridged," although they are as large as most scholars, let alone the casual browser, wishes to handle. In any case, print is a fallible medium for calculating language, at heart a spoken phenomenon. As the linguist Jean Aitchison has said, the "mental lexicon" will always far outweigh the printed lexicon, however supposedly all-encompassing that may be. Written dictionaries, as she puts it, can only "dodder along behind [spoken] language."[35] Real language goes far too fast for the lexicographer to capture every word, never mind every nuance. "The real difference between a book dictionary and the mental lexicon is that the latter contains far, far more information about each entry. All book dictionaries are inevitably limited in the amount they contain, just because it would be quite impracticable to include all possible data about each word . . . [It] is unlikely that anyone has ever assembled the total range of knowledge which could be brought together about any one dictionary entry."[36] But dictionaries are made and decisions have to govern their content. Size aside, how is one to judge just what makes up the lexis? When does a word "enter the language"? Are some occurrences "better" than others? How many occurrences have to be counted to establish a word? What people count as members of the linguistic community: only adults? children? debilitated speakers? There is a theory that given that there are a finite number of morphemes and a finite number of morpheme combinations then there must be a finite number of words, but that sum is infinitely huge and no dictionary can ever approach it.[37] In the end one is imprisoned in a a vicious circle: the lexis is the basis of the dictionary but the dictionary in turn has to be the basis of the lexis or at least a subset of that lexis. And on the lexicographer goes.

America vs. England

While the dictionary *qua* dictionary remains a constant term, for which a variety of reasonably similar definitions are proposed and generally understood, it is important to note the differences, both in style and content, of British and American dictionaries, or more properly, dictionaries of British English and American English. Oscar Wilde's suggestion that the two nations have "everything in common . . . except, of course, language"[38] is perhaps less true today than a century ago (English may be the world's dominant language, but it is American English, not the "mother tongue," that rules) but any analysis of the countries' respective dictionaries shows that there is a still a good deal of truth in his line. The lexicography of British English has always been primarily an élitist pursuit, its makers scholars and its consumers the middle classes and their betters. While the popular tradition has gradually gained ground, it has remained secondary. Dictionaries in England are for study, they represent an adjunct to the language rather than the sole repository of its rights and wrongs. A new edition of a British English dictionary may be criticized for its inclusion of certain neologisms, or more likely for its exclusion of others, but there are rarely any worries over the moral or aesthetic responsibilities behind such choices. The situation in America is very different. As Béjoint notes,

> Lexicographical prescriptivism in the US is exactly as old as the making of dictionaries, because of the role played by the dictionary in a society characterized by a great deal of linguistic insecurity. It has always had only one objective: not so much to preserve the language from change, as

was the case in other countries, but firmly to indicate good usage— which, for all the earlier period of American history, was British usage.[39]

The acknowledgment of this "linguistic insecurity" is not intended to be anti-American. The very same term can be found in a number of American writers on lexicography, typically Sidney Landau.[40] It is a phenomenon that underpins the whole world of popular dictionary making, as powerfully in France or Germany as in America. The industrial revolution, along with the social revolutions in America and France, and their lesser successors of 1848, all pushed toward a desire for greater public awareness. This came through educa- tion and through self-improvement and in both cases the perfection of one's language was seen as vital to the process. It is perhaps ironic that Frederick Fur- nivall, who so dedicated himself to the improvement of "working men," helped found a dictionary that was the ultimate in scholarly exclusivity, but there were many others—Chambers, Funk, Larousse—who provided a much felt need. And nowhere more so than in the United States. Both Europe, Britain included, and America saw great social changes, but the United States experi- enced an extra factor. For Europe there was some population movement, but it was internal, from the country to the town. America, thanks to its policy of unfettered immigration, represented a golden land for tens of thousands who chose to cross the ocean. It was these new arrivals, determined to advance their social position, who turned to the lexicographers and the grammarians for aid. The scholarly niceties of the historical dictionary were irrelevant: what an immigrant wanted to know was whether his usage and pronunciation were right or wrong. What was in the dictionary, says Landau, "was venerated as the unquestioned truth."[41]

Thus the American dictionary developed as an all-purpose reference book, as much an encyclopedia as a dictionary per se. For many people, immigrants and others, it represented the primary if not the only source of information. A typ- ical dictionary might offer sections on place names, foreign quotations, Amer- ican colleges, proofreaders' marks, vocabulary tests, and much more besides. Such material had once adorned British dictionaries too, but not for more than a century. As will be seen, it was the decision to drop much of this information that so enraged the critics of *Webster's Third New International.* The dictionaries' parallel uses, as linguistic etiquette books, meant that while encyclopedic material might be included, there were far less obsolete or "literary" terms than one might find in a British equivalent, that taboo terms were exactly that, as were racist ones, and that the word list worried far less about etymology than it did about usage.

The importance of the dictionary in the average American home today cannot be underestimated. Some 87 percent have a dictionary, even if all other information comes from a television screen. Compiled with the average reader in mind, they are, as Béjoint suggests, far more "user-friendly" than a European volume. "The American dictionary, on the whole, is not a remote object to be handled only by an élite; it is designed for use by the general public in all sorts of everyday situations."[42] It is also accorded enormous respect. So great is this rigid reverence that the linguist Allen Walker Read has suggested that rather than confer culture upon individuals, the real effect is to have had a positively "malign effect"[43] on American culture.

The writer John Algeo, suggesting that only the Bible is similarly revered, has coined the term "lexicographicolatry" for the concept.[44] That, again like the Bible, the book became "more venerated than used . . . mattered little. A literate household without a dictionary (and it mattered not what dictionary) was as badly exposed as a shoe salesman without his pants."[45] The whole concept is epitomized in the use of a single, all-encompassing phrase: *the dictionary,* characterized by Rosamund Moon as "UAD: the Unidentified Authorizing Dictionary, usually referred to as 'the dictionary,' but very occasionally as 'my dictionary.'"[46] As McDavid notes, the actual publisher—Random House, Merriam-Webster, OUP—is of marginal interest. In such remarks as "Is it in the Dictionary?" or "Look it up in the Dictionary" the dictionary is as monolithic an entity as is "The Bible," and carries for believers a similar weight of intrinsic authority.

Like so much else in postwar culture, the American style has gradually overtaken the British. The historically oriented pages of the *OED* remain immune, but the "college dictionary" style, pioneered in the United States, began moving into the British marketplace with the publication of the *Hamlyn Encyclopedia World Dictionary* (1971), based on the *American College Dictionary* and, more importantly, the *Collins Dictionary of the English Language* (1979). The Hamlyn was not particularly successful, but the Collins opened the way for money-spinning imitators, including even one from Oxford, the *Encyclopedic English Dictionary,* a determinedly trendy publication replete with 200 pages of non-lexicographical information, including a few pages on ecology.

One final aspect of American lexicography that must be mentioned is the sheer commercialism of the enterprise. One might, at a pinch, term the struggle over alleged plagiarism that was fought out between Thomas Blount and Edward Phillips *c.* 1660 as a "dictionary war," but it took the rivalry between the publishers of Noah Webster and Joseph Worcester to bring the public in on the fun. The American dictionary is always first and foremost a commercial object. It is advertised, promoted, and generally boosted as the latest, the best, and above all the biggest. Not that they pioneered any of these self-promoting encomia: one need only glance at the prefaces composed by British lexicographers of the seventeenth and eighteenth centuries to see that, but American publishers gave the practice a newfound devotion. The equation of quantity and quality is very much a phenomenon of the New World, even if the precise computations that lie behind the quoted figures are sometimes less than obvious to the lay observer. Depending on the counting system the same dictionary, advertised as boasting 155,000 entries, may actually offer but 80,000. Once again, Britain, at least in the sphere of popular and "concise" dictionaries, has more than caught up. Size matters.

Plagiarism

One aspect of the dictionary that Rey-Delbove's list does not include is originality. There is a good case for regarding the history of lexicography as the history of an infinite palimpsest. As Sidney Landau states at the very head of his brief history of the subject, "The history of English lexicography usually consists of a recital of successive and often successful acts of piracy."[47] Each dictionary draws upon its predecessors, displays its own additions, whether stylistic or lexical, and waits until a new dictionary or new generation overlays it with fresh contributions, which in turn will be subsumed as new lexicographers attempt to pin down the latest version of a given language. Like Isaac Newton, the lexicographer can, or should, declare to his forebears, "If I have seen further . . . it is by standing on the heads of giants." "To steal from one author is plagiarism," remarked the Hollywood ne'er-do-well Wilson Mizner (1876–1933), "if you steal from many, it's research." On that basis nearly every general-purpose dictionary is "research." The question remains: is it plagiarism too?

To take Mizner's definition more seriously than perhaps he meant it, one can see what has been termed plagiarism[48] as a twofold concept: "one author," or out-and-out plagiarism, and "many authors," or scholarly derivation from previous sources. Lexicography offers examples of both. It is surprising, given the huge number of dictionaries, that there seems to have been less "one author" plagiarism than might be expected. The hagiographers of certain pivotal figures have excoriated as "plagiarists" those who acknowledged the excellence of their work by integrating it into their own, but this is often unfair. The main instance that emerges here is that of Thomas Blount and Edward Phillips, whose works appeared respectively in 1656 and 1658. There are, undeniably, a good many similarities, and Blount was perhaps justified in his howls of fury. But in the end death cut short the argument and Phillips' work, entirely recast by a third lexicographer, went on to form the basis of a series of important advances in a new century. The work of an earlier author, John Rider, was allegedly stolen by another, Francis Holyoake. But Holyoake's accuser was not Rider, who was dead and in any case had pretty much abandoned the work that took his name as soon as the first edition was off the press, but the executors of yet another, even earlier, compiler: Thomas Thomas, whose work, they claimed, had been plundered by Rider himself. This argument too failed to take wing and petered out with no resolution. Indeed, no dictionary maker seems ever to have taken the ultimate step—a visit to court—to stop publication of another's work. Johnson too suffered alleged plagiarism, although he never complained. Not until Philip Gove, editor of *Webster's Third International* (1961), itself the source of even greater controversies (albeit unconnected with any form of literary theft), wrote about the marketing of Johnson's and Scott's dictionaries was battle joined on Johnson's behalf. According to Gove, Johnson was stripped bare by Joseph Nicol Scott, in his revision of Nathaniel Bailey's *Dictionarium Britannicum*. But Johnson in turn had worked, at least when he began, with a copy of Bailey open at his desk. Given the bitterness that informed the "dictionary war" between America's Noah Webster and Joseph Worcester, it is inevitable that plagiarism ranked among the mutual insults. But theirs was a battle of nationalisms as much as of literature, and if the Anglophile Worcester had really plundered the Anglophobe Webster, it is hard to see how this would have advanced his cause. Finally, although few of its compilers seemed to object, the collection of slang, especially in its first two hundred years, has often been as barefaced an example of repetitious copying as one might hope to see. Awdeley followed Copland, Harman Awdeley, Greene Harman, and Dekker Greene, and so it went. Given that that the "slang" of those early glossaries was essentially no more than a core glossary of criminal jargon or cant, it cannot be that surprising that one slang lexicographer copied his immediate predecessor. Nor are theirs real "dictionaries." Not until "B. E., Gent." offered his *New Dictionary . . . of the Canting Crew* (*c.* 1690) did "civilian" or "mainstream" slang begin to enter the picture.

"Many authors' plagiarism, what modern scholarship enjargons as "intertextuality," is another matter. A variety of linguistic "food chain," a lexical Pac-Man as it were, it lies at the foundation of lexicography. Setting aside the clay tablets of Sumer and Akkad, which cannot alas be linked to any developments that follow, the rest of lexicography, from Greece to Rome, Rome to Byzantium and then onward to the present day, can be seen as a continuous thread of lexicographical accretion. Certain figures, undoubtedly, were more seized upon than others. Calepino's monumental efforts ensured that his eleven-language *Dictionarium* (1502) directly influenced the whole range of European dictionary making for the next century and indirectly for even longer, given that those who absorbed his efforts would be absorbed in their turn. Similarly Charles Estienne's *Dictionarium Historicum, Geographicum, Poeticum . . .* (1553), became the sourcebook for a vast range of biographical and geographical dictionaries. Cooper, Thomas, Holyoake, and Phillips all benefited from his researches, and they were just the English representatives. But the history of lexicography makes it abundantly clear that every lexicographer looked backward. The language might have an infinite future; it sometimes appeared that the lexicographers looked to a near-infinite past. Rider, for instance, drew on Huloet, Pelegromius, Julius Pollux, and Thomas Thomas; Thomas had drawn on Cooper; Cooper took much of his material from Thomas Elyot and Robert Estienne (Charles' brother and author, with his *Thesaurus linguae latinae* [1532], of an even more popular sourcebook). All of these early lexicographers tell the same story, and often boast of it on their title pages or in their prefaces, either listing their sources or, like Rider, assuring readers that they had read, as it were on their behalf, the "learned workes of all the learnedst and best Dictionaries in England." How one regards such borrowings is very much a personal matter. Noting Philip Gove's attack on the Scott-Bailey dictionary, DeWitt Starnes and Gertrude Noyes observed that "As much as we may wish to overlook the fact, three unsavoury corollaries are implied in [Gove's] sketch of the development of the English dictionary: (1) in this early period lexicography progressed by plagiarism; (2) the best lexicographer was often the most discriminating plagiarist; and (3) a good dictionary was its own justification, whatever the method of compilation."[49] By the evidence of their joint work, which details without criticism a variety of "borrowings," Starnes and Noyes seemed less perturbed by such "unsavory" concepts than was Gove. And on the whole that refusal to be shocked by what is in the end a lexicographical *donnée* goes for most commentators.

Nor are modern lexicographers immune. Johnson takes pains to credit his own main influences—Bailey, Ainsworth, and Phillips, and the etymologists Junius and Skinner—although he backed their word lists (culled of course from centuries of earlier dictionaries) with his own reading as well as that of his amanuenses. Massive reading programs underpinned Johnson's English successor, the *Oxford English Dictionary,* but a trawl through those mighty volumes shows that the old ways were not forgotten. Aside from the oft-repeated notation "(J.)", indicating definitions plucked wholesale from Johnson himself, there are, *inter alia,* 1,306 citations from Henry Cockeram, 81 from Rider, 250 from John Kersey, and more than 5,000 from Bailey. Thomas Harman's *Caveat* (1567), which reproduced the entire recorded cant lexicon of its time, seems, in its 235 citations, to have been taken up in its entirety. Only Webster prefers to isolate himself from the trend. Like his peers, Webster drew on other researchers when amassing his word list, but that most religious of lexicographers allowed but a single credit when assessing his work: to "God Almighty." The *OED* is less self-denying: its most recent edition refers to Webster's various editions more than 5,000 times.

The sheer volume of dictionaries on offer today (perhaps 15,000 of various sizes and types dedicated to the English language alone) means that plagiarism remains a constant, although the theft these days might better be laid at the feet of commercial rather than scholarly imperatives. As John Algeo puts it in his article on American lexicography in the *International Encyclopedia of Lexicography,* "Many dictionary publishers are not overly committed to truth in advertising. Very often 'new' dictionaries are simply old ones cut down or padded out, and puffed up. The basic content of a dictionary is pushed into as many shapes and sold under as many variant names as the market will bear."[50] He too notes Gove's "unsavory" corollaries and admits that "today good lexicographers are more sophisticated about plagiarizing the competition, though they are just as aware of it. Moreover, they are no less industrious about reworking whatever sources they have a legal right to. Discrimination is still a virtue of high order in profiting from the model of previous dictionaries, and a good dictionary is still its own justification."[51] "Sophisticated" may, suggests Sidney Landau, be overgenerous. While early lexicographers, if sometimes grudgingly, acknowledged their sources, their twentieth-century successors are often less open. "The pressures of the marketplace dictate that every dictionary be 'new.'" But paradoxically, "a really new dictionary would be a dreadful piece of work, missing innumerable basic words and senses, replete with absurdities and unspeakable errors, studded with biases and interlarded with irrelevant provincialism."[52] It is such a dedication to newness, adds Landau, that undermined the quality of Noah Webster's original 1828 *American Dictionary.* Only the excellence of his definitions (and in time the commercial expertise of the Merriam Brothers) rendered such blunders unimportant. Like the historian, who cannot conjure up a pristine "new" version of history, but must add to what has gone before, the lexicographer cannot simply throw out a word store that has accrued over centuries. Nor is this necessarily to be seen as bad. Oliver Wendell Holmes, writing in 1858 as *The Autocrat of the Breakfast Table* (and as it happens a fan of Webster's rival, Joseph Worcester), is all for recycling:

"When I feel inclined to read poetry I take down my Dictionary. The poetry of words is quite as beautiful as that of sentences. The author may arrange the gems effectively, but their shape and lustre have been given by the attrition of ages." Such "newness" that does appear in a dictionary is not therefore the substitution of one fresh-minted vocabulary for an old, outmoded one, but is derived from fresh research, dealing perhaps with etymologies or changes in usage, or more usually from the most basic addition in a dictionary—that of new words. In the end any lexicographer has to face a basic fact: how many ways can there be of defining a given word? No reputable dictionary would simply reproduce material stolen from a predecessor, but it is inevitable, and generally accepted, that just as the language demands that the word list must, while gradually expanding, remain relatively stable, so too must the definitions included in that list.

More recently, Frederic Dolezal, writing in 1986, has put what for this discussion must be the final word.

> The early evolution of the English Dictionary has been considered as (1) an example of received and passed along tradition; (2) a tangled chain of influence and borrowing; (3) a loose conglomeration of word lists waiting for the imprimatur of authority from Samuel Johnson; and even (4) a sequence of clever and not so clever plagiarists . . . I would like to suggest another approach which I hope might bring a unified version of the development of the English Dictionary. Namely, if we viewed the English Dictionary as a single text, then the different "authors" of the successive dictionaries would more felicitously be called "editors."[53]

For Dolezal, if the language is a continuum, then anyone who chooses to write a dictionary based upon it is welcome to select and compile as he or she desires. Just what the public requires from its dictionaries will be considered in the final chapter, but all those who have faced that oft-repeated complaint, "It isn't in the Dictionary," should enjoy this riposte:

> We all know that people have a penchant for demanding more from a dictionary than can be delivered; by viewing the ENGLISH DICTIONARY as a single edited and re-edited text, we can at least answer misbegotten demands for "correctness" etc. with our own documented claims about the nature of the printed text. When confronted by the authoritarian "Is it in the dictionary?" we can clear a bit of breathing space, as it were, by a rejoinder, "Do you mean the dictionary of all possible occurrences that

are recognised by the ideal speaker of Language L to be members of Language L; or do you mean some particular, derivative, unabridged but somehow, nevertheless, limited dictionary?"[54]

Obscenity and Taboo

As the bearer of the linguistic law, the lexicographer is never more priestlike than when his dictionary is seen as a literally definitive statement of the moral and ideological values of the society in which it is used. As one can see in Johnson or Webster, whose definitions of such terms as "Tory" and "Whig," "liberty" and "freedom" are redolent of their own attitudes, the lexicographer is in a privileged position, able at will or whim to impose his beliefs on a world programmed to accept them. There is, however, another extensive area over which the lexicographer holds sway: that of taboo language, whether oaths, obscenities, or those terms, usually relating to sex and excretion, which, popular fallacies aside, need in no way actually be "dirty." Until recently such language has been strictly off-limits, although the reticence was in itself a relatively modern phenomenon. This refers, of course, to the mainstream dictionary maker. The compilers of slang dictionaries, from the sixteenth-century glossarists through to today's slang lexicographers, have traditionally, by the very nature of the vocabulary with which they deal, taken a more catholic viewpoint. To *wap* and to *niggle,* both meaning to have sexual intercourse, or more properly, since they come from the slang vocabulary, to fuck, appear in Thomas Harman's *Caveat* (1565). *Fuck* itself appears first not in a slang work, but in a bilingual dictionary, John Florio's *Worlde of Wordes,* where it is cited as one of the English synonyms for the Italian *fottere. Cunt* can be found in Francis Grose's *Classical Dictionary of the Vulgar Tongue* (1796), although he prints it "c**t" and defines it, in a phrase that defies a whole database of isms, as "a nasty name for a nasty thing." Farmer and Henley's late-nineteenth-century work and Eric Partridge's successor of the mid-twentieth both offer a state-of-the-art slang vocabulary, although Partridge, afflicted by a somewhat embarrassing coyness, is wont on occasion to take refuge in Latin, typically the retreat behind "*membrum virile*" for penis, when defining some lubriciously slangy synonym. For all his devotion to inclusiveness, Partridge seems to have found the listing of such terms hard going: "My rule, in the matter of unpleasant terms, has been to deal with them as briefly, as astringently, as aseptically as was consistent with clarity and adequacy; in a few instances, I had to force myself to overcome an instinctive repugnance."[55] Like the slang lexicographers, the dialect collectors, whether the Englishman Joseph Wright in 1907 or the American Frederick Cassidy eighty years later, are also accorded a license denied their mainstream peers. Like slang, dialect lies on the linguistic margin; so long as it makes no effort to infiltrate the center, then it can be safely, if reluctantly, left to its own coarse devices.

But for the mainstream compiler, the selection of the word list was far more limited, whether by choice or societal pressure—although the role of the lexicographer as priest meant, automatically, that what was included was "good" and what excluded "bad." It should be noted, however, that just as "priestly" lexicography is very much a fact of the seventeenth century and beyond (for all that it existed much earlier as a theory) so too is the division of language into the "acceptable"/"forbidden" dichotomy a product of that era. Prior to the seventeenth century, and in some cases well beyond it, the language of what was in fact (but would not be named until the nineteenth century) "standard English" was taken as a single entity. Its users might take up more or, more generally, less of what was on offer, but the vocabulary can be seen as a single receptacle, in which might be found the words of the English language, as calculated at a given moment in time. In fairness, this receptacle consistently excluded slang, but it is worth pointing out that so many of the basic terms of sex and excretion landed in the slang dictionaries not through linguistic causes, but by a process of *faut de mieux.* Early slang was essentially cant, that is the professional jargon of the begging and criminal classes. It was only when the formerly standard words, typically *arse, bollocks, shit,* and similar terms, were excluded from "polite" vocabulary that, wandering unclaimed and abandoned by standard lexicography, they were given a home among the slang terminology.

The concept of "obscenity" is very much a modern one. The common law offense of "obscene libel," which underpinned British censorship until the midnineteenth century, is an eighteenth-century construct; prior to that the ecclesiastical courts held sway over errant publications, and the sins they judged were those of blasphemy, sedition, and even heresy, but not of "dirty words." Overly credulous as to religion, they saw no need to tremble before the plain language that described common bodily parts and natural functions. When attitudes changed, at the start of the eighteenth century, new laws had to be promulgated. It took time: in the prosecution of James Read and Angell Carter in 1707 for publishing *The Fifteen Plagues of a Maidenhead,* the defendants were able to escape judgment by pleading successfully that the court, the Queen's Bench, had no right to try cases of obscene libel. The book, said the judge, is "bawdy stuff . . . [but] there is no law to punish it." When Edmund Curll, the least of whose literary crimes was pirating the work of the lexicographer Robert Ainsworth, was prosecuted in 1725 for similar breaches of literary taste, it took four years, and a new law, before he could be properly sentenced. A full-scale

"Obscene Publications Act" would not emerge until 1857 (its modern successor dates from 1959), but by then the concept of "obscenity" was firmly in place and dictionaries, as well as other books, duly suffered the effects of its fearful censorship.

The early glossaries and vocabularies of Old and Middle English (from the eighth to fourteenth centuries) are untroubled by such problems. Indeed, as Gabriele Stein has pointed out,[56] it is often from these early lists that today's historical dictionaries draw their first-use citations for such words. Aelfric, c. 1000, defined the Latin *testiculi* as "beallucas," the Middle English progenitor of today's *bollocks,* now strictly confined to the slang lexicon. The mid-fourteenth-century *Mayer Nominale* defines *piga* as "a balloke code," adding *cod,* another standard word turned latterday slang. *Virilius,* meaning penis, is defined in the MS Cotton Cleopatra A III as "pintel," a term condemned by the *OED* as "vulgar." *Anus* is simply "arse," while the Latin *vulva,* used for the female genitals, is widely translated as "cunt," other possibly than the modern "motherfucker" *the* taboo term of the last two centuries.

The word lists that underpin the English-English dictionaries of the early seventeenth century do not offer "obscenities" but this reflects their broader intention as much as any attempt to censor the vocabulary. Cawdrey, Cockeram, and their peers and immediate successors were assembling, in their "hard-word" dictionaries, lists of terms that were seen as enhancing the vocabulary of those who aspired to greater linguistic sophistication. If they omitted terms that would later be characterized as taboo, then they also omitted vast numbers of plain and simple words. Neither extreme was relevant to their purpose. Not until the eighteenth century, and John Kersey's much-expanded revision of Edward Phillips' *New World of Words* (1706), would dictionaries start attempting true comprehensiveness. Ironically it is also with the eighteenth century that one sees the dedicated exclusion of the allegedly obscene. There were a number of impulses for this shift, but one must have been the example, so important to those who pontificated upon the English language, of the Académie Française's *Dictionnaire,* published in 1694. This resolutely excluded any taboo words and set the standard for generations of French lexicography. Those who persist in the *canard* as regards the "dirty," sexually libertarian French, should note that the French equivalents of even such nontaboo sexual language as *phallus* did not appear in the popular *Petit Larousse* until 1974 (although *prepuce* had been there since 1961), while *masturbation* had to wait another two years. But imitating France was not enough. While the end of puritanism and its censorship had delighted many, what were perceived as the excesses of the Restoration court became increasingly repugnant. Even earlier than the Read and Carter case cited above, the playwright and poet Sir Charles Sedley, a royal favorite, found himself at the heart of the earliest prosecution for "obscene libel" when in 1664 he and some some friends appeared, "inflam'd with strong liquors," on the balcony of the Cock public house in Bow Street, Covent Garden. From here they proceeded to lower their breeches and "excrementiz'd in the street," following this display with a shower of bottles which they had, during their drinking bout, filled with urine. They also berated the crowd that gathered below with a variety of blasphemous speeches. It was this latter that constituted the "obscenity" although Sedley, on paying his fine, remarked that he was surely "the first man that paid for shitting."[57]

Sedley's friend John Wilmot, earl of Rochester, was deemed even more arrogantly distasteful. His play *Sodom: or, The Quintessence of Debauchery* (1684) is a paean to excess, in which a cast of characters named King Bolloxinion, Queen Cuntigratia, General Buggeranthos, Princess Swivia, the maids of honor Cunticula and Clitoris and the like copulate ceaselessly, in a whirligig of incest, bisexuality, and random perversions. Sodomy, of course, is the pleasure of choice. Rochester, says Margaret Drabble "wrote more frankly about sex than anyone in English before the twentieth century,"[58] but such frankness was proving an embarrassment. Those who were starting to agitate for an English Academy and for an authoritative version of the English language, would not have wished to see the picturesque margins of that language included. John Dryden, while a friend of Sedley and the one-time protégé of Rochester, would not have allowed his patron's works into any contemporary canon. By the time of Johnson, in whose *Dictionary,* if only by default, the task of establishing that linguistic authority would be vested, there was little chance of seeing the taboo terms given parity with their "respectable" coevals. Johnson himself may have claimed that "drinking and fucking" were life's great pleasures, and, according to Boswell, privately talked "the plainest bawdy"[59] but such unbuttoned liberties were singularly absent from his *magnum opus.* Johnson's immediate predecessor, Nathaniel Bailey, had been less circumspect. Drawing on the *Etymologicon Linguae Anglicane* (1671) of Stephen Skinner (as expanded by Thomas Henshaw), he chose to include some taboo vocabulary, including *fuck,* which in his *Dictionarium Brittanicum* (1730) he attributed to a "Dutch" origin. Backing off somewhat, he added the note: "a term used of a goat." But Bailey sank beneath the might of Johnson and the eighteenth century saw only one further attempt to include taboo terms in a mainstream work: *The New and Complete Dictionary of the English Language* (1775) by the Reverend John Ash (1724?–79). Ash, a Worcestershire parson, is best known and posthumously teased as such in the *OED* for his etymology of *curmudgeon* which he claimed derived "from the French *coeur:* unknown, and *méchant:* a correspondent." This was an awful blunder: Ash had copied Johnson who had appended to his own "prescientific" etymology (from the French *coeur méchant:* wicked heart) the comment "unknown correspondent." Ash did, however, include a number of taboo terms, again copied, this time from Bailey. Perhaps his most important long-term effect was to serve as a justification for America's early lexicographers, Samuel Johnson, Jr. and the Rev. John Elliott, whose *Selected Pronouncing and Accented Dictionary* (1800) managed, despite their many protestations as to the need for an obscenity-free language, to include the undoubtedly coarse *foutra.* Faced by a torrent of criticism, they blamed their error on the hapless and long-dead Ash.

Writing in 1721, in *An Accidence to the English Tongue,* the first grammar written in America, Hugh Jones, professor of mathematics at William and Mary College in Virginia, laid down that "None of *good Manners* use *nasty Expressions,* and *foul vulgar Terms,* which are *nauseous* and *odious;* for (particularly) *Obscenity* betrays a *corrupt Heart* void of Reason, and Goodness." His comments set the pattern for American lexicography. They also reflected the predictable moral stance that stemmed from the fierce puritanism that informed much of colonial and post-Revolutionary New England. Unlike in England there had been no evolution of eighteenth-century common law to bring obscenity under the legal umbrella, but nineteenth-century Federal law paralleled that of England when in 1873, sixteen years after Britain's first Obscene Publications Act, the "vice campaigner" Anthony Comstock managed to have passed what was christened The Comstock Act (1873), known properly as U.S. Code: Section 1461, Title 18. This banned "every obscene, lewd, lascivious, or filthy book, pamphlet picture, paper, letter writing, print, or other publication of an indecent character" from the U.S. mails and served as the touchstone of Federal obscenity law for the remainder of the century. It was not abandoned until 1915, after which date the establishing of obscenity standards was turned over to the Supreme Court. A lack of laws, however, was no bar to a proliferation of linguistic squeamishness. By the early nineteenth century Professor Jones' puritan impulses had been diluted: the threat of damnation was now merely one of social ostracism. "Leg" caused particular offense: euphemisms included "limb," "extremity," and "bender." "Stomach," "corset," "trousers," "sweat," and "sneeze" were among many "unmentionables" of the time. "Cock" had been "rooster" since the late eighteenth century. American lexicographers, reflecting their society as they must, eschewed such outlawed bluntness. None more so than Noah Webster. Among the many accusations that he ranged against his *bête noire,* the English Samuel Johnson, was that of allowing a wide range of terms that ought, in any decent lexicon, to have been automatically excluded. Webster represents, even more than does Johnson, the lexicographer as lawgiver. By contemporary British standards Johnson had purged the language, but British standards were not Webster's and his dictionary, pioneering an independently "American" language, had no time for Johnsonian laxity. In this he both instructed and reflected his compatriots. It was irrelevant that he had declared in 1817 that "the business of the lexicographer is to collect, arrange, and define, as far as possible, *all* the words that belong to a language, and leave the author to select from them . . . according to his own taste and judgement."[60] This, after all, was a man who had bowdlerized the Bible, producing an edition in which, as his granddaughter recalled, "the words *stink, suck, dung,* [and] *belly* . . . fell before his hand."[61] Subsequent editions of "Webster," as published by the Merriam Brothers, have stuck firmly to its founder's tenets. The *Third International* edition of 1961 faced much outraged criticism, but not for its "obscenity:" the "four-letter words" remained conspicuous only in their continued absence. In fairness to its editor, such terms, including *fuck,* had been researched and written up, but were excised at galley stage by Gordon J. Gallan, then president of Merriam-Webster.

With Johnson's work regularly apostrophized as "the Dictionary" until its replacement in that role by Oxford's great multivolumed tome a century and a half later, and the word police of Victorian rectitude setting their heavy imprint on nineteenth-century literature, taboo language largely vanished from mainstream English dictionary making. Richard Chenevix Trench, laying out his plan for the ideal English language dictionary in 1857, declared, like Webster, that the lexicographer must be all-encompassing in his selection of the word list. Those who put his plans into action, Sir James Murray and his team of Oxford lexicographers, were less self-contradictory than Webster, but they too fell short of all-inclusiveness. The fault, once again, was that of the religious superstitions that underpinned the mass market of Victorian moral values. It was not personal religion: Murray was as devout a Christian as ever Webster was, but he was far more of a professional—his own beliefs would never have impinged on the demands of lexicographical accuracy. It was the larger world to which, however reluctantly, he had to make acknowledgment. Writing in 1934 Allen Walker Read was less than tolerant: "It is to the lasting shame of Murray and [Henry] Bradley that their linguistic sense was not strong enough so that they could dissociate themselves from the warped outlook of their age."[62] It might be noted, however, that this denunciation comes in a lengthy piece devoted to the history of the word *fuck* from which the word itself is sedulously excluded. But Murray, while constrained by his audience to omit both *fuck* and *cunt*, had still included such terms as *arse, piss, shit,* and *turd;* those who consulted a late-nineteenth-century edition of "Webster" for such lemmas would have searched in vain.

The twentieth century has finally seen a return of the dictionary to the standards of the eighth: the majority of English language dictionaries, or at least the larger ones, give regular house room to what for so long were taboo terms. The second edition of the *OED,* for instance, offers *motherfucker* and *cocksucker,* both of which tend still in the United States to be restricted to specialist slang dictionaries. While the searching of dictionary pages to check that such terms are there may well be as absurd (if as time-honored) a pursuit as checking them to ensure that the selfsame terms have been omitted, it is interesting to see the manner in which such material has gradually made its way back into English and American dictionaries. Ex–*American Heritage Dictionary* lexicographer Reinhold Aman, now editor of *Maledicta: The International Journal of Verbal Aggression,* has done just that, summarizing his findings in volumes VII–X of his journal. Those who wish to chase down the gradual admission of such terms, as well as such medical or sex-specific terminology as *smegma* or *dildo,* should consult his detailed studies. Aman has also discovered the problems that can emerge when theory turns to practice: convicted in 1994 for sending supposedly abusive communications to his estranged wife and to her lawyers, he served a year in California's Lompoc Prison. From his point of view he was simply using the language of which he is a known expert. The courts were less tolerant.

Perhaps the most absurd example of such squeamishness is the absence of the resolutely standard English term *sexual intercourse* from virtually all American college dictionaries. Writing in 1985 Sidney Landau notes that only the *Random House College Dictionary* dares take on the term.[63] Taboo by proxy appears to be as scary as the real thing. As Henry Béjoint has noted, there are a number of articles but as yet no book dealing with the appearance or nonappearance of such terms in the dictionary; quoting Aman and Read among others, he adds only that "the conclusions of those papers are that all dictionaries have tended to be puritanical and that they are slowly changing." The frequency or lack of it of such terms can also be seen in the electronic environment. The spell-checker that accompanies the database on which has been collected much of the research for this book is distributed by Houghton-Mifflin, joint publishers of the *American Heritage Dictionary* which, at least in its first edition of 1969, was judged to be an enormous leap toward linguistic liberality (it was the first American dictionary to allow, *inter alia,* an entry for *fuck,* although later editions appear to have been bowdlerized). Of the twelve terms officially laid down by the Federal Communications Commission in 1973 as "filthy words," seven (*fuck, shit, piss, fart, cock, tits,* and *ass*) cause no hiccup in the checking process, while five (*cunt, motherfucker, cocksucker, turd,* and *twat*) bring the program to a temporary halt.

All that said, the old religious bugaboos are still as powerful as ever. Less so in Britain, where evangelistic fundamentalism is still a mercifully marginal activity, but massively so in America, where the religious right and its conservative bedmates include dictionaries in their campaigns for increased censorship and the obliteration of "secular humanism." In many cases local censors are able to override national standards, particularly in Texas where all schoolbooks have to be approved by the state and, as a result, the Educational Research Analysts, otherwise known as husband-and-wife team Mel and Norma Gabler, have successfully seen the *American Heritage Dictionary,* among many other publications, purged in the name of "decency." That Texans, who revel so noisily in their macho image, appear to be frightened of finding taboo words in their dictionaries, is just one of many absurdities that arise from such censorship. Texas is not, however, alone. The magazine *California English* (Jan.–Feb. 1980) quotes instances of the banning in various American states of such otherwise respectable volumes as the *AHD, Webster's New World* (student edition), the *Random House Dictionary,* the *Doubleday Dictionary,* and so on. Self-appointed "concerned" parents, school boards, and their allies object to such terms as "hot" (in a sexual sense), "horny," "crocked" (drunk), "knocker," "nut," "tail," "ball," and even "bed" (in the definition of which Webster's *New World* makes a reference to "bed" as a euphemism for sexual intercourse). Under such philistine dictatorships slang dictionaries, such as Robert Chapman's *New Dictionary of American Slang* (1986), are banned virtually sight unseen. That the lexicographers themselves justify their cowardice by stating, as did David Guralnik, editor of *Webster's New World* (1970), that "the terms in question are so well known as to require no explanation" is specious. So too, among many others, are "dog" and "cat" but *WNW* manages to find room for them. Nor, it should be noted, are the censors invariably moralists: commerce will have its noisy say as well. An illustrative sentence in Webster's *Second New International* (1934) suggesting that "electricity had replaced gas" was excised from the reprint after vociferous complaints from the gas industry. The facts were irrelevant. Similarly, Philip Gove's decision in Webster's *Third* to exclude capitals from all headwords enraged those who owned such trademarks as Frigidaire or Kleenex. That such terms were in many uses generic and that each was properly capitalized in the etymology was irrelevant. Copyright lawyers sprang into lucrative action: once more amendments had to be made.

This prefatory chapter inevitably begs some questions. The most important of which reflects, coincidentally or otherwise, the same question begged by so many lexicographers, priestly or not: where do the users of dictionaries fit in, what do they want from the word writers and their books, and to what extent must those wants be heeded? It is an important question, never more so than today, when the deferential, ordered society that could accept the linguistic diktats of a Johnson or a Webster has long gone. It was a question that was already pushing its way forward at the end of the eighteenth century and has made itself felt with increasing rowdiness ever since. It was not, however, so vital a concept when dictionary making began, some four millennia in the past, and, important or not, it must wait to be answered until the story of those earliest of "dictionaries," and all that followed, has been pursued.

1

The First Lexicographers
and the First "Dictionaries"

In June 1900, the lexicographer James Murray, editor of the *New English Dictionary* and that year's Romanes Lecturer at Oxford, noted that "The English Dictionary, like the English Constitution, is the creation of no one man and of no one age . . . Its beginnings lie far back in times almost prehistoric. And these beginnings themselves, although the English Dictionary of today is lineally developed from them, were neither Dictionaries, nor even English."[1]

That Sir James, then still simple Dr. Murray, was right is beyond argument. But the history of lexicography, like any history, demands some fixed points, and for the development of what we call the English Dictionary there can be established a pivotal moment around the mid fifteenth century. It is the composition, if not yet the actual publication, of the *Promptorium parvulorum clericorum,* the supposed product of the anchorite monk Galfridus, or Geoffrey the Grammarian. This work, which seems to have been written around 1440, and appeared in print about fifty years later, is generally seen as the earliest English dictionary. It was in fact an English-Latin dictionary—a purely monolingual English lexicon would not arrive until 1604—but its importance is that for the first time there appeared a dictionary that placed the English first and the Latin translation after. But dictionaries, however seemingly venerable, do not spring fully formed from nowhere. One need only glance at Geoffrey's preface to see a number of acknowledgments, all pointing to those sources, some specified, some general, which underpin his creation. Some are relatively recent, others can be traced back into antiquity. The nature of lexicography is that each new dictionary draws to a greater or lesser extent on its predecessors. The *Prompto-rium,* which sets "proper" English dictionary making on its eternally unfinished journey, conforms absolutely to type. With that in mind, it is worth looking at a number of those sources and noting how, as Sir James Murray pointed out, the nascence of today's lexicography is indeed "far back in time."

Lexicography, the writing of dictionaries, is as old as written language. It dates back to Sumerian, the language spoken by the tribes who from the fifth to the second millennium B.C. occupied southern Mesopotamia, an area situated between the rivers Tigris and Euphrates that roughly equates with modern Iraq. By 3000 B.C. the inhabitants of such Sumerian city-states as Erech, Kish, and Lagash were both militarily and economically powerful and culturally sophisticated. They produced pottery and metalwork of a high standard, and probably invented cuneiform or "wedge-shaped" writing. This writing was developed for inscription, with a sharpened reed, upon the clay tablets that were the basis of the wide-ranging Sumerian bureaucracy as well as of a written culture that produced such works as the religious *Epic of Gilgamesh* (c. 2750 B.C.). By 2500 B.C. the world's first libraries were being set up in Shuruppak (modern Fara) and Eresh (Abu-Salbikh). Within these libraries, in which the "books" were in fact collections of cuneiform-covered tablets, were found Sumeria's remarkably extensive collections of word lists. It was a culture in which the concept of order permeated every aspect of life. To the Sumerians an object existed only if it had a name; thus these word lists were nothing less than a register, in the most literal sense, of the known world.

A non-Semitic culture, Sumeria had for its main rivals the Semitic tribes of Akkad or Agade, their northern neighbors. And it was the conquest of Sumeria by Akkad, around 2340 B.C., that led to what, in the loosest possible sense, can be termed the world's first ever "dictionary." The triumphant Akkadians, who had traditionally been viewed by the Sumerians as a culturally inferior tribe, believed that as well as simple conquest, the best way of taking over Sumeria was to assimilate the national culture. Among the aspects of that culture they absorbed was one of its most basic artifacts: the cuneiform language, and with it the vitally important word lists for which it was used. And it was this assim-ilation that made necessary the world's first attempts at written translation, and with them what can be termed pioneer lexicography.

In its earliest incarnation lexicography was not a monolingual discipline. The words that appeared in the first collections were not defined in their own terms and their own language, as, say, are those incorporated in today's *OED* or *Webster.* They were bilingual word lists, intended, quite simply, to make one language comprehensible to those who spoke and read another. While Sumeria and Akkad used the same cuneiform script for writing, the languages represented by that script were quite different. Akkad was a Semitic culture, and its language was Semitic, like Hebrew or Arabic, and used inflection, in which a single word is altered to denote the changes grammar demands in a given context. Sumerian, a non-Semitic language, appeared *sui generis.* It seemed to have no links to any other language, although subsequent researches have posited links with the Dravidian languages of Southern India. It is an agglutinating language, in other words one that works from a list of basic word elements, which are combined as required to form words. Thus what the Sumerians called a "giant caterpillar," using the relevant elements, the Akkadians called simply "a dragon," and Sumer's "mouse of destruction" was Akkad's "rat." These distinctions point up a further cultural difference, which spilled over into language. While the Sumerians concentrated on order, the Akkadians preferred observation and explanation.

To bridge the gap, culturally and linguistically, the Akkadians compiled their own versions of what was an extensive collection of Sumerian word lists and in doing so created these pioneering bilingual dictionaries. Such a dictionary would offer the old Sumerian term, a note on its pronunciation, and an Akkadian translation. There are even polyglot lists, found in marginal areas such as Anatolia and northwest Syria, in which Hittite and even on occasion Hurrian and Ugaritic translations are appended. The lists themselves comprise tens of thousands of entries. There were nine major groups in all. Between them they offered lists of occupational terms, of kinship terms, of terms covering a variety of human activities, and so on. The *HAR-ra* (Sumer) = *hubullu* (Akkad) list, for instance, comprised 24 tablets, on which were inscribed over 9,700 separate entries. These included legal and administrative terms, trees and wooden artifacts, reeds and reed artifacts, pottery, hides and copper, other metals, domestic and wild animals, parts of the body, stones, plants, birds and fish, textiles, geographic terms, and those for food and drink. Other tablets offered lists of synonyms and antonyms, of both simple and compound cuneiform logograms (single letters representing whole words). Later on there also developed a series of lists which reversed the process, explaining Akkadian words to Sumerian speakers.

On a day-to-day basis the lists were used primarily for the training of future scribes and as such make it clear that this earliest style of lexicography is the precursor of a long-lasting tradition: the use of dictionary making as an adjunct to the education of the next generation of scholars in the classical texts of their predecessors. (This philosophy is a persistent one in lexicography, and it can be

seen again in Rome and Byzantium, in the "hard word" dictionaries of the seventeenth century, and even in the *OED,* which can, to some extent, be viewed
as an undertaking dedicated to helping in the reading of the great English-
language works of the previous millennium.) Such lists would be read in the
eduba, a Sumerian term translated by Akkadians as "tablet house."

There was no doubt, certainly in the scholarly atmosphere of the *eduba,* that
while Akkad might now possess the political power, culture was still very
much in Sumerian hands. Sumerian was still the language of privilege. "A
scribe who does not know Sumerian—what kind of scribe is he" ran a contemporary proverb. Education, at least at its higher levels, was carried out in
Sumerian, which may not have delighted the young Akkadian scribes. There
was a good deal of basic copying, which must have been tedious. A contemporary verse suggests:

> *If you have learned the scribal art, you had recited all of it,*
> *the different lines, chosen from the scribal art,*
> *(the names of) the animals living in the steppe to (the names of) artisans*
> *you have written (but) after that you hate (writing).*[2]

It was a magnificent undertaking, but as far as the growth of lexicography is
concerned, it stopped short when, *c.* 1750 B.C., Sumeria and Akkad were swal-
lowed into a greater single entity, that of Babylonia. Ideally, one would be able
to trace the Sumerian/Akkadian legacy through to Greece, where in the second
century B.C. there is a resurgence of lexicographical efforts, but facts stand in
the way of theory. The link, as far as current scholarship can discern, is simply
not there.

Where, however, the lexicography of old Babylonia does reach forward to a
newer world can be seen in style, rather than substance. It developed further the
concept of using the dictionary as a way of helping contemporary scholars grasp
the works of their esteemed predecessors. As Snell-Hornby suggests, the relationship between Akkadian and Sumerian was much like that between English,
or any other "vulgar" tongue, and Latin some three thousand years later.[3] It is
that of "cultural domination." In both cases it was necessary for the scholar to
gain a working knowledge of the "dead" language in order to study the texts
that still dominated the culture in which he lived. As far as English went, until
Cawdrey's *Table Alphabeticall* of 1604 bilingual lexicography was the rule. And
even after that Latin-English / English-Latin dictionaries would continue to
appear. Latin also formed the base of such polyglot works as Calepino's *Dictionarium,* compiled originally sometime during the late fifteenth century, which

began appearing in 1502. Indeed, it was the plan for another classical dictionary, a Greek lexicon which would back its definitions with historical citations, alongside the recent developments in German philology, that lay behind the creation of the *OED* itself. And as far as the techniques of that lexicography are concerned—the concept of defining one word in terms of variety of synonyms—the same system (which is still central to dictionary making) was already at the heart of the relationship between the columns of Sumerian terms and the parallel lists in the language of Akkad.

The final link between the word lists of 2500 B.C. and the world of modern lexicography is the role of the dictionary, whether on clay tablets or the printed page, in the schoolroom. The student poring over Stanbridge's *Vocabula* in some chilly late-fifteenth-century English classroom was not that far removed from his peer, studying in somewhat warmer conditions, three millennia in the past. Both young men would be duty-bound to learn the older language as a passport to proficiency in their own.

Other empires came and went, but as far as lexicography goes, the period from the second millennium to the fourth century before Christ is silent. That silence is broken by two men, representatives of yet more empires, respectively those of Greece and Rome. Whether it was yet lexicography per se is arguable. As Worcester remarked, "It is doubtful whether the ancient Greeks and Romans ever wrote what would properly be called *dictionaries* of their respective languages."[4] Nonetheless their influence, if as nothing else then as men who concerned themselves with the study of words as words, cannot be discounted.

Greek lexicography emerged to take on a specific task: the interpretation of the first ever works of classical Greek literature, Homer's *Iliad* and *Odyssey,* which are believed to have appeared during the eighth century B.C. Homer, as Plato noted in *The Republic* "educated Greece," but for that education to take effect, it was necessary that his vocabulary, much of which had grown unintelligible in the intervening four hundred years, should be made accessible.[5] To fulfill this task, some form of interpretation was necessary and once again one sees early lexicography as a means of passing on the scholarly and cultural torch. As would reemerge 1,500 years later, with the accretion of explanatory translations written above the less comprehensible words in a variety of Latin manuscripts, this early Greek lexicography took the form of elucidating the opaque words, or γλῶσσαι ("glossai") for modern readers. Nor was Homer the only subject of such γλῶσσογραφοι ("glossographoi"), or gloss writers. Classical Greece had no one, all-encompassing language, and a range of specific dialects were used to delineate the various literary genres. Thus tragedies might be composed in Attic, but the lyric interludes that interspersed them would be in Doric. Once again, this gave rise to the need for *glossai,* this time to deal with the dialectal differences. A third source of analysis was ancient law, the language of which was invariably obscure. Another was practical: the texts were by no means perfect copies of the original; as they had passed from one generation of scribes to the next they had picked up a variety of errors and corruptions. These all had to be discovered and either replaced by what was hoped was the original word, or annotated by *scholia* or marginal notes. Punctuation, or more likely a lack of it, had to be worked out and inserted. Finally, Greek fascination with philosophizing about language made the provision of textual addenda even more alluring.

Unsurprisingly, the history of these early *glossai* is virtually lost. The names of a few authors and of a number of their works reappear in later books, but of the originals there are but fragments. One knows only that there existed glossaries dealing with Homer, with the medical pioneer Hippocrates, with various dialects, with half-forgotten plays and with the long-dead, but still renowned speeches of great orators. Most of these early works were produced at the philological school of Alexandria, which flourished between the fourth and third centuries B.C. This in turn was allied to the celebrated Library of Alexandria, the half million–plus volumes of which were traditionally said to have included those amassed by Aristotle and purchased by King Ptolemy II Philadelphus. Without the Library and the dedication of its scholars, it is unlikely that any of the texts that form the corpus of today's classical Greek studies would exist.

The Alexandrian glossaries were of various types: some alphabetical (a technique that cannot have lasted long, since it had to be reinvented for the glossaries of the eighth and ninth centuries A.D.), some based on the appearance of the glossed words in the text under consideration, some by semantic fields and so on. The first dictionary proper would appear to be that compiled by Aristophanes of Byzantium (257–180 B.C.), head of the Library *c.* 200 B.C. and the most famous philologist of his era. His dictionary, entitled *Lexeis* (Words), was part of a literary oeuvre which included the first critical editions of Homer, Hesiod, Pindar, and Anacreon, the regularization of Greek accents, and the creation of a set of special signs which could be appended to manuscripts as indicators of passages which were considered in some ways different to the rest of the original text.

The *Lexeis* was organized in several ways, typical of which is a section ordered by related classes, rather as a modern thesaurus is compiled. Thus Aristophanes gathered together a number of terms under the group "Designations of Ages." Typical entries included "*Brephos:* [a child] just born," "*Paidion:*

[a child] nourished by the wetnurse;" *"Paidarion:* [a child] walking and starting to talk." Like many of the dictionaries that came after it, the *Lexeis* was frequently amended, expanded, and generally brought up to date.

Aristophanes was succeeded in the Library by Aristarchas of Samothrace (*c.* 215–*c.* 143 B.C.), who ran the institution from 180 to *c.* 145 B.C. Aristarchas followed his predecessor in his development of many branches of learning and is widely acknowledged as the originator of professional scholarship. Indeed, Aristarchas himself may have composed a grammar, but no more than fragments survive, usually in the form of notes on classical authors which have been attached to a few manuscripts. Better known is his work as a commentator on Homer, Aristophanes, and other literary figures.

In many ways Aristarchus' greatest legacy was not a manuscript, but a man. His pupil Dionysios Thrax or Dionysius of Thrace lived from *c.* 170 to *c.* 90 B.C. As author of *Techne Grammatike* or "The Art of Letters," he is responsible for laying out the earliest surviving authoritative work on Greek grammar. As a professional himself, Dionysius was later a teacher of grammar and literature at Rhodes. He may well have been far more prolific, but this is his only surviving work. Dionysius' was the first formal Greek grammar, its guiding principles being the ability to distinguish the genuine from the false, an art he cited as the highest calling of the grammarian. The book starts out with a definition of the parts of the subject, of which the noblest, he declares, is the criticism of poetry. He then deals with parts of speech, declensions, and conjugations. He ignores syntax and style.

A short book, but a highly important one, the *Techne* would remain a standard work for many centuries. Indeed, it might be said to have become the basis of every Greek textbook that schoolboys, in England and elsewhere, would face until the year 1000. Its influence spread even further when around 400 A.D. it was adapted into Syriac and then Armenian by the Oriental scholars based at Nisibis and Edessa. These translations were almost unique: very few Western works were deemed worthy of such treatment. And from Greek grammars its influence spread to their Latin equivalents and then, since the Latin formulations inevitably were those chosen by the first grammarians of modern Europe, to the "modern languages." Its influence is further underlined by the number of scholars, both contemporary and subsequent, who felt it necessary to add their glosses and commentaries to Dionysius' original labors. Dionysius was forced into exile sometime around 145–144 B.C. when Emperor Ptolemy Euergetes II, the short-lived ruler of Alexandria, began a persecution of Greek literary men. He does not appear again in extant records.

. . .

The first of the great Roman grammarians was L. Aelius Stilo, who went into exile at Rhodes *c.* 100 B.C. It was possibly there that he may have met Dionysius Thrax, and acquired from him his knowledge of Alexandrian scholarship.

Whatever the truth, Aelius is the first Roman scholar recorded as using the conventional critical signs of the Alexandrians, as originally worked out by Aristophanes of Byzantium. Among his contributions to learning was an authoritative list of the genuine—rather than merely attributed—works of Plautus, whose supposed production far outstripped the plays he actually wrote and whose texts had become substantially corrupt after centuries of alteration. Aelius' pupil Marcus Terentius Varro (116–27 B.C.) also attempted to set out the Plautus canon, and the study of Plautus led both lexicographers to another fundamental function of their craft: the interpretation of "hard words."

A poet, satirist, antiquarian, jurist, geographer, scientist, and grammarian, Varro was perhaps the most prolific writer of his era. (St. Augustine would later wonder quite how a man who claimed to have spent so much of his time reading the works of others could have produced so many volumes of his own). In all he is supposed to have written more than 600 titles and according to Quintilian he was "the most learned of Romans," Nicknamed "Reatinus" after his birth at Reate in Sabine territory, his life mingled solid scholarship with somewhat less centered involvements in the political ups and downs of his time. As a young man, like the sons of many well-off Romans, he studied in Greece, in his case under Antiochus of Ascalon, a Skeptic who ran the Academy. One of his fellow pupils was allegedly the future orator Cicero, although he was somewhat younger. The two men certainly did know each other—then or later—for Varro dedicated his major work, *De lingua Latina,* to his friend. Cicero, in turn, dedicated to Varro the second edition of his *Academica.*

Varro returned to Rome in 81 B.C., aged thirty-five. Initially opposed to Julius Caesar—he fought for Caesar's rival Pompey in Spain during the civil war—he judiciously changed his allegiance once Caesar had won. In 47 B.C. he was named as the putative head of the public library whose creation Caesar was contemplating and was commissioned by Caesar to start collecting books. In 43 B.C. fortune swung against Varro, when he was proscribed by Mark Antony, but he escaped this official sentence of death and lost not his life but merely some property and books.

Of Varro's massive oeuvre only *De re rustica* ("on farming") survives complete; there also exist six books out of the twenty-five of his *De lingua Latina* ("on the Latin language"), and some 600 fragments of his *Saturae Menippeae* ("Menippean satires"). He died, perhaps unsurprisingly, with pen in hand.

Although the rest of Varro's works are lost, it is possible to list at least their titles, and a little of the topics they cover. The *Hebdomades* ("sevens"), or *Imagines* ("portraits") was a collection of character sketches of well-known Greeks and Romans. Each sketch had its own colored portrait of the subject, and each boasted an accompanying epigram. Other works include the antiquarian treatise *Antiquitates rerum humanarum et divinarum* ("human and divine antiquities"): this was a historical encyclopedia, dealing with the history of Rome and of its religion; *De gente populi Romani* ("on the Roman nation"), concerning the prehistory and early chronology of Rome; *De vita populi Romani* ("on the way of life of the Roman people"), concerning the history and style of Roman society; *Disciplinae* ("studies"), on the liberal arts (grammar, dialectic, geometry, arithmetic, astronomy, medicine, and architecture), and *De philosophia,* a treatise on philosophy.

For the lexicographer, Varro's major contribution is in *De lingua Latina* ("on Latin"). Primarily a detailed study of grammar, it included notes on syntax as well as many etymologies. That the majority of these last were gloriously, absurdly inadequate, no more disqualified his work from lexicographical acclaim than such blunders would undermine the popularity of many later works. The book, of great importance in its author's lifetime and immediately beyond, vanished into obscurity once Rome had fallen. It was not until the eleventh century that *De lingua Latina,* along with a number of other important texts such as *The Golden Ass* of Apuleius and the *Histories* of Tacitus, was rediscovered by the monks of Monte Cassino, the mother monastery of the Benedictines, under their abbot Desiderius (1058–87). All these texts, representing the new outburst of interest in the classics, would be revived as central to the emergent culture of humanism. Such figures as Petrarch and Boccaccio were aware of them. In 1355, after obtaining a manuscript containing *De lingua Latina* on a visit to Naples, Boccaccio actually copied out Varro's efforts so as to pass them on to his fellow writer. His work was absorbed into Ambrosius Calepino's *Dictionarium,* the great polyglot work that dominated sixteenth-century dictionary making, and thence into the Latin-English dictionaries and the monolingual English volumes that followed them.

Varro was not the only Roman to be absorbed into the works of a later civilization. Verrius Flaccus (*fl.* 14 A.D.), "a man famous for his powers of instructing, etc."[6] was the author of *De significatione verborum* ("on the meaning of words"), a vital source for Calepino and after him such English lexicographers as Sir Thomas Elyot, Thomas Thomas, Baret, Rider, Holyoake, and Gouldman. It focuses on the explanations of obscure and "hard" words. Verrius was a freedman under the emperor Augustus and rose to become tutor to Augustus' grandsons. He was celebrated for the fine ancient books he gave out as prizes to favored pupils. His own lost discussion of language and grammar drew heavily, as was the tradition, on his predecessors, in his case the authors of the Republic. He was also interested in chronology, and erected a stone calendar in his native town, Praeneste. Of the original work only 70 of a total of 128 parchment leaves survive: letters after M are lost. What remained was reissued in a lexicon compiled by Sextus Pompeius Festus in the second century A.D. and gaps in this text were further supplemented from the abridgment of a letter by Paulus Diaconus in the eighth century.

The precise moment at which the focus of Roman imperium shifted from the seven hills of Rome to those of Constantinople is notoriously hard to pin down. The cultural shift, both from Greece and Rome, is equally slippery, but there is no doubt that among the preoccupations of Byzantine scholarship lexicography had an important place. Once again, the lexicographer works as baton carrier, taking over his segment of the race with his explanation of the now-obscure vocabulary of past masterpieces, and by his efforts passing on knowledge to a new generation. The purpose of the Byzantine lexicon is very much to act as a repository of learning, offering the scholar a means of better understanding and appreciating the classical texts which he or his peers are rediscovering, preserving, criticizing, and above all handing on. The language, Attic Greek, was at least five hundred years out of date; it was, in fact, a foreign tongue, for all that the Byzantine readers and writers were themselves ostensibly Greeks. It is a lexicography of the élite, unashamedly so, but it can also be seen as prefiguring the "hard word" compilations of the seventeenth century.

Further similarities to a later era can be seen in the way in which the Greek scholars of Byzantium believed that the ultimate in literary perfection was Attic prose, the language of Athens of 500–300 B.C. There was a "conscious desire on the part of educated Greeks who regretted the reduced state of their country to restore dignity and self-respect by nostalgic imitation of the language that had been written in the days of their great ancestors of classical Athens under Pericles and Demosthenes."[7] The sources of seventeenth-century dictionaries reflect in a similar way this desire to return to a mythologized classical past, or at least in this case to the classics as rediscovered by the Renaissance. England's lexicographers may not have been lacking in self-confidence as regarded their own language, but they were catering to a class, the aspirant bourgeoisie, who wanted their culture to be backed by a solid stratum of classical scholarship. In both cases dictionary makers looked steadfastly backward at age-old texts. A further factor in the renewed interest in these texts for Byzantium was the wholesale transference of the old papyrus texts onto a new medium, the parchment codex. Between the second and fourth centuries virtually the whole body of classical literature underwent such "rewriting."

Spurred on by these cultural beliefs, there emerged many such lexicographers, their efforts spanning much of the first millennium, busying themselves to perpetuate the lives of the classics; by the time Western Europe was ready to reassume its cultural supremacy, they in their turn had become the sources for a whole new world of dictionary making. One cannot list them all, but a few of the more important are undoubtedly worthy of mention.

One of the earliest is Julius Pollux (180–238). A Greek sophist and grammarian of Naucratis in Egypt, Pollux had taught the Roman emperor Commodus (a somewhat unstable figure whose announcement that he was the reincarnation of Heracles would lead to his swift assassination). His contribution to lexicography was the *Onomasticon,* literally a "list of proper names" and one of "a large number of lexicographical guides . . . composed for the aspiring writer."[8] It offered an extensive Greek vocabulary, including many synonyms and antonyms. Its arrangement was similar to that favored by Aristophanes of Byzantium in his *Lexeis.* The version that survives is a much-shortened one. Pollux covers a wide range of subjects, and offers a selection of vital information regarding the ancient world, especially in the areas of music, the ancient theater, and the Athenian constitution. It has, *inter alia,* some 33 discrete terms of abuse for a tax collector. Its printed version was by the printer Aldus Manutius (Aldo Manuzio), whose edition appeared in Venice in 1502. A Latin edition came out in 1542, edited by Rudolphus Gualtherus at Basel. It was thus available to influence such English lexicographers as Withals, whose own *Shorte Dictionarie for Yonge Beginners* (1553) eschewed the usual alphabetical sequence for something much more thematic.

Another such guide, long lost to the modern world, was by Pollux's contemporary Phrynichus. This too aimed to help the aspirant Greek scholar, but in this case by citing some four hundred specific expressions—all of which were to be avoided.

Quite how important Hesychius of Alexandria (*fl.* fifth century A.D.) was among his peers remains debatable. But his work has survived, albeit drastically abbreviated and as much through luck as judgment—since it was never an especially popular lexicon—and that in itself gives him a place in lexical history. A Greek lexicographer, Hesychius was a colleague of Theodosius the

Grammarian, author of the *Canons,* a list of grammatical forms of Greek nouns and verbs, accompanied by many complex rules. Hesychius wrote a short lexicon or glossary, explaining a variety of uncommon words and technical terms. It exists only in one badly preserved fifteenth-century manuscript, itself an abridgment of the original document. As Hesychius is the first to admit in his dedicatory letter, his is a compilation of earlier works. That said, he claims to have added a large amount of material through his own research. Its importance today is in its inclusion of some extremely rare terms, thus preserving a range of vocabulary that had often been superseded in daily use by more accessible homonyms. Such words make it especially useful when looking at Greek dialects and inscriptions. Hesychius' lexicographical work also included his abridgment of the appealingly named *Periergopenetes* ("impecunious students"). This second-century work, by Diogenianos, was itself drawn from a larger work by Pamphilos, which had appeared a century earlier. Hesychius himself was edited in the early sixteenth century by Marcus Musurus.

Hesychius' work appears to have had one main contemporary rival, a lexicon that appeared in the Middle Ages, but which may well have been written by Bishop Cyril of Alexandria (d. 444), a man otherwise notorious as the instigator of the Christian mob who murdered the pagan mathematician, astronomer, and philosopher Hypatia in 415.

With the appearance of another Christian cleric, Photius (*c.* 810—*c.* 891), one meets a man who is widely accepted as the most important figure in Byzantine classical studies. Like so many of these early lexicographers "his biography is obscure at the points where we should most like to have information"[9] but certain details can be set down. Despite the fact that he would in time twice become Patriarch of Constantinople—in 858 and 877—and in that role be one of the central figures in the promotion of the growing schism between what would become the Eastern (Greek) Orthodox and the Roman Catholic churches, his elevation within the hierarchy came relatively late. Indeed, he was still a layman a week before his first appointment to the patriarchal throne and, so he claimed, accepted the honor much against his will. Prior to this he enjoyed a distinguished career as a civil servant and *c.* 855 was sent on an embassy to the Arabs. His first patriarchate lasted for nine years, after which he fell from grace and went into exile for the next ten. Then in 877, he was returned to popularity as suddenly as he had been deposed and resumed his role as patriarch, for nine years more. Then, again, he was deposed. He died before he could be offered the throne for a third time.

Photius is as celebrated a scholar as he is a theologian, and his most important works were penned prior to his becoming Patriarch. His education is unknown; it was presumably first-rate, since he came from a good family and would have drawn on the prestige offered by his uncle—the patriarch Tarasius. Whether he enjoyed relations with any one especially gifted teacher is equally unknown. Certainly he showed himself to be interested in a number of diverse topics from a relatively early age. What is known is that so far above his contemporaries was Photius rated that one hostile commentator put it about that he, like Faust, had made a pact with the Devil, in this case in the form of a Jewish magician, surrendering his religious faith in return for knowledge and worldly success. Such smears notwithstanding, Photius did win himself a position at court, where as well as gaining the trust of the emperor he managed to run something of a private literary club. Prior to his leaving to negotiate with the Arabs over the return of prisoners of war, he composed for his brother, another Tarasius, a list summarizing all the books that he and his friends had been reading, with an emphasis on those that had been discussed when Tarasius had been unable to attend.

This summary, known as the *Bibliotheke* ("library," or literally and originally, "a box that contains papyrus rolls") or the *Myriobiblos* ("vast compendium"), contains 280 accounts of books read (usually called codices). The summaries vary in size, running anywhere from a couple of lines to seventy-plus pages. Detail varies, but most have a synopsis of the text. As Reynolds and Wilson suggest, Photius appears to have been the inventor of the book review. A little over half the books are theological; the remainder are Greek prose writers, ranging from classical authors to near contemporaries. In the years that followed many of the manuscripts were destroyed and without the *Bibliotheke* one would have no idea that they had ever existed. For instance, of the thirty-three historians he cites, the works of twenty have vanished forever.

In the realm of lexicography Photius compiled a work of which the short title is the *Lexicon,* and which, properly translated, is the "Alphabetical list of words which lend particular elegance to the compositions of orators and prose writers." It was a book which Photius obviously felt himself obliged to write: he had suggested in the *Bibliotheke* how useful such a volume would be. For more than fifteen hundred years it seemed that the *Lexicon* was as lost to posterity as many of the works cited in the *Bibliotheke,* but in 1959 the first complete copy was discovered in an obscure monastery in Macedonia. Once again, like many of these early dictionaries, designed to help scholars appreciate otherwise impenetrable works of classical Greek, it is as valuable for its mention of otherwise unknown works as for the actual definitions or translations of difficult words. The main aim of this lexicon was to bring together a number of other works of a similar kind; thus while he incorporates a number of quotations from the poets, it is possible that he did not actually read the works himself. Nor was this his only lexicon; it appears that he compiled at least two others. A final proof of his interest in "correct" language comes in his treatment of the letters he received from his friends. As well as acknowledging the communication he seems to have been unable to resist writing back to correct their grammar.

While Photius and his peers and successors, typically Arethas (c. 860–c. 935), the late-ninth-century archbishop of Caesarea, all played their part in keeping classical Greek culture alive, and to a greater or lesser extent perpetuated contemporary lexicography, the supreme example of Byzantine dictionary making is the *Suda* or *Souda* (from Greek *he Souda*: the fortress), a work of unknown authorship which appeared around the end of the tenth century. Despite what might appear to be a simple task of translation, the word *Suda* was assumed by later commentators to be the name of an actual person, usually rendered as "Suidas." This misapprehension began with later Byzantine writers, and continued until well after World War II. "For Attic phrase in Plato let them seek, | I poach in Suidas for unlicens'd Greek" remarks Pope in the *Dunciad* (1728),[10] and the assumption was still going strong when DeWitt Starnes and Gertrude Noyes repeated it without modification in their *Renaissance Dictionaries* (1954).

All that can be stated of the authorship of the *Suda* is that it was prepared by a group of scholars. They were building not merely on the long-term work carried out by a succession of Byzantine predecessors, but on that set in motion by the emperor Constantine VII Porphyrogenitus (905–59), something of a scholar himself. Constantine ruled nominally from 913–59, but between 919 and 944 was forced into virtual retirement by the usurper Romanus I. During this lengthy interregnum he turned, among other pursuits, to the compilation of various manuals of state. Apart from any governmental function, these quasi-encyclopedic documents, based on a wide range of historical sources, fulfill the continuing role of such collections in preserving old texts that otherwise might have vanished. This tenth-century tradition was continued by a new emperor, John Tzimisces (969–76), and it was probably during his reign, or possibly that of his successor, Basil II (976–1025), that the *Suda* appeared. The date can be further narrowed down through a couple of references, by no means complimentary, to the patriarch Polyeuctus (956–70), whose career is noted as being "in our own time."

The *Suda* is a mixture of both dictionary and encyclopedia. It is a huge work, running to 2,785 printed pages in the edition published in 1928, and containing some 30,000 entries. Of these a disproportionate 5,000 deal with the works of Aristophanes and the *scholia* that accrued to them. A lesser proportion, but still a notable one, is that devoted to Homer. The immediate source of much of the material can be seen in the works of Constantine, no more than fifty years old themselves. His efforts, or those of an unknown team that he assembled, provide many quotations from the Greek historians. Indeed, it has been suggested that one of Constantine's writers may have moved on to working on the *Suda* and taken his knowledge and his sources with him. Older by far, but central to the work, are the literary biographies, which seem to have been extracted directly from Hesychius, albeit in a much reduced form, since the *Suda* was drawing on an epitome of his work, rather than on the original text. Other sources include the *Palatine Anthology* (a unique tenth-century anthology, the first copy of which was later discovered in the library of the Count Palatine at Heidelberg), which the authors appear to have consulted directly, and extracts from the works of a wide range of historians, grammarians, and biographers. Not all the material is completely accurate, some is downright mistaken, but although the *Suda* is by no means an example of the highest scholarship, it remains a fascinating compilation.

Given the essentially carnivorous nature of lexicography—each dictionary snacking, as it were, on one or more of its predecessors prior to moving on to display its original researches—much of what has been described, at least in the areas of Greece, Rome, and especially Byzantium, would be incorporated in the earliest English, or more properly Latin-English and English-Latin dictionaries. Filtered through successive dictionaries, the works of Varro or the *Suda,* however indirectly, are as important to the lexicography of the fifteenth century as they were to that of their own era. Dictionaries continued to eat up material which had come before, and if the efforts of three great empires were considered suitably palatable, no less appetizing were the more recent publications of medieval Europe, especially the bilingual dictionaries and grammars of such scholars as Hugo of Pisa, Papias the Lombard, Joannes Balbus or Giovanni Balbi and Isidore of Seville. All these men were essentially working from one standpoint: the need to take on board the developing shift of their text from Latin, the traditional language of learning, to the "vulgar" (as in "common," thus the "vulgar tongue"), local language, e.g., English, French, and so on. To help themselves they began creating "vocabularia," lists of words arranged not in alphabetical order, but by conversational topics (rather like today's phrasebooks for tourists).

Among the earliest of such compilers was Isidorus Hispalensis, or Isidore of Seville (*c.* 570–636), later canonized as St. Isidore, whose best-known work is the self-explanatory *Originum sive etymologiarum libri* ("books of origins or etymologies"), a book designed as a wide-ranging vade mecum by which the newly converted people of Spain might gain access to every aspect of their new, Catholic faith. Essentially an early encyclopedist rather than a lexicographer, elements of Isidore's work were still absorbed into the dictionaries of later years. His main influence can be found in the *Catholicon Anglicum*, but his efforts have also been incorporated in Hugo of Pisa's *Derivationes* and subsequently in Baret's *Alvearie* and Huloet's *Abecedarium*. Other English lexicographers such as Rider and Holyoake both acknowledge him: the latter cites Isidore for the etymologies of *equus, expertus,* and *Februarius*. Modern scholars have been less kind, and Leighton Reynolds and Nigel Wilson dismiss his work as an "encyclopaedic compilation of ancient knowledge and nonsense [which] was to become a standard work of reference in the libraries of the Middle Ages."

Hugo of Pisa, otherwise known as Ugucio or Ugutio, was the professor of ecclesiastical jurisprudence at the university of Bologna in the late 1170s, before moving on to become Bishop of Ferrara from 1178 to his death *c.* 1212. He is the author of the *Derivationes magnae sive dictionarium etymologicum*. His work provided an important source of for the mid-fifteenth-century English-Latin dictionary *Promptorium parvulorum,* and he is cited as such in the preface. As ever, Hugo looked to his antecedents, in his case the *Elementarium doctrinae erudimentum* of Papias, published *c.* 1053. There are many manuscript versions of the *Derivationes,* but no printed edition.

Giovanni Balbi, Johannes de Balbis, Joannes Balbus or, with reference to his hometown of Genoa, Johannes Januensis, comes somewhat later in the chronology (he died in 1298) but his work depends largely on that of Hugo, and before him, as did Hugo's own, on Papias. Like Hugo, Balbi is cited in the *Promptorium* as one of the "auctores, ex quorum collecta sunt vocabula hujus libelli" ("the authors from whom the vocabulary of this little book has been collected"). His dictionary, the *Catholicon* or *Summa,* was completed in 1286; its first printed edition was published in 1460 in Mayence (Mainz) by the pioneer printer Johannes Gutenberg. There were many subsequent editions. As well as Papias and Hugo, the work draws on "multis diversis doctorum texturis elaboratum atque contextum." Its printed edition runs to 700–800 folio pages. The work is divided into four prefatory sections on "Orthographia," "Ethimologia," "Diasintastica," "Prosodia," or spelling, etymology, syntax, and prosody or the study of versification. Then comes the dictionary itself, mixing words and proper names (of both places and people) in alphabetical order throughout the text. Basically an encyclopedic dictionary, and as such a repository of information both lexicographical and non-lexicographical, it was one of the most sought-after books of the fifteenth century and the pivotal medieval (rather than classical) dictionary.

As the product of a scholar of the disdained thirteenth century, Balbi's work appalled the humanist Erasmus, who dismissed it as yet another example of the century's academic mediocrity. Later scholars felt much the same. But for all the inelegance of its text, and the errors which Balbi makes, it still has the kudos of being the first Latin dictionary to appear after the fall of the Roman Empire and the effective destruction (or at least dispersal) of the language. And, carping aside, it was good enough for his contemporaries, and in time for the author of the *Promptorium parvulorum,* who refers to and quotes from it throughout his own dictionary, and even later for Thomas Thomas, whose Latin-English *Dictionarium* appeared in 1587. One final point, perhaps the most important that should be made as regards Balbi's efforts, is that if the substance of the *Summa,* or at least the fifth section, which contains his "dictionary," can essentially be described as the assembling of a variety of material that was already, if not always known, then certainly available, then the style was far more his own. Neither Hugo nor Papias offered consistent alphabetical order, running from start to finish. Balbi did. And as Laurent Bray has suggested, in so doing Balbi moved away from the church-dominated systems seen in his predecessors to a more modern scheme, as demanded by an increasingly secular readership.[11] That a late-thirteenth-century book should still be seen as worthy of a new edition in 1460 underlines the needs that Balbi addressed. There would be twenty more printed editions by 1500. Not only was it the most important work of its era, it also served as the basis of lexicographical developments through to the sixteenth century. Subsequent lexicographers "extracted Balbi's words just as one takes stones from mediaeval ruins in order to create new buildings."[12]

Two final figures, or more properly one final figure and one final family, ought to be considered here. Both appear rather later in the chronology, but both drew extensively on the past and in their turn had a substantial influence on English as well as European lexicography.

Ambrosius Calepinus, or more often Calepino (1435–1511), must stand as one of the most single-minded lexicographers ever. His entire working life was dedicated to creating the *Dictionarium ex optimis quibusquam authoribus studiose collectum . . .* which appeared initially in 1502 and ran to dozens of editions, coming out time and time again for the next two hundred years. He went blind in the effort.

The dictionary was first published in 1502 at Reggio in northern Italy, and was dedicated to the senate and people of Bergamo, the nearest town to

Calepino's home of Calepio. There then followed a series of editions (1510, 1515, 1520, and 1531), each printed in a different Italian town. These first editions were in Latin only, but as the sixteenth and then seventeenth centuries passed, the *Dictionarium* expanded, both in content and in languages. Hebrew, Greek, French, Italian, German, Spanish, and English were all added; there were at least sixteen editions, all coming from the famous Aldus press, between 1542 and 1583; in 1609 the French writer Passerat published an octoglot edition, and there were many more. It was especially popular in France, where the Latin version began appearing in 1514. A French vocabulary was added to the *Pentaglottos* (five-language) edition of 1545 and some fifty-four editions appeared in France between 1568 and 1599. The largest *Calepine* of all was its ultimate edition, in which each entry covered no less than eleven languages. One only needs leaf through this massive folio, as thick as two volumes of today's *OED* and on substantially larger pages, every entry a marvelous combination of fonts and typography, to sense the breadth of the learning and appreciate its influence. Latin editions appeared in England from its initial publication, although English as such was not included until the ten-language editions that started with that of 1585.

The *Calepine,* as it became known, was thus the most influential dictionary of its period. It is cited in many subsequent works and such English lexicographers as Rider, Baret, Withals, and especially Thomas Thomas and, very likely, Sir Thomas Elyot were deeply indebted to Calepino's work. As DeWitt Starnes has noted, "During the whole period of the Renaissance scarcely an important dictionary was published which did not reflect directly or indirectly the influence of Calepine."[13] It also served as a bridge to the past. On his title page Calepino listed his sources, announcing that they were, naturally, "optimis authoribus" (by the very best authors) and listing the names of Nonius Marcellus, Pompeius Festus, M. Varro, Pedianus, Servius, Donatus, Perottus, Laurentius Valla, Tortellius, Suidas, "aliisque compluribus." As had happened previously and would often reoccur throughout lexicographical history, one can see the way in which the accepted classics or quasi classics of the past are mustered to give authority to the putative classic of the present day.

Calepino's major influence appears to have been the twenty-four chapters of the *Lexicon de partibus aedium* of Franciscus Grapaldus, which had been published in 1494. Although Grapaldus' work translates as the "lexicon of the parts of a house," and each chapter duly begins with a discussion of just such a vocabulary, the author rarely restricts himself to so narrow a vision. Thus his chapter on the "Apotheca" or wine shop moves briskly from the shop to the wine cellar and then to "the terms signifying the various types of vessels used to contain wine, the kinds of wines, the colors and flavors, grapes and other fruits and plants from which wine is made, testing of wine (*vini probatio*) for dilution, the wholesome and pleasurable uses of wine, and so forth. Treated in a similar manner is 'Gynaecium' (Book II, Chapter 5), the part of the house designed for women. This term suggests at once looking glass (*speculum*). Then follow rouge (*pupurissum*) for the lips and cheeks, ceruse, or white lead, for the neck and breast; medicines (*tetanothra*) to smooth wrinkles in the face; ointment (*psillothram*) to remove superfluous hair; an instrument (*volsella*) to pluck hairs from the body or face; instruments for trimming and for curling the hair; soap, perfume, and jewelry; also cradles (*incunabula*), and the feeding and training of children."[14] As well as concrete terms Grapaldus adds many more general discussions of his subjects.

The original *Dictionarium,* in its Latin format, depends heavily on expounding etymology. It is in alphabetical order, although this is somewhat modified in that derivatives are always placed after the root word, irrespective of perfect A–Z order. Parts of speech are specified and citations, from the authors listed above, are placed as illustration of use and meaning. As was the contemporary way, there is a good deal of what modern lexicography might term extraneous matter. A variety of proper names, whether of people (both real and mythological), places, or things, are to be found among the headwords, listed in the proper alphabetical order. As Starnes adds, "The Calepine was thus at once a dictionary abounding in grammatical and etymological information and an encyclopedia especially instructive about men and matters of antiquity." Calepino also included brief discussions of most of the individual letters of the alphabet. The practice was imported to England by Richard Huloet, in his *Abecedarium* (1552), although as Gabriele Stein has pointed out, there was some precedent for these mini-essays in such Latin-English dictionaries as the fifteenth-century works *Medulla grammatice* and *Ortus vocabulorum.*[15]

Just as did America's modern "Webster," "Calepine" became a generic term for "dictionary." It can be seen in French, in the phrase *"Cela n'est pas dans son calepin"* ("That's beyond his understanding") and in English, in "bring anyone to his Calepin": to bring one to the utmost limits of his information. Like the dictionary itself, the term persisted through the seventeenth century and one finds the diarist John Evelyn using it as late as 1662. But it was as a sourcebook that the Calepine seems to have had its greatest influence. Lexicography is de facto plagiaristic; few sources have been so eagerly plundered as Calepino.

Like Calepino, the Estienne family (the French translation of the Latin *Stephanus,* under which surname some members are also known) is somewhat removed from the main characters of this chapter, but its influence, especially that of Robert Estienne, would be substantial come the sixteenth century. The family occupations of scholarship and printing had been founded when Henri Estienne (d. 1520) came to Paris from Provence and founded a printing house. His son Robert (1503–59) was printer to King François I. Exiled to Geneva because of his Calvinist faith, he was taken on as printer to John Calvin himself. Among his other productions, Robert Estienne compiled the *Thesaurus linguae latinae* (1532), acknowledged as the foremost Latin dictionary of the sixteenth century. Subsequent editions appeared in 1538 and 1539 and the *Thesaurus* was hugely influential on the Latin-English dictionaries of the era, typically on Thomas Cooper's *Thesaurus Linguae Romanae et Britannicae* (1565), largely modeled on the French original.

Robert's son Henri (*c.* 1531–98) worked mainly in Geneva, following his father as a leading printer, although he traveled regularly in Europe. Henri Estienne was a classicist of renown, whose own *Thesaurus Graecae Linguae* appeared in 1572. He was also a satirist: the *Apologie pour Herodoe* mocks contemporary France and especially what he saw as Catholic credulity. The *Dialogue du nouveau françois italianisé* (1578) is a satire on the corruption of France by Italy. It is to Henri Estienne that the coinage of the quote/cliché *Si jeunesse savait, si vieillesse pouvait* is credited. The last of the relevant Estiennes is Robert's brother Charles (1504–64). He was a doctor and scholar but perhaps ill-suited to running the family business, which he duly inherited from his brother. It failed, and he died in a debtor's prison. Charles Estienne did, however, make one important contribution. In 1553 there appeared his lengthily titled *Dictionarium historicum ac poeticum, omnia gentium, hominum, locorum, fluminum ac montium antiqua recentioraque, ad sacras ac prophanas historias poetarumque fabulas intelligendas necessaria, vocabula . . . complectens.* Generally dismissed by his contemporaries as a mediocre work, especially when compared with his elder brother's efforts, this *omnium gatherum* of literary, historical, and geographical information was constantly rewritten, augmented, and above all plagiarized. Many of the earliest historical, biographical, and geographical dictionaries owed their origins to a trawl through Charles Estienne.

With the exceptions of Calepino and the Estiennes, who are undoubtedly full-fledged lexicographers in their own right and who have been placed here simply because of their influence on their English contemporaries and successors, all these scholars, whether considered above or for whatever reason left unremarked, form what might be called the protolexicographers. Their task is less that of defining words than of translating them, their primary aim to make accessible those treasures of past literature that underpin contemporary culture. Each work, as is the lexicographical way, builds upon its predecessors. Only the scribes of the Sumerian *edubas* stand on their own, though they too fulfill what would become the traditional role; indeed their antiquity gives them pride of place, even if one cannot, sadly, trace any legitimate continuity between them and their Greek, Roman, Byzantine, and early "European" successors.

As stated already, the first English dictionary "proper" is the *Promptorium parvulorum,* the "treasure house of words for the young." From the *Promptorium* onward the thread that is already apparent grows even stronger, and the line from that mid-fifteenth-century work to the present day can be traced from dictionary to dictionary. It has thirteen citations in the *OED,* three of them fittingly under the headword "ABC." Before reaching the *Promptorium* itself and dealing with other dictionaries that emerged during the fifteenth century, there are still a number of sources to mention. These, however, are almost all home-grown, stemming from English authors and compilers, and as such can be considered, along with the *Promptorium* itself, in a chapter of their own.

2

The Middle Ages: Putting It in Order

E nglish lexicography is generally accepted as beginning sometime around the early eighth century. Like the Greeks before them, the writers of early medieval England created glossaries, noting and explaining the *glossa* (from the Greek for a "hard" or "special" word) and adding an explanation to the manuscript being studied. As manuscripts were repeatedly copied, the glosses would be copied with them. After a while the glosses and manuscripts began to be separated: the monastery scribe would copy the manuscript by itself and then attach to it the relevant glossary, known as the *glossae collectae:* "collected hard words." As Sir James Murray explained:

> In the process of time it occurred to some industrious reader . . . to collect out of all the manuscripts to which he had access, all the glosses they contained and combine them in a list. In this compact form they could be learned by heart, thus extending the vocabulary at his command, and making him independent of the interlinear glosses, they could also be used in . . . school-teaching . . . Such was one of the fountainheads of English lexicography.[1]

Not that these proto "dictionaries" of the Middle Ages were strictly what we see as dictionaries—alphabetically arranged wordbooks, the cousins, as it were, of the encyclopedia (which might be described as an alphabetically arranged themebook). Although alphabetization had been known by the compilers of the Alexandrian glossaries that appeared 250 years before Christ, their knowledge had not spread West. The grammarians of the early Middle Ages were only beginning to experiment with such a scheme—which ran in any case in the face of quite antithetical theories of ordering—and it took several hundred years to develop fully. Thus the very earliest history of English dictionary making is as much about style—the basic order of the words that were listed—as it is about content—the vocabulary that made up the lists.

This process can be seen in the contents and arrangement of the four oldest surviving glossaries, which stand at the very head of English word collecting. Each is named for the library in which it is held: the *Leiden,* the *Epinal* and the *Erfurt* (two complementary works, the latter filling the gaps in the former), and the *Corpus* (held in Corpus Christi College, Cambridge). Generally regarded as the pioneer among them is the *Leiden,* the date of which, after some argument, has been placed in the early eighth century. It was probably compiled at St. Gallen in Switzerland and its basic vocabulary was Mercian (the language of the south Midlands) plus some elements of Kentish dialect. Arranged in two-column pages, the glossary is a collection of smaller glosses, each in the most basic alphabetical order—first letter or "A-order." All the words beginning with A were duly grouped together, but beyond the first letter there was no effort at classification; the user was forced to work through each entire section to discover the single word required.

Each section is headed by the text, almost always of an ecclesiastical work, from which it has been taken. Because all sections refer back to the text as written, the words are in inflected forms, i.e., the way they appear in that text, rather than in proper "dictionary form." Thus verbs may appear in tenses other than in the present and in forms other than the infinitive; nouns may be plural as well as singular. As well as the text-based material, there are also entries that must be assumed to come from other class glossaries, since here the nouns, always nominative, have a far more orthodox "dictionary" feel. The assumption is that they have already been processed.

Paradoxically, while the *Leiden* takes pride of place in lexicographical history, it is not in fact the oldest of these four old glossaries. That honor goes to the *Corpus,* cited by W. M. Lindsay, who edited it in 1921, as "England's oldest dictionary." But the very basic level of the *Leiden* glossary's alphabetization, and the fact that the work is broken down into a number of discrete lists, has caused the *Corpus* to cede it its position as the veteran. The *Corpus* itself has made notable progress in ordering its glosses. Probably not an original work, it is composed of two glossaries, both based on interlinear glosses, marginalia and on other, precreated glossaries. The first deals mainly in Hebrew and Greek words, and offers very little Old English. The second interprets Latin headwords by Latin or Old English definitions. Between them the glossaries run to 8,712 words. The first offers A-order only, but the second, and that which brings Old English to the fore, has AB-order, a sort on the first and second letters.

The rule of alphabetical order took time to grow. Gradually, as glossary followed glossary, one can watch the system that is taken for granted today developing. The first three-letter, ABC-order has been traced to a 94-page tenth-century manuscript in the Harleian Collection in the British Library. (MS Harley 3376.) It contains 5,563 entries, which end at the letter F, in the bulk of which both headwords and explanations are in Latin, although there are also some 1,500 definitions in Old English. Occasionally the scribe has even gone onto the fourth letter, ABCD-order. This level of sophistication is as far as Old English ordering goes. Other glossaries follow, but proper alphabetization does not fall into place until the Anglo-Norman period, starting with the Conquest of 1066.

Even then the rule was not all-encompassing. As late as the sixteenth century the hegemony of the alphabet could still find challengers. John Withals' *Shorte Dictionarie of English and Latin for Yonge Beginners* (the best-selling dictionary of its period) appeared in 1554 still defiantly proclaiming its thematic arrangement and offering, *inter alia,* times of the year, days of the week, the names of planets, winds, "serpents, woorms and creepinge bestes."

The apparent lethargy as regards sorting was due to the innate conservatism of those scholars who wished, as was then traditional, to promote an ordered, thematic world view. These men, known as the Schoolmen or Scholastics, based their disciplines on those pioneered by Flavius Aurelius Cassiodorus (who lived *c.* 490–*c.* 585 and wrote widely on Christian history and matters theological and bureaucratic as well as preparing a grammar), St. Isidore of Seville, and above all on St. Thomas Aquinas (*c.* 1225–74), "the quintessential encyclopedist of Roman Catholic thought."[2] Just as their peers in Islam, such as Ibn Qutayba (828–89) and Al Khwarizimi (*fl.* late tenth century), had set out a world view strictly in terms of its relationship to the precepts of the Koran, so did the Schoolmen attempt to order their world on the basis of the Bible. Given the importance of Greek learning, especially as far as science was concerned, neither religion could work on absolutely theological lines. It was important to synthesize the two traditions to provide a proper world order. This the Arabs had achieved in such works as the fourteenth-century Egyptian scholar Al-Nuwairi's massive 9,000-page work, *Nihayat al-'Arab Fi Funun al-Adab* ("The Aim of the Intelligent in the Art of Letters"). The Christian equivalent is Aquinas' unfinished but still substantial *Summa theologicae* (1273), "the culmination of Scholastic philosophy, the harmonizing of faith and reason and in particular the reconciliation of Christian theology with Aristotelian philosophy."[3] All this duly worked to provide as seamless as possible a world picture.

Assembling words in alphabetical order ran contrary to this: instead of keeping chunks of related information in a single area, the relevant words were spread across the alphabet, thus fragmenting rather than concentrating the theme. This was not the academic way. As Tom McArthur puts it, it "must have seemed a perverse, disjointed and ultimately meaningingless way of ordering material to men who were interested in neat frames for the containing of all knowledge."[4] But as knowledge grew and with it access to learning, sorting on the alphabet gained strength. The concept of amassing *omne scibile* ("all that is knowable") which underpinned the Scholastics' work could not survive in this themeless world. The thirteenth-century Schoolmen had as little chance of fixing the bounds of knowledge as would have the eighteenth-century lexicographers of fixing the bounds of language, however much they might wish otherwise. Yet, although modern dictionary users have become accustomed to alphabetical order rather than grouping by subject, there is still a case for considering such an arrangement as downright destructive of intellectual gain: why break up a topic into such tiny morsels, spread willy-nilly (other than alphabetically) through a fat volume? But technology, as ever, provided the impetus for change, and the development of printing, the cultural antithesis of the Schoolmen, with its emphasis on individual letters rather than on words, let alone themes, became the basis of information processing. A to Z became the order of the day. In the end it had one fundamental appeal: everyone knew it. In parallel to this was another aspect of learning, although in this case absolutely supported by the Schoolmen, which was equally encouraging of dictionary making. Whatever version of the "vulgar tongue" might be spoken in your country, the élite language, the language of academe and of the church, the language that mattered, was Latin. And just as the scholars of Byzantium created word lists to help understand the texts of ancient Greece to which they turned for intellectual validation, so did those of the Middle Ages begin creating the prototype dictionaries, *vocabularia* (vocabularies) or *nominales* (noun books) that helped them absorb and interpret their chosen texts, in this case primarily those of Rome.

Scholasticism was a construct of the past by the late fifteenth century, and by 1604, when Cawdrey produced the first English-English dictionary, the alphabet was the dominant form of listing. Its name, the *Table Alphabeticall,* is not mere coincidence. Cawdrey was proclaiming his own modernity. That said, Cawdrey still had to include a detailed explanation of his technique in his address to his "gentle readers." As he told them, "If thou be desirous . . . rightly and readily to vnderstand and to profit by this Table, and such like, then thou must learn the Alphabet, to wit, the order of the letters as they stand, perfectly without booke, and where every letter standeth."[5] Still mired in the Latin legacy, the letters I and J and U and V continued to be undifferentiated in most seventeenth-century dictionaries, and once the compiler strayed from the basic term, strict alphabetical order often foundered as compounds and derivatives were added to the list. Thus Thomas Blount, in his *Glossographia* (1656), places "epidemy" before "epidemical" and "nugatory" before "nuga-tion." Similarly these lexicographers still tended to what is known as *dégroupe-ment:* the allotting of a separate headword to each sense or compound. Thus John Kersey's revision of Edward Phillips' *New World of Words* (1706) has fifty discrete entries for "angle." On the whole seventeenth-century dictionaries averaged around 8 percent alphabetical errors in the word list, although some, like Blount, cut this back to 4.5 percent, while others, like Coles, reached 11 percent. By the time Samuel Johnson produced his *English Dictionary* in 1755, such aberrations had been largely eliminated, although even the doctor's work was not foolproof: for instance, *hodmandod* precedes *hodge-podge.* Some compil-ers, while following the alphabet, used it in surprising ways. Henry Cockeram's *English Dictionarie* (1623) offers not one but three alphabetical lists: one cites the "choicest" current vocabulary, the second a list of common words and their more learned synonyms, and the third has proper names, especially those of "Gods Goddesses, Giants and Devils, Monsters and Serpents, Birds and Beasts, Rivers, Fishes, Herbs, Stones, Trees, and the like."

That themes as much as the alphabet still had a major influence on early lex-icography is well illustrated in the works of perhaps the first English lexicog-rapher to have a recorded name. Abbot Aelfric (the Grammarian) lived around the early eleventh century and combined his ecclesiastical duties with work as an author and translator. Attempts have been made to link him with rather more illustrious clergymen, notably the roughly contemporary archbishops of Canterbury and York, both named Aelfric, but it would appear that he was indeed an abbot, although an important scholar too.

His links to the hierarchy probably developed through his works being so frequently used as referees in matters of theological argument, especially in the area of transubstantiation, toward which doctrine he was especially hostile. Aelfric was himself taught by a secular priest, with barely any knowledge of Latin, an experience which left him, somewhat ungratefully, with a lifelong disdain for such figures: "There was no-one who could write or understand Latin letters until Dunstan and Aethelwold revived learning," he declared in the Latin preface to his own grammar. Aelfric himself was for a while a pupil of Aethelwold (908?–984, bishop of Winchester, pioneer of British monachism and later canonized), which may make him a monk of the abbey of Abingdon, since Aethelwold was abbot there *c.* 954. When Aethelmaer, eorlderman of Devonshire and the great patron of West country monasticism, finished the abbey he was building at Cerne, he asked Aelfheah (954–1012), Aethelwold's successor as archbishop, to staff it with monks. Aelfheah sent Aelfric, by now "a monk and a mass-priest," to take charge of the new foundation. In 1005 he took over as abbot of Eynsham, another new foundation created by Aethelmaer. Aelfric remained on good terms with Aethelmaer and his son Aethelweard and much of his work was done for them. He wrote on theological doctrine and education, but his main works were translations and compilation.

Aelfric's main theological works are two books of homilies. Each contains forty sermons, translated from a variety of Latin originals. They were designed for use on Sundays and saints' days and are regularly interwoven with Aelfric's own emphatic opinions on various theological controversies. He often found himself opposed to the orthodox version as proposed by Rome. That the homilies were used by the Church in England as established doctrine only emphasizes Aelfric's importance as a theologian. Some pieces were still being reprinted and cited as theological authority in the early seventeenth century.

His *Dictionarium Saxonico-Latino-Anglicum* ("A Latin Grammar and Dictionary") appeared sometime during the early eleventh century. It was written for and dedicated to the boys of England and based on the grammars of Priscius (Priscian) and Donatus; it won Aelfric the nickname "Grammarius": the Grammarian. The dictionary runs to some 3,000 Latin words, each translated by one or more Saxon synonyms. The first printed version was published in Oxford in 1659 by the Anglo-Saxon scholar William Somner (1598–1669); a fragment of a twelfth-century edition was found by the bibliomane Sir Thomas Phillips (1792–1872) and published in 1838. The dictionary consists of thirty groups of words, covering a variety of topics. They deal with agricultural implements, ecclesiastical affairs, man, his relations and the parts of the body, food and drink, the house with its parts and what they contain, ships and their parts, and the names of birds, beasts, herbs, trees, colors, clothes, weapons, games, and certain heavenly bodies. Another grammatical work was the *Colloquium,* a dialogue written by Aelfric and edited by his disciple Aelfric Bata. An amusing reading book designed to teach the correct speaking of Latin to young scholars, it contains descriptions of the everyday life of men employed in various occupations: for instance a plowman, a king's huntsman, and a monastic scholar.

For Aelfric theology and scholarship were always intermixed, typically noting in the Saxon introduction to his *Homilies,* "men have need of good instruction, especially at this time, which is the ending of the world." There is a similar mixture to be found in his Latin preface to the dictionary:

> For I know that many will censure me for condescending to turn my mind to such studies, as the translation of an "art of Grammar" into English; but I conceive that such reading should be adapted to the use of boys, not of old men. I know that words can be interpreted many ways, but I follow a plain interpretation, in order to avoid giving disgust. If however our interpretation mislikes any one, let him say so when he will, we are content [to teach] as we have learnt in the school of the venerable prelate Æthelwold, who trained many in good ways. It must be known however that the art of grammar in many parts cannot easily be rendered into English . . . yet I think, as I have already said, that this book may be of use to young beginners. I marvel greatly that many shorten syllables in prose, which are short in metre, whereas prose is free from the laws of metre . . . yet I think it is better to invoke God the father reverently by lengthening the syllable, because God must not be subjected to the art of grammar.

Aelfric's motives are further explained in the Saxon preface:

> Young men should learn wisdom; it is the business of elders to instruct them; for by learning faith is preserved, and everyone that loves wisdom shall be happy . . . How should there be a supply of wise teachers for the people of God, unless they have been trained in learning while young? And how should faith be strong, if learning and teachers fail?

And he goes on to entreat those who copy his work to do it "exactly," noting darkly, with the moral confidence of one who is used to laying down religious law: "Heavy will be the guilt of the false copyist, unless he correct his blunders."

A vocabulary list of a century later works on very much the same basis, this time making its way through eighteen topics, each of which holds a number of subgroups. These include God, heaven, the angels, sun, moon, earth, and sea; man, woman, and their bodies; blood relations, professional and trades people; diseases; such abstract terms as "impious" and "prudent"; fishes; beasts; household equipment; and so on. The list has no author, but his humanity passes through the ages. After group 18, general terms, he stops writing, pausing only to remark: "We ne magon swa eah ealle naman awritan ne furor geencan," which can be paraphrased as "That's enough; I can't think of any more names to put in."

This list, of some 1,300 words, has been the subject of some confusion. It appeared in Wright's *Volume of Vocabularies* (1857) under the neutral title "Anglo-Saxon Vocabulary." Elsewhere, however, it has been cited as "Aelfric's Glossary." For a while it was also associated with a "lost" vocabulary that was supposedly once owned by the painter Peter-Paul Rubens. Current researches, spearheaded by Gabriele Stein, have given it a new name, the "London Manuscript," based on the majority of the original being held in the British Library, London.[6]

The flow of vocabularies continued to appear. Among them were a variety of anonymous Anglo-Saxon vocabularies and one labeled "Semi-Saxon." They show the gradual development of lexicographical technique, but for a more substantial influence (or certainly a weightier biography) one needs turn to Alexander Neckham or Necham (1157–1217), whose work was also published by Wright. Gossip once suggested that Neckham was the foster brother of King Richard I, the Lionheart. This may not be so, but certainly he was born in St. Albans on the same night as the future monarch. His mother acted as Richard's wet nurse and suckled both babies. He was educated in St. Albans, and can thus occasionally be found under his alternative name: Alexander de Sancte Albano. When still a young man he took charge of a school at Dunstable, an outstation of St. Albans Abbey. At some stage he had moved to Paris to study at the school of Petit Pons, an institution celebrated for the subtlety of its disputations (exercises in which parties formally sustain, attack, and defend a question or thesis, as practiced in the medieval schools and universities), and by 1180 he is noted there as being a distinguished teacher, for all that his pupils had given him the punning nickname *Nequam* ("wicked").

Neckham returned home in 1186, spent a year as head of the Dunstable school, and then applied to be head of that in St. Albans. The abbot, Warin, another aficionado of the pun, replied, *"Si bonus es, venias; si nequam, nequam"* ("If you are good, come; if wicked, do not"). Neckham did not get the job. After this he possibly took up a post as prior of St. Nicholas, Exeter, but no proof of this exists. He certainly did become an Augustinian canon and in 1213 became abbot of Cirencester. It is also possible that he made a trip to Rome with Walter de Grey, the bishop of Winchester, but in a work written in his old age—*De Laudibus Divinae Sapientiae*—Neckham states that his advancing age renders such journeys, which he would have liked to make, no longer feasible. Aside from his scholarly and ecclesiastical duties, much of the remainder of his life was spent at court. He died at Kempsey, Worcestershire, in 1217, and was buried at Worcester. Pun-prone to the last, his nickname, Nequam, is inscribed upon his tombstone, where it appears as part of his epitaph.

Neckham was a widely knowledgeable scholar, whose Latin was generally considered as superior to that of many contemporaries. Among his works is *De naturis rerum* ("of the nature of things"): a popular prose work on natural science, often quoted by Thomas More, among others. In it Neckham mixes the contemporary knowledge of the natural sciences with anecdotal illustrations. A verse version of *De naturis, De Laudibus Divinae Sapientiae* ("in praise of divine wisdom") omitted some anecdotes and added some new material. He produced a translation of Aesop's *Fables* and *De Contemptu Mundi* ("of the contemplation of the world") a verse work on monasteries.

His lexicographical work is contained in *Reportarium vocabularum,* a treatise on grammar, and *De Utensilibus,* a vocabulary of kitchen implements. The first work was widely respected, even if the alchemist Roger Bacon (1210–*c.* 1292), otherwise known as Dr. Mirabilis and the inventor of spectacles, demurred, saying that although "in many things he wrote what was true and useful, he neither has nor ought to have any title to be reckoned an authority."[7]

De Utensilibus, "a kind of vocabulary in the form of a reading book"[8] was described by Thomas Wright in his *Volume of Vocabularies:*[9]

> Neckham . . . begins with the kitchen, describes its furniture and implements and their several uses, and treats of the articles of foods and of the methods of cooking them. He then turns to the possessor of the house, describes his dress and accoutrements, when remaining at home or riding abroad, and introduces us . . . to his chamber and to its furniture. The chamber-maid is next introduced to us, with her household employments; and we are taken to the poultry-yard, with a chapter on the cooking of poultry and fish, and on the characteristics of good wine. We are next taught how to build a feudal castle, to fortify it, to store and to defend it; and this leads naturally to the subject of war in general, and to arms, armour and soldiers. From this we return to matters of a more domestic character—to the barn, the poultry-yard, and the stable, and to . . . weaving. The occupations of the country follow, and the author explains the construction of carts and waggons, the process of building an ordinary house . . .

Neckham goes on to deal with farming and its necessary implements, with navigation and ships, and the stores they carried, and finally "the tools, qualifications, and duties of a medieval scribe, the operations of the goldsmith, and a copious enumeration of ecclesiastical furniture, complete this curious treatise." And, as part of his notes on navigation, Neckham presents what must be one of the earliest references to the use of the magnetic compass.

All not so very "curious," perhaps, but at the time Neckham's listing of a relatively wide, but still specialized vocabulary, almost a list of dedicated jargon rather than a part of mainstream English, is a relatively rare production. On the whole vocabularies, however much they offered their definitions on a basis of related groups, still looked at a wider spread of general material. Dedicated or "class" glossaries would become increasingly common by the turn of the sixteenth century, and would contribute largely to the development of the new monolingual dictionaries of the seventeenth century.

Johannes de Garlandia, known in England as John of Garland, lived from *c.* 1180 to *c.* 1250. He was variously a theologian, chronologist, alchemist, versifier (but not a real poet), and above all a grammarian. Garland's name has always led to a good deal of confusion, which was not properly resolved until the mid-nineteenth century. Spelled variously De Garlandia, Garlandius, Garlandus and Gallandus, it has been associated with the twelfth-century French writer Gerlandus, with one John the Grammarian (either eleventh or thirteenth century), and with others. One source has suggested a link to the Clos de Garlande or Gallande, site of one of the most ancient schools of the University of Paris. Back on this side of the channel Garland has been tied, in Prince's *Worthies of Devon* (1810), to the Garland family, resident at Garland by Chumleigh, Devon. There were a number of noted Garlands in London at approximately the same time as the lexicographer: one John Garland was prebendary of St. Paul's *c.* 1200, another was sheriff of London in 1212.

However, as Garland himself sets down in his poem *De Triumphis Ecclesiae,* his mother was English, and only his nurse was French. That said, the same poem goes on to state his preference for France. As to his father, he makes no mention. He began his studies at Oxford, under the natural philosopher John of London. From there he moved to Paris, where he studied under Alain de Lille (or Alanus de Insulis, 1114–1203), one of the most illustrious scholars of his age and known popularly as "Doctor universalis." De Lille wrote, among other things a "Commentary on the prophecies of Merlin" and offered his own— invariably grim—predictions for the future of England.

When Count Raymond VII of Toulouse was forced to allow the establishment of a University at Toulouse in 1229, Garland was one of the professors selected for the faculty by its founder, the papal legate Romanus de Sancto Angelo. Garland taught at Toulouse for three years, during which time he amended what were apparently mistakes in the local estimation of the proper

dates for Easter, but after the death of the chancellor, Bishop Fulk or Folquet of
Marseilles, in 1231 the university began to decline. The faculty was no longer
paid and the students gradually dispersed. Many of these problems could be
traced back to the institution, *c.* 1229, of the Inquisition in the area, a move
that was deliberately set up to crush what was seen as the excessive independence of southern France and the Albigensian heretics who thronged there. As
Thomas Wright notes it was an increasingly anarchic era, however much such
anarchy might be justified.

> The violence of the French governors and the atrocities committed by the
> inquisitors had produced everywhere a spirit of resistance and the more
> resolute of the old national party, taking refuge in the woods and other
> hiding places, and in some of the castles and strongholds, where they
> were probably joined by many who sought only the opportunity of plun-
> dering and living riotously, prowled over the country, plundering their
> enemies and revenging themselves on all the papal agents and French
> who fell into their power.[10]

Given that Garland's university was unequivocally allied to the Papacy, its
teachers and students were automatically suspect, and even in actual danger of
their lives. Prudently, Garland chose to leave: he was apparently one of the first
to do so. Setting sail up the Garonne he found himself promptly turned over to
a band of outlaws by the boatman he had hired to help him escape north. Garland was detained and was on his way to the dungeons of the fortress of Castel-
Sarrasin, near Moissac, when an unspecified, but presumably melodramatic
"appearance in the heavens" caught his captors' interest. At the same time a
party of pro-Papacy troops arrived and rescued him. Further adventures followed, but Garland survived them all and arrived back in Paris in either 1232
or 1233. He remained there until his death. Garland maintained a high reputation as a teacher throughout his life and Roger Bacon, who had attacked
Neckham, was happy to join in the positive chorus. Another scholar, Erasmus,
was less impressed and later sneered at Garland as being no more than the best
of a singularly bad lot. Granted he knew a great deal, but in an age of such limited information, that was a dubious attainment at best. Nor was Erasmus
alone. In his preface to the *Promptorium,* the Victorian editor Thomas Way refers
to another document, the *Merarius.* He dismisses it as a "little relic of barbarous
Latinity . . . which seems suited to darken knowledge than to initiate," and
ascribes it to the hapless Garland.

But Erasmus' criticism was nearly three centuries in the future and in his lifetime Garland was happily content with his own reputation. He wrote widely, expounding on most aspects of the subjects that he taught and covered alchemy, mathematics, music, and grammar. His largest work was the poem *De Triumphis Ecclesiae* ("of the triumph of the Church").

It runs to 4,614 elegiac lines split into eight books. The overriding theme is the Crusades, but it starts with the crossing of the Red Sea and continues through to the preparations for the most recent crusade, being made almost as he wrote by Ferdinand of Castile. Only Ferdinand's premature death prevented the crusaders from their departure. As he tells his story Garland writes on a wide variety of early British legends, on French Merovingian history, on the Third Crusade, the Albigensian Crusade (one of the results of which was the establishment of the University of Toulouse), the Crusade of Louis IX, and much besides. Hugely discursive, Garland will step abruptly out of the narrative to offer a number of "sidebars," typically those on medieval siege strategy or popular methods of weather forecasting. It's a conceited, self-important, and above all not very good poem, as much as anything a vehicle for its author to show off the breadth of his learning, but for historians it does have the advantage of including many dates. It also offers such biographical details as exist regarding its author. The poem points up Garland's undoubted linguistic facility: he rejoices in puns, plays on words and special rhymes, including what scholars termed *versus retrogradi:* verses that read backward as well as forward.

It is for his grammatical works that Garland earns his place here, and they were many and varied. Among their titles are *Dictionarius scolasticus* (printed 1508), including phrases useful for scholars, plus a review of the contemporary trades of Paris and state of the city; *Dictionarius cum Commento:* mainly a study of sacred vestments and ornaments; *Compendium Grammatice* (printed 1489); *Accentarius sive de Accentibus; Liber Metricus de Verbis Deponentialibus* (printed 1486), some of which reappears in the *Promptorium;* and the *Synonyma* and *Equivoca,* a pair of works usually printed (e.g., the 1494 edition published by Wynkyn de Worde) with a commentary by Geoffrey the Grammarian. This last pair were very popular, more than likely becoming stock schoolbooks of the period. The printers Richard Pynson and Wynkyn de Worde produced a number of editions from 1494 to 1518; some of the material reemerges in the *Catholicon Anglicum* and the *Ortus vocabulorum.*

His two most important grammatical works are the *Cornutus,* or *Distigium* or *Scolarium Morale* and the *Dictionarius ad res explicandas* (1240?). The former (printed 1481) is essentially devoted to advising young students. A rhyming

tract with an interlinear gloss in English and Latin, it is 161 lines long. As
noted by Starnes, the *Distigium* forms "a vocabulary listing vocables associated
with these topics: the names of animals; a house and furnishing of a house; the
parts of the body; a mill and objects associated with it; a blacksmith's shop;
instruments of the household and farm, including distaff, spindle, plow, and
wagon; musical instruments; various artificers, such as cobbler, tailor, dyer, tanner, mason, and carpenter; species of trees; dress materials; and various classes
of people."[11]

This was hardly a departure from the norm. Garland had followed what was
by then current lexicographical practice, to be found in a succession of bilingual vocabularies appearing from the tenth to the fifteenth century. It was the
basic method of teaching, whether of Latin or of a "vulgar" tongue, and would
remain that way until the late sixteenth century. Only John Stanbridge's *Vulgaria* would offer a popular alternative.

The *Dictionarius ad res explicandas* is rather more widely consulted than was
the *Distigium*. It was apparently never printed until the nineteenth century,
although there are a number of extant manuscripts, both in England and
France. Despite its title, this is not a dictionary as such. Like Neckham's *De
Utensilibus,* and indeed like many such teaching vocabularies, it is more a piece
of heavily glossed and annotated fictional prose. There are no headwords and
definitions; rather the reader would read the text and refer where appropriate to
the notes and interlinear glosses. The aim of the book, so Garland explains, is
to help the young scholar amass a vocabulary of necessary words. Starting with
those that cover parts of the human body, he moves on to

> trades and manufactures, to the house of a citizen and its furniture, to the
> author's own wardrobe, to an ecclesiastical library, to the occupations and
> employments peculiar to women, to a fisherman and a list of fish, to a
> fowler and wild fowls, and to plants, herbs, and fruits.[12]

Garland's lists gradually expand to create a *promptorium,* or treasure house of
words, a concept that would be taken up, some two centuries later, both as a
book and a title by the Norfolk monk who may or may not have been named
Geoffrey the Grammarian. It would also be adopted, in some part, as source
material. Geoffrey's *Promptorium parvulorum* (c. 1440) cites the *Dictionarius* as an
authority on thirteen occasions.

Nor is Garland's advice limited to the bare facts. One French gloss, dealing
with glove makers, advised students to beware of their trickery and fraud. It is
not, in the end, a particularly outstanding work, and Erasmus' jibes were prob-

ably valid. But it survived, for two hundred years, resisting such rivals as appeared until the *Promptorium* finally displaced it. And like Neckham's work, and indeed like that of other compilers of vocabularies, the *Dictionarius,* whether deliberately or otherwise, lets the reader see the way the world in which he lived was changing. If one looks at the earliest Anglo-Saxon vocabularies they delineate a simpler world. For instance there are but a few words dealing with a man's house: a hall might be mentioned, along with a bedroom and perhaps a kitchen. By the Anglo-Norman era, things have changed. Neckham's lists, published in the twelfth century, offer a much more sumptuous picture; a century later Garland takes the process even further.

To quote Thomas Wright once again:

There is hardly any subject connected with medieval life which does not receive some light . . . We here see our forefathers in all their positions of relationship, position and occupation, from infancy to old age; we are introduced to the child in the nursery, and to the boy at his school; we see him in the clothes he wore, and with the arms that he carried to [the] wars which absorbed so much of medieval life; we learn in minute detail how he lived, what was his food and how it was prepared, and what he drank; we see the industrious housewife . . . we witness . . . games and amusements . . . and we even penetrate into the retired study of the scholar.[13]

Last in this list of the medieval compilers of vocabularies is Walter de Biblesworth, a country gentleman who owned manors in Essex and Hertfordshire. His birth date is unknown, and his death can only be ascribed to the period between 1277 and 1283. His fame rests on two poems. One of these is a supposed dialogue between Biblesworth and his friend Henry de Lacy, earl of Lincoln (1249–1312). De Lacy was poised to depart on a Crusade, but was torn between his religious duties and his affections for a certain lady. So great were the latter that he was loath to depart for the Holy Land. Biblesworth, pressing the moral strictures of one whose own emotions are not at stake, urges him to go. The Crusade in question is that of Edward I, which set off in 1270 and among whose members was Biblesworth himself. His other poem is *Le treytyz ke moun sir Gauter de Bibelesworthe fist à ma dame Dyonisie de Mounchensy, pur aprise de language* . . .("The treatise which Sir Walter de Biblesworth has made for Lady Dionysia de Mounchensy in order for her to learn the language . . ."). Lady Dionysia was a Kentish heiress, the daughter of William de Monchensy, baron of Swanscombe. She married Hugh de Vere, second son of the fifth earl of Oxford. Whether the book was for her benefit or, as Wright suggests,[14] for children, is unknown. Certainly she had no offspring of her own. While offering no major advances in lexicography, Biblesworth's treatise does illustrate an aspect of English sociolinguistic life. French, which a century earlier would have been the language of privilege and thus that of choice among the aristocracy, was here treated as a foreign language which it was necessary to learn. English, which had been very much the tongue of the conquered masses, had permeated into the upper classes who, since the Conquest, had dominated society.

Wright's collection includes a wide range of vocabularies, as well as several Latin and Anglo-Saxon glosses. Not all of them can be discussed here but one more, however, ought to be mentioned, before moving on to the four major works that dominate fifteenth-century lexicography. This is the *Pictorial Vocabulary*.[15] Wright attributes it to the late fifteenth century; later scholarship has roughly confirmed this, setting its probable date as 1500. Among its approximately 2,500 entries are 70 illustrative sketches, of the most basic quality. Wright suggests that they have been inserted to fill what would otherwise have been blank portions of the manuscript. He also suggests that the pictures were inserted to focus the reader's mind on his task, a view that seems less than feasible. Illustrated dictionaries did crop up occasionally before the twentieth century, but on the whole they were rare; had Wright seen some of today's products he would presumably have appreciated that in the *Pictorial Vocabulary*, as in more recent publications, the pictures were included simply to help the reader understand the words in question. Whatever the rationale, however, the unknown penman's efforts are distinctly rough edged. That said, they have a certain charm, offering a distant view of *inter alia* a church, a chapel, a crown, a dragon, and a cloaca or privy, this last edifice sporting a gothic exterior behind which is hidden what today's slang would term a "three-holer."

As a succession of scholars have found, listing the precise chronology of the most important examples of fifteenth-century lexicography has proved far from simple. Nineteenth-century writers, typically Britain's Henry Wheatley and America's Joseph Worcester, whose lists of dictionaries still provide the basic facts, offer four important works. The *Promptorium parvulorum*, the *Catholicon Anglicum*, the *Medulla grammatice*, and the *Ortus vocabulorum*. Both authors gave pride of place to the *Promptorium*, followed by the *Catholicon*. The *Ortus*, it was assumed, was part of the *Promptorium*, and was attributed to the same author. As far as the *Medulla* was concerned, this was viewed as no more than an alternative title for the *Promptorium*. This was a fair assumption: both the 1449 and 1508 editions of the *Promptorium* have as their subtitle "The Medulla grammatice." Listing citations in his *Dictionarium* (1587, and the standard work for the next quarter century), Thomas Thomas regularly refers to the "Medull." or "Medull. Gram." when in fact he means the *Promptorium.* By the mid-twentieth century DeWitt Starnes cut back some of the confusion when he suggested that "the term *Medulla grammatice* has, unfortunately, two distinct applications: (1) to fifteenth-century manuscript versions of a Latin-English dictionary, never printed, or, if so, with modifcations and change of title; (2) as an alternate title to the printed editions of the . . . Promptorium Parvulorum."[16] Current scholarship, as represented by Gabriele Stein, sets down the *Medulla,* when it has not been requisitioned as a subtitle, as a very late fourteenth-century work, which thus predates its peers.[17]

The *Medulla grammatice* (the "Marrow of Grammar") has no particular author. Given that there exist some sixteen manuscripts bearing this name, it is hardly surprising. One must assume that a variety of individuals—teachers, clergy, a selection of unknown clerks—all put in their bit, changing and augmenting the basic vocabulary. As Gabriele Stein points out, "it was the first and thus *the* comprehensive bilingual lexicon of the time, of which many copies were in circulation." And she suggests that in the absence of a widely accepted generic term for what we now call a dictionary, "any comprehensive bilingual word list might have been referred to as the *Medulla.*" Running to some 17,000–20,000 words, depending on the manuscript, the *Medulla* draws on a number of *glossae collectae,* glosses from classical texts and from the Bible. Additional material was apparently gleaned from a number of class glossaries or *vocabularia.* It is sorted in ABC-order.

It is possible that at least one of the men who compiled the *Medulla* is also responsible for the second of the fifteenth-century dictionaries, the *Ortus vocabulorum.* This "Garden of Words," far from being merely a part of the *Promptorium,* was not only a work in its own right, but also one that predated its better-known successor. Quite when it was written is unknown, the current view tends to *c.* 1430, but it was not printed until 1500, by Wynkyn de Worde, Caxton's successor and the printer of a number of other word lists. This printed version claimed in its title to offer its readers "almost all the things that are in the Catholicon, the Breviloqus, the Cornucopia, the Gemma vocabulorum and the Medulla grammatice, together with an exposition in the vernacular English." Of these works the *Catholicon* is the thirteenth-century Italian original rather than the fifteenth-century English successor and was compiled by Johannes Balbi; the *Breviloqus,* written by Guarinus Veronensis, was printed at Basel in 1480; the *Cornucopia sive linguae Latinae commentarii*

(printed 1489) was compiled by Nicolas Perottus (or Perotti), a bishop of
Siponto who died in 1480; and the "exposition" is a popular, if unascribed
vocabulary which was also one of the sources for the *Medulla*.

The *Ortus* was reissued in 1502 by another London printer, Richard Pynson.
Its blurb is nothing if not enthusiastic: as the compiler suggests in his *Prologus*,
this dictionary is not unworthily called "the garden of words" because,

> just as in gardens are found abundance of flowers, of herbs, and of fruits
> with which our bodies are strengthened and our spirits refreshed, so in
> this work are diverse words accommodated to beginners desirous of the
> pleasures of learning. With these words they may furnish the mind, adorn
> their speech, and finally, if the fates permit, grow into very learned
> men . . . Here in alphabetical order they may easily find whatever words
> they desire. The inflection and gender of nouns and the conjugation of
> verbs they will learn by a letter subjoined to such word. A work useful
> and profitable to all desirous of a knowledge of arts and sciences; and on
> account of the exposition of English speech, especially necessary to the
> realm of England. Hurry, therefore, all Englishmen, and spare not your
> small coins. Buy this volume while you can get it good cheap.

Presumably enough Englishmen did hurry, because there would be another
ten editions of the *Ortus* by 1533.

Fifteenth-century lexicography draws to its close, and to its climax with a
pair of dictionaries that for the first time set their headwords in English and
their definitions in Latin. The *Catholicon Anglicum* ("The Universal Remedy,"
or, more literally, the "universal purge") was printed in 1483. Shortly afterward, in 1499, came the *Promptorium puerorum* ("A treasure house of words for
children") otherwise known as the *Promptorium parvulorum sive clericorum* ("A
treasure house for the young or for clerks"). The *Promptorium* was written, however, as early as 1440, and as such ought to be considered first. Generally translated as a "storeroom" or "treasure house," the term, which in classical Latin
had meant a repository, in medieval England meant the department of a
monastery or similar institution whence stores were distributed; in a monastery
it was the responsibility of the cellarer. In the first critical edition of the *Promptorium* its editor, Albert Way, suggested that its probable author was one Galfridus Grammaticus or Geoffrey the Grammarian, a Dominican monk of Lynn
Episcopi in Norfolk, the county in which he had been bred, if not actually born.
An "ankyr" or hermit, Geoffrey had voluntarily had himself locked into his cell
for life, able to emerge only on the explicit instructions of his abbot. His

monastery held an order of Black Friars or Friars-Preachers and had been founded during the reign of Edward I by one Thomas Gedney. The books he used would have been available either in the monastery's own library, or in those of other monasteries of the Order. It has been suggested that Geoffrey was not in fact the author, and that the *Promptorium* was composed by one Richard Frauncis, another Black Friar, and another man versed in the dialects of East Anglia. This theory, advanced on the basis of a written note found in one printed edition of the book, was quickly discarded, not least through the unequivocal attribution to Geoffrey offered by Bale, Bishop of Ossory and himself an East Anglian, who left readers of his *Catalogue of the Writers of Great Britain* (1557) in no doubt as to his opinion. Other literary biographers, notably John Pits (who called Geoffrey "a good and simple man") and Archbishop Tanner, concurred.

Way confirmed this attribution in his edition, printed for the Camden Society in 1865. A subsequent scholarly edition, prepared by A. L. Mayhew and published by the Early English Text Society (EETS) in 1908 (Extra Ser. CII), holds the line. Mayhew is not wholly happy with Geoffrey's background, but concludes, "whatever may have been his patronymic, we may confidently ascribe to the Dominican recluse of Lynn, Galfridus, designated from his special studies 'Grammaticus,' the laborious achievement of the first English-Latin dictionary." This belief is duly enshrined in the *DNB*. Only DeWitt Starnes, in 1954, chose to reject the popular theory. That the compiler came from Lynn is in no doubt, and that his work was composed around 1440 is equally likely, but as to his real name, there is "no conclusive evidence that the recluse of Lynn . . . bore the name Galfridus Grammaticus. In the present stage of our knowledge we can only say that the real name of the compiler of the first English-Latin dictionary is not known."[18]

Like the casual destruction wreaked by the *OED,* when at a given headword it crushes years of cheerfully accepted popular theorizing with a tersely dismissive "etymology unknown," this rebuttal of a century's presumptions is disappointing, but all too probably correct. In truth, it does not affect the importance of the *Promptorium* itself. As Way set out in the very first paragraph of his Preface:

Whether we regard the Promptorium Parvulorum as an authentic record of the English language in the earlier half of the fifteenth century, as illustrative of the provincial dialects of East Anglia, or as explanatory of the numerous archaisms of a debased Latinity that pervades early chronicles and documents, its value can scarcely be too highly estimated. If, on the

other hand, we take into consideration the curious evidence which it sup-
plies to those who investigate the arts and manners of bygone times, it
were difficult to point out any relic of learning at the period equally full
of instruction, and of those suggestive details which claim the attention
of students of medieval literature and antiquities in the varied departments of archeological research.

The *Promptorium,* already sixty years in manuscript, was published for the
first time in 1499 by Richard Pynson. It is in the colophon of this edition that
the work is first subtitled the "Medulla grammatice." Other editions followed,
issued by both the other major contemporary printers: Wynkyn de Worde (in
1510) and Julian Notary (also 1510). De Worde also published a combined volume that offered the *Promptorium* and the *Ortus,* which, he makes clear, he saw
as complementary works. In his preface *ad lectorem* he advises "And yf ye can not
fynde a laten worde, or englysshe worde accordynge to your purpose in this
present boke [the *Promptorium*] so shall ye take *Ortus vocabularum,* the wyche is
more redyer to fynden a latyn word after the ABC . . ." He also suggests that
the *Ortus* is "most necessary for chyldren."

Conveniently, the author of the *Promptorium* gives an extensive list of his
sources, less to puff his work, one feels, than to establish his intellectual credentials. As one might imagine, they comprise the best of his predecessors:
Balbi's *Catholicon,* Hugo of Pisa, William Brito (a Welsh monk who died at
Grimsby in 1356, and whose pertinent work is the *Summa,* which deals with
the "hard words" found in the Bible), Alexander Neckham and the *Miravalen-
sis in Campo Florum* (a large vocabulary of obscure Latin terms). John of Garland
is cited for his well-known *Dictionarius scolasticus* and *Distigium,* as well as for
the *Commentarius Curialium,* the *Libellus misteriorum qui dicitur Anglia que fulget*
and the much-maligned *Merarius,* all of which are attributed to his researches.
It was Garland, nearly two centuries earlier, who had already likened a word list
to a *promptorium.* Finally, he cited Robert Kylwarbi or Kilwardby, the archbishop of Canterbury and composer of a treatise on Priscian (*fl.* 500), the
author of *Institutiones grammaticae* and eighteen other works, all rich in classical
citations and hugely popular during the Middle Ages, and sufficiently well
known to give the eighteenth-century catchphrase: "to break Priscian's head: to
speak or write bad grammar." Kilwardby was a native of England, educated at
Paris and then Oxford. He became provincial of the Dominicans in England,
and thus presumably an important figure to the Dominican of Lynn Episcopi,
before serving as archbishop of Canterbury between 1272 and 1278, at which
point he was made a cardinal by Pope Nicholas III. He moved to Italy, only to

die shortly afterward at Viterbo, the victim, it was widely rumored, of a poisoner. Nor were these all of the compiler's sources. There were, as he adds, *"aliis libris et libellis inspectis et intellectis."*

Writing in his "Preamble," the author is agonizingly self-deprecatory, calling himself "ignorant and unsophisticated, better suited to learn than to teach," and stressing the extent to which his work is no more than the collected precis of the earlier efforts of better men than himself. He has occasionally sought counsel from his betters, but only rarely essayed a pronouncement of his own. But, grieved by the prevailing barbarism, and pitying the destitution of the young clerks he saw around him who "thirsted for knowledge like harts to the water brooks, and in vain sought for guides, so that like wild asses they fainted in sobbing and sighs," he decided to offer his own advice. For otherwise, "according to the lament of the prophet, the young children ask bread and and no man breaketh it unto them!" And he ends his preamble with a heartfelt plea from one whose quality of work was dependent on his own skills of copying and correction:

> I humbly with prayers entreat all pedagogues, teachers and masters, that when they have examined this little work, they will approve what may by God's assistance have been rightly written, and will piously correct and emend what is written ill or erringly; since humble grammarians and boys may look on this short volume, as on a mirror, and find freely and immediately the common words which belong to the Latin tongue; besides many may without a blush glean behind the reapers' backs, who from age or any other cause are ashamed to learn what they know not. Whosoever therefore shall in this rude work discover any either profit or comfort for themselves, let them give thanks to God, and mercifully intercede for me a sinner.

The author protests far too much. Not only has his work been preserved as one of those that has been honored as the "first" English dictionary, but the *Promptorium* was a genuine breakthrough in lexicography. It may be, as less charitable critics averred, that he did little more than take the *Medulla grammatice* and reverse the headword-definition order, placing the English word at the head and Latin as its explanation, but if that was "all" he did, then no one had done it before and "Geoffrey," or whoever the compiler may have been, was far from the simple monk that he pretended to be.

The *Promptorium* lists approximately 12,000 words. They are in alphabetical order (AB- or ABC-order; I and J and U and V are undistinguished), with the nouns (*nomina*) and other parts of speech listed first, followed by the verbs (*verba*). Each English word is "translated" by one or more Latin words, whose gender and declension are noted. Often he adds more English synonyms and paraphrases and, before moving onto the Latin definition, throws in an English explanation first. The English used is the dialect of East Anglia: brought up in Norfolk the author would have known no other. (The fifteenth century had no "standard English.") But the *Promptorium* is by no means simple hackwork. Its compiler does far more than simply take old dictionaries and vocabularies and invert them. As the multiplicity of his sources illustrate, he has done his own extensive research.

The *Catholicon Anglicum* was written in the latter half of the fifteenth century. There are only two manuscripts in existence, one that in the nineteenth century was held by Lord Monson and one in the British Library (ADD MS 15,562). Lord Monson's manuscript is dated 1483, but the British Museum's version may well be earlier. The work was not printed until 1881, when Sidney J. H. Herrtage edited it for the EETS. No scholar has ever been able to pin down the scribe who assembled the *Catholicon,* unlike the *Promptorium,* which for many years was presumed to have a named author. The best guess, which has been generally accepted, is that proposed by Albert Way and later expanded upon by Sidney Herrtage: that the writer came from the northeast, specifically the northern part of the East Riding of Yorkshire. This regionality was noted by H. B. Wheatley, who stressed that if the *Promptorium* was a product of East Anglia, and the *Catholicon* one of the northeast, then the likelihood was that these two works are merely the survivors of a far greater range of dictionaries. Certainly, compared with the sixteenth century, the period seems particularly ill-served by its lexicographers. Perhaps subsequent wastage, rather than contemporary absence, is the cause. As Wheatley points out, "It seems hardly probable that other districts were behind their neighbours in the production of these most necessary books."[19]

Like the author of the *Promptorium,* the compiler of the *Catholicon* turned predictably to the current state of the lexicographical art when setting out to create his own version. Thus one finds among other sources: William Brito, Balbi's *Catholicon,* Papias, and Isidore of Seville. John of Garland and Hugo of Pisa are especially important. The compiler has followed Garland's habit of supplying not simply one synonym as a definition, but as many as he can gather. Links can also be traced to the *Medulla grammatice.* And once again like the *Promptorium,* the title of the work was hardly unique. Balbi's *Catholicon* was the first of the breed, but the name had become especially popular in France, where the first ever French-Latin vocabulary, printed in 1487, was entitled the *Catholicon parvum.* Other French works included the *Catholicon abbreviatum* and the Breton-Latin-French *Catholicum* of 1499.

The English *Catholicon* is a substantially smaller work than the *Promptorium,* listing only 8,000 words compared to the other's 12,000. Of these, 2,000 terms were not listed in the earlier work, a statistic which indicates that the two compilers had no knowledge of each other's efforts. They might, of course, have been especially saintly figures, but the odds on one lexicographer noting the appearance of a rival work and not casting even the most cursory glance across its headwords are slim. Whoever the *Catholicon's* compiler, his sources, methods of collection, and general technical treatment of headwords and definitions conform to rather than advance current practice. Given that, unlike Latin, English had yet to generate a sufficiency of texts for the lexicographer to draw upon properly, it must be assumed that, like the *Promptorium,* the *Catholicon* has depended to a great extent on the taking of previously itemized Latin-English entries and reversing them. However, in his use of a mass of synonyms—taking this principle far further than any other contemporary—and in his attempt to show the differences between the various Latin usages—providing, as it were, a form of thesaurus—the author made with his small book a genuine and important advance in lexicographical method.

Yet as the fifteenth century drew to its close, and all the signs made it clear that dictionary making had undoubtedly taken steps toward modernity, the old *glossae collectae* and *vocabularia* were far from dead. Not only had they provided invaluable resources for the compilers of dictionaries proper, but they also had a role in teaching, especially of the young, which was far from redundant. They were not, however, of a uniformly high standard. Introducing his *Volume of Vocabularies,* Thomas Wright noted that:

> It can hardly be doubted that the manuscripts of these vocabularies . . . were written by schoolmasters for their own use; and we cannot help being struck by the large proportion of barbarous Latin words . . . and by the gross blunders with which they abound . . . Many of the Latin words are so disguised and corrupted that we can hardly recognise them, and in some cases the schoolmaster has actually mistaken the genders. It is thus clear that the schoolmasters of the fifteenth century were very imperfect scholars.

It was, presumably, to counter this that the century from 1373 saw the foundation of three great schools: Winchester, Eton, and Magdalen (in Oxford). It was at the last of these three, which like Magdalen College itself was founded by William of Waynflete, that what Beatrice White has termed "a humble, indigenous movement towards improved methods of teaching Latin" was begun.[20] This system was fostered by a number of talented teachers, starting with the first Informator or head teacher, Anwykyll, who held the post from 1481 to 1487, and moving through a succession of Latinists such as John Stanbridge, Robert Whittington, and the future Cardinal Wolsey, who held the post of Informator for six months in 1498.

Prior to Magdalen's foundation, the basic grammar as doled out to schoolboys was the *Ars Minor*, written by St. Jerome (*c.* 342–420). The saint was revered as one of the four "Doctors of the Church," but his work was a millennium old already and something fresh was definitely required.

Anwykyll took it upon himself to create a new grammar and in 1483 published the *Compendium totius grammatice*. Issued either as an addendum or as a separate work was his *Vulgarea quaedam abs Terentio in Anglicam linguam fraducta*. This is a collection of useful phrases from Terence and is the first attempt by an English teacher to create a dedicated vocabulary to help readers find their way through what might otherwise be the tortuous language of a specific Latin work. What Magdalen began, Eton would follow. *Floures for Latine Spekynge* (1534), another treatment of Terence, was compiled by Nicholas Udall (1504–56), author of the doggerel play *Ralph Roister Doister* (1541) and a headmaster celebrated for flogging, among many others, the author Thomas Tusser. It was of the sadistic, if scholarly Udall that Tusser recalled,

> *From Paul's I went, to Eton sent*
> *To learn straightways the Latin phrase,*
> *Where fifty three stripes given to me*
> *At once I had.*
>
> *For fault but small, or none at all*
> *It came to pass that beat I was.*
> *See, Udall, see, the mercy of thee,*
> *To me, poor lad.*

In the end Udall's affection for the erotic potential of the birch proved excessive. He was dismissed and jailed in the Marshalsea—although he was eventually rehired by another great scholastic foundation. As John Chandos notes, "After . . . the notorious Eton flogger had been convicted of paederastic offences against the boys in his charge, this record did not prevent his becoming, later, having served a term of imprisonment, not only a successful literary pundit, but headmaster of Westminster School."[21]

In 1488 Anwykyll was succeeded as Informator at Magdalen by the usher, John Stanbridge. And while Anwykyll had reformed the teaching of Latin grammar, his successor revolutionized it. Stanbridge appears an exemplary figure. In the words of the chronicler Anthony à Wood,

> This John Stanbridge was a right worthy Lover of his faculty, and an indefatigable Man in teaching and writing, as it may appear by those things that he hath published, very grateful to the Muses and publick concerns. The last of which he consulted more than his own private interest, and when in his old age, he should have withdrawn himself from his profession (which is esteem'd by the generality a drudgery) and have lived upon what he had gotten in his younger Years, he refused it, lived poor and bare to his last, yet with a juvenile and cheerful Spirit.[22]

Stanbridge was born in Heyford, Northamptonshire, in 1463. Aged twelve he went to Winchester, and thence to another of William of Waynflete's foundations, New College, Oxford. He became a Fellow in 1481. He then moved to Magdalen School and held the post of Informator from 1488 to 1494. In April 1501 he became master of the Hospital of St. John at Banbury. At the same time his brother (or perhaps just a near relative), Thomas Stanbridge, was master of the grammar school there. As well as teaching Sir Thomas Pope, Founder of Trinity College, Oxford, Thomas Stanbridge pioneered his relation's new grammar, to such an extent that when two new schools were founded in Manchester and Cuckfield, their statutes pay special attention to the way grammar was taught at Banbury school, "wiche is called Stanbrige Gramyer." In February 1507 John Stanbridge was appointed vicar of Winwick, near Gainsborough, and in August 1509 he was collated to the prebend of St. Botolph's in the cathedral of Lincoln. Since the church records note that his successor, Oliver Coren, took office on September 8, 1510, it must be assumed that Stanbridge died on or slightly before that day.

Stanbridge wrote and published two grammatical works: the *Vocabula* and the *Vulgaria* (literally "common things," thus "common words") appeared in 1496 and 1508 respectively. Editions continued to appear through the next century—seventeen of the *Vocabula* between 1496 and 1631 and seven of the *Vulgaria* from 1508 to 1529—and both works were expanded and revised in the seventeenth century by Thomas Newton and by John Brinsley. By lasting so long, the *Vocabula* can be seen as keeping alive the essentially medieval tradition of the vocabularies and *nominales* into a period of quite different lexicography. They can also be seen as the precursors of another "teaching dictionary": John Withals' *Dictionarie for Yonge Beginners*.

The *Vocabula* is very typical of the sort of vocabulary or protodictionary that had been appearing ever since the earliest Anglo-Saxon examples. It is arranged in topics—parts of the body, diseases, the table and things associated with it, a range of occupations that include those of the baker, the carpenter, the smith, the mason, the goldsmith, and the cobbler, the world of agriculture and the countryside, of weapons, and of musical instruments. Readers of John of Garland, of Alexander Neckham, or even of Aelfric would have recognized much of what Stanbridge had collected. Indeed, Stanbridge had turned, like his predecessors, to the classics, and he lists among his authorities Pliny, Cato, Columella, and the *Cornucopia* of Nicholas Perottus. However, whether he actually read those works, or simply judged that if they had been good enough for his more recent peers, then they were quite good enough for him, is a matter that must be left open.

"Vulgar" began by meaning common things, and thus the common (i.e., non-Latin) language, but by the time of Whittington, Stanbridge's successor at Magdalen and editor of his own *Vulgaria* (1520), the word had been adapted in schools to mean those English sentences set for translation into Latin. Stanbridge's *Vulgaria* appeared in 1508. Similar to today's foreign language phrasebooks, as used by the world's tourists, the *Vulgaria* proved very successful. Not only did schoolboys use them enthusiastically, but undergraduates at Oxford were equally keen. The book is perhaps best known for Stanbridge's preface, in which he commends his youthful readers:

> *All lytell chyldren besely your style ye dresse.*
> *Unto this treatyse with goodly aduertence*
> *These latyn wordes in your herte to impresse*
> *To hende that ye may with all your intelligence*
> *Serue god your maker holy vnto his reuerence*
> *And yf ye do not*
> *the rodde must not spare*
> *You for to lerne with his sharpe morall sence*
> *Take how good hede*
> *and herken your vulgare.*

But threatened thrashings or otherwise, what Stanbridge appreciated was that if you wanted children to learn, it helps if they have at least a modicum of interest in what is being taught. There is something alive about this treatment of an ostensibly "dead" language that positions Stanbridge's efforts very far indeed from the Latin grammars that still hold sway today, with their "allies attacking the ramparts" and "slaves retreating from the line of battle." Any schoolboy, whether of the fifteenth or twentieth century, might have penned some of the "typical" sentences below.

"Syt awaye or I shall gyue the a blowe." "He hath taken my boke fro me." "Thou stynkest." "Lende me the copy of thy latyn and I shall gyue it the agayne by and by." "The latyn is full of fautes." "I haue blotted my boke." "The chyldren be sterynge [stirring] about in the maistres absence." "Let me alone or I shall complayne on the." "It is euyll with us whan the mayster apposeth us." "I am fallen in the maysters conceyte. I haue gete the maysters fauoure," "I hadde leuer go to my boke than be bete," "I am the worst of all my felowes," "I was beten this morning. The mayster hath bete me. The mayster gaue me a blowe on the cheke. I fere the mayster," and "My gowne is the worste in all the scole."

Stanbridge moved on from Magdalen to enjoy his ecclesiastical preferment, but his successors maintained the grammatical revolution. His pupil Robert Whittington took over as Informator, and duly produced his own *Vulgaria.* And Magdalen produced a number of other grammarians, notably John Holt, Thomas Wolsey, and William Lily or Lilly. Holt, once the teacher of Thomas More, wrote the *Lac Puerorum, or, Mylke for Children* (1497). His inclusion of child-friendly illustrations advanced Stanbridge's process into new areas of adaptability to the minds of those at which it was aimed. Wolsey, who would also encounter Sir Thomas More, but in a distinctly less amicable relationship, was author of the *Rudimenta Grammatices & docendi Methodus.* The book was written for use at the school in Ipswich where he had himself been educated as a boy, but the debt to Stanbridge and Magdalen is undeniable. In the preface he even credits his predecessor as Informator, albeit obliquely. Finally Lily (1468?–1522) was the first high master of Colet's new school: St. Paul's in London. He had followed Colet at Magdalen and had probably been charged with assembling the earliest nucleus of St. Paul's boys who, when their building in St. Paul's Churchyard was finally completed in 1512, would move into the new school. One of England's first ever Greek scholars, his grammatical work is best seen in the *Grammatica Rudimenta,* the earliest surviving edition of which is dated 1527, and which continued to appear well into the eighteenth century. Like all these Magdalen grammarians, Lily too was aquainted with More, with whom he translated Greek epigrams as well as a treatise on the art of divination through interpreting throws of the dice.

Stanbridge's system was hugely influential in schools, but in the context of mainstream lexicographical advance it represents a backwater. The vocabularies and *nominales* from which his work, especially the *Vocabula,* drew its origins, were rooted in the Middle Ages. That they provided inspiration, and important basic material for the new generation of dictionaries is equally true, but as the new century proceeded these roots would vanish beneath new systems and techniques. Stanbridge's efforts might suit schoolchildren; the world of scholarship, still the primary user of the dictionary, demanded something rather more advanced.

3

The Move from Latin

B y the turn of the fifteenth century alphabetical order had been properly established and there had developed a regular flow of first Latin-English and then English-Latin glossaries; the production of such vocabularies, which were paralleled by similar compilations across Europe, dominated the sixteenth century. The flow of major dictionaries increased, and, while not yet "lexicographers" in the modern, professional sense of the term, there were emerging a number of linguistic authorities.

The sixteenth century was remarkably fruitful in the production of dictionaries. Production started slowly, leaving the field to the still recent *Promptorium parvulorum* and the *Ortus vocabulorum* which went respectively into eight and ten editions before their popularity petered out during the 1530s. "Herken your vulgare," admonished John Stanbridge, and in many ways his comment could stand as the leitmotif for the next century's lexicography. There were still no English dictionaries as such, but that was simply because, as the century began, there was still no English. Not, anyway, in the world of schoiarship. The unlettered obviously spoke English, or a mongrel version thereof, blending the remnants of Anglo-Saxon with Norman French. And in everyday speech and in popular literature so too did most people, from the aristocracy down. But scholarship, in England as on the Continent, was the still the province of Latinists. However, as the century progressed the intrusion of the vernacular, the national versions of the "vulgar tongue," whether English, French, Italian, or whatever, began to break down the Latinists' grasp on learning. The vernacular, with its roots in the Latin *verna:* a homeborn slave, was, as its etymology implies, a despised form of communication, but as the century progressed it became a dominant one. The sixteenth century may begin with new editions of dictionaries that were still rooted in the Latinate past; it ends but four years away from the work that would signify the all-English future.

Not that Latin simply vanished overnight. In some countries it persisted well into the eighteenth and even the nineteenth century. Aside from ecclesiastical Latin, which still serves today as the "official language" of Roman Catholicism, there are dozens of instances, general and particular, of Latin survivals. Peter Burke, writing in his essay "Heu Dominae, Adsunt Turcae," shows how Latin was used for scientific and philosophical treatises, for teaching, and for learned works of all sorts and even, if rarely, for imaginative fiction.[1] While Renaissance scholars were pioneering their respective vernaculars, it was also common to find their works translated from the vernacular in which they had been written *back* into Latin, itself the far from moribund vernacular of the scholarly community. Outside scholarship Latin found a role as a convenient *lingua franca,* mainly among diplomats who had no other tongue in common, but also lower down the social scale. Burke recounts tales of eighteenth-century travelers in central Europe who found innkeepers, otherwise unable to speak any but their own, incomprehensible language, who could be talked to quite satisfactorily in Latin. Thus Latin lingered, but in the lexicographical context its power was waning. The sixteenth century might produce some fine Latin-English and English-Latin works, but the trend was increasingly away from the classics and toward a language all could speak.

The sixteenth century saw Latin give way to vernacular languages all across Europe. England was no exception. While not quite the "golden age of the English language," as touted by nationalist romantics, it is undoubtedly a pivotal period for the development and ascending domination of the vernacular. When the century begins, English is still a marginal language, far less popular than its European peers. Even more critical, notes Jürgen Schäfer, "and this was of serious concern for patriots, English was a backward language . . . far removed from the impressive literary achievements of Italian."[2] The poet John Skelton wrote ruefully, "Our natural tonge is rude | And hard to be ennuede [envied]." Yet, after this "period of agonizing linguistic uncertainty"[3] everything had changed. As the century ended another writer, Ralph Holinshed, could celebrate English: "There is no one speache vnder the sun spoken in our time, that hath or can haue more varietie of words and copie of phrases."

. . .

In considering the dramatic development of English, three factors must be taken into account: the intellectual Renaissance, the ecclesiastical Reformation, and the economic expansion of England as a mercantile power. The arrival of the printing press, invented in Germany by Johannes Gutenberg and pioneered in fifteenth-century England by William Caxton, occasioned a "communications revolution" that would not be paralleled until the advent of mass-market computing in the late twentieth century. The print culture of 1500 was as undeveloped, and as open to exploitation, as the computer culture of today. And if the early Latin publications might be compared to the "mainframes" of the 1950s and 1960s—arcane, few in number and purpose—built for the exaltation of an élite "priesthood" (in those days almost literally so)—then the new publications of the sixteenth century, increasingly substituting English for Latin texts, can be seen in the same light as the desktop machines of the 1980s and beyond.

The press also drove the pace and direction of change. The entire print production throughout Europe in the years between Gutenberg's invention (*c.* 1436) and 1500 had been approximately 35,000 items. The bulk of them, unsurprisingly, were in Latin. The next 140 years would see 20,000 items printed in England alone, and these were all English-language works.[4] The effect was twofold: the increased literacy offered by these books helped promote a rising middle class; and that same middle class made it clear that, unlike the denizens of academe, they wanted their reading in the vernacular. Caxton and his successors were businessmen, but they also saw the interdependent possibilities of promoting both their books and the national culture. Printing Malory and Chaucer made money and underlined England's literary abilities. Latin did not wholly vanish, but those who used it were keen to dismiss the debased forms of the last few centuries and promote what they saw as the purity of classical Latin. The most fundamental "rebirth" of the Renaissance was that of the classics. Such intellectuals as Thomas More, Thomas Elyot, and later Francis Bacon looked backward to the Latin of an older, more cultivated period. And if they persisted in choosing it over the still emergent vernacular, then it was because they saw it in a greater and more sophisticated literary style than English could yet offer. Indeed, when Elyot or Ascham first essayed a work in English, their decision remained slightly tentative, and their prefaces are rather apologetic. But Latin, while respected, was no longer the ultimate authority.

The individual took pride in his achievement and he questioned the predominant position of Latin as the language of knowledge and learning. In Italy, France, and England the struggle for the recognition of the vernacular became a public debate and a national issue which in the seventeenth century was to result in the compilation of the first monolingual dictionaries . . . The most outstanding characteristic of sixteenth-century English lexicography, compared to that of the preceding century, is its turning towards the spoken vernaculars.[5]

That debate would not end until the seventeenth century, when the final struggles over the usefulness or otherwise of what became known as "inkhorn terms" took place. Indeed, it may not have ended then: in the mid-twentieth century one could still find George Orwell extolling the beauties and clarity of non-Latinate English over what he decried as an overly ornate alternative. But in the sixteenth century there was less an argument than a slow change. At the same time one can see Latin increasingly excluded from mainstream discourse, but at the same time invading the vernacular vocabulary to an ever greater extent since "the more one wanted to talk about higher things in the lower languages, the more one had to import the only material there was"[6]—and that material was then (and in many cases remains to this day) based on Latin and, to a lesser extent, Greek.

The rise of a literate middle class and its embrace of the vernacular over the classics was a pan-European phenomenon. The Reformation of the 1530s and Britain's increasing importance as a maritime, trading power were not. And both of these tended to encourage the growth of English as a statement of its speakers' individuality and isolation, both chosen and enforced, from the rest of Europe. Latin, the language of Papist Rome and of its agents in hostile Spain, was seen as tainted, however elegantly the likes of Thomas Elyot might pen it.

Of all the lexicographers to be encountered here, Sir Thomas Elyot (1490?–1546) is probably the grandest figure and the most deeply involved in a world beyond pure scholarship. Certainly he played a major part in national life, as a courtier and ambassador as well as a humanist intellectual of the caliber and influence of such peers as Thomas More or, across the Channel, Erasmus.

Sir Thomas Elyot (or Eliot) was born in Wiltshire, the son of Sir Richard Elyot, a lawyer. Some claims existed for his having been born in Suffolk, and this spurious theory lasted for at least nine editions of the *Encyclopaedia Britannica*. But Elyot's paternal grandfather, Michell Elyot, came from Coker, near Yeovil, and the family remained anchored to the West Country.

Richard Elyot must have been born about the middle of the fifteenth century. He began practicing as an advocate late in the century and in 1503 was created commissioner for Wiltshire, responsible for collection of "aids" required by the king to pay for the knighting of the Prince of Wales and the marriage of his daughter Margaret to the king of Scotland. Later that year he became serjeant-at-law and attorney general to the Queen Consort. In 1509 he was justice of assize for Wiltshire, a post he retained until his death. He continued to rise in the law, becoming a judge of common pleas in 1517. He died in 1522. Richard married some time in the 1480s. His wife's name is unknown, but she appears to have been the niece of Sir Thomas Fynderne, who in 1461, as a supporter of Lancaster in the Wars of the Roses, had been executed and had forfeited his estates. Their son Thomas was born around 1490. His childhood, otherwise unremarkable, has one recorded incident: a visit with his father to Ivy Church, near Salisbury, where a gigantic skeleton, allegedly 14'10" long, had been unearthed. Alongside it, apparently, lay "a booke therein of very thicke parchment all written with capitall Romane letters. But it had lien so long that when the leaues were touched they fouldred to dust. Sir Thomas Elyot, who saw it, iudged it to be an Historie."[7] This was not Elyot's only brush with West Country antiquity. Sometime later, according to Holland's edition of William Camden, "I haue heard that in the time of King Henrie the Eight there was found neere this place a table of mettall as it had been tinne and lead commixt, inscribed with many letters but in so strange a character that neither Sir Thomas Elyot nor Master Lilye, Schoole-maister of Paules, could read it and therefore neglected it. Had it been preserved, somewhat happily might have been discovered as concerning Stoneheng which now lieth obscured."

Thomas Elyot was educated at home. Oxford and Cambridge claimed him later, but in fact both universities were experiencing a period of relative decline, and his father saw no benefit in his attending either. His father's circle of friends, who included the physician Thomas Linacre, the educators John Colet and William Lily, and the clergyman Hugh Latimer, doubtless provided an adequately intellectual atmosphere. He studied Latin, Greek, and medicine (notably the works of Galen, Hippocrates, Avicenna, and other experts). His medical studies were directed by "a worshipful physician" who was probably Linacre himself, head of the college of physicians, an acclaimed Greek scholar and the translator of Galen.

In 1511 he became Clerk of Assize on the Western Circuit. In 1522 his father died, leaving him a substantial estate; a year later so too did his seventeen-year-old cousin Thomas Fynderne who also bequeathed Elyot much landed property. Thomas' father, Elyot's uncle William Fynderne, fought the will and Elyot paid heavily to defend his title. The suit lasted eighteen months and cost £100. Fortunately it was heard before Cardinal Wolsey, who appeared to prefer the young man and duly judged in his favor. He underlined his partiality by making Elyot clerk to the Privy Council, although he offered no salary. Preferment continued. By 1527 Elyot was sheriff of Oxfordshire and Berkshire, and in that position struck up a friendship with another influential figure: Thomas Cromwell, the future Lord Chancellor. But status was not matched by income and in 1530 Elyot lost his clerkship "without any recompense, rewarded only with the order of Knyghthode, honourable and onerouse, having moche lasse to lyve on than bifore." He appealed to Wolsey for a new job, and was given a variety of unspecified duties at court. A fee of forty marks was attached, but Elyot was never paid. He alleged a conspiracy by rivals at court, and called his financial position "the most damnable vice and most against injustice." Whatever the truth, Wolsey fell from power in 1529 and such advantages Elyot might have gained from his patronage vanished with him. Fortunately, there were no disadvantages. Elyot was promptly appointed as one of those commissioners, in his case for Cambridgeshire, who investigated Wolsey's affairs.

In 1530 Elyot married Margaret Abarrow, the daughter of a Hampshire gentleman, and in 1531 published his first work: *The Boke called the Gouernor.* Prudently dedicated to Henry VIII, it was a treatise on the education of statesmen, dealing particularly with the moral and social duties of princes. It is the earliest treatise on moral philosophy in the English language. As well as philosophizing, Elyot was also promoting his parallel agenda: as a humanist who saw his intellectual stimulus in antiquity, and not in the more recent Middle Ages, he saw English, with its roots in Anglo-Saxon, as less sophisticated than other European languages. To remedy this he determined to extend the national vocabulary. His opponents jeered his "strange terms" but the King, who enjoyed linguistic innovation, was a supporter.

His Highnesse benignely receyuynge my boke, whiche I named The Governor, in the redynge therof sone perceyued that I intended to augment our Englyshe tongue wherby men shulde as well expresse more abundantly the thynge that they Conceyued in theyr hartis (wherfore language was ordeyned), hauynge wordes apte for the pourpose, as also interprete out of greke, latyn, or any other tonge into Englysshe, as sufficiently as out of any one of the said tongues into an other. His Graec also perceyued that through out the boke there was no terme new made by me of a latine or frenche worde, but it is there declared so playnly by one mene or other to a diligent reder that no sentence is therby made derke or harde to be understande.

Henry even tolerated Elyot's attacks on the vices of the upper classes and Elyot praised him for showing intelligence and restraint where lesser men "lyke a galde horse abidynge no playsters, be alwaye gnappynge and kyckynge at suche examples and sentences as they do feele sharpe or do byte them . . ."

The Governor was fantastically successful, outselling any other volume of the era, including More's highly influential *Utopia*. It was the first book in English to be written on education and, apart from any other characteristics, it shows how well its author managed to combine the old Latin and the new English traditions. Reprinted three times almost at once, its printer could barely meet the demand. Eight editions would follow over the next fifty years. One of its charms was its size: it was octavo (later editions were even smaller) and as such much easier to read, let alone carry, than the usual massive folios. It was also highly influential and while no direct proof can be offered, must have made its mark on such similar works as Budaeus' *De l'institution du Prince* (1547), dedicated to Francis I; John Sturm's *De educandis erudiendisque Principum* (1570), dedicated to Duke William, brother of Anne of Cleves; the anonymously written *Institucion of a Gentleman* (1555) and Harry Peacham's *The Compleat Gentleman* (1622).

Aside from its role as a manual for princes, *The Governor* stands, in the developing world of English lexicography, as the stimulus of neologisms and as a "kind of English dictionary" in itself.

Besides being part of an unfinished work on politics, a handbook of education and ethics for the sons of English gentlemen, an approximate imitation of Plato's Republic, and a prince's mirror for Henry VIII, the Governour was intended to serve as a kind of dictionary of new and useful words in English for the benefit of Elyot's countrymen. This effort to augment the English vocabulary is not confined to the Governour alone, but figures in all of Elyot's writings, and is the principal motive behind the series of translations he made of foreign books. He was particularly concerned to build up the English language for use in the more technical fields of learning, where it was least developed—in moral philosophy, political theory, and medicine.[8]

Elyot's work is emblematic of the desire of sixteenth-century English intellectuals, as patriotic and nationalistic as any of their peers, to enhance the national culture. Like the London literati of the late seventeenth century, whose desire to "fix" the language (the result of which would be Samuel Johnson's *Dictionary*) was impelled by what they saw as the threat of the French *Académie* and similar institutions, they sought to counter what were seen as European advances by the proclamation of the excellence of the English language and the culture it sustained. And as humanists, their standards harking back to those of classical antiquity, they wanted to establish in their own tongue a standard that would equal that of their respected antecedents. Finally, they wished to cater for the emergent bourgeoisie, bringing them through a purer English the fruits of centuries of knowledge, hitherto locked away in foreign languages. The fact that Elyot wrote in English, since as an accomplished scholar he could equally easily have chosen Latin, underlines his desire to back his mouth with his money.

To fulfill this ambition Elyot studded his text with neologisms and he has been termed "the most deliberate and conscientious neologizer of the period."[9] As noted above, while others may have queried his "strange termes," Henry himself understood the scheme perfectly. Typical of his neologisms are such staples of subsequent English as *execrate, involve, superstitiously, exactly, articulate, emulation, aggravate, activity, audacity, beneficence, clemency, democracy, education, equability, frugality, implacability, imprudence, liberty of speech, loyalty, magistrate, mediocrity, sincerity,* and *society.* Somewhat more "strange" are *adminiculate, adumbration* (in the sense of shading in painting), *annect, applicate, decerpt, falcate, humect, illecebrous, ostent,* and *provect.* Virtually none of these latter have lasted, but they too were proof of a conscious effort to bring English into the modern world. The popularity of *The Governor* undoubtedly helped promote such terms, but Elyot was aware that only continuous usage would fulfill his aims. He planned for a trickle-down expansion of the language. From his own text to his learned readers, who would ideally take up the terms themselves, and thence to the mass reading public and, finally, into the commonly spoken word. To help the linguistic proliferation he added simple definitions of his new terms. He also tended, as seen in the second edition, of 1537, to eliminate Latinisms and substitute vernacular synonyms. Thus, typically, the "fortitude and magnanimitie" of the 1530 edition have become "strength and courage" seven years later.

The success of *The Governor* prompted a similar success for its author. As an outstanding scholar and a self-proclaimed monarchist, Elyot was brought ever nearer to the center of things and although Henry never declared it as such, he was rewarded by being made ambassador to the court of the Holy Roman Emperor Charles V. In this post he was described by Chappuys, the imperial ambassador to England and as such his opposite number, as "Master Vuylliot, a gentleman of 700 or 800 ducats of rent, formerly in the cardinal's service, now in that of the lady [Anne Boleyn] who has promoted to this charge."[10]

Elyot's main task was to obtain Charles V's assent to Henry's much-desired divorce from his wife Catherine of Aragon. At the same time he was deputed to help Stephen Vaughan, the English agent at Antwerp, to search for the heretical theologian William Tyndale, whose translation of the Bible into the vernacular had so appalled the ecclesiastical authorities. (According to Jürgen Schäfer, Tyndale was also the author of one of those glossaries upon which the next century's dictionaries would draw.[11]) The king, who saw Vaughan as overly partial to Tyndale, viewed Elyot as more reliable. He appears to have been right: while subsequent biographers have praised Vaughan for his tolerance, Elyot is generally seen as a dubious figure, who "consented to be employed in the main work of trepanning Tyndale to gratify the King's evil passions."[12] But Elyot, who arrived in Antwerp in December 1531, was no more capable than Vaughan of persuading the dissident to return to England. Tyndale remained in the Low Countries until 1535, when the emperor had him arrested; he was strangled and burnt at the stake a year later.

After Antwerp Elyot moved on to Ratisbon, which he reached in March 1532. Despite his commission, he was unable to see Charles, who had fallen from his horse, an accident, as Elyot wrote to the duke of Norfolk, "which almoste grievith me as moche as the Emperors fall grievith him." Elyot was an entertaining correspondent, whose letters to Norfolk give a vivid picture of the towns through which he passed.

Wormes "for the more part and allmoste the hole, is possessid with Lutherians and Jewes," Spires [Spier] "kepith yet their faith well, [although] one thing I markid, suche as were lovers, divers of them hadd theire paramors sitting with theim in a draye which was drawen with a horse trapped with bells, and the lovers, whipping theim, causid theim to trott and to draw theim thurghoute everie strete, making a grete noyse with their bells; the women sate with theire heddes discoverid, saving a chaplet or crounet wrought with nedil wark. I hadd forgoten to tell that there were grete hornes sett on the horsis heddis I suppose it was the tryumphe of Venus, or of the Devil, or of bothe."

Nuremberg was "the moste propre towne and best ordred publike weale that ever I beheld," an opinion that may have been helped by the fact that the town Senate sent Elyot "thirty galons of wyne, twenty pikes, thirty carpes, a hundred dasis [dace], with sondry confectiones." And "One thing liked me well (to shew your Grace freely my hart). All the preestes had wyves; and thei were the fayrist women of the towne . . ." He was also shown the stocks of harness, ordnance, and corn, all of which hugely impressed him. "The provision of grayn I am aferd to reherse it for jeoperding my credence."

But if he succeeded as a letter writer, he failed as a diplomat. Back at court in the spring of 1532 he was forced to tell the king that Charles was dead-set against the proposed divorce (and Crofts suggests that "like all high-minded men" so too was Elyot). Henry was less than pleased. Desperate to improve the situation Elyot turned to Chappuys, trying hard to enlist him, and thus his imperial master, in Anne Boleyn's cause. He was also worried, as ever, by his own finances. Abroad he had complained that his 20s. per diem allowance was only half of what he was actually forced to spend as befitted an embassy for "the second King in Christendom" and at home he tried, in vain, to have himself released from his position as sheriff of Cambridgeshire—which he had been given for a second time. It was very expensive and as he wrote to his friend Cromwell (on November 18, 1532) "If the king should appoynt me, then I am more undone."

By 1533 Elyot had abandoned diplomacy for that occupation in which his talents had already been amply proved: writing. He began producing a variety of texts—mainly religious, philosophical, or political. Of them all, the most interesting to modern readers is undoubtedly *The Castel of Helth* (1534), which stemmed from Elyot's youthful study of Greek and oriental physicians and from his enduring friendship with Linacre. Dedicated to Cromwell, the book, in context, can be termed a manual of "alternative medicine."

> The intent of my labour was that men and women readyng this worke and obseruyng the counsayles therin should adapte therby their bodies to receiue more sure remedie by the medicines prepared by good physicions in dangerous sicknesses, thei kepyng good diete, and infourmyng diligently the same physicions of the maner of their affectes, passions, and sensible tokens. And so shall the noble and moste necessarie science of phisicke, with the ministers therof, escape the sclaunder whiche they haue of long tyme susteyned.[13]

Certainly it infuriated the medical establishment. One physician sneered that "Syr Thomas Elyot is becometh a phisicion and writeth in phisicke, which besemeth not a knight; he mought have ben muche better occupied." Elyot fought back in a lengthy rebuttal: "Truely, if they wyll call hym a phisicion

whjiche is studiouse about the weale of his countrey, I wystaufe [vouchsafe] thei so name me, for dyuryng my life I wyll in that affection alwaie continue . . ."
He defended his suggestions that diagnoses on "uncertayne tokens of urines and other excrementes" were not invariably correct and pointed out that he promoted good diet and preventive, rather than curative, medicine. Finally "if physicions be angry that I haue written physicke in englishe, let them remember that the grekes wrate in greke, the Romains in latin, Auicenna and the other in Arabike, which were their own proper and naturall tongues." And notes that although some of these were "Paynims or Jewes" they surpassed "us christians" in that they made no effort to keep those who wished to study medicine from learning about it.

He also discussed his own health problems, offering his cure for a cold that had, for the last four years, apparently defeated the doctors, who could only advise warm headgear. After checking in Galen,

> I perceyued that I had ben longe in an errour. Wherfore first I dyd throwe away my quylted cappe and my other close bonettes, and onely dyd lye in a thynne coyfe, . . . and ware a light bonet of veluet only. Than made I oxymel after the doctrine of Galen, sauynge that I boyled in the vynegar rootes of persely and fenell with endyue, cichory, and betayne, and after that I hadde taken it thre dayes continually, euery day thre sponesful in the mornynge warme, than toke I of the same oxymell, wherein I had infused or steapid one dramme of Agaryke and halfe a dramme of fyne Reubarbe, the space of iii dayes and iii nyghtes. Whyche I receyued in the mornynge, eatynge noo meate vi houres after, and that but a lyttel brothe of a boyled henne, wherof ensuyd viii stoles abundant of choler and fleume. Soone after I slepte soundly and had good appetite to eate. After supper I wolde eyther eate a fewe colyander sedes prepared, or swalowe downe a litel fyne mastyx, and forbeare wyne and dranke only ale, and that but lytell and stale and also warmed. And sometyme in the morninge woulde take a perfume of Storax Calamitae, and now and than I wolde put in to my nosethrilles eyther a leafe of grene laurell or betaine, or water o maiorame bruised, which caused the humour to distill by my nosethrilles. And if I lacked storax, I toke for a perfume the ryndes of olde rosemary and burned them, and held my mouth ouer the fume closynge myne eyes; afterwarde to comfort my stomake and make it strong, sometyme I wold eate with my meat a litel white pepper grosse bruysed, sometyme Galens electuary made of the iuice of quinces called Diacytonites, somtyme marmalade of

quynces or a quynce rosted. And by this diete I thanke almighty god, unto whome onely be gyuen all glory, I was redueed to a better state in my stomache and head than I was xvi yeres before, . . .

The public voted with their purses: the *Castel of Helth* was reprinted ten times up to 1595.

Despite his earlier failure, the king had not given up on Elyot and in 1535 sent him once more in pursuit of Charles V. He chased the emperor first to Barcelona, then on his expedition to Tunis and finally caught up with him in Naples. It was there that he learned from Charles himself that his old friend Thomas More had been executed. By 1536 Elyot had returned home and found himself facing a couple of problems. The first stemmed from a recent decree which had called for the surrendering of any privately owned copies of "Papist" sermons, especially that which Archbishop Fisher had preached in 1509 on the death of Lady Margaret, the mother of Henry VII. Based on John xv:26 it was deemed decidedly popish.

Elyot, keen to cover his back, wrote promptly to Cromwell admitting that while he had a large book collection, and that he had bought the Fisher sermon, he had long since lost it. He further assured Cromwell that he accepted Protestantism and that he utterly rejected "the pompouse authoritie of the Bisshop of Rome." He also asked once more, and as vainly as ever, for proper payment for his years of diplomatic work. More problematical was his long friendship with the recently executed Thomas More. Once again, in autumn 1536, Elyot wrote to Cromwell, seeking to clear his name. Given the frequency with which heads were rolling, one must sympathize with his determination to keep his own, but his disavowal of what had been an intimate friendship does his probity no favors. "I therefoe beseche your goode Lordship to lay apart the remebraunce of the amity between me and Sir Thomas More, which was but *usque ad aras* [literally "as far as the altar"], as is the poverb, consideryng that I was never so moche addict unto hym as I was unto truthe and fidelity toward my sovereigne lord as godd is my juge." The proverb in question is taken from the answer supposedly given by Plutarch to Pericles when refusing the request of a friend to give false testimony on his behalf. "Usque ad aram amicus sum," he declared, a phrase translated as "I'm a friend, but not a perjurer before God."

And referring back to the Fisher sermon, Elyot stresses that "I have in as moche detestation as any man lyving all vayne supersticions, superfluouse ceremonyes, sklaunderose ionglynges, countrefaite mirakles, arrogant usurpacions of men callid Spirituall, and masking religious, and all other abusions of Christes holy doctrine and lawes."

For what would prove to be the last ten years of his life, Elyot continued to fulfill his role as a local dignitary in Cambridgeshire and concentrated on his literary ambitions. In 1536 or 1537 he began researches for his *Dictionarie*. A new edition of *Pasquyll the Plaine* (a study of the judicious use of freedom of speech that he had originally written in 1533) followed in 1540, and the same year saw *The Defence of Good Women*.

The publication, also that year, of *The Image of Governance, compiled of the Actes and sentences notable of the moste noble Emperour Alexander Seuerus, late translated out of Greke into Englyshe by syr Thomas Elyot, knight, in favour of nobylitie* managed to provoke a new controversy. It was widely claimed that Elyot had simply forged this allegedly Greek work and passed it off as his own. There were lengthy debates, attacks, and rebuttals. There was no real solution, although such Elyot partisans as H. H. S. Crofts are in no doubt as to the truth.[14] In July 1545 Elyot produced his final work, *A Preservative agaynste Deth*. It was dedicated to Sir Edward North, chancellor of the Court of Augmentations, which collected money from the revenues of the suppressed monasteries, and contained passages from Scripture and from the Fathers.

Thomas Elyot died on March 26, 1546. He was buried in the church at Carleton, Cambridgeshire. A large monument was erected to his memory, but it had vanished within a century. It was probably destroyed as part of the Puritan destruction of "idols." He left no children and his widow Margaret remarried, to James Dyer, who succeeded her first husband as the local MP. She died in August 1560.

All other works aside, it is for his *Dictionarie* that Elyot is best remembered. *The Dictionarie of Syr Thomas Eliot, knight* was published in 1538. It was, as Sir James Murray pointed out in his Romanes lecture of 1900, the first ever English reference work to employ the word "Dictionary" in its title.[15] The century would still see an *Alvearie* and an *Abecedarium*, but they would prove aberrations. From Elyot onward, the generic term for an alphabetically arranged, defined word list would be "dictionary." It had been two years in the making and would stand as the first of a series of dictionaries which would appear over the next fifty-odd years, illustrating the shift from the old *Promptorium* and *Ortus* to the next century's *Table Alphabeticall* and beyond. Indeed, so keen was Elyot to emphasize his distance from the essentially medieval bases of those earlier works that he completely ignored them in his preface. He cites many sources, primarily classical, but neither of these, his immediate predecessors and works of which he was presumably aware, is acknowledged. Paradoxically, given the impetus to English writing that Elyot had given in *The Governor,* the dictionary is a Latin to English work, but the methods he used would be adapted by lexicographers of the vernacular too.

As DeWitt Starnes explained:

> Elyot's . . . ideal, inspired by the new learning, was to compile a dictionary that would exemplify classical Latin and the English idiom of his own day. It should be obvious that his ideal of classical Latinity was but partially realized and that his lexicon, like many later ones, still contains a goodly amount of medieval matter. Nevertheless, under the influence of Continental predecessors, he laid the foundation for a system of lexicography in England, a foundation on which his successors continued to build during the sixteenth century. This system involves the alphabetical arrangement of terms to be defined; the giving of grammatical information; the use, on a limited scale, of quotations from standard Latin authors to establish meaning and usage; the occasional citation of authorities; and the insertion of much mythological, biographical, and historical matter. This system, with all its shortcomings, may be regarded as the beginning of modern Latin-English lexicography.[16]

Strictly speaking, the work that Elyot published in 1538 is the third Latin-English dictionary, but in his eyes, and in those of his European peers, neither the *Promptorium parvulorum* nor the *Ortus vocabulorum* were worthy of the name. The author Ludovicus Vives, a visitor to England in the 1520s, had pointed this out in his treatise *De tradendis disciplinis* (1531), when he dismissed those two fifteenth-century dictionaries as "the mere vocabularies of schoolboys." He called for the creation of something better. Elyot had already asserted his credentials as a lexicographer with *The Boke called the Gouernor;* now he took up this new challenge. He began researching in 1537. This work was hugely augmented when reports of his efforts reached the king, who promptly threw open the royal library to aid Elyot's researches. It meant recasting the book, and in the event publishing a lengthy corrigendum in the first edition, but it made for a much better work.

As assiduous a courtier as ever, Elyot dedicated the book to King Henry and in his *Proheme* explains his method. Not only does he include words as such, but also a large amount of what would in modern eyes be termed extraneous material, better suited to an encyclopedia. Nor, in these sections, does he affect the distanced role of the scholar. His entry on the Scots is typical. Other than the headword, the definition is devoted, in Latin and in an English translation, to the words of St. Jerome, who declares, "Whenne I was a boye, I sawe in Fraunce, scottes, a people of Britayn, eate mennes flesshe: and whanne they founde in the forestes herdes of swyne, beastes and cattayle, the wolde cutte the buttockes of the boyes, whyche kepte theym, and also the womens pappes, and toke that to be the moste deyntie and delycate meate."

As the equally opinionated Dr. Johnson's efforts would make clear, two centuries later, the Scots seem to fare badly in lexicographical terms. No wonder Scottish lexicography, as practiced by Chambers and others, established itself as an autonomous branch of the art. It might also be noted that Elyot, eschewing the sixteenth century's equivalent of political correctness, included "paynymes" and "detestable heretykes"; their language too, loved or loathed, was all part of the greater whole.

> I . . . aduentured to make a generall collection by the order of letters of all notable countrays, cities, mountains, and ryuers, with theyr true descriptions, boundes, the names and natures of sundry beastes, foules, serpentes, and fysshes: the declaration of a great number of herbes, trees, fruites, gummes, precyouse stones and metalles, whiche before me were neuer of any man (that I can here of) declared and sette forthe in englyshe: The true definitions of all syckenesses and kyndes of maladyes, whyche commonly doe happen to men, with the cause wherof they procede: Fynally the names of most notable personages, who from the fyrst man Adam untyll thre hundred yeres after the incarnation of Christe . . .
>
> I haue not omytted fables and inuentions of paynymes, for the more easy understandyng of poetes. I also thought it necessary to enterlace the detestable heretykes, with theyr sundry heresyes, concernynge the substance of our catholyke faythe iustly condemned by the hole consent of all true chrysten men, to the intente that those heresyes beinge in this wyse diuulgate, may be the sooner espyed and abhorred . . . I haue sette out the computation of tyme callid Chronography, wherin it appereth how longe the persons were eyther before the incarnation of Christe, or howe longe after. Also I haue declared the auncient coynes, weyghtes, and measures, conferryng them with those whiche be currant and usuall amonge us. I haue planted in Prouerbes, callyd Adagia, such as be founden in authours, with theyr expositions. Also the proper termes belongyng to phisyke and surgery, and other dyuers and sundry artes and scyences . . .

Like many of his successors, Elyot based his belief in the excellence of his own efforts on what he felt were the failings of earlier works. In listing these criticisms he both underlines those failings, and simultaneously manages to parade his own erudition in reading so many classical predecessors:

> I well perceyued that all though dictionaries had ben gathered one of an other, yet nethelesse in eche of them ar omitted some latin wordes interpreted in the bokes whiche in order preceded. For Festus hath manye whiche are not in Varros Analogi: Nonius hath some whiche Festus lacketh: Nestor toke nat all that he founde in them bothe. Tortelliuse is not so abundant as he is diligent: Laurentius Valla wrate only of words which are called elegancies, wherin he is undoubtedly excellent; Perottus in Cornucopie dyd omitte almost none that before him were written, but in wordis compounde he is to compendiouse; Fryere Calepine (but where he is augmented by other) nothyng amended but rather appaired that which Perottus had studiousely gathered . . .

Nor was he always so confident himself. But with royal encouragement, and his own best efforts, he had indeed produced a work that surpassed, as he hoped, everything that had gone before.

> Whan I consydred all this I was attached with an horrible feare, remembryng my dangerous enterprise (I being of so smal reputation in lernyng in comparison of them whom I haue rehersed) as well for the difficultie in the true expressynge the lyuely sence of the latine wordes as also the importable labours in serching, expending and discussing the sentences of ancient writers. This premeditation abated my courage, and desperation was euen at hand to rent al in pieces that I had written had nat the beames of your royal maiestie entred into my harte . . . wherwith my spirite was reuyued and hath set up the sayle of good courage, and under your graces gouernance, your highnesse being myn onely mayster and styrer [steerer] of the shyppe of all my good fortune, I am entred in the goulfe of disdaynous enuie, hauynge fynished for this tyme this symple Dictionarie, wherin I dare affirme may be founde a thousande mo latine wordes than were togither in any one Dictionarie publyshed in this royalme, at the tyme whan I fyrste began to write this commentarie, which is almost two yeres passed . . .

He goes on to apologize for his errors, to trust that with his dictionary, "[M]enne beinge studious may understande better the latine tunge in syxe monethes than they mought haue doone afore in thre yeres withoute perfyte

instructours, whyche are not many, and suche as be are not easy to come by"
and, as oleaginous a courtier as ever, promises that,

> For my parte I render most humble thankes unto your maiesdtie for the
> good estimation that your grace retayneth of my poore lerning and hon-
> estie, promysynge therfor to your highnes that duryng my lyfe naturall
> I shall faythfully employe all the powers of my wytte and body to serue
> truely your maiestie in euery thynge wherto your mooste excellent iudge-
> ment shall thinke my seruyce conuenient and necessary. In the meane
> tyme and alway, as your bounden seruant, I shal hartily pray unto god to
> prospere your hyghenes in all your vertuouse procedynges, grauntynge
> also that your maiestie may longe raigne ouer us, to the incomparable
> comforte and ioye of all your naturall and louynge subiectes. Amen.

As far as the sixteenth century was concerned, Elyot's was the "modern" dictionary that circumstances demanded. It was based in the needs of scholarship
for a Latin-English dictionary, no doubt, but the English it used acknowledged
the advances in the vernacular and the swelling ranks of those who were now
consuming the books pouring from the English-language presses of Caxton's
successors. It would run to eight editions, and would be wholly absorbed in
Thomas Cooper's *Thesaurus Linguae Romanae et Britannicae* (1565).

A typical contemporary response can be seen in Richard Sherry's dedicatory
epistle to his *Treatise of Schemes and Tropes* (1550), where he pays tribute to

> [The] ryght worshipful knyght syr Thomas Eliot, which first in hys dic-
> tionarye as it were generallye searchinge oute the copye of oure language
> in all kynde of wordes and phrases, after that setting abrode goodlye mon-
> umentes of hys wytte, lernynge and industrye aswell in historycall knowl-
> edge, as of eyther the Philosophies, hathe herebi declared the plentyfulnes
> of our mother touge, loue toward hys country, hys time not spent in van-
> itye and tryfles.[17]

There were negative responses too: the "strange termes" that had been complained of in *The Governor* were attacked once more when they appeared in *The
Dictionarie*. What was seen as the overembellishment of English, usually by the
incorporation of Latin-based neologisms, had been a problem since the fourteenth century. What were called "aureate" (golden) terms had been employed
by a variety of writers. The practice was sometimes mocked, but the larger language debate was not yet so involved as to cause any real controversy. The mid-

sixteenth century saw a very different situation. What Elyot and his backers might see as positive enrichment, was decried as affectation by those who deplored the tainting of "pure" English by Latin. "Inkhorn terms" (coined 1543 and meaning self-consciously learned or bookish words; the inkhorn was a small portable vessel which held writing ink) or "dark words" became the subject of a bitter argument. Scholars such as Roger Ascham and Sir John Cheke opted for purity. To them English was self-sufficient and there was no need for these new terms, with their roots in Latin, Greek, Hebrew, and Arabic. "I am of this opinion," wrote Cheke to Sir Thomas Hoby in 1561, "that our own tung shold be written cleane and pure, unmixt and unmangeled with borowing of other tunges." Sir Thomas Chaloner, to whom John Withals dedicated his dictionary, declared that the users of inkhornisms were "archdoltes [and] foolelosphers [who] plainely thynke themselfes demygods, if lyke horseleches thei can show two tongues" and compared the insertion of Latinisms to the placing of "a gold rynge in a sowes nose." Even more virulent was Thomas Wilson, whose *Art of Rhetorique* (1553) was a sourcebook for Shakespeare. After savaging the users of inkhorn terms he appended a fake letter, in which he included such supposed absurdities as "mundane, capacity, clemency, verbosity, and relinquish." His supporters doubtless applauded, but all these, and many more besides, have survived.

This debate over "inkhorn terms" would last into the next century and beyond. But the supposed purity of Anglo-Saxon was debatable at best, and the simple fact that learning was equated with Latinism made it inevitable that many people, desirous of parading their own cleverness, would opt for such words. The next century would see a number of "hard-word" dictionaries, geared to making such terms accessible. And before that there would appear the works of a number of schoolmasters, typically Richard Mulcaster, Edmund Coote, and William Bullokar, whose books were geared toward introducing these terms at what he called the cutting edge of language learning: the classroom.

If Palsgrave, William Salesbury, and later Florio, offered bilingual dictionaries that gave the speakers of French, Welsh, or Italian the opportunity to augment their knowledge of English (see Chapter 4), then the dictionary published in 1552 by John Veron offered a new twist on the development of vernacular-to-vernacular works. His *Dictionariolum puerorum, tribus linguis, Latina, Anglia, et Gallica conscriptum* was in essence an English translation of a slightly earlier work, Robert Estienne's *Dictionariolum puerorum Latino-Galicum* of 1542. Indeed, as the titles make clear, Veron simply added a third language to Estienne's Latin-French original, inserting the English phrases and sentences between the Latin and French ones. However, Veron's efforts, while generally faithful to his source, are not utterly slavish. Scholarly analysis of the text shows that he may well have used an English dictionary, based on Latin-English lexicography.[18] The preferred candidates are the *Ortus vocabulorum,* or the more recent *Dictionarie* of Sir Thomas Elyot.

Quite why Veron produced a dictionary in the first place is far more confusing. An enthusiastic Protestant controversialist who would suffer imprisonment for his pains, he had been born at or near Sens, in France, and styled himself "Senonensis." After studying at Orleans *c.* 1534 he moved to England in 1536. He attended Cambridge University, but did not graduate, then began work as a tutor. By 1548 his devotion to aggressive Protestantism was in full swing. In that year he published *Certyne litel Treaties set forth by J. V. for the erudition and lernyng of the symple and ignorant peopell,* an omnibus work that included four tracts, entitled "The Five abominable Blasphemies contained in the Mass," "The Byble the Word of God," "No Human Lymmes the Father hath," and "The Mass is an Idol." In 1550 he moved to Worcester and began publishing translations of Protestant texts, notably the works of the Swiss theologian Zwingli. In 1551 he was made first deacon and then a priest. On January 3, 1552 he became rector of St. Alphage, Cripplegate in London.

Nearly two years later, on August 16, 1553, Veron was committed to the Tower of London as a seditious preacher. This followed an affray at Paul's Cross which also involved another militant Protestant, John Bradford (1510?–55) who would be executed on the orders of "Bloody" Queen Mary in June 1555, and who comforted a fellow martyr as the flames were lit, "Be of good comfort, brother, for we shall have a merry supper with the Lord this night." Paul's Cross, within the precincts of St. Paul's cathedral, had once been the site of an annual folk moot and had long served as the platform from which all the great occasions of state had been announced; by the sixteenth century the Cross, a wooden, lead-covered pulpit, served as a contemporary "Speaker's Corner," later described by Thomas Carlyle as the "Times newspaper of the Middle Ages." Political and religious speeches were given regularly and Henry VIII had commanded that Catholicism should be "preached down" from its steps. As well as Veron, such distinguished divines as Latimer, Ridley, Gardiner, Coverdale, and Laud all preached there. In 1553 Queen Mary's fervent Catholicism had replaced Henry's Reformation zeal and it was now Protestantism that was officially the object of the Paul's Cross preachers. That Veron's sermon resulted only in imprisonment should be seen as lucky.

But survive he did and while in the Tower he published a translation of Bullinger's pamphlet "A Dialogue between a Libertine and a Christian." On release, following the accession of Queen Elizabeth in 1558, he became a full-time preacher at Paul's Cross and in 1559 prebendary of St. Paul's. He enjoyed a number of other ecclesiastical appointments prior to his death, in bed, in 1563. For all his fiery youth and contentious maturity, Veron appears to have enjoyed a certain degree of clout. Certainly when attacks were made on his character, their authors were forced to do public penance. In October 1559 he preached before the queen herself, and among the various anti-Anabaptist tracts that he wrote, one was dedicated to Elizabeth.

None of which explains his indulgence in lexicography. One can understand his allegiance to promoting the language of his native France, albeit a far less Protestant country than, say Germany, but the compilation, or translation, of a dictionary seems slightly out of character. Nor, despite his book being aimed at the young, was he a schoolmaster. But whatever the cause he appears to have picked up a copy of Estienne's bilingual original and added the English dimension. The similarities of the two works, and the acknowledged origins of Veron's efforts, have led to some confusion in its title. Some authorities credit Veron alone, but given that the title page states openly that the work is Estienne's, with English additions by Veron, the current attribution is to both men.

In 1575 a revised edition apeared, edited by Rodolphus Waddington, a schoolmaster at Christ's Hospital. Waddington also stressed the origins of the work, although his edition carried a new title: *A Dictionary in Latine and English, heretofore set foorth by Master Iohn Veron, and now newly corrected and enlarged For the vtilitie and profit of all young students in the Latine tongue, as by further search therin they shall finde.* In his preface Waddington explains some of Veron's motivation. Noting the importance of learning foreign languages for the purposes both of expanding one's knowledge and in the pursuit of trade, and giving credit to "that learned Knight Syr Thomas Eliot" and to Thomas Cooper (whose work, which took Elyot as its basis, had appeared in 1565), he points out that such scholarly works "cannot be comprised in any smal volume fitte in price or bulke, for young students."

Therefore that worthy French Printer Robert Steuens, thought good to draw a short Dictionary into Latine and French for the use of his countrey schollers, wherunto Maister Iohn Veron Senouois, likewise a French man, and a painefull preacher of Gods Gospell here amongst us, desiring to promote our youth in the Latine tongue, wherein he was very skilfull, added the English. These Bookes being all sold, and the meaner [poorer] learned youth of this land wholly unprouided, I was intreated by one desirous to further learning, to ouer looke and augment the same . . .

After deprecating his own abilities as compared to those of his predecessors, and explaining how only his national duty had overcome his natural reticence, Waddington added that in his edition he had chosen to omit the French, preferring to use the available space for increasing the word list. He dedicated his efforts to "the toward youth of my Cuntrey, to whom I wish such furtherance in learning as they may therby not only attaine both praise and aduancement in the true understanding of Gods truth, whereby they may the more faithfully serue, our Queene and common weale heere, but also assure themselues of euerlasting praise and euerlasting aduancement in Christ Jesu."

Although Sir Thomas Elyot, in the title of his own work, set down the term "dictionary" as the synonym of choice for a defined, alphabetical word list, and the older Latin *dictionarium* can be found in England on a wide range of works, dating back to those of Aelfric and later Garland, it remained for a few years more one of many. Indeed, Elyot's own work was swiftly rechristened: its later editions were known as *Bibliotheca Eliotae:* Eliot's library. Looking back from 1600, wordbooks are variously entitled alvearies, cure-alls (the *Catholicon*), dictionaries, gardens (the *Ortus*), glossaries, handfuls (the *Manipulus*), marrows (the *Medulla*), lexicons, woods (the *Synonymorum sylva*), treasure houses (the *Promptorium* and a number of thesauri), vocabularies, and common things (the *Vulgaria*). In 1552, an exceptional year for lexicography—there had already been the Veron-Estienne and a new edition of Elyot—there appeared yet another variation: the *Abecedarium Anglico-Latinum, pro tyrunculis,* compiled by Richard Huloet or Howlett.

Huloet is, alas, an opaque figure of whom very little is known. His *DNB* entry refers to his birth at Wisbech, Cambridgeshire. No precise date is offered. Two contemporaries appear in the book: it is dedicated to his patron, Thomas Goodrich, bishop of Ely and lord chancellor of England, while an entry mentions one "Lillius" as a former teacher. It may be assumed from this that Huloet had probably been a pupil of William Lily, the first high master of St. Paul's School. In his "Peroration to the English reader" Huloet states that in the making of his book he has "emploied my industrye, laboure, and dilygence almoste these tenne yeres passed." This presumes that he began work in the early 1540s; his sources, as far as can be worked out, indicate a somewhat later date, since the majority can only be traced to the latter part of the decade, although it has been suggested[19] that homage was paid to many of them almost by rote. He describes himself as a "simple craftis man" and "amongst all the most vnlerned and least knowinge."

The dedication to Thomas Goodrich brought from Thomas Fuller, in his *Worthies of England,* a comment that cast a less than positive light on its author's profession:

> Some will condemn him of indiscretion, in presenting so low a subject to so high a person, as if he would teach the highest statesman in the land to spell aright. Others will excuse him, his book being though of low, of general use to the common people, who then began to betake themselves to reading (long neglected in the land), so that many who had one foot in their grave had their hand on their primer.[20]

The original *abecedaria* were works from which children could learn the alphabet. Huloet aimed his work at the same juvenile audience, *tyrunculis* or young beginners, but in the context of what he produced, it took on a slightly altered meaning: an English-Latin dictionary for the young. Two aspects stand out at once: it is the first bilingual dictionary of the sixteenth century to set the headwords in English and the equivalents in Latin. It also offers its users more English words than any predecessor. A third innovation is Huloet's notes on the individual letters of the alphabet, although this sort of discussion, which has its origins in Calepino, can also be found in earlier Latin-English dictionaries. Finally, while previous dictionaries had largely confined their headwords to the briefest statement, usually a single word, Huloet's headwords can run to substantial sentences in which, after a lengthy English preamble, the Latin synonym appears almost as an afterthought. For instance, the headword that begins "stipulation" runs to ninety words, within which the term is defined in English, before one reaches the Latin *stipulatio.* "Crampe" is almost as long and, like many other entries, offers an English definition as part of the headword before concluding with the Latin term.

A further edition of Huloet appeared in 1572. Its full title runs *Huloet's Dictionarie, newly corrected, amended, set in order and Enlarged with many names of Men, Townes, Beastes, Foules, Fishes, Trees, Shrubbes, Herbes, Fruites, Places, Instruemnts, etc. And in eche place fit Phrases, gathered out of the best Latin authors. Also the frenche thereunto annexed, by which you may finde the Latin or Frenche of anye English woorde you will.* It was edited by the poet, antiquary, and historian John Higgins (*fl.* 1570–1602), who would also translate Adrian Junius' *Nomenclator.* Higgins' own works included *The Flowers, or Eloquent Phrases of Latin Speech* (its coauthor was the flogging grammarian Nicholas Udall), and a history of early Britain, *The Mirror for Magistrates.* The revision of Huloet, which took him two years, was his first book. As the title indicates, Higgins' main innovation was the addition of French terms, to augment the English and Latin of the original.

For those who hoped that "dictionary" had become the primary synonym for an alphabetized, defined wordbook, there would be distinct disappointment following the appearance of *A Shorte Dictionarie of English and Latin for Yonge Beginners* by John Withals, another vague figure who is best described as "probably a schoolmaster."[21] The word is correct, and the running head, "A littell Dictionarie for children," underlines it, but as readers would discover, Withals' book harked back far more directly to the *vocabula* and *nominales* of the Middle Ages, than to more recent publications. It was the best-selling dictionary of the century, and at that stage the best-seller of all time, running to thirteen editions. It lacked the intellectual éclat of Elyot, another best-seller, but its 6,000 headwords, arranged in a thematic order that could be traced back to the Schoolmen, and particularly to such of their successors as Grapaldus,[22] obviously met a widespread need. It was also cheap and small, which made it ideal for the mass educational market. The title page of the first edition described the work as "very necessary for children" and nearly eighty years of consistent selling make it clear that Withals was right.

In his dedication to the diplomat Sir Thomas Chaloner (1521–65), an established author and poet in his own right (and a contributor to Higgins' *Mirror for Magistrates*), Withals describes his dictionary as:

[A] thinge written by me to induce children to the latine togue, not moued thereto with the desire of vaine glory but with a feruente affeection and loue I beare unto my countrey. I haue resorted to the most famous and ancient Authours, out of the whiche, as out of cleare fountaines, I haue drawen as diligently as I could the proper names of thinges conteyned under one kynde, and disposed them in such ordre, that a very childe beyng able to reade, may with little labour profitely imprinte them in memory; whiche shall not be onely profitable for them nowe in their tendre age, but hereafter when they shalbe of more judgement and yeres, it shalbe unto them a singular treasure: for the lack whereof they shall be compelled, as I haue herde many profounde clerkes both in disputacion as also in familiar communication to use in steede of the proper and naturall woorde, a paraphrase or circumlocucion.

Above all he was convinced that his decision to reject alphabetical order, and to offer a series of developing themes, was, as a later editor, William Clerk, put

it in his preface: "the fittest order and the fittest method for yong beginners."[23]
A–Z order was too advanced for the young, and *"children* must be fed with
Milke, and led by the hands, till they be apter for stronger meats, and to goe
alone."[24] Thus, the table of contents, which begins with "the sky" and ends
with "a journey with the appurtenances" offers the names of birds, fishes, "ser-
pentes, woorms and creepinge bestes," "four-footed beastes" (including "an
oliphant [*elephas*]" and a "drumbledare [*dromedarius*]"; "beasts that labour";
"Heardesmen, haywardes, shepheardes, with such other as keepe cattel"; "the
tillage of lande with the instrumentes of husbandrie"; "the vineyard, with that
belongeth"; the names of wines; "the partes of housinge"; "the ewrie, with vessels, instrumentes and other that longeth to the ewrie (*domus aquaria*)";
"clothinge or apparell"; "instrumentes of musicke," and much more. Somewhat
surprisingly for a children's book, Withals also offers the terminology of "The
Stewes, with baudes, harlottes and theves," but the words and phrases so listed
would have offended very few. The schoolboy searcher intent on the time-
honored pursuit of scouring of a dictionary for its "dirty words" would have to
look to the fledgling slang glossaries that were just making themselves known.
As well as the themes, there are "certain phrases for children to use in familiar
speech" ("It is hard for a man to counterfeit madness," "He is never well but
when he is playing the knave"), and a selection of Latin tags and proverbs,
taken from "the best authors."

By 1616, the date of the last edition (subsequent impressions appeared in
1623 and 1634), the title was much embellished. Withals' "little Dictionarie"
was now *A Dictionarie in English & Latine deuised for the capacity of children, and
young Beginners. At first set foorth by* M. *Withals,* with Phrases both Rhythmi-
cal and Prouerbial: Recognised by Dr. *Euans; after by* Abr. Fleming: *and then by*
William Clerk. And now at this last impression enlarged with an encrease of
*Words, Sentences, Phrases, Epigrams, Histories, Poeticall Fictions, and Alphabeticall
proverbs;* with a compendious *Nomenclator* newly added at the end. *All composed
for the ease, profit and delight of* those, that desire instruction, and the better perfection of the Latin tongue. *Initio facillima et optima sunt discenda.* B.R. Printed
at *London* by *Thomas Purfoot* 1616.

Of these new editors, Dr. Lewis Evans (*fl.* 1574) was a religious controversialist. His outspoken statements in favor of Roman Catholicism earned him
the enmity of Bishop Grindal and he fled to Antwerp. While there he published *The Betrayal of the Beastliness of the Heretics* (1565), an attack on the
bishop. On his return to London he was promptly arrested. His friends extri-
cated him from jail, and at their urging he reversed his position, writing *The
Castle of Christianity, detecting the long erring state, as well of the Roman church, as of*

the Bishop of Rome, together with the defence of the Catholic faith* (1568). It was, as was noted, "as full of ill language against the Roman Catholics as the other was full of good for them." The Catholics fought back, sending out rumors that Evans had fled to Antwerp again or, better still, was dead. In fact he was in Oxford. He responded with another anti-Papist tract, *The Hatefull Hypocrisie and rebellion of the Romishe Prelacie* (1570). In 1574 there appeared his version of Withals. His last recorded appearance is a letter to the duke of Leicester implying that he was in financial trouble. He is not heard of again.

Abraham Fleming (1552?–1607), whose own *Short Dictionary in Latin & English* was published in 1586, worked on the revisions of a number of lexicographers. As well as his expanded edition of Withals, he revised Baret's *Alvearie,* revised and augmented Waddington's edition of the Veron-Estienne, and added a "dictional" index to the John Higgins' translation of Junius' *Nomenclator.* He was a poor poet, but a first-rate antiquary. Born in London around 1552 and educated at Cambridge, he was another of these clergymen who delivered their militant opinions at Paul's Cross. He was for a while chaplain to the Countess of Nottingham and Rector of St. Pancras, Soper Lane, London. He died in 1607, on a visit to his brother Samuel, the rector of Bottesford in Leicestershire.

Some fifty-nine works have been found, including his revision of Withals. Fleming does not appear to have been especially particular as to his labors. Among them are translations of the classics, religious tracts, an edition of Holinshed's *Historie of England,* and a translation of John Caius' *Of English Dogges.* He also penned a pamphlet telling of "A Straunge and Terrible Wunder wrought very late in the Parish Church of Bongay . . . the fourth of this August 1577, in a geat tempest of violent raine, lightning and thunder . . . With the appearance of a horrible-shaped Thing, sensibly perceived of the people then and there assembled," a short history of earthquakes, based on an earlier work by Frederick Nawse, and "The Diamond of Deuotion, cut and squared into six severall pointes, namelie: 1. The Footpath of Felicitie, 2. A Guide to Godlinese, 3. The Schoole of Skill, 4. A Swarme of Bees, 5. A Plant of Pleasure, 6. A Grove of Graces. Full of mainie frutifull lessons auailable vnto the leading of a godlie and reformed life."

Of all the sixteenth-century lexicographers, Thomas Cooper (1517?–94) might be considered the most purely scholarly. Born in the slums of Catte Street, Oxford, the son of a very poor tailor, Cooper took himself from the literal rags of his youth to the splendid vestments that would signify his appointment as the university's vice chancellor and in due course as the Bishop of Winchester. He managed to have himself educated as a chorister at Magdalen College School, where the grammarians Stanbridge, Whittington, and Lily had all taught Latin, and showed himself so able a pupil that he was elected to Magdalen College itself. After graduation he worked as a teacher, before becoming his old school's headmaster.

A Protestant believer, he had intended to join the Church, but the accession of the fiercely Catholic Queen Mary dissuaded him from so open a confession of his faith. Instead he began practicing as a doctor in Oxford. In 1545 he took over the writing of the late Thomas Lanquet's *Chronicle of the World.* Its author, who had died aged only twenty-four, had covered the period from the Creation to the year 17 A.D. Cooper spent the next four years reaching the reign of Edward VI. His section ran to three times the length of his predecessor's work. The work was published in 1549, now renamed *Cooper's Chronicle.* It is a compendious volume, if occasionally somewhat fanciful. For instance for the year 1452 it is noted that "one named Johannes Faustius fyrst founde the crafte of printinge, in the citee of Mens . . ."

When another edition, with new material by a third writer, appeared in 1559, Cooper was much annoyed and promptly set about publishing a further two editions of his own work. They appeared in 1560 and 1565. At same time as he compiled the *Chronicle,* he had also been working to complete his revision of Thomas Elyot's *Dictionarie* of 1538, to be called the *Biblioteca Eliotae.* It appeared in 1548. A further edition, *Eliot's Dictionary, the second time enriched and more perfectly corrected by Thos. Cooper . . . ,* came out in 1559.

With the queen dead and her Protestant successor safely placed on the throne, Cooper finally managed to take his orders and soon gained a reputation as a zealous preacher. He also began work on his magnum opus: the *Thesaurus Linguae Romanae et Britannicae,* which appeared in 1565. So delighted was Queen Elizabeth with his work that she announced that she wished to promote its author as high as was in her power.

His private life was less enviable. His wife, Amy, bored perhaps by his endless ferreting among the manuscripts, was notoriously generous with her sexual favors. So celebrated was one particular affair, with the canon of Christ Church, that her lover was bound over to avoid her company, and a contemporary satire, detailing the amours of various Oxonian worthies and lovingly reproduced by Anthony à Wood, devoted some fifteen innuendo-laden verses to Amy Cooper's dalliances. The hapless Cooper turned a blind eye. He was similarly forbearing when, as John Aubrey put it, his wife, "irreconcileably angrie with him for sitting-up late at night so, compileing his Dictionarie . . . threw it into the fire and burnt it. Well, for all that, the good man had so great a zeale for the advancement of learning, that he began it again."[25] Hearing of this new persecution, the university authorities offered to arrange a divorce, but long-suffering Cooper rejected their aid. The couple would never part, and Amy Cooper is duly included, alongside their daughters Elizabeth and Mary, in her late husband's will.

An innocent at home he may have been, but Cooper was as enthusiastic as any contemporary in embracing the religious controversies of the time. In 1562 he began involving himself in theological debate, and when Bishop Jewel published his pamphlet "Apology of the Private Mass," Cooper hit back with "An Answer in Defence of the Truth against the Apology of the Private Mass."

Whether through his queen's patronage or not, Cooper continued to climb the ladder of clerical success. In 1576 he became dean of Christ Church and was vice chancellor of the university for several years. He was dean of Gloucester in 1569 and bishop of Lincoln a year later. His "Brief Exposition of the Sunday lessons" (1573) was placed, by order of Archbishop Parker, in every church, as the ideal way of explaining church ritual to the laity. He reached the peak of his career with his appointment in 1584 as bishop of Winchester. Much noted, as Anthony à Wood points out, "for his learning and sanctity of life," he held the post until his death ten years later. It was during his tenure that the slang term "Winchester goose," meaning syphilitic bubo, is first recorded. The stews of Southwark, host to such diseases, were part of his diocese.

In 1589 he returned to the religious fray when he became involved, as a determined representative of the Establishment, in clashes with author of the Martin Marprelate tracts. Seven of these had appeared between 1588 and 1589, attacking clergy "with coarse wit and invective."[26] Cooper fought back with the deeply grave "Admonition to the People of England, wherein are answered not only the slanderous untruths uttered by Martin the Libeller, but also many other crimes by some of the brood, objected generally against all Bishops and the chief of the Clergy purposely to deface and discredit the present state of the Church" (1589). Marprelate replied with a cheeky new pamphlet entitled, "Ha'ye any work for the Cooper?," and followed it with a successor, "More Work for Cooper," which was found in Marprelate's press when it was seized by the authorities.

Cooper has been accused of excessively severe persecution of the Catholics in Hampshire, which fell beneath the Winchester diocese. His defenders reject this charge, pointing out that in 1581 Parliament had passed an anti-Catholic act and that 1588 was the year of the Armada and of intense anti-Spanish and thus anti-Catholic feelings. A return of 1582 claims that Hampshire's 132 recusants make it the third most pro-Catholic county after Yorkshire and Lancashire. Various priests and five laymen were executed there, quite possibly on Cooper's orders. That said, Cooper appears to have had other ideas as to punishment. He seems to have approved of an early form of transportation, suggesting in a letter that "an hundred or two of obstinate recusants, lusty men, well able to labour, might by some convenient commission be taken up and sent to Flanders as pioneers and labourers, whereby the country would be disburdened of a company of dangerous people and the rest that remained be put in some fear." Cooper was also very enthusiastic in the putting down, as commanded by the queen, of "prophesyings" in his area.

Thomas Cooper died on April 29, 1594; he is buried in Winchester Cathedral. A monument, since lost, described him as *"munificentissimus, doctissimus, vigilantissimus, summe benignus egenis."*

Tracts and pamphlets apart, the *Thesaurus* is Cooper's great work, with his revision of Elyot proving a useful way station. A century later, Francis Gouldman, writing his historical introduction to his own *Copious Dictionary in Three Parts* (1664), recalled Cooper's role.

> Sir Th. Eliot, an able Lawyer, and every way a famous Scholar in those days first brake the Ice as to our English Tongue, with great pains Compiling a Latine and English Dictionary called his Bibliotheca, in the Reign of King Henry the Eighth, to whome it is Dedicated. This work Thomas Cooper, in the beginning of the Reign of Edward the Sixth, Augmented and Enriched with Three and thirty thousand Words and Phrases, besides a fuller account of the true Signification of Words; farther declaring, That there was a complaint of innumerable Faults in Eliot, by too strict following Calepine, the mistakes of Impressions, or his own hast and oversight. Afterward the Reverend and Learned Cooper, Bishop of Lincoln, reserving still as a Foundation Eliot's and his own former Labours upon him, and making great use of Stephen's [Estienne's] Thesaurus . . . put forth his Thesaurus linguae Romanae & Britannicae, about the year 1565.

Martin Marprelate was less kind, observing during their quarrel that "His Lordship of Winchester is a great Clarke, for he hath translated his Dictionarie, called Cooper's Dictionarie, verbatim out of Robert Stephanus his Thesaurus, and ill-favoured too, they say!"[27] He challenged Cooper's character, calling him "a monstrous hypocrite, for he is a very duns [dunce], not able to defend an argument, . . . he will cog [sl.: cheat] and face it out, for his face is made of seasoned wainscot, and willie as fast as a dog can trot."[28] Poor Cooper was furthermore "a sodden headed Asse,"[29] "Tom Tubtrimmer"[30] and "old soaking student,"[31] and a "sicly Schoolemaster, being also as unlearned as a man of that trade and professsion can be."[32]

Praise or vituperation aside, what is most important about Cooper's lexicography, whether as a reviser of Elyot or on his own behalf, is his willingness to cut what he saw as dross and to replace it with the purer Latin of the classical period. Elyot and his predecessors had been far more tolerant of barbarous "modern" Latin, while Cooper preferred the example of Robert Estienne, of whose work he had observed, "The greatness [size] is the onely inconvenience of that Golden Work." Whether his adoption of the title "Thesaurus" was in deliberate homage to Estienne, whose own *Thesaurus* appeared in 1552, is unknown, but one cannot but note the fact. At the same time he trimmed much of the encyclopedic matter, typically the myths and legends of bygone men and creatures and details of faraway flora and fauna, which had enlivened earlier editions. These were either shortened, or dropped completely.

Like his hero, Cooper produced a dictionary notable for its "greatness" but as Gabriele Stein points out, it is quality and not quantity that makes Cooper's work important.[33] He is simply better ordered than any lexicographer who has come before. Accepting that consistency is the mark of the best dictionaries, Cooper has attended properly to the minutiae. He has stripped out the proper names, still inevitable, and placed them in a separate appendix; his headwords and the definitions that accompany them gain added clarity from different fonts; he included special spacings and symbols to put across other important information. He is not, however, immune to self-indulgence. Where Elyot appears to have had a problem with the Scots, his reviser apparently had one with the Welsh. After setting out on a perfectly reasonable definition, "The countrey of Wayles on the west syde of Englande . . .," he suddenly lurches off:

This haue I here put, not beuase I thynke it is vnknowen to any Englysh man, but to take an occasion to clere my selfe of an vniust and false suspicion, that by malicious and naughtie tongues hath been spredde of me, as though I should not beare good mynde vnto that country, and that I haue wrytten against it in [my] Chronicle . . .

And on he runs for forty lines of wounded self-justification. Perhaps Marprelate's jibes struck deeper than Cooper's few and dignified rejoinders admitted.

But Cooper's abilities far outweigh such aberrations, especially when it comes to the translations that explain the various Latin headwords. These often offer a range of synonyms, drawn from a variety of languages. Each of these illuminates the term and, for the latter-day scholar, offers an insight into a wide range of Elizabethan idioms. As DeWitt Starnes points out "Transforming foreign definitions into the vernacular was Cooper's special effort and his pride."[34]

Peter Levins is another of those dictionary makers whose biography must remain a shadowy sketch. Born at or near Eske, Yorkshire, he appears at Magdalen College in 1552 and in 1557 was elected probationer fellow on "a Yorkshire place" (i.e., a closed scholarship).[35] He became a full fellow in 1559 but abandoned his fellowship a year later. What became of him thereafter is unknown, other than that he taught at a grammar school and practiced medicine. The date of his death is not recorded, but in the years that remained Levins published two books: A *Pathway to Health* and the *Manipulus Vocabulorum.*

"So many Dictionaries of Latin and English (gentle Reader) haue now beene of late by diuers sundrye writers set forth, that except some kind of Noueltie should bring delite to the persuers . . . it should be but a vaine thing."[36] The "Noueltie" that makes what H. B. Wheatley terms "a very curious little work"[37] is that the *Manipulus Vocabulorum,* or "handful of words," is England's first rhyming dictionary. As its title page declares, it is "A Dictionarie of English and Latine wordes, set forthe in such order, as noneheretofore hath ben, the *English* going before the *Latine,* necessary not onely for Scholers that want varietie of words, but also for such as use to write in English meetre." To that end the work is broken down into nine sections, listed according to the final syllable of a word—the prerequisite of a rhyme—and arranged by vowels and diphthongs.

Reading Levins' preface, which with its "Note for the vse of the booke" offers readers the most lucid explication to date of both a lexicographer's intent and a dictionary's operation, it is clear that his aims are as much sociological as intellectual. Like Withals before him, he is aiming at the "young beginner," and, equally importantly, at the poorest of such neophytes. Levins' is the clearest statement yet of a lexicographer's desire not merely to augment existing knowledge, but to implant it among those who would otherwise be denied such help. The "hard-word" dictionaries of the next century would also target those whose learning their authors wished to improve, but those putative readers were the emergent middle classes. Levins was interested in a different class. Other lexicographers, typically Huloet, had provided for "greter students" and offered "great and costly" works, "ful of phrases and sentences fit for them that vse oration and oratorie." Levins had no such aspirations. His dictionary "is onely stuffed full of words, and the vse thereof fit for them that are not yet come to better exercises."[38] With his focus unequivocally upon the unlearned poor, Levins can be seen as a precursor of that later champion of mass education, John Wesley.

Levins' other recorded work, *A Right Profitable Booke for all Disease, called the Pathway to Health,* appeared in 1587. Based, no doubt, upon his experiences as a doctor, it too deals with language. In its preface Levins defends himself against those who criticize him for writing in vulgar English rather than scholarly Latin, noting that those who feel this way are simply masking their desire to hide useful knowledge, in this case of one's health, from the majority of people. This is not merely foolish, it is actively malicious and "exceeding damnable and devilish."

Next in the sixteenth century's litany of dictionary production is a volume apostrophized by H. B. Wheatley as "one of the most quaint and charming of all the early Dictionaries."[39] This is *An Alvearie: or triple dictionarie* (1573), compiled by John Baret. It comprised English, French, and Latin words. His *Quadruple Dictionarie,* an expanded edition adding Greek and "newlie enriched with a varietie of wordes, phrases, proverbs and divers lightsome observations of Grammar," appeared, posthumously, in 1580. John Baret, or Barrett, was Fellow of Trinity College, Cambridge, where he received his B.A. in 1544–5 and an M.A. in 1558. He is said subsequently to have taught in London and possibly to have traveled abroad. He received an M.D. from Peterhouse, Cambridge, in 1577, though there is no evidence that he ever practiced medicine. His will was proved in 1578.

Baret is best appreciated in his own words. In his dedicatory letter to Lord Burghley (1520–98, chief minister to Elizabeth I), he explains the genesis and gestation of his book.

About eyghtene yeares agone, hauing pupils at Cambridge studious of the Latin tongue, I vsed them often to write epistles and themes togither, and daily to translate some piece of English into Latin, for the more speedy, and easie attaining of the same. And after we had a little begunne, perceyuing what great trouble it was to come running to mee for euery word they missed, (knowing then of no other Dictionarie to helpe vs, but Sir Thomas Eliots Librarie, which was come out a little before) I appoynted them certaine leaues of the same booke euery day to write the English before ye Latin, and likewise to gather a number of fine phrases out of Cicero, Terence, Caesar, Liuia, &c. and to set them vnder seuerall Tytles, for the more ready finding them againe at their neede. Thus within a yeare or two they had gathered togither a great volume, which (for the apt similitude betweene the good scholars and diligent Bees in gathering their wax and hony into their Hiue) I called then their Aluearie, both for a memoriall by whom it was made, and also by this

name to incourage other to the like diligence, for that they should not see
their worthy prayse for the same, vnworthily drowned in obliuion.

Baret and his pupils intended their efforts for their own use only, but the
Alvearie's fame spread and inevitably there were calls for its wider publication.
Baret being "both vnwilling, and halfe ashamed to haue our rude notes come
abrode vnder the viewe of so many learned eyes, and especially finding no lea-
sure from my prefixed studies for the polishing of the same, vtterly denied their
request." His reluctance did not last long, however. In London Baret was
offered the financial backing of Sir Thomas Smith, principal secretary to Queen
Elizabeth, "that noble Theseus of learning and comfortable patron to all students," and of Alexander Nowell, dean of St. Paul's. With his costs ensured,
Baret sought out a team of writers, employing both a number of his former
pupils, now dispersed around the inns of Court, and various other helpers, writing according to his instructions.

The dictionary, which aimed to offer its readers a three-way means of moving
between English, French, and Latin, is notable, among other things, for its
author's mention of "hard words" on both the title page and in his preliminary
address "To the Reader." "Hard words," meaning in lexicography scholarly,
classic-based terms rather than simple English words drawn on Anglo-Saxon,
are usually associated with the monolingual dictionaries of the next century,
when in his manual *Youth's Behaviour* (1663) Francis Hawkins could define a dictionary as simply "a Lexicon, a Book wherein hard words and names are mentioned and unfolded," but Baret used the term in exactly the same way. He
concentrates on the "hard words," explaining that he "thought it not meete to
stuffe this book" with "common easie words." He also chose to exclude obsolete
terms and to offer more substantial etymologies than many earlier lexicographers, even if too many appear to have been taken uncritically from Calepino
and Estienne. Baret also had his own particular ideas on spelling, reflecting rue-
fully that "We may still wonder and find fault with orthographie (or rather
cacographie in deed)" but accepting that it was up to "the learned Universities"
to amend the system. He was less than happy too with traditional alphabetical
order and apologizes for using it. Each letter is given a short essay, and few are
spared censure. He regrets the proliferation of the redundant *e* at the end of so
many words, sympathizes with those who have to discern between the *g* of "gin-
ger," "begin," and "Giles," and thinks that one could exist quite happily without *w*. He is especially worried by the letter *c,* of which he observes, "This letter
troubleth me woorst of all, and maketh me to woonder howe it got this third
place of honour, or how it hath so absurdely thus long usurped that dignitie . . ."

The second edition, which appeared in 1580, was embellished, as was the wont in a number of dictionaries, typically Cooper's, by a number of dedicatory verses in praise of the compiler. Baret had been dead two years, but he would have doubtless appreciated the following, by "Thos. M." (probably Thomas Mulcaster) whose lengthy epistle begins:

> *When Barret liude, yt first this worke did frame,*
> *In sort you see, with long and tedious toile,*
> *A Beehive hee, did deeme it best to name,*
> *Because like Bee he manie a yeere did moile . . .*

The final Latin-English dictionary of the century appeared in 1587. The *Dictionarium Linguae Latinae et Anglicanae,* compiled by Thomas Thomas (1553–88), the first official printer to the University of Cambridge, quickly established itself as a standard popular work. Five new editions of what was known as the "Thomasius" had appeared within a decade, and the book continued to enjoy reprints until 1644. The 1615 edition was further expanded by the *Lexici Latino-Anglici Paralipomena* of Philemon Holland.

Thomas was born in the city of London on Christmas Day 1553. He was educated at Eton and, as a scholar, at King's College, Cambridge. Appointed a fellow in 1574, he took his B.A. in 1575, and an M.A. in 1579; a year later he began studying theology. He was appointed printer to the university in May 1582 but no publications appeared until 1584. This delay was caused by professional jealousy: the Stationer's Company, who by royal appointment controlled all matters concerning the press, decided that his printing was an infringement of their privileges and seized his press and materials, notably a half-printed work by William Whitaker (1548–95), a Cambridge divine and master of St. John's College. Thomas had his rights restored only after the university vice chancellor and several heads of houses petitioned Lord Burghley. Thomas, who according to Martin Marprelate was known as "the puritan printer," lived less than thirty-five years. His press delivered some seventeen books, but it was working on his own dictionary that seems to have proved overly stressful. It appeared in 1587; shortly afterward Thomas contracted a fatal disease. He died in early August 1588 and was buried on August 9.

Thomas' work drew on a number of sources, notably Thomas Cooper and most importantly the French humanist Gulielmus Morelius, whose *Verborum Latinorum cum Graecis Anglicisque* had appeared in 1583. From Morelius he borrowed new techniques for the illustration of punctuation, an area of lexicography that had been largely ignored, at least by its English practitioners. He also copied Morelius in omitting the old divisions of letters into "A *ante* B," "R *ante* O" (i.e., words that began ab- or ro-), and so on.

By the late sixteenth century it might generally have been assumed that alphabetical rather than thematic order would finally have taken over in mainstream lexicography. Other than John Withals, the major compilers duly bear this out, but in the last new English-Latin dictionary of the century, John Rider's *Bibliotheca Scholastica,* the thematic system, albeit much amended, reappears.

Like so many contemporary dictionary makers, John Rider (1562–1632) was a clergyman and teacher. Born in Carrington, Cheshire, he was educated at Jesus College, Oxford, from where he graduated in 1583. That year he became rector of South Ockendon in Essex (another lexicographer, Francis Gouldman, had this living later). His main efforts were devoted to teaching and to the compilation of his dictionary, which was published in 1589. From 1597 to 1615 Rider was rector of Winwick, Lancashire, but he rarely visited his parish. At the same time he was made dean of St. Patrick's Cathedral in Dublin and in 1612 bishop of Killaloe. Rider chose to live the rest of his life in Ireland, where among other pursuits he encouraged the study and use of the Irish language. He died on November 12, 1632. Among his publications are the "Letter concerning the News out of Ireland, and of the Spaniards landing and present state there." Other than for compiling his dictionary, Rider is best remembered for his long controversy with the militant Jesuit Henry Fitzsimon (1566–1643). As a senior Protestant cleric, Rider was incensed by Fitzsimon, who set himself up in Dublin as an enthusiastically proselytizing Roman Catholic. So zealous was Fitzsimon that in 1599 he was jailed, and languished for five years in Dublin Castle. It was during that time he engaged with Rider, among others, both head-to-head and in pamphlets. Rider's case is outlined in "A friendly caveat to Ireland's Catholickes, concerning the Daungerous Dreame of Christs corporall yet invisible presence in the Sacrament of the Lord's supper," published in 1602. They battled on until 1603, when James I ordered Fitzsimon's release. He spent the next twenty-six years in exile, including a period as chaplain to the imperial army, engaged in the early period of the Thirty Years' War.

The *Bibliotheca Scholastica* was published in 1589. It was "a double Dictionarie. Penned for all those that would hauve within short space the use of the Latin Tongue, either to speake or to write" and would appear in a number of subsequent editions, including the supposedly "plagiarized" revision edited by Francis Holyoake in 1617. It is worth noting that unlike most lexicographers, who remain jealous of their creation long past its first edition, Dean Rider did his job, published his work, and decamped to Ireland. He paid no further attention to the book, and the seventeenth-century editions, even though he was alive to witness most of them, bear the name "Rider" more as a trademark than as a guarantee of authorship.

The dictionary is dedicated to Sir Francis Walsingham (1532–90), whose duties as principal secretary to Elizabeth I included running her domestic intelligence service, among the triumphs of which was the detention and eventual execution of Mary, Queen of Scots. It is prefaced by Latin verses inscribed to the earl of Sussex and William Waad (1546–1623, the ambassador to Portugal and later Clerk to the Privy Council), both of whom had helped finance the project. Rider also acknowledged help from his parishioners in Bermondsey (where he had worked briefly, possibly in the late 1580s) and his friends in and around Banbury. In the usual piece of lexicographical self-aggrandizement he claimed to have 4,000 more words than any predecessor, and furthermore that this was the first dictionary in which English terms preceded the Latin. While his word count may well be valid, the latter claim does not hold up: Huloet, Withals, and Simon Pelegromius all predated him, and all set the non-Latin language first. The much older *Catholicon Anglicum* had also reversed the classical order, but in fairness it was not printed until the nineteenth century. What Rider could claim, however, was the publication of a work in which for the first time the entire English-Latin section came before the Latin-English one. Among his sources, Rider drew heavily on his immediate predecessor, Thomas Thomas. Thomas Fuller, in his *Worthies of England* (1640) declared that he "borrowed his saddle and bridle" from the Thomasius.[40] But Rider's was generally seen as the better work and John Underhill, the bishop of London, underpinned the distinction with this couplet: *Quantum Thomasio Calepinus cedere debet | Tantum praeclaro Thomasius ipse Ridero.* ("As much as Calepino had to give way to Thomas, so did Thomas to his superior, Rider.")

Rider, perhaps more than anyone before him, establishes his proposed audience quite definitively. He also makes it clear that, despite a preface in which he mouths the usual pieties regarding his unfitness even to carry the books of those who have worked before him, he is satisfied with what he has done and more than happy to be judged upon it. The title page declares his book to be "Verie profitable and necessarie for Scholers, Courtiers, Lawyers and their Clarkes, Apprentices of London, Traveliers, Factors for Marchants, and briefly for all Discontinuers within her Maiesties Realmes of England and Ireland. *Compiled by* Iohn Rider, *Master of Artes, and preacher of Gods word.* First reade me; With others conferre; Then censure me. Read the Preface, Learne the vse."

The *Bibliotheca* falls into three parts: the English-Latin dictionary, a second English-Latin dictionary, arranged by topics (Birds, Colors, Fish, Numbers, Stones, etc.), and finally a Latin-English dictionary. The whole work is prefaced by detailed "Directions for the Reader" in which Rider explains his method and warns intellectuals that they should not forget his primary audience: "the vnlearned." Each section, even the thematic one, is arranged alphabetically. Like Cooper, Rider has planned his work well; it is, according to Stein, "one of the most ambitious lexicographical undertakings in the sixteenth century."[41] Its clarity, and thus ease of use, whether as to the page layout as a whole, or to that of individual entries, has advanced substantially. However, unlike many contemporaries, Rider has chosen to ignore the usual illustrative examples and citations from approved classical authors.

The *Bibliotheca Scholastica* reappeared in 1617, now embellished with a "Dictionarie Etymologicall," compiled by Francis Holyoake (1567–1653). Holyoake (or Holyoke) was a teacher and clergyman, the rector of Southam, Warwickshire and a member of Convocation, the legislative synod of the Church of England. An outspoken royalist, he became the target of Parliament troops, to such an extent that he and his family were ejected from their house, "his wife being so ill-used so as to hasten her death."[42] His estate, worth £300 a year, was sequestered and he and his family forced to subsist on charity for the rest of his life. Holyoake died on November 13, 1653.

This did not, however, hinder his dictionary making and by the time a fourth edition of what was ostensibly Rider's work appeared, in 1633, so substantially had it been altered and expanded that it appeared under Holyoake's name and had a new title: *Dictionarium Etymologicum Latinum.* Two editions on, in 1640, it was declared to be *"compositum et absolutum a Francisco de Sacra Quercu"* (Francis of the Holy Oak). Thomas Holyoake (1616?–75) took over before his father's death but he too died before he could publish and his revision appeared posthumously under the name of Francis' grandson Charles as *A Large Dictionary in Three Parts.*

An analysis of the various editions reveals the extent to which the Holyoakes had moved on from Rider's original, but accusations of plagiarism were made. Not, of course, by Rider himself but by the executors of Thomas Thomas, from whose book Rider himself had borrowed so liberally. Fuller comments somewhat smugly, "Such plagiaryship ill becometh authors or printers; and the dove being the crest of the Stationers' arms, should mind them, not (like rooks) to filch copies one from another" and implies that the subsequent revisions were caused not by any intellectual ambition, but by the desire to refute these allegations.[43]

In the end, as Starnes points out, "Rider" can be seen as the ultimate repository, or at least the current way station, of English lexicography. All that has gone before can be found within his pages and his own researches have pushed the system even further forward:

The major source . . . of Rider's Bibliotheca scholastica . . . was the Latin-English dictionary of Thomas Thomas [and if] we remember that Thomas was based on Cooper and Morelius, and Cooper on Elyot and Robert Stephanus and Frisius, and also that Rider supplemented the matter from Thomas by Pelegromius' Synonymorum sylva, Gualtherus' Latin edition of Julius Pollux' Onomasticon, the Huloet-Higgins, Baret, and Junius, we may agree that Rider's dictionary is an epitome of the "learned workes of all the learnedst and best Dictionaries in England." Rider's own contribution was somewhat more than that of a mere compiler: he distinguished levels of usage as respects the Latin vocabulary, made a superior collection of Latin synonyms, and, by his collection of class names, incidentally revealed the riches of Thomas's Dictionarium. The compilation thus made was destined to continue, with little change, in the Rider-Holyoke dictionaries through the seventeenth century.[44]

4

Vulgar Tongues

A s far as the sixteenth century was concerned, mainstream lexicography means Latin-English and increasingly English-Latin dictionaries. But there was another side to the period's dictionary making in which Latin was far less important. This was the world of the bilingual or polyglot vernacular dictionary.

The making and merchandising of dictionaries was primarily subject to the period's ongoing cultural developments, but there was another impetus, one in which academic debate was incidental, and the down-to-earth requirements of commerce infinitely more important. The needs of traders were definitely not intellectual. They spoke the vernacular and those with whom they traded did the same. There developed a need for "translation manuals," or bilingual dictionaries, to service the mutual needs of these merchants. The polyglot dictionaries that began with the three-language *Introito a porta* (originally published as an Italian-German dictionary by Adam von Rottweil in 1477 and expanded to three languages in 1513) and climaxed in the eleven-language editions of Calepino's superb *Dictionarium* were geared precisely to that situation. Other polyglot compilations included the *Introductio quaedam utilissima* (published in Rome in 1510) which offered Latin, Italian, French, and German and was based on the *Introito;* the *Introductio*'s descendant, the *Dictionnaire de huict languages* (Greek, Latin, Flemish, French, Spanish, Italian, English, and German; nine editions by 1580), and the *Sex linguarum* (Latin, French, Spanish, Italian, English, and German) which appeared in 1537 and ran to twenty editions by 1600. There were also more immediate reasons for a trader to pick up at least the basics of another language. During the Peasants' Revolt of 1381, according to the *Chronicle of London,* many Flemings lost their heads, "namely they that koude nat say Breede and Chese, But Case and Brode."[1]

It was another, much more restricted book, designed to address this same need for bilingualism that is the first new dictionary to appear in sixteenth-century England, beating Sir Thomas Elyot by eight years. *Lesclarcissement de la langue françoyse* by Jehan or John Palsgrave appeared in 1530. It had developed as a by-product of the peace treaty drawn up in 1514 between Henry VIII and Louis XII of France. Built into the provisions of that treaty was an arrangement for Louis to marry Mary, Henry's sister. Among the retinue that accompanied Mary to France was a tutor especially selected to help her learn her new husband's language. This teacher was John Palsgrave, born in London *c.* 1480, who had followed his education at Corpus Christi College, Cambridge with a spell gaining his M.A. at the University of Paris. Already well respected as a French teacher, he held a church office—as prebend of Portpoole, attached to St. Paul's, London—at the same time as he was deputed to help the king's sister. So successful was the trip to France that Mary would always express her indebtedness to Palsgrave. The marriage was less successful. Louis was dead within a year and Mary, along with her tutor, came home. On her return to England the newly widowed queen petitioned Cardinal Wolsey to offer her former tutor a variety of livings, and in due course he appointed Palsgrave to a succession of churches in Leicester and East Anglia.

Palsgrave's fame as a French teacher mounted and by 1617, when he paid a visit to Louvain, he was sufficiently well known to be the subject of correspondence between Erasmus and Thomas More. At Louvain he studied law and the classics, but it was as a French speaker and teacher that he was most valued, and in 1523 he entered into a contract with the London printer Richard Pynson for the printing of sixty reams of paper at 6s. 8d. a ream; a further contract specified the printing of 750 copies of a work that would explain the rules of French grammar to English readers. Pynson undertook to print both sides of a sheet every day and Palsgrave promised in return not to leave him waiting for copy. The work in question was *Lesclarcissement de la langue françoyse.*

Not only did Palsgrave have a contract with his printer, but he also had the official backing of the king. This "privilege" can be read in the dictionary's forematter, and states, in part:

> Where as our trusty and ryght welbeloued subiecte maister Johnn Pals-graue . . . hath made a boke entituled and called/Lesclarcissement de la langue Francoyse/whiche euidently appereth vnto vs . . . to be very neces-

sarye/profitable and expedient/as well for the bryngyng vp of the youth of
our nobylite/as for all other maner parsons our subiectes to attayne the
parfyte knowledge of the frenche tong . . . [we] haue liberally and
benignely graunted vnto the sayd maister Palsgrave our fauorable letters
of priuilege/convernyng his sayd boke . . . for the space and terme of
seuen yeres next and immedyatly after the date hereof enswyng. Straytly
chargyng and commandyng/all maner our subiectes/boke sellars . . . that
they ne none of them/nother print nor cause to be prynted/nother within
this our realme/nor elswhere out of our realme any nombre of bokes/after
the copy of the sayd Lesclarcissement . . . vpon payne of our hysh displea-
sure and confiscation and forfaycture of all maner suche bokes/outher
printed or bought.

Henry's affection for Palsgrave continued through his reign. In 1525 he was
hired as tutor to the king's bastard son by his mistress Elizabeth Blount: Henry
Fitzroy, the duke of Richmond and Somerset, then six years old, had just been
appointed lieutenant-general of areas north of the River Trent. For this task
Palsgrave was allotted three servants and an annual stipend of £13/6/8d. Palsgrave's name is on a number of documents issued by the Council of the North
and in 1529 he wrote to the king about his pupil, assuring him "that according
to my saying to you in the gallery at Hampton Court, I do my uttermost best
to cause him to love learning, and to be merry at it; insomuch that without any
manner fear or compulsion he hath already a great furtherance in the principles
grammatical both of Greek and Latin." In a letter to Lady Elizabeth Tailboys he
quotes the king as saying "I deliver unto you . . . my worldly jewel; thou Palsgrave, to bring him up in virtue and learning."

For all his reputation and his royal connection, Palsgrave was by no means
prosperous. In a letter to Thomas More, written in 1529, he thanked him for
his friendship and support, promised his own absolute loyalty, and added, "I
beseech you for your accustomed goodness to continue until such time that I
may once more tread under foot this horrible monster, poverty." It was apparently an ongoing problem: he wrote to Sir William Stevynson complaining
that to pay his debts, to stay alive, and support his aged mother he had but
£92 per annum from his various livings. Stevynson asked Palsgrave's old
pupil, Mary, to help get him out of trouble. By 1533 he had taken another
degree, this time at Oxford, then moved on to a living in London and subsequently, in 1545, to a place as the rector of Wadenhoe, Northants. He stayed
there until his death, sometime before August 4, 1554[2] (although Wheatley
suggests September 12).[3]

Lesclarcissement de la langue françoyse is the first French-English dictionary to appear on either side of the Channel. An earlier attempt had been made to deal with the two languages, but it was more a phrasebook than a dictionary. William Caxton's *Vocabulary in French and English* (c. 1483) is a series of dialogues and there is no trace of the alphabetical order and the arrangement by headwords that is generally assumed to imply a "proper" dictionary. Palsgrave's work was "originally intended to be a kind of dictionary for the use of Englishmen seeking to acquire a knowledge of the French tongue. In this respect it has been superseded by later works, but it is now used in England for another purpose, as one of the best depositories of obsolete English words and phrases; and it is of the greatest utility to those engaged in the study of the English language from the times of Chaucer, Gower and Wiclif to those of Surrey and Wyat."[4]

It falls into three parts.

> The book, although written by an Englishman, was the first attempt to reduce the French language to grammatical rules. It is a most interesting and curious volume, and includes, what is in fact the principal portion of the work, an English-French vocabulary, in which the words are divided under the heads of substantives, adjectives, pronouns, verbs, adverbs, etc., and are then arranged in alphabet under those heads. The table of words is very full, and occupies more than half the work.[5]

In addition to this was a pronunciation guide. While the table of words is indeed "very full," it does not contain the entirety of contemporary English and thus Palsgrave's promise, offered in the dictionary, to include "all the wordes in our tong" is not fulfilled. Yet, as Gabriele Stein has noted, in terms of lexicographical development *Lesclarcissement* is valuable for three aspects. It is a genuine vernacular-to-vernacular dictionary—there is no Latin, simply English to French; Palsgrave's examples of use are based on everyday conversation (this had already been seen in such teaching vocabularies as Stanbridge's *Vulgaria,* but dictionaries proper had always turned to the classics for their usage examples), and he manages to deal with those parts of speech other than simple nouns in a far more sophisticated, and thus reader-friendly manner than any predecessor had done.[6]

In timing and content, *Lesclarcissement* would seem to be an important work, yet very few copies were printed at the time and of these only three have survived; two now held by the British Museum, and but a single copy in the whole of France. The reason for this scarcity can be traced to Palsgrave's jealousy of his own position. To distribute the dictionary openly and widely would be, as it were, to distribute the tricks of his trade. He was London's foremost French teacher: this was not a position he wished quietly to abandon. Wheatley offered his explanation, in an anecdote:

> In Ellis's Original Letters (3rd series, vol. ii. p. 214) is a letter from Stephen Vaughan to Thomas Cromwell, which throws some light upon the cause of the extreme scarcity of this book. He says that he had tried to prevail upon Palsgrave to let him have a copy, but he would not; and Vaughan insinuates that, perhaps, if Cromwell will apply for a copy, Palsgrave will not be able to refuse him; and goes on to say, "I perceyve that Palsgrave hathe willed Pynson to sell none of them to any other person then to suche as he shall comaunde to have them, lest his proffit by teching the Frenche tonge myght be mynished by the sale of the same to suche persons as, besids hym, wern disposed to studye the sayd tongue. If I had one, I wolde no lesse esteme it then a jewell, wherfore I hartely pray youe to healp me to one, and for the same I shall send youe some other thing to youe of much more value."[7]

Indeed, Palsgrave was always a parsimonious writer. He claimed in the preface to *Lesclarcissement* to have written two similar works before—but they were never printed and no manuscripts survive. They were supposedly presented to Queen Mary of France and the duke of Suffolk. His other works include a translation of William Fullonius' Latin *Comedy of Acolastus,* designed to be used in schools: "translated into our English tongue after such manner as children are taught in the Grammar Schools, first word for word . . . and afterwords according to the sense . . . with admonitions . . . for the most perfect instructing of the learners . . ."; plus *Annotationes verborum, Annotationes participiorum,* and *Epistolae ad diversos.* If there were other works, they have been lost.

As is clear from Palsgrave's *Lesclarcissement,* the bilingual vernacular-to-vernacular dictionary played an important part on the evolution of sixteenth-century lexicography. The second of the period's bilingual lexicons, William Salesbury's *Dictionary in Englyshe and Welshe* (1547), "moche necessary to all suche Welshemen as wil speedlye learne the englyshe tongue, thought vnto the kynges maiestie very mete to be sette forth to the vse of his graces subiectes in Wales."

The outstanding Welsh scholar of his day, Salesbury (1520?–1600?) was adept in nine languages. He was educated as a Catholic but converted to Protestantism while at Oxford. He published an anti-Catholic pamphlet in 1550 and on the accession of the fiercely Catholic Queen Mary was forced to retreat to his house in Wales, where he conducted a good deal of his life in a secret room accessible only by climbing up a large chimney. Salesbury is remembered today both as the pioneer of comparative philology and as a champion of the Welsh language. Unlike many contemporaries, both English and Welsh, who could see no point in preserving this rapidly declining tongue, he regarded it as just one more vernacular, as worthy of note as English, French, or Italian. To that end he compiled his *Dictionary*.

Salesbury's other works included *Oll Synwyr Pen Kembero* (1546), a collection of Welsh proverbs. If the printing date is correct this is the earliest printed book in Welsh. (Another work, a Welsh almanac, might slightly predate it, though this too is probably by Salesbury.) A year later he published a *Calendar of Months and Days*. Like the 1546 almanac, of which it was presumably a revised edition, this is lost. His major work, aside from the dictionary, is his translation of the New Testament. This was commissioned under an act of Parliament (5 Eliz. cap. 28) which called upon the Welsh bishops to prepare a vernacular version of all or any part of the Bible and the Book of Common Prayer. Salesbury was given the task, and a time limit of four years. The book was duly published on October 7, 1567. He had two helpers, but he wrote 330 folios to his companions' 54. He continued to work with one of them, Richard Davies, bishop of St. David's Abergwili, with whom he produced many tracts, pamphlets, Biblical translations, and the like. However they parted company *c.* 1576, following a dispute over the etymology of a single word. Salesbury never really returned to Biblical writing or translation; he did however produce a Welsh botanology and books on rhetoric and poetry. He was also deeply involved in scientific and antiquarian studies. He died in or around 1600.

Salesbury's *Dictionary* runs to some 7,000 Welsh headwords, the majority of which, though by no means all, have a definition in English. Not only are the languages in the vernacular, but the headwords are very much of the vernacular, in other words there are few "hard words" or "strange termes" derived from literature, philosophy, or similar learned concerns. The word list stems from the everyday spoken languages of both races. His introduction and pronunciation guide is in Welsh, and is far removed from the stilted apostrophes of Elyot's courtier prose. "As none as an idiot would expect . . ." he declares, before citing some obvious construction. And he ends it with a jolly couplet: "Learn English speech until you age! | Wise he, that learns a good language!" It was a popular book, and created sufficient interest in Welsh for Salesbury to be called upon to write a sequel. This, *A playne and a familiar Introduction, teaching how to pronunce the letters in the Brytishe tongue,* appeared in 1550.

The last, and perhaps most important of the century's transvernacular wordbooks is John Florio's *Worlde of Wordes* (1598). But Florio, while outstanding, was not alone and it is worth mentioning three more works, all of which appeared, as did Baret's *Quadruple Dictionarie,* in 1580. The *Synonymorum Sylva* ("the wood of synonyms") had originally been compiled *c.* 1537 as a Flemish-Latin dictionary by the Flemish author Simon Pelegromius. He had died in 1572, but an author known only as "H.F." had translated the Flemish section into English, thus creating an English-Latin work. Its lists of synonyms, with the English arranged alphabetically, each headword or phrase with its English and in many cases Latin equivalent, proved very popular. There were four further editions by 1632. The other important publication of 1580 is *A Treasurie of the French tong* by Claudius Hollyband, a work that was reviewed and reissued as *A Dictionarie of French and English* in 1593. It is also possible that Hollyband either drew on or perhaps even was himself the author of an otherwise anonymously compiled *Dictionarie French and English* of 1571, accepted as the first French-English dictionary. It had been preceded by Palsgrave's *Lesclarcissement,* but Stein points out that whereas Palsgrave compiled his word list on the basis of his own mother tongue, in his case English, Hollyband, or his anonymous precursor, began with the foreign language, and worked backward.[8] Finally there was the arrival in England, almost three quarters of a century after its first edition, of Calepino's *Dictionarium* (see Chapter 1), now expanded to ten languages: Latin, Hebrew, Greek, French, Italian, German, Spanish, Polish, Hungarian, and English.

Conveniently, but nonetheless accurately, John Florio, the last lexicographer to place his work on the literary market of the sixteenth century, can be seen as summarizing in his person and in his achievements the character of all that had gone before. He is "the representative humanist of the Elizabethan Age . . . in all respects one of the most learned and prodigious scholars of the Renaissance . . . He may be fairly called the *uomo universale* of English Renaissance scholarship: translator, teacher, secretary, lexicographer and encyclopedist, stylist, interpreter, book collector, philologist, and philosopher."[9]

John Florio, "an Englishman in Italian," was born *c.* 1553. His father, Michael-Angelo Florio, a Florentine Protestant with his own origins in Siena, had fled to London during the early 1500s in order to avoid religious persecution. There he became preacher to his fellow expatriates. He found patronage from Archbishop Cranmer and from Sir William Cecil, later Lord Burghley, but they dropped him, as did his congregation, after he was faced with charges of gross immorality. Some of this supposed immorality was less than dramatic—the preacher had arranged to be paid five pounds a month for his efforts, and had complained when his parishioners failed to pay a single penny; he had also accused them of finding his anti-Papal sermons too strong and of reneging on their Protestantism. However there was a further lapse, allegedly of some otherwise unspecified "fornication," which was a good deal more serious. Bereft of his congregation and his patrons, Florio set up as a teacher of Italian, and as such was possibly employed by the earl of Pembroke, William Herbert. He wrote, *inter alia,* a history of the life and death of Lady Jane Grey and his own *Apologia* (1557). Like many outspoken Protestants he left England on the accession of Queen Mary and it was during his stay abroad that his son John was born, either in Piedmont or Savoy. With Mary dead and Elizabeth's accession restoring England to Protestantism, the Florios returned to London where they lived, at least for a time, off Upper Thames Street. John Florio attended Magdalen College, Oxford, matriculating in 1581. He boosted his income by working as a tutor in foreign languages to Emmanuel Barnes, son of Robert Barnes, the bishop of Durham and was "a teacher and instructor of certain scholars in the university."[10]

In 1578 Florio's first successful publication appeared: *I. Florio His firste Fruites: which yeelde fimilliar speech, merie Prouerbes, wittie Sentences, and golden sayings. Also a perfect Induction to the Italian, and English tongues, as in the Table appeareth. The like heretofore, neuer by any man published.* The book takes the form of a series of forty-four Italian-English dialogues, graded from easy through to hard, supposedly used by two gentlemen wandering through London. They talk of the Court, suggest entertainments, consider the personality of Queen Elizabeth (who is hugely praised), and generally comment on everyday life in the city. Florio also, in a dedicatory request to his patron, the earl of Leicester, asks for protection from malicious critics. This may stem from the content of Dialogue xv: "To speake of England." In it Florio discusses his adopted country. He is by no means wholly complimentary, for all his earlier currying of favor with the queen. He clearly sees himself as a sophisticate among boors, as a subtle Italian and as such superior to the gross Britons. He sees them as overindulgent and attacks their excesses of food and drink, the lax upbringing of their children, and their publication of "lewd" literature. This somewhat puritan stance extends throughout the dialogues; there are several literary extracts—all of which have a moralizing edge.

This book, and its successor, *Second Frutes,* are very typical of a type of teaching manual used at the time, often for French. Dialogues were created on various topics, typically food, which had been a staple of such works since the thirteenth century. They included some guidance on grammar, but their vocabularies were more important. In that respect they both prefigure today's phrasebooks and look back to such vocabularies as those created for teaching Latin by John Stanbridge and others. Florio's early works include a translation of the Italian writer Ramuzio (1578), which was dedicated to Edmund Bray, the sheriff of Oxfordshire, and a collection of Italian proverbs (1582), dedicated to Sir Edward Dyer.

Between 1583 and 1585 Florio was employed at the French embassy by the ambassador Michel de Castelnau, lord of Mauvissière. There he worked as the tutor to Castelnau's daughter Katherine Marie (the goddaughter of Mary, Queen of Scots and Catherine de Medicis), as well as as acting as an occasional interpreter. During his stay at the embassy, in Butcher Row, an alleyway off the Strand, the household also played host to the Italian philosopher Giordano Bruno, whose heretical beliefs had forced him to flee Italy. It was at this time that Florio appears to have married, although no wife is officially recorded, and had children. Of these the first three—Joane born *c.* 1585, Edward in 1588, and Elizabeth 1589—all died; only Aurelia, who appears in his will, survived him.

In 1591 appeared *Florios Second Frutes, To be gathered of twelue Trees of diuers but delightsome tastes to the tongues of Italians and Englishmen. To which is annexed his Gardine of Recreation yeelding six thousand Italian Prouerbs.* It was dedicated to his new patron, Nicolas Saunders of Ewell. As the title indicates, the "Garden of Recreation" is a collection of 6,000 Italian proverbs and in his introduction Florio commends the importance of such sayings; they are "the pith, the proprieties, the proofes, the pureties, the elegancies, as the commonest so the commendablest phrases of a language." Once again he offers a series of dialogues, many of which refer back to the collected proverbs. One of the protagonists is named Aurelio (presumably a nod to his daughter). This time the dialogues play down life at Court and substitute more homely interests. There is a morning call, games of tennis, chess, "primero" (a card game), and "tables" (backgammon). They swap proverbs on traveling and love, run down the state of contemporary literature, and enjoy a variety of general gossip. There is also a meal: six at table with capon, rabbits, hen, chickens, goose, woodcocks, "snites" (snipe?), larks, quails, partridges, pheasants, and a venison pasty to eat; one guest gets stomachache and Florio in an authorial aside criticizes the "tipling and swilling." However, compared with the earlier volume, the *Second Frutes* lacks an overly puritan tone. This may have resulted from a change in Florio's character; it may also have stemmed from his being more confident. Certainly the dozen years since *First Frutes* appeared had seen a marked improvement in his fortunes. From a being a jobbing tutor he was now at the heart of London's literary scene, a position that would be further enhanced by his next publication, his first dictionary, the *Worlde of Wordes.*

In 1603 appeared his greatest non-lexicographical work: his translation of Montaigne's *Essays,* "Or Morall, Politike and Millitarie Discourses," which had actually been finished since 1598. He must have circulated his work in progress among his smart friends, since in 1600 Sir William Cornwallis announced that "Montaigne now speaks good English. It is done by a fellow less beholden to nature for his fortunes than wit, yet lesser for his face than his fortune. The truth is, he looks more like a good fellow than a wise man, and yet he is wise beyond either his fortune or education." Cornwallis (d. 1631?), a member like Florio of London's literary coterie, was himself a devotee of the French essayist, writing his own essays in hopeful imitation of the master. Michel de Montaigne (1533–92) is largely regarded as the inventor of the essay form, and the French originals of his work appeared between 1580 and, posthumously, 1598. A typically mordant comment runs, "Nothing is so firmly believed as that which we least know."

Florio's translation typifies his general, slightly overblown style: he often embellishes Montaigne's simpler, and more elegant prose, using three words where the original requires just one. But French precision could often only be rendered by English diffuseness, and Florio's translation brought him much well-deserved fame. It also enabled him to add a number of words to English, e.g., *its* (the genitive neuter pronoun: Florio was the first to use it), *entraine, conscientious, endeare, tarnish, comporte, efface, facilitate, amusing, debauching, regret, effort, emotion* (for which he is not cited in the *OED*), and more. In the end, however, Florio's cannot be considered an accurate translation. He used a different style, he incorporated many additions; as Francis Yates put it, "He made, in fact, such a bad translation that it is nearly an original work, not Montaigne, but Florio's Montaigne."[11] A comparison of the two texts shows the extent to which Florio has superimposed himself on the original, especially when it comes to finding English equivalents for Montaigne's coinages. Thus for Florio "maistre Jean" becomes "Sir John Lacklatine," "les basques et les Troglodytes" (terms which were used to illustrate types of obscure languages) become "the Cornish, the Welsh, or Irish." There are also some terrible howlers, the most blatant of which is Florio's slipshod reading of *poisson* (fish) as poison.

All of which, while valid, cannot undermine the essential importance of Florio's work. It was hugely influential: the hapless Walter Raleigh read it in the Tower, the playwrights Ben Jonson and John Webster both acknowledged their debt; it was the favored reading of the smart and the well connected, both men and women. Florio, never loath to advance his interests, prefaced the first edition with tributes to not one, but six aristocratic patrons. By the time the second edition appeared, in 1611, these lesser mortals had been replaced by Queen Anne herself, to whose son Prince Henry he had been, since 1603, the tutor and to whose person he was made reader in Italian at a salary of £100 per annum. By the time of the posthumous third edition of 1632, all dedications had been replaced by a verse: "For, he that hath not heard of *Mountaine* yet | Is but a novice in the schools of wit." In 1685 Florio's translation was ousted by that of Charles Cotton, but it was republished in 1885 and can still be found.

The book may even have touched Shakespeare. The theory that the playwright is parodying Florio in the verbose Holofernes of *Love's Labours Lost* lacks proof—his acquaintance Robert Greene was a similarly unlikely candidate—but Shakespeare almost certainly drew on Florio's version of Montaigne for Gonzago's description of his ideal state as set out in *The Tempest.* In 1838 a supposed Shakespeare autograph edition of the Montaigne was bought by the British Museum for £140. The signature was presumed to be genuine, but proved to be an eighteenth-century fake.

Florio's career continued to prosper. In August 1604 he was appointed gentleman extraordinary and groom of the privy chamber. And as noted by Giovanni Torrio, who edited the edition of 1659, "In the Year 1611 John Florio set forth a second Edition of his Italian and English Dictionary, which for Variety of Words was far more Copious then any extant in the World at that time. This, notwithstanding being defective, and other Dictionaries and Italian Authors coming to his Hands, he collected out of them an Addition of many thousand Words and Phrases, relating to Arts, Sciences, and Exercises; intending (if he had lived) a third Edition, which he left behind him in a very fair Manuscript, perfected and ready for the Presse." This revision was, unsurprisingly, dedicated to his latest patron, the queen, and even paraded her name in its new title: *Queen Anna's New World of Wordes.*

This partiality for his aristocratic and better still royal connections, and his inability to resist concocting lengthy and bombastic prefaces to display them, brought him a good deal of mockery. John Donne included him in *The Courtier's Library*—a catalog of imaginary books by real-life authors, in which he satirized their pretensions. Florio's volume was no. 15:

> The Ocean of Court, or, The Pyramid, or the Colossus, or the Bottomless Pit of Wits: in which, by sixty thousand letters sent and received by the Milords of every Nation invariably in the vulgar tongues to avoid display, anything that can be propounded is propounded on the subject of toothpicks and nail-parings. Collected and reduced into a corpus and dedicated to their individual writers by John Florio an Anglo-Italian: the chapter headings of those included in Book I are contained in the first seventy pages; the diplomas of Kings with their titles and the attestations of licensers in the next one hundred and seven pages; poems in praise of the Author in Books I-XCVII, which follow.

In 1617 his first, anonymous wife died and he was married again, to one Rose Spicer. He remained a successful courtier for two more years until the queen's death of dropsy in 1619. From there on it was as if his celebrity had never been. James I and his queen had abandoned all but the most formal of relations thirteen years previously and Anne's favorites were unlikely to survive her death. Florio duly lost his place at Court and spent his final years in poverty, living in Fulham. He did manage to obtain a pension by petitioning the secretary of state, Sir Francis Windebank (1582–1646): he was promised £100 per annum for the rest of his life, but it appears never to have been paid. There are records of his writing begging letters to Court in 1621, when arrears had reached £250, and again in 1623. Meanwhile, he worked steadily toward a third edition of his dictionary. It was never finished: Florio died, a victim of the plague, in October 1625. He left his Fulham house to his wife and his books to the earl of Pembroke, whose father may once have employed his own. His will is sadly indicative of the bitterness of his last years:

As for the debts that I owe, the greatest, and onelie is upon an obligatory writing of myne owne hand, which my daughter Aurelia Molins with importunity wrested from [me] of about three-score pounds, wheras the truth, and my conscience telleth mee, & soe knoweth her conscience, it is but Thirty foure pounds or therabouts, But let that passe, since I was soe unheedy, as to make and acknowledge the said writing, I am willing that it bee paid and discharged in this forme and manner, My sonne in law (as my daughter his wife knoweth full well) hath in his hands as a pawne a faire gold ring of mine, with thirteene faire table diamonds therein enchased which cost queene Anne my gracious Mistresse seauen and forty pounds starline [sterling], and for which I might many tymes haue had forty pounds readie money, upon the said ring my sonne in the presence of his wife lent mee Tenne pounds, I desire him and pray him to take the overplus of the said ring in parte payment, as also a leaden Ceasterne which hee hath of myne standing in his yard at is [*sic*] London-house that cost mee at a porte-sale fortie shillings, as also a siluer caudle cup with a couer worth about forty shillings which I left at his house being sicke there; desiring my sonne and daughter, that their hole debt may bee made up, & they satisfied with selling the Lease of my house in Shoelane, and so accquitt and discharge my pore wife who as yet knoweth nothing of this debt.

Florio's outstanding achievement, *A Worlde of Wordes, Or Most copious, and exact Dictionarie in Italian and English, collected by Iohn Florio,* appeared in 1598.

It runs to 46,000 headwords and is dedicated to the earl of Southampton, the earl of Rutland, and the countess of Bedford, all of whom had been his pupils. Southampton was actually his patron and employer, while Lucy Russell, the countess of Bedford, was the sponsor of a wide coterie of writers, including Jonson and Donne. Ostensibly an Italian-English dictionary, it was a pioneering, even revolutionary publication which introduced for the first time nonclassical citations and included both slang and obscenities. Irrespective of any other success, this work alone would make Florio into one of the most influential literary figures of the period.

The book, so Florio explained, had been conceived in the late 1570s when he saw an unfinished (and unpublished) manuscript by a gentleman of "worshipful account" and "well experienced in the Italian." By 1591, the year of publication of his *Second Frutes,* he was able to announce imminent publication of his dictionary: he would "shortly send into the world an exquisite Italian and English Dictionary and a compendious Grammar."

Although the *Worlde of Wordes* falls into the category of a vernacular-to-vernacular work, it is through Florio's English definitions that it stands preeminent. He describes his work as "most copious" and his definitions, in which he regularly offers a wide range of English synonyms for a single Italian headword, underline the extent to which he has fulfilled that promise. And copiousness of another sort can be seen in his addition of a number of hitherto unprinted, and unprintable, terms. While there is much more to A *Worlde of Wordes* than a few "dirty words," it is here that readers were first able to find "*Fottere,* to iape, to sard, to fucke, to swive, to occupy." Florio also offers "beak-nose" (*naso adunco*), "gear" (for both male and female genitals), the euphemistic "Mount-faucon" (the vagina) and the insults "shitten fellow" and "good-man turd." However, according to Starnes his same claim of copiousness reveals the extent to which Florio based his work on that of Thomas Thomas, which appeared in 1587.[12]

Florio, as defended by his biographer Francis Yates, would demur. As he points out in his address to the reader, his task was rendered doubly difficult by the fact that there was not much earlier work to guide him. He continues, "If any thinke I had great helpes of Alunno or of Venuti, let him confer, and knowe I haue in two, yea almost in one of my letters of the Alphabet more wordes then they haue in all their twentie . . ." He compares himself to a lone sailor. Unlike Elyot, Cooper, Thomas, or Rider, all of whom "had so many, and so great helpes," he worked solo: "I was but one to turne and winde the sailes, to use the oare, to sit at sterne, to pricke my carde, to watch upon the upper decke, boat-swaine, pilot, mate and master . . ." He cites the names of seventy-two authors whom he has read. This was generally accepted for many years, and critics have traditionally praised the breadth of his reading (the list was expanded to 249 titles for the edition of 1611). More recent skeptics, however, have wondered how much he really read and how much, in a manner increasingly found among contemporary dictionary makers, was the rote listing of sixteenth-century lexicography's "usual suspects." This may be true, but given that this was an Italian-English dictionary, Florio does appear to have done his own reading as far as Italian literature was concerned.

It was his confidence in this area, perhaps, that allowed him to acknowledge at least one model. As far as the field of Italian-English dictionaries went, he accepted that he did indeed have a predecessor, noting that "our William Thomas hath done prettilie." Thomas was the author of *Principal Rules of Italian Grammar* (1550), which included a *Dictionarie for the better vndrstandynge of Boccache* [Boccaccio], *Petrarcha and Dante.* In any case, he was himself no longer available for comment. Like so many outspoken Protestants Thomas had found himself in danger once Queen Mary came to the throne. Unlike the majority, who recanted or modified their views, went into hiding, or simply left the country, Thomas became increasingly radical. Whether or not, as was alleged, he planned the assassination of Bishop Gardiner is unknown, but in December 1553 he joined the rebellion of the diehard Protestant Thomas Wyatt. He offered his services to Sir Peter Carew, who had undertaken to lead the rebels in the West Country, but when Carew failed to muster sufficient support, Thomas was forced to flee. As the indictment against him read, he went "from county to county, in disguise, not knowing where to conceal himself, yet he did not desist from sending seditious bills and letters to his friends, declaring his treasonable intentions . . ." Thomas was captured before he could reach a safe refuge and on February 20 was imprisoned in the Tower. There he faced the rack, apparently in the hope that he might reveal some link between Wyatt and Princess Elizabeth, and it was possibly to avoid this torture that he attempted suicide "by thrusting a knife into his body under his paps."[13] The wound did not prove fatal, but betrayal did. A fellow prisoner, Sir Nicholas Arnold, alleged that Thomas had suggested the murder of Queen Mary herself, and it was on this evidence that he was condemned to death for treason. On May 18, 1554 he was taken to Tyburn and there hanged, drawn, and quartered, probably the only lexicographer to meet so gruesome a fate. His head was displayed on London Bridge and the remainder of his corpse at Cripplegate, where he had lived.

Politics aside, Florio's intention was to offer something far more substantial than a purpose-built glossary gleaned from three classics. His dictionary was to cater for the whole range of readers, from "new-entred nouices," who were still struggling with the rudiments of the language, through "well-forwarde students," who were well versed in Italian literature, to even the "most compleate Doctor." Whether, as advertised, Florio managed to include the full extent of contemporary Italian vocabulary is unlikely. But as he pointed out, "If any man aske whether all Italian wordes be here? I answer him, it may be no: and yet I thinke heere be as many as he is likely to finde . . . within the compass of his reading; and yet he may haue read well too." He stresses the variety of his own researches and adds, "If no other bookes can be so well perfected, but still something may be added, how much lesse a Word-booke?" No lexicographer, before or since, could honestly offer more.

Fêted by contemporary society for his wit and learning, Florio also faced his critics. Some of the most endearing passages in the "Address to the Reader" come when he takes his opportunity to fight back. Above the signature "Resolute John Florio," he denounces with a fine vituperation worthy of so literate a writer,

> Those notable Pirates in this our paper-sea, those sea-dogs, or lande-Critikes, monsters of men, if not beastes rather then men; whose teeth are Canibals, their toongs adder-forkes, their lips aspes-poyson, their eies basiliskes, their breath the breath of a graue, their wordes like swordes of Turkes, that striue which shall diue deepest into a Christian lying bound before them. But for these barking and biting dogs, they are as well knowne as Scylla and Charybdis . . . Who then are they that mispend all their leisure, yea take their cheefe pleasure in backbiting well-deseruers? I see and am sorie to see a sort of men, whose fifth element is malediction, whose life is infamie, whose death damnation, whose daies are surfeiting, whose nights lecherie, . . . and whose couches are Spintrie [devoted to "unnatural practices"]; whose thrift is vsurie, meales gluttonie, exercise cousenage, whose valour bragardrie, . . . or if it it come to action, crueltie; whose communication is Atheisme, contention, detraction, or pillardise, most of lewdnes, seld of vertue, neuer of charitie; whose spare-time is vanitie or villanie: yet will I not deale by them, as they doe by others.

His particular loathing is for "a tooth-lesse dog, that hateth where he cannot hurt, and would faine bite, when he hath no teeth. His name is H.S. . . . Let H.S. hisse, and his complices quarrell, and all breake their gals, I haue a great faction of good writers to bandie with me." Quite who "H.S." was remains a mystery. Two theories have been propounded: one that he was Henry (or Hugh) Stanford (or Stamford), who died in May 1607 and was the secretary to the earl of Pembroke. The other makes him one Henry Salisbury (1561–1637), author

of a Welsh grammar and an unpublished Welsh-Latin dictionary and another
who gained his patronage from Pembroke. Whoever he was, H.S. remained an
abiding obsession and Florio took him to task once more in 1599 when he
wrote a mock dedication to the tobacco seller and versifier Humphrey King in
his friend Thomas Nash's *Lenten Stuffe:*

> This fellow, this H.S. [has] made as familiar a word of I.F. as if I had bin
> his brother. Now *Recte sit oculis magister tuis,* said an ancient writer to a
> much-like reading grammarian-pedante: God saue your eie-sight, sir, or
> at least your in-sight. And might not a man . . . finde as much matter out
> of H.S. as you did out of I.F.? As for example, H.S. why may it not stand
> as well for Haeres Stultitiae, as for Homo Simplex? or for Hara Suillina,
> as for Hostis Studiosorum? or for Hircus Satiricus, as well as for any of
> them? And this in Latine, besides Hedera Seguace, Harpia Subata,
> Humore Superbo, Hipocrito Simulatore in Italian. And in English world
> without end. Huffe Snuffe, Horse Stealer, Hob Sowter, Hugh Sot, Hum-
> frey Swineshead, Hodge Sowgelder. Now Master H.S. if this doe gaule
> you, forbeare kicking heerafter, and in the meane time you may make you
> a plaister of your dride Marioram.

But H.S. and other critics were mere pinpricks. *A Worlde of Wordes* proved a
triumph and, for his contemporaries, his most important work. Posterity may
prefer Florio's *Montaigne,* but his peers esteemed his dictionary even higher.

In 1611 Florio offered its second edition. It boasted a new title—*Queen
Anna's New Worlde of Wordes newly much augmented by Iohn Florio, Reader of the
Italian vnto the Soueraigne Maiestie of Anna, Crowned Queene of England, Scotland,
France and Ireland, &c. And one of the Gentlemen of hir Royall Priuie Chamber.
Whereunto are added certaine necessarie rules and short obseruations for the Italian
tongue*—but it was essentially an expanded version of the original. As well as
the lengthy "Rules for the Italian Tongue," there were now 74,000 definitions
and a selection of adulatory verses from such as *Il Candido* (Matthew Gwinne,
who had also written for the 1598 edition), Alberto Gentili, a fellow teacher of
Italian, the poet Samuel Daniel, John Thorius, another refugee teacher, in this
case of Flemish, and the Spanish scholar James Mabbe, who also contributed
verses to Shakespeare's First Folio, and here offers the anagram: *Ioannes Florio |
Ori fons alieno.* Florio signed his preface, "Still resolute Iohn Florio."

Florio's revision trumpets the theory that bigger is better. He offers more
sources, notably a wide range of technical ones: there are now terms culled from
general knowledge, history, theology, botany, zoology, cooking, the art of war,

medicine, the theater, falconry, and more. His coverage of literature is wider, and he cites a high percentage of plays. He deals skillfully with the discrepancies and variations in use that may be encountered within a single author or between two of them, and thus comments on differences between Dante and Machiavelli when both men are using the same words in different contexts. He includes words from a number of Italian dialects. Taken as a whole, Florio's detailed, wide-ranging definitions make his work into as much an encyclopedia as a straight dictionary; as such it is perhaps the exemplar of its time. However, in common with his contemporaries, this knowledge sometimes strays into the fantastic and Florio offers without comment the names of imaginary beasts and the folkloric properties of many flowers. The whole effect is enhanced by Florio's facility not merely for translation, but for finding apt English equivalents for Italian places, customs, and the like. He also offers antiquarian notes, typically his lengthy discussions of religious sects, especially of the Jews. Indeed Florio himself, according to his father, may have had some distant Jewish blood.

In the third, posthumous edition of 1659, the dictionary was retitled yet again, this time as *Vocabolario Italiano & Inglese, A Dictionary Italian & English. Formerly Compiled by John Florio, and since his last Edition, Anno 1611, augmented by himselfe in His life time, with many thousand Words, and Thuscan Phrases. Now Most diligently Revised, Corrected, and Compared, with La Crvsca, and other approved Dictionaries extant since his Death and enriched with very considerable Additions. Whereunto is added A Dictionary English & Italian, with severall Proverbs and Instructions for the speedy attaining to the Italian Tongue. Never before Published. By Gio: Torriano An Italian, and Professor of the Italian Tongue in London.* This edition was reprinted in 1688 and 1690. Perhaps the most interesting aspect of the reprint was the reference to "La Crusca," in other words the Florentine Accademia della Crusca, publisher in 1612 of the *Vocabulario della Crusca,* a work that alongside the *Dictionnaire* of the Académie Française would have a profound influence on the direction of English lexicography.

By then, however, the vogue for bilingual dictionaries had passed. With their emphasis on the vernacular, they had moved the direction of lexicography away from the traditional concentration on Latin, the scholar's language, to the vulgar tongues, those of the general speaker. It was symbolic of this shift in direction that England's next major wordbook, which would appear midway between Florio's first two editions, would be the pioneer of an entirely new discipline: the monolingual dictionary.

If the bilingual dictionaries can be seen as the exotic end of the dictionary-making industry, then the grammars produced by a trio of schoolmasters,

William Bullokar, Richard Mulcaster, and Edmund Coote, represent a more prosaic but equally influential area.

Although viewed as less intellectually glamorous than lexicography, grammar was considered as important to the public as was full-blown dictionary making. Traditionally, the national successes of the future are seen as conditional on the current literacy of the young and the sixteenth century was true to the belief. As noted by R. F. Jones, "The recognition of the importance of the mother tongue and the desire to see it regulated and stabilized find clear expression in the various grammars of English and the grammatical treatises on it that were published during this period . . ."[14] Equally important was the extent to which these teachers appreciated the need for a proper English dictionary and, in the case of Bullokar and Mulcaster, either proposed that they themselves create one, or called for another scholar to undertake the task. Coote, while never properly accredited as a lexicographer, went ahead and, within limits, did it.

The earliest of the grammars, *Bullokars Booke at large, fore the Amendment of Orthographie for English speech* (1580) is, as its title proclaims, as much a plan for a new scheme of spelling as it is a grammar. But as well as promoting his new orthography, Bullokar also offered, as the full title reveals "a ruled Grammar, to be imprinted hereafter, for the same speech, to no small commoditie of the English nation, not only to come to easie, speedie, and readie entrance into the secretes of other Languages, and easie and speedie pathway to all Straungers, to use our Language, heertofore very hard unto them, to no small profite and credite to this our nation, and stay thereunto in the weightiest causes."

William Bullokar, whose namesake John would in due course produce a full-fledged dictionary of his own, was a teacher who lived from *c.* 1520 to 1590. During the reign of Queen Mary he served in the army, soldiering abroad under Sir Richard Wingfield and later Sir Adrian Poinings. He studied agriculture for a brief period, and temporarily involved himself in the law, but teaching, and more important the writing of his *Booke at Large,* soon dominated his life. He had, as he explains in the preface to the *Booke,* noticed as early as 1550, while still at university, the extent to which the sounds and names of the letters of the alphabet caused "quarels in the teacher and lothsomenesse in the learner."[15] By 1573, now a teacher, he noticed that the same problems remained as intense as ever and resolved to "restrain his owne businesse for halfe a yeare," laying his "privat doings aside," which his "abilitie was il able to bear" in order "to provide some remedie."[16]

A large part of that "remedie" was to be a reformed system of spelling, but his growing appreciation that he was not alone in such plans led him to bring the manuscript to a speedy conclusion and publish as fast as he could. To promote the book he began appearing in a variety of public places, where he gave a brief speech, advertising the book and its system. He also announced his intent to compile a proper dictionary, but it would never appear. Instead he busied the remainder of his life with a variety of works, all of which were rendered in Bullokar's new system of "tru orthographie." They included his version of *Aesop's Fables* (1585), "Short Sentences of the Wys Cato," a book on "Tully" (Marcus Tullius Cicero) which remained unpublished, a Psalter, and so on. Unfortunately the special characters this system required were unavailable at the average print shop. He also published a corrected version of his original pamphlet and stated that the original version should be burned. In 1586 he published a *Bref Grammar for English.* He promised a larger *Grammar at Large* but this did not appear, although Bullokar claimed that it "staieth from the print against my wil." He also promised his dictionary again, stating in verse: "Your good acceptance of thaez painz, | will caie me to set at hand, | too perfecting a Dictionary, | the third strength of this hand."

Richard Mulcaster (1530?–1611) was a widely respected scholar who was "eminent among the Oxonians for his rare and profound skill in the Greek tongue."[17] He was born in or near Carlisle to a family that could trace its line back to the time of William Rufus, when they were involved in repelling Scots invasions. Educated at Eton, where he encountered the grammatical expertise and the disciplinary enthusiasms of its headmaster, Nicholas Udall, he attended both Oxford and Cambridge universities. As well as classics he studied Hebrew, and made himself one of its foremost experts.

By 1559 he had arrived in London, where he worked as schoolmaster. He prospered in this career and when a new school, Merchant Taylor's, was founded in 1561 he was appointed its first headmaster. He stayed until 1586, having spent "nigh 26 years in harmless drudgery; yet though he felt the inconvenience, he was happy in the toil."[18] He was generally successful, although his dislike of the slightest criticism, even by his own governors, made him a prickly figure who had frequent fallings-out with his paymasters. In 1590 he became a clergyman, serving in a variety of livings before returning to teaching in 1596 as high master of St. Paul's School. He was a very influential teacher, albeit a harsh one. According to Fuller, he could be swayed.[19] "The prayers of cockering [pampering] mothers prevailed with him [although] the requests of indulgent fathers, rather increasing than mitigating his severity on their offending child." His habit was apparently to teach a lesson, then spend an hour catnapping at his desk while the pupils learned their lines. And "woe to the scholar that slept the while. Awakening, he heard them accurately; and *Atropos*

might be persuaded to pity as soon as he to pardon where he found just fault."[20]
Yet by contemporary standards Mulcaster was a revolutionary. His pupils
learned music and singing, and often performed masques before the Court and
queen; he insisted on the importance of physical education and emphasized the
right of girls to get as good an education as boys. He did not, however, advocate sending girls to grammar schools, but excused this double standard since
it "was not a thing used in my country." He also advocated a special system for
the training of teachers. He resigned in 1608, possibly overwhelmed by the loss
of his wife of fifty years, took up a last living, in Stanford Rivers, Essex, and
died on April 15, 1611.

As well as his grammar, he wrote some Latin verses which were prefixed to
Baret's *Alvearie* and *Positions, wherein those primitive Circumstances be examined,
which are necessary for the Training up of Children, either for Skill in their Book or
Health in their Bodie* . . . (1587); this was dedicated to Queen Elizabeth. *The
First Part of the Elementarie* appeared in 1582; no second part was ever published. It is a list of 8,000 "hard words" in English. There are no definitions.
These words were doubtless useful, but Mulcaster's long-term influence was in
his stressing of the intrinsic worth of English as English and his demands that
it should be used more widely. "But why not all in English, a tung of it self
both depe in conceit, & frank in deliuerie? I do not think that anie language, be
it whatsoeuer, is better able to vtter all argumets, either with more pith, or
greater planesse, then our *English* tung is, if the *English* vtterer be as skilfull in
the matter, Which he is to vtter: as the foren vtterer is."[21]

He also calls for a way of making the language more accessible to students.
He makes no promises himself but notes in the margin of the *Elementarie:* "A
perfit English dictionarie wished for."[22] He pursues this theme in his text:

> It were a thing verie praiseworthie in my opinion, and no lesse profitable,
> then praise worthie, if som one well learned and as laborious a man, wold
> gather all the words which we vse in our English tung, whether naturall
> or incorporate; out of all professions, as well learned as not, into one dic-
> tionary and besides the right writing, which is incident to the Alphabete,
> wold open vnto vs therein, both their naturall force, and their proper vse:
> that by his honest trauell we might be as able to iudge of our own tung,
> which we haue as we ar of others, which we learn by rule. The want
> whereof, is the onelie cause why, that verie manie men, being excellentlie
> well learned in foren speche, can hardlie discern what theie haue at home,
> still shooting fair, but oft missing far, hard censors ouer other, ill execu-
> tors themselues.

As his own contribution, he offers "The Generall Table," in which is set out his list of "hard words." A last quotation from Mulcaster emphasizes another aspect of his demands—unalloyed nationalism:

> For is it not in dede a mervellous bondage, to becom servants to one tung for learning sake, the most of our time, with losse of most time, wheras we maie have the verie same treasur in our own tung, with the gain of most time? our own bearing the joyfull title of our libertie and fredom, the Latin tung remembering us of our thraldom and bondage? I love Rome, but London better, I favor Italie, but England more, I honor the Latin, but I worship the English.

The last of this trio is Edmund Coote, whose *English Schoolemaster* appears in 1596. Little is known of his life other than that he graduated from Peterhouse, Cambridge in 1583 and was made headmaster of the grammar school at Bury St. Edmunds on June 5, 1596. He held the post for the next eleven months. *The English Schoolemaster* was remarkably successful—an edition published in Dublin in 1684 claims to be the forty-second, and it was still appearing in 1704—for all that he is consistently misnamed on the title page as "Edward" Coote. It is primarily a teaching manual, and of it Coote wrote that "I have so disposed the placing of my first book, that if a child should tear out every leaf as fast as he learneth, yet it shall not be greatly hurtful; for every new chapter repeateth and teacheth again all that went before." Alongside the grammar, catechism, prayers, and graces that were commonly incorporated in bilingual dictionaries, it offered a small vocabulary. But in contrast to those dictionaries there is no second language. Like Mulcaster before him, he offers simply a list of "hard words." Unlike Mulcaster, however, he "translates" each "hard word" by a simpler synonym. Coote's book does not boast the name, nor does he claim it—that accolade would be preserved for Robert Cawdrey, eight years later—but such a listing falls properly into a new category: it is in effect a prototype "modern" dictionary.

5

Slang: Part I

A lthough the sixteenth to eighteenth centuries saw the development of a new strain of specialist dictionaries, for example Levens' *Rhyming Dictionary,* Blount's *Law Dictionary,* and particularly John Harris' *Lexicon Technicum* (1704), which last would be enthusiastically cannibalized by many general lexicographers up to and including Samuel Johnson, the main concentration of nonstandard English lexicography could be found in the world of slang or, more properly at this stage, cant or criminal jargon. Appearing first as glossaries, then gradually expanding into larger volumes, this parallel vocabulary, as widely spread four centuries ago as it is now, gained its own, parallel lexicography. Indeed, nearly 150 years would pass between the appearance of the first attempt to codify, even marginally, the world of cant, and its inclusion, and then only in part, in a mainstream dictionary. The nature of mainstream lexicography, first concentrating on hard words, then aiming at elegance and authority, and still hoping, to a greater and lesser extent, to "fix" a standard for the English language, conspired to reject cant and its wider variation, slang. Dictionaries such as those of Cawdrey, Bullokar, and Cockeram could go through several editions and many revisions, but none would acknowledge what might be termed the truly "vulgar tongue." The aspirant bourgeoisie, for whom they catered, were not interested. Cant might play a leading role in popular literature, but not in the dictionary. Class, as ever, proved a determinant in England, and whatever might happen in the mainstream, cant lexicography was abandoned to a world of its own, a linguistic backwater, advancing only slowly, throughout the seventeenth and virtually the whole of the eighteenth century.

That said, it developed in much the same way as did mainstream dictionary making. Just as the glossaries that would form the bases of the early-seventeenth-century's "hard-word" dictionaries were appearing in ever-increasing numbers in publications that concentrated on "legitimate" preoccupations, such as cooking, archery, or medicine, so too were those which were concerned with the lowlife citizens of the Tudor world creating small vocabulary lists, either appended to a larger work, or forming a central part of the overall discussion. Indeed, Jürgen Schäfer, who cites several cant glossarists in his lists (see Chapter 6) makes no distinction between them and their mainstream peers.[1] But in whatever way these early slang lexicographers worked, the terminology they expounded was relatively narrow—the first example includes perhaps forty terms and that basic vocabulary would provide the core of at least a century's further glosses.

More important perhaps is the context on which these first slang collectors drew. Obviously slang did not simply leap into existence, fully formed and ready for collection, sometime in the early sixteenth century. The mid-nineteenth-century slang lexicographer John Camden Hotten, as keen as any other Victorian scholar to find antecedents in the classical and preclassical worlds, offers the readers of his *Slang Dictionary* (1859) an alluring, if somewhat fantastical picture of this "universal and ancient" species of language. "If we are to believe implicitly the saying of *the* wise man, that 'there is nothing new under the sun' the 'fast' men of buried Nineveh, with their knotty and door-matty looking beards, may have cracked Slang jokes on the steps of Sennacherib's palace; and the stocks [*sic*] and stones of Ancient Egypt, and the bricks of venerable and used up Babylon, may, for aught we know, be covered with slang hieroglyphics unknown to modern antiquarians . . ."[2] Indeed, as Eric Partridge remarks, the Phoenicians, the Greeks, and the Romans all undoubtedly had their own slangy speech.[3] Nor was slang monolithic. Athenian women, it has been noted, had their own specialized vocabulary. While some of its words may well have been inherited from the vocabulary of an earlier race, some, like much early slang, may have been deliberately devised to create a secret language, in this case one that was incomprehensible to male hearers.[4] So too, almost inevitably, did the Sumerians and their Akkadian conquerors. But if the vocabularies existed, the collectors did not. For them, at least in their English language incarnation, we must return to the relative modernity of the early sixteenth century.

Slang, as Hotten put it, "is the language of street humour, of fast, high and low life. Cant . . . is the vulgar language of secrecy."[5] And what the sixteenth-century slang glossarists collected was not slang, the casual, "alternative" language of the "civilian," but cant, the deliberately obfuscatory professional jargon of the contemporary underworld. The slang was there, of course, but for whatever reason, it remained outside polite or other inquiry until the late seventeenth century when "B. E., Gent." (no further identification has ever been offered) produced his *New Dictionary . . . of the Canting Crew* (*c.* 1690). There followed the anonymous *New Canting Dictionary,* essentially an expanded version of "B.E.," which appeared in 1725, and most importantly Captain Francis Grose, publishing at the very end of the century, turned his attention to its listing. By then, albeit guardedly, cant had begun to appear in mainstream works, first of all in Elisha Coles' *English Dictionary* (1676) and to a far greater extent in Nathaniel Bailey's *Dictionarium Britannicum* (1730).

Thus it is to the underworld that one looks in search of the very first glossaries, and one finds them not in England, but in continental Europe. Mencken mentions, without further detail, a collection of German cant, gathered *c.* 1420 by one Gerold Edilbach[6] but what is currently accepted as the earliest such collection appeared in Basel, Switzerland, *c.* 1450, entitled *Die Betrügnisse der Gyler* ("The Deceptions of Beggars"). It appears to have been the work of a clergyman, John Knebel, who picked up his material at a series of criminal trials. Three manuscripts survive; at some later stage it went into print and was still appearing as late as 1749, although no copies of that edition exist. This "beggar book" or "rogue pamphlet," as the genre became known, set out, as its opening lines explain, to inform the law-abiding citizen of "the deceptions which beggars and blind men practice, and especially all the dodges, as they call them, by which they make their living." Like its many successors, the *Deceptions* goes on to list the types of beggars, the tricks they use and the language they adopt to deceive the authorities and the gullible public. Like the Kentish magistrate Thomas Harman, two centuries later, the author provides a supposed "conversation" between two criminal beggars, putting their cant into context. This, he notes, is *rottwelshe* or beggar's patter. The German word comes from the Middle High German *rot:* a beggar and *welsch* or *wälsch,* which, cognate with one use of the English word *Welsh* means a "strange, outlandish language" (similar to slang uses of *Greek* or *Hebrew*).

The legal system boosted the cant lexicon once more a few years later, in France, when the trial of a group of Burgundian bandits known as the Coquillards gave an insight into its French variety when the published records of the proceedings included a glossary of roguish talk. *Coquillard* itself was cant, meaning a fake pilgrim: the *coquille* or shellfish (literally "mollusk") being the symbol of the genuine pilgrims who made the journey to St. James of Compostela (thus also the dish "coquille Saint Jacques"). Many European beggars pretended to piety. The Coquillard language was further celebrated by the dissolute poet François Villon (1431–1470?), one of their associates, who wrote a number of ballads in cant, although these were not properly translated until the nineteenth century. Cant collection returned to Germany in 1510 when an anonymous author, possibly the warden of a "spittal house" on the Rhine issued the *Liber Vagatorum* ("The Book of Vagabonds"). This was enormously popular, with editions in High and Low German, Low Rhenish, and Dutch. The Protestant reformer Martin Luther even contributed a foreword to that of 1528, admitting that "I have myself of late years been cheated and befooled by such tramps and liars more than I wish to confess."[7] John Camden Hotten published an English edition—*The Book of Vagabonds and Beggars, with a Vocabulary of their Language*—in 1860. The first printed "beggar book," it offered a glossary of *Rottwelsch* and a detailed list of 28 varieties of villain, a "dramatis personae" that would be seen again in many successors. Among the terms listed are *barlen:* to speak (from French *parler*); *fetzen:* to work (from German *fetzen:* tatters, the "uniform" that beggars used); *kabas:* the head (from Latin *caput*); *bosshart:* meat (from Hebrew *basar*), and *zwicker:* the hangman (from German *zwicken:* to pinch). The beggar-book tradition continued through the sixteenth century, with further titles appearing in France and Spain, where among others Cervantes took note of the world of villainy. It was hardly surprising that England, especially London, had its own variety:

> *And as we talked, ther gathered at the gate*
> *People as me thought of very poor estate*
> *With bag and staf, both croked, lame and blynde*
> *Scabby & scuruy, pocke eate flesh and rynde*
> *Lowsy and scalde, and pulled lyke as apes*
> *With scantly a rag, for to couer theyre shapes . . .*
> *Boys, gyrles, and luskysh strong knaues*
> *Dydderyng & dadderyng, leaning on their staues*
> *Sayng good mayster, for your moders blessyng*
> *Gyue us a halfpenny . . .*

Apostrophized here in what must stand technically as the first English "slang dictionary" (although really such a distinction must wait thirty or forty

years for Thomas Harman), Robert Copland's *Hye Way to the Spytell House,*
printed and published by its author sometime between 1517 and 1537 (Judges
opts for 1535–6 on the basis of its attacks on popery and its reference to a
statute concerning beggars of 1531),[8] it was this sordid crew who provided the
core terms of Britain's contemporary cant vocabulary. These were the professional mendicants, the wandering villains, the "sturdy beggars" whose activities came under the hostile scrutiny of a succession of Tudor poor laws. Among
them prospered the *roger* (pronounced with a hard *g* and as such possibly no
more than a synonym for the basic rogue), a wandering beggar who pretended
to be a poor scholar from Oxford or Cambridge, the *pardoner,* a mendicant posing as a seller of indulgences, the *ruffler,* a top villain who posed as a discharged
soldier (and might indeed have been one, though he had equally likely been a
former servant), but actually worked as an itinerant robber, and his female companion, the *dell.*

The Hye Way to the Spytell House, which translates roughly as "the quick route
to the charity clinic" (a *spytell house,* synonymous with a lazar house or poor hospital, was a form of charity foundation, dealing specifically with the poor and
indigent and especially with those suffering from a variety of foul diseases) is a
lengthy verse dialogue between Copland and the Spytell House Porter. The
clinic in question, while unnamed by Copland, is generally accepted to have
been St. Bartholemew's Hospital, London's oldest, founded in 1123. Trapped in
the hospital porch by a snowstorm, Copland strikes up a conversation with the
Porter, taking as their subject the crowd of beggars who besiege the Spytell
House, and discussing why some are allowed in and others rejected. Within
this framework Copland notes and the Porter describes the various categories of
beggars and thieves, as well as the tricks and frauds that are their stock in trade.
They further note the way folly and vice lead inevitably to poverty and thence
disease and finally, willy-nilly, to the Spytell House.

Copland's birthdate remains a mystery, but his known professional career as
a printer, bookseller, and stationer, as well as a collector of cant, covers the years
1508–47 (when he seems to have died). He worked primarily as an assistant to
the printer Wynkyn de Worde (d. 1535). De Worde, in turn, had been William
Caxton's principal assistant from 1476, when Caxton brought him to London
from his home in Worth, Alsace, until the master printer's death *c.* 1491.
Indeed Copland claimed to have worked for Caxton too: in the preface to his
book *Kynge Apollyon of Thyre* (1510) he states that he gladly follows "the trace
of my mayster Caxton, begyninge with small storyes and pamfletes, and so to
other," but given their respective dates, this relationship is more likely figurative than factual. There is no doubt, however, that Copland worked for Caxton's

successor. His first publication, *The Justice of the Peas,* appeared in 1515 and is effectively the third edition of a title that de Worde had already printed twice. De Worde too is regularly credited as "my mayster" and repaid the compliment in his will, where he left his assistant ten marks (£6/13s/4d).

By 1547 it would seem that Copland in his turn had taken on the role of London's leading printer, for all that this position had fallen upon him through chronology—de Worde had died in 1535—rather than any particularly outstanding talent. The author Andrew Borde, writing that year in *Prognostications, or, The Pryncyples of Astronamye,* mentions "old Robert Copland . . . the eldist printer of Ingland." Somewhat later, writing in his *Bibliographica Poetica,* the eccentric eighteenth-century antiquary Joseph Ritson described him as "the father of his profession" but this was overly generous. Indeed, critics have judged the dozen or so books which have been traced to his presses as generally run-of-the-mill as far as typographical expertise is concerned and the type he used, shared with his younger brother William, was allegedly old and worn, but he does boast one notable achievement. This was in the sphere of punctuation, an area of printing that was still reasonably flexible in his time: in *The xij Fruytes of the Holy Ghost* (1535) he uses the comma stop for the first time in a black letter book. Prior to that the virgule (a thin sloping or upright line occurring in medieval manuscripts either denoting the caesura or as a punctuation mark) or dash was the norm. This brother William overlapped with Robert, coming into his own *c.* 1549, after the latter's death. He may also have been that same William Copland who as church warden of St. Mary Bow donated a new bell, the Bow bell, which chimed fifth in the ring. It was heard every night at nine, cheering the London apprentices, who on hearing the Bow bell knew their day's work was over.

Like their typography, the content of Robert Copland's books, mainly translated from French originals, was unremarkable, with the exception of two volumes: the *Hye Way* and *Jyl of Breyntford's Testament,* "based upon a coarse popular tale"[9] and privately reprinted in 1871 by a lexicographer of far more substantial pedigree, Frederick Furnivall. Among the other titles, valuable more for their rarity than for their literary importance, are *The Kalendar of Shepeherdes* (1508), *Kynge Appollyn of Thyre* (1510), *A Goosteley Treatyse of the Passyon of our Lorde Jesu Chryste* (1532), *The Introductory to write and to pronounce Frenche,* by Alexander Barcley (1521), which includes Copland's own "The maner of dauncynge of base daunces," *The Rutter of the Sea,* a guide to navigation, listing "Hauors [Harbors], Rodes, Soundynges, Kennynges, Wyndes, Flodes . . . ," *The maner to liue well* (1540), *The Questionary of Cyrurgyens* (1541) and *The Seuen*

Sorowes that women have when theyre Husbandes be deade. Copland also contributed verses to Chaucer's *Assemble of Foules* (1530).

With its detailed exposition of villainy set carefully within a moral frame-work—Copland's *Envoi* adjures his readers (and presumably his subjects too) to "eschue vyce"—the *Hye Way* sets the pattern for a number of subsequent cant collections, none more so than those of the playwright Robert Greene. Greene is undoubtedly the most accessible of the sixteenth-century cant collectors, but there were others, and they should not be overlooked.

John Awdeley, also known as John Sampson and at times Sampson Awdeley, flourished *c.* 1559 to 1577. A printer's apprentice, then a full-fledged printer, his printshop in Little Britain was but a few minutes walk from St. Bartholemew's front porch, where Copland had quizzed the Porter for cant. Awdeley's output was reasonably predictable for his times: a variety of religious pamphlets and treatises, some sermons and studies of "algorism" (the decimal system) and of husbandry. As befitted a collector of cant Awdeley was not above the odd dip into sensationalism. His *Description of Swedland* (1561) concentrates on "the moste horrible and incredible tiranny of the second Christern kyng of Denmarke against the Swecians," while the broadsheet *Cox's Retraction* (1561) prints out "the vnfained retraction of Francis Cox, which he vttered at the Pillery in Chepesyde, and els where . . . being accused for the vse of certayne sinistral and Diuelish Artes." Further broadsides included "A monsterous chylde which was borne at Maydestone" and "The endes of ij presoners lately pressed to death in Newgate." He also penned in 1563 "The Epitaphe of Mr. Veron," memorializing the anti-Catholic polemicist and fellow lexicographer John Veron, author of the *Dictionariolum puerorum* ("the little dictionary for boys"), which dealt with English, French, and Latin.

Nor was Awdeley himself immune from the occasional clash with the authorities. In 1559 he printed a catechism, for which he was fined two shillings. He was regularly fined further sums for "printing other mens copies"—probably the popular ballads for which there was always a ready market—and in July 1561 he sacrificed fourteen pence for assailing one "Rychard Lante with unseemly words."

But his primary work, which would stand for the next century and more, was *The Fraternity of Vagabonds* (1561). "As wel of ruflyng Vacabondes, as of beggerly, of women as of men, of Gyrles as of Boyes . . . Confirmed for euer by Cocke Lorell." The status of this latter figure, Cock Lorel, called up to add his weight to the accuracy of Awdeley's researches, requires a comment. It veers between that of a simple linguistic construct and a semimythological flesh and blood villain. On the one hand this cant term means simply a chief rascal: *cock* meaning chief or leader and *lorel* or *losel* a rogue. The equivalent, perhaps of today's "Guv'nor" or "The Man." On the other hand the most common contemporary use of the phrase is as the proper name Cock Lorel, who may possibly have been a genuine person, and who certainly features largely in the literature of Elizabethan villainy. "A great rascal, but evidently a man of talents"[10] his first appearance is as the eponymous antihero of *Cock Lorel's Bote* (*c.* 1500), a work that relates directly to *Das Narrenschiff* (1494) by Sebastian Brandt (1457–1521) and its English version *The Ship of Fooles* (1508), translated by Alexander Barclay and printed by Wynkyn de Worde. Here Cock Lorel is a shipmaster (Samuel Rowlands, himself an adept of cant, opts for another classic villainous type: "a tinker") whose "crew" are a group of rogues drawn from the workshops and gutters of London. Together they "sail" the country, engaging in a variety of villainies. He appears in a number of works, always at the head of his marauding beggars, sometimes plotting against the State, on one occasion even entertaining the Devil to dinner. According to Rowlands, who lays out a generally fictitious "history" of the "canting crew" or criminal beggars, the real-life Cock Lorel's rule supposedly lasted from *c.* 1511 to 1533.

If Copland's interlarding of his text with cant can be cited as the first attempt at any such collection, then Awdeley's glossary is the first proper listing of the cant vocabulary. It is brief—its nine pages contain but forty-eight headwords, mixing the occupational names of beggars and rogues with those of sluggish and slovenly servants—but highly influential. One can see Awdeley's researches appearing time and time again, embellished and expanded no doubt, but still undeniably plucked from his files. The work falls into three parts: the first deals with rural villains, the second with their urban cousins and the third is Awdeley's list of "the xxv. Orders of Knaues, otherwyse called a Quartern of Knaues." These, however, were not villains as such, but ill-behaved servants— the original meaning of knave—who may or may not have descended into actual crime. Typical among them are the "Bawde Physicke . . . is he that is a Cocke [cook], when his Maysters meate is wyll dressed, and he challenging him therefore, he wyl say he wyll eat thye rawest morsel thereof him selfe. This is a sausye knave, that wyl contrary his mayster alway" and the "Esen Droppers . . . bene they, that stand under mens wales or windoes, or, in any other place, to heeare the secretes of a mans house. These misdeming knaves wyl stand in corners to heare if they be evill spoken of, or waite a shrewd turne." This latter section, while amusing, is very much tied to its time; indeed a number of the names, suggests Partridge, may well be nonce creations of Awdeley's own.[11] Whatever their provenance, they did not survive their putative coiner;

even the *OED,* often tolerant of the most ephemeral of long-defunct cant, omits them. Other than in *The Fraternitie* itself, and in Partridge's wide-ranging *Dictionary of the Underworld,* their last appearance was in Frederick Furnivall's reprints of the book, both for the EETS in 1869 and for the New Shakespere Society, where they appear in 1880 under the title "Rogues and Vagabonds of Shakespere's Youth."

Awdeley's lists of urban and rural miscreants, however, stayed the course. His own pamphlet can barely have sold out when its successor appeared, little more than five years later. Indeed, so similar was Thomas Harman's *Caveat for Common Coursetours,* that for many years it was believed to have preceded Awdeley, whose work in fact forms its heart.

Harman was the grandson of one Henry Harman, who was clerk of the crown under King Henry VII and was granted the estates of Ellam and Maystreet in Kent around 1480. Harman's father, William, expanded the family lands by buying another estate, that of Mayton or Maxton, also in Kent. Thomas himself, the heir to this not inconsiderable property, and certainly not the "poor gentleman" that he liked to style himself, lived nearby, in the town of Crayford. He remained in the country from 1547 until his death, the date of which remains unknown, but is presumed to have followed not so long after the appearance of his book. Never a well man, or so he claims, he preferred the fresh air of Kent to the less salubrious atmosphere of the metropolis. That said, Harman was more than happy to pursue the insalubrious side of language. He regularly probed the beggars who appeared at his door, swapping his food or money for their vocabulary. He knew his local villains so well that he lists them in his book: "Harry Smith, hee dryveleth when he speaketh" and "Richard Horwood, wel neer lxxx. yeare old, he will bite a vi. peny nayle asunder with his teeth and a baudy dronkard." He would also pay regular visits to London to double-check his information. He was not, however, immune to deception. On occasion beggars presumably fed him any old words in order to pick up their fee, but Harman had clout. He was a magistrate and, as he explains, was not above depriving some particularly mendacious traveler of his license, confiscating such money as he had and distributing it among the honest poor of his neighborhood.

Sometime before 1566 Harman had completed his labors: he had the manuscript of a substantial treatise on beggars and their ways, complete with a brief glossary and, as has been noted, a lengthy list, with less than flattering descriptions, of the individuals who made up his primary sources. While the book was making its way through the press he stayed at "the Whitefriars within the Cloister," an area near Fleet Street that within fifty years would be better known as Alsatia, a hotbed of crime and the spawner of much cant. The *Caveat* appeared either in 1566 or possibly a year later. No copy of the purported first edition has survived; the first available, and as such reprinted, yet again by Dr. Furnivall alongside the EETS edition of *The Fraternitie* in 1869, is dated 1567. Dedicated to his county neighbor, Elizabeth, countess of Shrewsbury, Harman's underworld vade mecum was an immediate success. So much so that two printers, Henry Bynneman and Gerrard Dewes, were fined by the Stationers' Company, which licensed all printing, for attempting to circulate pirated copies.

As he puts it in a burst of alliterative disdain, Harman offered his readers "the leud lousey language of these lewtering [loitering] luskes [idlers] and lasy lorrels [blackguards] where with they bye and sell the common people as they pas through the country. Whych language they terme Peddelars Frenche, a vnknowen toung onely, but to these bold, beastly, bawdy Beggers, and vaine Vacabondes . . ." He prefaces his work with an "epistle" to the reader, followed by some twenty-four small essays, each dealing with a different rank of villain, from the "upright man" (the leading rank of villainy) to the "counterfeit crank" (bedecked with repellent sores), and from the "dummerar" (feigning dumbness and claiming to have been mutilated by the infidel Turk for denying Mohammad) to the "fresh-water mariner" (whose "shippes were drowned in the playne of Salisbury"), and a list of some 114 terms. These are very briefly defined, usually with a single synonym. The book also features a number of woodcuts, notably those of Nicolas Blunt, an upright man, and Nicolas Genynges [Jennings], a counterfeit crank. In many ways the most fascinating section of the book, other than the list of long-vanished villains, is the cant dialogue that Harman offers, purporting to be between a pair of criminals. These wonderfully contrived exchanges, carefully laying all his favorite terms out on display, include, for example, "Maund of this morte whate bene peck is in her ken," and translates it, "Ask of this wyfe what goode meate shee hath in her house." Elsewhere he throws in the oath-ridden "Gerry gan the Ruffian cly thee," which becomes "A torde in thy mouth, the deuill take thee." And on they go. "By this lytle ye maye holy and fully vnderstande their vntowarde talk and pelting [worthless, contemptible] speache, mynglede without measure," promises Harman, but he acknowledges that cant is always changing and "as they haue begonne of late to deuyse some new termes for certien thinges, so wyll they in tyme alter this, and deuyse as euyll or worsse." To what extent such terminology baffled the contemporary "harman becks" or policemen, or indeed how much help they gained from the *Caveat*'s glossary, is debatable, but without Harman's translations such conversations would surely elude today's reader.

Certain of Awdeley's terms undoubtedly make their way into Harman's lists, but "honest Harman"—as Partridge described him[12]—moved a substantial distance beyond Awdeley's pioneering efforts. He may have hoped, as he states in his epistle, that his sociolinguistic efforts would provide a useful sourcebook for his fellow magistrates, as well as for interested members of the public, but the real beneficiaries of his manual were his lexicographical successors.

The first "borrower" was the playwright Thomas Dekker (1570?–1632). His birthdate is arbitrary, and while his death may have come in 1632, it might equally possibly have occurred nine years later. His *DNB* entry covers more than seven columns, but the actual biography, rather than the listing and analysis of his works, is frustratingly scant. At some stage, while still a young man, he picked up a working knowledge of linen drapery and shoe making, as well as of the less savory end of the law. He apparently knew the Low Countries, could certainly read Dutch, and may have fought in the Spanish wars. He began writing plays around 1598. But although his personal biography is generally lost in time, he remains one of the best chroniclers of Elizabethan life. An indefatigable eulogist of the city in which he lived, Dekker saw London as "the nurse of his being" and sets it at the heart of both plays and prose. Yet for all that Dekker himself had an intimate knowledge of the underworld—he suffered from a wearingly fluctuating income and was imprisoned for debt on several occasions, once for nearly seven years—his incorporation of cant, albeit accurate, is far from subtle. Typical is a scene from *The Roaring Girle* (coauthored with Thomas Middleton between 1604 and 1610 and premiered in 1611). Like some early-seventeenth-century episode of British television's *Minder,* that repository of modern-day urban slang, the authors are at pains to display their knowledge of the underworld. The "Roaring Girle" herself, Moll Cutpurse (the real-life pseudonym of the pickpocket Mary Frith who may, since she was alive at the time, have even seen the play), meets a fellow lowlifer and puts him through an interrogation:

Moll: And Tearcat, what are you? a wild rogue, and angler or a ruffler . . . ?

Trapdoor: I have, by the salomon, a doxy that carries a kinchin mort in her slate at her back, besides my dell and my dainty wild dell, with all whom I'll tumble this next darkmans in the strommel, and drink ben bouse, and eat a fat gruntling cheat, a cackling cheat and a quacking cheat . . .

All good stuff no doubt—no less than sixteen discrete cant terms in this brief example and the whole scene carries on in the same way—but it reads less like a feasible dialogue and more like a cursorily dramatized slang glossary, bereft only of alphabetical order and explanatory definitions.

Dekker's plays tend to be collaborative efforts; his prose pamphlets are solo creations. Perhaps the best known is his description of an outbreak of the plague, *The Wonderful Year, 1603,* but his rogue pamphlets, notably *The Bellman of London* (1608) and *Lanthorne and Candlelight* (published seven months later in the same year), point up his extensive knowledge of cant and its users. *The Bellman* was instantly successful, meriting Dekker's speedy follow-up. A fellow writer, William Fennor, surveying the state of cant lexicography in *The Counter's Commonwealth* (1617), noted Greene and Luke Hutton, author of *The Black Dog of Newgate* (a ballad devoted to the prison's mythical "black dog," supposedly the ghostly remains of a poor scholar, cannibalized by his fellow prison inmates), but preferred above both "the most wittiest, elegantest and eloquentest piece, Master Dekker (the true heir of Apollo) composed, called The Bellman of London" in which Dekker had "set for the vices of the time so vively, that it is unpossible the anchor of any other man's brain can sound the sea of a more deep and dreadful mischief." Viewed with so generous an eye, Dekker is indeed exemplary, but Fennor presumably saw no need to probe further. In fact Dekker borrows hugely from Harman (as he does from Greene). Where he surpasses his predecessor is in the story with which he surrounds his exposition of the vocabulary. Hardly surprising, since Harman was a magistrate and Dekker an accomplished playwright. But many of the characters are the same and Dekker's list of 27 major villainous types is essentially the same as Harman's 24. However, in fairness to Dekker, one should note that his aims in displaying this list were somewhat different from those of Harman. Where the magistrate wanted to alert his fellow law makers, as well as the "straight" public, to this hitherto secret world, Dekker was more interested in the language itself. His fascination, it appears, was with the fictional possibilities of such a lurid vocabulary. He was bearing witness, as it were, while Harman was briefing witnesses.

The pamphlet falls into two parts. Dekker begins with a country episode, in which, after some paragraphs in praise of country life, the author stumbles upon a country cottage where there are gathered a number of criminal beggars. They eat a meal and leave. In the cottage, playing host to the criminal crew, is an old woman who proceeds to inform him of the various types of rural villains (in effect repeating Harman's categories). Like Sherlock Holmes in *The Copper Beeches* ("It is my belief, Watson . . . that the lowest and vilest alleys of London do not present a more dreadful record of sin than does the smiling . . . countryside"), Dekker professes himself appalled by rural corruption and declares, "I have heard of no sin in the city but I met it in the village, nor any vice in the tradesman, which was not in the ploughman." It has been suggested that in his description of the beggars' gathering, Dekker was allegorizing the still-recent agrarian uprising of 1607, when one "Captain Pouch" led bands of Midlands peasants in rampages across the country, filling ditches, tearing down hedges, and breaking open the enclosures of formerly common land. How true this might be remains open to debate. Allegorical or otherwise, Dekker declares himself disillusioned and returns to town. Here he meets a new informant, the Bellman, "a man with a lantern and candle in his hand, a long staff on his neck, and a dog at his tail." The Bellman, who styles himself "the sentinel of the City, the watchman for every ward, the honest spy who discovered the 'prentices of the night,' " plays much the same role for Dekker as the Spytell House Porter did for Copland. In his turn he expounds his own, urban knowledge, running down the world of the London criminal classes for Dekker, and his readers.

So successful was *The Bellman of London* that Dekker quickly wrote and published the sequel *Lanthorne and Candlelight,* which echoed the title of a popular ballad of 1569 and reintroduced the Bellman. Much of the material reworks the original pamphlet, although on this occasion Dekker opts for an out-and-out glossary, Harman yet again, as well as a discussion of cant which claims to trace its origins back to the original dispersal of tongues at the Tower of Babel. As well as the Bellman, Dekker also introduced another character: the beadle of Bridewell, supposedly the Bellman's brother. This figure was taken up by another author, "S.R."—known either as Samuel Rid or Samuel Rowlands— who in 1610 issued a fictional rejoinder to Dekker: *Martin Mark-All, beadle of Bridewell; his defence and answere to the belman of London.* Rowlands/Rid made it clear that Dekker, for all his popularity, had simply plagiarized Harman and that in doing so had made no effort to bring up to date a glossary that had originally been composed a half century earlier. He also stressed what he claimed was his own superior knowledge of the criminal world:

I have thought good, not only to show his error in some places in setting down old words, used forty years before he was born, for words that are used in these days—although he is bold to call me an usurper (for so he hath done in his last round), and not able to maintain the title—but have enlarged his dictionary (or Master Harman's) with such words as I think he never heard of, and yet in use too, but not of our vain-glory, as *his* ambition is, but, indeed, as an experienced soldier that hath dearly paid for it. And therefore it shall be honour good enough for him, if not too good, to come up with the rear—I do but shoot your own arrow back again—and not have the leading of the van as he means to do, although small credit in the end will redound to either.

Rowlands then offers some 129 entries, of which ten are modernizations of Harman's usage and fifty-three are brand-new expressions.

Both *Beadle* and *Bellman* had their readers, but the flow of rogue pamphlets, with their concomitant vocabularies and glossaries, faded as the march of puritanism worked with increasing success to sideline such corrupting frivolities. In addition, the prominence of the criminal beggar, so central to late Elizabethan life, was much diminished. The pose of informative reformer, which had been adopted by Dekker and Greene, or of genuine sociological researcher, as taken by Harman, was no longer particularly relevant. Thus while mainstream dictionaries continued to appear throughout the seventeenth century, the world of cant lexicography was placed on hold until the Restoration. It was not until 1665 that it reemerged, with Frances Kirkman and Richard Head's *The English Rogue.* This, the life story of one Meriton Latroon (f. *latron:* a robber), "a witty extravagant," embellished with "a Compleat History of the Most Eminent Cheats of Both Sexes," included a seven-page glossary, drawing freely on Harman and Dekker, and the canting song, "Bing Out Bien Morts," which is dense with cant. Indeed, the glossary which follows it is essential for its understanding. It was not, as these four lines indicate, the simplest of ditties: "This Doxie Dell can cut bien whids | And wap well for a win: | And prig and cloy so benshiply, | All the Deuse-a-vile within . . ."[13] Nor was Latroon's life considered acceptable: it was banned for its indecency and circulated secretly, as one of the recognized "obscene publications" of its day. Eight years later came Head's solo offering: *The Canting Academy, or the Devil's Cabinet opened. Wherein is shown the mysterious and villainous practices of that wicked crew commonly known by the name of Hectors, Trepanners, Gilts, etc.* (1673).

This too is firmly rooted in Harman and his successors. It is also typical of the format within which late-seventeenth-century cant studies flourished: that of being addenda to genuine or semifictional biographies of notable rogues. It is a strange mishmash of a book, which throws together canting songs as well as some composed by "the choicest Wits of the Age," the oaths taken by professional criminals, "the vicious and remarkable lives of Mother Craftsby and Madame Wheedle," a number of "joviall paradoxes," and some suitably bloodcurdling "examples of Covetousness, Idleness, Gluttony and Lechery." Its most important feature was its glossary, the "compleat Canting Dictionary."

Although one can trace its direct line to Harman, Head was keen to stress the efforts he had made on his own account in the creation of this compilation:

"I can assure you (the helps extant being so inconsiderable) the pains I took in the Collection of new Words is unimaginable." He also notes his efforts in the field, underlining then as now the fundamental need of cant (even more so than slang) to keep moving on, keeping its villainous users a necessary step ahead of the authorities.

> I have consulted . . . what is printed on this subject, and have slighted no help I could gather from thence, which indeed is very little; the greatest assistance I had in this discovery was from *Newgate;* which with much difficulty I screwed out of the sullen Rogues . . . from these I understood, that the Mode of Canting alter'd very often, and that they were forced to change frequently those material words which chiefly discovered their mysterious practices and Villainies, least growing too common their own words should betray them. Here, in this Vocabulary or little Canting Dictionary, you have all or most of the old words which are still in use, and many new never published in print, and but very lately minted, such too which have passed the approbation of the Critical Canter.[14]

One extra aspect of the book is that like a traditional bilingual dictionary, Head offers Standard English–Cant/Cant–Standard English sections. For him cant is presented not merely as a parallel vocabulary, but a genuinely "foreign" one. But if in his selection of slang terms, for all his claims of originality, Head can be relegated to yet another borrower from Harman, Greene, Dekker, and others, his efforts had an influence of their own. The miscellaneous writer John Shirley (*fl.* 1680–1702) included a canting glossary in *The Triumph of Wit* (1688); it appears to have been stolen wholesale from *The Canting Academy.* Nor was Shirley immune to theft in his turn: *The Scoundrel's Dictionary* (1754) is little more than a reprint of his cant list. More important was Head's wider influence. Mainstream lexicographers had so far sedulously averted their gaze from cant and similar vulgarisms. But three years after *The Canting Academy* appeared that pattern changed, albeit briefly. Elisha Coles published his *English Dictionary* in 1676. In it was included pretty much all of Head's word list. Coles, unsurprisingly, felt it necessary to note in his preface his deviation from the orthodox. His justification is pleasingly pragmatic: " 'Tis no Disparagement to understand the Canting Terms: It may chance to save your Throat from being cut, or (at least) your Pocket from being pick'd." His innovation did not last. Cocker, whose work of 1704 borrowed extensively from Coles, excluded any such vocabulary (although later editions grudgingly reintroduced "some few, but omitted a multitude"), while in 1755 Samuel Johnson, loathing what he saw as naked vulgarity, had no truck with such material. Bailey, Johnson's immediate precedessor and sometime rival, did include some of the vocabulary, and offered a separate 36-page list (drawn probably on *The New Canting Dictionary* of 1725) in later editions of his *Universal Etymological English Dictionary*, but he was still the exception and by no means the rule. Cant, like slang, would be left primarily to its devotees for some time to come. A rare exception, and on the surface a surprising one, was *The Ladies Dictionary* by John Dunton of 1694. This work, which aimed at being "a *Compleat Directory* to the *Female-Sex* in all *Relations, Companies, Conditions* and *States* of Life," did include some cant vocabulary, essentially that referring to the ranks of female beggars, typically *autem-morts, kynchin-morts,* and the like. Its aim, presumably, was to acquaint its gentle readers with the varieties of female mendicants they might find at their doors.

Head, even more so than Dekker, lived the life on which his books commentated. As one critic sniffed, "His indelicacy pleased the public but he led a wild and dissipated life . . ."[15] He had been born *c.* 1637 in Ireland to a father who had eloped with his mother shortly after leaving Oxford and subsequently gained employment as a nobleman's chaplain. After accompanying his patron to Ireland, Head Sr. settled at Carrickfergus where, in 1641, he was murdered by Irish rebels. His wife and son, aged only four, fled their home and "after fearful sufferings"[16] arrived, via Belfast, back in England. Brought up in Plymouth, Head followed his late father to Oxford, but left quickly and apprenticed himself to a London bookseller. Here he wrote the presumably salacious *Venus' Cabinet Unlock'd,* then married and opened up his own shop in Little Britain, still a center of the literary world. It was not a success: its meager profits were promptly tossed away on the gambling tables and Head judiciously packed up and relocated in Dublin.

There he wrote a play, *Hic et Ubique, or the Humours of Dublin,* which, according to his biographer William Winstanley (in *Lives of the Most Famous English Poets,* 1687), was "acted privately with great applause." Armed with this success he returned to London in 1663 and had his hit printed, dedicating it to Charles, duke of Monmouth. He then took a house near Paternoster Row and attempted to rekindle his bookselling career. Unfortunately gambling remained both alluring and expensive; this second bookshop collapsed in its turn and Head was reduced to hackwork, knocking out such copy as was requested at 20/- a sheet. He remained a hack, suffering vertiginous ups and downs and "many crosses and afflictions" for what remained of his life, which ended, according to Winstanley, when in 1686 he drowned on a crossing to the Isle of Wight. John Aubrey, on the other hand, dispatches him ten years earlier, and sets the scene of his drowning off the shore near his childhood home of Plymouth. Aubrey noted that Head had recently been traveling with the Gypsies and in a less than flattering aside says that he "looked like a knave with his goggling eyes" and, somewhat mysteriously, that he could "transform himself into any shape."

Head's extensive output was firmly geared to the lower end of the reading market. Cant studies aside, his other books include a number of fictional "biographies" of notable villains, *Jackson's Recantation, or the Life and Death of the notorious Highwayman now hanging in chains at Hampstead* (1674), *The Life and Death of Mother Shipton* (1677), *News from the Stars* (1673, supposedly authored by Meriton Latroon), *O Brazil, or the Inchanted Island* (1675), *Madame Wheedle, or the fashionable Miss Discovered, Al-Man-Sir, or Rhodomontados of the Most Horrible, Terrible and Invincible Captain Sir Frederick Fightall* and a pamphlet in favor of liberty of conscience satisfyingly entitled *Moonshine* (1672).

Finally, among those for whom Thomas Harman provided so vital an inspiration, comes one in whom lexicography was very much an afterthought and the world from which his cant glossary was drawn of far more immediate import. John Hall, who is cited in the *DNB* simply as "criminal," was born at some undetermined date to poor parents in Bishop's Head Court, Gray's Inn Lane, London. Brought up to be a chimney sweep, he soon turned pickpocket. He was only intermittently successful and in January 1682 was convicted of theft at the Old Bailey, and whipped at the cart's tail. In 1700 he was sentenced to death for housebreaking but won a pardon, on condition that he emigrated to America within six months. He managed to desert the ship which was meant to take him to the colonies, and returned to crime. In 1702 he had a cheek branded and was jailed for two years for stealing a portmanteau from a coach. On his release he formed a burglary gang with Stephen Bunce and Richard Low. They were daring, successful housebreakers who were arrested several times, but never convicted. Hall had few scruples. On one occasion he broke into the house of a Hackney baker. Tossing his apprentices into the kneading trough, Hall grabbed the baker's baby granddaughter, threatening to put her in the bread oven if the baker did not hand over his cash. He did: some seventy pounds. In 1707, convicted for breaking into the house of Captain Guyon near Stepney the gang was finally sentenced to death. They hanged at Tyburn on December 12, 1707. Before his death Hall used his time in jail to compose *The Memoirs of the right villainous John Hall, the late famous and notorious robber, penn'd from his own mouth.* It appeared in 1708 complete with a glossary of thieves' terms. Connoisseurs of such terminology could note that even posthumously John Hall managed a final theft: this time from Harman's *Caveat.*

One last major figure remains of this pioneering period of cant and slang collection. It is Robert Greene, an habitué, albeit a slightly older one, of the same playwriting milieu as Thomas Dekker, a fellow writer with whom Greene shared a number of friends. And it is in Greene that one finds at last the most properly three-dimensional figure among these early pursuers and publicizers of the criminal vocabulary.

Robert Greene was born in Norwich sometime between 1550 and 1560. His main biographer, the Russian scholar Nicholas Storojenko, prefers the latter date, and suggests that his was "a very old and respectable family." Greene himself speaks of his parents as being respected for their gravity and the honesty of their life,[17] but Grosart, editor of his collected works, suggests that such claims erred to the spurious. Referring to the class gradations of such titles, he notes that Greene never signs himself R. Greene, Gent. ("Gentleman") but only R. Greene, Norfolciensis ("of Norfolk"), a geographical rather than a social title. That said, Greene matriculated at St. John's College, Cambridge in 1575, took his B.A. in 1578, then moved to Clare Hall, where he gained an M.A. He was incorporated, in other words given an *ex officio* membership, at Oxford in 1588, an honor that obviously pleased him, since he ostentatiously places the Latin *Utriusque Academiae in Artibus Magister* ("And Master of Arts of the Other University") on the title page of some of his works.

At some stage between the taking of his B.A. and M.A. Greene left England to travel abroad, certainly in Italy and Spain and probably in Poland and Denmark too. It was on these travels that the young Greene appears to have discovered new pleasures beyond those of Oxbridge academe. As Dyce censoriously remarks, "From the laxity of manners prevalent in some of those countries he seems to have acquired a taste for the dissolute habits in which he afterwards indulged."[18] It was not a lifestyle which Greene appears to have required any great urging to adopt. Nor was the contemporary university especially renowned for its piety. Huber, writing in *The English University,* claimed that university life was characterized not for its learning but by "immorality, impiety, dissipation and disreputable conduct." Writing in his posthumously published *Repentence* Greene recalled,

> For being at the Vniversitie of Cambridge, I light amongst wags as lewd as my selfe, with whome I consumed the flower of my youth; who drew mee to trauell into Italy and Spain, in which places I sawe and practizde such villainie as is abominable to declare. Thus by their counsaile I sought to furnishe myselfe with coine, which I procured by cunning sleights from my father and my friends, and my mother pampered me so

long, and secretly helped me to the oyle of angels [money used for gifts or bribes; the angel was a coin worth approximately 50p], that I grew thereby prone to all mischiefe: so that beeing then conuersant with notable braggarts, boon companions, and ordinary spend-thrifts . . . I became as a sien [scion] grafted into the same stocke, whereby I did absolutely participate of their nature and qualities.[19]

Such trips to Europe, while common among those who could afford them, were by no means viewed as a wholly positive phenomenon. Despite the influence of the Renaissance, which sprang from European origins and which can be seen in the work of such contemporary scholars as Sir Thomas Elyot, a generally anti-European feeling was growing during the latter half of the sixteenth century, fueled no doubt by the enmity between Anglican England and Catholic Spain. Lord Burghley in his *Ten Precepts* remarked, "Suffer not thy sons to pass the Alps, for they shall learn nothing there but pride, blasphemy and atheism" and the overall mood was summed up by the classicist Roger Ascham (1515/16–1568), whose career at St. John's had preceded Greene's by nearly fifty years. Writing in *The Schoolemaster* (1570) he condemned Italy as a "new Circe" turning once sober young men into dissipated swine. Ascham was all in favor of Italian as a language, but Italy itself was dangerous and corrupting. "I was once in Italie my self; but I thanke God my abode there, was but ix. dayes; And yet I sawe in that litle tyme, in one Citie, more libertie to sinne, than ever I heard tell of in our noble Citie of London in ix. yeare." His own supposed addiction to dicing and cock fighting, which some claim reduced his last years to poverty, was presumably overlooked in such observations. Not for nothing, therefore, was Greene reduced to "cunning sleights" to finance the trip. His conservative father might have banned it; fortunately for him his mother proved more liberal.

Greene returned to England, probably in 1580. The odds are that, indulgent mother notwithstanding, he had run out of money. Back home he found everything dull and uninspiring. "Being new-come from Italy (where I learned all the vilainies vnder the heauens), I was drowned in pride, whoredome was my daily exercise, and gluttony with drunkennes was my onely delight." He was less than cheerful and "ruffeled out [swaggered around; thus the cant *ruffler*: a mendicant beggar who poses as a returned soldier] in my silks in the habit of Malcontent, and seemed so discontent that no place would please me to abide in, nor no vocation cause mee to stay myelfe in . . ."[20]

To alleviate his ennui he also penned a ballad, now lost: "Youthe, seeing all his wais so Troublesome, abandoning Virtue and Learning to Vice, recalleth his

Former Follies with an Inward Repentence." Given his other comments on his mood, it seems unlikely that this was wholly sincere. He also wrote what is his first extant piece of prose: *Mamillia: a Mirrour or looking glasse for the Ladies of Englande.* This may have arisen from some frustrated affair, for its somewhat embittered subtitle claims to explain "howe Gentlemen vnder the perfect substance of pure loue, are oft inueigled with the shadowe of lewde lust . . ." *Mamillia* was registered with the Stationers' Company that year, although its first publication was in 1583.

It has also been suggested, on the basis of Thomas Rymer's *Foedera* (a multi-volumed collection of treaties and similar alliances made between Britain and foreign countries, appearing under various editors 1704–1830), that Greene took holy orders in 1576 and was duly appointed a chaplain to Queen Elizabeth, and given the rectory of Walkington in the diocese of York. Appealing though the paradox might be, Greene was a Cambridge undergraduate at the time.

In the end Greene chose to return to Cambridge where he worked toward his M.A., which was awarded on July 1, 1583. *Mamillia* was published in that year, and over the next twelve months Greene followed it with a number of other works, notably *The Mirror of Modestie, Arbasto, the Anatomie of Fortune, Morando, the Tritameron of Loue, Gwydonius,* and *The Carde of Fancie . . . wherein the Folly of . . . Carpet-Knights is decyphered."* In 1585 he began studying medicine and wrote an astronomical treatise, *Planetomachia: of the first part of the generall opposition of the seuen Planets: wherein is Astronomically described their essence, nature and influence . . .* For the title page of this work Greene styled himself "a student in Physicke." It was not a career in which he persisted.

Despite this apparent dedication to his work, Greene remained happily immured in pleasure and degeneracy, along with a growing circle of fellow writers who mixed hackwork with self-indulgence, and in the way of such ambitious young men worked and played equally enthusiastically as they awaited their moment of "discovery." Among this group, latterly christened the "University Wits," were Christopher Marlowe, playwright and possible government spy, who some still believe "was" Shakespeare; Thomas Nashe, whose first published work was a preface to one by Greene and who defended the dead writer from the scabrous attacks launched against him by his enemy Gabriel Harvey; Thomas Watson, one of the most celebrated lyric poets of the time, known as the "English Petrarch"; Thomas Lodge, author of *Rosalinda,* which Shakespeare used for the plot of *As You Like It,* and George Peele, one of his closest friends, and one who, as Greene lay dying, called on him to repent and abandon drink and debauchery.

He also began to mingle with London's actors, who persuaded him to start writing for the stage; it was an arena, they assured him, that would yield substantial profits. Greene even worked very briefly as an actor himself, appearing as "The Pinner" in *George-a-Greene, the Pinner or Pindar of Wakefield*. But his main role was "as an author of playes and a penner of love-pamphlets."[21] Gradually, Greene's earnings, and his fame, increased. His taste for "immorality," however, was not diminished. "Yong yet in yeares, though olde in wickednes . . . I grew so rooted in all mischiefe that I had as great a delight in wickednesse as sundrie hath in godlinesse, and as much felicitie I tooke in villainy as others had in honestie." There was, nonetheless, one brief flirtation with goodness, as he recounts in *The Repentence*. "Let me confesse a trueth, that euevn once, and yet but once, I felt a fear and horrour in my conscience, and then the errour of God's iudgementes did manifestly teach me that my life was bad, and that by sinne I deserued damnation, and that such was the greatnes of my sinne that I deserued no redemption." Visiting Norwich, his hometown, Greene, for whatever reason, found himself in St. Andrew's Church. There he was confronted by a hellfire preacher, whose sermon, so Greene claimed, "might have conuerted the worst monster of the world." Since Greene knew that "whosoeuer was worst, I knewe myselfe as bad as he," this sermon hit home. Greene duly determined to mend his ways before he was "wipte out of the booke of life."

The Repentence, of course, bears all the hallmarks of a deathbed conversion, notably a gross discrepancy between the lubricity of the life lived and the promises of reform occasioned by the fear of imminent death. Greene's response to his experience in St. Andrews sounds more like a man in the temporary grip of a raging hangover than a genuine move toward reformation. His friends obviously felt much the same. Greene had barely murmured "Lord haue mercie upon mee and send me grace to amend and become a new man!" when "I met with my copesmates [companions], but seeing me in such a solemn humour, they demanded the cause of my sadnes." On being informed that the playwright was suffering the throes of a guilty conscience (with or without the hangover) and had determined to seek the path of righteousness, "they fell vpon me in jeasting manner, calling me Puritan and Presizian . . . that by their foolish perswasion the good and wholesome lesson I had learned went quite out of my remembrance; so that I fel again with the dog to my old vomit . . ."

Greene did, however, return not long after to church, in this case for his own marriage, which occurred on February 16, 1586, when, according to Dyce, he married one Elizabeth Taylor, the daughter of a Lincolnshire squire. Storojenko prefers the name Dorothy, sets the date sometime in 1585, and claims that

Dyce's evidence, to be found in the marriage register of the Church of St. Bartholomew the Less in London (where Inigo Jones had been christened a decade earlier), refers to quite another couple. Nomenclature aside, the marriage was short-lived. Dorothy/Elizabeth made the fatal mistake, so Greene claims, of attempting to "perswade me from my wilfull wickednes."[22] This failed and "hauing spent vp the marriage-money which I obtained by her," Greene abandoned his wife and their young child. Quite when this desertion took place is arguable. Greene claims to have left her "at six or seven," a phrase that might mean after six or seven months, implying, since they had already a child, that the marriage might not have ever been one of choice, or simply, through so precipitate a decision, "at sixes and sevens." Elizabeth/Dorothy and the child sought refuge with her family in Lincolnshire; Greene returned to his degenerate life in London where he devoted himself to a twin-track existence, penning a succession of plays, almost invariably promoting the triumph of piety and good over debauchery and evil, and living a life in which "there would continue quaffing, carowsing and surfeting with me all the day long."

Greene was first and foremost a writer on demand. As John Clark Jordan notes, "Whatever literary form he took up, it was for exploitation; whatever he dropped, it was because the material or the demand was exhausted. He did what no man before him in England had done so extensively: he wrote to sell."[23] And Greene was undoubtedly good at what he did. His peers may have exceeded him for quality, but Greene's quantity was what made him popular. You name it—drama, poetry, romances, social pamphlets, treatises, even deathbed repentances—Greene could and did knock it out, and deliver to the deadline. As Nashe put it in his defense of his newly dead friend, *Strange Newes, of the Intercepting Certayne letters* (1592), "In a night and a day he would have iarkt [written, literally counterfeited] vp a pamphlet as well as in seauen yeare." Printers, it was said, would "pay him deare for the very dregs of his wit." Nor did this journeyman hack seem especially obsessed with fame. "He made no account of winning credite by his works," adds Nashe, ". . . his only care was to hauue a spel in his purse to coniure up a good cuppe of wine at all times." He wrote some thirty-eight works (although the manuscripts of others may have vanished, as did a variety of literature, during the Great Fire of London) of which twenty-eight appeared in his lifetime and ten more were attributed to him later. His eight plays were published after his death: the best known are *Orlando Furioso* (1594), *Frier Bacon and Frier Bungay* (1594, in which the real-life mage Roger Bacon, "Dr. Mirabilis," conjures up the Devil) and *James the Fourth* (1598). Perhaps his most important work, other than his four "rogue pamphlets," is the *Groats-Worth of Witte, bought with a Million of Repentance.* This autobiographical prose tract, which appeared in 1592, the year of his death, is, according to Storojenko, one of a pair of pamphlets (the other is *The Repentence*) composed when "lying on his death-bed, during the long and sleepless nights, Greene reflected much over his fate, and . . . was seized with sincere penitence for the wasted time of his youth and his misused life." The *Groats-Worth* tells the story of one "Roberto" (Greene himself) and his gradual decline into debauchery. The piece ends with an Address to his fellow playwrights; Greene cites Marlowe, Lodge, and Peele, urging them to use their brains for something better than the writing of plays. He also attacks those who turned him against religion and toward atheism. This may be a reference to the undoubtedly atheistic Marlowe, as Dyce suggests, but the villain of Greene's piece may, if Storojenko is right, be yet another Italian: the demonized political philosopher Niccolò Machiavelli, "Old Nick" himself.

Most importantly, Greene excoriates "the upstart Crow, beautified with our feathers, that with his *Tygers heart wrapt in a Players hide,* supposes he is as well able to bumbast out a blanke verse as the best of you: and being an absolute *Johannes fac totum,* is in his owne conceit the only Shake-scene in a countrey." Unsurprisingly, it has been assumed that this is an attack on William Shakespeare, newly arrived in London from the Midlands and looked down upon by the Wits as one who lacked the advantages of an Oxbridge education. Certainly it is the first ever mention of Shakespeare as a working dramatist. Whether Greene's attack hurt Shakespeare is unknown; more usefully, his prose romance *Pandosto* (1588), itself based on a Polish folktale, provided his greater contemporary with the plot for *A Winter's Tale* (1610). Indeed, Professor J. M. Brown, writing in *The New Zealand Magazine* (April 1877), suggests that Greene should be seen as "the father of Shakespeare—as far, at least, as an ordinary man may be said to be the father of a giant." He also suggests that Shakespeare paid Greene back, mocking him through the character of Bottom, in *A Midsummer Night's Dream,* and burlesqued both Greene and his sworn enemy Harvey in *Love's Labours Lost.* It has been further suggested that Greene's name was used by Virginia Woolf for the braggart Nick Greene, in her book *Orlando* (1928).

However substantial or otherwise may have been Greene's influence on Shakespeare, it is in the sphere of the popular "rogue pamphlet" that he is possibly best remembered now. The first such pamphlet, *A Notable Discouery of Coosnage* [cozenage, or trickery]. *Now daily practised by sundry lewd persons called Connie-Catchers* [confidence tricksters] *and Cross-biters* [swindlers] . . ." appeared in 1591. It was followed by *The Second part of Conny-catching* and the *Thirde and last Parte of Conny-catching,* all published in the same year. These in turn were followed by *A Dispvtation between a Hee Conny-catcher and a Shee Conny-catcher, whether a Theefe or a Whoore is most hurtful in Cousonage . . .*, *The Black Booke's Mes-senger* and finally *The Defence of Connycatching* "by Cuthbert Conny-catcher," all 1592. The proposed *Black Book* never appeared, nor did a tract entitled *The Con-nycatcher's Repentence.*

The essence of all these is the parading by Greene of what he claims are his firsthand reminiscences of and insider tips on the underworld and its language. Like some sixteenth-century precursor of today's *True Detective* magazine Greene gleefully peddles his downmarket sensationalism, larded with cant and anec-dote, but carefully quarantined with pious horror. Typical is the *Disputation,* in which readers are presumably meant to affect worthy horror, as does the author, at this discussion between the thief Lawrence and the "alluring Strumpet" Nan. But one cannot ignore Greene's obvious, approving fascination with the vil-lainies of which he writes, and especially his somewhat rueful observations on the power of sex, rendering the whore superior to the thief, despite his ostensi-bly greater skills. "You men theeues touch the bodie and wealth, but we ruine the soule, and indanger that which is more pretious than the worldes treasure. You make work only for the gallows, we both for the gallows and the diuel, I and for the Surgian too . . ."

Greene positions himself as a lone fighter against crime, protesting somewhat overenthusiastically the way in which he has risked the wrath of the coney catch-ers, and indeed his own life, by breaching their tavern bench *omertà* and reveal-ing their masonic secrets. But nothing is as important as getting out the story. He compares himself to the Roman hero Scaevola, who sacrificed his own hand in order to save Rome, claiming that despite their most bloodcurdling threats "these vultures, these fatall Harpies" will not still his tongue.[24] *Nascimur pro patria:* "We are born for the good of our country," trumpets the title page of each pamphlet, and Greene's ostentatiously public-spirited sentiments dominate every page. Greene also parades, in *The Second Part,* which in fact had probably been written at the same time as the first, a variety of "testimonials" from poten-tial coneys, whose money had been saved thanks to a timely encounter with his efforts: "Maisters, I boughte a booke of late for a groate that warnes me of Card-playing . . . I have foresworne cards ever since I read it";[25] another, who had not been so fortunate, meets Greene and sees his book: "Sir, said he, If I had seen this booke but two dayes since, it had saved me nine pound in my purse."[26] That the *Notable Discouery* in fact makes no mention of cardplaying is neither here nor there. This is the commercial world.

Like Thomas Harman, who similarly advertised his labors "for the proffyt of [my] naturall Countrey,"[27] Greene played the reformer's card, but unlike his forerunner, the deck he used was distinctly corrupt. Nor was Harman the only source on which he drew. Substantial pieces of information had appeared around forty years earlier when *A Manifest Detection of Dice-Play* was published sometime between 1544 and 1552. Detailing the activities of a typical coney catcher of his day, the pamphlet has, alas, no known author, but as Judges points out, the wealth of detail makes it clear that it was "obviously founded on personal knowledge."[28] It also provided material for subsequent researchers, Greene in the *Notable Discovery* being one of several who lifted large chunks from its text, often without bothering with even the most cursory revision.

Greene's works further resemble those of the restrained Harman, as Dr. Jordan has pointed out, in ways that exceed his simple pilfering of the earlier writer's glossary. When in *The Second Part* he rejects the criticisms of those who regret the absence of "eloquent phrases" in these pamphlets, he is echoing Harman's celebration of his own decision to employ "plain terms . . . Eloquence have I none; I never was acquainted with the muses; I have never tasted of Helcyon . . ." Instead he has preferred to write "simplye and truelye, with such usual words and termes as is amongst us wel known . . ."[29] Greene, naturally, offers a somewhat different justification for his plain language. Self-serving as usual he explains that he has deliberately rejected the florid niceties of which he is undoubtedly capable, since "a certain decorum is to bee kept in everie thing, Therefore I humbly crave pardon and desire I may write basely of such base wretches."[30]

Yet failings of style and motives can be ignored in the face of what Greene's pamphlets actually offer the collector or historian of cant. Rodomontade aside, Greene's lexicography is impressively systematic. In the *Notable Discovery,* for instance, he deals one by one with the varieties of fraud: "High Law: robbing by the highway side; Sacking Law: lecherie; Cheting Law: playing at false dice; Cros-biting Law: cosenage by whores; Coneycatching Law: cosenage by cards; Versing Law: cosenage by false gold; Figging Law: cutting of purses and picking of pockets; Barnard's Law: a drunken cosenage by cards." He then lists the essential "players" of each variety of fraud; thus when he expounds upon the "Cros-biting Law," "cosenage by whores," or what, in modern terms would be the "badger" or "murphy game," he lists the whore herself, here known as the *traffique,* the sucker or "coney," this time termed the *simpler,* and the *cross-biter,* who beat and robbed the unfortunate punter. The system is sustained through each type of trickery. Only when faced with what he calls the "Cheting Law" does Greene, otherwise so determined in his efforts to reveal every facet of villainy, show himself strangely reticent, and declares, "Pardon me, Gentlemen, for although no man could better than myself discover this law and his termes, and the names of their Chetes, Bar'd-Dice, Flats, Forgers, Langrets, Gourds, demies and many other . . . yet for some speciall reasons, herein I will be silent." It has been suggested that this silence stems from plain ignorance of all but the names themselves; more likely, surely, is that here was an area of fraud which Greene not merely knew but practiced, and saw no reason to reveal himself as an adept. Similar analysis is offered in *The Second Part,* where he deals with the Prigging Law (horse stealing), Vincent's Law (deceit at bowls), the world of the Nip (a cutpurse) and the Foist (a pickpocket), Lifting Law (larceny), Courbing Law (hooking items out of open windows), and the Black Art (lockpicking). He also appends nine salutary tales. *The Third Part,* which contains only tales and no glossaries, is essentially an addendum to its predecessors; he had exhausted his canting vocabulary but Greene appreciated the popularity of his pamphlets and saw no reason to turn off the supply.

Whether Greene wrote what would be the final "coney-catching pamphlet," *The Defense of Conny-Catching, or A Confutation of Those two injurious Pamphlets published by R.G. against the practitioners of many nimble-witted and muysticall Sciences,* remains unresolved. The author purported to be one "Cuthbert Cunnycatcher," a "Licentiate in Whittington College"—a joke aimed foursquare at the underworld: Whittington College being in fact Newgate Jail, its name taken from the celebrated Richard "Dick" Whittington, he of pantomime and actual fame; Whittington's executors had used his legacy to refurbish the prison in 1422. Cuthbert is furious, railing against this "cursed book of Conycatching" and reviling "this R.G. that had made a puyblike spoyle of so noble a science . . ." Not only has he revealed many secrets of the criminal fraternity, but he has missed out on a number of even grosser ones. Why persecute the poor coney catcher? There are many more despicable villains. In fact the book is low on hard information, it is basically a collection, like *The Third Part,* of more or less relevant tales. Perhaps the most interesting passage is that in which Cuthbert teases R.G., "Aske the Queene's Players if you sold them not Orlando Furioso for twenty nobles, and when they were in the country sold the same play to the Lord Admirals men for as much more. Was this not plaine *Conny-catching* R.G.?" This is a genuine enough gripe, but was there a real Cuthbert or, despite an elaborate rejection of the theory both by Grosart and by Professor H. C. Hart in *Notes and Queries* (10th series 4,5,9), was Greene the author of this pamphlet too? For all its pious indignation, "Cuthbert" is surely just one more way of milking a profitable genre. In the end, Greene was most likely as much the author of this refutation as he certainly was of the two pamphlets against which it pretends to rail. Teasing himself in print, revealing his own duplicities, it all seems totally in the character of a man who liked to sail close to the wind.

By 1592 excess was beginning to take its toll. In Storojenko's words, "Intemperence, licentiousness, an irreverence for religion, sometimes finding vent in coarse and revolting blasphemies" remained central to his daily round and the pieties of the coney-catching pamphlets were rarely reflected in their writer's actual life. He did pause, again only briefly, when in 1591 he published *A Farewell to Follie,* in which he promised to live a righteous life and henceforth devote himself to the promotion of morality. Whether or not he achieved this aim remains unproven; it had originally been registered in 1587 and was then, perhaps mimicking the postponed good deeds it recommended, put off. To quote Professor Storojenko again,

> The dissipated life which Greene led for many years gradually under-mined his constitution; and at last the prophecies of his friends, who had entreated him to leave off his carouses and orgies, which would sooner or later work his ruin, were fulfilled. After one of his drunken orgies, of which the leading features were pickled herrings and Rhenish wine, Greene was seized with indigestion and took to his bed. His broken down constitution was incapable of coping with sickness. Bad medical aid, the absence of attendance, and his extreme poverty, completed the rest. Deserted by his friends and boon companions, who were either in igno-rance of his condition, or else with unpardonable levity neglected to visit him, Greene expired, alone in a poverty-stricken room rented on credit of a shoe-maker. But his landlord and landlady proved themselves kind-hearted people, and showed a sincere interest in him. They and the woman with whom he had been living, were the only people that did not desert him during his illness.[31]

That woman, "a sorry, ragged queane," as his enemy Gabriel Harvey called her, and who has never been named, was the sister of a well-known villain, one Cut-ting Ball, who had recently perished on the Tyburn gallows. With her Greene had had a son, named Fortunatus, and nicknamed Infortunatus ("unfortunate") by Harvey. This infant scarcely survived his father and died in August 1593.

Greene's final effort, which was published after his death, is *The Repentence of Robert Greene Maister of Artes. Wherein by himelf is laid open his loose life, with the manner of his death . . .* The pamphlet was edited and published by Cuthbert Burbie, a printer with a shop in Poultry and who had helped in editing the *Third and last Part of Coney-Catching.* Burbie offered his own preface, crying up the catalog of debauchery and due repentance that he was peddling, and explaining that "although his loose life was odious to God and offensiue to men, yet forasmuch as at his last end he found it most griuous to himself (as appeareth by this his repentent discourse), I doubt not but that he shall for the same deserue fauour of both God and men." Burbie added that since he himself had "found this discourse very passionate and of wonderfull effect to withdraw the wicked from their ungodly waies" he had thought it a good idea to publish the tract. After all, he concludes, "by his repentence [others] may as in a glasse see their own follie, and thereby in time resolue, that it is better to die repentent than to liue dishonest."[32]

And indeed *The Repentence* is devotedly contrite. Whether genuinely heartfelt, or mawkish with terminal self-pity, Greene's apparent recantation is nothing if not fulsome:

> Oh I feele a hell already in my conscience, the number of my sinnes do muster before my eies, the poore mens plaints, that I have wronged, cries out in mine eares and saithe Robert Greene thou art damned . . . Now I do remember (though too late) I have read in the Scriptures, how neither adulterers, swearers, theeves nor muderers shall inherit the kingdome of Heaven. What hope then can I have of any grace, when *I exceeded all other in these kinde of sinnes?*[33]

But was this really Greene talking, or was it the old hack, letter-perfect unto the grave, grinding out the last few pence, offering his faithful audience the required deathbed/gallows-edge confession—as was expected of the lifelong degenerate? Professor Brown acknowledges the theatricality, but suggests that rather than being one last burst of crowd-pleased hackery, "the closest analogy is to that of the revival preacher, who, to make the picture of the present as telling as possible, sees and paints his past in its very blackest colours." Certainly, Greene's self-denunication established him as an "awful warning" for at least two generations.

The charitable Storojenko has no doubts:

> "The Repentance" consists of two parts. In the first, Greene gives a general review of his life, and breaks into bitter lamentations over his miserable fate. These laments, with which the first part is full, are the result of a boundless despair, which takes possession of the dying author whenever he fully realises the unfathomable abyss before him. These sobs of despair are interrupted by prayers to God and fits of tardy repentance . . . The second part contains a short autobiography of Greene, written with a view to turn others from following those pernicious paths through which

his own life had passed. Greene's autobiography stands unique among works of the same kind. Usually autobiographies and memoirs are written by people for the purpose of defending themselves in the eyes of posterity, showing their actions and motives in the best light possible. Greene's autobiography—the fruit of the exceptional state of mind he was in—is written for a diametrically opposite purpose. Having decided to lay bare the dissoluteness of his life for the instruction of his readers, Greene evidently took a morbid delight in representing himself, his actions, and all his motives in the foulest and most repulsive colours. If we are to believe Greene, his whole life was an endless round of intoxication, debauch, and blasphemy.[34]

Whether or not Greene was sincere in *The Repentence* it would seem that one deathbed reversal was genuine. On the eve of his death Greene was visited by one of his friends, who brought him a message from his long-deserted wife, telling him that she was well. This pleased the playwright, who asked whether he could see her once more before he died and confessed that his treatment of her had been far from acceptable. Whereupon, wrote Burbie, "feeling his time was but short, hee tooke pen and inke" and wrote her a letter to this effect:

Sweet Wife, as euer there was any good will or friendship betweene thee and mee, see this bearer (my Host) satisfied of his debt: I owe him tenne pound, and but for him I had perished in the streetes. Forget and forgiue my wronges done vnto thee and Almighty God haue mercie on my soule. Farewell till we meet in heauen, for on earth thou shalt neuer see me more.
   This 2 of September, 1592.
   Written by thy dying Husband.
   Robert Greene.

A somewhat less flowery and perhaps more accurate version of this letter, albeit recorded by the devotedly hostile Harvey, runs "Doll, I charge thee for the love of our youth and by my soule's rest, that thou wilt see this man paide; for if he and his wife had not succoured me, I had died in the streetes."

The next day, September 3, 1592, unvisited by his wife, but still nursed by the shoemaker's faithful consort, Greene died. He was thirty-two, a man, said his friend Chettle, "of indifferent years, of face amible, of body well proportioned; his attire after the habite of a scholler-like Gentleman, onely his hair was somewhat long." Harvey, hostile as ever, condemns him for wearing such long hair as was worn only by thieves and cutthroats, and said he was overly vain in wearing his M.A. robes. Nashe recalled his "jollie red peake [beard], like the spire of a steeple, cherisht continually without cutting, whereat a man might hang a jew-ell, it was so sharp and pendant." He also mentions a "very faire" cloak "of a goose-turd greene" and in his mocking response to Harvey, suggests that he could do worse than offer ten shillings for it. Greene's hostess-cum-nurse, Mis-tress Isam, out of affection placed a crown of bayleaves on his head. He was buried in the New Churchyard, near the hospital of St. Mary Bethlehem, better known as Bedlam.

A man who inspired both friendship and enmity in life, Greene when dead still polarized his acquaintance. Whether or not Shakespeare was hurt, or Mar-lowe converted by Greene's jibes, remains unresolved. But Greene's pen had already conjured up more concrete enemies, none more venomous than Gabriel Harvey (1550?–1631). Harvey was hardly immune from controversy, the *DNB* cites "an overweening estimate of his own attainments" and an "arrogant and censorious spirit," which threatened continually to overwhelm his undoubted abilities as an academic (dealing mainly in rhetoric) and as a penetrating judge of contemporary literature. His relations with Greene were consistently poor. When in 1590 his brother Richard attacked Greene, Nashe, and others of their set, for what he saw as their overenthusiastic interference in the controversy caused by the Martin Marprelate tracts (which had already involved a some-what more serious lexicographer, Thomas Cooper), Greene hit back with the unrestrained *Quippe for an Upstart Courtier,* in which he savaged the Harvey brothers, interspersing his literary comments with remarks as to their parent-age (their father was a self-made man, a rope maker of Saffron Walden). The row was still in full spate at Greene's death and Harvey spared no time in rush-ing round to Dowgate (a Thames-side street near the watergate where the river Walbrook, now lost, entered the greater river; it lay near today's Cannon Street Station), where Greene had died and questioning his landlady as to the manner of his final days. The landlady, who had no inkling of Harvey's true feelings, cheerfully regaled him with a variety of anecdotes. Harvey noted all, and promptly reproduced them in his *Four Letters,* savaging Greene as a "king of paupers, an arch-atheist, a base man, a dishonour to the stage," and making not the slightest effort to mask his exultant satisfaction at the playwright's death:

I was altogether unacquainted with the man, never once saluted him by name: but who in London hath not heard of his dissolute, and licentious living; his fonde disguisinge of a Master of Arte with ruffianly haire, unseemly apparell, and more unseemelye Company: . . . his apeish coun-terfeiting of every ridiculous and absurd toy: . . . his fine coosening of iuglers, and finer iugling with cooseners; hys villainous cogging and foisting; his monstrous swearinge and horrible forswearing; his impious profaning of sacred textes; his other scandalous and blasphemous rauinge; his riotous and outragious surfeitinge; his continuall shifting of lodg-inges; his plausible musteringe and banquettinge of roysterly acqaintance at his first coming, his beggarly departing in euery hostisses debt; his infamous resorting to the Banckeside, Shorditch, Southwarke, and other filthy hauntes; his obscure lurkings in basest corners; his pawning of his sword, cloake, and what not, when money came short; his impudent pamphletting, phantasticall interluding, and desperate libelling, when other coosening shiftes failed; his imployinge of Ball (surnamed Cuttinge Ball), till he was intercepted at Tiborne to leauy a crew of his trustiest companions to guarde him in danger of arrestes; his keping of the foresaid Balls sister, a sorry ragged queane, of whom hee had his base sonne Infor-tunatus Greene; his forsaking of his owne wife, too honest for such a hus-band; particulars are infinte;—his contemning of superiours, deriding of other, and defying of all good order?

He never envyed me so much, as I pittied him from my heart: espe-cially when his hostisse Isam with teares in her eies, & sighes from a deeper fountaine, (for she loved him derely) tould me of his lamentable begging of a penny pott of Malmsey; and, sir reverence how lowsy he, and the mother of Infortunatus were . . . and how he was faine poore soule, to borrow her husbandes shirte, whiles his owne was a washing: and how his dublet, and hose, and sword were sold for three shillings: and beside the charges of his winding sheete, which was foure shillinges: and the charges of hys buriall yesterday, in the New-churchyard neere Bedlam, was six shillinges, and four pence; how deeply hee was indebted to her poore hus-bande: as appeared by hys own bonde of tenne poundes: which the good woman kindly shewed me.[35]

To this Harvey added a sonnet, supposedly penned by his late brother John, which begins "Come fellow Greene, to thy gaping graue . . ." and continues "Vermine to vermine must repair at last."

Fortunately Greene was not friendless. The otherwise anonymous "R.B., Gent." produced *Greene's Funeralls,* an unabashed hagiography, bereft of a sin-gle critical line. A second, more telling defense was launched by Thomas Nashe, who supposedly had been encouraged by an intermediary pamphlet, published in December 1592, entitled *Kind-Hartes Dream,* by Greene's friend Henry Chettle, a fellow pamphleter and the editor of *A Groats-Worth of Wit.*

According to him, Greene's spirit had appeared in the night and laid a manuscript on his chest. In it Greene begged Nashe to rebut Harvey's vilifications,
since otherwise he could not rest easy in his grave.

"Having with humble penitence," Chettle makes Greene say, "besought pardon for my infinite sinnes, and paid the due to death; euen in my graue was I
scarse layde, when Enuie (no fit companion for Art) spit out her poyson, to dis-
turbe my rest. *Aduersus mortuos bellum suscipere, inhumanum est.* There is no glory
gained by breaking a deade mans skull . . . Yet it appeares contrary in some,
that inueighing against my workes, my pouertie, my life, my death, my burial,
haue omitted nothing that may seeme malitious . . . Awake . . . reuenge thy
wrongs, remember mine: thy aduersaries began the abuse, they continue it: if
thou suffer it, let thy life be short in silence and obscuritie, and thy death
hastie, hated, and miserable."

Nashe performed as requested, perhaps to hide his own guilt at not having
visited Greene during the latter's final illness, and, as antagonistic to Harvey as
any of the University Wits, duly counterattacked with *Strange News, of the Intercepting Certayne letters,* in which he addressed Harvey as a "filthy vaine foole" and
declared "open warres upon him and his brother."

Harvey came back with a detailed rebuttal, *Pierce's Supererogation.* Nashe,
now somewhat ashamed of his attack, made a fulsome apology in *Christes Tears
over Jerusalem* (1592), but when Harvey refused to be mollified, returned to the
attack with *A New Letter of Notable Contents.* Nashe reissued *Christes Tears,* this
time withdrawing his regrets and attacking the Harveys even more viciously.
Not until Gabriel Harvey retired to Saffron Walden, where he spent the rest of
his life, and it was ordered by authority that all the books written by both parties to the controversy should be seized and "that none of the same bookes be
ever printed hereafter" did the argument fade.

But by then Greene was long dead. Gone indeed to his "gaping grave" but
from there perhaps to join his fellow poets in some heavenly debauch. Or so
Thomas Dekker supposed, in *A Knight's Conjuring* (1607) when he visualized
the dead Wits, united once again:

> These were likewise carowsing to one another at the holy well, some of
> them singing Paeans to Apollo, som of them hymnes to the rest of the
> Goddes, whil'st Marlowe, Greene and Peele had got under the shades of a
> large vyne, laughing to see Nash (that was but newly come to their
> Colledge) still haunted with the sharpe and satyricall spirit that followed
> him here upon earth.

6

The Seventeenth Century: Hard Words

By 1600, the "inkhorn controversy" that had so exercised the literati during the middle decades of the previous century had largely ended. In black and white terms the inkhornists had won—their critics had largely fallen silent—but the reality was a compromise. Those terms that were seen as acceptable, and even useful, were absorbed quietly into the language; those that were deemed absurd or excessive were just as quietly dropped. The zealotry that pioneered the adoption of inkhornisms had faded, and so had the vociferousness of those who opposed them. There were few, however purist, who were willing any longer to oppose the inclusion in English of such terms as *scientific, major domo, function,* and *penetrate*. Likewise, the most dedicated advocate of an expanded vocabulary offered no objection to the rejection of *adminiculation* (rooting out), *cautionate* (caution), *deruncinate* (to weed), and *attemptate* (attempt). Not all died at once, but vanish they did. *Deruncinate,* for instance, has but one citation in the *OED,* and that is taken from another dictionary.

The new lexicographical buzzword was "hard words." First used as lexicographical jargon by John Baret in his *Alvearie* (1573), the term was recognized as meaning the new scholarly vocabulary, usually drawn from Latin and Greek but also from Arabic and Hebrew, which by then had been infiltrating standard English for thirty years. The "hard word" is the "inkhorn term," now rationalized, accepted, and shorn of its pejorative status. "Hard words" were still largely incomprehensible outside the scholarly circles that had taken them from the classics and introduced them to the vernacular, but the difference now was that not only were such words seen as a necessary part of English, but that for all their scholarly background, there was now a mass market eager and willing to take them on. It was for this market that the dictionary makers of the new century, with their series of "hard-word" dictionaries, most enthusiastically catered. As Sir James Murray has noted, these words were "unknown to, and not to be imbibed from, mother or grandmother. A work exhibiting the spelling and explaining the meaning, of these new-fangled 'hard words' was the felt want of the day; and the first attempt to supply it marks . . . the most important point in the evolution of the modern English Dictionary."[1]

Geared primarily to the explanation of "hard words" these dictionaries made no effort to deal with usage as do today's equivalents. Basing themselves on the word lists of the sixteenth century's Latin-English dictionaries, the aim of these all-English wordbooks was to transfer the whole current Latin vocabulary, already understood by scholars, into English. Such dictionaries were for the educationally insecure: nonscholars, the *nouveau riche* aspirants to a higher class—merchants, artisans, and the like—and the wives of already established gentry. Thus their dictionaries were heavily infused with Latin-derived terms. Above all their publication was intended to broaden the basis of the educated élite; the illiterate masses remained irrelevant. A typical dictionary would give the Latinized term plus a simpler synonym in English. Thus Cawdrey has: "*magnitude:* greatness; *ruminate:* to chew over again, to studie earnestly upon," etc. They were, one might suggest, not so much works of reference as the linguistic etiquette books of their period.

Although for many years the first compiler of a monolingual, English-English "hard-word" dictionary has regularly been announced as the Coventry schoolmaster Robert Cawdrey, he did have some antecedents, who may profitably be noted before his appearance. As seen in Chapter 4, the grammarians Richard Mulcaster, William Bullokar, and Edmund Coote all called for a monolingual dictionary of English. Bullokar promised such a dictionary, but came up with nothing beyond his grammar; Mulcaster called vociferously for such a work, but he too failed to deliver. He did, however, append "The Generall Table" to his own *Elementarie.* This did list "hard words," but they are left "untranslated." Only Edmund Coote, in *The English Schoolemaster,* actually lists "hard words" and then offers some form of "easy" definition. This list, brief though it is, must be considered as a precursor of Cawdrey's greater production.

The last possible challenger for Cawdrey's crown has received very little attention. His champion, Noel Osselton, has written of this early monolinguist in R. K. K. Hartman's *The History of Lexicography* (1987) and it is from his essay "The First English Dictionary? A Sixteenth-Century Compiler at Work" that this information is drawn. It was his investigation of MS Rawlinson Poet. 108 in Oxford's Bodleian Library that brought to light a work that seems to predate the established innovator. The manuscript, of course, is not a fully formed dictionary. It is, rather "a mere initial draft for a dictionary text, with the false starts, gaps, corrections and duplications which are to be expected when a compiler is feeling his way in a hitherto unattempted mode."[2] There is no accurate date for the material: it was written on the blank pages that remained in a manuscript written *c.* 1570, but it is definitely later than that. However, given each successive lexicographer's predilection for absorbing his predecessor's work into his own, it would appear that had the Rawlinson compiler worked subsequently to Cawdrey, then Cawdrey's word list would be part of this one. Osselton compared the two texts and found that this simply was not so. It would seem, therefore, that this fragment, containing 337 entries for the letter A and somewhat less for B, is an earlier work.

As an unfinished work, it is impossible to prove absolutely what were the compiler's intentions, but from what can be seen, while his word list is more extensive than that of Cawdrey (who has only 286 entries for A), his definitions are far more rudimentary. He is generally satisfied with a single word, e.g., *abase:* humble, *abolish:* destroy, *abrogate:* destroy, where Cawdrey offers a more substantial entry. Had it been finished, however, the proposed dictionary, based on the Rawlinson:Cawdrey ratio at A, would have been a larger work, totaling perhaps 3,000 entries, nearly 500 more than Cawdrey managed. However, as Osselton notes, Cawdrey has a disproportionately high percentage of terms under A: some 11.5 percent. Most dictionaries have only 6.5 per cent at A and on that basis the Rawlinson dictionary might have topped 5,000 headwords, making it similar in size to John Bullokar's *English Expositour* (1616).

Perhaps the most important point about Osselton's discovery was that the word list makes it clear that unlike the "hard-word" dictionaries that dominate the first half of the seventeenth century, this dictionary would, if concluded, have offered a large number of "easy" words as well. The Rawlinson compiler, a decade or more before Cawdrey, set about his task in a very different way to the man whose name would head the "first English dictionary." His use of ordinary as well as hard words was, as Noel Osselton points out, "entirely at variance with contemporary practice . . . Even with this provisional account of a fragmentary text . . . it may be seen that Cawdrey's choices were not self-evident even at the time: the English dictionary might very well have been more balanced in its vocabulary even from the start."[3] Like Cawdrey, the Rawlinson compiler offers *aggravate, agnition,* and *agony,* but unlike him he also includes such run-of-the-mill vocabulary as *age, alehouse, apple, apron,* and *arm.* Assuming that the dating to the late sixteenth century is correct, this fragment offers a breadth of vocabulary that would not be included in a published work until the early eighteenth century, with J.K.'s *New English Dictionary: Or, a Compleat Collection of the Most Proper and Significant Words, Commonly used in the Language.* One must not forget, of course, that this is only an unfinished fragment, and that "the curiously haphazard and illogical nature of some of his entries"[4] makes it possible that the compiler abandoned his labors because he realized that the task was beyond him, but the fragment remains an important sideline in lexicographical history.

So much for antecedents, proven and hypothetical. What is generally acknowledged as the first monolingual "English dictionary," *A Table Alphabeticall of . . . hard usual English Wordes . . .* "with the interpration thereof by plaine English words, gathered for the benefit & help of Ladies, gentlewomen, or any other unskilful persons. Whereby they may more easilie and better vnderstand many hard English wordes, which they shall heare or read in the Scriptures, Sermons, or elsewhere, and also be made able to vse the same aptly themselues" by Robert Cawdrey was published in 1604. A small, octavo book, it covered 120 pages and offered 2,500 headwords. It may be that Cawdrey and his immediate successors offered, in Allen Walker Read's dismissive phrase, "little more than enlarged spelling books for adults,"[5] but these guides to "hard words" were fulfilling a need. The advance of learning among the expanding middle classes was such that these adult spellers were, for better or worse, what the market wanted. This was a very pragmatic lexicography: it lacked the historical depth that the traditional range of citations "from the best authors" implies, etymology was ignored, and the definitions on offer were basic to the point of brevity.

For one who authored so pivotal a work Cawdrey is an unfortunately anonymous figure. All one knows is that he was born in Oakham, Rutland, *c.* 1580, and that he taught at Oakham Grammar School and later at a school in Coventry, a fact that he noted in the introduction to his other wordbook, *The Treasurie or Storehouse of Similies* (1600). One tiny piece of his biographical jigsaw can be deduced from his introduction to the *Table Alphabeticall:* the courtier Sir John Harington was once his "scholler (and now my singular benefactor)." Harington, as will be seen below, was something of a lexicographer in his own right, and the glossary he prepared for use with his translation of Ariosto's *Orlando Furioso* (1591) was one of those absorbed, if not into Cawdrey's *Table* itself, then into the work of some of his immediate successors. Another Harington, Lady

Anne, was one of the dedicatees of John Florio's translation of Montaigne. Presumably she was a relation, although the *DNB* names Sir John's wife as "Mary."

According to its compiler, the *Table Alphabeticall* was based upon three main sources: Edmund Coote's *English Schoolemaster,* Thomas Thomas' *Dictionarium Linguae Latinae et Anglicanae,* and the work of the otherwise anonymous "A.M.," a Dutchman whose translation of Oswald Gabelkhouer's *Booke of Physicke* had a glossary at its end. This work had been imported wholesale, although much of its "translation" was gibberish: no more than English endings put onto otherwise untranslated Latin words. The glossary, upon which Cawdrey drew, attempted to explain these bizarre coinages. On top of this, as has been noted, Cawdrey and his "hard-word" successors went back to the previous century's Latin-English lexicons and set about making their vocabularies available to monoglot English speakers.

They did not draw, however, purely upon the old Latin dictionaries of the previous century. As the late Jürgen Schäfer has pointed out, the early-seventeenth-century lexicographers could draw on a wide variety of glossaries, each one created as an addendum to all manner of specialist studies.[6] They too, by their very nature as "trade" or "professional" jargon, were "hard words." They were duly incorporated into the seventeenth-century dictionaries, although so prolific did such vocabularies grow, that they would in time find themselves corralled into specialist or technical lexicons. There are, Schäfer notes, more than one hundred such glossaries cited in the *Short-Title Catalogue* for the period 1475–1640.[7]

If Schäfer is right, and it is generally accepted that his work, coming nearly forty years after DeWitt Starnes and Gertrude Noyes set up the previous status quo in lexicographical history, does indeed paint a true picture, then these glossarists are the great unsung dictionary makers of the seventeenth century. They are a random group, but a very influential one. However, as Schäfer notes, they were driven mainly by personal interest in the topic at hand, and it is highly unlikely that they appreciated what they were doing as far as the development of dictionary making was concerned. "Even Robert Cawdrey . . . was not certain as to exact nature of his achievement: his *Table Alphabeticall* is in turn a spelling book, prepares children for Latin, helps the unlearned in understanding books and sermons and also encourages 'fine English clerks' and 'far-journeyed gentlemen' to banish 'affected rhetoric.' "[8]

As the titles of their works indicate, there is no set pattern to the glossarists. John Trevisa (1326–1412) was a translator and chaplain, whose list of legal terms, *De legibus legumque vocabulis,* appeared in 1480. Bartholemew Traheron

(1510?–1558?) was a fanatical Protestant who fled England to escape the stake and never returned. His *Interpretation of straunge wordes, vsed in the translation* [*sic*] *of Vigon* [Vigo] appeared in 1543; it lists medical terms. The cant collectors Thomas Harman and Thomas Dekker were respectively a magistrate and a playwright.

Many had substantial alternative careers. Robert Recorde (1510?–1558), a mathematician and physician, possibly to both Edward VI, and later Mary, offers "The exposition of certayne wordes, in *The vrinal of physic*" (1547). As an Oxford don Recorde taught mathematics, "which he rendered clear to all capacities to an extent wholly unprecedented," as well as rhetoric, cosmology, anatomy, music, and astrology, in all of which he was considered a foremost expert. As Fuller put it, "His soul did not live in the lane of a single science, but traversed the latitude of learning," and when it came to his medical writing "his judicious rules have reduced that harlot to honesty, and in a great measure fixed the uncertainty thereof."[9] By 1547 he was in London, working as a doctor. In this capacity he published *The Vrinal*. An active champion of the Protestant Reformation, Recorde was widely knowledgeable in all branches of natural sciences. A numismatist, he ran, for a while, the Bristol mint and was later appointed general surveyor of the mines and of money. He was probably the first English scientist to adopt the Copernican system (the earth circles the sun, rather than vice versa), but given the Church's antagonism to such "heresy," his writings on the subject were prudently restrained. Recorde, celebrated as the founder of English mathematical writing, was called by James Halliwell-Phillips "an oasis in an age deficient in science." He was the first to appreciate the importance of algebra. The first use of the word "sine" in England appears in his *Pathway to Knowledge, or the First Principles of Geometry* (4 vols., 1551–1602). He was also the first mathematical writer to use "=" for equals; the sign was taken from medieval manuscripts, where it stood for the Latin *est:* it is. His *Whetstone of Witte* (1557) has the first published use of the signs "+" and "−" for "plus" and "minus." Recorde's works remained standard textbooks for the next 150 years: Walter Scott's *Fortunes of Nigel* mentions the *Whetstone* as one of a usurer's two books—the other is the Bible. Yet despite such acuity with figures, Recorde's own computations were less successful. He fell deeply into debt and was confined in the King's Bench Prison in June 1558 and died there a month later.

Of the termes of venerie, in The noble arte of venerie or hunting was published by George Turberville (1540?–1610?) in 1575 as an addendum to his *Booke of Falconrie or hawking. For the only delight and pleasure of all Noblemen and Gentlemen . . .* A poet and epigrammatist, Turberville accompanied Thomas Randolph, England's ambassador to Russia, on his trip to the court of Ivan the Terrible in

June 1568. Turberville used the trip to write his first poems and to send home three letters on Moscow manners, noting in them "a people passing rude, to vices vile enclined." On his return to England in late 1559 he found himself popular, "esteemed a most accomplished gentleman, and his company was much sought after and desired by all men."[10] In 1587 he wrote *Tragicall Tales,* a series of ten tales of which eight were taken from Boccaccio. He may be the same George Turberville summoned to the Privy Council in June 1597 "to answer certaine matters," but if he was he survived.

Gervase Markham (1568?–1637), whose *Cheape and good husbandry for the well-ordering of all beasts, and fowles, and for the generall cure of their diseases* (1614) included "A short table, expounding all the hard words in this booke," rejoices in what to some may be the dubious title: "the earliest English hackney writer" or, as we have it, hack. An unrestrainedly prolific writer, Markham began his adult life as a soldier in Ireland and the Low Countries. Free of the army he turned to writing for his wages. Fluent in Latin, French, Spanish, and possibly Dutch, Markham wrote anything: poems and plays—in neither of which disciplines was he particularly successful—and theology, in which he steered a careful course between rival doctrines. Ben Jonson was contemptuous: "He was not of the number of the Faithfull, but a base fellow." Where he did shine was in his books on agriculture—which were highly praised—and as a trainer and owner of horses. He championed improved methods of horse breeding and horse racing, allegedly imported the first ever Arab horse into England, and owned many valuable steeds. One of his Arabs was sold to James I for £500. But even here, where he was on firm ground, Markham couldn't resist the temptation to extract the maximum profit from his writing. His books shamelessly repeat themselves; the titles might change but the text remains essentially the same. He compounded the situation by reissuing his unsold backlist under new titles. In July 1617 the London booksellers called a halt, forcing him to sign an undertaking that he would not produce any more works on treating sick horses or cattle. Among his books, which included treatises on archery, on cockfighting and angling (*The Pleasures of Princes,* 1615), agriculture, and a glossary of Anglo-Saxon words, was a 174-stanza epic poem on the *Revenge* and its captain, Sir Richard Grenville. Tennyson, whose subsequent treatment of the same topic is still a teacher's if not pupil's favorite, seems to have "borrowed" from Markham. "Sweet maister gunner, split our keel in twain" writes the sixteenth-century hack; the nineteenth-century poet laureate offers "Sink me the ship master gunner, sink her—split her in twain."

Markham is related to another glossarist, the courtier Sir John Harington (1561–1612). Harington's translation of Ariosto's epic poem *Orlando Furioso* appeared in 1591. Appended to the text was "An exact and necessarie table in order of alphabet, wherein you may readilie find the names of the principall persons treated in this worke, with the chiefe matters that concerne them."

Harington was the godson of Elizabeth I, with whom he and his family had briefly been imprisoned in the Tower by her sister Mary. His own father, John Harington Sr., had been Henry VIII's treasurer of camps and buildings. The elder Harington's first wife, Ethelreda, was Henry's illegitimate daughter; she had been brought up by the king's tailor, John Malte, as his own child. She died around 1554, at which point John Harington married Isabella Markham, Gervase Markham's sister. Their son, the younger John Harington, went to Eton and then Cambridge, where his main achievement appears to have been running up sufficient debts for him to be forced to request a friend to intercede with his father for help in their payment. Legal studies followed, but Harington was no more a lawyer than a scholar, preferring to hone his real talents: those of a wit and man of the world. In 1564 he married Mary Rogers, the daughter of a Somerset squire, but rather than dull him with domesticity "marriage only increased his exuberant spirits."[11] His epigrams began to be quoted and he paraded a caustic and often coarse wit. Typically, the first portion of *Orlando Furioso* to be translated was the risqué story of Giocondo: the queen reprimanded him for corrupting the minds of her ladies-in-waiting and banished him to his country house until he had finished the whole book. It was to this translation that he appended his glossary.

Elizabeth forgave him, not for the last time, and in 1592 paid a visit to his house Kelston, on her way to Bath. Harington was also appointed high sheriff of Somerset. In 1596 he returned to Court and promptly found himself in even deeper trouble when he published, under the pseudonym "Miascmos," *A New Discourse of a Stale subject, called the Metamorphosis of Ajax.* Three similar tracts followed: *Ulysses upon Ajax* by "Misodiaboles," *An Anatomie of the Metamorphosed Ajax* by "T.C. Traveller," and *An Apoligie: 1. or rather a Retraction, 2. or rather a Recantation, 3. or rather a Recapitulation, . . . 12. Or rather none of them.* It was all very labored humor: the initial pseudonym came from the Greek *miasma* or noxious smell, while *Ajax* equaled *a jakes* equaled the slang term for a privy, and *stale* referred to urine. The perceived indecency of this plea for the introduction of water closets was grudgingly accepted; the slur its text contained on the royal favorite the earl of Leicester was not. Harington was ordered to quit the Court "until he had grown sober." There was even talk of bringing him before Star Chamber, but this never happened. Future editions of the books were banned but the original *Metamorphosis* still went through three editions in a year. In 1598 Harington was back in favor once more, although he prudently stayed clear of the queen, preferring to accompany the earl of Essex on his ill-fated expedition to Ireland. Here he was knighted by the increasingly unpopular Essex, which infuriated the queen yet again, and he only regained her favor by returning to Somerset, writing up a detailed report on his commander's activities and delivering it to Elizabeth. He then declared his intention to avoid "any risk of shipwreck on the Essex coast" and added, "Thank heaven I am safe at home and if I go into such troubles again I deserve the gallows for a meddling fool."

Harington's last years continued his up and down existence. In 1602 he was back at Court, where he wrote an account of the last days of Elizabeth. He also began ingratiating himself with her successor, James VI of Scotland, to whom he gave a lantern which was so constructed that it represented the waning light of the old queen and the brightness of the new king. On it was a representation of the crucifixion, and the motto, usually attributed to the thief who died alongside Christ, "Lord, remember me when thou comest into thy kingdom." Harington also wrote a "Tract on the Succession to the Crown" which assembled a detailed refutation of the claims of the Infanta Isabella. In addition it saw off the arguments of the various religious factions and offered a number of hitherto unrevealed insights into the character of the queen. This was never published. James assumed the English throne without fuss and Harington, for all his efforts, went quite unrewarded.

Although Fuller believed that "he was a poet in all things save in his wealth"[12] and that he left a "fair estate," by now Harington was facing financial problems. Back at Kelston he began showering his influential friends with begging letters. His service in Ireland had been costly; a lawsuit had lost him one of his estates. In 1605, when Archbishop Loftus, the chancellor of Ireland, died, Harington suggested to the king that he would make an ideal replacement— not merely as chancellor, but as archbishop too. "I think," he wrote, "my very genius doth in sort lead me to that country." The king felt otherwise. Harington remained at Court, bemoaning the good old days of Elizabeth and eking out a living as tutor to the young Prince Henry. He remained in reasonably good favor until his death, aged fifty-one, on November 20, 1612.

In his prime Harington had been almost a licensed court jester, displaying what his cousin Robert Markham termed his "damnable uncovered honesty." To quote the historian Mandell Creighton, writing of Harington in the *DNB:*

He had a quick power of observation and was almost entirely destitute of restraint. Though desirous of pushing his fortunes, he had none of the qualities necessary for success. Elizabeth spoke of him as "that saucy poet, my godson" and he was generally regarded as an amusing gossip. He wrote easily and was certainly not a hero to himself. The most intimate facts of his domestic life afforded him materials for an epigram, and his frankness was entire. Hence he gives a living picture of life and society in his times and abounds in incidental stories which throw a great light on many prominent persons.

Last in this selection of glossarists in Philemon Holland (1552–1637). Holland has some claim to the title of actual lexicographer: not only did he provide three of the glossaries which were incorporated in the dictionaries of others, but in 1615 issued a supplement to the *Dictionarium Linguae Latinae et Anglicanae* by Thomas Thomas, entitled *Lexici Latino-Anglici Paralipomena.* Holland was born in Chelmsford, Essex. His father, John, had fled with Miles Coverdale, the Lutheran translator of the Bible from German to English, to escape persecution by Mary. On his return he became rector of Great Dunmow, Essex.

Holland was educated at Cambridge, where he was taught by the future Archbishop Whitgift, and later at Oxford. He studied medicine after university and in 1595 was awarded an M.D., a degree he was very fond of parading and which was probably awarded by a European or Scottish university. Around 1595 he moved to Coventry, the home also of Robert Cawdrey, where he spent the remainder of his life. There he conducted a small medical practice, but his main occupation was the study of classics. In 1608 he became usher of Coventry Free School and in 1627 the headmaster. He resigned in 1629 at the age of seventy-six. Holland suffered badly from poverty and illness in his last years. He had been awarded the freedom of the city in 1612 and from 1609 had been relying on the local authorities to help boost his income. They paid him £4 for his edition of William Camden's *Britannia.* In 1632 he was given a pension of £33 6s. 8d. per annum for the next three years, at the end of which Henry Smyth, president of Magdalene College, Cambridge, authorized him to receive regular charitable benevolence from the university in consideration of "his learning and worthy parts." Holland died of old age on February 9, 1637, after being bedridden for a year. He was eighty-five. He had never worn glasses and until his last illness was "most indefatigable in his study."

Holland was known to have one of the largest vocabularies in England. Fuller described him as the "translator generall" of his era, and adds that "these books alone of his turning into English will make a country gentleman a competent library."[13] In *The Dunciad* Pope talks of "the groaning shelves" bending under the weight of Holland's works.[14] Southey said that "for the service which he rendered to his contemporaries and to his countrymen, [he] deserves to be called the best of the Hollands." Among Holland's works was a translation of Livy's *History of Rome,* which he claimed to have written using only one pen, which was subsequently encased in silver by a lady friend. He composed a brief verse to celebrate the event: "With one sole pen I writ this book, | Made of a grey goose quill; | A pen it was when it I took | And a pen I leave it still." In 1601 he translated Pliny's *History of the World.* Other translations included works by Suetonius (a wit remarked, punning on the Latin author's name: "Holland with his translations doth so fill us | He will not let Suetonius be Tranquillus"),[15] Plutarch, Ammianus Marcellinus, and Xenophon. So exquisite was his handwritten version of Euclid's *Harmonica* that it was used by the typographer Baskerville when preparing his new Greek font. His supplement to the *Thomasius* (1612) drew heavily on his classical studies, and he added to its pages terms derived from Pliny, Cellinus, Festus, Celsus, and Paracelsus as well as from Balbus' *Catholicon* and the *Promptorium parvulorum.*

This supplement is directed to readers to perfect their knowledge of Latin grammar. In his address to the reader, Holland explains how for the past fifteen years "as often as he could find an idle moment in his medical work, he was drawn by some power (*nescio quo ingenij siue ductu ce impetu*) to the pleasant gardens of grammar and to the reading of historians and poets. When, in the reading of various approved classical authors, he had collected many words and phrases, not, so far as he knew, observed by lexicographers, it seemed to him worthwhile to arrange these in alphabetical order and to make a supplement to a dictionary. These observations, he thought, should be made available to posterity."[16] He had then permitted the printer of this new edition to append them to the original dictionary.

The first "hard-word" dictionary to follow Cawdrey's was *The English Expositour: Teaching the Interpretation of the hardest words used in our Language, with sundry Explications, Descriptions and Discourses* (1616). It was compiled by John Bullokar (*c.* 1580–*c.* 1642), a doctor of physic whose origins are uncertain, but who, at the time of his *Expositour*'s publication, lived in Chichester, where he was attached to his "singular good ladie, the Ladie Jane, Viscountess Montague." No relationship has ever been properly proved to the grammarian William Bullokar but the *DNB* suggests he might have been the "chyld" for whose benefit the older Bullokar translated various "short sentences" of "wyz Cato." Other sources suggest the men were brothers, while others still posit no relationship whatsoever. John Bullokar joins the ranks of the biographically "invisible" lexicographers, although one adventure has been set down: on a visit to London in 1611 he saw a dead crocodile. The *Expositour* was written "at the request of a worthy gentleman whose love prevailed much with him" in his "yonger yeares." His "little vocabulary" was published on October 17, 1616.

Two years later Bullokar published a life of Christ, rendered in six-line stanzas and rather melodramatically entitled *A true description of the Passion of Our Saviour Jesus Christ, as it was acted by the bloodie Jewes, and registered by the blessed Evangelists; in English Meetre.* Further editions of the *Expositour* appeared in 1621 and 1641; there was a fourth edition in 1656 "newly revised, corrected, and with the addition of above a thousand words, enlarged. By W.S." Subsequent revisions appeared in 1676 (by "A Lover of the Arts"), 1684, 1691, and finally in 1719, revised by R. Browne, "author of The English School Reform'd."

Bullokar had no doubts as to his audience. Like Cawdrey he aimed foursquare at those who wished to parade their learning, preferably through the shortcut that such a "translation manual" could supply. In his address "To the Courteous Reader" Bullokar explains that

> in my younger yeares it hath cost mee some observation, reading, study, and charge; which you may easily beleeve, considering the great store of strange words, our speech doth borrow, not only from the Latine, and Greeke, (and from the ancient Hebrew) but also from forraine vulgar languages round about us: beside sundry olde words now growne out of use, and divers termes of art, proper to the learned in Logicke, Philosophy, Law, Physicke, Astronomie, etc., yea and Divinitie it selfe, best knowen to the several professors there of. And herein I hope such learned will deeme no wrong offered to themselves or dishonour to Learning, in that I open the signification of such words, to the capacitie of the ignorant, whereby they may conceive and use them as well as those which have bestowed long study in the languages, for, considering it is familiar among best writers to usurpe strange words (and sometimes necessary by reason our speech is not sufficiently furnished with apt terms to expresse all meanings) I suppose withall their desire is that they should be understood; which I (knowing that *bonus quo communius eo melius*) have endeavoured by this Booke, though not exquisitely, yet (I trust) in some reasonable measure to performe . . .

The *Expositour,* "a curious little book which went through several editions,"[17] became enormously popular, especially after its 1663 revision by "A Lover of the Arts." This revision included a new section "serving for the translation of ordinary English words into the more scholastick, or those derived from other languages." This section was even more unashamedly devoted to producing a facsimile of learning. As Baugh and Cable note, "By means of this supplement a person might write in ordinary English and then, by making a few judicious substitutions, convey a fine impression of learning."[18]

Bullokar's was a popular work from the start, but among the spurs that impelled "A Lover of the Arts" to offer a revised and even more accessible guide to learning was the publication, in 1623, of a rival work: *The English Dictionarie or, an Interpreter of Hard English Words* by H.C., Gent. H.C. was properly Henry Cockeram, and his dictionary was characterized by Murray as "a deeply interesting little book."[19] Cockeram himself had no doubts, claiming somewhat arrogantly, "What any before me in this kinde have begun, I have not only fully finished, but thoroughly perfected." On either count, Cockeram was the first compiler to term his efforts an "English Dictionary."

Like other "hard-word" compilations, the dictionary's full title lays out its stall with no expenses spared: *The English Dictionarie: or, An Interpreter of Hard English Words.* "Enabling as well Ladies and Gentlewomen, young Schollers, Clark Merchants, as also Strangers of any Nation, to the understanding of the more difficult authors already printed in our Language, and the more speedy attaining of an elegant perfection of the English tongue, both in reading, speaking and writing. Being a Collection of the choicest words contained in the *Table Alphabeticall* and *English Expositour* and of some thousand of words never published by any heretofore." The usual groups—clerks, students, women, foreigners—are targeted and offered, temptingly, "the choicest words." Cockeram cites his immediate predecessors and potential rivals—he has no doubt that he has surpassed them.

He also pillaged them. Cockeram's word list drew on Cawdrey and even more so on John Bullokar. The original edition tended to abbreviate their definitions, but the revision of 1642 adds extra material to theirs. In fairness he accepts neither of them blindly, nor are they his only sources. He uses the *Thomasius,* as the most recent and the best Latin-English dictionary and the Rider-Holyoake, especially when he deals with proper names.

Henry Bradley's summation for the *DNB* notes that Cockeram's work "is a small pocket volume and, as the title indicates, does not profess to contain all the words in the language, but only those which specially require explanation. The second part, which occupies half the volume, may be called a dictionary for translating plain English into fine English, giving the ordinary words in alphabetical order, with their equivalents in the pompous literary dialect affected by writers of the period." It was this section that would be copied by "A Lover of the Arts." Cockeram had little time for such "pompous literary dialects" and notes that only reluctantly has he included "the fustian termes used by too many who study rather to hear themselves speake than to understand themselves."

He continued, in his introduction, to explain his method, which was "plaine and easie, being alphabeticall, by which the capacity of the meanest may soon be inlightened."

> The first Booke hath the choicest words themselves now in use, wherewith our language is inriched and become so copious, to which words the common sense is annexed. The second Booke containes the vulgar words, which whensoever any desirous of a more curious explanation by a more refined and elegant speech shall looke into, he shall there receive the exact and ample word to express the same: Wherein by the way let me pray thee to observe that I have also inserted (as occasion served) even the *mocke-words* which are ridiculously used in our language, that those who desire a generality of knowledge may not bee ignorant of the sense, even of the fustian termes used by too many who study rather to bee heard speake, than to understand themselves. The last Booke is a recitall of severall persons, Gods, Goddesses, Giants and Devils, Monsters and Serpents, Birds and Beasts, Rivers, Fishes, Herbs, Stones, Trees, and the like, to the intent that the diligent learner may not pretend the defect of any helpe which may informe his discourse or practice. I might insist upon the generall use of this worke, especially for Ladies and Gentlewomen, Clarkes, Merchants, young Schollers, Strangers, Travellers, and all such as desire to know the plenty of the English . . .

From a purely lexicographical viewpoint perhaps the most important aspect of Cockeram's work, as it is of Cawdrey's and Bullokar's, is the extent to which, in his attempt to create a list of "hard words," he has gone back to the sixteenth century's Latin-English dictionaries to provide the word list. On the more general social level, their work did what it aimed to do: to introduce a wider public to a more sophisticated vocabulary. The playwright John Ford offered these congratulatory lines to Cockeram: "For my part I confesse, hadst thou not writ, | I had not been acquainted with more wit | Than our old English taught: . . ." and adds "The benefit is generall."

One more point should be added here: the extent to which women were specifically targeted by these "hard-word" dictionaries. Women had often been dedicatrices of dictionaries: Walter de Biblesworth wrote for Dionysia de Munchensy, Florio for half a dozen aristocrats and later a queen. The difference now was that women as such were the object of lexicography. Cawdrey's work is dedicated to five aristocratic women, the sisters of his old pupil Sir James Harington, but the title page also commends the book to "Ladies, Gentlewomen, or other vnskillful persons." Bullokar, whose *Expositour* is dedicated to Viscountess Montague, suggests that his dictionary "will not prooue altogether vngratefull" to the "greatest Ladies and studious Gentlewomen," while Cockeram wishes to enable "Ladies and Gentlewomen," as well as foreigners, "to the more speedy attaining of an elegant perfection of the English tongue." Their successor Thomas Blount includes "the more-knowing Women" (and "less-knowing Men") among his potential readers. These dictionaries were of enormous importance to women who wished for education. Prior to their publication there had simply not been a means for a woman, however enthusiastic, to gain the sort of education that her brother or father saw as his right. These subtitles may seem patronizing and sexist today; at the time they provided a gateway to much-desired and otherwise inaccessible information. By the Restoration of 1660, these references had been dropped, nor would they be included in any new dictionary until in 1702 "J.K." notes that his *New English Dictionary* is "chiefly designed fore the benefit of young Scholars, Tradesmen, Artificers, and the female sex." Whether, as Sir James Murray asks, "this was owing to the fact that the less-knowing women had now come upsides with the more-knowing men; or that with the Restoration, female education went out of fashion and women sank back again into elegant illiteracy" remains unresolved.[20]

The "hard-words" tradition reaches its climax in the work of two men, Thomas Blount and Edward Phillips. And, falling cheerfully into the pun, in their case the "hard words" can be found not simply as a lexicographical technicality but also as the basic currency of a bitter argument between the two. Given the nature of lexicography—each dictionary maker building on the work of his predecessors to create his own work, and then in turn being subsumed in the dictionaries that follow—it is surprising that there are no more cries of "Plagiarist!" And if one looks over the list of successive lexicographers that had accumulated by the mid-seventeenth century, each following upon the last, there would appear already to have been an infinity of opportunities for such allegations. Yet while lexicographers might have muttered to themselves, their intimates or their booksellers, any such complaints seem so far to have been suppressed. Perhaps they realized too well the dangers of casting the first stone. Dictionary makers might well boast of their offering more words and more definitions than those who came before, but they seem to have restrained themselves from commenting on those who followed on. Only among the cant collectors, where the vocabulary was infinitely smaller and thus more obviously passed from list to list, did such allegations fly. Of course in many cases the predecessor was long dead. And it is when the lexicographers turn from "the best authors" of a classical past, to setting down the "hard words" of contemporary language, that tempers start to fray.

There had been problems with Holyoake's revision of Rider in 1617, but one protagonist had long since abandoned the field, while the other, long dead, was represented only by his executors. Their threatened suit came to nothing. But not every lexicographer chose to ignore what he saw as theft. Not until the American "dictionary wars" of the mid-nineteenth century did the problem receive so dramatic an exposure as in the clash between Blount and Phillips, whose respective works, Blount's *Glossographia* (1656) and Phillips' *New World of English Words* (1658), show the "hard-word" tradition at its peak.

Thomas Blount was born in Bordesley, Worcestershire in 1618. His was a cadet branch of the ancient Blount family. He was called to the bar and soon afterward succeeded to considerable properties in Essex and Warwickshire. He was a zealous Roman Catholic, which caused him problems in practicing the law under the strictly Puritan Commonwealth, but he still managed to maintain an enthusiastic amateur interest. Certainly he was happy to hand out free advice to the tenants of his manor at Orleton. He also signed his dictionary "Barrester." However, with no need to make a living, he gradually abandoned the law for literature, returning to his law books only as sources for his researches into legal jargon, a task he performed for "nothing but his own satisfaction."[21] He was also a devotee of national histories, studying those of Turkey, France, Spain, and Italy. He was a reasonable Latinist, spoke French tolerably, and had a smattering of Greek and other tongues. Although he was not personally involved, the Popish Plot of 1678 and the anti-Catholic agitation that followed it meant that as a Catholic Blount had to flee his home. He contracted palsy in 1679 and died on Boxing Day of that year, supposedly of apoplexy. By then, according to his friend the chronicler Anthony à Wood, quoting his last letter from Blount, he had abandoned all reading other than that of religious tracts.

Blount was a widely recognized intellectual whose writings include both general and lexicographical works. Among the former are *Boscobel: or the History of His Most Sacred Majesties most miraculous preservation after the battle of Worcester* (1660), a Catholic Almanac, treatises on bankrupts, on Booker's Telescopium Uranicum and on the Blount family, and a list of Roman Catholics who lost their lives fighting for King Charles I in the Civil War. In addition to the *Glossographia* and to his rejoinder to Phillips' alleged plagiarism, he wrote a number of language-related books. These include *The Art of making Devises,* "treating of Hieroglyphicks, Symboles, Emblemes, Aenigmas, Sentences, Parables, Reverses of Medalls, Armes, Blazons, Cimiers, Cyphres and Rebus, translated from the French of Henry Estienne, lord of Tossez" (1646) and *The Academie of Eloquence,* "containing a compleat English Rhetorique exemplified, with *Common places* and *Formes* digested into an easie and methodical way to read and write fluently, according to the *mode* of the present times, together with letters, both Amorous and Moral, upon emergent occasions" (1654). In 1670 there was published *A Law Dictionary* "interpreting such difficult Words and Terms as are found either in our Common or Statute, Ancient or Modern Lawes. With References to the several Statutes, Records, Registers, Law-Books, Charters, Ancient Deeds and Manuscripts wherein the words are used; and Etymologies, where they properly occur." Otherwise known as the *Nomolexicon,* this jargon dictionary would provide the core vocabulary for a number of later imitations.

Glossographia, "or a Dictionary, Interpreting all such Hard Words, Whether Hebrew, Greek, Latin, Italian, Spanish, French, Teutonick, Belgick, British or Saxon; as are now used in our refined English Tongue. Also the Terms of Divinity, Law, Physick, Mathematicks, Heraldry, Anatomy, War, Musick, Architecture; and of several other Arts and Sciences Explicated. With Etymologies, Definitions, and Historical Observations on the same "appeared in 1656. Further editions were published in 1661 (this claims 500 new words, but the book does not seem to get any bigger: perhaps it was simply a puff) and in 1670 (with "many additions," perhaps 400 words in all), 1674, and 1681.

It is an ambitious book. Like every other compiler of "hard-word" dictionaries, Blount borrows widely from his predecessors, especially the Latin-English dictionaries of the previous century, but he casts his net wider than does Cawdrey or Cockeram. Possibly drawing on John Minsheu's polyglot *Ductor in Linguas,* Blount found material in a variety of other languages, both ancient and modern. Like Cawdrey he aimed at "the more-knowing women and the less-knowing men" but he also hoped to attract "the best of Schollers" and "all such as desire to understand what they read." Identifying with his putative readers, he claimed that despite his own wide reading in French, Latin, and Greek, as well as other tongues, he still often felt himself "gravelled in English Books." He wanted to find out the proper meanings of words and, assuming that this was not his problem alone, to share his findings with others via this dictionary. He also wanted to explain the jargon of tradesmen, shopkeepers, cooks, and similar workers. He explains this last desire in his note "To the Reader":

Nay, to that pass we are now arrived, that in London many of the Tradesmen have new Dialects; The Cook asks you what Dishes you will have in your Bill of Fare; whether Ollas [stews], Bisques, Hachies, Omelets,

Bouillons, Grilliades, Ioncades [junkets], Fricasses; with a Haugoust [a highly seasoned dish], Ragoust, etc. The Vintner will furnish you with Montefiascone, Alicante, Vornaccia, Ribolla, Tent [vino tinto], etc. Others with Sherbet, Agro di Cedro, Coffa, Chocolate, etc. The Taylor is ready to mode you into a Rochet [a surplice], Mandillion [overcoat], Gippon [short jacket], Justacor [a waistcoat with sleeves], Capouch [cowl], Roqueton, or a Cloke of Drap de Bery, etc. The Shoo-maker will make you Boots, Whole Chase, demi-Chase, or Bottines, etc. The Haberdasher is ready to furnish you with a Vigone [vicuna hat], Codeck [woolen hat] or Castor [beaver hat], etc. The Semstress with a Crabbat, Toylet, etc. By this new World of Words, I found we were slipt into that condition which Seneca complains of in his lifetime; When men's minds begin to enure themselves to dislike, whatever is usual is disdained: They affect novelty in speech, they recal orewarn and uncouth words: And some there are that think it a grace, if their speech hover, and thereby hold the hearer in suspence, etc.

For a man who in two years will be self-righteously, if justifiably, embroiled in a battle with an alleged plagiarist of his own work, Blount is somewhat disingenuous when he declares:

To compile and compleat a Work of this nature and importance, would necessarily require an Encyclopedie of knowledge, and the concurrence of many learned Heads; yet that I may a little secure the Reader from a just apprehension of my disability for so great an undertaking, I profess to have done little with my own Pencil; but have extracted the quintessence of Scapula, Minsheu, Cotgrave, Rider, Florio, Thomasius, Dasipodius, and Hexam's Dutch, Dr. Davies Welsh Dictionary, Cowel's [sic] Interpreter and other able Authors for so much as tended to my purpose.

This may be true, but it is the absences that are conspicuous. Blount's is the first English dictionary to offer citations, but as Starnes and Noyes point out, he carefully fails to mention his real sources: the Rider-Holyoake and the work of Thomas Thomas, whose earlier efforts provided around 58 percent (so Starnes and Noyes calculate) of the whole.[22] He has also drawn heavily on the equally invisible John Bullokar, though he does get credited at specific entries. Blount took many words from John Rastell's *Terms of the Law* (1667) but in his defense, this was a book that he had himself edited. Once again, one sees in the word list a direct throwback to the sixteenth-century Latin-English dictionaries. Finally, in this list of inconsistencies, Blount is not wholly honest in some of his citations. He attributes them, for instance, to Francis Bacon or Thomas Browne, but it appears that he has not read the original work himself. Instead he has found the word in a Latin dictionary, traced its use to the relevant book, and then credited it to the author in question as their coinage. Too often, it seems, Blount seems to be using secondary sources and claiming them as his own firsthand reading. In his defense, note Starnes and Noyes, this technique may have been developed to offset the inevitable attacks on what effectively are his neologisms, even if they are drawn from Latin originals.[23]

In a wider perspective, Blount is a dedicated lexicographer who sees the value of what he is doing. For all that he uses so many secondary sources he is certainly no hack. He also appreciates that there is no real end to his nor to any fellow lexicographer's task, and worries that his "labour would find no end, since our English tongue daily changes habit." It is for this reason, perhaps, that he turned so frequently to earlier dictionaries, rather than attempting to plow ever onward through what must have seemed limitless original texts. Not until Furnivall and Murray assembled the team of readers who amassed citations for the *OED* would such a task be essayed, and even then a good deal went unconsidered. His refusal to fall prey to the fantasies of "fixing" the language that dominated much of eighteenth-century lexicography, and to appreciate its essentially organic and ever-expanding growth, make him a definite "modern" in his field. That said, he is under no illusion as to the importance of the individual lexicographer in determining what, in any given dictionary published at any given time, "the language" is. The "genius" of each dictionary maker, and the character of each word he considers, will help him come to a satisfactory conclusion as regards what goes into a word list and what does not.

Like his forerunner Sir Thomas Elyot, Blount was an enthusiastic neologizer. He rejects those conservatives who criticize such novel terms, pointing out that "our best modern Authors . . . have both infinitely inriched and enobled our Language by admitting and naturalizing thousands of foreign words . . ." His own definitions, whether of new or old words, add to his dictionary's appeal. They can be quirky, even aphoristic, as would be Johnson's a century later. Typical are "Hony-Moon, applyed to those married persons that love well at first, and decline in affection afterwards; it is hony now, but it will change as the moon" and "Ventriloquist . . . one that has an evil spirit speaking in his belly, or one that by use and practice can speak as if it were out of his belly, not moving his lips."

Blount's is the first monolingual English dictionary to offer etymology. Like the Latinists, whose etymologies often erred to the fanciful if not actually absurd, Blount's suggestions lack the benefit of the developments in philology that would bear their finest fruit in the *OED,* but one must credit him for the effort. Three examples suffice: The name *Arthur* is supposedly "a British word composed of *Arth,* which signifies a Bear, and *grw,* which signifies a man (*Vir*). So *Arthur, quasi* a man that for his strength and terror may be called a Bear." *Druids* "took their name from *drus* [Greek], an Oake, because they held nothing more holy than an Oak . . . or because they were wont to exercise their super-stition in Oaken groves . . ."[24] A *shrew* is "a kind of Field-Mouse, which if he go over a beasts back, will make him lame in the Chine; and if he bite, the beast swells to the heart, and dyes . . . From hence came our English phrase, I beshrew thee, when we wish ill; and we call a curst woman a Shrew."[25]

Of Blount's sources, the majority have been mentioned elsewhere, but one fig-ure, John Cowell, deserves a brief diversion. Cowell (1554–1611) was born in Ernsborough, Devon and educated at Eton and then King's College, Cambridge, where he was advised by his tutor Richard Bancroft (later archbishop of Canterbury) to devote himself to civil law. This he did, and rose to become the university's vice chancellor between 1603 and 1604 and, thanks to Bancroft, vicar-general in 1608. This glowing career was marred when he published *The Interpreter,* "a booke containing the signification of Words: Wherein is set forth the true meaning of all . . . such words and termes as are mentioned by the Lawe-writers or Statutes . . . requiring any Exposition." Dedicated to Bancroft, who had helped with its production, this dictionary of legal jargon appeared in 1607 to no particular response. But antimonarchist readers discovered that, inadver-tently, Cowell had gone too far. Under headings of "King," "Parliament," "Pre-rogative," "Recoveries," and "Subsidies" he noted that the English monarchy was an absolute monarchy and Parliament only existed out of the king's "goodness in waiving his absolute power to make laws without their consent."

Given the ever-increasing tensions between Parliament and the king, this was not a sentiment calculated to endear the author to MPs. The Commons was furious and in 1610 members asked the Lords to join them in directing King James' attention to these passages. A conference was arranged under Francis Bacon but before it could take place the earl of Salisbury announced that King James himself had summoned Cowell and disavowed his doctrine, a gesture which enraged the ultramonarchical Cowell. The irony was that for all his pro-monarchy beliefs, the king too felt that Cowell had trespassed on matters that lay beyond even the most favorable public commentator. He was called before the council of state in March 1610 and ordered to "answer some other passages of his book which do as well pinch upon the authority of the king, as the other points were derogatory to the liberty of the subject . . ." But Cowell did not budge and "could not regularly deliver what grounds he hath for the maintaining of those his propositions."[26] The result was Cowell's being turned over to the custody of an alderman and the book being burned by the common hangman on the basis that it insulted the king and Commons; it was officially banned and a proclamation stating this was read in public. Cowell resigned his professorship in May 1611 and died five months later. His book was reissued, quite unchanged, in 1637; further editions, including one edited by Thomas Manley, whose law dictionary would so enrage Thomas Blount, appeared until 1727.

Thomas Fuller suggests that Cowell's problems really arose through the professional jealousy of Sir Edward Coke, a lesser lawyer but a more powerful man, who led the attacks.[27] Coke invariably described his rival as "Dr. Cowheel" and Fuller punningly observes "a *cow-heel* (I assure you) well dressed is good meat that a cook (when hungry) may lick his fingers after it." Coke, of course, is pronounced "cook."

Two years after Blount's work had been published there appeared a new dictionary, by the latest lexicographer of "hard words": Edward Phillips, a nephew of the poet John Milton. Its full title reads *"The New World of English Words:* or a General Dictionary, Containing the Interpretations of such hard words as are derived from other Languages; whether *Hebrew, Arabick, Syriack, Greek, Latin, Italian, French, Spanish, British, Dutch, Saxon,* &c. their Etymologies and perfect Definitions: Together with All those Terms that relate to the Arts and Sciences; whether *Theologie, Philosophy, Logick, Rhetorick, Grammer, Ethicks, Law, Natural History, Magick, Physick, Chirurgery, Anatomy, Chimistry, Botanicks, Mathematicks, Arithmetick, Geometry, Astronomy, Astrology, Chiromancy, Physiognomy, Navigation, Fortification, Dialling, Surveying, Musick, Perspective, Architecture, Heraldry, Curiosities, Mechanicks, Staicks, Merchandise, Jewelling, Painting, Graving, Husbandry, Horsemanship, Hawking, Hunting, Fishing,* &c. To which are added The signification of Proper names, Mythology, and Poetical Fictions, Historical relations, Geographical Descriptions of most Countries and Cities of the World; especially of these three Nations wherein their chiefest Antiquities, Battles and other most Memorable Passages are mentioned; as also all other Subjects that are useful, appertain to our English Language. *A Work very necessary for Strangers, as well as our own Countrymen, for all persons that would rightly understand what they discourse, write or read."* It had dedicatory epistles to Sir William Paston (of the *Paston Letters*), Sir Robert Bolles, and Edward Hussy.

Like all the "hard-word" lexicographers, Phillips was keen to stress his efforts in making the delights of English available to a wider audience.

The Preface to this work, in which the author endeavours to deduce the history of the English language, is remarkable for the vein of manly sense and propriety which runs through it. [He] stickles warmly for the honour of his native tongue, guarding equally against those pedantic and over-subtle reasoners on the one hand, who would deny it the name of a language, because it is not an original speech of itself, but made up of terms borrowed from various nations; and the frantic innovators on the other hand, who regard all novelty as an improvement, and would cherish every term which fashion offers to their acceptance, however contrary it may be to all admissable rules in its mould and composition, and however alien in its nature to the genius of the language into which it claims to be incorporated.[28]

This first edition offered readers some 11,000 entries, an increase on Blount which can be mainly accounted for by the inclusion of proper, historical, and mythological names. The primary source for these entries is Charles Stephanus' (Estienne) *Dictionarium Historicum Geographicum, Poeticum . . .* (1533), whose many editions made it a sourcebook for such English compilers as Cooper, Thomas, Holyoake, and others. Phillips also uses Cockeram, John Bullokar, Rastell's law dictionary, and Cowell's *Interpeter.* But his chief source was Blount's *Glossographia.* This wholesale plagiarism, as it would soon be condemned, was compounded by the prefatory "Advertisement to the Reader," an essay largely devoted to Phillips' denigration of Blount. To balance this Phillips included a list of the experts whom he had supposedly consulted when preparing his work, typically Elias Ashmole for "antiquities," Ralph Greatorex for mathematical instruments, and "Mr. Taverner" for fishing. Whether any of these experts really were involved is debatable: some even disowned the whole work. And at no point at all does Phillips ever acknowledge his debt to Thomas Blount.

Edward Phillips (d. 1696?) was born in August 1630 in the Strand, near Charing Cross. His father, also Edward, worked for the Court of Chancery, his mother, Anne, was the only sister of the poet John Milton. Phillips Sr. died in 1631; Edward's younger brother John, destined to become one of the era's better known hack writers and scurrilous controversialists, was born shortly after his father's death; their elder sister died in infancy, eliciting from her uncle the poem that begins "O fairest flower, no sooner blown than blasted." Anne Phillips then married her husband's friend and fellow worker in Chancery, Thomas Agar, by whom she had two daughters, Mary and Anne.

Edward and John were educated by their uncle John Milton. When Milton returned from a trip to Italy in 1639 Edward began daily lessons, in the classics, in modern French and Italian literature, and in divinity and mathematics, at his lodgings near St. Bride's Churchyard, Fleet Street. When Milton moved to "a pretty garden house" in Aldersgate Street, Edward began boarding with him. He stayed with his uncle until the age of twenty, moving with him through a succession of homes. After coming down from Oxford without a degree he began looking for work either as a private tutor or in a bookseller's. Although his time at Oxford had turned him violently against his uncle's political, religious, and moral attitudes, the two remained friends. Edward regularly visited Milton and was able to read *Paradise Lost* as it was being written. When in 1659 he brought out a new (nineteenth) edition of Joannis Buchler's *Sacrarum Profanarumque Phrasium Poeticarum Thesaurus* he added two original essays in Latin, in the second of which he wrote the first printed words of praise offered to Milton's work, which "is reputed to have achieved the perfection of this kind of poetry [i.e., epic]."

Phillips began publishing in his own right in 1653: his first effort was a poem prefixed to Henry Lawes' *Ayres*. Five years, and a number of verses and prose works later, "after many years' labour"[29] he published his dictionary, *The New World of Words*. That same year he also published the elaborately titled *Mysteries of Love and Eloquence: or the Arts of Wooing and Complementing;* "as they are managed in the Spring Garden, Hide Park, the New Exchange and other Eminent Places. A Work, in which is drawn to the Life the Deportment of the Most Accomplisht Persons, the Mode of their Courtly Entertainments, Treatments of their Ladies at Balls, their Accustom'd Sports, Drolls and Fancies, the Witchcrafts of their Persuasive Language in their Approaches, or other more Secret Dispatches. And, to compleat the Young Practitioner of Love and Courtship, these following Conducive Helps are chiefly insisted on: Addresses, and set Forms of Expressions for Imitation, Poems, Pleasant Songs, Letters, Proverbs, Riddles, Jests, Posies, Devices, A-la-mode Pastimes, a Dictionary for the making of Rimes, four hundred and fifty delightful Questions, with their several Answers. As also Epithets, and Flourishing Similitudes, alphabetically collected, and so properly applied to their several subjects, that they may be rendered admirably useful on the sudden occasions of discourse or writing. Together with a New Invented Art of Logick, so plain and easie, by way of questions and answers, that the meanest capacity may in a short time attain to a perfection in the ways of arguing and disputing." A second edition appeared in 1699 as *The Beaux' Academy*. Blount seems not to have noticed, but in aim, if not in content, Phillips' book echoes his own *Academie of Eloquence*. Its preface was addressed to "The youthful gentry." "The whole is entertaining, but often licentious"[30] and stands as a tribute to Phillips' rejection of Milton's puritan values. "The book is put together with conspicuous ingenuity and profligacy, and is entitled to no insignificant rank among the multifarious productions, which were at that time issued from the press, to debauch the manners of the nation and to bring back the king . . . [The whole book is] interspersed . . . with veins of vulgarity and obscenity, and the author apparently never misses an occasion of saying what he would have called severe things against Puritans and hypocrites."[31] How useful Phillips' work proved to be is debatable; one can but wonder at the effect of such "set Forms" as "You walk in artificial clouds, and bathe your silken limbs in wanton dalliance," "Report could never have a sweeter air to fly in, than your breath," and "Would I were secretary to your thoughts."

In 1660 Phillips took over the writing of Baker's *Chronicle,* a task on which he worked until the edition of 1684. This too exasperated Thomas Blount, and their spat over the *Chronicle,* a history of the monarchs of England, appeared in 1641, written by Sir Richard Baker (1568–1645), a religious historian whose debts had led him to a miserable death in the Fleet Prison. Phillips' volumes were ostentatiously pro-monarchist, although with the Commonwealth still dominant he judiciously included some rote praise of Oliver Cromwell and the occasional attack on the Stuarts. All this vanished with the post-Restoration editions and the book became a staple of country-house libraries. The *Spectator* notes it as part of the fictional Sir Roger de Coverley's regular reading, while it appears in Henry Fielding's novel *Joseph Andrews* (1742) as a book owned by Sir Thomas Booby.

In October 1663 Phillips became tutor at Sayes Court, near Deptford, to the son of John Evelyn, the diarist. Evelyn describes him as "a sober, silent and most harmless person, a little versatile in his studies, and understanding many languages, especially the modern." He was "not at all infected by his uncle's principles, although he was brought up by him." In 1665 he moved to Wilton as tutor to Philip Herbert, the future seventh earl of Pembroke and scion of a family who seem consistently to have been involved with dictionary making. He was used, *inter alia,* "to interpret some of the Teutonic philosophy to whose mystic theology the earl was much addicted." He temporarily abandoned tutoring in 1672 and a year later, when his stepfather Agar died, he was left £200 to be used for an annuity or to set himself up in some form of money-making employment. In September 1674 he obtained permission to print his *Theatrum Poetarum,* a critical index of the names of poets of all countries, although the lists are mainly British. Many subsequent critics believe Milton himself was involved, either in passing on his opinions, or even in the actual writing. Winstanley's later *Lives of the English Poets* (1687) is largely a copy of Phillips' efforts.

In September 1677 Phillips entered (possibly on Evelyn's recommendation) the service of the earl of Arlington in Euston, Suffolk, who wanted "a scholar to read and to entertain him sometimes." He also taught languages to the earl's nephew Henry Bennet and the earl's ten-year-old daughter, who was already married to the earl of Grafton. In 1678 he dedicated the fourth edition of the *New World of Words* to her. Around two years later he returned to London and "married a woman with several children, taught school in the Strand near the Maypole, lived in poor condition, though a good master; [and] wrote and translated several things merely to get a bare livelihood."[32] Phillips continued to write for the rest of his life. His main works were editions of Milton's *Letters of State* and his own *Life of Milton,* which appeared in 1694. He also used Milton's notes to prepare the *Tractatulus de modo formandi voces derivativas Linguae Latinae* (1682) and *Enchiridion Linguae Latinae, or a Compendious Latin Dictionary . . . for all learners* (1684). He died sometime around 1696.

Describing Edward Phillips, his biographer Godwin summarizes him as

> a being of a mild and gentle nature, irreconcilable to the exercise of almost every degree of severity. Once, in the beginning of manhood, he was seduced into a desertion and almost a defiance of his uncle; but he soon repented and from that time . . . continued to see him almost daily. It would not be too great a refinement to say, that this temporary apostasy arose out of the mildness of his disposition. It seemed to him that tenets of his uncle were too severe; he shrank from the severe and simple firmness of a republican creed. When he saw the gay votaries of the family of Stuart, his gentleness soon inclined him to pity a monarch in exile . . . It is the same temper . . . that fills him with reverence towards exalted minds . . .

Faced by the Edward Phillips' dictionary, so imitative of his own, and so speedily published after it, Thomas Blount was naturally furious. To add to his rage, it seemed that Phillips had also plagiarized another of his works, the revision of Rastell's *Law Dictionary.* Thus he writes to Anthony à Wood on March 14, 1670: "I am much discouraged in my so fancied scrutiny of words [the *Glossographia*], since I am lately assured my last dictionary [*Rastell*] is at the press surreptitiously, being trancrib'd, mutilated, and disguis'd with some new title, and this by a beggarly half-witted scholar, hir'd for the purpose by some of the law booksellers, to transcribe that in four or five months which cost me twice as many years in compiling . . ."[33] However, here he was wrong. Not Phillips but Thomas Manley (1628–90), more usually associated with political pamphleteering, actually compiled this work, entitled *Nomothetes,* and although he did indeed look at Blount, he, like Blount, drew on the earlier *Interpreter* by Cowell. But in this rapidly escalating quarrel the facts were secondary. In 1672 Blount attacked Phillips in his *Animadversions upon Sir Richard Baker's Chronicle and its continuation* (1672). He cites eighty-two errors, but Godwin describes this as "in every respect an insignificant performance": Blount's main criticism was of Phillips' misspellings, so this was hardly substantial stuff.

In *A World of Errors Discovered in the New World of Words* (1673) Blount shows himself far more enthusiastically aggrieved. Whether or not his rage was justified, it was certainly not pretended. More than four centuries on, one can feel the indignation still crackling off the page, as he asks the reader:

> Must this then be suffered? A Gentleman for his divertisement writes a Book, and this Book happens to be acceptable to the World, and sell; a Bookseller, not interested in the Copy, instantly employs some Mercenary to jumble up another like Book out of this, with some Alterations and Additions, and give it a new Title; and the first Author's out-done, and his Publisher half undone.
>
> Thus it was with my *Glossographia,* the fruit of above Twenty years spare hours, first published in 1656. Twelve Months had not passed, but there appeared in Print this *New World of Words, or General English Dictionary,* extracted almost wholly out of mine, and taking in its first Edition even a great part of my Preface; onely some words were added and altered, to make it pass as the Authors legitimate offspring. In these Additions and Alterations he not seldom erred, yet had not those Errors been continued, with new supplies to a Second and third Impression, so little was I concerned at the particular injury, that these Notes (in great part collected from his first Edition) had never reproached his Theft to the World.

He attacks the frontispiece—"wherein are sculped our two famous *Uniuersities,* Pictures of . . . our most Learned Men of the last Age, with a Scholar of each University" and his title page which "affirms the work *to be very necessary for strangers, as well as for our own Countrymen:* As if our Author intended the World should believe his Book to be the *Factotum* of all *Great Britains* learning, and himself the Parent of so immense a Production." Despite Phillips' listing of *his* sources, Blount, who is far from blameless in this area, pooh-poohs the likelihood of his actually having read them all; nor is he impressed by the list of expert consultants "whereby the Author would at least obscurely insinuate, that those Learned Persons had contributed to or assisted him in it, thereby to advance his reputation; but I believe nothing less, having heard some of the chief of them utterly disown both the Author and his Work."

But his deepest cri de coeur seems to be reserved for the scholar's nightmare: that his efforts will not be properly appreciated: "What then will *Strangers* think of it; what our own *Countreymen?* They will say, *Canis festinans caecos parit catulos:* That such a Dictionary cannot be hudled up in Eight or ten Moneths, nor without much industry and care, though the Author be never so learned."

After this, Blount goes on to list Phillips' supposed errors. A number of these, he claims, occur when Phillips has copied his, Blount's, errors, whether of learning or of bad printing, without double-checking them. Thus he has perpetuated, through plagiarism, the same mistakes. These misprints had been corrected by the edition of 1696. But Blount's real fury comes when he details the errors that he attributes to ignorance and/or inaccuracy. Talking directly to the reader, whose complicity he assumes, he sets them out as targets of his scorn:

Rosemary . . . he omits the singular use of it in adorning a piece of roast beef.

Mac "An Irish word signifying as much as *son* in English or *Fitz* in Welsh." I see our author is no Britain nor Frenchman; else he would have understood that *Fitz* is borrowed from the French, not Welsh.

Bigamie "The marriage of two wives at the same time, which according to Common Law hinders a man from taking holy orders." Here our Author speaks some truth, at peradventure: For he that marries two Wives at the same time commits Felony, and the punishment of Felony is death which (suppose it be by hanging) may very well hinder him from taking holy orders—I find he does not understand the word.

Emergent "An Emergent occasion is taken for a business of great consequence." Well guessed!

Franchise Royal "Is where the King Grants to a person and his heirs to be quit? or the like." To be quit, of, God knows what.

Gallon (Spanish) "A measure containing two quarts." Our author had better omitted this word, since every Alewife can contradict him.

To Grown   "The Foresters say, a Buck growneth." But what it means you must learn elsewhere; for this is all of the word.

Lungis   (French) "A tall slim Man, that hath no length to his heighth." Quasi, A low gross Man that has no thickness to his bulk.

None of a Day   "The third quarter of a day, from Noon till Sun-set." Where then shall we find the other three-quarters? He should have said from Noon till the Sun be half-way down.

Pathopep   (Greek) "An expression of a Passion, in Rhetorick it is a figure by which the mind." We are left to guess at the rest; for so he leaves it. And Pathopep is an unknown word of his New World.

Quauer   "A measure of time in Musick, being the half of a Crotchet as a Crotchet the half of a Quaver, a Semiquaver, &c." What fustian is here? Just so, two is the half of four, and four the half of two; and Semiquaver is explicated by a dumb "&c".

How much the readers agreed with, how much they even cared for this splenetic, even pedantic outburst, cannot be properly estimated, but both Wheatley and Godwin suggest that Blount might have been protesting somewhat too vehemently. "Blount very much overestimates the injury he has received," says Wheatley and more importantly adds, noting Blount's sneers at Phillips' "needless inclusion of many trivial words," that "it shows how little of the real use of dictionaries was understood."[34] Far from trivializing the word list, Phillips was in fact opening out the "hard-word" tradition; a process that would be extended even further in the revision of his work in 1706. In Godwin's view, "Much caution ought always to be preserved in listening to a charge of plagiarism. Very often it has happened for such a charge to be advanced, without any foundation, but the fretful impatience and self-importance of an author . . . To be arraigned and reproached is in some cases one indication that a man is not destitute of merit." And he goes on to make the general point, which every lexicographer must face:

Of all works a Dictionary is most exposed to the charge of plagiarism, and is therefore the the work against which such a charge should least be credited upon a surmise or allegation only. How shall I contrive not to define a word in the same manner, as some certain writer has done before me? Or am I under any such obligation? If he has defined it well, am I obliged to define it ill? Every dictionary-maker, great or small, will of necessity place other dictionaries before him, when he sits down to work, and will take his definition from one or other of them, when he finds that they have done it so, that he cannot mend it [do it any better].

Godwin, Phillips' biographer, is naturally on his side, and notes after considering the arguments, that "in the two redoubted champions now before us, Blount is severe and repulsive, while Edward Phillips is as evidently amiable and conciliating, with a certain portion of occasional, yet censurable, negligence." Certainly in the fourth edition of 1678 Phillips adds a new, justificatory preface in which, says Godwin "his gentle spirit felt an invincible repugnance to the fencings and woundings of controversy." He writes that,

As on the one part I am sufficiently conscious not to have been wanting in my utmost industry; so on the other side, as to whatever oversights or omissions may possibly have escap'd, through the prescription of overruling interests, and for want of that profound leisure and vacancy which is absolutely requisite for the bringing of any laborious undertaking to mature perfection, I shall easily submit to the reasonable animadversions of the candid and judicious; and for the Errors of the Press, which, where exact attendance cannot be given, may be expected to be not a few, I have thought it sufficient, though the addition, omission, or mistake of one letter, may oftentimes very much pervert or alter the sense, to take notice only of the most material of them, well knowing how rational and obvious it is, for any person that hath put off the Pedant, and is not blinded by prejudice, to make a distinction between a Printers and an Authors mistake.

Blount died in 1679 and Phillips in 1696 and their quarrel died with them. So too would the "hard-word" tradition, giving way as the century proceeded to new questions, notably those of etymology. In 1706, however, a new edition of Phillips' work appeared, edited by John Kersey. It is technically a revision, but the changes are so extensive that it is effectively a new work. Its full title, displaying even more areas of vocabulary than Phillips' original, is "The New World of Words: or a Universal English Dictionary, CONTAINING An Account of the Original or Proper Sense and Various Significations of all Hard WORDS derived from other Languages; whether *Hebrew, Arabick, Syriack, Greek, Latin, Italian, French, Spanish, British, Dutch, Saxon,* &c. as now made use of in our

English Tongue. Together with A brief and plain Explication of all Terms that relate to the Arts and Sciences, either Liberal or Mechanical, viz. *Grammar, Rhetorick, Logick, Theology, Law, Metaphysicks, Ethicks, Natural, Philosophy, Law, Natural History, Physick, Surgery, Anatomy, Chymistry, Pharmacy, Botanicks, Arithmetick, Geometry, Astronomy, Astrology, Cosmography, Hydrography, Navigation, Architecture, Fortification, Dialling, Surveying, Gauging, Opticks, Catoptricks, Dioptricks, Perspective, Musick, Mechanicks, Statics, Chiromancy, Physiognomy, Heraldry, Merchandise, Maritime* and *Military Affairs, Agriculture, Gardening, Handicrafts, Jewelling, Painting, Carving, Engraving, Confectionery, Cookery, Horsemanship, Hawking, Hunting, Fowling, Fishing,* &c. To which is Added The Interpretation of Proper Names of Men and Women, that derive their Original from the above-mention'd Ancient and Modern Tongues, with those of Writs and processes at Law; Also the *Greek* and *Latin* Names of divers forms of *Animals, Plants, metals, Minerals,* &c. and several other remarkable Matters more particularly express'd in the Preface. *Compiled by* EDWARD PHILLIPS, *Gent.* The Sixth Edition, Revised, Corrected, and improved; with the Addition of near Twenty Thousand Words, from the best Authors, Domestick and Foreign, that treat of the several Subjects: *By J. K. Philobibl. A Work very necessary for Strangers, as well as our own Country-men, for all persons in order to the right understanding of what they Speak, Write or Read.*"

It was "made out of the most approved Authors . . . far the largest of any hitherto extant." The total word list now ran to 38,000 headwords. Kersey's preface explains:

The whole has been carefully Revis'd . . . and it was judg'd expedient to leave out all Abstracts of the Lives of Eminent Persons, Poetical Fictions, Geographical Descriptions . . . in regard that they are already treated of at large in several particular Dictionaries. In the room of these are inserted near Twenty Thousand hard Words and Terms in all Arts and Sciences . . . to which are added many Country-Words, and such as are us'd in our ancient Latin Writers, old Records . . . Also the *Greek* and *Latin* names of many sorts of Beasts, Birds, Fishes, Insects, Plants . . . The Magistrates and Officers of the Grecian and Roman Empires . . . Besides a summary View of Religious Orders and other Remarkable Things in England, and our American plantations.

The changes in style are as important as those of content. Kersey's work is as much of its period, the dawning of the Enlightenment, as Phillips' was of his, the waning of the Renaissance. The clearest indication of this is in the deletion of the old encyclopedic material, the pages of copy drawn from medieval and classical myths and legends, which had been a mandatory part of any major dictionary for centuries. In their place came new technical vocabularies, based not in legend, but in state-of-the-art modernity. Aside from Cowell's *Interpreter,* revised in 1701, and the legal terms listed in both Phillips and Blount, Kersey drew on John Harris' *Lexicon technicum* "or, a Universal Dictionary of Arts and Sciences, Explaining not only the Terms of Art, But the Arts Themselves." Published in 1704, this was an early, if not the earliest dictionary of trade jargon. Country words, whether of general dialect or describing specific agricultural processes, came from John Ray's *Collection of Words Not Generally Used* (1674), itself acknowledged as the first full-scale dialect dictionary, and John Worlidge's *Systema Agriculturae* (1669).

What remains is a blend of Phillips, who concentrated on "hard words," and Kersey's own additions, which focused on the more general vocabulary. This latter appears to have been taken from the groundbreaking *New English Dictionary* (1702) by "J.K.," initials that are presumed to be those of Kersey himself. But J.K. is best known for his devotion to "easy" rather than "hard" words, and it seems that if anything proves the connection, then it is Kersey's promotion of such terms in his revision of Phillips. Otherwise Kersey tends to expand Phillips' definitions, but makes one major omission: etymology, which Phillips tried hard to include, has been completely ignored.

Blount and Phillips were still embroiled in their slugging match when in 1676 the schoolteacher Elisha Coles (1640?–1680) added his installment to the tale of "hard-word" dictionaries. He was a nephew of an earlier Elisha Coles (1608?–88), a dissenting theologian under the Commonwealth and clerk to the East India Company subsequent to the Restoration. He left Magdalen College, Oxford without a degree and in 1663 began teaching English to the young and to foreigners and "continued in that employment with good success in Russell Street, near Covent Garden." From here, in 1677, he was appointed a teacher at Merchant Taylors' School (following in the footsteps of Richard Mulcaster) and in 1678 at Galway School in Ireland. He died on December 20, 1680 and was buried in Galway. According to Anthony à Wood, Coles was "a curious and critical person in the English and Latin tongues, did much good in his calling, and wrote several useful and necessary books for the instruction of beginners."

Apart from the *Christologia, or a Metrical Paraphrase on the History of Our Lord and Saviour Jesus Christ* (1671), a grotesque piece of verse, more doggerel than poetry, all of Coles' work dealt with teaching. Other than his dictionary he published the *Compleat English Schoolmaster;* "or, the most natural and easie method of spelling and reading English, according to the present proper pronunciation of the language on Oxford and London" (1674), *Syncrisis, "or the most natural and easie method of learning Latin, by comparing it with English"* (1675), *Nolens, Volens, or, you shall make Latin, whether you will or no,* "containing the plainest directions that have yet been given upon that subject" (1675), and *The Young Scholar's best Companion,* "or an exact guide or directory for children and youth from the ABC to the Latin Grammar, comprising the whole body of the English learning." In 1677 he also produced *A Dictionary English-Latin and Latin-English, containing all things necessary for translating of either language into the other,* a work that remained the basis of Latin teaching for the next century. He also wrote a pioneering essay in shorthand: *The newest, plainest and best Shorthand* (1674), "containing (1) A brief account of all the Short-hands already extant, with their alphabets and fundamental rules. (2) A plain and easie method for beginners, less burthensome to the memory than any other. (3) A new invention for contracting words, with special rules for contracting sentences, and other ingenious fancies, both pleasant and profitable to all, let their character be whose or what it will." It ran to ten editions by 1707. Coles was not the first experimenter in shorthand, but he was the first to suggest different positions—above, below and on the line—for the shorthand characters. The system was not adopted until 1692, when it was explained fully in Abraham Nicholas' *Theographia.*

An English Dictionary "Explaining The difficult Terms that are used in Divinity, Husbandry, Physick, Phylosophy, Law, Navigation, Mathematicks, and other Arts and Sciences. Containing Many thousand of Hard Words (and proper names of Places) more than are in any other English Dictionary or Expositor. Together with The Etymological Derivatives of them from their proper Fountains, whether Hebrew, Greek, Latin, French, or any other Language. In a Method more Comprehensive, than any that is extant" was published in 1676. It runs to around 25,000 words, more than in the fourth edition of Phillips, which appeared in 1678, but his definitions are usually short and often run to no more than a single word or phrase.

Coles, consciously or otherwise, left no opportunities for accusations of plagiarism; but he made no effort to disguise his lack of respect for those who came before him. As he stated in his preface, "Not that I am ignorant of what is already done. I know the whole succession, from Dr. Bulloker [*sic*] to Dr. Skinner; from the smallest volume to the largest folio. I know their difference and their defects. Some are too little; some are too big; some are too plain (stuft with obscenity not to be named), and some so obscure that instead of expounding others they have need themselves of an Expositor. The method of some is foolish, and supposes things to be known before they are explained." He also touted the size of his word list. "The addition that is made to the number of words in former authors of this kind, is almost incredible (considering the bulk) being raised from seven in the Expositor to almost thirty thousand here, which are some thousands more than are in Mr. Blount's Glossographia or Mr. Phillips' World of Words."[35]

Starnes and Noyes suggest that Coles made a number of important advances in the techniques of dictionary making.[36] He retains and augments lists of "old words," i.e., those used by Chaucer, Piers Plowman, etc., although he removes what he sees as the foolish inclusions of others, typically "*fidicula:* a falling vulture; *eviration:* a yielding (i.e., gelding), and *lungis:* a tall slim man that hath no length to his height," a term that especially irritated Thomas Blount. Coles also opted, less sensibly, to throw out *ejaculation:* a yelling. He defines many dialect terms—only Stephen Skinner's *Etymologicum Linguae Anglicanae* (1671) had previously chosen to note them and he concentrated on the Lincolnshire vocabulary amid which he lived; he expands the "encyclopedic" aspects of the dictionary by including the names of the market towns of England and the cities and towns of Europe; he also extends the treatment of proper names and offers the stories that accompany those of classical figures. But it is in his expansion of the bases of his word list that he is most innovative. As well as dialect terms, he offers a higher volume of technical language or jargon; he lists whole groups of related words together—other dictionaries would offer simply a noun, a verb, an adjective, or some other part of speech and leave them as representative of all the others. His intention, he explains, is to improve the ease of access to the word list. He is also the first mainstream lexicographer to acknowledge the importance of slang, or at this stage cant or criminal slang. His cant vocabulary may be little more than a reworking of Richard Head's *Canting Academy* (1673) but at least Coles has appreciated its importance, even if he sees it as social rather than linguistic: " 'Tis no Disparagement to understand the Canting Terms: It may chance to save your Throat from being cut, or (at least) your Pocket from being pick'd."

There would be no more "hard-word" dictionaries. John Kersey would revise Phillips in 1706, while the anonymous *Glossographia Anglicana Nova* (1707) would be considered by some so similar to Blount—in its content as well as in its title—that it has been listed as effectively a revision too. But by the eighteenth century the job of the "hard-word" compilers had been completed. As one followed another, absorbing and then expanding on each successive word list, the language gradually expanded and the end of the century saw a vastly increased number of those who had access to what had once been élite, Latinate vocabularies. The dictionaries too were also gaining in sophistication: etymologies were becoming the norm, even if they were far from consistent and often downright fantastical; there were guides to pronunciation, spelling, and similar aspects of the language. At the same time the "encyclopedic" aspects of the dictionaries—one of the longest hangovers from the "Scholastic" lexicography of the Middle Ages—were progressively cut down. In their place came crisper definitions and wider vocabularies.

As Starnes and Noyes summed up the century, these lexicographers "made their way along a devious path with many excursions into tempting bypaths but with slow progress towards their goal."[37] Their works "are strongly marked by the personalities and predilections of their authors—a feature which, while constituting part of their charm, is also a measure of their imperfection." Much of their efforts turned on establishing what was still a new and unrefined art and lexicography became as much a matter of the form as of the content of the works it produced. Their primary interest might have been the study and definition of the words themselves, the bedrock discipline of their profession, but there were other areas to be considered. What exactly was a dictionary, and what should and could it contain, most especially when compared to another emerging reference genre: the encyclopedia; and having created the product, who then would purchase their dictionaries, and what did those buyers hope to find? Above all, as lexicography moved gradually toward becoming a full-fledged profession, what did the job description really entail?

The period is pivotal to English dictionary making. One tradition—the sixteenth-century pedagogical style—was replaced by the "hard-word" compilations, which in turn drew on the Renaissance interest in the classics, in fine writing, and in elegant speech. What might be termed the U vocabulary was notably classical—undoubtedly elegant, but inevitably excluding the uneducated mass. Dictionaries boasting "common" rather than "hard" words would not begin appearing until the early eighteenth century and even these were not aimed at the mass public. That audience would finally be addressed by the Methodist preacher John Wesley, whose deliberately downbeat dictionary, authored "by a Lover of Good English and Common Sense," appeared in 1753.

The seventeenth century closes with a flourishing vernacular English not merely in place, but also widely accessible. The next stage of dictionary making, the "fixing" of that English, would dominate the eighteenth century, even if the concept would prove a vain one.

7

The Seventeenth Century:
Variations and Themes

If the predominant mode of seventeenth-century lexicography is the "hard-word" dictionary, it is not the only one. Other forms of dictionary were published, some bringing a trend to its end—the thematic vocabularies of Bathe, Comenius, Ray, and Greenwood—while others continued a tradition—the various English-Latin and Latin-English dictionaries, or those which translate one vernacular into another—and finally others still initiated a new direction—the etymological works of Skinner and of the anonymous compiler of the *Gazophylacium Anglicanum.*

The medieval tradition of "vocabularies," which persists into the early sixteenth century with the works of Stanbridge and his successor Whittington, and which can be found in John Withals' highly popular *Shorte Dictionarie for Yonge Beginners,* is still flourishing in the seventeenth century and even tiptoes into the very earliest years of the eighteenth. While none are dictionaries as such, their arrangement, by themes rather than alphabetical order, and the vocabularies they offered to their readers, made them all very popular and as such they must be seen as a part, if not a central one in this context, of the development of English words.

The launchpad for these latterday vocabularies is the *Janua Linguarum* ("the Gateway of Tongues") which was published in 1611 by William Bathe (1564–1614), rector of the Irish college at Salamanca, Spain and a man who, according to Anthony à Wood, was "endowed with a most ardent zeal for the obtaining of souls, and was beloved of, and respected by, not only those of his own order, but of other orders, for his singular virtues and excellencies."[1] This paragon wrote *A Brief Introduction to the true Arte of Musicke* in 1584, before publishing his Latin-Spanish vocabulary. It reached England in 1617, as a Latin-English manual. It was used to help in the teaching of Latin and it was alleged by one contemporary scholar that with its help a dedicated learner could absorb as much Latin in three months as other methods imparted in three years. It contained around 5,000 words, arranged into twelve "centuries," with the word list fitted into 1,200 statements or sentences. Each individual century was based on a given topic, ranging from abstract concepts—justice, fortitude, temperance—to the concrete aspects of daily life.

Bathe's *Janua,* while widely popular, proved a disappointment to one reader, John Comenius or Komensky (1592–1671), the bishop of Moravia and a widely respected educational reformer who saw universal education as the panacea for all human ills. He also believed that rather than cram young minds with grammar, one should "follow the footsteps of nature" and bend the teaching to the child's mind, rather than, as was (and still largely remains) traditional, the other way round. Comenius' response to Bathe was to produce his own work, *Janua Linguarum Reserata* ("The Gate of Tongues Unlocked"), in 1631. The first edition was printed in Latin and German; later that year an English, French, and Latin edition appeared and in time every European language was included. Comenius' work largely resembles that of Bathe: he has the thematic arrangement in 100 chapters ranging from the origins of the world and the elements through to death and burial and Providence, God and the angels, and uses sentences, in his case 1,058 of them, to transmit the vocabulary.

Comenius' work was popular, but its author was apparently as unsatisfied with it as he had been with Bathe's effort. In 1657 he brought out a further revision of the concept: the *Orbis sensualium pictus* ("The Illustrated World of Things We Can Feel"). This is not the first wordbook to include pictures, that tradition technically began with a Latin–Middle English vocabulary of the fifteenth century (see Chapter 2), but it was by far the most influential and can be seen as the sourcebook of every illustrated encyclopedia, and indeed dictionary and illustrated textbook that has followed. To jump forward into the world of computer-based analogy, Comenius, it can be claimed, is the founder of multimedia education.

As he had in the *Janua,* Comenius uses the chapter format—there are 151 of them—and displays the usual range of vocabularies. The pictures that accompany them work to augment the book's accessibility. "The Museum," for instance, is suitably illustrated by a book-lined room and a scholar poring over a volume on his worktable. A series of numbers are printed next to many of the pictured objects and these numbers are duly attached to the vocabulary list printed beneath the illustration.

Comenius, like Bathe before him, was published in England, where he was seen as a modernizer. The works of the two native-born vocabulary makers, while appearing later in the seventeenth century, reflect an earlier tradition of vocabulary. The naturalist John Ray, FRS (1627–1705) is better known today for his *Collection of English Proverbs* (1670) but in 1675 he published his own vocabulary: the *Dictionariolum Trilinguae,* a small volume in English, Latin, and Greek. Subsequent to its fourth edition it was renamed *Nomenclator Classicus, sive Dictionariolum.* It too was divided into chapters (32 of them). It lacks the innovation of pictures, but its divisions—"Of Stones and Metals," "Of Herbs"—retain a predictable format. Unsurprisingly, for a talented naturalist whose work would be superseded only by Linnaeus and Darwin, Ray is especially strong on the names of plants and animals. Less well known, but highly influential, is Ray's *Collection of Words Not Generally Used* (1674). Eighty-four octavo pages long, it was divided into two "Alphabetical Catalogs" dealing respectively with the southern and northern counties, the latter list being twice as long as the former. Ray also gives fifteen pages of bird names, fifteen of fishes, and thirty-five referring to the mining and processing of minerals. A second edition, omitting the birds and fishes, appeared in 1691. Ray's lexicographical collection stemmed from the same researches that underpinned his more celebrated botanical works. As he traveled the country in search of species, he picked up and recorded the everyday dialect speech of the country people he met. The two forms of research, suggests the writer Jo Gladstone, were intrinsically linked. "The English dialect—collecting tradition . . . was an integral part of the empirical impetus that also fired the natural sciences."[2] Ray would give the technical English and Latin names for, say, a given species of grain, in his botanical works, while listing the dialect term for the same specimen in the *Collection of Words.* There was another important factor in Ray's collecting, given the period in which he worked. The execution of Charles I and the establishment of a republican Commonwealth had "turned the world upside down." Ray's researches began only at the very end of the period, in 1658, but they reflected contemporary concerns about authority. As Jo Gladstone explains, "Who here is the child, the reader intended to be educated by the dictionary? Who here is the expert, the one who understands the language that is being imparted? Who here commands the words being taught—the language with which to control the rural environment?"[3] Two centuries on, Joseph Wright's *English Dialect Dictionary* would function as a repository of a dying lexicon; it dealt, in the end, with nostalgia, with what today would be a "heritage" culture: dialect has not survived the mass media. Ray worked in a very different mold: a republican himself, who regretted the Restoration of 1661, his collection is of living, contemporary language. Its speakers, the peasants and country folk, were not seen as part of the traditional power structure. By setting down their language, the *Collection of Words* underpinned the questioning of authority; it was "an implicitly oppositional code."[4] Such "political" lexicography, at least of a nonconformist bent, would not survive the eighteenth century. The lexicography remained political, and perhaps even intensified such interests, but in the hands of Samuel Johnson it moved emphatically to the right. Dialect, as a nonstandard lexis, was largely banished from the influential mainstream dictionaries.

Last of these vocabularists is the schoolmaster James Greenwood (d. 1737) whose *London Vocabulary* appeared *c.* 1700. Further editions followed for the rest of the century. The book aimed to give schoolchildren a basic Latin vocabulary, so that thus equipped they could progress to more serious work. Greenwood did use pictures, noting in his preface that

> I have made choice of the most Natural and Entertaining that the subject is capable of; and distributed Matters into such an Order that the Learner may . . . understand the things themselves which they express, with their Order and Dependence upon one another. And the better to fix both upon the Memory of the young Readers, and to give them as clear an idea of what they earn I have caused little Draughts and Pictures to be made of such Things as are known and distinguished by their outward Shapes with references to the Words that mention them.

He arranged his lists in thirty-three chapters, each dealing with a given topic and listing the words that refer to that topic. As usual, the chapters cover the concrete and abstract, the divine and the more mundane. To facilitate the learning process, the English words run down one side of the page, while the Latin equivalents are placed in a parallel column. When a term is illustrated it is followed by the same number that appears on the picture. Starnes and Noyes note the chapter entitled "Of Judicial Matters," in which there are two complementary illustrations.[5] One is of a courtroom, with the judge, his law book, a barrister, and a witness all numbered and cross-referenced to the text. The other shows the jail yard. Here the student can observe the gallows, and on it the dangling corpse of the thief, attended by "Jack Ketch" the hangman.

The *London Vocabulary* cost only one shilling and proved very popular. It doubtless helped thousands of boys to learn the basics of Latin. The last, twenty-sixth edition was published in 1816, and it crossed the Atlantic in 1787 to start a parallel life in America.

Greenwood was also responsible for another best-seller, his *Essay towards a practical English Grammar* (1711), a book that was praised by Isaac Watts, the educator and hymn writer of "O God our help in ages past" among others, as showing "the deep Knowledge, without the haughty Airs of a Critick." It was at Watts' suggestion that Greenwood published an abridged version of his grammar, entitled *The Royal English Grammar* and dedicated to the Princess of Wales. The appearance almost simultaneously of two rival grammars led in 1712 to the publication of a mocking pamphlet, attacking all three under the title "Bellum Grammaticale; or the Grammatical Battel Royal."

All these vocabularies, however innovative and popular they may have been, must ultimately be viewed as a sideline of mainstream lexicography. That they helped introduce new words to the basic word stock is undeniable, and in their way they had the same effect as the "hard-word" dictionaries, which also drew heavily on Latin, but their logical development pointed toward a new type of reference work, the encyclopedia. The argument that encyclopedias are in themselves merely a thematic branch of lexicography may well be valid, but that discussion is not the purpose of this book.

While seventeenth-century scholarship was no longer restricted to those whose fluency in Latin rivaled that in English, scholars still used the language and the classics retained the respect they had always had. Thus the flow of Latin-English and English-Latin dictionaries, while much diminished by earlier standards, was far from dammed. A number of works appeared to maintain a tradition that, in the end, lay behind the all-English dictionaries that dominated the century's lexicography.

The *Dictionarium minus: A Compendious Dictionary* by Christopher Wase appeared in 1662. Wase (1625?–1690) was educated at Eton and King's College, Cambridge, where he became a fellow. This fellowship was lost when Wase, whose sympathies were ostentatiously royalist, published in 1649 a translation of Sophocles' *Electra,* which he dedicated to Princess Elizabeth. He compounded his error when he undertook to deliver a letter, supposedly from King Charles, to the provost of king's. The authorities could not tolerate such open dissent and Wase was expelled from Cambridge. He fled England, only to be captured at sea and returned to Gravesend jail. He managed to escape, fled successfully this time and joined the Spanish army to serve against the French. Taken prisoner once more, he was released and returned to England where, rather than having to face jail yet again, he benefited from a calmer atmosphere to become tutor to the eldest son of the earl of Montgomery. He worked as a teacher from 1655 and in 1671 became a superior beadle-at-law and, against the vociferous opposition of Dr. John Fell who headed the university press, printer to the University of Oxford. It was this Dr. Fell, a generally unpopular man, who inspired Thomas Browne's doggerel lines, ostensibly a translation of a Martial epigram, "I do not love thee Dr Fell, | though why I cannot tell . . ." It was in 1674, during Wase's term of office, that fellows of All Souls attempted to leaven their normally unarousing intellectual diet with the printing of what was then Europe's best-selling piece of pornography: the *Sonetti Lussuriosi* of the sixteenth-century wit Pietro Aretino and their accompanying *Posizioni* or "Postures," illustrations by the master engraver Marcantonio Raimondi depicting the more imaginative methods of sexual intercourse. As the sheets appeared on the university's press in the Sheldonian Theatre so too did Dr. Fell. Enraged, he destroyed all the material, threatening the errant dons with expulsion. Wase himself survived in his job and died on August 29, 1690.

A Copious Dictionary in Three Parts by "the industrious and learned" Francis Gouldman appeared in 1664. Gouldman was a clergyman who held the same living in South Ockendon, Essex, that had been held by his lexicographical predecessor, John Rider. He was sequestered, i.e., banned from holding services and taking income, under the Commonwealth, but was restored to favor after the Restoration. The *Copious Dictionary* ran to four editions between 1664 and 1678. In the third, published in 1673, the "Hebrew Roots and Derivatives" were added to the text. The dictionary fell into three parts: "1. The English before the Latin . . . 2. The Latin before the English . . . 3. The Proper Names of persons, places, etc. Together with Amendments and Enlargements."

Gouldman prefaced his work with an extensive discussion of his aims. In short these were to gather together those Latin dictionaries that had preceded his and to amend their faults: of style, of content, and of structure. He made no pretense as to originality, and it is possible to trace his work's origins as far back as Varro and Verrius Flaccus. His aim, as he stresses, is clarity:

> As to the adding this Dictionary after others that have been well reputed and are useful, Let it be considered, That they were written one after another, and that was no hindrance to their Authours pains or others acceptance: yea others of late in other Countries have been and are still adding new to old: and who can fix the time when such Works are at the height of all desirable or possible Perfection, where Hercules's Pillars may be placed with a Ne plus ultra? Nay, it will appear by what followeth, that even the latter Dictionaries have been defective: Moreover they, as

hath been represented, had their Amendments and Increase by successive Endeavours and Editions, raising them to that pitch wherein they stand.

To achieve his own work he has improved English spelling, amended, increased, and properly ordered the headwords (he claims to have added 10,000 more to any previous effort); he has removed "Multitudes of Faults amended in the Words, both Latin, Greek, Hebrew and English" and ensured that "The Sense which was sometimes unintelligible, and sometimes lame and defective, is now made Entire and Plain, so far as brevity would permit." As the layout demonstrates, while dividing the book conceptually into three parts, he has unified those three parts in each headword. Thus Gouldman's entry for "dog" first offers "dog" (in Gothic type) "or bitch, Canis"; this is followed by thirty-eight dog-related terms, both general and specific: e.g., a little dog or whelp, a fierce dog, a swift dog, that hath a collar on his neck, an old dog past the best; a spaniel, a bloodhound, a terrier, a Mastiff or band-dog, etc.; there are then the related verbs: to bark like a dog, to howl, to set dogs on, to cry like a young whelp. Finally comes an alphabetical list of dog names, e.g., Blab, Blackfoot, Blanch, Close-biter, and more. This system continues throughout the work.

Gouldman's preface also offered a history of lexicography, taking it from its origins, which as he saw it dated back to Rome, to the work of his most recent predecessor, Christopher Wase. Other prefaces and introductions had made their references to the past, usually in order to parade the author's learning, and his superiority to what has come before. Gouldman boasts too—his entire dictionary is posited as an improvement on past efforts—but he gives a more comprehensive overview than most. For the first time lexicography is seen as a continuing, consistent discipline. Gouldman's predecessors were not, of course, lexicographical professionals in any but the loosest sense, nor really was Gouldman himself, but reading his history one sees, as never before laid out, the pursuit of lexicography as a proper profession.

A Large Dictionary in Three Parts "The English before the Latin, the Latin before the English, the proper names of persons, Places and Other Things necessary to the Understanding of History and Poets" was published in 1676–7. Its author Thomas Holyoake was the only son of Francis Holyoake, the much-maligned reviser in 1617 of John Rider's *Bibliotheca Scholastica*. A royalist, Holyoake was chaplain of Queen's College, Oxford, when the Civil War broke out. When Oxford became Charles I's garrison town, Holyoake duly rallied to his monarch's colors. He was made captain of the Civil War's equivalent of the Artists' Rifles—a foot company made up exclusively of scholars. Fittingly he was awarded his degree of Doctor of Divinity in the field, at the express command of the king. When Oxford surrendered, Holyoake returned to civilian life, working as a doctor under the Commonwealth. He died on June 16, 1675, of a high fever. His dictionary appeared a year later prefaced by essays written by his son Charles and by Thomas Barlow, the bishop of Lincoln. Of Thomas Holyoake's dozen children one, Henry (1657–1731), is worth a slight digression. He was headmaster of Rugby School and "despite the smallness of his salary and other disadvantages, he raised the school from insignificance, and was the first to engage an assistant master."[6] He died unmarried in 1731 and was buried alongside his dictionary-making father and grandfather. Among other bequests he left £30 to the daughter of "Widow Harris," his "tripe-woman." While at Rugby he was noted for his persecution and ultimate expulsion of Edward Cave, who would turn out to be his most famous pupil. Cave, who would become the publisher of the *Gentleman's Magazine* and Samuel Johnson's printer, was born "in reduced circumstances" in the family home, known as Cave's Hole. His father was a younger son, bereft of any inheritance and forced to work as a cobbler. Cave was eligible for Rugby and duly attended the school, but was expelled, despite Holyoake's admission that the boy had university potential, for allegedly robbing Mrs. Holyoake's henhouse and helping his fellow students cheat at their work.

"Judicious and accurate" Adam Littleton (1627–94) published the *Linguae Latinae Liber Dictionarius Quadripartitus,* his contribution to the century's English-Latin dictionaries, in 1678. Littleton was born on November 2, 1627, the son of the vicar of Halesowen, Worcestershire. He was educated at Westminster School and as a scholar of Christ Church, Oxford. Like many contemporary lexicographers, Littleton preferred the king to Parliament, and in 1648 he temporarily lost his place at the university for the poem "Tragi-Comoedia Oxoniensis" which ridiculed Parliament's official visitor to Oxford. In fact the scurrilous verses may well have been penned not by Littleton but by fellow undergraduate John Carrick. Whatever the truth, he was readmitted in 1651 and after graduating spent the rest of the decade teaching before setting up his own school at Chelsea. In February 1669 Littleton became rector of Chelsea. Soon afterward he took a degree in divinity and became Charles II's chaplain, enjoying a variety of livings before his death on June 30, 1694. At one stage he was promised the headship of Westminster, but it never materialized. Littleton was married three times, on the third occasion to an heiress, although it was reported that there was little of her fortune left when her husband died. If this was so, the money was not squandered on riotous living, but on books. Littleton was primarily a classicist, but he was also a capable mathematician, skilled in oriental languages and rabbinical learning. He collected books from Europe,

Asia, and Africa "to the great impoverishment of his estate." The writer Jeremy Collier, best known for his campaigning against the alleged "immoralities" of the stage, claims that Littleton's attainments won him the title "The Great Dictator of Learning" and that he was charitable to a fault, "easy of access, wonderfully communicative of his rare learning and knowledge, facetious and pleasant in conversation, never ruffled with passion . . . endued with a strong habit of body made for noble undertakings of a clean and venerable countenance."[7]

As its title indicates, the *Linguae Latinae Liber Dictionarius Quadripartitus* is "A Latine Dictionary, In Four Parts," notably "English-Latin, Latin-Classical, Latin-proper and Latine-Barbarous." It is dedicated to King Charles II. Like Gouldman, Littleton has set out to correct the errors of the dictionaries that preceded his. His has eliminated the errors of the past, added "several Thousands" of new headwords, improved the supply of etymologies, and generally cleaned up the blunders and inconsistencies of those who predate him. Above all, "in all Four Parts, many things that were utterly impertinent and cumbersome to School-Institution and to the true uses of Learning," are laid aside. In a novel departure he adds "The most usual Christian Names of men and Women Rendered into latine" as well as three pages of "Nick-Names."

Littleton's note "To the English Reader" is best paraphrased by DeWitt Starnes:

The compiler explains that, though he has traveled all along in the "Old beaten Road of Alphabet," as the method most conducive to the study of youth, he has made amendments and supplements and the like so that in matter and manner of handling it his book is "as free from Incroaching upon any others Copyhold, as any that has been writ in English of the king since Thomasius his time." His great aim, he insists, has been "to carry the purity of the Latine Tongue throughout," not to take things or words upon trust, to avoid transcribing the mistakes of others, and wherever possible to get more certain information from the authors themselves. Littleton's laudable aim of compiling a classical dictionary, emphasized here and upon the title page, is hardly attained. He follows too closely some of his immediate predecessors; he prepares the way, however, for Ainsworth, who more nearly realizes this purpose. After these remarks, the compiler makes pertinent comment on each of the four parts of his dictionary. In the English-Latin part he has endeavored to present English as it is now spoken, together with suitable Latin. As a result he has supplied "several Thousands of Words and Proprieties formerly wanting" . . . "Idiotisms" (idioms?) and proprieties of speech have been enlarged; old-fashioned words, such as abarstick . . . and circumlocutions, such as "the inward top of the finger next to the Nail," have been thrown out.

In the "Latine-Classick" "besides the Etymology, Signification and Use of each word," other things are supplied: parts of speech are indicated; the Hebrew is continued throughout; primitives are put in capitals; words taken from the Greek are noted with an asterisk and those peculiar to a particular science are marked with an obelisk; synonyms are designated by an equal sign, and antonyms (antithetae) by a special symbol. "In giving Etymons, wherein we have been obliged to be the larger by other Examples rather than our own Judgment . . . we have endeavoured to be close and pertinent; as resolving no great matter of learning to lie in forced and affected derivations, unless they be brought to some true measures of Analogy. The Significations of words are adjusted, as near as might be to the present English expression, and deduced orderly along; beginning either with that which is the most natural and proper importance, or with that which is most ordinary and common. The use, more especially of Verbs, is represented in such pertinent Instances, as to show at once their Grammatical Construction and Government, together with the Latin Propriety or Phrase."[8]

Littleton concludes his preface with a final boast: "Let it suffice thee, Reader, that thou hast here the whole body of the Latine Tongue with all its natural and genuine branches, delivered to thee; whereby thou mayst be inabled to speak and write Latine by the same authority as the Romans themselves missest here, and meetest with elsewhere, thou must know that they being but corruptions and abuses of Latine, are better let alone than taken notice of." Starnes is less impressed, noting that while the author has made certain improvements on Holyoake and others, "notwithstanding his aim to the contrary, [he] has copied their mistakes."

All other aspects aside, Littleton's dictionary has long been known as the source of what had best be termed a lexicographical "chestnut." Tradition has it that during the compilation Littleton addressed the Latin word *concurro* ("to meet, to assemble") to his assistant. The assistant, assuming, from the similarity of sounds, that the English followed the Latin, asked Littleton, "Concur, I suppose, Sir." His master replied tetchily, "Concur! condog!" Fearing to challenge his master's voice the assistant duly entered "condog" into the manuscript as one of the meanings of *concurro*. It duly appeared in the first edition, and again in the *Cambridge Dictionary,* a wholesale reproduction of

Littleton, in 1693. But it was expunged from all later editions of Littleton proper. Another version of the story, much embellished, is attributed to a slightly later Latin lexicographer, Robert Ainsworth. However, since Ainsworth's work did not appear until 1736, and nowhere contains "condog," it is hard to understand quite why. For a final deflation of the tale one need only glance at the *OED,* which cites *condog* as early as 1592, when it is used by John Lyly in *Galathea.* It is "conjectured to be a whimsical imitation of concur (cur = dog); but no evidence has been found of its actual origin." Henry Cockeram has it in 1623 and there is yet another citation, in 1649, before Littleton joins the party. Regrettably, as Starnes notes, "we must abandon the pretty fiction."

A second edition of Littleton appeared in 1684 and another in 1704. However, this was labeled as the fourth edition, since an irregular printing had appeared in Cambridge in 1693. The anonymous authors made no reference to Littleton, but it was generally acknowledged to be the effective third edition. To confuse matters further the edition of 1715, a reprint of the 1704, and like it displaying Littleton's name as author, is also labeled the "fourth edition."

Strictly speaking, Robert Ainsworth, whose *Thesaurus Linguae Latinae compendiarius* "or, a Compendious Dictionary of the Latin Tongue, designed principally for the use of the British Nations" appeared in 1736, falls outside the chronology of this seventeenth-century survey, but as what might be termed the "last of a line," he deserves inclusion. There would be other Latin dictionaries after his, but they would represent another, more specialized lexicography. The great compilations of the nineteenth century would undoubtedly surpass their predecessors, but their audience would be a specialized one, that of the university and the schoolroom, rather than of the larger world.

Ainsworth was born in 1660 in Woodyale near Manchester. He was educated in Bolton and later kept his own school there before moving to London *c.* 1698 and becoming headmaster of "a considerable boarding school" at Bethnal Green. He moved the school to Hackney where it prospered, and thence to various of London's "villages." By 1724, when he was elected a fellow of the Society of Antiquaries (there is an encomium in the first volume of the Society journal *Archaeologia*), Ainsworth had made enough money from his various schools to retire. Like a number of other dictionary writers, typically Budaeus and Robert Recorde, Ainsworth was also a numismatist and he made a large coin collection, gleaned alongside other small curiosities "procured at a small cost" from the London dealers. By 1743, thanks to his teaching and his collecting of both words and coins, he was a well-known figure. His fellow antiquary Thomas Hearne (1678–1735) notes:

Mr. Aynsworth formerly kept a boarding school and had a very flourishing
school. His wife is dead but he had no children. He is not in orders. He was
born in Lancashire, in which county he is about making a settlement,
being down there at present, for the poor forever, having no relations but
at a great distance. He hath been said to be a nonjuror. I think he is rather
a Calvinist . . . He hath a very great collection of coins. A maid servant
robbed him of many gold and silver ones. Dr. Midleton Massey is well
acquainted with him. He is well spoken of in Westminster school.[9]

Ainsworth was also acquainted with the pioneer Methodist Charles Wesley.
It is unknown whether his lexicographical labors inspired those of Charles'
brother John, whose own, very different dictionary appeared in 1753, but
Thomas Jackson, author of Charles Wesley's life, notes that "among those who
visited Charles at this time [May 1738] was the learned Mr Ainsworth, author
of the Latin Dictionary which bears his name. He was venerable through age,
and attended the methodist meetings for prayer and spiritual converse, in the
spirit of a little child." Writing in his *Journal* for May 12, 1738, Charles Wesley professed himself much moved at the sight of "Mr Ainsworth, a man of
great learning, above seventy, who, like old Simeon, was waiting to see the
Lord's salvation, that he might depart in peace. His tears, and vehemence, and
childlike simplicity, showed him upon the entrance of the kingdom of heaven."
A couple of weeks later, on May 24, Wesley reports that "I was much pleased
today at the sight of Mr Ainsworth; a little child, full of grief and fears, and
love. At our repeating the line of the hymn 'Now descend and shake the earth'
he fell down as in an agony."

Ainsworth died on April 4, 1743, aged eighty-two. He was buried at Poplar,
where a memorial, which he composed for himself and for his wife, reads:

> *Rob. Ainsworth et Uxor ejus, admodum senes*
> *Dormituri, vestem detritam hic exuerunt,*
> *Novam, primo mane surgentes, induturi.*
> *Dum fas, mortalis, sapias, et respice finem,*
> *Hoc suadent manes, hoc canit Amramides.*
> *To thy Reflection, mortal Friend,*
> *Th' Advice of Moses I commend;*
> *Be wise and meditate thy End.*

Aside from his lexicography Ainsworth was a notably progressive educator,
both for his own time and for many years to come. While teaching at Bethnal

Green he wrote "a very suggestive pamphlet" entitled *The most Natural and Easie Way of Institution:* "containing Proposals for making a Domestic Education less Chargeable to Parents and more Easie and Beneficial to Children. By which Method, Youth may not only make a very considerable Progress in Languages, but also in Arts and Sciences, in Two Years."[10] It appeared in 1698.

It is a remarkably forward-looking proposal, the basic tenet of which was Ainsworth's rejection of the current method of teaching languages—through their grammar—and his substitution of a system that he extended even to the classics. "I believe," he writes in his preface, "the Latin Tongue may be learn'd so far forth as to understand very well a Roman Author, to write Latin correctly and speak it fluently, and a considerable Knowledge attained in Arts and Sciences, by little Children, by the Proposals following, in two years time at most, and that with ease and pleasure, both to Master and Scholar."

Ainsworth goes on to outline a point-by-point proposal for carrying out his plan.

> Proposition (1) That a convenient House be taken, a small distance from London, with a large Garden and other Conveniencies. (2) That there be two Masters, whereof one to be capable of teaching Latin, Greek and Hebrew: The other, at least, to understand Latin and speak it fluently, to be well skilled in Logic, Rhetoric, Geography and History, and that he write a good Hand. (3) That Latin be made a Living Language in the Family, i.e. that no other language be us'd in presence of the Boys. (4) That one or both the Masters continually be present with the Pupils, whether Reading, Writing, Translating, or Playing from 7 in the morning till 8 at night. (5) That there be no Rods, or any kind of Punishment, but that a generous Emulation be carry'd on by Rewards to which use the parents shall allow—per Annum of which they to have an Account Monthly in a Latin Epistle, by which they may be inform'd both of their proficiency and Diligence, from time to time. (6) That the number of Pupils exceed not Twelve. (7) That they read English well, and that their Master take care to Improve it. (8) That they be not younger than Six, nor older than Eleven Years of Age. (9) That their Authors, and Masters, be their Grammar, Dictionary and Phrase-book. (10) That nothing be impos'd upon them as a task.

It does not appear that Ainsworth ever put his theories fully into practice, although one must hope that some permeated into the less experimental atmosphere of his London schools.

Ainsworth chose not to place his name on the title page of the first edition of this pamphlet, but he did add it to his dedication to Sir William Hustler, MP for Northallerton and a close acquaintance. And at the end he advertised that "Such as desire to discourse the Author on these Proposals, may hear of him at the Booksellers, or at the Marine Coffee House in Birchin Lane," after "Change, who can inform them of Undertakers." A second edition, slightly revised, came out in 1699; another, also called a second edition, was pirated by the notorious printer Edmund Curll in 1736. This was the least of Curll's crimes: he is best remembered as one of those who most impelled the authorities to establish literary censorship in England when in 1725 he was tried for the publication of *De Usu Flagorum in re Medica et Venerea* by John Henry Meibomius MD (a supposed manual of flagellation, but far more of a tedious medical textbook) and a new edition of Europe's current pornographic best-seller *Venus dans le Cloître, ou la religieuse en chemise* (Venus in the Cloister, or the Nun in her Smock). Alexander Pope, with whom he conducted a running battle, coined the term "Curllicism" to denote his iniquities.

Around 1714 a group of publishers approached Ainsworth with their plan for creating a new "Compendious English and Latin Dictionary." Ainsworth was keen, but the usual problems of compilation were accentuated by his age, and by his weakening eyes. Dr. Samuel Patrick was engaged to revise the copy once the first twelve sheets had been struck off the press. Patrick (1684–1748) was the second master at Charterhouse school. Late in life he became a doctor of law and also took holy orders, although he received no preferment. According to the *DNB* he "appears to have been . . . deeply read in the classics and ignorant and oblivious of most other matters."[11] Ainsworth was paid £666 17s. 6d. The book was envisaged as a schoolbook, hence no doubt the choice of author, but it gradually expanded into a wider market, especially through the addition of citations.

Ainsworth's Latin dictionary followed the pattern of many of its immediate predecessors. As laid out in the subtitle, it offered "The English Appellative Words and Forms of Expression before the Latin; in which will be found some thousand English Words and Phrases, several various Senses of the same Words, and a great number of proverbial Expressions, more than in any former Dictionary of this kind, all carefully endeavoured to be rendered in proper and classical Latin." He also included a number of proper and Christian names, "The ancient Latin Names of the more remarkable Persons and Places occurring in the classic Authors, with a short Account of them both historical and mythological; and the more modern Names of the same Places, so far as they are known, collected from the most approved Writers, to which are added 1. The

Roman Calendar, much fuller than any yet published. 2. Their Coins, Weights, and Measures. 3. A Chronology of the Roman Kings, Consuls, and more remarkable Events of that State. 4. The Notes of Abbreviation used in ancient Latin Authors and Inscriptions. 5. A short Dictionary of the more common Latin words occurring in our ancient Laws . . ."

Licensed by King George II, the work was dedicated to the "Very Learned" Richard Mead, the royal physician. Ainsworth included a Latin address to all lovers of pure Latin; and a lengthy preface in which he outlined the history of Latin-English lexicography and laid out a detailed plan of the new dictionary. By the time a new edition was required, Ainsworth had been forced into retirement, and Patrick and a new editor, Dr. John Ward, prepared the text, which appeared in 1740. Ainsworth received £250, £101 11s. 9d. went to Dr. Patrick and £25 5s. to Dr. Ward. There were seven further editions by 1829, when it lapsed.

Ward (1679?–1758) was a former clerk in the Navy Office who in 1710 had resigned in order to open a a school in Tenter Alley, Moorfields. Two years later he became one of earliest members of a nameless society composed of divines and lawyers who met to discuss the civil law or the law of nature and nations. In 1720 he was chosen to be professor of rhetoric at Gresham College, which had been founded in 1579 by Sir Thomas Gresham for the delivery of public lectures on Divinity, Music, Astronomy (Christopher Wren gave these under the Commonwealth), Geometry, Physics, Law, and Rhetoric. These Gresham lectures had led, in 1645, to the founding of the Royal Society for the Advancement of Natural Science, abbreviated today to the Royal Society. In 1723 Ward became a member of the Royal Society (Isaac Newton was president) and 1752 he became one of its vice presidents. In 1735 he was elected to the Society of Antiquaries, where presumably he met Robert Ainsworth; he became its vice president in 1743. Among Ward's many honors was that of being among the founding trustees of the British Museum.

Like the Latin-English dictionaries, the transvernacular and polyglot dictionaries of the sixteenth century intrude for a while into the new era. Once again, their publication signifies the end, rather than the beginning, of a trend, but their word lists reemerge in some of the century's mainstream works.

Calepino's polyglot *Dictionarium,* first published in England in 1585, had at its most expansive offered its readers eleven languages. The *Hegemon eis tas glossos, id est Ductor in Linguas, the Guide into Tongues* by John Minsheu, which appeared in 1617, was another massive polyglot, comprising English and ten other languages: Welsh, Low Dutch, High Dutch, French, Italian, Spanish, Portuguese, Latin, Greek, and Hebrew. It is the first English book to be printed by subscription, or at least the first one to carry a list of its subscribers: 174 are noted. As briefly apostrophized by the *DNB,* Minsheu "was poor, was married and had children."[12] He lived in London and made his living as a teacher of languages. Never wealthy, Minsheu found his lexicographical labors regularly halted for lack of cash, but he was equally regularly bailed out by generous friends such as the historian and antiquary Sir Henry Spelman (1564–1641), whose own glossary of legal terms appeared in 1638. While in Cambridge in order to finish off his Spanish dictionary Minsheu made many friends, some of whose names appear on his subscription list. He moved to Oxford to revise the *Ductor in Linguas,* but despite a certificate granted in 1610 by the university authorities saying that the "Dictionary" or "Guide" was worthy of publication, no one there subscribed. Minsheu appears to have been a laborious student who, it seems, worked himself to death. His finances were not improved by his assiduity in having his polyglot definitions checked by "a troop of scholars and foreigners."[13] Paying them ensured that he ran himself "into many and great debtes, unpossible for him ever to pay . . ."

As well as his polyglot work, Minsheu also specialized in Spanish and in 1599 had published a *Dictionary in Spanish and English* and a *Spanish Grammar.* Around 1617 he added a *Vocabularium Hispanico-Latinum et Anglicum copiosissimum.* In all these books Minsheu drew heavily on those of Richard Perceval (1550–1620) whose *Bibliotheca Hispanica,* "containing a Grammar with a Dictionarie in Spanish, English and Latin" had been published in 1591. As a young man Perceval infuriated his father by marrying one Joan Young, the daughter of an impoverished Dorset gentleman "with whom he had no fortune," and having "ruined himself by his riots, he was now left to recover himself by his wits." He moved to Spain, lived there for a while, and on his return was recruited through family connections by Lord Burghley, chief of domestic intelligence, who used him as a spy. Perceval is credited with deciphering the papers that in 1586 gave first news of the forthcoming Armada. This work gained him preferment at Court, notably as secretary to the Court of Wards. This improvement in Perceval's fortunes pleased his father, who left him an estate worth £1,700 a year. He was MP for Richmond, Yorkshire between 1603 and 1604, during which time he was involved in negotiations for the union of Scotland and England. When his patron Burghley died, Perceval lost his London jobs, but he was sent to Ireland as Registrar of the Court of Wards in 1616. He sold off the bulk of his estates and reinvested his profits in lands near Cork. He died in Dublin on September 4, 1620.

In Wheatley's opinion, Minsheu's work was "of so important and valuable a character that it marks an era in the history of Dictionaries"[14] but today it is probably most useful for those studying contemporary Elizabethan English. Joseph Worcester, writing three centuries later, notes that Minsheu undertook to explain the etymologies of most of the words included but, according to Sir John Hawkins, only managed 14,173 of them, thus, declared Hawkins, "the work must be deemed not sufficiently copious."[15]

One etymology Minsheu did attempt was that of *cockney,* and, however fanciful the remainder may be, in its first sentence he sets down an etymological cliché that has ever since been associated with the inhabitants of London's East End:

A Cockney or Cockny, applied only to one borne within the sound of Bow-bell, that is, within the City of London, which tearme came first out of this tale: That a Citizens sonne riding with his father out of London into the Country, and being a novice and merely ignorant how corne or cattell increased, asked, when he heard a horse neigh, what the horse did his father answered, the horse doth neigh; riding farther he heard a cocke crow, and said doth the cocke neigh too? and therefore Cockney or Cocknie, by inuersion thus: incock, q. incoctus i. raw or vnripe in Countrymens affaires.[16]

Less widely ranging, but equally important to seventeenth-century lexicographers, was *A Dictionarie of the French and English Tongues* (1611) by Randall Cotgrave. Cotgrave's biography is minimal: he was born in Cheshire and educated as a scholar of St. John's College, Cambridge *c.* 1587. He was subsequently made secretary to William Cecil, Lord Burghley, to whom he dedicated his book. He also presented a copy of the first edition to Prince Henry, the son of James I, from whom he received £10. As Henry Bradley describes it in the *DNB,* his dictionary, "although not free from ludicrous mistakes, was, for the time at which it was published, an unusually careful and intelligent piece of lexicographical work, and is still constantly referred to by students, both of English and of French philology."[17] Cotgrave was forced, on at least one occasion, to buy his own copies of the book. He paid 11s. apiece, and requested payment from the person to whom he gave them since "they cost me who have not been provident enough to reserve any of them, and therefore am forced to be beholden for them to a base and mechanicall generation that suffers no respect to weigh down a private gain." Fifty years later, on Shrove Tuesday 1661, the diarist Samuel Pepys gave a copy to "My lady Jemimah" at "Mr Crew's" (John Crew, Baron Crew of Stine). Later that day he was "very merry" and ate the best fritters of his life.[18] A second edition appeared in 1632, and Cotgrave died in 1634.

Given the mongrel nature of the English language, lexicographers quickly realized the need for establishing the etymology or roots of a given word. European writers such as Balbi and Calepino had shown the way, and such Latin-English dictionaries as those of Thomas Cooper and Thomas Thomas attempted to give some word origins. Cawdrey's *Table Alphabeticall,* the first published monolingual English dictionary, makes an attempt to include the most basic indications of a word's origin. For those terms which have their roots in Greek, Cawdrey inserts a bracketed *g* after the relevant entry. Blount offered etymologies, as did Phillips and Coles, but viewed with hindsight honed on the new developments of nineteenth- and twentieth-century philology, their efforts often appear as lamentably poor, even plainly absurd. Etymology would take on greater importance, if not always greater accuracy, in the eighteenth century, but the seventeenth does have a number of works upon which most of the mainstream lexicographers had no choice but to draw.

Some of these reflected what might be termed a backlash against the main thrust of contemporary lexicography: the classically based "hard-word" dictionaries. Scholars such as Sir John Cheke began demanding a return to the use of Anglo-Saxon and the late sixteenth and seventeenth centuries do see a revival in Anglo-Saxon studies. The fruits of this appear in such works as William Camden's history of the English language, *Britannia* (1586), as well as Verstegan's *Restitution of Decayed Intelligence* (1605), Davies' *Welsh-Latin Dictionary* (1632) and Sumner's *Dictionarium Saxonico-Latino-Anglicum* (1659). Two works, however, stand out.

What Wheatley terms "Dr Skinner's valuable Etymological Dictionary," the *Etymologicon Lingua Anglicanae,* appeared in 1671.[19] The named author, Stephen Skinner (1623–67), died before it was finished, but his manuscript was completed by Thomas Henshaw.

Skinner was born in London and educated at Oxford, where he graduated in 1639. A royalist, he left England shortly afterward, seeking to avoid the incipient Civil War. He served overseas, probably in Ireland. Back in Oxford in 1646, he took his B.A. and M.A. that year, and went on to study medicine at Leyden (1649) and Heidelberg (1653). During his travels he visited France, Germany, Italy, and the Netherlands, staying in a number of princely courts and making a wide circle of friends among Europe's intellectuals. On his return to England he began practicing as a doctor and in 1664 was made an honorary fellow of the Royal College of Physicians. He was based in Lincoln, where he died of a malignant fever in 1667. As well as his etymological dictionary, he left a number of philological treatises; edited by Thomas Henshaw they appeared as *Etymologicon Linguae Anglicanae.*

Skinner seems to have taken almost all his definitions from Edward Phillips, although he carefully avoids admitting to his predecessor's contribution and the link was not properly established until Albert Way, the editor of the *Promptorium parvulorum,* noted it in 1855. Indeed, the only mentions of Phillips by Skinner are determinedly negative: "[He] is asleep; he is miserably ignorant; the definition is a figment of the author's imagination" and the like. Skinner is undoubtedly flawed, but he has one point in his favor. Dr. Johnson used him extensively and notes in his preface: "For the Teutonick etymologies I am commonly indebted to Junius and Skinner, the only names which I have forborn to quote when I copied their books, not that I might appropriate their labours or usurp their honours, but that I might spare a perpetual repetition by one general acknowledgement . . ."[20] Skinner's stablemate "Junius" is Francis Junius (born François Du Jon, 1589–1677), "one of the most learned of philologists."[21] His *Etymologium Anglicanum,* although written much earlier, did not appear until it was published by the Anglo-Saxon and Gothic scholar Edward Lye (1694–1767) in 1743. In the interim it had been among those papers which Junius had bequeathed to Oxford's Bodleian Library. Lye's edition was prefaced by his own Anglo-Saxon grammar.

The second major etymological dictionary of the seventeenth century is the anonymously edited *Gazophylacium Anglicanum* "Containing the Derivation of English Words . . . Proving the Dutch and Saxon to be the prime Fountains. And likewise giving the similar words in most European Languages, whereby any of them may be indifferently well learned and understood. Fitted to the capacity of the English Reader, that may be curious to know the origin of his mother-tongue." It appeared in 1689 and again two years later. *Gazophylacium* dates to the fourteenth century and means strongbox or treasure chest; it comes from two Greek words: *gaza:* treasure and *phylassein:* to guard.

The anonymous author is enjoyably candid as to his motives, explaining in his preface that, "The chief reason why I busied myself herein, was to save my time from being worse employed . . . I have many things to alledge in defence of the weakness and inequality of this performance; as mainly its being collected at divers times, and in haste, because of my other more necessary business, as also, its being printed from a foul copy, and the like; which first may have alter'd the style, and the two last let many things pass muster, which, upon more mature deliberation, would not." And he adds a note explaining his method: "Observe that all along through the book, that word is set next to the English, from which I have judged it most likely to be derived; and the synonymous words of the other European languages follow: which shews, I have left it to the opinion of the Reader, to draw it from which he pleases. Moreover, by a curious reading hereof, any of the European languages may be indifferently well learned."

If one accepts that an assessment of current etymological theory gives a good indication of current lexicographical sophistication, then this extract from the preface offers a view of the way seventeenth-century wordmen saw the bases of their researches.

> The Confusion of Languages at Babel (for before it, all the then World spoke one and the same Dialect, supposed to be Hebrew) gave Rise to all the several Languages in the Universe; of which the primitive Language of this Nation was one; and, had it not been corrupted, perhaps as good and intelligible as the best; but being so alter'd by the aforesaid Accidents, it has quite lost its primitive Glory, as well as that of the French and other Nations.

So extensive is that corruption, and so mongrelized the old purities of Britain's native speech that

> when I look'd an hundred or an hundred and fifty Years only behind me, I could scarce imagine it ever to have been the Language of my Ancestors, or even of the country I was born in, 'tis so chang'd through Commerce, Correspondence, Travellers, and such like Accidents: Much more may you imagine it to be alter'd in a thousand or two thousand Years, by Conquests, Invasions, Transmigrations of the Government: So that . . . it is brought to what we now find it, even a Composition of most, if not all the Languages of Europe; especially the Belgick or Low-Dutch, Saxon, Teutonic or High Dutch, Cambro-British or Welsh, French, Spanish, Italian, and Latin; and now and then of the Old and Modern Danish, and Ancient High-Dutch; also of the Greek, Hebrew, Arabick, Chaldee, Syriack and Turckick.

Wheatley calls this "a curious and interesting Etymological Dictionary . . . though some of the etymologies are very absurd."[22] He cites as examples "Hasle-nut, from the AS. Haesl-nutu, the Belg. Hasel-noot, or the Teut. Hael-nux, the same; all perhaps from our word haste, because it is ripe before wall-nuts and chestnuts"[23] and "Hassock, from the Teut. Hase, an hare, and Socks; because hair-skins are sometimes worn instead of socks, to keep the feet warm in winter."[24] Wheatley does not wish, however, to mock for mockery's sake and undermines his critique with the remark that "It would not however be fair to judge the book from these extracts."[25] In the end the *Gazophylacium* is substantially indebted to Skinner, both in its etymologies, which are often imported wholesale, and for its inclusion of dialect terms, which again seem to have been copied, although they are now defined in English rather than in Latin.

8

The Early Eighteenth Century

E ighteenth-century lexicography was dominated by the growing desire to create what might be termed a "national language," a standard, fixed, refined
language that could stand with any in the world, especially that of France, where
such standards were already in place. It was assumed that language development,
in flux for several hundred years, had now reached a plateau of perfection. From
there it could only move in one direction: downhill. The intelligentsia, determined to avoid such a decline, believed, rightly or not, that by setting English in
linguistic aspic change could be arrested. There were a number of methods of carrying this out: for the lexicographers it meant the construction of a new type of
dictionary. "Hard words" were no longer enough. What was need was an all-
encompassing lexicon, what Noel Osselton has termed "a scholarly record of the
whole language."[1] Such aspirations would come to a climax in 1755, in the two
folio volumes of Samuel Johnson's *English Dictionary*.

One more piece of the jigsaw, however, was to be added before contemporary
lexicography reached this peak. The previous century's determination to compile and explicate "hard words" had been essentially accomplished by midcentury, when Blount and Phillips published their rival works, but there remained
another aspect of the language to be incorporated into the dictionaries: what
might be termed "easy words," i.e., the general vocabulary of spoken, rather
than literary or scholarly English. The task of adding such material to the basic
word list fell to a number of lexicographers, and the century has more than a
dozen dictionaries before Johnson's. Two men, however, stand out as preemi-

nent: John Kersey and Nathan or Nathaniel Bailey, who between them provide five of the new works. Neither Kersey nor Bailey seems to have been much concerned with lexicographical theory: the scholarly *Sturm und Drang* that underpinned Johnson, demanding that the language be in some way "fixed," rolled over or ran beside their efforts. Instead they seem simply to have got on with making their dictionaries, rather than worrying about the status of the terms they listed. "They were not . . . 'academic.' Throughout, their aims were populist and commercial, uninfluenced by any desire to outdo the Frenchies and save the national honour."[2] Both men, however, would have a substantial influence on Johnson, especially Bailey, whose *Dictionarium Britannicum* (1730), in a special edition interleaved for the purpose of manuscript additions, provided the backbone of his successor's researches.

Neither John Kersey nor Nathaniel Bailey, alas, has left much biographical detail. Kersey was the son of the mathematician John Kersey the Elder (1616–90?), whose treatise on algebra had become a recognized authority on the subject. His own dates are unknown. Kersey began his recorded career with the much expanded 1708 edition of Edward Phillips' *New World of Words* (see Chapter 6). However, as has been seen, there is a strong argument to attribute to him a previous work, *A New English Dictionary,* published in 1702 under the initials "J.K." It has never been possible to prove completely that John Kersey and "J.K." were one and the same—Wheatley is dubious,[3] Starnes and Noyes, although sympathetic, ultimately remain on the fence[4]—whatever the truth, and the evidence must point toward a confirmation of Kersey's role, this dictionary took a new step forward: the Latinized terms that had dominated earlier works were largely discarded, and in their place came the vocabulary of popular, everyday speech, making this, quite literally, an *English* dictionary.

J.K. brought together two traditions, both of which flourished in the seventeenth century: the "hard-word" dictionaries, and the grammars and spellers, which had forgone "hard words" in favor of those that could most easily be taught to the young. "The importance of this work . . . ," say Starnes and Noyes, "lies in its introduction into the English dictionary of the bulk of the English language—that is, of the essential words of daily speech, writing and reading . . . If J.K. could not at a single step close the gap between the two traditions and produce a modern dictionary with its tolerant inclusiveness and service to all types of people, he at least called attention to the forgotten words and the forgotten class of readers."[5]

In the tradition of dictionary prefaces, J.K. lists his predecessors and notes their failings. He judges that Elisha Coles, who in fairness had added dialect, slang, and a number of technical terms to the word list, still depended too heavily on a classical bias which accepted terms "which are scarce ever us'd by any ancient or modern Writer, even in a Figurative, Philosophical, or Poetical Sense." Even the dialect inclusions were "hard words" of their type and "a plain Country-man, in looking for a common English Word, amidst so vast a Wood of such as are above the reach of his Capacity, must needs lose the sight of it, and be extremely discouraged, if not forc'd to give over the search . . ."

In his dictionary J.K. was determined to list "the genuine and common significant Words of the *English* Tongue" that are so conspicuously absent from Coles and many like him. It was all well and good for such authors to pack their books with as wide a range of exotica as they could find, but in his labors he had preferred "to make a Collection of all the most proper and significant *English* Words, that are now commonly us'd either in Speech, in the familiar way of Writing Letters, &c.; omitting at the same time, such as are obsolete, barbarous, foreign or peculiar to the several Counties of England; as also many difficult, abstruse and uncouth Terms of Art, altogether unnecessary, nay even prejudicial to the endeavours of Beginners, and unlearned Persons, and whereof seldom any use does occur." A vocabulary composed of hard words, in the end, promoted affectation. There was no place in his English English Dictionary for those words that "were viciously introduc'd into our Language by those who sought to approve themselves Learned rather by unintelligible Words than by proper Language."

J.K.'s collection runs to approximately 28,000 words: few had ever appeared in an English dictionary, but most were to be found in contemporary spellers and elementary grammars. Thus, as Dr. P. W. Long suggests, this dictionary can be seen as an antecedent of the college and school dictionaries that begin with Wesley and flourish in the nineteenth century and beyond.[6] J.K. attempted to offer more substantial material, but like the spellers, which had the excuse of concentrating on the way a word was spelled, and not what it meant, his definitions often err toward the terse. This may have have stemmed from laziness or authorial inadequacy but it is, paradoxically, "an embarrassing fact in dictionary-making that the easiest words most persistently defy definition."[7] A second edition appeared in 1713, with only 21,000 headwords but including lists of given names (many of them the bizarre quasi-Biblical forms adopted by the Puritans, the more fanatical of whom employed not merely Charity, Mercy, and Patience but also Fight-the-good-fight-of-faith, Search-the-Scriptures, and Job-raked-out-of-the-Ashes) and nicknames.

J.K. remained a staple reference work, praised by Isaac Watts in his *Art of Reading and Writing* (1720) as the ideal basic dictionary. Later, in a note that was printed in successive editions of the dictionary, Watts declared that despite the appearances of Bailey's much larger work, "which may be very entertaining and useful to Persons of a polite education, yet for the bulk of mankind, this small one of J.K. is much more convenient; and I wish it were in the hands of all young persons, to acquaint them better with their mother-tongue."

There is no doubt that Kersey wrote the *Dictionarium Anglo-Britannicum,* "or a General English Dictionary, comprehending a brief, but emphatical and clear explication of all sorts of difficult words, that derive their original from other Ancient and Modern Languages; and also of all terms relating to Arts and Sciences both liberal and mechanical, . . . to which is added a large collection of Words and Phrases, as well Latin as English, made use of in our Ancient Statutes, old Records, Charters, Writs, and Processes at Law, never before publish'd in so small a volume: besides an interpretation of the proper names of Men and Women, and several other remarkable particulars mentioned in the preface. The whole work compil'd and methodically digested for the benefit of young students, tradesmen, artificers, foreigners, and others, who are desirous thoroughly to understand what they speak, read, or write. By John Kersey, Philobibl." (1708). It has no new material to offer, but it is the first ever abridged English dictionary, and thus launches a tradition that persists today in the *Shorter, Concise,* and other Oxford dictionaries, the many "college dictionaries" of America, and all their varied peers.

Writing in the preface, Kersey states that

This work must needs be of great use to . . . all persons who are desirous to inspect the vast treasures of our English tongue, which is so superlatively eminent, even above most other European languages, for its copiousness, elegancy, variety of phrases, and other admirable beauties: but if any are for making a more strict search into the imnost recesses of this imperial mine, they need only have recourse to the last edition of Phillips's Dictionary set forth by us, with very large additions and improvements, an. 1706, where they'll find the various sorts of rich Oar [ore] amply display'd in their natural Order and Position.

Among the dictionary's users was the young poet Thomas Chatterton, who killed himself while still in his teens; he discovered much of the archaic vocabulary he preferred in Kersey's pages. A great consulter of wordbooks, he also used Skinner's *Etymologicon Linguae Anglicanae,* Verstegan's *Restitution,* and the works of Kersey's successor, Nathaniel Bailey.

Bailey's first work *A Universal Etymological English Dictionary,* appeared in 1721, his more influential one arrived nine years later. "Of the compiler," says the *DNB,* "nothing is known except for the fact that he belonged to the 7th Day Baptists . . . and kept a boarding school at Stepney, where he died on 27 June 1742." An advertisement included in the first edition states "Youth Boarded, and taught the Hebrew, Greek and Latin languages, in a Method more Easy and Expedient than is common . . . by the *Author* of this *Dictionary.*" Despite this attempt to boost his finances, Bailey was first and foremost a professional lexicographer whose life was devoted to making dictionaries. As well as those cited here, he authored the *Dictionarium Domnesticum* (1736); the *Dictionarium Rusticum, Urbanicum & Botanicum* (1704) has no signature but is generally credited to Bailey. His influence was profound. Bailey is the first lexicographer really to lay out the language as it is, taboo words, slang, and all. He also offers usage guidance, notes on word stress, pronunciation, and so on. He was one also of the first dictionary makers to aim for comprehensiveness and his major work, the *Dictionarium Britannicum,* actually contains more definitions than that of Johnson. It would become the basis for the Doctor's own epochal effort and would run to thirty editions in all. Like Johnson, Bailey was backed by a group of booksellers, notably Charles Rivington and A. Bettesworth, who would go on to form the "New Conger" (*B. E.'s Dictionary of the Canting Crew* defines *Conger* as "a Set or Knot of Topping Book-sellers of London"), a trade association aimed at breaking the monopoly of the "Old Conger" that preceded them.

The scope of Bailey's first dictionary is displayed in the full title: *A Universal Etymological English Dictionary* "Comprehending The Derivations of the Generality of Words in the English tongue, either Antient or Modern, from the Antient British, Saxon, Danish, Norman and Modern French, Teutonic, Dutch, Spanish, Italian, Latin, Greek, and Hebrew Languages, each in their proper Characters. And Also A Brief and clear Explication of all difficult Words . . . and Terms of Art relating to Anatomy, Botany, Physick, . . . Together with A Large Collection and Explication of Words and Phrases us'd in our Antient Statutes, Charters, Writs, Old Records, and Processes at Law; and the Etymology and Interpretation of the Proper Names of Men, Women, and Remarkable Places in Great Britain: Also the Dialects of our Different Counties. Containing many Thousand Words more than either Harris, Phillips, Kersey, or any English Dictionary before Extant. To which is Added a Collection of our most Common Proverbs, with their Explication and Illustration. The whole work compil'd and Methodically digested, as well for the Entertainment of the Curious as the Information of the Ignorant, and for the Benefit of young Students, Artificers, Tradesmen and Foreigners . . ."

Bailey has never been accorded the degree of reverence allotted his successor and rival, Samuel Johnson, but on the basis of sales his was the most popular and representative dictionary of the century. The Prime Minister Earl Chatham, while hardly an "Artificer" let alone a "Foreigner," supposedly read it twice, from cover to cover. Bailey's importance is summarized in Edward Horwood's preface to the 1782 edition, which exalts the lexicographer as "one of God's creatures . . . by his divine benevolence, originally predestinated to this great and useful end." Johnson is, of course, admirable, but

> The Character of Bailey's Dictionary hath long been deservedly established and through a series of many years hath acquired a just reputation, which the numerous competitors we have lately seen hath not been able to eclipse . . . The peculiar and unrivaled Excellence of this Work is the definition and explanation of many hundred technical terms, which belong to respective Sciences, which are not found in other Dictionaries. Particularly are the terms in Anatomy, Physic, Natural Philosophy, and the Mathematics concisely and familiarly illustrated in this Thesaurus. In short, its principal excellence is, that it is a Scientific Dictionary . . . The Etymological part is written in plain and easy language, the hard and obscure words not rendered harder and obscurer by a studied pomp and ostentation of diction, but everything is treated with perspicuity as well as erudition, Mr. Bailey possessing a happy method of communicating his ideas.

Bailey amasses around 40,000 headwords, a couple of thousand more than Kersey's revision of Phillips. Among them were "several 1000 *English* Words and Phrases, in no *English* Dictionary before extant." He included proverbs, some ninety in all, as well as a good deal of dialect (from Kersey and before him Coles) and cant and reinstates a variety of obsolete words that had been dropped in more recent dictionaries. But Bailey's great importance is his promotion of etymology as an integral part of the dictionary, a role that, certainly in major dictionaries, it has never lost. Somewhat boastfully he claimed to be the first lexicographer to take this step, "except what Mr Blount has done in his Glossographia, which is but a very small Part, and those of a *Latin* derivation chiefly, besides a small extract of Dr *Skinner's Etymologicon*." But he goes on to admit that in fact he has copied the efforts of others, and name-checks Somner, Camden, Verstegan, Spelman, Casaubon, Thomas Henshaw, Skinner, Junius, Menagius, Minsheu "and other great Names and approved Etymologists . . ."

Bailey's second dictionary, *The Universal Etymological English Dictionary,* appeared in 1727. Backed this time by a single publisher, Thomas Cox, who would also publish the *Dictionarium Britannicum,* it was billed as the second volume of the 1721 work, but appears rather to have been issued to pave the way for the more influential *Dictionarium*. Other than "some thousands of Words not in the former Volume, with their Etymologies and Explications," Bailey's revised work covered much of the same ground as did its predecessor. He dealt again with proper names, anatomy, and orthography, although the title page no longer offered dialect or proverbs. There was, however, "The Theogony, Theology, and Mythology of the Egyptians, Greeks, Romans, &c. being an Account of their Deities, Solemnities, Religious or Civil, Oracles, Auguries, Hieroglyphicks, &c. necessary to be understood: especially by the Readers of English Poetry."

Bailey's preface explains that this volume contains the material for which he had no space in volume one plus that which he has subsequently picked up through his own researches and through contributions from "Persons of generous and communicative Dispositions." He also prompts readers to note his extensive use of woodcut illustrations. His accentuation of words make this the first dictionary to do so, although spellers and and grammars had been inserting accents, as punctuation guides, for some time. According to Starnes and Noyes, this move comes from the popularity of Thomas Dyche's *Guide to the English Tongue* (1709) and from the public's desire to know how properly to pronounce all the new technical terms Bailey was including.[8] He modified a number of etymologies, preferring to categorize them as "uncertain" rather than guessing and getting it wrong.

The word list included a number of extra "hard words," and longer definitions, but its main interest is in the large technical vocabulary, an area that was expanded even further in the third edition of 1737. Bailey includes the jargon of heraldry, horsemanship, navigation, military science, and law. The third edition also included a much enlarged cant vocabulary "for the Satisfaction (but not the Imitation) of the Curious." Unlike the original, 1721 dictionary, these terms were no longer scattered alphabetically through the text, but unified in a 36-page "supplement." Most of the material simply replicates Head's *New Canting Dictionary* (1725), the latest dedicated cant collection.

After Bailey's death in 1742 there were two more editions, notably the fifth (1760) in which the editor, James Buchanan, included illustrative citations on the pattern of Dr. Johnson—many indeed were straight lifts from Johnson's dictionary. Buchanan was the author of *Linguae Britannicae vera Pronunciatio,* "or, A New English Dictionary" (1757); and an "Essay towards establishing a Standard for an Elegant and Uniform Pronunciation of the English language" (1766).

In 1730 appeared Bailey's crowning achievement, "the greatest lexicographical work yet undertaken in English,"[9] the *Dictionarium Britannicum* "Or, a more

Compleat Universal Etymological English Dictionary than any Extant. Containing Not only the Words, and their Explications; but their Etymologies . . . Also Explaining hard and technical Words, or Terms of Art, in all the Arts, Sciences, and Mysteries following. Together with Accents directing to their proper Pronuntiation, shewing both the Orthography and Orthoepia of the English Tongue . . . Illustrated with near Five Hundred Cuts . . . Likewise A Collection and Explanation of Words and Phrases us'd in our antient Charters, Statutes, Writs, Old Records and Processes at Law. Also The Theogony, Theology, and Mythology of the Egyptians, Greeks, Romans &c . . . To which is added, A Collection of Proper Names of Persons and Places in Great-Britain, with their Etymologies and Explications. The Whole digested into an Alphabetical Order, not only for the Information of the Ignorant, but the Entertainment of the Curious; and also the Benefit of Artificers, Tradesmen, Young Students and Foreigners . . . Collected by several Hands, The Mathematical Part by G. Gordon, the Botanical by P. Miller. The Whole Revis'd and Improv'd, with many thousand Additions, By N. Bailey, Philologos."

This would be the working base for Johnson, whose interleaved copy held his additions and amendments. In it Bailey demonstrates the extent to which his professionalism has moved lexicography into a new world: as in his earlier works he displays the English language in as far as possible its entirety, accepting dialect, slang, and technical jargon. One area that would not be included in Johnson was that of the taboo terminology that Bailey, keen on comprehensiveness, offered users. Among others he has *shite,* "to ease Nature, to discharge the Belly," and *fuck,* with a full etymology, although the definition, *Foeminam subagitare,* remained for classicists only. The word list aside, his directions on usage and other guidelines brought out once more the extent to which Bailey was moving lexicography forward. Its 48,000 headwords take the best from the two volumes of the *Universal Etymological English Dictionary* and add some extra material. The more esoteric words are dropped, while others have near-encyclopedic entries. "Gothick Building," for instance, has a 200-word entry, plus subsections for "Antient" and "Modern Gothick Architecture" and space for Bailey's own opinions, e.g., "Antient Gothick Architecture . . . [is] exceeding massive, heavy and coarse." Much of this material was plucked from a new work, Ephraim Chambers' pioneering *Cyclopedia, Or, An Universal Dictionary of Arts and Sciences* (1728). Aside from eliminating the transient proverbs, and dividing the categories of proper nouns—the mythologic and legendary ones are in the main text, the historical and geographical are in a separate list—Bailey's major innovation is in his building up of "word families" arranged in orderly fashion with all derivations and related expressions, a policy that prefigures the massive linked collections that appear classically in the *OED*.

The second edition of 1736 offered "numerous Additions and Improvements," and credited a collaborator on the etymologies: "T. Lediard, Gent. Professor of the Modern Languages in Lower Germany." The headwords now number 60,000. Bailey adds a preface, which he had neglected six years earlier, in which he traces the history of language since Babel. Preeminent among the world's many tongues is, unsurprisingly, English, a language which "has been compar'd to the River *Nile,* in that it preserves a Majesty, even in Abundance" and which, unlike French and Italian, is "of a masculine quality." It is also "the closest, clearest, most chaste and reserv'd in its Diction . . . and also the most just and severe in its Ornaments and also the honestest, most open and undesigning." The partiality for personal reflection that was seen in the earlier edition is extended with the reintroduction of proverbs. Not only does Bailey cite the original phrase, but adds his own facetious addendum, e.g., *"Maidens must be true and meek | Swift to hear, and slow to speak.* This us'd to be the advice of mothers to their daughters in former days: but the most seem to be of another mind nowadays, and to think nothing is prettier than to let their *Tongues run before their Wit"* and *"Pride goes before, | Shame follows after. Or, Pride goes before a Fall.* It generally happens so." Nor was he always so terse: *A Rolling Stone gathers no Moss* needs 125 words of moralizing explanation, plus Latin, Greek, French, and Italian versions of the same concept.

Bailey's dictionary has now become a monster, packed full of words and information. The question remains, however, is the work, in the strictest of senses, still a dictionary? Not only are the proverbs reinstated, but Bailey now includes the "Iconology of the Ancients," mixing legends, historical facts, interpretations, and so on, gleaned from a vast range of sources both factual and fantastic. It all makes for wonderful reading, especially the etymologies, but "when so much colourful material is incorporated, the more pedestrian tasks of the lexicographer are naturally neglected, and the result is an 'all-purpose' reference book rather than a fine dictionary."[10] Chambers' declaration in his *Cyclopedia* that "the Analogy between a *Dictionary* and a History is closer than People may at first imagine . . ." has proved too alluring and Bailey's last work, completed six years before his death, is fascinating, certainly, but ultimately a somewhat self-indulgent encyclopedia rather than a simple wordbook.

One last Bailey must be noted, the *New Universal English Dictionary,* which appeared a few months after Johnson's *English Dictionary,* in 1755. According to its title page it had been extensively revised by a new compiler, Joseph Nicol Scott. Scott, a dissenting minister and physician, was born *c.* 1703 in Hitchin,

Staffordshire, the son of Thomas Scott, an independent minister. By 1725 he had become his father's assistant at the Old Meeting, in Norwich, but his increasing interest in Arianism led to his dismissal—a terrible blow to his father, "one of the holiest and most benevolent men upon the earth"[11]—who died aged sixty-six in 1646, "permanently unhinged"[12] since the rift. Scott gained a Sunday lectureship at the French church of St. Mary the Lees in Norwich to which he initially attracted large crowds. He published his sermons, which, *inter alia,* promoted the belief in the ultimate and total annihilation of the sinful. He then moved to Edinburgh to study medicine, and subsequently to Felsted in Essex when an admirer, a Mr. Reynolds, bequeathed him an estate there. He lived out his life in Essex, dying in 1769.

Scott was no lexicographer and the publication of this revised version of Bailey was strictly a booksellers' scheme, designed to challenge Johnson's success. Thus they used Scott as a name that the public would recognize. He wrote the preface and corrected a number of those entries of which he had knowledge (medical and religious), but probably did no more real "revision." The "Scott-Bailey" is bigger than Johnson, 65,000 entries to Johnson's 40,000, and manages to cram itself into a single volume. It also cost half the price. Where the book betrays its publishers' motives is in its unabashed theft from Johnson. The "elaborate Mr Johnson" is duly credited as a source, but the extent of what critics have termed unabashed theft is naturally bypassed. As Philip Gove, later editor of *Webster's Third International* and who in 1940 analyzed Scott's appropriations, put it, "To be charitable, one may say it is modeled on Johnson."[13] In fact Gove's essay is rather less than forgiving, referring to "the indebtedness of a servile but dully alert mind," to "downright copying" and to the fact that "the Bailey-Scott Dictionary owes its principal merit largely to Johnson's involuntary contribution."[14]

Scott himself, aware no doubt that his stratagems were all too transparent, mounted the pulpit to declare in his preface that the compilation of a dictionary is as much a spiritual as a secular task, saying that "Words are the Medium . . . thro' which we come at TRUTH." He attempts to preempt possible attacks by denying any out-and-out plagiarism: "We . . . are not mere Copyists from others; . . . not taking Things upon Trust, as is too often done; but having traced them up to the *Fountainheads . . .*" Gove, at least, finds this hard to swallow and points out that "A glance at any page of Bailey will reveal that line after line is rankly plagiarized from Johnson."[15] Nor is the pious Scott above snapping at the hand that has dictated so many of his entries. In what has to be seen as a sneer at Johnson's orotund phraseology, he notes, "As to our Style, we have chosen the plain and unadorned; as best suiting Works of this Nature; and indeed the *florid* Diction is an artifice too often used to cover a *poverty* of Thought . . . Wheras our chief Ambition has been to advance the Truth; and not to amuse our Readers with *historic Romance,* and *scholastic Jargon . . .*"

What Scott in his own defense and Gove as counsel for the prosecution both overlook, and which Starnes and Noyes, among others, make clear,[16] is that Johnson himself had already borrowed substantially from Bailey. He may not have ransacked the *Dictionarium Britannicum* to the extent that Scott plundered the *English Dictionary,* but as Allen Riddick notes, "In his initial uncertainty Johnson appears to have relied fairly heavily on the dictionaries of his predecessors, notably the *Dictionarium Britannicum.*"[17] and Johnson himself, in his preface, declares that "many words yet stand supported only by the name of Bailey, Ainsworth, Phillips."[18] It is also arguable that by contemporary standards Scott felt his tip of the hat toward Johnson was quite sufficient and that, over and above such borrowings, there is a good deal of material over which the most ardent Johnsonian has no claim.

Only a virtual line-by-line comparison, for which there is no space here, can properly lay out the differences and the similarities between the two books. History, for whatever reason, has favored Johnson, and while the *OED* has more than 5,700 citations from Bailey, Johnson's contribution is so massive that, aside from a similar amount of quotations from nonlexicographical works, borrowings from his dictionary are signified by a simple (J.). Johnson's status as a public figure, his scholarship, his powers of self-promotion and even his longevity (he outlived Bailey by forty-two years), undoubtedly helped. But in the end it is the quality of his work, as will be seen in the following chapter, that most impressively proves his superiority.

The flow of eighteenth-century dictionaries prior to Johnson was by no means restricted to the efforts of Kersey and Bailey. There are also the works of B. N. Defoe (*A Compleat English Dictionary,* 1735), J. Sparrow (*A New English Dictionary,* 1739), and James Manlove (*A New Dictionary,* 1741) as well as the anonymous *Pocket Dictionary* (1753). Francis Junius' *Etymological Dictionary* or *Etymologium Anglicanum,* upon which Johnson relied so heavily for his etymologies, was published in 1743.

Given his influence on Bailey, whose second volume of the *Universal Etymological English Dictionary* owes something to the *Guide to the English Tongue* (1709), it is worth giving a little more space to *A New General English Dictionary,* compiled by Thomas Dyche, with the help of William Pardon, in 1735. Pardon remains an anonymous figure other than in his name, but Dyche was born in Derbyshire and thence moved to London. In 1708 he was keeping a school near Fetter Lane, and by 1710 was headmaster of the free school at Stratford Bow. Nine years later he attempted to expose in print the peculations of one John Ward of Hackney "in discharge of [Ward's] trust in repairing Dagnam (Dagenham) Breach." Dagenham Breach was originally a 400-foot gap in the Thames Wall, which had caused a large mudbank to gather in the river, thus endangering shipping. It was not repaired until an act of Parliament, passed in 1714, ordered the work. Ward duly carried it out, and what remained was a 1,000-acre lake, which was promptly taken over by East London's anglers. The tradition of "whitebait dinners," attended by Cabinet Ministers and held at the Ship Inn in Greenwich on or near Trinity Sunday originated in this work. The original dinners were held in Dagenham, by the commissioners supervising the repairs. The custom began when the prime minister was invited to join the meal. It lapsed in 1894. Quite what Ward's alleged "peculations" were has been forgotten, but he sued Dyche for libel in June 1719 and won himself £300 in damages. Dyche died sometime between 1731 and 1735 and left a family who are mentioned in the dedication to his *Spelling Dictionary.*

Dyche is responsible for three major works. The two-part *Guide to the English Tongue* had amassed forty-eight editions by 1774 and was still appearing in 1830. Its most important aspect was Dyche's interest in proper pronunciation and his desire for the child to avoid "vicious Pronunciation." It was prefaced by a verse by the poet laureate Nahum Tate (1652–1715), dedicated to "my ingenious Friend the Author," and one by another, lesser versifier, John Williams: "This just essay you have perform'd so well | Records will shew 'twas Dyche first taught to spell." Dyche followed the *Guide* with *The Spelling Dictionary,* "or a Collection of all the Common Words . . . Us'd in the English Tongue; And of the most usual Proper Names; With Accents, directing to their true Pronunciation" (1725). It is less a dictionary proper than an extension of the *Guide.* In it Dyche suggests various spelling reforms, such as the dropping of the *-ck* ending and its alteration to a simple *-c* (e.g., logick to logic, physick to physic, etc.), the reducing of *-ll* to *-l*, *-our* to *-or* (e.g., authour to author), and the dropping of the final *e* unless it is necessary to lengthen a syllable. Many of these innovations were duly adopted.

Ten years later Dyche produced a real dictionary: *A New General English Dictionary* "Peculiarly calculated for the Use and Improvement Of such as are unacquainted with the Learned Languages. Wherein the Difficult Words, and Technical Terms made use of in Anatomy, . . . Are not only fully explain'd, but accented on their proper Syllable, to prevent a vicious Pronunciation; and mark'd with Initial Letters, to denote the Part of Speech to which each Word peculiarly belongs. To which is prefixed, A Compendious English Grammar . . . Together with A Supplement, Of the Proper Names of the most noted

Kingdoms, Provinces, Cities, Towns, Rivers, &c. throughout the known world. As Also Of the most celebrated Emperors, Kings, Queens, Priests, Poets, Philosophers, Generals, &c. . . . The Whole Alphabetically digested, and accented . . ." It ran to eighteen editions between 1735 and 1794, including a French one in 1756.

Unlike Bailey and Johnson, Dyche and Pardon's effort was consciously downmarket. Bailey could have the intellectuals, but they had another target group: "The Whole is intended for the Information of the Unlearned, and particularly recommended to those Boarding-Schools, where *English* only is taught, as is the Case commonly among the Ladies, by a careful Use whereof I doubt not but the Teachers will soon find the Benefit from the Improvement their Scholars will insensibly make, not only in Orthography, or true Spelling, but in Writing coherently and correctly, the Want whereof is universally complained of among the Fair Sex." This was a dictionary geared to those whose intellectual demands were limited: "Derivations and Etymologies are entirely left out: First, because of their Uncertainty, . . . secondly, upon account of their Uselessness to those Persons that these Sort of Books are most helpful to, which are commonly such, whose Education, Reading, and Leisure, are bounded within a narrow Compass; and therefore such Helps and Hints, as were judged more universally beneficial, are substituted . . ." In many ways this can be seen as a "hard-word" dictionary for the mass market. Its basic entry takes a relatively complex word, then explains it in a simple, educational definition. Unlike the "hard-word" dictionaries, however, Dyche and Pardon offer, as did their more intellectually driven peers, a good deal of technical terminology and encyclopedic material, albeit reduced to the simplest of definitions. They include a "Compendious English Grammar": nine pages of tiny print which discuss various aspects of grammar and suggest how useful grammatical information is in a dictionary. A second edition appeared in 1744 adding 3,000 new terms, most of which deal with the market towns of England and Wales and list such details about each as their MP, the market day, the distance from London, and the like. Subsequent editions added more words, and by the final "much revised" edition of 1794 the old 20,000-strong word list had reached 30,000 words, many of which dealt with the vocabulary of natural history.

Dyche's preoccupation with providing a dictionary geared to the mass rather than the élite market is reflected in another book that appeared soon after his: *The Complete English Dictionary*, "Explaining most of those Hard Words, Which are found in the Best English Writers. By a Lover of Good English and Common Sense," appeared in 1753. Its compiler, determined to leave no one in doubt as to the excellence of his work, appended to his title a note: "NB: The Author assures

1. Sir James Murray (1837–1915)

2. The *Promptorium parvulorum* (?1440)

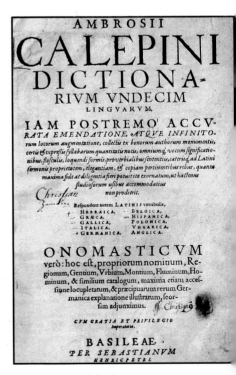

3. The *Medulla grammatice* (mid-fifteenth century)

4. The *Catholicon Anglicum* (1483)

5. Ambrosio Calepino, *Dictionarium . . .* (1502)

6. John Withals, *A Shorte Dictionarie . . .*
(1529). Illustration shows a later edition.

> A
> DICTIONARY
> IN ENGLISH AND LA-
> TINE; DEVISED FOR
> the capacitie of Children,
> *and young Beginners.*
>
> At first set forth by M. *Withals,*
> with Phrases both Rythmicall and
> Proverbiall: Recognized by D! *Evans* ;
> *after by* Abr. Fleming : *and then
> by* William Clerk.
>
> And now at this last Impression enlar-
> ged with an encrease of *Words, Sentences,
> Phrases, Epigrams, Histories, Poeticall
> fictions,* and *Alphabeticall Proverbs* ;
> With a compendious Nomenclator
> newly added at the end.
>
> Corrected and amended in divers places.
>
> *All composed for the ease, profit, and delight of*
> those that desire Instruction, and the better
> perfection of the Latine tongue.
>
> *Initio facilima, & optima sunt discenda. B. R.*
>
> Printed at *London* by *Thomas Purfoot.*
> 1634.

7. Thomas Thomas, *Dictionarium . . .*
(1587)

> ILLVSTRISSIMO
> DOMINO FRANCISCO, BARONI
> *VERVLAMIÆ,* SVMMO ANGLIÆ
> CANCELLARIO, AVGVSTISSIMO
> IACOBO MAGNÆ BRITANNIÆ,
> FRANC. ET HIBER. REGI A SANCTIO-
> RIBVS CONSILIIS, ALMAE MATRIS
> Academiæ Cantabrigiensis olim alumno dig-
> nissimo, nunc Patrono benignissimo.

8. A detail from a page of John Florio,
A New World of Words (1599)

> Fossina, *a little* Fóssa. *Also a long pole
>   to bob for Eeles.*
> Fósso, *as* Fóssa.
> Fóssola, *as* Fóssa.
> Fossoláre, *as* Fossáre.
> Fóssole, *a kinde of disease in a mans
>   eies.*
> Fóstu, *for* Tù fósti, *thou wast.*
> Fottárie, *iapings, fuckings, swiuings.*
> Fottènte, *fucking, swiuing, sarding.*
> Fóttere, fótto, fottéi, fottúto, *to iape, to
>   flucke, to sard, to swiue.*
> Fotterígia, *a cramp-fish.*
> Fótti, *I doe or make the.*
> Fótti, *iape thow.*
> Fottistério, *a bawdy or occupying-house.
>   Also the mistery of fucking.*
> Fottitríce, *a woman occupier.*
> Fottitóre, *a man occupier, a iaper, a swi-
>   uer, a sarder. Also a rammer.*
> Fottitúra, *a iaping, a fucking, a sarding.*
> Fottiuénti, *wind-fuckere, stamels.*
> Fottúta, *as* Fottitúra.

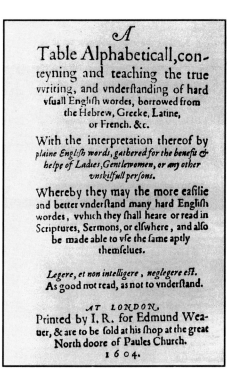

9. Robert Cawdrey, *A Table Alphabeticall*
(1604)

> A
> Table Alphabeticall, con-
> teyning and teaching the true
> vvriting, and vnderstanding of hard
> vsuall English wordes, borrowed from
> the Hebrew, Greeke, Latine,
> or French. &c.
>
> With the interpretation thereof by
> *plaine English words, gathered for the benefit &
> helpe of Ladies, Gentlewomen, or any other
> vnskilfull persons.*
>
> Whereby they may the more easilie
> and better vnderstand many hard English
> wordes, vvhich they shall heare or read in
> Scriptures, Sermons, or elswhere, and also
> be made able to vse the same aptly
> themselues.
>
> *Legere, et non intelligere, neglegere est.*
> As good not read, as not to vnderstand.
>
> *AT LONDON,*
> Printed by I. R. for Edmund Wea-
> uer, & are to be sold at his shop at the great
> North doore of Paules Church.
> 1604.

10. Sir Thomas Elyot (?1490–1546)

11. John Florio (c.1553–1625)

12. Samuel Johnson (1709–84)

13. Samuel Johnson, *A Dictionary of the English Language* (1755)

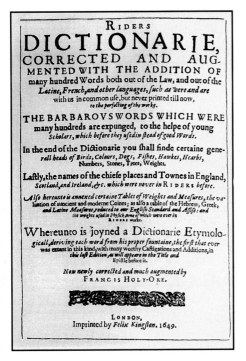

14. Holyoake's revision of John Rider, *Bibliotheca Scholastica* (1649)

15. Edward Phillips, *The New World of English Words* (1658)

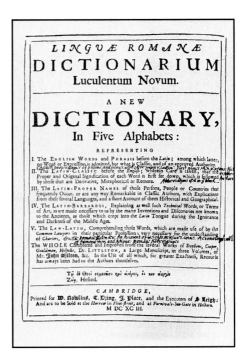

16. John Baret, *An Alvearie or Triple Dictionarie* (1673)

17. Adam Littleton, *Linguae Romanae Dictionarium* (pirated edition 1693)

18. Robert Copland, *The hye way to the Spyttell hous* (c.1535)

19. Thomas Harman, *A Caveat or Warening for Commen Cursetors* (1567)

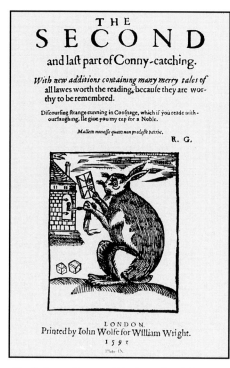

20. Robert Greene, *The Second and last part of Conny-catching* (1592)

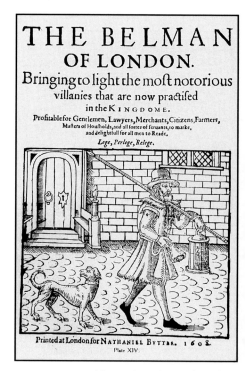

21. Thomas Dekker, *The Belman of London* (1608)

22. Francis Grose (*c.*1730–91)

23. James Hardy Vaux (*c.*1783–185?)

24. Eric Partridge (1894–1979)

25. Noah Webster (1758–1843)

26. Joseph Emerson Worcester (1784–1865)

27. Frederick Furnivall (1825–1910)

28. Henry Bradley (1845–1923)

you that he thinks this is the best English Dictionary in the World." That author, it transpired, was more usually known as the Methodist pioneer John Wesley, whose life is generally recalled in contexts other than the lexicographic. However, his drive for mass literacy, and the dictionary he provided to fuel it, laid the groundwork for the flood of popular, rather than scholarly dictionaries that began emerging, especially in America, during the nineteenth century.

John Wesley (1703–91) actually knew Johnson, who found him a good conversationalist, but "never at leisure," and for all that Wesley had a similar educational background—Oxford University—and a similar appreciation of English literature and reverence for the Christian religion, the two men could not have been less similar. The pious, self-denying Wesley would never have been elected to Johnson's Club. He had his own coterie, which had developed at university. Along with his brother Charles and George Whitefield (later to break away and found his own Methodist splinter group) he exhibited such piety, some might say priggishness, that their circle was nicknamed the "Holy Club." Another nickname was the "Methodists" and it was this name that Wesley embraced when in 1738 he opened the first Methodist chapel, in Bristol.

Wesley's own works would run to some thirty-four volumes, and he never faltered in his belief in the importance of literacy. "Reading Christians," he declared, "will be knowing Christians." But while he and other Methodist leaders might be as cultured as any of their educated peers, the vast majority of their followers had enjoyed no such privileges. Working- and lower-middle-class, they were badly educated, if at all. Wesley aimed to change all that and urged his followers to read. It was suggested that they put in five hours a day on their books—which must have comprised most of their available free time—and in 1740 he set up the the Methodist Book Room in London. Each chapel had a permanent display of books and traveling Methodist preachers never set off on a journey without stocking up with cheap reading matter. Foremost among such books and pamphlets were Wesley's own writings. Over the years he amassed as much as £40,000 from sales of his books and to those critics who caviled at such commercialism he replied that people would gain far more value from a book for which they had paid, than from something handed out for free. And as Richard Altick has suggested, "This argument is not as ingenuous as it seems; quite probably Wesley's publications, for which a small fee was charged, were more respected by the people to whom they were addressed than the free tracts which were to be broadcast the length and breadth of England."[19] Louis B. Wright makes a similar point: "While Pope and Johnson held in succession the dictatorship in the narrow circle of letters, Wesley preached salvation and intelligence to the teeming proletariat and lower middle-class. What Wesley said about books meant infinitely more to his followers than did Dr. Johnson's ponderous dicta. Although Wesley left no impress upon the literary development of the age, he did powerfully influence the developing literary taste of a large segment of the British and even the American public."[20]

As well as offering his own efforts, Wesley tried to make at least what he felt were the acceptable literary classics available to the "common reader." In 1743 he produced an edition of Bunyan's *Pilgrim's Progress,* offering it in a pocket-sized format at fourpence a copy. In 1763 he condensed *Paradise Lost.* Other works included *A Concise Ecclesiastical History, The Concise History of England, A Collection of Moral and Sacred Poems* (1744), and his *chef d'oeuvre,* the *Christian Library:* "Consisting of Extracts from, and Abridgements of, the Choicest Pieces of Practical Divinity which have been published in the English Tongue" (1749–55). Like everything Wesley produced, all these had been subjected to a strict Methodist filter: less a censor than a bowdlerizer, Wesley cut, compressed, even rewrote in order to ensure that his followers were always being imbued with Methodist ideology, whether overtly theological or not. That said, he was still offering people who would otherwise have experienced little or no "culture" an insight to a wider world. Intolerant of what he termed "the superfluity of words" he aimed to put over concepts "in the plainest dress: simply and nakedly expressed, in the most clear, easy and intelligible manner."[21] Writing in 1764 to the Rev. Samuel Furly, he emphasized that "Clearness, in particular, is necessary for you and me, because we are to instruct people of the lowest understanding. Therefore we, above all, if we think with the wise, yet must speak with the vulgar. We should constantly use the most common, little, easy words (so they are pure and proper) which our language affords . . ." Thus if he changed the original text, it was as much to make the writing intelligible to those not otherwise learned as to propagandize. Ironically, as is often the way, Wesley's followers were more fanatical than was their leader. While Wesley was wont to interlard his sermons with quotations from all sorts of writing, those who promoted his views tended to exclude genuinely popular literature. Few general works found their way into the chapel book displays, where the faithful were more likely to have to choose between "the exegetical volumes of approved divines and such items, sufficiently described by their titles, Divine Breathings of a Devout Soul, Collings' Divine Cordial for the Soul, Heaven Taken by Storm, Young's Short and Sure Guide to Salvation, Baxter's Call to the Unconverted, and the same author's Shove for a Heavy-arsed Christian."[22] All those drawbacks notwithstanding, Wesley's scheme was a resounding success. While the mass of common non-Methodists remained restricted to the Bible, the Prayer Book, and perhaps an almanac and a few issues of prototype "partwork" history of England, their

Methodist peers were, by comparison, highly literate. By 1789 there were 56,000 of them and together they made up the most concentrated group of lower-class literates in the country.

Wesley's *Complete English Dictionary* was very much part of his overall plan. As he puts it in the preface, "As incredible as it may appear, I must avow, that this dictionary is not published to get money, but to assist persons of common sense and no learning to understand the best *English* authors: and that, with as little expence of either time or money, as the nature of the thing would allow." He had deliberately eschewed the classicisms of the seventeenth-century "hard-word" dictionaries and all technical and jargon terms. What he aimed to do, in just 144 pages, was to explain "most of those hard words which are found in the English writers." In his context "hard," fittingly, was used not as lexicographical jargon, but to mean exactly what it said: words that were used in literature but which would confuse the simple reader. As to his remarks on the excellence of his work, his cynicism might surprise those who assume that Christian is automatically at odds with Mr. Worldly-Wise. "I have so often observed, the only way, according to the modern taste, for any author to procure recommendation to his book is, vehemently to commend it himself. For want of this deference to the publick several excellent tracts lately printed, but left to commend themselves by their intrinsic worth, are utterly unknown or forgotten. Whereas if a writer of tolerable sense will but bestow a few violent encomiums on his own work, especially if they are skilfully ranged in the title-page, it will pass thro' six editions in a trice; the world being too complaisant to give a gentleman the Lie, and taking it for granted, he understands his own performance best." Having justified his position he added that "this little dictionary is not only the shortest and cheapest, but likewise, by many degrees, the most correct which is extant at this day. Many are the mistakes in all the other *English* dictionaries which I have yet seen. Whereas I can truly say, I know of none in this; and I conceive the reader will believe me: for if I had, I should not have left it there. Use then this help, till you find a better."

Wesley's followers undoubtedly appreciated his work, but later commentators have been less charitable. Wheatley, firmly on the side of élitist academe, sniffs, "Although called a dictionary, it is nothing more than an alphabetical list of words with explanations"[23] and writing later on "John Wesley's English Dictionary"[24] adds:

We cannot agree with the compiler in the estimation of his book. There is no explanation of the origin of the words, and the definitions are usually neither very clear nor very correct. It is rather too bad to have a hard word explained by a harder one—as in this instance "An abscess, an impostume." The following entry is not very explicit from a Natural History point of view—"An ortolan, a very dear bird."; and the reader who came upon some allusion to the changing hue of the chameleon, would not be much enlightened by the following, "A chameleon, a kind of lizard, living on flies."

Wheatley is cruel, but not wholly wrong. Wesley's word list—at 4,600 words the shortest since Cawdrey—appears to have been his own work, and presumably suited his purposes, but for all his talk of clarity all too many definitions are indeed execrable. "*A Felucca:* a sort of boat"; "*Literature:* learning"; "*A Madrigal:* a song"; "*Pantaloons:* a sort of trousers." It is hard to discern the practical use of these. They might serve for parrot learning, but they hardly imparted knowledge. Unsurprisingly, there are neither etymologies nor usage notes. Like other, more mainstream lexicographers, Wesley was not above pursuing his own interests. One, of course, was religion. He is unashamedly *parti pris:* "*The Millennium:* the thousand years during which Christ will reign upon earth"; "*A Puritan:* an old strict Church of England man"; "*Purgatory:* a place where the papists fancy departed souls are purged by fire"; "*Methodist:* one that lives according to the method laid down in the Bible." But he also includes medical terms (he had written *A Primitive Physick* in 1747 and cared for the physical as well as the spiritual health of his flock) and some musical ones. There are a number of "naturalized" French terms which might turn up in literature, as well as some specimens of colloquialism, slang, and dialect, all intended to help his traveling preachers relate to their audience: "*cully:* one that is apt to be made a fool of"; "*bilk:* to cheat"; "*beck:* a little brook"; "*mope:* a stupid, heavy person"; "*scruse:* to squeeze or press hard."

A second edition appeared in 1764; reprints followed in 1777 and 1790. None of them approached the slightest sophistication—that of 1777 included 300 new terms, mainly stolen from Johnson, though the Wesleyan method comprehensively removed any Johnsonian embellishments—but that was not the point. Wesley served his immediate purpose and in the longer term proved, if proof were wanting, that the popular dictionary, shorn of academic apparatus, could fulfill an increasingly vital lexicographical need. It was one that would be soon addressed in full measure both in Britain, especially through such "Scottish lexicographers" as William and Robert Chambers, and in America by Funk and Wagnalls and their many rivals.

The compilation and definition of word lists, while central to eighteenth-century lexicography, was not its sole concern. Thomas Dyche, typically, had been fascinated by spelling reform, and his was a preoccupation that touched a number of lexicographers. The exemplar would be an American, Noah Webster, whose *American Spelling Book* (1783) would have far-reaching effects on his nation's orthography. Another American, Benjamin Franklin, also made his suggestions, in an essay published in 1768. In England there were a number of schemes, and Johnson naturally tackled spelling, as he did other aspects of the language. However, one figure stands out: James Elphinston (1721–1809), who in his enthusiasm "distanced all his predecessors in his work of murdering the English language."[25]

Elphinston was born in Edinburgh, the son of an Episcopalian clergyman. After attending Edinburgh University, he became tutor to the son of Lord Blantyre, while still barely seventeen himself. Aged about twenty-one he toured France and the Low Countries with the historian Thomas Carte (1686–1754), before returning to Scotland and, since "his worldly circumstances . . . rendered it necessary for him to employ his talents,"[26] he took up another tutoring job. In 1750 he reappears in a new guise: superintending the publication of a Scottish edition of Johnson's journal *The Rambler*. This work brought him into contact with Johnson, and they became occasional correspondents. Johnson later observed that Elphinston was "fit for a travelling governor [a tutor]. He knows French very well. He is a man of good principles and there should be no danger that a young gentleman should catch his manner, for it is so very bad that it must be avoided."[27] He later remarked that "he has the most inverted understanding of any man I have ever known."[28] Elphinston's "manner" was obviously not a little neurotic. The writer Robert Dallas (1754–1824), whose generally affectionate memoir was published in the *Gentleman's Magazine,* recalled his "singularities, some of which were undoubtedly foibles":

> The colour of his *suit* of clothes was invariably, except when in mourning, what is called a drab; his coat was made in the fashion that reigned, when he returned from France, in the beginning of the last century, with flaps and buttons to the pockets and sleeves, and without a cape: he always wore a powdered bag-wig, with a high toupee, and walked with a cocked hat and an amber-headed cane.[29]

Nor was Elphinston the most socially comfortable of men.

> When any ladies were in company whose sleeves were at a distance from their elbows, or whose bosoms were at all exposed, he would fidget from place to place, look askance, with a slight convulsion of his left eye, and

never rest until he approached some of them, and, pointing to their arms say, "Oh yes indeed! It is very pretty, but it betrays more fashion than modesty!" or some similar phrase; after which, he became very good-humoured.[30]

In 1753 Elphinston published his first essay at language studies: *An Analysis of the French and English languages.* That same year he left Edinbugh for London and set up a school at Brompton (near Knightsbridge). This school was moved to Kensington in 1763, at which point Elphinston published *Education, a Poem in Four Books,* "a composition devoid of merit, and apparently designed as an advertisement for his academy."[31] He also prepared a grammar but this too lacked real substance. Elphinston gave up teaching in 1766 and shut the school. Johnson dined with him once or twice while the academy was still going and remarked in the patronizing tone that seems to mark all his references to his acqaintaince, "I would not put a boy to him who I intended for a man of learning, but for the sons of citizens who are to learn a little, get good morals, and then go to trade, he may do very well."[32]

In 1782 the former dominie produced a new book: a translation of the works of the Latin epigrammatist Martial. Poor Elphinston, his efforts, four years in the production, were the subject of almost universal ridicule. His brother-in-law William Strachan, the King's Printer, subscribed £50, with the promise that were Elphinston to suppress the book, there would be £50 more. Johnson apparently lacked the heart to say so but the actor David Garrick was less fearful and begged him not to publish. Elphinston was undaunted and went ahead regardless. The reponse was unrestrainedly savage. Dr. Beattie, writing to Sir William Forbes, remarked, "Elphinston's Martial is just come to hand. It is truly unique . . . a whole quarto of nonsense and gibberish . . . It is strange that a man not wholly illiterate should have lived so long in England without learning the language." Robert Burns, writing in 1788, addressed Elphinston:

> *O thou whom poesy abhors,*
> *Whom prose has turned out of doors!*
> *Heardst thou that groan? proceed no further;*
> *'Twas laurell'd Martial roaring murther.*

Elphinston hit back with his rebuttal, *The Hypercritic,* but his translation was not rescued.

He then turned to a fresh pursuit, the formulation of a new system of spelling. This appeared in two books: *Inglish Speech and Spelling* (1787) and *Inglish Ortho-*

ggraphy epittomized, and Propriety's Pocket Diccionary (1790). "A life spent actively in the cause of Religion, of Virtue and of Learning . . . cannot fail to be replete with instruction and interest," said the *Gentleman's Magazine*[33] but Wheatley, in his overview of "English Heterographers" gives Elphinston less kindly treatment, talking of "absurdities" and of his "hideous looking language."[34] An example, drawn from the dedication to King George III that prefaces *Inglish Speech and Spelling* proves Wheatley's point all too well:

> Yoor Madjesty, emmulous no les ov preceding dhan ov contemporary glory, and finding glory only in dhe improovement ov mankind, haz dained not merely by pattronage ov dhe sblimest music and by dhe institucion ov a British Acaddemy, to raiz rivals to dhe moast exquizite artists of anticquity, but by fixing Inglish Speech in Inglish Ortho-ggraphy to secure dhe unfading luster ov Truith . . .

As Wheatley remarks, "It is difficult to understand what the author means in this passage, and it must have puzzled the King." Other works followed, all written in Elphinston's new system. Typical is *Forty Years Correspondence between Geniusses ov boath sexes and James Elphinston* (1791–94). It is notable that here, as in other books, Elphinston cheerfully parades his spelling theories—the letters of the "Geniusses" were all translated into the new spelling—other than in one instance: that of his own name. Elphinston died in 1809. He left a wife, his second, and a son. His spelling system, unsurprisingly, did not survive him.

If spelling can be seen as a technical branch of lexicography, then the work of John Harris, D.D. is lexicography applied to technique, in this case that of a variety of what can loosely be termed "sciences." Harris (1666?–1719) worked somewhat earlier than most of those who have preceded him in this chapter and his single dictionary, the *Lexicon Technicum,* "or, a Universal English Dictionary of Arts and Sciences, explaining not only the terms of Art but the Arts themselves," appeared in 1704. A second edition followed in 1708–10 while in 1744 a supplement was prepared by "a society of gentlemen." Various dedicated glossaries, as noted in Chapter 6, had appeared during the sixteenth and early seventeenth centuries, and had played an important role in the "hardword" dictionaries that followed soon after, but Harris' was the first full-fledged work of its sort. As such it can be seen, just as Wesley's *Complete English Dictionary* is the precursor of "popular," nonacademic dictionaries, that the *Lexicon Technicum* was the founder of the specialist or "subject-field" dictionary tradition, opening up a path that leads directly to today's many dictionaries of professional or occupational jargons. In the shorter term, it provided a core technical vocabulary for such lexicographers as Bailey and Johnson. And Harris has lasted: the *Lexicon* still accounts for nearly 1,000 citations in the *OED*. Typical of the subjects he covers are seamanship, astronomy, medicine, botany, geometry, masonry, architecture, and ordnance.

Harris was a divine, hence his "D.D.," and a scientific writer and topographer. After winning a scholarship to Trinity College, Oxford he was employed in various minor ecclesiastical appointments before being taken up by Sir William (later Lord) Cowper, Lord Keeper of the Great Seal and later the Lord Chancellor, who made Harris his chaplain and a prebendary of Rochester Cathedral. This was in either 1707 or 1708. The second volume of the *Lexicon Technicum* is dedicated to his benefactor—the first went to Prince George of Denmark. Among his livings was that of St. Mildred, Bread Street, London, where he was severely persecuted by the rector, the Reverend Charles Humphreys, who in 1716 attacked him in a pamphlet: "The Picture of a High-Flying Clergyman." As well as his clerical career Harris was a practicing scientist and was elected a Fellow of the Royal Society in April 1696. Two years later he delivered the Boyle lectures in St. Paul's Cathedral, their topic being "the Atheistical Objections against the being of God." Around the same time he began giving a series of free public lectures on mathematics at the Marine Coffee House in Birchin Lane. These talks had been instituted "for the public good" by Sir Charles Cox, MP. Harris continued the lectures in 1702 and 1704; in 1703 he taught a variety of mathematical topics from his house at Amen Corner "where any person might be either boarded or taught by the month." From 1709 to 1710 he was secretary of the Royal Society; he was also probably its vice president, although no specific dates can be found. Around 1711 he was employed by group of London booksellers to compile *A Collection of Voyages and Travels* (which was later improved by Dr. John Campbell). Other works included an "Astronomical Dialogue between a Gentleman and a Lady, wherein the Doctrine of the Sphere, uses of the Globes, and the Elements of Astronomy and Geography are explained. With a description of the Orrery" (1719) and a sermon, published in 1715, "The British Hero, or a discourse shewing that it is the interest, as well as the duty, of every Briton to avow his loyalty to King George on the present important crisis of affairs." He also wrote a *History of Kent* in 1712. It was not a major work and in any case it appeared posthumously. Harris died, "in absolute poverty," on September 7, 1719 and was buried in the church near Norton Court, in Kent, the home of his long-time patron Mr. John Godfrey. Despite the importance of his dictionary, and the fact that he was well enough known for his name to be sought and used in congratulatory blurbs for the title pages of other men's books, Harris had never prospered. He was "culpably improvident and was generally in distress" declares the *DNB*.[35]

The last of the important pre-Johnsonian dictionaries was published, like Harris' *Lexicon,* early in the century. And its author, like John Wesley, is more usually found in quite another occupation. Edward Cocker (1631–75), best known for his mathematical textbook, on which he drew at least in part on the elder Kersey's efforts, supposedly issued a dictionary in 1704. One says "supposedly" since the authenticity of the dictionary was hardly helped by its putative compiler having been dead some twenty-nine years. Even its editor, John Hawkins, had been in his grave for twelve. Nonetheless it has been accepted that the editor was, if not *the* Cocker then at least *a* Cocker, most likely his son. Whatever its origins, the dictionary manages to combine virtually all of its recent predecessors and, as one critic notes, "here . . . the fine art of borrowing . . . reaches its zenith, and the author's own contribution sinks to a minimum."[36]

Cocker's English Dictionary was subtitled as "Interpreting The most refined and difficult words in Divinity . . . To which is Added An Historico-Poetical Dictionary . . . Also the Interpretation of the most usual Terms in Military Discipline. Likewise the Terms which Merchants and others make use of in Trade and Commerce . . . by Edward Cocker, the Late Famous Practitioner in Fair Writing and Arithmetick. Perused and Published from the Authors Correct Copy by John Hawkins." Beneath this was a picture of Cocker in flowing wig and gown, and the verses "Cocker, who in fair writing did excell | And rithmetick perform'd as well. | This necesary work took next in hand, | That Englishmen might English understand." It was published by Bettesworth, one of the "New Conger" who were associated with Bailey. Less skeptical than Starnes and Noyes, Wheatley makes no comment as to Cocker's involvement, calling his work "a most curious little volume, containing much amusing information related in a very quaint manner, although the historical portion is not very trustworthy, for instance Praxiteles is called 'a famous Statuary in Italy; said to be the inventor of Looking-glasses, which he first made of silver.' "[37]

Cocker, who is best known today in the phrase "according to Cocker," which, like its successor "according to Hoyle," implies an agreement with a given set of rules and regulations, was a man whose career and reputation went through a number of changes. In his lifetime he was first a schoolmaster, then an engraver, and finally a master calligrapher. Those who praised him for these abilities did not, apparently, suspect his talents as a lexicographer and even his association with mathematics seems to have arisen after, rather than during, his lifetime.

He was born as far as can be ascertained in 1631, probably in Northamptonshire. By 1657 he was in London, living near St. Paul's Churchyard and teaching writing and arithmetic "in an extraordinary manner."[38] So admired were his abilities that in 1661 Charles II ordered that he should be given a gift of £150. In 1664 he was confident enough to advertise the imminent foundation of a public school for the teaching of writing and maths. After a brief stay in Gutter Lane, Cheapside, he left London and by 1666 had moved to Northamptonshire. Samuel Pepys knew him: on August 10, 1664, wishing to have tables engraved upon his new "sliding rule" and finding that no other craftsman was up to the job, he "found out Cocker, the famous writing master, and got him to do it." Pepys spent an hour watching Cocker at work, marveling at his ability to engrave such tiny marks. He was full of admiration: "I find the fellow, by his discourse, very ingenuous; and among other things, a great admirer and well read in all our English poets."[39] Two months later, on October 7, Cocker presented Pepys with "a Globe of glasse and a frame of oyled paper . . . to show me the manner of his gaining light to grave by, and to lessen the glaringnesse of it at pleasure." He paid Cocker a crown "and so, well satisfied, he went away."[40] Pepys' fellow diarist John Evelyn cites him in *Sculptura* (1662) as the supreme English calligrapher and as such equal to the best in France or Italy. He owned a large library of rare manuscripts and scientific books. Cocker died suddenly, aged forty-four, in 1675.

Like his career, Cocker's writings fall into three areas. In the first, calligraphic, there are some twenty-three books, ranging from *The Pen's Experience* (mid-1650s) to *The Competent Writing Master* (pre-1675). His mathematical works include *Cocker's Arithmetick* (1678), on which his reputation as a mathematician rests. Finally come various miscellaneous works, among which is the dictionary. Cocker's reputation for calligraphy, while most uncontrovertibly his own, barely survived his death. In its place came a new image, that of master mathematician. The phrase "according to Cocker" enters the language and his rules are seen as those to follow. His dictionary, whatever its provenance, never made any substantial mark.

Cocker's reputation began to deteriorate in the nineteenth century when A. De Morgan, in *Arithmetical Books* (1847), suggested that his *Arithmetick* was forged by John Hawkins, "with some assistance, it may be, from Cocker's papers." Hawkins had succeeded Cocker at the latter's school near St. George's Church, Southwark. His own works were *Clavis Commercii* (1689) and *The English School-Master Compleated* (c. 1692). Hawkins also "persued and published" *Cocker's Decimal Arithmetic* (1685), itself a decade posthumous. Cocker's lexicography came under fire in 1884 when H. B. Wheatley asked in the journal *The Bibliographer* "Who Was Cocker?" Wheatley's central point was that since both the "author" and "editor" were dead, the real creators of *Cocker's Dictionary* were the London Bridge booksellers, their eyes on the profit that could be made by exploiting the two men's names and reputations. He underlined his theory by asking why, if the dictionary's manuscript was so outstanding, it had been lying unnoticed for thirty years. This was backed up by Sir Ambrose Heal in *English Writing Masters and their Copy-Books, 1570–1800* when he attributed the *Dictionary,* the *Arithmetick* and the *Decimal Arithmetick* to this same group of profit-oriented booksellers. But Heal added a new twist: in his view the author was not Hawkins, who like Cocker was dead, but rather Edward Cocker, Jr. (1658–1723), like his father a writing master and scrivener. Starnes and Noyes are unconvinced and opt for the booksellers, backed possibly by a hack lexicographer. They also note that "in any case it is paradoxical to debate the authorship of a work which has no original material."[41] In the end the "ghostly author" and his "ghostly editor"[42] represent more of a curiosity than a genuine contribution to dictionary making.

The dictionary itself is divided into four vocabularies: general ("hard words"), historico-poetical, military, commercial. The author notes that he needs the third and fourth because "in this War-like Age, we often encounter with Military Terms in our Gazzets and other publick news, several of them newly invented, and which few or none have yet taken notice of in Print, and are little understood by many" and trade is "now . . . extraordinarily improved and enlarged with Foreign Nations and Merchants [are now] making use of words in Traffick not commonly apprehended." In all they total 22,000 headwords.

"Cocker" stole everything. His historical preface is an abridgment of Edward Phillips; the hard words come from Coles; his etymologies are taken from the *Gazophyllacium* and Skinner (although he was hardly exceptional in that); the historico-poetical proper names also come from Phillips, and thus before him from Charles Stephanus / Estienne. The military material is plucked directly from Sieur de Guillet's *Les Arts de l'Homme de l'Epee* (1673, published in England as *The Gentleman's Dictionary,* 1705) and the trade terminology from a short commercial dictionary published in Edward Hatton's *Merchant's Magazine.*

In its second edition, published in 1715, all these vocabularies had been merged into one, and there is now an anonymous reviser listed on the title page, although the preface is still ostensibly signed by Hawkins. New terms include cant (taken from Coles, who in turn reproduced Richard Head) and archaisms (which are grudgingly accepted with a comment that while "some Dictionary-makers [i.e., Coles] may have liked them 'Mr Blount' says that he 'expressly shunned' them" and in any case no-one else read or was interested in them").

The anonymous reviser's last innovation was a section entitled "Historical remarks upon the Lives and Actions of Emperors, Popes, Kings, . . . both in the former and latter Ages of the World, With Brief Observations upon the reign of every English Monarch . . . Also a short View of what is Considerable in every county of England and Wales." "This material no doubt reflects a wave of nationalism resulting from foreign victories, the union with Scotland, the spread of news sheets, the increase in road-building and consequently in travel in all parts of the islands. 'Descriptions of Great Britain,' road maps and itineraries, lives of the English kings, and formal histories abound, . . . Such is the avid curiosity about things English which the reviser aims to satisfy."[43] And this material, which like everything else was stolen, appears to have been tacked on to the dictionary as an afterthought. Nothing of this type appears prior to the letter H, a problem which the compiler overcomes by putting all monarchs whose names begin with the earlier initials under K for "King" or Q for "Queen."

"Cocker," coming at the beginning of the century, is hardly representative of the trends in lexicography that typify the period. Epitomized by Bailey, but underlined by Kersey and brought to fruition by Johnson, the lexicographer was now a real professional. It was, as Starnes and Noyes note, a "dictionary-conscious age."[44] If the previous century had been one of individual exploration, as much in its lexicography as in other areas of life, this one required a respite from such comings and goings. In its place the movement was toward stability, in language as much as elsewhere. Cocker may very possibly have been a specious dictionary maker, but the phrase to which he lent his name was of greater import than its subject. The dictionary, along with other aspects of society, had to obey rules. It too must be prepared, as Johnson would attempt, figuratively if not factually, "according to Cocker."

9

Samuel Johnson: The Pivotal Moment

A side from any internal, linguistic considerations, the great impetus to British lexicography as the eighteenth century opened derived not from social but from patriotic impulses. No sooner had English emerged as a self-sufficient language than its advocates found themselves looking to Europe where vernaculars had been not only fostered but in addition rendered properly disciplined through the agency of a deliberate policy of refinement. These developments, it was noted, sprang from an institution that while by no means new, had reappeared in Europe after centuries of hibernation. It had not, however, seen a similar resurgence in England.

The concept of "the Academy" as the repository of intellectual excellence dates back to *c.* 380 B.C. when Plato founded his school near an olive grove sacred to the hero Akademos on the west side of Athens. The actual school lasted in a variety of incarnations until the Roman general Sulla sacked it, along with the rest of Athens, in 86 B.C., but the concept would never vanish. For the modern world it came back in the form of two foundations, both of which would have a major influence on English intellectuals: Florence's Accademia della Crusca and France's Académie Française. The Florentine foundation emerged in 1582, the date of Mulcaster's *Elementarie,* and dedicated itself to maintaining "Italian culture," even though "Italy," as a political unity, would not appear for nearly three centuries. Among its successes was the publication, in 1612, of the *Vocabulario della Crusca,* an Italian dictionary which concentrated on extensive citations from contemporary literature and which aimed, amid much controversy, to purify the language. By 1738 it had reached a fourth edition, and the original single folio volume had expanded to six.

The Académie Française was founded in Paris on January 2, 1635 by Cardinal Richelieu, who brought together a number of the era's most distinguished men of letters with the express intention of setting down fixed rules for the French language. The group had originated around 1630, as a collection of self-appointed tastemakers who met at the house of the grammarian Valentin Conrart. They included the poets Jean Gombauld and Antoine Godeau (who was also bishop of Bresse) and the critic Jean Chapelain. Richelieu turned their informal meetings, designed to criticize rather than create literature, into the Establishment of French letters. There were forty members—the number has never changed—known to a culture that instinctively appreciates rather than distrusts its intellectual élite as the "Forty Immortals."

The Académie was a notably conservative body, preferring to champion established forms rather than encourage innovation. Its primary interest was the codification of the French language, and as laid down in Article XXIV of its Constitution, the creation of a dictionary within which that code could be enshrined. The writing of the dictionary was substantially influenced by the grammarian Claude de Vaugelas (1585–1650), whose works were devoted to stating the rules of French diction, the basis of which, he claimed, was simply the usage of the royal court. As far as the proposed dictionary went, it was very much modeled on the Italian work and its original plan, as laid down by Chapelain, called for the reading of "all those dead authors who wrote the purest version of our language."[1] Armed with such writers it would be both possible and desirable to set down in perpetuity what in French was good, what bad and what unacceptable.

Work began in 1639, directed by Vaugelas. It took fifty-five years to complete, with the researchers constantly submitting their material to the members of the Académie for extensive debate. Only the *Deutsches Wörterbuch* of the Brothers Grimm took longer—122 years—while the compilers of the *OED* worked marginally faster. The work was split between two departments, but neither worked as quickly as had been hoped. It took nine months to complete A (it was revised in 1672) and other letters demanded similarly lengthy attention. As almost happened with the *OED* when its original editor, Herbert Coleridge, died suddenly, the death of Vaugelas in 1650 nearly put paid to the project. The death of Richelieu in the same year was equally deleterious. But the compilers struggled on until 1672 when, on finishing the preliminary writing, it was decided, given how much time had passed, to submit the entire text to a full-scale revision. This was done by 1680, at which point printing began.

In 1694, at last, the finished work was presented to the king to whom it had been dedicated.

It was then and has remained above all a usage dictionary rather than a philological one; "its chief concern is to give words acceptable from a literary point of view."[2] To this end it undergoes regular revision, but unlike its later peer, the *OED,* it prescribes language, rather than describes it. Supposedly representative of a vocabulary suited to an "honest man" (where "honest" means educated, conservative, and bourgeois), it excluded archaisms, technical jargon, slang, working-class colloquialism, and neologisms. But even the *honnêtes hommes* nodded occasionally and examples of all these did creep in, albeit carefully marked as outsiders. Ironically Vaugelas, who was charged with "fixing" the language, made it clear, as would Johnson, that such hopes were to be dashed by the intrinsic mutability of the topic, and that the best a lexicographer could do was set down the language as it was at a given time, but the *dictionnaire de l'Académie* was, and still is, synonymous with setting language in stone.

If the effect of the *dictionnaire* on France was to confer on the national language the degree of gravitas desired by the project's founder, then its effect across the Channel was to appall the London literati. From the mid-seventeenth century onward, when it might be said that with the publications of Blount and Phillips, the task of the "hard-word" dictionaries was effectively completed, those who concerned themselves with language were more and more intent upon taking this newly confident, exuberant vernacular English and knocking it into shape. To achieve this task the intellectuals looked to Europe: they saw the Accademia and the Académie and determined to follow suit.

England's attempt at an Academy might be said to date to 1572, when the Society of Antiquaries was founded by Archbishop Parker and started meeting at the house of Sir Robert Cotton, the famous collector. Whether it would have turned from antiquity to language is unknown—the society languished with the accession of James I in 1603. Before that there were suggestions for a society, never named, that would bring together such figures as Sir Edward Coke, Sir Kenelm Digby, Sir Henry Spelman, Inigo Jones, Ben Jonson, and Sir Henry Wotton, but it came to nothing. The launch of the Académie Française rekindled such projects, and the process was much accelerated after the Restoration. Typical of the suggestions that began to appear was a pamphlet, *New Atlantis . . . Continued,* in which the author envisioned an academy "to purifie our Native Language from Barbarism or Solecism, to the height of Eloquence by regulating the termes and phrases thereof . . ." The author of this work was named only as "R.H., Esquire," a figure who may very well have been the scientist Robert Hooke (1735–1803). Nothing came of this scheme, but the impetus toward an Academy, and with it the purification of English, grew fast. In 1664 John Dryden wrote a dedication to his play *Rival Ladies* in which he took time to declare himself "Sorry, that (Speaking so noble a Language as we do) we have not a more certain Measure of it, as they have in France, where they have an Academy erected for the purpose . . ."

As Tom McArthur points out, the nearest equivalent to an English Academy was the Royal Society of London for the Improvement of Natural Knowledge, founded in 1662.[3] The Royal Society was primarily devoted to scientific inquiry, not language, but, shortly after Dryden's plea, in December 1664 the Society adopted a resolution stating that as "there were persons of the Society whose genius was very proper and inclined to improve the English tongue, Particularly for philosophic purposes, it was voted that there should be a committee for improving the English language . . ." The committee of twenty-two, which met at the home of Sir Peter Wyche, included such figures as Dryden, John Evelyn (who actually visited the Accademia), Thomas Sprat, and Edmund Waller. Evelyn, failing to attend the initial meeting, sent a letter explaining what he felt should be done: among his suggestions were the compilation of a grammar, spelling reform, which should concentrate on eliminating superfluous letters, and the compilation of a "Lexicon or collection of all the pure English words by themselves; then those which are derivative from others . . . then, the symbolical: so as no innovation might be us'd or favour'd, at least, 'till there should arise some necessity of providing a new edition, & of amplifying the old upon mature advice." Evelyn further suggested separate collections of dialect, archaisms, technical jargon, and so on. Finally the best of the classics, and even some modern European works, should be translated so as to help offer models of elegant style. None of this bore fruit. The Royal Society remained a mainly scientific organization: language was not a major concern, and after three or four meetings the committee quietly dispersed.

The concept, however, was not abandoned. In his *Essay upon Projects* (1697) Daniel Defoe had this to say: "The *English* tongue is a Subject not at all less worthy the Labour of such a Society than the *French*, and capable of a much greater Perfection . . . The Work of this Society shou'd be to encourage Polite Learning, to polish and refine the *English* Tongue, and advance the so much neglected faculty of Correct Language, to establish Purity and Propriety of Stile, and to purge it from all the Irregular Additions that Ignorance and Affectation have introduc'd." He suggested that such a society should be composed of thirty-six members: "twelve to be of the nobility, if possible, and twelve private gentlemen, and a class of twelve left open for mere merit . . ." These men who "should preside with a sort of judicature over the learning of the age" would be "the allowed judges of style and language, and no author would have the impudence to coin without their authority." Once this system was set in place, "it would be as criminal . . . to coin words as money." Joseph Addison, editor of the *Spectator,* was similarly inclined. Writing in issue 135 he claimed that usage queries could not be settled without "something like an Academy, that by the best authorities and rules drawn from the analogy of languages shall settle all controversies between grammar and idiom."

In 1712 the most powerful call yet for an English Academy was published when Jonathan Swift issued his eloquent *Proposal for Correcting, Improving and Ascertaining the English Tongue,* in the form of a letter to the earl of Oxford, the Lord Treasurer of England. Swift had already assailed what he saw as the corruption of the language in a piece in the *Tatler* (no. 230, 1710), when he published what he claimed was an actual letter, "received . . . from a most accomplished person." In this letter, which in fact seems remarkably phony, he finds such words as *bamboozle, uppish, the hipps* plus the abbreviations *phizz, incog, tho'* and *couldn't.* Such terminology, a mixture of the slangy and the colloquial, ought, Swift claims, to be subjected to an annual "*index expurgatorius* [that will] expunge all words and phrases that are offensive to good sense." Now, writing "in the name of all the learned and polite persons of the nation," he complained that "our language is extremely imperfect; that its daily improvements are by no means in proportion to its daily corruptions; that the pretenders to polish and refine it have chiefly multiplied abuses and absurdities; and, that in many instances it offends against every part of grammar." He was especially incensed by innovations and noted that "I have never known this great town without one or more *dunces* of figure, who had credit enough to give rise to some new word, and propagate it in most conversations, though it had neither humour nor significancy." What he proposed, as an agent of this vital reform, was an Academy.

A free judicious choice should be made of such persons, as are generally allowed to be best qualified for such a work, without any regard to quality, party, or profession. These, to a certain number at least, should assemble at some appointed time and place, and fix on rules, by which they design to proceed. What methods they will take, is not for me to prescribe . . . The persons who are to undertake this work will have the example of the French before them to imitate, where these have proceeded right, and to avoid their mistakes. Besides the grammar-part, wherein we are allowed to be very defective, they will observe many gross improprieties, which however authorized by practice, and grown familiar,

ought to be discarded. They will find many words that deserve to be
utterly thrown out of our language, many more to be corrected, and perhaps not a few long since antiquated, which ought to be restored on
account of their energy and sound.

He ends, in a typically challenging manner, "If genius and learning is not
encouraged under your Lordship's administration, you are the most inexcusable
person alive."

For all its vehemence, and its reflection of the views of many of his peers,
Swift's was not a unanimously welcomed proposal. Nor was the opposition, as
might have been presumed, purely intellectual. An immediate rebuttal came
from the Whig historian and pamphleteer John Oldmixon (1673?–1742) who
dismissed Swift's demands on the premise that the *Proposal* was no more than a
piece of Tory intemperance. Most of his 35-page essay was an attack on Swift
himself; he had nothing as such against an Academy. He was less impressed,
however, by the idea of a "fixed" language, remarking sarcastically, that "I
should rejoice with him, if a way could be found to *fix our Language for ever,* that
like the *Spanish* cloak it might always be in fashion." Furthermore, he quotes
extensively from Swift's own *Tale of the Tub* (1704) to show that he was far from
immune to vulgar language. It did not require Oldmixon, however, to see the
Proposal fail. It may be, as contemporaries believed, that had Queen Anne lived
a little longer, she might have backed the idea; as it was she did not, and her
successor George I was not interested. Determinedly philistine, His Majesty,
whose English was never of the best, had famously declared, "I hate all Boets
and Bainters," and the emotion was presumably extended to literary reformers
too. The Academy was not to be.

For all its vehemence, Among those who disdained an Academy, and indeed objected to the idea of
"fixing" English, was Samuel Johnson, a freelance writer and critic, but still a
relative unknown. As he would write, in 1755:

Those who have been persuaded to think well of my design, require that
it should fix our language, and put a stop to those alterations which time
and chance have hitherto been suffered to make in it without opposition.
With this consequence I will confess that I flattered myself for a while;
but now begin to fear that I have indulged expectation which neither reason nor experience can justify. When we see men grow old and die at a
certain time one after another, from century to century, we laugh at the
elixir that promises to prolong life to a thousand years; and with equal
justice may the lexicographer be derided, who being able to produce no

example of a nation that has preserved their words and phrases from mutability, shall imagine that his dictionary can embalm his language, and secure it from corruption and decay, that it is in his power to change sublunary nature, or clear the world at once from folly, vanity, and affectation. With this hope, however, academies have been instituted, to guard the avenues of their languages, to retain fugitives, and repulse intruders; but their vigilance and activity have hitherto been vain; sounds are too volatile and subtile for legal restraints; to enchain syllables, and to lash the wind, are equally the undertakings of pride, unwilling to measure its desires by its strength.

And he added, voicing the other side of that nationalism that sought to create an Academy to help English rival French, that were an Academy to be created, "English liberty will hinder or destroy" it. But these remarks must be seen in context. They come in the preface to Johnson's magnum opus, a work that in many ways would satisfy both the "academics" and the "fixers," without properly fulfilling the desires of either party: *A Dictionary of the English Language* by Samuel Johnson, A.M.

The demand for an authoritative English Dictionary had always been intertwined with those urging the establishment of an Academy. Richard Mulcaster had suggested such a work in the 1580s and a century later the need seemed even greater. The editor of Skinner's *Etymologicon* (1671) voiced an increasingly popular mood, at least among intellectuals, when he hoped that one day England would follow Italy and France not just in the establishment of an Academy but also in the compilation of a national dictionary. And other figures, already demanding an Academy, wanted a dictionary too.

John Evelyn's letter to the Royal Society Committee on language included a call for "a more certaine Orthography" and an authoritative grammar and lexicon. Dryden, in the dedication of *Troilus and Cressida,* stressed the need for authority, noting that "propriety must first be stated, ere any measures of elegance can be taken"; in 1693 he bemoaned the absence of "a tolerable dictionary, or a grammar; so that our language is in a manner barbarous." In 1724, an anonymous pamphlet, "The Many advantages of a Good Language," worried yet again as to the absence of a good dictionary: such a work would correct the many failings still to be found in English and "bring it into method, with an account of the Derivations, and Senses and Uses of Words." In 1747 the theologian William Warburton (1698–1779) noted the lack of a standard for English, "for we have neither GRAMMAR nor DICTIONARY, neither Chart nor Compass, to guide us through this wide sea of Words." There were other intellectuals devoted to the scheme, including Addison and Pope, both of whom went so far as to compose a list of possible authorities. The poet Ambrose Phillips (1675?–1749), another of that circle, issued his *Proposals for printing an English Dictionary in Two Volumes in Folio*. In it he promised to explain the whole language by giving correct spellings, proper etymologies, clear definitions of the different meanings of a single word, and illustrations of the levels of usage. He also promised to include proverbs, jargon, and archaisms. Phillips' plan was never more than that, but it might have served as a blueprint for the man who finally achieved that which others had merely dreamed: Johnson himself.

Yet before Johnson, and indeed while the doctor was still working on his own great creation, there appeared the work of another lexicographer: Benjamin Martin (1704–82), whose *Lingua Britannica Reformata* was published first in 1749 and again, just a year before Johnson's *Dictionary,* in 1754. Martin was born in Worplesdon in Surrey and began life as a plowboy in the hamlet of Broadstreet. Relinquishing so unrewarding a job, he set himself up as teacher of reading, writing, and arithmetic in Guildford; in his spare time he taught himself mathematics, becoming an ardent champion of the Newtonian system. A legacy of £500 allowed him to buy "books and philosophical instruments" and he began touring Britain, lecturing on natural philosophy. These lectures brought him a wide circle of friends, many of whom are listed in the twenty-six columns of "subscribers" to his *Bibliotheca Technologia,* "or, Philological Library of Literary Arts and Sciences" (1737, 1740), "a very skilful and comprehensive compilation"[4] in which Martin laid out the current state of science under twenty-five subheadings. By now he had settled in Chichester, where he kept a school and began inventing and producing optical instruments. His main product was the pocket reflecting microscope, costing one guinea. He also gained a reputation as a maker of spectacles.

In 1740 Martin moved to Fleet Street, taking a house three doors below Crane Court (in which the Royal Society, where his hero Newton often lectured, had its headquarters between 1710 and 1780). There he began manufacturing "Hadley's Quadrant And Visual Glasses" with much success. Aside from his dictionary, Martin wrote widely, publishing a wide range of popular scientific books. Between 1755 and 1764, he was the editor-publisher of *Martin's Magazine,* dedicated to King George III and described in the *Gentleman's Magazine* as a "New and Comprehensive System of Philosophy, Natural History, Philology, Mathematical Institutions and Biography." The magazine was less a journal than a collection of essays; it was announced as running to fourteen volumes, but no more than seven appeared: two on mathematical institutions (1759, 1764), two on philosophy (1759, 1764, including essays on the world's religions and on geography), two on the natural history of England (1759, 1763, with descriptions of each county, plus its natural curiosities and a map), and one volume of the biographies of mathematicians and philosophers.

Of his other works, which dealt variously with Newton, geometry, navigation, optics, and many related topics, two stand out. *The Philosophical Grammar* (1735) is divided into four parts: I Somatology; II Cosmology; III Aerology; IV Geology. "The whole extracted from the writings of the greatest naturalists of the last and present age, treated in the familiar way of dialogue, adapted purposely to the capacities of the youth of both sexes, and adorned and illustrated with a variety of copperplates, maps, &c., several of which are entirely new, and all easy to be understood." The other, published in 1746, is *An Essay on Electricity* . . . "being an enquiry into the nature, cause, and properties thereof, on the principles of Sir Isaac Newton's theory of vibrating motion, light and fire, and the various phenomena of forty-two capital experiments . . ." Martin's suggestion that "This subtle matter or spirit appears to be of an elastic nature, and acts by the reciprocation of its tremors or pulses, which are occasioned by the vibrating motion of the parts of an electric body excited by friction" presages nineteenth-century scientific opinion.

In 1781, aged seventy-seven, having retired from active management of his business, he became bankrupt—the managers to whom he had turned over the business had proved incompetent—and in his desperation attempted suicide. The details of his attempt, which failed, are not known, but according to the *DNB* the wound he sustained proved fatal. He lingered into the new year, dying on February 9, 1782. His valuable collection of fossils and curiosities was auctioned at the lowest of knockdown prices.

Since Martin had no lexicographical experience it might at first seem unlikely that he should have provided Britain's first response to the Académie's project. But his scientific preoccupations make it an entirely logical act. After all, another scientist, Robert Hooke, seems to have been equally interested in language reform. Like many contemporaries Martin believed that it was time for the English language to be properly codified. To accompany that scientifically recast language, there should be a dictionary of similar efficiency. Nothing of the sort existed as yet; as he put it in the introduction to his own work, "The article of English Dictionaries, especially, has been so far from anything of a progressive improvement, that it is manifestly retrograde, and sinks from its low apex, from bad to very bad indeed." He goes on to lay out the requirements of a "genuine English Dictionary" and suggests that his work answers them entirely. "He thinks that it is much the most perfect of its kind, though he will not go so far as to say that it is without faults," notes Wheatley, who judges it to be "a valuable work, but partakes more of the quality of an Encyclopedia than a Dictionary."[5]

In the event, Martin's efforts would be surpassed in every respect by those of his successor, Johnson, but he contributed one important new stage to dictionary making: a plan. Proposing his *Lingua Britannica Reformata,* he laid out the following structure.

I. UNIVERSAL;   Containing a Definition and Explication of all the Words now used in the English Tongue, in every Art, Science, Faculty, or Trade.

II. ETYMOLOGICAL;   Exhibiting and Explaining the true Etymon or Original of Words from their respective Mother-Tongues, . . . and their idioms, . . .

III. ORTHOGRAPHICAL;   Teaching the True and Rational Method of Writing Words, according to the Usage of the most Approved Modern Authors.

IV. ORTHOEPICAL;   Directing the True Pronunciation of Words by Single and Double Accents; and by Indicating the Number of Syllables in Words where they are doubtful, by a Numerical Figure.

V. DIACRITICAL;   Enumerating the Various Significations of Words in a Proper Order, viz. Etymological, Common, Figurative, Poetical, Humorous, Technical &c. in a Manner not before attempted.

VI. PHILOLOGICAL;   Explaining all the Words and Terms, according to the Modern Improvements in the Various Philological Sciences, viz: Grammar, Rhetoric, Logic, Metaphysics, Mythology, Theology, Ethics, &c.

VII. MATHEMATICAL;   Not only Explaining all Words in Arithmetic, . . . according to the Modern Newtonian Mathesis; but the Terms of Art are illustrated by Proper Exercises, and Copper-Plate Figures.

VIII. PHILOSOPHICAL;   Explaining all Words and Terms in Astronomy, Geography, Optics, . . . according to the latest Discoveries and Improvements in this Part of Literature.

To which is prefix'd an Introduction, Containing a Physico-Grammatical Essay "On the propriety and Rationale of the English Tongue, deduced from a General Idea of the Nature and Necessity of Speech for Human Society; a Particular view of the Genius and Usage of the Original Mother Tongues, the Hebrew, Greek, Latin, and Teutonic; with their respective Idioms, the Italian, French, Spanish, Saxon, and German, so far as they have Relation, to the English Tongue, and have contributed to its Composition."

Martin followed this by a detailed and properly planned preface. In one area he did follow tradition: prior to extolling his own work, he roundly condemned the efforts of all who had preceded him.

The published dictionary ran to 24,500 words, mixing general vocabulary, "hard words," and, as one might expect, some technical language. In many aspects of his work, his self-congratulation is not without justification: he offers a simpler system of spelling and a clearer guide to pronunciation than any predecessor. His etymologies are less acceptable—they are by no means consistent and he tends to overlook Germanic in favor of Latin origins. As did Johnson's, the word list draws mainly on Nathan Bailey, and Martin mimics many of his source's definitions. However, he introduces a new method: instead of separate entries for each word, all homonyms are gathered beneath a single headword, then numbered to indicate their different senses. And it is with his definitions that, as Starnes and Noyes put it, "we arrive at the outstanding innovation of Martin, the reform of the Definition. He writes earnestly on the need for such reform, explains his own method of building definitions, and even specifies sources."[6]

A Critical and accurate Enumeration and Distinction of the several Significations of each respective Word must be allow'd by all to be indispensably the chiefest Care of every Writer of Dictionaries. And yet nothing is more certain, than that all our English Dictionaries are more notoriously deficient in this important Particular than in any other; . . . This grand Defect it has been been my principal Care to supply, and indeed was the greatest Motive to my undertaking this Work. And that I might acquit myself more perfect herein I laid before my Amanuensis *Ainsworth's* Latin Dictionary and French Dictionary; where, in the English Part, as the Authors were obliged to consider every different Sense of an English Word, . . . this Task was by that Means greatly facilitated; and by a careful Collection and Addition such others as the common Dictionaries, Glossaries, and Popular Speech supplied, 'tis presumed we have attain'd to no inconsiderable Perfection and Success in this most Essential Part of our Work.[7]

Yet despite what Starnes and Noyes term an "intelligent and progressive prospectus" Martin fails.[8] The printed dictionary, the plan of which is so carefully enunciated, never really lives up to the theory behind it. That its major innovation is the 108-page-long "Physico-Grammatical Essay" only underlines that premise. His topics: "man's physical and mental endowment for receiving and communicating ideas; alphabets ancient and modern; the history of England with specimens of the language at various periods; a study of the individual letters and of vowels and consonants; a sketch with paradigms of Hebrew, Greek, Latin, Italian, French, Spanish, Portuguese, German, Saxon, and modern English grammar; and a discourse on etymology . . ." are all well covered and "Martin's treatment of these topics is much broader and more advanced than that of any predecessor."[9] Indeed those who persisted in believing that the language could be "fixed" could have learned from his comments:

> [The] pretence of fixing a standard to the purity and perfection of any language, . . . is utterly vain and impertinent, because no language as depending on arbitrary use and custom, can ever be permanently the same, but will always be in a mutable and fluctuating state; and what is deem'd polite and elegant in one age, may be accounted uncouth and barbarous in another. Of this truth none I think can doubt, as we have such numerous instances of it in the fore-going part of this essay, to which perhaps two or three centuries may add as many more. And Addison, Pope, and [James] Foster [1697–1753, preacher and controversialist] may appear to our posterity in the same light as Chaucer, Spenser, and Shakespear do to us; whose language is now grown old and obsolete; read by very few, and understood by antiquarians only.

But none of this proved sufficient. Like Bailey before him, Martin would be overwhelmed by the advent of a new lexicographer. In some ways Johnson was as inexperienced as Martin—his previous writings had not included a dictionary, nor had he shown any special interest in broadening his range. But circumstances drew Johnson toward lexicography and the profession, and its new practitioner, would benefit enormously from the move.

In the event it was commerce rather than culture that underwrote the creation of the much-demanded English Dictionary. A group of booksellers had backed Nathaniel Bailey in his lexicography, now another group turned to Samuel Johnson and asked him to do much the same task. They were led by Robert Dodsley, who, according to Boswell, had already approached Johnson with a similar idea some time before.

> I have been informed by Mr. James Dodsley, that several years before this period, when Johnson was one day sitting in his brother Robert's shop, he heard his brother suggest to him, that a Dictionary of the English Lan-

guage would be a work that would be well received by the publick; that Johnson seemed at first to catch at the proposition, but, after a pause, said, in his abrupt decisive manner "I believe I shall not undertake it."

On this occasion Johnson must have responded differently. By now he was tiring of his work for Edward Cave's *Gentleman's Magazine*—where since 1738 he had been, *inter alia,* the Parliamentary correspondent—and yearning for a freelance life. His finances were wretched: there was a little work, but he had been forced to sell off his few valuables to keep himself out of debtor's prison. He had considered abandoning writing and turning to the law. Cultural considerations aside, this offer, with its promised fee of 1,500 guineas (£1,575), must have seemed like a prayer granted. In April 1746 he wrote the "Scheme" of the work, which he presented to Lord Chesterfield, the arbiter elegentiae of the period, for his approval and possible patronage. He obtained the former, and duly dedicated a revised "Scheme," now entitled a "Plan," to his lordship. Patronage, which meant financial security, was not forthcoming. A few weeks later, on June 18, he contracted with Dodsley and others to write the book that would become his *Dictionary of the English Language.* He was then in his thirty-eighth year. His career to date had been respectable, but hardly distinguished. Born in Lichfield, the son of a bookseller, he had attended Oxford before returning home to try his luck at schoolmastering. He married, and began writing, mainly translations. When teaching failed, in 1737, he departed for London, setting off with his equally hopeful, equally penurious pupil David Garrick. In 1738 he began writing for the *Gentleman's Magazine.*

Edward Cave (1691–1754), whose magazine provided Johnson with his "break" and which later joined happily in puffing his *Dictionary,* was one of the great pioneers of journalism. Expelled from Rugby by its headmaster, the lexicographer Thomas Holyoake (see Chapter 7), Cave moved to London and, after a spell clerking, became an apprentice printer. After learning the trade and working on some small papers, Cave became sufficiently competent to be made Clerk of the Franks, the official responsible for those letters which were carried free once an approved signature or "frank" had been affixed. With the connections this job created he began running newsletters, bringing country news to London. In 1731, after surviving a prosecution for breach of privilege, he set up as a printer and launched the *Gentleman's Magazine,* the title of which gives the first use of "magazine" as a collection of disparate information rather than as a repository for military matériel. He wrote as "Sylvanus Urban, Gent." By 1739 circulation had reached 10,000 a month, far outstripping its rivals, the gossipy, inaccurate sheets of the period. By the mid-1740s it was 15,000. He launched coverage of parliamentary debates in 1732; Johnson was his correspondent until 1743. The two men remained intimates, and when Cave died on January 10, 1754, his hand was clasped in Johnson's. Cave could have had an even more successful career as a pioneer of the industrial revolution. In 1740 he bought a spinning machine and had a mill set up near the Fleet River. Had the enterprise been properly managed, Cave could have predated James Hargreaves of "spinning jenny" celebrity, but his heart was not in it and the project languished. A similar fate befell his water wheel, designed to run a carding machine, in Northampton. A friend of Benjamin Franklin, he mounted one of Franklin's lightning conductors on his office at St. John's Gate, Clerkenwell. Next to it were four portable cannons of Cave's invention. Shoulder-mounted and capable of firing cannonballs or bullets, they too could have earned him a fortune.

Johnson's fee was no fortune, but it revolutionized his finances, at least for a while. Thus newly enriched with his advance, he took a lease on 17 Gough Square, set among the alleyways that lead off Fleet Street. He hired an assistant, one Francis Stewart, who would become the first of the six amanuenses, "mostly Scottish, mostly impoverished Grub Street hacks,"[10] who would help in the laborious work of copying, clipping, filing, sorting, and the other quotidian tasks necessary to compilation.

Stewart, the son of an Edinburgh bookseller, was paid 12s. a week. It is possible that he was already working for one of the booksellers with whom Johnson had contracted; certainly he was immediately deputed to start copying passages that Johnson had already marked up for citations. With his bookselling experience "Frank" Stewart as Johnson called him, "an ingenious and worthy man," took over much of the day-to-day business, exhibiting a greater skill in that area than did his employer. Much of this work involved keeping a variety of creditors at bay. Stewart, "a porter-drinking man" (according to his contemporary, the slang collector Francis Grose) was seen as more worldly wise than Johnson, and he was probably the source of such cant terms and gambling jargon that the *Dictionary* contains. He vanishes from the project in 1752, either through death or resignation.

Alongside Stewart, Johnson hired Alexander Macbean, whom he once declared, perhaps overkindly, to be "a man of great learning." Macbean had worked on Chambers' *Cyclopedia,* which must have made him a valuable figure, but it seems that he was better as a copyist than as a source of originality. His brother William, the only one of the amanuenses to survive Johnson, worked on the *Dictionary* too, and later attempted to create his own supplement. He worked on this private project for many years but it was never published. When Alexander died, on June 25, 1784, Johnson wrote to Hester Thrale: "He was very pious.

He was very innocent. He did no ill." A fourth amanuensis, Robert Shiels, a journeyman printer and a man of very "acute understanding" was not without talents. He produced a poem in praise of Johnson's early play *Irene* and later, after finishing his *Dictionary* work, produced an authoritative work on the lives of English poets. Unfortunately the booksellers credited it to the better-known Theophilus Cibber (1703–58, son of the writer Colley and grandson of the sculptor Caius Cibber). Shiels died in December 1753, and never saw the *Dictionary* published. Another man, the otherwise anonymous Maitland, also worked for Johnson.

All these were Scots; V. J. Peyton was the sole English amanuensis. Johnson seems to have been especially fond of him, a theory enhanced by an anecdote that tells how on March 12, 1750 Johnson stood bail for Peyton's wife, Mary, who had been bound over to appear at the next quarter sessions and to keep the peace as regards another woman, one Mary Humphreys. No further detail is known, although J. L. Clifford established that the magistrate in the case was the novelist Henry Fielding, author of *Tom Jones*. Johnson would look after Peyton for many years, employing him on the fourth edition and giving him the occasional gift of money. He paid for both Peyton's and his wife's burial.

Although Johnson's own fee was seemingly large, in fact he was still forced to look elsewhere to boost his funds while the project progressed. He was responsible for his own subsistence, plus that of the amanuenses, and for purchasing paper, books, pens, and ink, and similar necessities. Debts were never far away, including one to his milkman, who supposedly threatened to have him arrested. When the milkman, plus attendant bailiffs, arrived at his door Johnson barricaded it with his bed and waited out his pursuers, who were forced to leave empty-handed: "Depend upon it, I will defend this my little citadel to the utmost." He continued to produce freelance work, and write for his own magazine, *The Rambler,* which he had founded in 1750, partly for money and partly as a "relief" from lexicography.

While the amanuenses were largely deputed to what must indeed have been lexicographical drudgery, Johnson himself took on the more creative task of preparing the definitions and the etymologies. He also selected the quotations that would provide the citations of usage, marking up what he felt were suitable writers in volumes taken either from his own shelves, or from friends who were happy to contribute a book to the greater work. The books were then passed to the amanuenses, who copied each citation onto a slip, in a method that prefigures that adopted in the next century by the compilers of the *OED*.

The books concerned can be seen in the quotations that run through the *Dictionary*—they cover writers from Philip Sidney (1554–86) to Alexander Pope (1688–1744); older manuscripts were less easily available, many were secreted in the libraries of the great country houses. In addition certain general sources were employed. For etymologies he used Skinner and Junius; for technical terms he looked to Chambers' *Cyclopedia,* Harris' *Lexicon Technicum,* Quincy's *Lexicon Physico-Medicum,* and similar specialized volumes. In the time-honored manner Johnson consulted his lexicographical predecessors: Ainsworth, Phillips, and above all Nathaniel Bailey. It is well attested that he had prepared an interleaved copy of Bailey's *Dictionarium Britannicum* and consulted it extensively, especially during his early researches. But according to Alan Reddick the idea, as propounded by Johnson's first biographer, Sir John Hawkins, taken up by Boswell and thence by many others, that Johnson either wrote citations on these blank pages, or inserted tens of thousands of slips between them, simply doesn't hold water.[11] There was insufficient space to amend each word with one, let alone several quotes; and one can barely consider the "chaos" of so many slips, however carefully arranged, staying properly filed in this single, albeit substantial volume. It must be assumed, rather, that Johnson's use of Bailey was for his word list (in the event it exceeded his own) and as he stresses in his preface, there are many words that are validated by no more than Bailey's name.

Johnson is credited as the pioneer of proper citations, but the lexicographers of Greek and Latin were offering them two centuries earlier and, more recently, the Academicians of Italy and France had also done it. Indeed, compared with those researchers, who had the time and the numbers to get everything as right as possible, Johnson's use of his sources was nothing if not cavalier. In all he amassed 116,000 quotations to cover 40,000 headwords. As he admitted in prefaces to the later editions, some quotations were compressed and others modified. This was an understatement. If Johnson didn't like a quote, he changed it. He would omit an opening phrase or amputate a conclusion and if a phrase didn't convey the meaning he required, he had no scruples in rewriting it. Nothing was sacred. One reason, as J. L. Clifford notes, might have been the saving of space, but often "it was also a question of taste. When Johnson disliked the style of an author, he did not hesitate to improve it. After all, he was using earlier authors merely as a means of providing evidence of the proper usage of words."[12] It was a glorious conceit, but it made for what he believed his readers wanted.

The preliminary work appears to have been finished by late summer 1750. With his word list and his "card file" of quotations properly copied onto slips and sorted as to the word they illustrated, Johnson began what he and he alone could achieve: defining the words and giving them an etymology. As far as the myth of the *Dictionary* is concerned, it is of course for these definitions, or what is in fact a small proportion of them, that Johnson's work is most celebrated.

His idiosyncratic animadversions on "oats," "excise" (which nearly landed him jail for defamation), "Grubstreet," and most celebrated of all "lexicographer" are to be found in every dictionary of quotations. They are enjoyable and deserve their fame. They also make it clear that however much discipline Johnson had brought to his profession, in comparison to today's dictionaries, his was a freewheeling, buccaneering affair, with plenty of room for the writer's personality to shine through. Such individuality is rare today; aficionados are best directed to the work of the late Eric Partridge, and he, of course, was dealing in slang, not standard English. Some of these popular Johnsonian remarks, however, typically that in which he defines oats as "a grain, which in England is generally given to horses, but in Scotland supports the people" were by no means "all his own work." Writing in the *PMLA* in 1937, Lane Cooper has outlined the origins of this definition, tracing what has been seen as an anti-Scottish jibe, back to Burton's *Anatomy of Melancholy* (1621), to one John Major, in his *History of Greater Britain* (1521), and beyond him to the medieval physican Galen and thence to the Latin historian Pliny—all of whom compare bread made from oats with that, generally considered superior, which is made from wheat.[13] And, more recently, Johnson's predecessor Bailey had defined the word in 1721 as "forage for horses . . . and sometimes provision for men." In none of these was there any nationalist aspersion, and although in later years Johnson supposedly told Boswell that he had indeed been aiming to "vex" the Scots, he may have been pandering to a self-image that had not yet been in operation when he was working on the *Dictionary*. And as Cooper points out, would he really have set out to annoy his own amanuenses, the majority of whom were Scots?

What is perhaps more interesting is the less obvious way in which Johnson allows his personality to invade his pages. Robert De Maria has pointed out the way in which Johnson has pushed forward his own views, notably on religion, which he sees as paramount in human affairs.[14] As Noah Webster would do seventy years later in his *American Dictionary,* Johnson used his work to promote a personal program. The *Dictionary* is no tract, but as he skewed individual quotations, so too does Johnson skew his choice of sources. For instance, the political theorist Thomas Hobbes, who had his own attitudes to dictionary making, is never chosen himself; only in quotations in which he is systematically refuted does he make an appearance. At the same time, many of the political writers Johnson uses are also pillars of the High Church. In this there can be no doubt that he is deliberately standing in the way of progress. As Rod Mengham has remarked, "His choice of texts . . . compose a hierarchy among the branches of knowledge in which revealed religion is given an importance far greater than the achievements of human reason."[15] Johnson is consciously misrepresenting the contemporary intellectual atmosphere to drive home his own point. In the end,

> Johnson's ulterior purpose in compiling the Dictionary is to make it a channel for moral instruction, as well as means of inducing its readers to recognize the authority of the Christian religion . . . Dictionary-making is a more or less conservative undertaking; in Johnson's case, it supplies a pretext for reinforcing the political status quo, religious authority and cultural authoritarianism. Its technical criteria are designed to exclude insubordination, dissent, subversion—everything that offers to destabilise verbal meanings and social values . . .[16]

There is another aspect to this conservatism. It is possible, suggests De Maria, to break up the whole book into such topics as Death, Judgement, Happiness, Freedom, Money, Education, and so on.[17] It is as if Johnson saw the *Dictionary* as his essay at the *omnium scibile* so desired among the Schoolmen. Certainly his work as cataloger of the Harleian Library, with which he had been occupied immediately prior to starting the *Dictionary,* had imbued him with respect for the great scholars whose manuscripts were included on its shelves. More recently, he had the example of Ephraim Chambers' *Cyclopedia.* Thus one finds large chunks of what Johnson saw as useful material spread around the citations. Typically he reprints a good deal of John Locke's *Essay concerning Human Understanding,* a book which espoused the principle that language, far from susceptible to being fixed, remains fluid. "Our language," states Johnson, "is yet living, and variable by the caprice of everyone that speaks it . . . and [parts of it] can be no more ascertained in a dictionary than a grove, in the agitation of a storm, can be accurately delineated from its picture in the water."

The desire to fix English was, of course, one of the great motive factors behind the agitation for the sort of authoritative dictionary that Johnson was commissioned to produce. And Johnson, at one stage, undoubtedly believed that such "fixing" was within his grasp. But as he explains in his preface, actual research, rather than intellectual theory, had utterly dashed that belief. He is constitutionally incapable—witness the selective quotation, the tampering with other writers—of resisting the temptation of "fixing," but he admits himself defeated. The idea was undoubtedly alluring at the outset, but "I have indulged expectation which neither reason nor experience can justify."[18] We laugh, he adds, at the promises of an elixir that guarantees eternal life, "and with equal justice may the lexicographer be derided, who . . . shall imagine that his dictionary can embalm his language, and secure it from corruption and decay, that it is in his power to change sublunary nature, or clear the world at once from folly, vanity and affectation." He notes that "academies have been instituted" in the hope of so doing, but that like his efforts, theirs have failed, proclaim what they may. That said, "I have devoted this book, the labour of my years, to the honour of my country, that we may no longer yield the palm of philology to the nations of the continent."[19]

By the start of 1755 the *Dictionary* had been ready for some time, but Johnson's desire to affix his degree, which after many years of pleading by Johnson and his friends was finally been awarded by Oxford in February 1755, held up the final impression of the title page. This done, printing was completed and on April 15, 1755, and for some days afterward, there appeared in the London press this advertisement:

A Dictionary of the English language: in which the words are deduced from their originals and illustrated in their different significations by examples from the best writers. To which are prefixed a History of the Language and a Grammar. By Samuel Johnson, A.M.

Reviews were mixed, but generally favorable. Few would match the verse encomium that Johnson's friend and former pupil David Garrick, now a theatrical superstar, published in the *Public Advertiser,* the *Gentleman's Magazine,* and elsewhere. An orgy of nationalist pride, it declared:

> *Talk of war with a Briton, he'll boldly advance,*
> *That one English soldier will beat ten of France;*
> *Would we alter the boast from the sword to the pen,*
> *Our odds are still greater, still greater our men . . .*
> *First Shakespeare and Milton, like gods in the fight,*
> *Have put their whole drama and epick to flight . . .*
> *And Johnson, well arm'd like a hero of yore,*
> *Has beat forty French, and will beat forty more!*

The idea that Johnson, singlehandedly, had "beat" the Forty Immortals of the Académie Française was a constant theme. In the *Gentleman's Magazine* another friend, John Hawkesworth, called for due honors to go to Johnson, "who alone has effected in seven years what the joint labour of forty academicians could not produce to a neighbouring nation in less than half a century." The preface, he added, "is written with the utmost purity and elegance; and though it is only an avenue to the dusty deserts of barren philology, it abounds with flowers that can shoot only on poetic ground; it delights the passenger without detaining him by the way." Others were more tempered, noting a variety of errors, but generally preferring not to harp on them: Johnson's achievement outweighed the carping of less accomplished men.

The remarks of the economist Adam Smith stand for many others:

> Mr Johnson . . . has made a very full collection of all the different meanings of each English word, justified by examples from authors of good reputation. When we compare this book with other dictionaries, the merit of the author appears very extraordinary . . . The merit of Mr Johnson's dictionary is so great, that it cannot detract from us to take notice of some defects . . . These defects consist chiefly in the plan, which appears to us not to be sufficiently grammatical. The different significations of a word are indeed collected; but they are seldom digested with general classes, or ranged under the meaning which the word principally expresses. And sufficient care has not been taken to distinguish the words apparently synonymous . . . we cannot help wishing that the author had trusted less to the judgement of those who may consult him, and had oftener passed his own censure upon those words which are not of approved use.[20]

Particularly gratifying must have been the comments of the Marquis Nicolini, president of the Accademia della Crusca. Johnson's work will be "a perpetual Monument of Fame to the Author, an Honour to his own Country in particular, and a general Benefit to the republic of Letters throughout all Europe."[21] Indeed Europe was more generous to Johnson than he, or at least his claque, were in return. His preface, and the *Dictionary* itself, were frequently printed abroad, and positively reviewed, while in France Voltaire proposed in 1778 that the Académie should completely make over their own *dictionnaire* on Johnson's model. As it would in England, Johnson's influence persisted in Europe well into the next century.

Some, however, did vent their feelings. Just as Swift's plans for an Academy had been dismissed as Tory propaganda, so too was Johnson attacked by the Whigs for his supposed Tory bias. There was, of course, some justification for this. Johnson's definition of Tory: "one who adheres to the ancient constitution of the state, and the apostolical hierarchy of the church of England" jibed badly with that of Whig: "a faction." Even if he included the etymology of Tory: "derived I suppose from an Irish word meaning savage," he more than balances it with a damning quote from Swift as a citation for Whig, plus the uncomplimentary etymology. Thus one of his most hostile critics was Thomas Edwards, a hardcore Whig who accused the *Dictionary* of being no more than "a vehicle for Jacobite and high-flying tracts." This attack came in a letter, of which Johnson was presumably ignorant, but in the party political atmosphere of the period it cannot have been unique.

The general reader, who had no recourse to journalistic pontification, occasionally had the chance to face the lexicographer himself. One, a lady, asked how he could have defined *pastern* (properly the part of a horse's foot between the fetlock and the hoof) as the "knee of the horse" and was given the candid response: "Ignorance, Madam, pure ignorance." An equally celebrated anecdote tells of a literary lady who praised him for his restraint in excluding "naughty" words.[22] According to Johnson's friend Sir Herbert Croft, whose own lexicographical plans would be aborted through lack of interest, he replied, "No, Madam, I hope I have not daubed my fingers. I find, however, that you have been looking for them." In the way of dictionary "criticism" Johnson occasionally met those who triumphantly pointed to a word they knew and he had omitted. But Johnson had never pretended to absolute inclusion of every single word and the language naturally had more to offer than his 40,000 headwords.

Sometimes his generalizations were embarrassingly easy to overturn. The classic example is that laid out by Johnson in the Grammar section, where he states that the letter "H . . . seldom, perhaps never, begins any but the first syllable in which it is always sounded with a full breath, except in heir, herb, hostler . . ." The radical MP John Wilkes, whose own writing, notably issue 45 of his journal *The North Briton,* would bring him untold problems a few years later, couldn't resist exploding Johnson. Correcting his statement, Wilkes declared that "The author of this remark must be a man of a quick *appre-hension,* and *compre-hensive* genius; but I can never forgive his *un-handsome be-haviour* to the poor *knight-hood, priest-hood* and *widow-hood,* nor his *in-humanity* to all *man-hood* and *woman-hood.*" In later editions, abashed but by no means defeated, Johnson grudgingly acknowledged that "sometimes" H could begin middle or final syllables.

But the worst criticisms came too late to mar Johnson's success. The anonymous author of a collection of old Scottish verses, published in 1786, promised that the next age "will pronounce his work, what it really is, a disgrace to the language." He excoriated him for poor examples, inadequate etymologies, and misquotation and suggested that "any schoolmaster might have done what Johnson did. His *Dictionary* is merely a glossary to his own barbarous works." Johnson had "very small learning," was "without taste," and in the end that "the very worst writer in the language . . . whose works are true *pages of inanity,* wrapt in barbarism, should set up for a judge of our language; are all ideas to excite laughter." Only the passionately Anglophobe H. L. Mencken, writing in 1945, managed greater bile when he savaged "Samuel Johnson . . . the grand master of all the pedantic quacks of his time. No eminent lexicographer was ever more ignorant of speech-ways than he was."[23] But Mencken had his own ax to grind, and he was blessed with 160 years' worth of hindsight.

More immediate, and of much greater moment to Johnson, was the response of his putative patron, the earl of Chesterfield. Writing in Dodsley's magazine *The World,* on November 28, 1754, Chesterfield reported:

> I heard the other day with great pleasure from my worthy friend Mr. Dodsley, that Mr. Johnson's English Dictionary . . . will be published this winter . . . I had long lamented that we had no lawful standard of our language set up, for those to repair to, who might chuse to speak and write it grammatically and correctly: and I have as long wished that either some one person of distinguished abilities would undertake the work singly, or that a certain number of gentlemen would form themselves, or be formed by the government into a society for that purpose . . . Many people have imagined that so extensive a work would have been best performed by a number of persons, who should have taken their several departments of examining, sifting, winnowing (I borrow this image from the Italian *crusca*), purifying, and finally fixing our language, by incorporating their respective funds into one joint stock . . . I think the public in general, and the republic of letters in particular, greatly obliged to Mr. Johnson for having undertaken and executed so great and desirable a work . . . if we are to judge by the various works of Mr. Johnson, already published, we have good reason to believe that he will bring this as near to perfection as any one man could do. The plan of it, which he published some years ago, seems to me to be proof of it. Nothing can be more rationally imagined or more accurately and elegantly expressed.

All pleasant enough, and elegantly expressed itself, if a little condescending, but hardly the stuff of controversy. Yet Johnson took serious offense. Johnson and Chesterfield had first crossed paths in 1746, when the lexicographer approached the lord in the hope of gaining valuable patronage. Intermediaries showed Chesterfield the still unfinished "Scheme" for the work and the two men met. Chesterfield professed himself impressed and when the revised "Scheme," now entitled a "Plan" appeared, duly dedicated to Chesterfield, Johnson was rewarded with a gift of £10. That however was all. Tradition has it that Johnson visited Chesterfield on a number of subsequent occasions, only to be ignored or turned away. The effect of this was to sever relations between the two. Whatever hopes Johnson might have had, he had abandoned them sometime earlier. Dodsley, however, still believed there was cash to be gained from Chesterfield and informed him that the *Dictionary* was on the verge of publication. At which point he penned the notice above. To the disinterested observer it was at worst a gratuitous puff, but to Johnson it was infuriating. The implicit presumption that Chesterfield, who had long since snubbed him, was now claiming to have been the guiding light behind his work was unbearable. As Sledd and Kolb noted, "Dodsley . . . had stupidly given Johnson the double opportunity to acquit himself of ingratitude and to teach the most zealously elegant gentleman of the age a lesson in manners. Johnson did both."[24]

On February 7, 1755 Johnson penned his own letter, which also appeared in *The World*. It climaxed in a celebrated paragraph:

> Is not a Patron, my Lord, one who looks with unconcern on a man struggling for life in the water, and, when he has reached ground encumbers him with help? The notice which you have been pleased to take of my labours, had it been early had been kind; but has been delayed till I am indifferent, and cannot enjoy it; till I am solitary and cannot impart it; till I am known, and do not want it. I hope it is no very cynical asperity, not to confess obligations where no benefit has been received, or to be unwilling that the Publick should consider me as owing that to a Patron, which Providence has enabled me to do for myself.[25]

Whether Johnson wounded him or not, Chesterfield, true to type, betrayed no such emotion. Instead he displayed the letter on a table, and read it out to Dodsley, remarking at the "severest passages," observing how well they were expressed and saying, "This man has great powers." Johnson was not mollified and made, in due course, a couple of remarks calculated to offend: "This man . . . I thought to have been a Lord among wits; but, I find, he is only a wit among lords." And when in 1774 Chesterfield's *Letters to His Son* were published, he said that "they teach the morals of a whore, and the manners of a dancing master." Chesterfield was dead by then, but while still alive had hit back, at least in a letter, with a description of Johnson (as was presumed) as "a respectable Hottentot." The affair inevitably petered out, and it is unlikely that there was any effect on the reputation of the *Dictionary*. Indeed, in a more skeptical age one might even wonder whether Dodsley, far from being obtuse as some scholars have suggested, knew exactly what was going on and quite deliberately fostered the row in the hope of boosting sales. If he did, it was a futile gesture. The *Dictionary,* while widely praised, was at £4.10s. beyond the average pocket. It took ten years to sell even four thousand copies (and that sum may be exaggerated by 1,000). As copies languished on booksellers' shelves a new scheme was proposed: the publication of a second edition, in 165 weekly parts for sixpence a part. Those who were willing to pay 1/- would need wait only half the time. Serialization might work for novels, where readers enjoyed the sort of cliff-hanging breaks that ninety years later would have Dickens' devotees queuing up in anticipation of a new episode, but for a dictionary, a practical work that was of use only as a whole, it was a foolish concept and not a success. Far more lucrative was the octavo abridgment which was launched in 1756. It sold 40,000 copies at 10/- each over the next thirty years.

A third edition of the folio appeared in 1765; it was nearly identical with the first, but when the fourth edition appeared in 1773 it was found that Johnson had made extensive changes. This, it has been accepted, is in many ways the *Dictionary* that Johnson had always desired. The revision had taken a year's steady work, starting in mid-1771. Helped by two of his old amanuenses— V. J. Peyton and (probably) William Macbean—he set about bringing the book up to date. The amanuenses appear to have started by including a good deal of the material that had been excluded from the original edition, but Johnson often chose to reject their suggestions. Much of the "encyclopedic" material that had made for such lengthy definitions in certain, usually technical areas, was abridged. In its place came 2,500–3,000 new quotations, usually adding even more substance to the moral and religious theses that underpinned the book. Definitions and etymologies were all considered and in many cases amended.

Johnson died in 1784, but editions of his dictionary continued to appear well into the new century. Of these editions the best known were those of Henry Todd, published in 1818, an abridged version of Todd, edited by Alexander Chalmers in 1820, and the American Joseph Worcester's subsequent edition of Chalmers' Todd, which appeared in 1827. But perhaps the most interesting was one that in the event did not appear. Planned by Johnson's friend Sir Herbert Croft, not only would it have served as an embellishment of Johnson's master work, but it would also have been the first work of reference to be called *The Oxford Dictionary.*

The *Gentleman's Magazine* of August 1787 (volume LVII, part II) printed a lengthy missive from "the Gentleman employed upon a New Dictionary of the *English* Language." The gentleman in question was the Reverend Sir Herbert Croft (1751–1816), an earnest if eccentric figure, whose life, as itemized in the

DNB was both "hampered by pecuniary pressure" (despite his title the family income had devolved upon another, more fortunate branch) and further hindered by a "volatile character, which prevented him from adhering to any definite course of actions." Croft obtained the living of Prittlewell in Essex, but the bulk of his life was spent either in Oxford, where he undertook literary or lexicographical researches, or on the Continent, fleeing his creditors. One such journey followed a mere forty-eight hours after his second marriage, although the resultant stay in Paris brought him into contact with Charles Nodier, primarily a dilettante but also, on occasion, a lexicographer. The ins and outs of Croft's life are too many for proper delineation here, but its main thrust, when unpursued by debt, was in "busying himself in the collection of materials for his proposed English dictionary, which he proposed calling *The Oxford Dictionary* after the University where he conducted much of his research." This dictionary was intended to revise and indeed replace that of Johnson. Like his predecessor Croft prepared a "Plan," which was laid out both in a number of letters to the *Gentleman's Magazine,* and in a 51-page "Letter to the Rt. Hon. Wm Pitt concerning the New Dictionary of the English by the Rev. Herbert Croft." Written in March 1788, it concentrated on pointing out the defects of Johnson's *Dictionary.* In it Croft explained that he had already amassed 200 quarto volumes of manuscript for his own work. By 1790 he was claiming to have found 11,000 words omitted by Johnson, three years later he claimed 11,000 more, "as used by the highest authorities." His intention was to publish a four-volume work, at twelve guineas the set, but it would never happen. As the *DNB* explained, "The undertaking which Croft persecuted, it must be readily acknowledged, with great energy, involved him for many years in labours entirely unremunerative . . ." His official renunciation of the scheme, pleading an almost complete lack of subscribers, was published in the *Gentleman's Magazine* in 1793. In 1802, apparently oblivious to the current state of war, he left once more for France, where he was arrested as an Englishman but freed once the authorities were apprised of his status as a *littérateur.* He spent the rest of his life in Amiens and Paris, surviving thanks to the support of Charles Nodier.

Croft was an odd figure whose writings included a number of bizarre publications, among them a proposed new system of punctuation, a free sheet entitled the *Literary Fly* (10,000 copies were distributed on January 18, 1779), a memoir of the poet Young (which is included in Johnson's *Lives of the Poets*) and *Love and Madness,* which was based on letters written by the suicidal poet Thomas Chatterton, which to his shame Croft had obtained through trickery. All this said, Croft was no fool. He had some real linguistic knowledge, so much so that the chemist Joseph Priestley, who had been planning his own study of English, was happy to turn over his papers to Croft, to be included in the proposed *Oxford Dictionary.* But in the end his timing was bad and his labors pointless. There would be an *Oxford Dictionary,* but it would be the work not of this eighteenth-century eccentric, but of an infinitely more dedicated and capable man.

Giving the Romanes lecture in June 1900, Sir James Murray, who as editor of the *New English Dictionary* was currently shepherding the letters I, J, and K through the presses, opened his talk by suggesting that for many people "the Dictionary" meant simply Johnson's work of 1755, an authority as fixed as the Bible or the Prayer Book. Sir James' lecture, of course, was intended to explode this myth and trace lexicography back to much earlier origins. Today "Johnson" has been long superseded, in Britain by Murray's own dictionary and in America by Webster, but the myth persists. Before Johnson lexicography was composed of a number of developing strands. In his work these strands were united, setting standards for whatever has followed. Before moving on to the dictionaries that succeed him, whether in England or in what was soon to be a rival center of dictionary making, the newly freed states of America, it is worth pausing to consider just how far the legend matches the facts. Johnson set himself a number of tasks when he commenced the *Dictionary:* the first, as called for by his intellectual forebears, was the fixing of the language; in addition to this were the bringing up to date of a variety of lexicographical "technicalities," notably his treatment of definitions and etymologies.

Since Murray's lecture, in which he credited Johnson with raising lexicography "altogether to a higher level,"[26] Johnson has continued to enjoy much congratulation. Starnes and Noyes praised his professionalism, while D. J. Greene describes the dictionary as "a very great and serious achievement in the history of the study of the English language. It is . . . a most important landmark in the development of English, from a set of unimportant dialects spoken by a small group of islanders on the fringe of civilization, to a great world language."[27] Mencken, as noted above, was hostile, but while Baugh and Cable drew back from the chorus of unalloyed enthusiasm they did not condemn Johnson outright. They state that "judged by modern standards it is painfully inadequate. Its etymologies are often ludicrous. It is marred in places by prejudice and caprice. Its definitions, generally sound and often discriminating, are at times truly Johnsonian.[28] It includes a host of words with a very questionable right to be regarded as belonging to the language"[29] but they too accept the size of Johnson's "great achievement" which was "justly so regarded." They also appreciate the extent to which he exhibits the language "much more fully than ever . . . before" and note, as does virtually every commentator, his use of citations to an unprecedented extent.

It is in the area of citations, of course, that Johnson stands unrivaled, at least in 1755. He chopped them and changed them, used them selectively to drum home his own moral agenda and generally showed their learned authors only scant respect, but no predecessor had ever amassed so many illustrative quotations. For quantity, if not always quality, he cannot be undone. But as to the bigger picture, was Johnson truly an innovator, or, as Sledd and Kolb ask, to what extent did Johnson's published *Dictionary* live up to the ideals he proposed in its plan? Was he an original, or was he simply the agent of a bookseller's scheme, aping the European academies, and reiterating, rather than revolutionizing, the lexicographical techniques of his English predecessors?

Certainly the structure of the work is wholly traditional. The preface, followed by the word list itself, plus the History and the Grammar were dyed-in-the-wool staples of lexicographical method; they can all be seen in seventeenth- and eighteenth-century works. As for the quality of the history and grammar, they might not have been the "contemptible performances; [the] reproach to the learning and industry"[30] of the nation as dismissed by Horne Tooke, but they were hardly exceptional. Nonetheless the Académie borrowed from the history and if the grammar was run-of-the-mill, it was sufficiently interesting for Bishop Lowth to commence his own in-depth study. The truth appears to be that Johnson was not especially interested in either and he concludes the grammar with an unashamed cop-out: "Thus have I collected rules and examples, by which the English language may be learned, if the reader be already acquainted with grammatical terms, or taught by a master to those that are more ignorant. To have written a grammar for such as are not yet initiated in the schools, would have been tedious, and perhaps at last ineffectual." Now, we hear him *sotto voce,* let's cut to the chase.

His preface is much more important. Even the usually antagonistic Tooke liked it. To quote Sledd and Kolb, "The Preface . . . is one of the finest things that Johnson ever wrote, a moving personal document and an excellent statement of the aims, methods, and difficulties of one kind of eighteenth-century lexicography."[31] But they qualify this praise, adding that "Its excellence cannot be rightly understood, however, if it is read . . . in isolation from its historical context; for the basis of its merit is not originality." In "an age of dictionaries of all kinds" Johnson's contribution, in their eyes, was simply *primus inter pares* and its preface, while admirable, undoubtedly reflects another famous declaratory preface, that written by Ephraim Chambers for his *Cyclopedia.* Both men acknowledged the influence of the Academies, but both were essentially solo performers and John-son might well have echoed Chambers when he declared that these "Royal, Impe-rial, Caesarian and Ducal Academies [have] Splendid Names, pompous Titles but [are] rarely productive of Fruits answerable thereto! Many of our private Clubs might vie with their Academies; and much of the Conversation at certain Coffee-house Tables, with their Conferences."[32] They wished to rival the Academies, but saw no need for an English equivalent. And, like Johnson, Chambers felt no embarrassment in pointing out that his work, performed by one man and in a fraction of the time taken by the intellectual teams of Italy and France, was quite up to scratch.

As far as definitions are concerned, one need only observe the extent of his revisions for the fourth edition to appreciate that Johnson was never fully satis-fied with his efforts. Nonetheless they are, especially for the nonprofessional, the most widely quoted aspect of the *Dictionary.* He has been attacked not just for the idiosyncrasies that in some eyes taint his defining, but for the awk-wardness of some of the definitions, especially when turning to the simpler words. Classic examples are *"Network:* any thing reticulated, or decussated, at equal distances, with interstices between the intersections" and *"Cough:* a con-vulsion of the lungs, vellicated by some sharp serosity. It is pronounced *coff."* But while "it is customary to laugh at the ponderous way Johnson defined sim-ple objects . . . at least he did not avoid the task."[33] In the end, one can agree with Johnson himself: "To interpret a language by itself is very difficult; many words cannot be explained by synonimes, because the idea signified by them has not more than one appellation; nor by paraphrase, because simple ideas cannot be described."[34]

As far as "fixing" the language is concerned, Johnson grew to appreciate the futility of such a plan. He acknowledged, in the preface, that the lexicographer should be one of those who "do not form, but register the language; who do not teach men how they should think, but relate how they have hitherto expressed their thoughts." No doubt he believed this, although his more opinionated def-initions, especially those regarding politics, and the religious agenda that per-meates the whole book rather militate against such professed openhandedness. Indeed, he only abandoned his original intentions after several years' work, driven to accept the realities of the language with which he was dealing. One must admire him, in the end, for admitting that he had been mistaken. He was also echoing a growing belief among lexicographers who, unlike the high-flown theorists of academe, actually worked on dictionaries. His immediate predecessor, Benjamin Martin, had made his position amply clear. And Ephraim Chambers, with whose opinions Johnson so often concurred, had said:

"The Dictionary-writer is not supposed to have any hand in the things he relates; he is no more concerned to make the improvements, or to establish the significations."[35] He might be a historian by default, but it was for historians proper to deal with that side of the work. As Sledd and Kolb put it: the Lexicographer "had enough to do to keep the minutes of the language, someone else might call the meeting to order."[36]

The concept of improving or refining the language was very much intertwined with the belief that it could be "fixed." Johnson aimed to help with this process, but to what extent the *Dictionary* achieved this aim is hard to tell. Johnson was not, as would be his American descendants, producing a prescriptive work. However personalized his definitions may have been, he is not, for all his linguistic self-confidence, actually telling people that A is good and B bad. He made changes in spelling, but many of these had already been established; he certainly paid substantial attention to usage—to a greater extent than any lexicographer before him—and his dictionary and the opinions on language it contained would be a model for his successors. How much any of this actually influenced the standards of British speech is less clear. Since he resisted marking punctuation, it cannot be said that he influenced the way the language sounded; his Grammar was insufficiently original to credit it with any major influence; he barely deals with syntax.

In the wider world, outside that of his professional and intellectual peers, Johnson had little effect. Like the majority of lexicographers—Wesley is a notable exception—he neither understood nor cared for the masses. As Horne Tooke put it, "Nearly one third of this Dictionary is as much the language of the Hottentots as of the English; and it would be no difficult matter so to translate any one of the plainest and most popular numbers of the Spectator into the language of that Dictionary, that no mere Englishman, though well read in his own language, would be able to comprehend one sentence of it."[37] In Johnson's defense, many of his sources, which helped dictate his word list, were dedicated to "hard words"; and Johnson incorporated their selections. Bailey, his eighteenth-century rival, may have included common language but Phillips, who is cited next to Bailey as a major influence, was the "hard-word" tradition personified.

Where Johnson is more culpable, at least with the benefit of hindsight, is in his judgments on those words that were socially acceptable and those that were not. Among those that he wished to see consigned to linguistic purgatory were *bang* (beat, thump), *to belabour, blackguard, to budge, to cajole, to coax, to con* (study, commit to memory), *conundrum, to doff, doings, to dumbfound, fuss sb., gambler, glum, ignoramus, job sb., lead* (as in to take the lead), *pat* (fit, convenient), *posse, scrape* (difficulty), *sensible* (reasonable, judicious), *shabby, sham, shambling, simpleton, slim* (slender), *spick and span, squab* (plump and flat), *to squabble, stark* (as in stark mad), *tiff, touchy, trait, transpire, to volunteer, width,* and up to 800 more. In this context it is surprising that he found no problems with "mob," which Swift abhorred. In any case, Johnson's withdrawal of his imprimatur does not seem to have had any great effect. These words and several hundred others similarly rejected seem to have survived perfectly well. One whole group of words that Johnson rejected out of hand were those described as dialect. Given the linguistic conservatism that pervades his work this is hardly surprising, but even Johnson acknowledged a few, mainly Scottish terms. In this, as in many other matters, his decision influenced his successors, and there are few dialect terms to be found in such works as those of Kenrick, Ash, or Sheridan. Those who sought such vocabularies turned instead to such dedicated publications as Francis Grose's *Provincial Glossary* (1787) and the many county-specific lists that began to emerge during the nineteenth century and which would form the basis of Joseph Wright's *English Dialect Dictionary.*

Johnson attempted, with the help of Skinner and Junius, to deal more thoroughly with etymology than any predecessor. Quantitatively he may have succeeded, but the quality of his work was less impressive. Lord Macaulay dismissed his efforts, calling him "a wretched etymologist," but in fairness Johnson was hamstrung from the start. He looked at the best authorities, and duly incorporated their work in his, but the best authorities of the period would not stand the test of time. The revolution in etymology that would come with Sir William Jones' researches into Sanskrit was still thirty years in the future. The developments in German philology, which would be seen in the methodology of the *OED,* were even further distant. There is no point, as Sledd and Kolb point out, "in patronizing learned men who merely shared the errors of their times."[38]

Bereft of such latterday advances, eighteenth-century etymologies were based on twin theories: the "mutation of letters," which basically accepted that in any context any letter could mean and sound whatever it was necessary for it to mean and sound, plus a complex historical concept known as "the wanderings of the people" which took its origins from Bible stories and the beliefs of ancient historians. It was during these wanderings that a supposedly original, unifying tongue gradually broke down into separate groups and subgroups of language. "The etymologists rouse admiration," note Sledd and Kolb, "both for their learning and for the ingenuity with which they bring into a single story the adventures of Shem, Ham, Japhet, the Homeric heroes, the Phoenicians, Gomer, Odin, Hengest, Horsa, the Scythians, and the Druids."[39]

Linguistic patriotism was very important: it could overcome a good deal of contrary fact. Thus Benjamin Martin could explain, "We are told also by Cluverius and other geographers and historians that the ancient Germans, Gauls, Spaniards, and Britains [*sic*] were all call'd by the name of Celto-Scythae; and further that they had all one language and differ'd only in dialect; and many of the learned have thought that this ancient German, Celtic, or as it was most commonly call'd, Teutonic language was an original one, or one of those we have deriv'd from the confusion of tongues at Babel; yea, some have gone farther, and insist on its being the vernacular tongue of Adam, his family and descendants." Such a pronouncement lacks the slightest proof, but it seemed to satisfy even the most learned authorities at the time.[40]

Talking to Boswell, many years later, Johnson declared himself essentially satisfied with his work: "I knew very well what I was undertaking—and very well how to do it—and have done it very well." Despite all the criticisms that can be made, it is hard not to agree with him. He had responded to the dreams of the intellectual élite, the perceived demand of an increasingly literate public and to the commercial imperatives of the booksellers and in his idiosyncratic, often self-indulgent way transcended them all to produce a work that, at least in his native country, would not be surpassed, albeit often rivaled, for 150 years.

"Scarcely any man," he was to write in his Preface to Rolt's *Dictionary of Trade and Commerce,* "publishes a book, whatever it be, without believing that he has caught the moment when the publick attention is vacant to his call, and the world is disposed, in a particular manner, to learn the art which he undertakes to teach"; but he himself had done what others merely hoped to do . . . The forty French, at least in the judgment of Englishmen—and Scotsmen—had been well beaten.[41]

And as Robert Burchfield has pointed out, "In the whole tradition of English language and literature the *only* dictionary compiled by a writer of the first rank is that of Dr Johnson." It may well be, he adds, that had Dryden, who had his own take on language, or Macaulay, albeit no admirer of dictionary makers, turned their hands to the task "the result would very likely have been as beguiling, and as influential."[42] But neither man did, and the palm remains with Johnson.

In any pivotal moment, and the publication of the *Dictionary* is undoubtedly that, there is the question of viewpoint: is the occasion the climax of the old or the gateway to the new? To what extent was Johnson's work a case of launching a rearguard action in defense of older, absolute values, and to what extent did it work to glorify what was still the relatively newly confident English vernacular? For all Johnson's achievements his work is ultimately backward looking. As a literary artifact, if one accepts Peter Conrad's theory, the whole *Dictionary* "is Johnson's necropolis," a labor carried through "because it coincided with his deepest imaginative and emotional conviction, that it is our responsibility . . . to mourn and in so doing to remember." To define, to etymologize is to open "the grave inside the word [and] since the entries are lapidary inscriptions or funerary tablets, the whole language amounts to a family plot."[43] As a sociocultural artifact, it stands determinedly in the way of progress. A definition, declares Johnson, "is the only way whereby the meaning of words can be known, without leaving room for *contest* about it." Contest, debate, argument—if we dispute the meaning of words, then we dispute that of the world in which they are currency. In Johnson's conservative worldview this cannot be tolerated.

In purely lexicographical terms the *Dictionary* brings together the traditions of centuries, refines them, and in so doing offers a work that stood as an authority from the middle of the eighteenth century to the beginning of the twentieth. But the paradox is that in perfecting the past, Johnson also stands as its last-ditch defender. He sets the scene for the next chapter in lexicography, but he does not advance toward it. Nor indeed does he wish to. The great tome is a bastion of conservatism and if Johnson acknowledged that "fixing" the language was an impossibility, such pragmatism does not appear to have diminished a lingering desire to "fix" society. His work, so successful in encapsulating what had gone before, was ill-suited to the world around it, an increasingly scientific world in which, as regards lexicography, such self-indulgent solo performances as Johnson's would become increasingly alien. Johnson regrets, in his preface, that he dreamed as a poet but woke as a lexicographer, yet he still managed to allow the poet a good deal of leeway in his work. The future would demand only the lexicographer. Johnson was authoritative, but the image of his *Dictionary* is epitomized in a celebrated scene in Thackeray's *Vanity Fair.* On leaving Miss Pinkerton's academy for young ladies the emancipated young Becky Sharp is presented with a copy (the 10s. octavo) of Johnson. Her first gesture is to toss it away. It is a renunciation of the past and a step into the new world. The world delineated by he whom Miss Pinkerton terms "The Great Lexicographer" was collapsing. Becky's hero is Napoleon, rather than her mentor's Johnson. Linguistic authority, epitomized by Johnson's work, was in free fall. From now on, Rod Mengham suggests, the Johnsonian dictionary "is suddenly rendered useless, its respect for fixed definitions, stable order, classification, made redundant."[44] As Anthony Burgess notes, "That great book now seemed to be a dog walking on its hind legs and, moreover, walking backward."[45] Johnson's successors learned from Johnson what not to be, but it would take more than a century, and the development of a whole new approach to philology before the dictionaries suited to this new world would start to appear. And before approaching those new dictionaries, it is necessary to quit Europe and move west, to witness the emergence of a new and energetic center of dictionary making: America.

10

America: The Years Before Webster

G iven the endless thread that runs through the history of lexicography, it is satisfactorily fitting that the first homegrown American lexicographer should be called Samuel Johnson, Jr., whose *School Dictionary* was published in 1798. But before looking properly at this transatlantic Johnson, and those of his successors who predate the first truly great American lexicographer, Noah Webster, it is necessary to look backward for moment.

English is America's national language today and has been ever since independence was declared in 1776. Yet if one looks back to the earliest days of colonial America, the success of English seems as much a matter of luck as of judgment. As Allen Walker Read points out, the pattern of exploration was such that the French, who held vast tracts of the interior, the Germans, who had flooded to Pennsylvania and thence to the Midwest, and the Dutch, who had substantial settlements around the Hudson valley, might any one of them have bid for linguistic preeminence.[1] Yet all these bowed to English, the language of the chain of states running along the eastern seaboard, and while they might continue to speak their own languages at home, society, especially as regards the demands of trade and commerce, demanded that they be bilingual. Even the American Indians, whose own tribal languages, known to the seventeenth century as the "American Language," predated any European incursion, were happy to take on English—a useful esperanto that overrode the complexities of intertribal communication. All these languages, and those of the successive waves of immigrants who arrived in the New World, would vastly enrich the dominant tongue, and go on to make "American English" a very different creature from its ancestor "English English," but they were and remain second-class citizens. James Fenimore Cooper, writing in 1828, the year of *Webster's Dictionary,* summed up the situation: "If the people of this country were like the people of any other country on earth, we should be speaking at this moment a great variety of nearly unintelligible patois; but in point of fact, the people of the United States . . . speak, as a body, an incomparably better English than the people of the mother country."[2] Cooper was naturally patriotic, but English—American English—ruled, and still rules the linguistic roost. Whether Spanish, already expanding dramatically, will one day go so far as to overthrow English is a matter for the twenty-first century.

The concept of "American English," unsurprisingly, seems to have been coined by Noah Webster, who wrote in 1789 of "the American tongue,"[3] and eleven years later published in the *Monthly Magazine and American Review* an essay "On the Scheme of an American Language." A fiercely patriotic linguist, Webster wrote presciently of the "future separation of the American tongue from the English" and called for "a system of our own, in language as well as government."[4] Both would come to pass, and Webster would be the great moving agent of the division, but just as the English system of government dominated the colonies, so too did the English language, and with it the English dictionary.

The earliest dictionaries to appear in independent America were neither American nor were they the best of what was available in England. Samuel Johnson's *Dictionary of the English Language* (1755) was not imported until 1818, by which time it had reached its eleventh edition. It was printed, as was common, in a companion volume to Walker's *Principles of English Pronunciation,* a work whose practical guidance made it much more popular than Johnson's sonorous pronouncements, which would come to serve, as much as anything else, as a convenient butt for Webster's work-in-progress. Various editions of Johnson, notably Todd's revision of 1818 (which was in 1827 revised itself by an American, Joseph Worcester) and Chalmers' subsequent abridgment, continued to appear until Webster finally rendered them obsolete in 1828. However, the Johnson tradition, somewhat modified, would be carried on by the same Joseph Worcester. Other major dictionaries appeared, typically the "Scott-Bailey," but even that, which ranged wider than most in its inclusion of the marginalia of the English vocabulary, paid no attention to developments in the colonies. The history of the American dictionary prior to the Revolutionary War was simply that of its English cousin.

Even in its choice of imports, however, the new nation made what would become its predominant lexicographical feature clear from the start. The scholarly dictionary, consciously geared to an intellectual élite, was never as popular as more easily accessible works. American lexicography then as now was mainly prescriptive: English dictionaries, especially those of the Johnson/Bailey mold, appealed to the intellectually secure; the colonists and the émigrés who flooded in constantly to swell their numbers were less grounded. What they wanted was not to be told what was in the language, but what might be the best way of using it: what was acceptable, and what was not. Thus many of the dictionaries that appeared prior to 1800 concentrated on spelling and pronunciation and it was this educational aspect of his work that would contribute to Noah Webster's popular success. Of the imports, four works stand out, written by John Entick, William Perry, Thomas Sheridan, and John Walker.

Entick's *New Spelling Dictionary of the English Language* had appeared in England in 1764 and had been revised in 1787. It offered readers a mixture of encyclopedic information, specifically a "List of all the Cities, Boroughs, Market-Towns and Remarkable Villages in England and Wales" and "a Succinct account of the Heathen Gods, Goddesses, Heroes and Heroines, etc. deduced from the best authorities." It backed this up with a guide to spelling. It was from Entick, an American best-seller, that Webster would derive much of his method.

Entick (1703?–73), "a bookseller's drudge,"[5] styled himself "the Reverend Entick" although there is no proof as to his ever having taken holy orders. A schoolmaster by trade, his first publication, *Speculum latinum* (1728), was designed to make Latin intelligible even when a teacher was "perplexed with a very dull boy." When in 1755 he began writing for the antigovernment journal *The Monitor* at an annual salary of £200 he proved so enthusiastic a critic that in November 1762 his house was entered and his papers seized. Undaunted, Entick fought back with a suit, claiming £2,000 in damages. He settled for £300. The first edition of the *New Spelling Dictionary* appeared in 1763; it sold, as did each of its successors, 20,000 copies. In 1771 came a second dictionary: *A New Latin and English Dictionary.* Entick spent most of his life as a writer, mainly for the bookseller Edward Dilly (1732–79). It was no doubt thanks to Dilly's extensive trade with America that the speller made its way across the Atlantic. Entick died, still in authorial harness, on May 22, 1773.

With Entick, one learned to spell the language; with another series of dictionaries, notably those produced by William Perry, Thomas Sheridan, and John Walker, one learned how to pronounce it. While Johnson had set his seal on etymology and citation, he had avoided delineating pronunciation and in the fifty years that followed the *Dictionary*'s first edition there appeared a number of dictionaries that dealt primarily with his omission. All these were exported to America, where they proved even more successful. Typical was William Perry's *Royal Standard English Dictionary* (1775), which was published in America in 1788 and touted as "The First Work of the Kind printed in America." The claim was true: this was the first dictionary to be printed there rather than imported. Dedicated to the American Academy of Arts and Sciences, it offered a dictionary and a system of pronunciation "intelligible to the weakest capacity" plus a grammar of English Scripture, a list of proper names in the Bible, together with their pronunciation, the names of principal cities, rivers, and other features of the known world, the names of ancient and modern philosophers, poets, statesmen, and their pronunciations. It ran to 30,000 words in 596 double-columned pages. Perry also wrote a spelling dictionary, *The Only Sure Guide to the English Tongue.*

Thomas Sheridan's two-volume *General Dictionary of the English Language* (1780) was, in George Krapp's words, "the first pronouncing dictionary to acquire what, for lack of a better term, may be described as social distinction."[6] The social fears that permeated late-eighteenth-century American society were a paradise for lexicographers. No pronouncing dictionary of the period was impartial: each offered its own particular variation and users had to make their choice: Perry, Sheridan, or later Walker. "Neither among professional writers on the subject, nor among the conscientious lay speakers of the language," says Krapp, "was there any inclination merely to follow nature."[7] People wanted to be told what to do, and having chosen their guru and established through his advice their social credentials, they were loath to see him traduced by a rival system. It was this attitude that seventy years later would be one of the main factors impelling the ferocities of the War of the Dictionaries, in which the ultrapatriotic Webster was pitted against the Anglophile Worcester. In the longer term one can see the seeds of the best-selling "how to" guides that do so well in America but almost invariably founder in the U.K.

Sheridan happily set himself up as a arbiter, doubtless well aware of the commercial advantages to be gained by adopting such a posture. Not everyone approved: the puritan Webster, unsurprisingly, deplored the whole idea, equating it with that same corruption that he adduced to every British institution, especially the stage and the court. In fact this was unfair: Sheridan was not aiming to create some kind of élite pronunciation, but given his background his own pronunciation, upon which he based his dictionary, doubtless reflected the speech of those he regarded as socially correct. Sheridan's original work was published in England (by Johnson's publisher Dodsley) in 1780 and exported to America, but it was the revised version, edited by Stephen Jones (first published in Britain in 1798) and printed and published in Philadelphia in 1806 that was the real success. Retitled *A General Pronouncing and Explanatory Dictionary of the English Language for the Use of Schools, Foreigners learning English, etc.* "In which it has been attempted to improve upon the plan of Mr Sheridan," it immediately established itself as one of the staples of American speech. Jones (1763–1827), the nephew of the celebrated Welsh nonconformist clergyman and educator Griffith Jones (1683–1761), was a noted journalist and freemason. As well as the revision of Sheridan he was editor of the *Biographica Dramatica* or "a Companion to the Playhouse" (1812).

In some ways Sheridan (1719–88) earned his fame by proxy. His son Richard Brinsley Sheridan (1751–1816) became, as author of *The Rivals* and *A School for Scandal,* one of his country's most celebrated playwrights. Thomas Sheridan was best known as an elocutionist, although like his son, he had a professional involvement with the stage. His father, also Thomas (1687–1738), had been an intimate of Jonathan Swift, who became godfather to the younger Thomas. Born in Dublin, and educated at Trinity College, he defied his father's wishes for him to become a teacher, preferring to pursue a career on stage, a dream that had begun at Trinity when he starred there in his own play, *Captain O'Blunder, or, The Brave Irishman.* Persevering at his calling, he performed at Drury Lane before returning to Dublin to manage the Theatre Royal. The low point of this appointment came when one Kelly, a young man from Galway and too drunk to know better, began insulting the actresses and when told to be quiet by Sheridan, threatened awful vengeance. The audience promptly took sides and what was known as "the Kelly riot" devastated the theater. Kelly was jailed and fined £500. Sheridan promptly bailed him out and generously managed to have the fine waived. When one of the audience, Miss Frances Chamberlaine, wrote a poem in his praise, Sheridan had himself introduced and eventually married her. This didn't prevent him inciting a second riot when he censured what he felt were inappropriate lines from a popular play. After this he returned to England, where he was seen by some as a rival to Garrick himself. After a brief return to Dublin he was back in England once more, acting behind him and a new career as an elocutionist in progress. When he was offered £200 to prepare a pronouncing dictionary by the earl of Bute, Samuel Johnson, a friend, was most affronted. The friendship swiftly lapsed into insults. Johnson, said Sheridan, had "gigantic fame—in these days of little men." "Sherry," remarked the doctor, "is dull, naturally dull, but it must have taken him a great deal of pains to become what we now see him. Such an excess of stupidity is not in nature." Despite his honors, Sheridan was plagued by debts and in 1764 took his family to Blois "to bid defiance to his merciless creditors." Back in England he boosted his funds by giving dramatic readings. He died on August 14, 1788. His nephew, James Knowles (1759–1840), continued the lexicographical tradition with his *Pronouncing and Explanatory Dictionary* (1835), a work on which he only started work at the age of seventy.

As a lexicographer "Sheridan deserves great credit . . . although the fact of his being an Irishman was much against him."[8] This latter impediment came home when in 1790 there appeared the anonymously authored *Caution to Gentlemen who use Sheridan's Dictionary . . .* The author claimed that Sheridan had managed to impart his Irish brogue to his work, illustrated this by citing various errors in Sheridan's pronunciation system, then stated that "his Dictionary, in itself, is not worth sixpence. It derives its only merit from the rules of pronunciation; and in this respect the author is indisputably entitled to the praise of originality. But his errors are so numerous, and so very pernicious in tendency, that the book may be considered rather as a national disgrace than ornament." Fortunately for Sheridan, America was less fastidious.

The last of these important pronunciation dictionaries, the *Critical Pronouncing Dictionary and Expositor of the English Language,* was published by John Walker in 1791. Its prefatory Essay on the Principles of English Pronunciation was "by far the most elaborate and discriminating discussion of pronunciation that had so far appeared in an English Dictionary."[9] It brought him an immediate and lasting success and established him as a major authority on pronunciation for the next half century. As seen above, Walker was regularly bound together with Johnson as a single volume. Editions such as John Longmuir's *Walker & Johnson Combined* (which also offered a reprint of Joseph Worcester's list of English dictionaries) appeared as late as 1864. Dedicated to David Garrick, it became one of the best selling and most popular of all English dictionaries. Not every American liked it, however. Perhaps predictably, Noah Webster, writing in 1829, a year after his own *American Dictionary* had been published, described it as "one of the greatest evils our language has ever suffered."[10]

Like Sheridan, Walker (1732–1807) was an actor turned elocutionist and like him he worked in both Dublin and London, where he was a member of Garrick's company at Drury Lane. He specialized in taking the second lead in a variety of tragedies. His Brutus (in Shakespeare's *Julius Caesar*) was much admired. In January 1769 he abandoned the stage and joined James Usher (1720–72), like him an enthusiastic convert to Roman Catholicism, in establishing a school at Kensington Gravel Pits (now Notting Hill Gate). His teaching career was short-lived, and in 1771 he began giving the lectures in elocution that finally brought him success and the friendship of such luminaries as Johnson and Edmund Burke. He published the "Plan" of his *Dictionary* in 1774; the dictionary itself appeared seventeen years later. His *Dictionary of the*

English Language, "answering at once the purposes of Rhyming, Spelling and pronouncing" appeared in 1775; retitled *The Rhyming Dictionary* it was regularly reprinted throughout the nineteenth century. Walker died on August 1, 1807 at his home in Tottenham Court Road, London.

It was the popularity of Walker and his peers that underpinned the comment by a writer in the *Gentleman's Magazine* that in the Southern states "novels and useful histories are the best articles to be considered here after Dictionaries."[11] Such popularity was not confined to the South. Even without Webster's exhortations, it was logical that on commercial grounds alone Americans would soon start producing their own dictionaries. It was also logical, given the potential readership, that these dictionaries would at first represent the educational rather than the intellectual side of lexicography. As George Krapp observes, "The beginnings of American lexicography are . . . rather humble, reflecting the needs and conditions of popular education, not the high life of Sheridan and Walker."[12]

As noted above, with neat synchronicity the first native American lexicographer, author of *A School Dictionary* (1798), was named Samuel Johnson, Jr. The great-nephew of yet another Samuel Johnson, the first president of King's College, New York, now Columbia University, he was born on March 10, 1757. After attending Yale University (then College) he married and in 1786 settled in Guildford, Connecticut, where he remained until his death on August 20, 1836. He was "a tall, spare, old gentleman with piercing eyes and rounded shoulders."[13] Johnson worked as a teacher, following his father into the profession, although their family had traditionally been associated with cloth making since in 1707 an earlier Samuel Johnson had been granted land to build a clothiers. Johnson, "the luminary of learning to the region around,"[14] taught the three Rs, plus grammar and geography. Among his pupils was the future poet Fitz-Greene Halleck (1790–1867). As well as teaching he pioneered the cultivation of fruit trees, studied genealogy, showed himself to be a skilled calligrapher, and kept a notebook filled with his favorite literary quotations.

Johnson's motivation to dictionary making seems to have emerged from a period, some years earlier, when Connecticut took up the idea of finding an alternative vernacular to English. This idea, prefiguring the nationalism that impelled such as Noah Webster to push for a properly American English, variously advocated French, Latin, and even Hebrew as possible substitutes. Young people, carried away by their enthusiasms, preferred French while their elders, naturally drawn to the Bible, opted for Hebrew and the state saw an upsurge in the naming of children on Biblical lines. Academics chose Latin. Johnson set himself up to counter this linguistic vagabondage, and "fought, not with empty trumpets like Joshua at Jericho, but [with] a sober little book that should mayhap show mothers how to call their children and give mongrel folks from Europe something to be guided by."[15]

Johnson's career was summed up by his biographer, Henry Pynchon Robinson, in one of his *Guildford Portraits* (1907). One of the half dozen verses should suffice to give the flavor:

> *Indeed, he is recalled by not a few*
> *To whom he had imparted all he knew.*
> *Or would have, had Fortune to him brought them*
> *And in other ways this teacher taught them;*
> *A lexicon, for instance once he made*
> *This rare remembered present passing shade.*

A School Dictionary was a slim 24mo. volume of 198 pages with a vocabulary of around 4,100 words. It ran to just one edition, of which there are but four surviving copies: three in America and one in the British Library. Johnson's object was "not to afford either entertainment or instruction to persons of education . . . [but] to furnish schools with a dictionary which will enable youth more easily to acquire a knowledge of the English language . . . Should it answer this purpose, his design will be accomplished, and his ruling passion (that of being serviceable to youth) highly gratified." He called it his "little companion." The majority of its vocabulary was collected from "Authors of established reputation." It not only included "familiar and obsolete words" but "others really useful, such as are not easily and generally understood by children: a knowledge of which is necessary in order to read good authors to advantage, and without which no person can either write or speak our language with purity and elegance." His aim was to create a dictionary that would fit "into the compass of a sizeable and cheap school book so that the spelling, pronunciation and definition of the way may be easily obtained."[16]

To what extent he achieved these aims is debatable. J. H. Friend is unimpressed: Johnson's book "can scarcely have been helpful to schoolchildren with its relatively few entries, meager definitions, crude orthöepy, rudimentary grammar and curiously uneven word list."[17] Certainly it was an inconsistent work, with space for such headwords as *cap-a-pie, belles lettres,* and *bon-mot* [sic] but none for *newspaper, ocean,* and *population.* The spelling also varies; it can hardly have been helpful for schoolchildren to find not just "arbor" and "fervor," but also "honour" and "odour." As Steger notes, "This dictionary shows no innovations and no improvement on previous English works. It is nothing more than a synopsis, a compendium of existing works, minus a number of their merits, lacking in individuality and following the beaten path of lexicography."[18] All true enough, but Steger omits one achievement that cannot be taken from Johnson: he wrote what, for better or worse, was America's first-ever homegrown dictionary. And for that he must take his place, however marginal, among the immortals of lexicography.

Johnson also seems to have had problems with some of his definitions. Examples include *bemused:* "overcome with musing"; *chymistry:* "the act of separating bodies with fire"; *lout:* "to bow awkwardly"; *mizzy:* "a quagmire, a shaking meadow." But in fairness, he had never set out to emulate his namesake. Using his experiences as a teacher, he intended to remedy a basic want in American schools: a suitable dictionary. In that, whatever his failings of detail, Johnson seems to have succeeded. His book lacked the lexicographical sophistication of such British imports as Walker or Sheridan, but he had a very different audience in mind. And his success may best be judged from the fact that two years after this first ever American dictionary, Johnson, now with a coauthor, the Rev. John Elliott, published a successor: *A Selected Pronouncing and Accented Dictionary* (1800).

Elliott came from "a line of respectable and pious ancestors"[19] and like his coauthor attended Yale before turning to a career in teaching. His early-seventeenth-century ancestor John Eliot [*sic*] had evangelized among the American Indians and Elliott, in the family tradition, was ordained a pastor in 1791 and ministered to the Congregational Church of East Guilford, Connecticut until his death on December 17, 1824. A fiery, persuasive preacher, he expanded the congregation, bringing in 335 new worshipers during a series of revivals. He was elected a fellow of Yale in 1812, and the theological department there received a financial bequest, known as the Elliott Fund. An earnest, rectitudinous small-town clergyman, he was, according to one affectionate memoir, "a tall, very thin and slim man. His legs, always draped in black stockings and small clothes, seemed too slender to hold him up. How neatly he was always draped, not a spot or wrinkle on his garments! What a broad-brimmed hat he wore, renewed just once in two years . . . He was a fine scholar, a genuine lover of study, a capital preacher, a wise and shrewd man, never trying to be rich or known, but well known . . . He was the life and soul of the village library, and ready for every good work."[20] At his funeral his prudence, judgment, solemnity, and pious devotion were duly celebrated. It was Elliott who pushed for the moral line that pervades the joint production.

In this dictionary, as in its predecessor, Johnson, joined by Elliott, was aiming at education and not "entertainment." He was also focused foursquare on his young audience. However, one new element did appear: nationalism. In *A School Dictionary* Johnson had simply hoped to provide children with a dictionary and thus enhance their learning. Now, as the preface states, he was working specifically in an American context.

> The Education of youth in a free republic is a matter of the highest importance. The increasing attention which has been paid to this interesting subject in our country, for several years past, affords just grounds of congratulation, and joy, among the friends of order, virtue and religion. Great improvements have already been made upon former systems, but to complete the cycle of useful Schoolbooks, a Dictionary of suitable size seemed very requisite.

Nor were Johnson and Elliott simply concerned with providing a word list. Quality, especially moral quality, was to be noted. Not only were other dictionaries far too expensive, but the pair had observed their contents and found them insufficiently censored: "Many words there found are highly offensive to the modest ear and cannot be read without a blush. To inspire youth with sentiments of modesty and delicacy is one of the principal objects of early instruction; and this object is totally defeated by the indiscriminate use of vulgar and indecent words." Despite this moral tone, their dictionary included *foutra* (fuck), which, as the Italian *fottere,* had first been included in a dictionary two hundred years earlier in John Florio's *Worlde of Wordes* (1598). They categorized it as "a low vulgar word" but its appearance in a work aimed specifically at schools brought them a good deal of criticism. According to their definition, the term was "French," but that traditional passing of the linguistic buck allowed them no excuse. Writing in the *American Review* the reviewer noted that

> There is another word to which, at first, we thought these gentlemen had the exclusive right. We cannot soil our page with the transcription of it: it is to be found under the letter F, and is called French, but we were sure no French dictionary would admit a word so shockingly indecent and so vulgar . . . Nor did we think it possible that it should find its way into any English dictionary; but turning to Ash [*The New & Complete Dictionary of the English Language,* 1775], whose purpose it appears to have been to insert every word written or spoken in our language, we there found it. We hope, however, that neither the authority of the reverend pastor [Elliott], or even of his learned colleague, will be sufficient to give it currency. Observing, from the definition of this word in Ash, which they

have literally copied, that he does not understand the meaning of the term, we sincerely hope that they may have the same apology; for ignorance would here afford them some excuse as men of decency and piety, though none as lexicographers.[21]

Supposed breaches of taste aside, this dictionary is very similar to Johnson's earlier work, but for its larger vocabulary: some 9,000 words in 223 pages. Once again there are problems with definitions, some of which are embarrassingly banal, e.g., *ball:* "any round thing"; *ballad:* "a trifling song"; *balloon:* "a kind of ball, a vessel to traverse the air," while others show an unashamed partiality that would not have seemed alien amid the pages of Johnson's British namesake: *anti-Christ:* "one who opposes Christ; the Pope."

As stated, Johnson and Elliott set out to provide for an American audience and the real innovation of their work is that for the first time homegrown American, rather than simply imported English words are included. This is expressed by the inclusion of Indian-based terms (*tomahawk, wampum*), American place names (*Cincinnati*), and the American usage of originally British words (*Capitol, federal, freshet*). They also note that some words, as used in America, "are the same or somewhat similar in pronunciation, but different in spelling and signification." They include "some vulgar errors in pronunciation corrected," e.g., "cowcumber/cucumber," "chimbley/chimney," "winegar/vinegar," and "widder/widow."[22] Once again the *-our* and *-or* spellings appear at random, as do the suffixes *-ection* or *-exion.* Although their technique thus showed little advance on Johnson's earlier effort, and as such still fell some way behind more sophisticated British dictionaries, Johnson and Elliott had, with their pioneering inclusion of Americanisms, taken a giant step forward. American English, rather than English English, had emerged almost literally from the backwoods, to take its place in dictionary making for the first time.

A second American-made dictionary also appeared in 1800: *The Columbian Dictionary of the English Language* by Caleb Alexander. It offered "many new words, particular to the United States, and many words of general use, not found in any other English dictionary." Like its predecessors it concentrated on spelling and pronunciation and was "calculated to assist foreigners . . . and to be used as a school book." Johnson/Elliott had included Americanisms, Alexander was the first native lexicographer actually to parade them as a selling point.

Born on July 22, 1775, Alexander was brought up on his father's farm in Northfield, Massachusetts. His great-grandfather, John Alexander, had emigrated from Scotland and had, with twelve others, purchased land from the Indians on which to found the town. It was in memory of this that Alexander himself was widely known as "the old Scotchman." As an adult he was "thick set, and about five feet nine or ten inches in height. He was slightly lame, and walked in a manner that would indicate that one leg was slightly shorter than the other. His face was full: broad, of rather florid complexion, and expressive of reflection and intelligence. His manner evidenced a benevolent spirit, and yet he was distinguished for strength of purpose . . . he was not particularly communicative, except on some special occasions, and then he would make himself highly interesting."[23] He was educated first at Dartmouth and then at Yale. He appears to have been something of a rebellious youth, but calmed down. A letter from his Dartmouth principal, Wheelock, advocating his acceptance at Yale, mentions him as one who was "the subject of God's saving mercy . . . The change appearing in the youth was very great, as, before it, he was considerably of the wild order; but ever since, as far as I have seen or heard, he has adorned his Christian profession by a truly religious and exemplary conversation."[24] He was ordained pastor in 1778 and worked in a number of Massachusetts towns. He also spent some time as a missionary in western New York State.

In 1803 Alexander became preceptor of the Fairfield Academy in Fairfield, Massachusetts. Here he was highly successful, although he was unable to turn his academy into a college, despite his best efforts. He had better luck on moving to another academy, that of Chilton in Oneida County, and was duly offered the chance of becoming the first principal of the new institution, renamed Hamilton College. He turned it down. This rejection was more than likely due to his continuing financial problems. It appeared, for whatever reason, that neither church nor academe could fulfill his expectations as to a salary. He regularly abandoned his pastoral work through lack of what he saw as sufficient payment and moved elsewhere, hoping for a better offer. He did settle, for four years, as principal of yet another academy, that of Onondaga Hollow, but this job didn't last and he moved again, this time to found a theological seminary in Auburn. That year he took up a secondary occupation: farming. For the rest of his life, which ended on April 12, 1828, he worked as a preacher, a teacher, and a missionary, as well as writing regularly in the theological press.

The *Columbian Dictionary* has 556 pages and offers 25,700 headwords, approximately three times the number in Johnson/Elliott, although this expansion is largely due to Alexander's allotting every change in meaning a new headword. In order to keep the price down all words ending in -*ness* and nearly all those ending in -*ly* were omitted. It offers a mix of hard and common words. As well as including Americanisms, typically *cent, dime, dollar, Congress, Congressional, lengthy,* and *minuteman,* and offering the local spellings of such words as *chequer/checker, sponge/spunge, calendar/Kalendar,* Alexander displays his patriotic aspirations in his desire to offer an American system of pronunciation. "Could any means be used," he asks in his advertisement, "or any plan devised, to alter and unite Americans in giving similar sounds to all the vowels and consonants and their various combinations, the event would be happy." He admits that such a system may be hard to enforce in the face of established regional practice: "In spite of the most learned dissertations and the best rules, some would pronounce *tune,* others *tshone,* some *tuesday,* others *tshosday,* some *vol-um,* others *vol-yum . . .* and each would have his admirers and followers," but he hoped nonetheless to do "a little to fix a *uniform* and *permanent* standard of pronunciation, no pains have been spared in dividing and accenting the words according to the practice of the most *approved* and *polite* speakers."[25] Krapp acknowledges that his efforts were at least "more than any other dictionary maker would have attempted to do . . . but his dictionary was too traditional and imitative to acquire significance as an historically important document."[26]

Others, notably a contemporary writing in *The Portfolio* (1801), were less tolerant.

> One Alexander, a presbyterian preacher, at a little village in Massachusetts Bay has published a ridiculous book which he calls "A Columbian Dictionary." This work, a disgrace to letters, is a disgusting collection of every vicious word or phrase, chosen by the absurd misapprehension, or coined by the boors of each local jurisdiction in the United States. It is a record of our imbecility. A map and journal of our tottering and imperfect step in the walks of literature. God forbid that any man who has the memory of his ancestors in his heart, or a spark of English spirit, glowing in his veins, or one trace of English style in his memory, should ever recur to this blind *Columbian* guide! Possessing Johnson's and Walker's Dictionaries, the first filling the mind with the most energetic, and elegant words, and the second filling the tongue to the most accurate and courtly pronunciation, scholars will hardly consult the secretary Alexander, nor on his authority adopt wigwam words, or pronounce coquette, *kokwet,* according to the new-dangle gibberish of this village schoolmaster.

Another, writing in the 1801 edition of the *American Review and Literary Journal,* took particular exception to the word *lengthy,* which he describes as "undoubtedly the growth of the wigwam . . . a vicious, fugitive soundrel and True American word. It should be hooted by every elegant English scholar, and proscribed from every page." *Lengthy,* which began life referring to prolix, tedious speechifying, rather than physical extent, has in fact a highly respectable pedigree: John Adams, a future president, uses it in 1759, Benjamin Franklin in 1773, and Tom Paine in 1796; its first English use comes, via Southey, in 1812.

These criticisms, while undoubtedly impassioned, are perhaps a little unfair. For instance, whatever might be meant by a "wigwam word," *wigwam* itself isn't even in Alexander's word list. What neither reviewer managed to note was that for all his boasting, there are barely a dozen "words not found" in other dictionaries. Perry and Walker had already covered the vast majority of recent neologisms. But facts never mattered much in a good controversy and such sentiments, equally robust, would reemerge time and time again, never more so than in the 1860s War of the Dictionaries, when the élitist Anglophilia of Joseph Worcester's supporters clashed so vociferously with the patriotic populism of those of Noah Webster. American lexicography, so intertwined with national and social aspiration, promoted the most excited emotions almost from its very beginning. Political Correctness was two centuries in the future, but the products of the White European Male, dead or otherwise, disturbed the intellectually insecure as much then as they would later. What was seen as the need for their defense, as quoted above, caused similar flutters of apprehension. In a general swipe at all such efforts, the *Monthly Magazine* declared that other than "technical and scientific terms . . . any other species of American words are manifest corruptions and to embalm these by the lexicographical process would only be a waste of time and abuse of talents."[27] As Krapp put it, "It was enough . . . to arouse violent opposition at this time if one merely announced one's intention of making a dictionary specially for America and for Americans, for the animosities which center about innovations in language are likely to be stronger than the facts themselves warrant."[28] Two American dictionaries appeared in 1801: *A Key to the English Language; or a Spelling, Parsing, Derivative and Defining Dictionary* by William Woodbridge, and *The Young Ladies' Pocket Companion* by Henry Priest. Neither made any great lexicographical advance. Woodbridge, the first principal of the Phillips-Exeter Academy, and of the Young Ladies Academy in Medford, Massachusetts, was born to a poor family, who traced their ancestors through a long line of English dissenting preachers. Woodbridge attended Yale, but not until he had worked as a teacher, and as a clerk in his brother's store. He had some commercial acumen and might well have stayed in trade if a merchantman in which his current savings were tied up hadn't gone down. Still impoverished, he paid his way through Yale by teaching, and specialized in the foundation of a succession of girls' schools. He was sufficiently accomplished to be chosen as the first preceptor of Phillips-Exeter when it opened in May 1783. He stayed there until 1788, when ill health forced him to retire. The remainder of his life was devoted to teaching and missionary work and, *c.* 1800, to compiling his dictionary. While his own work was unexceptional, its relative insignificance did not preclude his heated opinionating on that of others.

C. C. Baldwin, the librarian of the American Antiquarian Society, noted in his diary entry for February 20, 1834 that he had been visited that day by the aging Woodbridge.

> He is in his 80th year . . . [and] has the airs and dry humor of an old pedagogue about him. I laughed heartily to hear him complain of the innovations that have been introduced into the system of education. "When," said he, "will people be done trying experiments? There are several conceited fops now at work attempting to palm off upon the community their crude and impracticable schemes in the work of instruction. There's Noah Webster, old as he is, is as full of changes as the moon. Do but look at his productions. I have been striving for more than half a century to put down his spelling book. But *cui bono?* It is in use everywhere. And there is his great dictionary, which he calls his *opus magnum.* What is it but a great evil, *mega biblon, mega kakon.* But, alas, *tempora mutantur et nos mutamur in illis.* We can make no progress in the great work of education until we return to the point from which we have diverged, but *hic labor, hoc opus est,* and I fear it is now too late to accomplish so desirable an object."

Henry Priest's contribution to these early dictionaries was aimed, as his prefatory letter to "Young Ladies" makes clear, directly at the girls apostrophized in his title. It mixes hard words and a certain amount of encyclopedic matter, concentrating on "Arts, Sciences, Geography, Heathen Mythology, etc." A small book, with just 2,600 headwords, it was aimed at the members of his own academy, in New York. Three years later appeared *An English Orthographical Expositor* by Daniel Jaudon, Thomas Watson, and Stephen Addington. It ran to four editions and offered 7,000 headwords. Geared to the needs of the young, it aimed to give spellings rather than informative definitions and borrowed from both Walker and the British Johnson.

The succession of dictionaries linked to the school market continues well into the nineteenth century, and other than Noah Webster (himself a teacher by profession), whose first lexicographical work appeared in 1806 and whose major dictionary was published twenty-two years later, it is the educators who for many years dominate the field. As George Krapp has said, "Unlike the sewing machine, the dictionary was not an American invention. But if America cannot claim the dictionary by right of discovery, she may be said to have made at least the popular English Dictionary peculiarly her own by right of use and occupation."[29] Typical among them are Abel Flint (1766–1825), whose *Spelling, Pronouncing and Parsing Dictionary* appeared in 1806, Burgess Allison (1753–1827), author of *The American Standard of Orthography and Pronunciation* (1815), William Grimshaw (1782–1852), author of *An Etymological Dictionary* (1821) and *The Ladies' Lexicon* (1829), and Thomas Gallaudet (1787–1851), far more celebrated for his work for the deaf, whose *School and Family Dictionary* appeared in 1841.

Two works, and their authors, can be singled out for a little extra consideration. *A New Critical Pronouncing Dictionary of the English Language* by Richard Coxe was published in 1813. Coxe came from a famous family: his father William was well known as a horticulturalist while his grandfather, Daniel Coxe, had been doctor first to Queen Catherine, wife of Charles II, and then to Queen Anne. Daniel had been Governor of St. Bartholomew's Hospital before moving to what was then the province of West Jersey in 1687. He built a house at Burlington, as well as what was probably the state's first pottery. Richard Coxe attended Princeton (its youngest ever student to that date), and left with his degree of B.A. at sixteen. Other than compiling his dictionary, he spent his entire life, until his death in 1865, as a lawyer.

The flavor of his work can best be enjoyed by setting out its long and self-aggrandizing title, worthy of comparison with the most boastful of the seventeenth-century "hard-word" compilations:

A New Critical Pronouncing Dictionary of the English language, containing all the words in general use, with their significance accurately explained, and the sound of each syllable accurately expressed: among which will be found several hundred terms, with their acceptions and derivations, which appear to have been hitherto omitted by the best lexicographers; also a variety of the technical terms of medicine, law, commerce, arts and general science: the whole interspersed with critical and philological observations and references to the respective authorities. To which will be affixed Mr Walker's Principles of English Pronunciation: a nomenclature of the names of distinguished persons and places of antiquity: comprising a sketch of the mythology, history and a biography of the ancients, from the most authentic sources: a chronological table of remarkable occurrences, from earliest ages to the present time: containing whatever is worthy of record as discoveries, inventions, etc etc. Compiled from authors of the most approved reputation, with considerable additions by an American Gentleman.

A glance at the dictionary as published reveals that, alas, much of this was simple bombast and that for sheer hot air, the preface is even worse. Johnson, suggests Coxe, has done an adequate job, but he, Coxe, will take it upon himself to remedy the doctor's faults. "But as the Sun is the only source of that light, by which we are enabled to perceive the spots upon its surface; so it is solely by adhering with the utmost inflexibility to the plan proposed, and in a considerable degree executed by this profound lexicographer Dr Johnson that we have ventured to assume upon ourselves the responsibility of endeavouring to repair his faults and supply his deficiencies."

Few were fooled. Sidney Willard, reviewing the dictionary in *The General Repository & Review,* no. 4, 1813, does not spare his target. The dictionary "begins with a lofty march of mock majesty, that seems to betray the aspirations of an ambitious youth to reach the real dignity and grandeur of the greatest English lexicographer" but its promise is not sustained and Willard states that "When we find such evident marks of a want of a consistent, preconceived plan, and of carelessness, and haste in execution, we cannot think that learning has gained much by this addition to the number of dictionaries, and do not believe that any scholar, who has much reputation to lose, will allow himself willingly to be the person entirely, or principally responsible for the *Compilement* or *coacervation* or *heaping up,* as the word is explained in the dictionary." Coxe offers around 54,000 words. It is a big book, of some 941 pages, of which the introduction alone covers 85. There is also a reprint of Walker's pronunciation guide; a classical dictionary, and a table of events. Coxe, having presumed to set himself above Johnson, calmly appropriates his word list and commits the cardinal sin of reproducing his errors, without any attempt to update them. He then compounds his mistakes by adding a good many errors of his own making.

Like Burgess Allison (whose 390 pages included 23,400 headwords), Coxe assembled a much larger work than had hitherto been published in America. Still aimed at schools, it was far more comprehensive than the sort of dictionaries that were current in education. What lets it down, apart from the unfulfilled arrogance of its author, is its lack of organization. But as Krapp points out, from this increase in size, "one may infer that the making of dictionaries in America was growing in dignity at least as a commercial undertaking."

Aside from any lexicographical attainments, the last of these early American dictionary makers must be included for one simple fact. Unlike any predecessor, or indeed nineteenth-century successor, Susanna Rowson (1762–1824) was a woman. And unlike her generally austere contemporaries, whose lexicography was very much an extension of their educational activities, Rowson had led a far more wide-ranging life. She was born in Portsmouth, England, the only daughter of Lieutenant William Haswell, RN (d. 1805) and his wife Susan (née Musgrave) who died in childbirth. Before or certainly shortly after Susanna's birth her father had moved to New England, where he began working as a customs officer in Boston. He returned in 1766 to collect his daughter and take her to his new home on the promontory of Nantucket Beach, Massachusetts. Here Haswell remarried, to one Rebecca Woodward, by whom he had three sons. Susanna was a devotee of reading from an early age—she had supposedly consumed Dryden, Virgil, Pope, Homer, Shakespeare, and Spenser by the age of ten. As a young intellectual she attracted the attention of James Otis, the lawyer and statesman, who took her under his wing as his "little scholar." The War of Independence brought problems for the Haswells. As an officer of the British crown Lieutenant Haswell could not take the oath of allegiance to the colonies and his home and property were confiscated. He and his family were briefly held as prisoners of war, then moved around New England until, in 1778, they returned, impoverished and jobless, to England. Here Susanna worked as a governess for the duchess of Devonshire until her marriage, in 1786, to William Rowson, a hardware merchant and trumpeter in the Royal Horse Guards. That same year she published her first novel, *Victoria,* a two-volume work, backed by a number of subscribers, among whom was the actress Sarah Siddons. Its characters, apparently, were taken from her own circle. The book was dedicated to the duchess of Devonshire, who repaid the compliment by introducing its author to the Prince of Wales. He too must have enjoyed her work, since shortly afterward he bestowed a pension on her still impoverished father. In 1788 she published a second novel, *The Inquisitor, or the Invisible Rambler.* This took up three volumes and was consciously modeled on Sterne. It appeared in America in 1794.

In 1790 Rowson published *Charlotte Temple, or a Tale of Truth.* It would be her greatest success and was arguably Britain's first ever "best-selling" novel. Its first printing, of 25,000 copies, sold out in a few years and the reprint was equally popular. It appeared in America, with editions printed in every major city and in 1835 was translated into German. Its success in America, where it was seen as a popular classic, outstripped its popularity even in England. It is a melodramatic tale, which like her first novel is allegedly based on fact. Like most best-sellers *Charlotte Temple* failed to impress the literary critics. Among others William Cobbett "assailed Rowson's books with coarse vehemence"[30] in a piece entitled "A Kick for a Bite." Apart from writing a number of school-books Susanna Rowson never abandoned fiction. As well as her best-seller, the success of which would never be repeated, she wrote among other titles *Rebecca, or the Fille de Chambre* (1792, an autobiographical novel), *The Trials of the Human Heart* (4 vols., 1795), and *Reuben and Rachel, or Tales of Old Times* (2 vols., 1798), *Sarah, or the Exemplary Wife* (1812), *Charlotte's Daughter, or the Three Orphans* (a sequel to her early hit, published posthumously in 1828). In addition to *Americans in England,* the play in which she gave her final performance, she wrote *The Volunteers* (1793, a farce inspired by the recent whiskey insurrection in West Pennsylvania), *The Slaves in Algiers* (1794, an opera), and *The Female Patriot* (1794, a farce). She also wrote poetry, judged by the *DNB* as "more fluent than strong," which is scattered through her works, and she composed one popular song: "America, Commerce, and Freedom."

By the standards of her time Rowson can lay some claim to being ranked among the early nineteenth century's generation of feminists. Her novels, for all their melodrama, "combined the traditional didactic seduction plots with a more feminist treatment of women's situation. Acknowledging the power of sexuality and the dangers of women's economic dependency (especially dependency on those who prove unreliable),"[31] her writing presages the "women's fiction" genre that emerged later in the century, "read by women, written by women and centred on women's experiences."[32] It dominated the American fiction market of the period. Among her pupils was Eliza Southgate Bowne (1783–1809), a well-known letter writer and one of her country's earliest feminists, who stated, *inter alia,* "I may be censured for declaring it as my opinion that no one woman in a hundred married for love" and that "I do not esteem marriage essential to happiness." Thus, one suspects, the sentiments of a teacher whose experiences had been somewhat wider than those of the majority of her peers.

Despite her success Rowson did not profit—she received a fee, the booksellers made the money—and even as her work was selling heavily on both sides of the Atlantic, she and her husband were facing poverty. When William Rowson duly declared himself a bankrupt Susanna turned to acting in the hope of boosting their income. Based in Edinburgh, she appeared in a number of plays, often acting alongside her sister, before in 1793 deciding to return, with her husband, to America. There she found work in a number of big-city theaters, playing such parts as Lady Sneerwell in Sheridan's *School for Scandal* and Mistress Quickly in Shakespeare's *Merry Wives of Windsor.* Her career culminated in Boston in 1797 with her performance in her own play, *Americans in England.* It ran to three performances, hardly an epic run, but they were all well received.

That same year, Rowson opened her first girls' school, in Federal Street, Boston. It had but a single pupil, the daughter of her backer, Mrs. Samuel Smith. There would be no other pupils for the whole term: staid Boston was deeply suspicious of a woman who had been not only a novelist but an actress too. Indeed, she was also, from 1802 to 1805, a journalist, editing the *Boston Weekly Magazine* and contributing to various other periodicals. But such suspicion gradually broke down and the school became increasingly popular, even if, in 1799, Mrs. Rowson committed a new revolutionary act: the installation of a piano in the schoolroom. A piano teacher, Mr. Lamont, was hired and the piano became increasingly popular, to such an extent that it replaced the spinets and harpsichords that up till then had been the staple instruments in schools. The school moved on a number of occasions, growing ever more popular until in 1811 it settled on Hollis Street, Boston. Here it remained until the headmistress left, a victim of failing health, in 1822. She died on March 2, 1824.

The Spelling Dictionary, her contribution to lexicography, appeared in 1807. It is the most user-friendly of children's dictionaries, more a speller than a dictionary proper. Backed by a decade's teaching, she wanted to abandon the normal parrot-learning that dominated schools, through which system a child might have a large vocabulary, but not the slightest idea of what many of the words actually meant. Since such mechanical learning was "a very serious evil," and "to study the Dictionary, even the smallest of Johnson's or the common one of Perry's [was] so laborious a task,"[33] she determined to offer a useful alternative, better tailored to the child's wants and abilities. She offered a selection of "spelling lessons," none of which involved more than a dozen or so words, drawn from her own teaching practice. She hoped that this sort of "dictionary" was far more suited to the young mind than the more demanding tomes that were currently available. "Children study with more cheerfulness, when the lesson is short and determined" and she hoped that ease of learning would lead to better learning and thus a better preparation for the sort of studies and amusements they would encounter as they grew up. "I do not say that all these consequences will arise from the study of my little book, but if it in the least contributes to the advancement of so desirable an end, I shall have attained my purpose." And she concludes, "It is my fixed opinion, that it is better to give the young pupil one rational idea than fatigue them by obliging them to commit to memory a thousand *mere words.*"

11

America: Noah Webster and Joseph Worcester

The concept of a genuinely American English had been growing ever since the War of Independence, and the materials for the creation of that English had been developing for much longer. The pure geographical distance from England meant that colonial English was gradually moving away from its origins, and the influx of immigrants from non–English speaking countries, while bowing to the preeminence of the English language, inevitably stamped its linguistic differences on the dominant tongue. However, geography apart, this remained a period of standardization, in language as in other concerns, and while America might wish to set up her own distinct variety of English, like those who felt similar concerns back in London, her intellectuals were just as keen to legislate for a "fixed" or "standard" language.

The idea of an "American Academy," while not as old as the English parallels, dates back to the early eighteenth century, well before independence. In 1721 Professor Hugh Jones of William and Mary College noted in his grammar, *An Accidence to the English Tongue . . .* that since "*our Language* seems to be *arrived* at its *Crisis,* or highest Pitch . . . it is to be wished that a Publick *Standard* were fix'd; as a *Touchstone* to true *English,* whereby it might be regulated." These sentiments reflected those across the Atlantic, and while equally popular in academic theory, remained just as unrealized in linguistic practice. There would still be a number of attempts at standardization. Writing in the *Royal American Magazine* of Boston in 1774 "An American" addressed "the Literati of America" with his demand for the establishment of an "American Society of

Language." Such a society would "correct, enrich and refine" the language and advance America toward "the summit of learning." The future president John Adams suggested, in 1780 and in terms reminiscent of Dean Swift's *Proposal* of 1712, that a "public institution for refining, correcting, improving and ascertaining the English language" should be established by Congress. Congress was unresponsive, but Adams was undaunted, declaring that were Congress to act first, Britain's "king and parliament may have the honor of copying the example." In 1788, while American minister in London, he contacted the eccentric but earnest amateur lexicographer Sir Herbert Croft, whose own fantasies ran to a revised and improved edition of his friend Samuel Johnson's *English Dictionary*. Croft was easily converted to the plan, and believed that it had a better chance of success in America than in England, adding that "deservedly immortal would be that patriot, on either aside of the Atlantick, who should succeed in such an attempt."[1] Events rejected such immortality and Adams' academy proved as illusory a project as did what Croft had called the *Oxford Dictionary*.

New York's Philological Society, formed in 1788, numbered the young Noah Webster, always an advocate of linguistic reform, among its members but that did not save it from early extinction, nor advance its variation on the academic theme. Even a grand procession through the streets of the city on July 23, 1788, with the members dressed in subfusc and their secretary bearing a scroll on which were inscribed the principles of a Federal language, had no effect. Nor did the views, among others, of the lexicographer Caleb Alexander, who called for linguistic uniformity, albeit admitting that such a hope was largely unattainable. Further plans for a national cultural academy were frustrated by the fiercely held independence of individual states: federalism came a definite second to the policy of states' rights, but there was one very near miss. This nearest example of an American Academy was founded on October 20, 1820 in New York, and called the American Academy of Language and Belles Lettres. Its officers included John Quincy Adams, another future president, two justices of the Supreme Court, and other senior professional men. Membership covered the states, being drawn from the great and good of each. There was no official sponsorship nor financial backing. The Academy, "impressed with importance of Literature to the moral habits, character and happiness of individuals," wished among things "to control its irregularities and prevent its divisions."[2] Opinion was canvassed among the nation's leading men, most of whom offered their backing. John Jay, John Adams, Chief Justice John Marshall, and President-to-be James Madison all approved. Unsurprisingly they saw the Academy, as had their British peers, as a force for linguistic conservatism. Others, swayed perhaps by Noah Webster's vocal campaigning within his own constituency, hoped that through the Academy there might develop the much desired "American language." Webster himself told William S. Cardell, the Academy's main proponent, that such an organization, while not without merit, would be useless until it had an authoritative dictionary, similar to that on which he was himself working, to back its pronouncements. Just as equivocal was Thomas Jefferson, who rejected the Academicians' offer of the honorary presidency, although he allowed himself to be made an honorary member. He approved of the development of a language that emphasized the differences between America and Britain, but as a dedicated anti-Federalist, deplored the idea of a national linguistic authority. Less eminent, but perhaps more immediately influential was Edward Everitt, writing in the Boston-based *North American Review.* Boston vs. New York rivalries were to be expected, but his piece probably did more to undermine the Academy than any other criticism. His argument was simple: the very fact that membership, from officers downward, was spread so widely, militated against the institution's effectiveness. As regarded fine words and "vast ultimate objects," the Academy was unimpeachable but as to the practicalities, there was not a "single practical hint . . . by which these objects are to be obtained. There is in fact nothing wanting to this academic institution, but the single fact of being an academy and until something is done to make it one, we shall rest in the unpleasant conclusion that Mrs. Glass, author of that renowned precept 'first catch a turbot,' has lived and written in vain."[3] Whether through this onslaught or, more likely, through the general indolence of the majority of its members, the Academy collapsed in 1822.

Attempts to form an Academy would persist throughout the century, but with little more success. The success of Webster's dictionary and the establishment of a strong tradition of American lexicography did much to fulfill desires for a homegrown language, for all that there would remain a substantial body who still saw London as the sole repository of linguistic authority and derided the notion of an "American Academy" as a contradiction in terms. Academies of one sort or another were proposed in 1868, the same year as the American Philological Society was founded, and in 1894, when a bill backed by General Lew Wallace (author of *Ben Hur*) called for the "promotion of literature, art, science and invention." Wallace proposed a committee of twenty-five eminent figures who would meet regularly in the newly built Library of Congress to pontificate on American culture. He gave this body no name, suggesting they should find their own. The plan came to nothing: its unabashed élitism being condemned as "un-American" by the egalitarians of the media. As the Chicago *Tribune* put it, America produced "not . . . immortals but mortals, and any one mortal is as good as any other mortal as long as he lives."[4] It was ironic that the Academy, first proposed as a means of affirming America's individuality, should now be seen as a threat to that same characteristic. There would be other on-and-off attempts to resuscitate the academic ideal, but they petered out. The desire for "authoritative rulings," as Allen Walker Read put it, was part of the same insecurity that holds " 'the dictionary' . . . in superstitious awe."[5] In 1800, however, "the dictionary," as a purely American creation, was barely in existence, and the theories of an Academy can be abandoned in favor of tracing the practical ways in which that thriving American institution began moving toward its present-day status.

Of the two strands that can been seen in the wavering enthusiasms for an American Academy, the putative "fixing" of the language is of increasingly lesser importance, while the real interest is reserved for the establishment of what would become "American English." Just as in England the demands for such a standard had been linked to national pride, notably the need to rival France and its academicians, so too did the newly independent colonists see that the establishment of an "American" language would similarly distinguish their country from its immediate rival: England. As can be seen from the preceding chapter, there had been some small effort by lexicographers to incorporate Americanisms into their work. But aside from the sprinkling of words in such dictionaries as that of Caleb Alexander the effort had been marginal—and often much maligned. The term "American language" was coined by Noah Webster, and it is to Webster that one must turn to see the way in which that language was nurtured, developed, and finally set firmly on its feet.

Hagiographers and family memoirists aside, Noah Webster has received a generally bad press. Samuel Johnson, who has maintained a much better image, was certainly a difficult man. Yet he consistently comes over as a wit and, compared with his American successor, a sophisticate. Modern views of Webster are summed up succinctly, if somewhat flippantly, by Bill Bryson who has written that "Noah Webster . . . was by all accounts a severe, correct, humorless, religious, temperate man who was not easily liked, even by other severe, religious, temperate, humorless people. A provincial schoolteacher and not-very-successful lawyer from Hartford, he was short, pale, smug, and boastful. (He held himself superior to Benjamin Franklin because he was a Yale man while Franklin was self-educated.) Where Samuel Johnson spent his free hours drinking and discoursing in the company of other great men, Webster was a charmless loner who criticized almost everyone but was himself not above stealing material from others . . ."[6] H. L. Mencken, usually so keen to back anyone who has shown themselves, like him, to be vocally antagonistic toward England, had to admit that for all his achievements, Webster "was not only a pedagogue but also a Calvinist, and a foe of democracy." A contemporary, Thomas Jefferson, infuriated by Webster's importuning of himself, Washington, and Franklin for a puff for his spelling book, dismissed him as "a mere pedagogue, of very limited understanding and very strong prejudices and party passions."[7] Elsewhere he has been seen as a crank, a pedant, and a humorless monomaniac. All of which, however, is in the end a sidebar to his lexicography. What matters are his achievements in the making of the most important American dictionary of the period and the impetus that this and his other works give toward the formation of the truly American language. His personality, like that of any other lexicographer, undoubtedly impinges on his work, but one must view the life as an adjunct to his work and view it, as the legal jargon says, "without prejudice."

Noah Webster was born on October 16, 1758 in the village of West Hartford, Connecticut. His ancestor John Webster had left England in 1635 and was among those who founded the settlement in which his descendant lived. He was also a member of the colony's administration. The statesman Daniel Webster (1782–1852) was a distant cousin. Webster's father, also Noah, was a farmer of relatively limited education whose holding of ninety acres provided the sole means of support for his wife, three sons, and two daughters. He was a justice of the peace and a deacon of the parish and ruled his family through the precepts of the austere Calvinism that he professed. Such fundamentalism, it will be seen, would influence the lexicographer as much as it did the boy. Webster worked on the farm until he was fourteen, attending the local school where the only textbooks were the Psalter, the New Testament, and Dilworth's spelling book. Family legend claims that he was always interested in words, and even took his Latin grammar into the fields, although whether this was, as claimed, a sign of the scholar in embryo, or merely an attempt to catch up on undone homework, is not known. In 1774 he entered Yale, still very much a fledgling institution. Here he learned Latin, Greek, and Hebrew and in June 1775 joined a parade of students who cheered the visiting General George Washington.

He graduated from Yale, aged twenty, and returned home. He had considered the law, but there were no obvious openings. It was a period of deep recession: the country was still fighting for its independence and the outcome was by no means certain. Webster's own independence was more assured: his father allegedly gave him a few dollars and told him to take it and start his own life. He left home promptly and began the first of a number of teaching jobs before setting up his own school at Sharon, Connecticut. It was in response to what he saw as the deficiencies both in his pupils and the current textbooks available to them that he composed his first work: *A Grammatical Institute of the English Language* "comprising an easy, Concise, and Systematic Method of education, designed for the Use of English Schools in America." It supposedly reflected John Calvin's *Institutio* (1536), which had established the basic tenets of his creed. It offered a spelling book, a grammar, and a reader. The latter parts of this tripartite volume, while initially successful in themselves, were destined for relative obscurity. Not so the speller, which was republished on its own in 1788. This spelling book would be one of the greatest publishing success stories of the century, going on to be one of the best-selling, if not *the* best-selling nonfiction work in America, rivaled only by the Bible. It became "not only a universal textbook in the schools and the master book on spelling everywhere, but a standard article of commerce and, like sugar and salt, was kept in the stores along with the gingham and the calico."[8] The "Blue-Back Speller" was an indissoluble adjunct of American childhood. It took over from the previous favorite, Dilworth's *Aby-sel-pha* (from which Webster himself had learned to spell), although, as Mencken puts it, Webster was "sufficiently convinced of its merits to imitate it, even to the extent of lifting whole passages."[9] Given Webster's subsequent establishment of Johnson as his whipping boy, it is ironic to find him declaring in his introduction, "I have generally made *Dr. Johnson's* dictionary my guide, as in the point of orthography this seems to be the most approved authority in the language." A year later, as Read notes,[10] he denied his mentor, attributing his influences to Entick, the declared source of his *Compendious Dictionary.*

Initially published simultaneously by 209 companies, Webster turned the rights over to Hudson and Co. of Hartford, Connecticut for the fourteen years from 1818. In his letter proposing the deal he noted that annual sales had averaged out at around 250,000 copies. Subsequent sales figures are even more astounding: by the mid-1840s there had been sold some 30,000,000 copies of what since 1829 had been called the *Elementary Spelling Book* and the steam presses of its new publishers, George F. Cooledge & Bro., were turning out 525 copies every hour—5,250 a day. By 1869 the total sales topped 62,000,000 and a century after its publication that total had reached 80,000,000. The vast profits this generated did not, alas, trickle down to the author. He had sold the rights in a one-off deal. However, the success gave Webster a distinction that would also be accorded his great predecessor: becoming an eponym. The *OED* dates this to 1874 but according to Allen Walker Read *Websterian* emerged in 1790.[11] *Johnsonian* does not appear for another twelve months.

Webster was hardly the first American to consider spelling reform. His most important predecessor had been Benjamin Franklin, whose *Scheme for a New*

Alphabet and a Reformed Mode of Spelling had been published in 1768. The scheme involved the introduction of a whole new alphabet, in which each sound would be represented by a single letter. This would obviously require more than the current twenty-six letters, and Franklin actually had a purpose-built font cut to include six new characters[12]—although it was never used. In 1783, while preparing his *Grammatical Institute,* Webster had mocked such plans, but three years later he had changed his tune. After considering Franklin's plans he wrote to him offering his own alternative, and requesting that should Franklin approve, he would show the plan to Congress. In response Franklin disinterred his own *Scheme,* but Webster rejected it as overly radical. The introduction of new characters was "neither practicable, necessary nor expedient."[13] Despite this, he still desired some reform of American spelling and laid it out in an appendix to his *Dissertations.* In this he urged the exclusion of all superfluous letters, typically the *u* of "honour" or "flavour." This would be adopted, but the omission of the silent *a* in "bread" or the *e* in "give" would appeal only to a tiny minority. Such spelling might equate with pronunciation, as Webster felt all orthography should, but while it sounded right, once written down, it simply looked too bizarre to be accepted. The idea of substituting *ee* for *ea* as in "mean" or "speak," and replacing *ch* by *k* in "character" or "chorus" was no more popular.

Not all of these suggestions were Webster's own. English spelling had been in flux for many years, and there had been a succession of attempts to refine it, by no means all of them as extreme as that of James Elphinston (see Chapter 8). The inclusion/deletion of the redundant *u,* for instance, had been a problem for Shakespeare, whose plays offer both versions. But Webster's scheme ran directly counter to that of Johnson, and in so doing, it ran contrary to the established usage in England. This was linguistic revolution: Webster justified his scheme on many grounds, usually of utility and efficiency, but above all he saw it as the best possible means of promoting his primary interest: the pushing forward of the autonomy of American English.

> A capital advantage of this reform in these States would be that it would make a difference between the English orthography and the American. This will startle those who have not attended to the subject; but I am confident that such an event is an object of vast political consequence. The alteration, however small, would encourage the publication of books in our own country. It would render it, in some measure, necessary that all books should be printed in America. The English would never copy our orthography for their own use; and consequently the same impressions of

books would not answer for both countries. The inhabitants of the present generation would read the English impressions; but posterity, being taught a different spelling, would prefer the American orthography.

Besides this, a national language is a band of national union. Every engine should be employed to render the people of this country national; to call their attachments home to their own country; and to inspire them with the pride of national character. However they may boast of Independence and the freedom of their government, yet their opinions are not sufficiently independent; an astonishing respect for the arts and literature of their parent country, and a blind imitation of its manners . . . turns their attention from their own interests, and prevents their respecting themselves.[14]

By the time he published his *Compendious Dictionary* in 1806 Webster had drawn back from some of his more extreme principles, although his patriotism was as rampant as ever. The ridicule that had greeted his earlier proposals, as much as any intellectual decision, had forced him to reconsider. The dropping of the redundant *u* had survived, and would become one of the great differences, to this day, between American and English spelling; he also dropped the archaic *k* from such English words as "musick" or "logick" (despite some initial jibes England would soon follow suit), and substituted *k* for *que* in such terms as "cheque," "masque," and "risque." This last was also adopted as regular American spelling, as was his decision to reverse the French-influenced *re* in "centre," "theatre," and "metre." Only the dropping of the final *e* from "medicine" or "examine" proved too much for his fellow countrymen to accept. That said, he was not wholly consistent. One finds "traffick" and "almanack," as old-fashioned a spelling as any English equivalent. Nor did he abandon spellings that today seem somewhat absurd: "ake" (as well as the established "ache"), "croud" (and "crowd"), "gillotin" (there is no mention of "guillotine"), "iland" (plus "island"), "tung" (with "tongue") and "lepard" (with "leopard"). The spelling of "wimman" and "wimmen" (which he included alongside the conventional "woman" and "women") would not return to lexicography until the *Feminist Dictionary* of 1983 (although the two dictionaries had somewhat different agendas: Webster based his spelling on etymological theory; the feminists on a desire to rid the language of "men").

Income aside, the immediate result of the spelling book was to concentrate the schoolteacher's mind on the possibility of schemes for a more general reformation of the language. These schemes can best be seen in his *Dissertations on the English Language,* the published version of a series of lectures which he delivered between 1785 and 1786 in the major cities of the Northeast. Only in

Philadelphia, where civic pride forbade the citizens to allow a provincial from
New England to dictate *their* pronunciation, did he receive a wholly unsympa-
thetic hearing. His own attitude to pronunciation was to eschew that set out in
earlier dictionaries or by university authorities, preferring what he saw as cultivated usage (by which he meant that of New England). As he declared in the
preface to his *Dissertations,* "The most difficult task now to be performed by the
advocates of pure English is to restrain the influence of men learned in Greek
and Latin but ignorant of their own tongue."

The *Dissertations* represent Webster's shot at establishing himself as the foremost advocate of a solely American language. His suggestions echoed those of
the anonymous author who, in his contribution to the *Royal American Magazine*
in January 1774, had called for "a plan for perfecting the English language in
America" and of the future President John Adams, who in a letter to Congress
of September 20, 1780 noted that rather than America imitating England, as
had been the practice, the future would see a reverse. The New World would be
setting the standards and "the population and commerce of America will force
their language into general use." Webster took up these ideas and called for the
establishment of a proper American standard, which should be taught in
schools across the country. Unlike élitist England, there should be no hint of
class domination in this, the standard should be that of all Americans. Two
hundred years later Webster appears as the most prescient of seers, but at the
time his concept of "Federal English" was largely pooh-poohed. Just as the criticisms of Johnson that he voiced in the *Compendious Dictionary* would be seen as
lèse-majesté, so were the theories that underpinned the *Dissertations.* The young
men of New York's Philological Society (formed "for the purposes of ascertaining and improving the *American Tongue*")[15] might back him, but they had little
influence and their society, of which he was the leading light, foundered within
a year. Franklin, to whom he had dedicated the *Dissertations,* was at best equivocal, putting off formally accepting the honor and, when he did, suggesting
that its donor would best be occupied in purging the language of its growing
burden of "Americanisms."

In 1806 Webster moved from simple spelling into full-scale lexicography
when he published *A Compendious Dictionary of the English Language.* He had
taken some steps toward compiling a school dictionary as early as 1800, but
had abandoned them in pursuit of a work that could be used in addition by
adults. As well as the word list and Webster's directions as to spelling and pronunciation it offered international tables of money and of weights and measures, divisions of time as regulated in the classical world, a list of U.S. post
offices, the population and the exports of the United States, and "new and

interesting" chronological tables of events and discoveries. Its 408 pages held 40,600 headwords.

It was not a particularly innovative work, nor, in fairness, did Webster claim it to be one. He explains in the introduction that "The following work is an enlargement and an improvement of Entick's [1764] spelling dictionary which public opinion, both in Great Britain and the United States, has pronounced the best compilation of the kind. His selection of words, his orthography, pronunciation, and definitions undoubtedly justify this preference. To his list of words which is *the* most complete I have added about *five thousand* others, which have been mostly collected from the best writers, during a course of several years reading. The purchasers of this Compendious will therefore find the list of words by far the most complete of any vocabulary extant." What he did claim, however, was how much more efficient was his work than that of Samuel Johnson. In a letter of 1807 he claimed to have read more extensively than Johnson and that the "correctness of his definitions" surpassed that of his predecessor or any lexicographer since.

This mood can be seen writ larger in the introduction, where Johnson is the butt of a wide-ranging attack. Johnson had failed; he, Webster, would finally do the job of dictionary making properly, would knock Johnson from his perch and would be recognized as the world's next great lexicographer. Most important, he would compile an *American* dictionary. There were those who still saw American culture as inferior to that of Europe, but they were irrelevant. "Men who take pains to find and to exhibit to the world, proofs of our national inferiority . . . are certainly not destined to decide the ultimate fate of this performance."[16] Webster had no fears as to his intellectual or his physical abilities. In the job of dissolving "the charm of veneration for foreign authorities" no effort could spared. The *Compendious* was thus no more than a way station, a necessary one no doubt, but it was merely a "trial balloon"[17] for the real thing.

That said, the nationalistic saber rattling of Webster's introduction is reflected to some extent in the word list itself. While the vast majority of its contents were plucked straight from Entick, Webster claimed that the 5,000 new words were all products of life in America. This new vocabulary included a variety of jargon terms, derived from the local vocabularies of law, agriculture, industry, and so on; there were political terms, provincialisms and localisms, Indian loanwords, and American proper names. If he was attacked for allowing what others might condemn as "barbarisms" into the word list he defended himself in the way that the moral arbiter, faced with questions as to his or her own probity, always has: he explained that although others might be indeed be at risk from such terminology, it was the duty of the lexicographer to include it, so as to warn and protect the unwary reader. Webster also maintained his anti-Johnson stance by deliberately ignoring a number of words that Johnson had included in 1755 but which he now deemed did not belong in the language. By including such words as *fishify* (to turn to fish, found in *Romeo and Juliet*), *jackalent* (a simple sheepish fellow), *param-citty*, and *jeggumbob*, Johnson had "transgressed the rules of lexicography beyond any other compiler." Webster was equally appalled by Johnson's admitting "vulgar words and offensive ribaldry," notably the loathsome *foutra*. If Johnson justified such inclusions as part of Britain's national vocabulary, that simply meant that the "national language as well as national morals are corrupted and debased." When he does venture to include the supposedly risqué, he is deliberately vague, e.g., *sodomy:* "a crime against nature." Webster's innate puritanism can best be seen not in his lexicography but in the bowdlerized version of the Bible that he published in 1833. He had started "the most important enterprise of my life" in 1821. A specimen section was offered to the Andover Theological Seminary in 1822 but the experts thought he had gone too far and he abandoned the project, concentrating on the *Dictionary* until in 1830 he returned to the Bible. His version retained every incident but changed words ad lib, offering thousands of alterations, every one dedicated to euphemism and absolute decency. Typical is the story of the self-abusive Onan who, rather than "spill his seed" "frustrates his purpose." Testicles become "peculiar members," and female genitals, and even wombs, are conspicuous only by their absence. He also changed much Biblical poetry into prose. Although Webster's Bible had its brief success—it was adopted by the State of Connecticut in 1835 and endorsed by Yale University—his sheer pedantry and his refusal to leave unaltered even those parts acknowledged to be "decent" alienated many readers. After the second and third editions appeared in 1839 and 1841 Webster's version vanished.

Webster saw English, certainly as codified by Johnson, as an old, decaying building, struggling to maintain itself in the face of the advances of time. Johnson had not, in fact, "fixed" English, but Webster vilified him for supposedly trying. "A living language," he declares, "admits of no fixed state nor of any certain standard of pronunciation by which even the learned in general will consent to be governed . . . lexical change will follow cultural change . . . in the vocabulary of a language permanence is not always good and change not always bad."[18] In the way of the self-ordained moralist there was, as ever, a good larding of hypocrisy. His strictures against Johnson's alleged "fixing" are quite at odds with his own desire to purge the language of "vulgarisms." In Webster's eyes, suggests Friend, "one might not legitimately seek to fix the language but clearly one had a moral duty to cleanse it."[19] Thus the *Compendious* purged such terms as *fart, turd,* and the bulk of the then common sexual and excretory vocabulary; even *cullion:* a testicle, which is included in Entick, is cut. Johnson and Webster never show themselves more conservative than in the biases that underpin their word lists: Webster's sexual squeamishness, the product of his cramped religiosity, is his equivalent of Johnson's unashamed political partiality and both form a continuous thread that does nothing to improve either man's work.

A more general attack, aimed at English dictionaries in general rather than at Johnson in particular, can be seen in his preface to the *Dictionary for Schools* (1807), an abridged version of the *Compendious:*

> Some of them contain obscene and vulgar terms, improper to be repeated before children, others abound with obsolete words, or terms of art, which are of no use to common people; some of them are extremely faulty in the manner of marking their accent, making no distinction whatever between the long and short vowels; all of them contain some words not used in this country, or not in the same sense as in Great Britain; and what is very important, all of them are deficient in a multitude of words which are sanctioned by the best usage.

He also notes that "two nations, proceeding from the same ancestors, but established in distant countries, cannot long preserve a perfect sameness of language." America speaks English, but it is *American* English and therefore needs a dictionary of its own. Webster's most prescient comment, however, came in the preface to the original work. Whether or not it was mere bombast or heartfelt belief, he was, give or take a few decades, absolutely right. In fifty years, he prophesied, American English "will be spoken by more people than all the other dialects of the language, and in one hundred and thirty years, by more people than any other language on the globe, not excepting the Chinese."

As Friend has observed, this early effort was very much a test bed for the greater work of 1828 and "it is obvious that Webster's reputation would have reached no such heights if it had been based entirely on [the *Compendious*]."[20] Mencken, generally pro-Webster, describes this groundbreaking effort as "full of the author's crotchets and prejudices, and many of its proposed reforms in spelling were so radical and grotesque that even their author later abandoned them, but despite all these deficiencies it showed wide learning and hard common sense, and so opened the way for the large 'American Dictionary' of 1828,"[21] while another critic, George Krapp, added "On the whole this first dictionary . . . is interesting more as showing the directions to which his mind was turning than as realizing in the treatment of detail any new ideas."[22] Nor was this first essay in lexicography especially well received. Americans were essentially conservatives as regarded their language: Johnson and Walker may have largely ignored their emergent culture, but they had the appeal of established authority. It was not only Jefferson who saw Webster as a jumped-up Yankee with much to say but little worth hearing. Colonial insecurity was far from fully vanquished and Europe still inspired a disproportionate degree of awe in those who, barely thirty years earlier, had been Britain's subjects. In addition Webster faced the bizarre, but deeply held belief, on both sides of the Atlantic, that there was no need for any more words, especially not from the barbarians of the United States. One Captain Basil Hall, an English traveler in America, visited Webster and asked why he felt the need for any linguistic innovations. Webster suggested that American neologisms were a valuable addition to the English vocabulary. Hall was unimpressed and declared loftily that Webster was wrong: "There are words enough already." That many of the alleged neologisms were in fact, had the critics bothered to check, well-established Anglicisms, was irrelevant to those who chose to decry his efforts. Webster might justifiably bemoan the "utter ignorance of men of letters in our country respecting the *amount* and *utility* of my improvements"[23] but he was destined to spend the next twenty years in the wilderness, fighting his corner, plowing the profits from his *Spelling Book* back into his researches and moving headword by headword and page by page toward the completion of the all-American dictionary that, whether they wished it or not, he had promised his countrymen would be delivered.

In 1810 Webster announced his new project in a *Prospectus of a New and Complete Dictionary of the English Language.* It comprised five major aims: "1. To comprehend all the legitimate words in the English language . . . with perspicuous and discriminating definitions, exemplified by authorities . . . ; 2. To contract the size of the work within the smallest compass that is consistent with the comprehensiveness of the design and by reducing the price considerably below that of Johnson's larger work, to render it more accessible to men of small property; 3. To exhibit the true orthography and pronunciation of words . . . ; 4. To explain obsolete words [in] a separate department of the work; 5. To deduce words from their primitive roots . . . This part of the work will be new, and will offer results singularly novel and interesting . . ."

It would be fifteen years before Webster would finish his work, ironically in England rather than in America. It was, naturally, an emotional moment, but in character, Webster permitted himself a second's pause, then returned to normality. As he recalled later, "When I finished my copy, I was sitting at my table in

Cambridge, England, January 1825. When I arrived at the last word I was seized with a tremor that made it difficult to proceed. I, however, summoned up strength to finish the work and then, walking about the room, I soon recovered."[24] The intermediary period was by no means easy. Like Johnson he was beset by money problems. There were the funds from the *Spelling Book* but they were insufficient by themselves. He circularized the great and good soliciting support, noting that he was not requesting money—he envisaged costs of $10,000 and the real outlay would be nearer $25,000—"for my *own sake*" but to help in the creation of a design that would be "the most interesting to literature of any ever undertaken in America" and infinitely more worthy of investment than "a party or a despicable newspaper."[25] Those to whom he wrote obviously felt otherwise, and nothing was forthcoming. Nor would it ever be, however many times Webster appealed to them during the lifetime of the project.

Given its size, some 70,000 entries, every one written in Webster's own hand, and its importance to contemporary lexicography, the fifteen years it took for the *Dictionary* to be written is not so long a period. Unlike Johnson he had no amanuensis, only a proofreader after the printing was completed. This was the poet and geologist James Gates Percival, who was equally well known for his linguistic abilities. Webster felt himself slowed by lack of proper funding— he moved house from New Haven to Amherst in search of cheaper accommodation—but he was also forced to take some time at the outset to improve his knowledge. The *Compendious* had, in the end, been like so many dictionaries the sum of its predecessors. What he envisaged now was a radical step forward. If he was, as he wished, to see off Johnson, it was necessary to best him on every front. To remedy Johnson's perceived errors was easy, to increase the word list and render it more "American" was also feasible; where Webster had a greater struggle was in the area of etymology. He determined to establish "the truth" as regarded the origins of language. He had covered the first two letters of the alphabet before he realized that his etymological knowledge was simply inadequate for the task. He stopped work and devoted the next ten years to remedying his deficiencies. Aside from the etymologies that would appear in the *Dictionary,* the fruits of this labor were concentrated in the unpublished *Synopsis of Words in Twenty Languages.* This thesis, in which he attempted to lay out the relations of words possessing the same cognate or radical letters, drawn from some twenty Middle Eastern and European languages, and which underpins the *Dictionary* etymologies, remains entombed in vaults of the New York Public Library.

With the etymological research finished, Webster returned to preparing the text and by 1821 had reached H. Financial pressures had slightly eased: his children had left home, and the *Spelling Book* was selling in increasingly lucrative quantities, although Webster's income derived from the one-off sale of rights: he made no royalty deals. In 1822 he was able to move back to New Haven and two years later he sailed for England, hoping there to put the finishing touches to his work and possibly to interest a British publisher in it. In this he failed, but he did finish his work in the library at Cambridge. He returned home with his manuscript and began arranging for the printing, which finally began on May 8, 1827.

The *American Dictionary of the English Language* was published on April 21, 1828. Its two large quarto volumes covered approximately 1,600 unnumbered pages. It cost $20.00 and the initial print run was 2,500. As well as laying out the dictionary's aims on the title page, Webster inserted this quotation: "He that wishes to be counted among the benefactors of posterity, must add, by his own toil, to the acquisitions of his ancestors." The preface stated that while he had initiated the *Dictionary* in no more than the hope of amending the errors of previous lexicographers, he had expanded his aims as the work progressed and now intended, by purifying the language, "to furnish a standard of our vernacular, which we shall not be ashamed to bequeath to *three hundred millions* of people who are destined to occupy . . . the vast territory within our jurisdiction."[26] He also stressed the importance of his work as an *American* dictionary: "It is . . . necessary that the people of this country, should have an American Dictionary of the English language; for, although the body of the language is the same as in England, and it is desirable to perpetuate that sameness, yet some differences must exist."[27] He quotes with pride the range of his American sources—Franklin, Washington, Adams, Jay, Madison, and many others—and compares them favorably with any literary élite. He writes at length on his etymological studies and claims that he has taken great steps in all the various branches of dictionary making: rules of spelling and pronunciation, the inclusion of homegrown American language, and in definitions and etymology.

As far as the spelling and punctuating are concerned, Webster had laid down his opinions on these "technical" aspects of the language in a number of previous works. His attitudes to spelling had fluctuated: he had started off looking to Johnson, then moved radically in the direction of wholesale reform, and then begun a steady process of moving back to a more moderate stance. It is that later position which can be seen in the *American Dictionary*. His underlying principle remained that of economy, thus his insistence on abandoning what were seen as redundant letters. Thanks to his etymological studies he was also looking back, seeing what might be seen as obscure terms as the basis of modern spelling. Thus if, as he believed, *women* is based on *wifmen* it was logical that the correct spelling should be *wimen,* although he accepts the more usual version. Similarly if *bridegroom* came from the OE *guma,* then the word should properly be *bridegoom.*

Webster, said James Murray in 1900, "was a born definer of words"[28] and the consensus is that Webster's definitions are the great glory of his work. He was, however, subject to the limits that restrict any lexicographer—those of the current state of knowledge. Webster's reference sources were minimal compared with those, for instance, of the *OED* and he cannot be blamed for that. Nor can he be blamed for working solo. Johnson's amanuenses do not appear to have added particularly to his store of information, but such isolation, compounded by what must have been the still primitive state of American libraries and bookstores, cannot have helped.

"One must admire, nonetheless," writes George Krapp, "both the courage and skill of Webster in his definitions. He was not afraid to attack any term, nor did he fail to give a definition that was clear, and true at least to the elements of the subject defined."[29] Webster liked getting to the bottom of a definition, taking the word apart and seeing, as it were, how it worked. His own wide range of interests was very important for defining: as well as a lexicographer he was a grammarian, an essayist, a newspaper editor, an educator, a lawyer, a politician, a farmer, and a scientific observer. He wrote widely, his topics including pestilential diseases, the rights of neutrals, the operations of banks and insurance offices. He contributed to learned journals, and was a member of learned societies. In his definitions, adds Krapp, he "reveals a clearness of mind, a soundness of judgment and catholicity of interest that puts him intellectually in the same class with [Benjamin] Franklin." Yet there was still a degree of provincialism. Webster gives far too great an importance to New England, that area in which he had always lived. New England, which had been less welcoming to European immigrants than other areas, had been seen as the home of the purest American pronunciation, and Webster had taken local usage as the basis of his own standards. But this was supposed to be an American dictionary, not a New England one, and his more sophisticated critics disdained such parochialism.

It has also to be noted that however venomously Webster had attacked Johnson, he was far from reticent when it came to "borrowing" from the earlier work. He stresses that of course Johnson's book is riddled with errors, but, he explains in his preface, "a considerable part . . . is well executed; and when his definitions are correct and his arrangement precious, it seems to be expedient to follow him." Not for nothing have later generations deplored the Pecksniffian aspects of Webster's personality. His lack of humor is also notable in at least one borrowing. After inserting his own definition of *oats*—"a plant of the genus Avena, and more usually the seed of the plant . . ." he cannot resist appending Johnson's version. Unfortunately he attempts awkwardly to recast it: "the meal of this grain, *oatmeal,* forms a considerable and very valuable article of food for man in Scotland, and every where oats are excellent food for horses and cattle." As J. H. Friend says, "Johnson . . . would have enjoyed the humourless sententiousness of this reformulation of his joke,"[30] but he also notes that Johnson himself, as has been subsequently proved, was not in fact its originator.

As far as Americanisms are concerned, Webster had been touting his concept of an American tongue for thirty years; he was not likely to abandon it now. His pride in the citations he drew from local writers is displayed in the preface but it has been noted that for all his boasting, the number of Americanisms is far less extensive than might be assumed. There are certainly some native American words: typical are Indian terms such as *sachem, wigwam, squash, pow-wow, moccasin, moose, toboggan;* those derived from France: *bureau, cache, levee, portage, prairie;* from Holland: *boss, cruller, Santa Claus, waffle;* from Germany: *pretzel, (saur)craut;* and Spain: *coyote, mescal, tequila.* There are notes of the way in which Americans use English words in a new context and with a variant meaning: *backwoods, bluff, clearing, divide.* Politics provides *selectman, big chief, gerrymander,* while the domestic and educative sides of life give *apple butter, bobsled, log-cabin, johnny-cake, conestoga wagon, campus, yankee, senior* (fourth-year student), *junior* (third-year), and *squatter.* But in a 70,000-strong word list these make up the smallest of proportions and the bulk of Webster's material has no especial qualification as "American." Likewise, while he opts wherever possible for a local citation, the quotations he uses are as likely to back up a quotidian English term as to unearth and display a new American one.

Nor did Webster ever suggest that in promoting an American tongue he was actually proposing that such a tongue should replace English. He respected the differences, which had hitherto been largely overlooked, but, even in the determinedly aggressive pronouncements of his youth, he never advocated absolute segregation. Indeed, his dictionary was happily accepted by English users. The first English edition was of 3,000 copies—500 more than the American one— and 140,000 copies had been sold by the early 1870s. The United States spoke American English: it was a different brand but it was still English. In 1841 he sent a copy of the second edition to Queen Victoria; his covering note held the hope that "genuine descendants of English ancestors born on the west of the Atlantic, have not forgotten either the land or the language of their fathers." It was all a far cry from the post-Revolutionary hothead of the 1780s.

Writing of Johnson's etymologies in his preface, Webster declared that "whole scheme of deducing words from their original is extremely imperfect."[31]

But if Webster had been praised, rightly or not, for his definitions, the etymologies that followed them have generally been seen as an unparalleled disaster. It was to these that George Krapp referred when, writing a century later, he
described Webster's *Dictionary* as "the most significant contribution to the
growth of English lexicography between Dr. Johnson and the first volume of
the New [Oxford] English Dictionary" but nonetheless as "only partially successful . . . the book was broadly conceived, but in parts executed with an inadequate scholarship and with a stubbornness of personal conviction that
seriously impaired the noble design." Indeed, suggests Krapp, Webster's original work was far from an "American classic, and if it were not for elaborate publishers' revisions of Webster's work, revisions with which he had nothing to do,
but which nevertheless did retain what was genuinely good in the Dictionary
of 1828, Webster's name would probably be unknown in the land."

Had those revisions not been made, Webster might, in the face of advances
from European philology, have been more of a joke than the institution that he
has become. He had worked assiduously on developing his own theories of language, but quantity and quality are not invariable bedfellows and in this area
of his researches Webster was disastrously off-key. He believed that there had
been a single ur-language, from which all the rest had emerged: "before the dis-
persion; the whole earth was of one language and of one or the same speech."
This language he christened Chaldee. It was a belief that could only exist if,
like Webster, one accepted unquestioningly that every word written in the
Bible, rather than being an agglomeration of fact, fantasy, and fable, conveniently constructed to promote a particular sect, was actually true. James Murray claimed that Webster "had the notion that derivations can be elaborated
from one's own consciousness."[32] This is overcondemnatory. Webster believed
they had a real root: Chaldee. Of the language that really is at the root of so
many English words, Anglo-Saxon, he had little or no knowledge.

Webster was no fool, and ten years of scholarly research underpinned his theories with substantial foundations. The tragedy was the extent to which they
rested on the sands of his basic misapprehensions. Webster's etymologies were
based on the setting down of the major "radical words"—the basic units from
which all languages originally derived. He made lists of words in various languages that had similar meanings and which looked alike in their consonants.
But he overlooked the vowels, feeling that "little or no regard is to be had to
them, in ascertaining the origin and affinity of languages." More dangerously,
he derided Sir William Jones (the most innovative English-speaking philologist of the era, whose methods were to contribute substantially to the methodology of Murray's *New English Dictionary*). "It is obvious," he wrote, "that Sir

W. Jones had given very little attention to the subject [of etymology], and that some of its most common and obvious principles had escaped his observation."[33] As will be seen, only Horne Tooke, whose etymologies rivaled even Webster's for their farfetchedness, showed himself equally bloody-minded.

As Sledd and Kolb put it, in a passage of devastating disdain:

> The basis of his etymologizing was simple fantasy. Accepting the scriptural account of the dispersion, he believed that "the primitive language of man," spoken by "the descendants of Noah . . . on the plain of Shinar, . . . must have been the original Chaldee," and that "all the words of the several great races of men, both in Asia and Europe, which are vernacular in their several languages, and unequivocally the same, are of equal antiquity, as they must have been derived from the common Chaldee stock."[34] Thus the native element in modern English consists of "words which our ancestors brought with them from Asia," and the Danish and Welsh loans are also "primitive words," derived from the language of Japheth and his descendants.[35] Webster could believe all this forty years after Sir William Jones, twenty after Schlegel, a dozen after Bopp, and half a dozen or more after the first volumes of Jacob Grimm, he could believe it after actually reading Jones . . . For such invincible ignorance, it is best to attempt no excuse; and if one looks for redeeming features in Webster's practice as a dictionary-maker or in other aspects of his theory, some of the praise which usually is given him begins to appear a little strained.[36]

James Murray's condemnatory remark on Webster's derivations takes its lead from the undeniable fact that he appears to have felt, like so many folk etymologists, that if two words looked alike and had vaguely similar meanings, then they must be related. But not only had he ignored Jones, but he chose to bypass more recent developments, set down in the Grimm Brothers' groundbreaking *Deutsche Grammatik,* in which concrete phonetic rules and laws were established. It was another area that betrayed his innate provincialism. That he was probably unable to read German is insufficient excuse. By 1850 the new philology had crossed the Atlantic and Webster's theories were rendered obsolete. By then, however, Webster himself was dead. Like Columbus, who died never fully accepting that he had found the New World (rather than what he believed to be a back route to Cathay), Webster would never realize the extent of his errors. He died in blissful ignorance: four years before his death he was still happily pronouncing that the Germans, while "the most accurate philologists in

Europe [are] wholly deficient."[37] It was not until 1864 that Webster's etymologies were put right, thanks to a German scholar, C. A. F. Mahn, who had been commissioned by G. & C. Merriam. The 1864 revision, which he supervised, is thus known as the Webster-Mahn. As Friend points out, "Though souvenirs of . . . Webster's original formations can still be found in the definitions of the Merriam dictionaries that continue to bear his commercially valuable name, it would be hard to detect any trace of his linguistic meanderings."[38]

Sledd and Kolb are not alone in their attack, but neither they nor anyone else who excoriated the hapless Webster admit of one important factor: Webster's religion and the importance it had in every aspect of his life, not least the standards he attempted to convey through his dictionary. Even Mencken, who says that he was not alone in his overreliance on Holy Writ,[39] cannot really let him off. Johnson was religious too, but his religion, which also comes out in his *Dictionary,* was High Anglican, a more tolerant and supple faith than the fundamentalist Calvinism that was Webster's creed. It is that agenda which has to be taken into account when assessing his work, especially his etymologies.

In April 1808 Webster was "born again" as a Calvinist and in July 1809 published in *The Panopolist* his *Reasons for Accepting the Christian and Calvinist Scheme.* It has been suggested that this espousal of fundamentalist religion alienated a number of those who might otherwise have backed his *Dictionary* with their cash. True or not, far more important is the effect his decision had on his work. The *American Dictionary* has traditionally been paraded as an exemplar of its author's nationalism; as suggested by Rollins it is far more a profession of his personal beliefs, which in his case meant his religious faith.[40]

However much he paraded his distaste for Johnson, Webster's book, like his predecessor's, is as a much a statement of his personal philosophy as it is a simple work of reference. His dictionary making, as does Johnson's, represents the supreme example of the lexicographer as personality and as self-proposed cultural legislator. There would of course be other dictionaries, whether prescriptive or descriptive, geared to setting out the rules of language, but these would be the product of teams. Johnson and Webster were the last, and greatest, individuals to bring down the lexicographical tablets of the law and reveal them to the people. Thus, just as did Johnson, Webster set out to propound his version of politics, society, and religious dogma. It runs, like Johnson's, as a subtext through the language of his definitions and the choice of his citations. The semiologist will attribute similar motives to any lexicographer, and such as Thomas Elyot undoubtedly had a point to make, but these men of the modern world, with a potential audience far greater than Elyot's intellectual élite (for all that he helped expand it), were infinitely more open in their schemes.

As a citizen of a new nation which based its society on a written Constitution, Webster could not fail to appreciate the overriding importance of words. It was vital that they should be defined properly. As early as 1788 he was calling for studies that would "show how far truth and accuracy are concerned in a clear understanding of words."[41] Ironically, his opponents saw his attempts at linguistic reform as subversive: what was good enough for the past should suffice for the present, but Webster took the opposite stance. Only by refining the language, by purifying it of its many errors and corruptions could the status quo be sustained. He was a patriot, no doubt, but as Mencken observed, no special friend of democracy, let alone of the freedoms he would have considered (and indeed defined) not as liberty but as license. He saw Jefferson, who in turn was no great admirer of Webster, as his absolute antithesis; the "father of American liberalism" is not one of those local heroes of whom Webster boasts and whose words are used for citations. Webster's main concern "was not to celebrate American life or to expand independence [but] to counteract social disruption and reestablish the deferential world order that he believed was disintegrating."[42] To misunderstand the true meaning of a word was to pave the way to social disorder. Thus the dictionary takes especial care with such key terms as *free, equal, democrat, republican, love,* and *laws.* Freedom, other than in subjection to divine laws, was absurd; it is seen as "violation of the rules of decorum" and "license." Equality was out of the question: unsurprisingly, despite being one of the contributors to the radical Hartford constitution of 1814, Webster stood foursquare against universal male suffrage. Like Johnson's defining of Whig and Tory, Webster equated a Democrat with "a person who attempts an undue opposition or influence over government by means of private clubs, secret intrigues or by public popular meetings which are extraneous to the Constitution." Republicans, on the other hand, were "friends of our representative Governments . . ." As for love, "the love of God is the first duty of man . . ." Laws existed simply to "enjoin the duties of piety and morality." Injunctions toward such submissiveness can be found throughout the *Dictionary.* Duty, as might be presumed, is highly valued: do what you are told and ask no questions might have been Webster's credo. As for education, it was a concept that in Webster's world had no relation to learning; education was "instruction and discipline," it would fit the young for their future stations. And while a general education was "important" a religious one was "indispensable." The fear of the Lord, as he often declared, quoting the Book of Common Prayer, was the beginning of wisdom.

As far as his etymologies are concerned, Webster's entire scheme was based on religion. Viewed with hindsight his theories are ludicrous but if Krapp is correct[43] his aims were spiritual rather than philological and it was spiritual rather than phonological truths that interested him: "No part of my researches has given me more trouble or solicitude than that of arriving at the precise radical significance of moral ideas, such, for instance, as hope, love, favor, faith." Like Plato, he believed that "the truth of a word, its original root value, is equivalent to the truth of the idea it conveys."[44] But, while this may have been the original meaning of etymology, it was not that understood by modern philologists. Webster, however, had, as Rollins put it, "no choice but to write Christian etymology."[45] What did the theories of some fallible German intellectual matter if Christ had, via the Bible, pronounced otherwise. With the invincible ignorance of the true believer he let his work be dominated by the concept that were the Bible, even in a single syllable, to be found wanting, then society would collapse. To Webster the Bible was literal truth: God gave language to Adam, languages were confused at the Tower of Babel, and the ones that survived were split into three tribes—those of Ham, Shem, and Japhet— of whom the Japhetic represented the tongues of the modern inhabitants of Northern Europe.

Finally, as Rollins points out, while one might assume that so lengthy a task would elicit from most authors a list of helpers, influences, and sources, Webster offers none of these. Nor, for all that he has so often been associated with militant nationalism, are there any "paeans to American freedom, celebrations of the heroes of the Revolution, or . . . other spread-eagle statements."[46] Instead, as the product of a religious movement "whose major concern was social control, not the nationalistic fervour of the late eighteenth century,"[47] the *American Dictionary of the English Language* was dedicated to God.

The criticisms quoted above come almost entirely from twentieth-century sources. The contemporary response to Webster's efforts was predictably mixed. Scotland's *Quarterly Review* was less than friendly. After praising his industry, and itemizing the complimentary remarks made elsewhere, its reviewer professed his disappointment and stated that in his own opinion, "the general execution of his work is poor . . . The mere perusal of his Preface is sufficient to show that he is but slenderly qualified for the undertaking. There is everywhere a great parade of erudition, and a great lack of real knowledge; . . . we do not recollect ever to have witnessed . . . a greater number of crudities and errors, or more pains taken to so little purpose."[48] It savaged his etymologies, pointed out every howler and ended by commenting that "Dr Webster's quartos were hardly worthy of being reprinted in England." The London *Times,* however, was more generous, declaring that "We can have no hesitation in giving it our decided opinion that this is the most elaborate and successful undertaking of the kind which has ever appeared." The *English Journal of Education* cited Webster as "the greatest lexicographer that has ever lived." The *Westminster Review*, while equivocal as to certain technicalities, still proclaimed it to be "a work of admirable practical utility" and one in which the etymologies in particular would "provide much that will enlighten and inform the most profound of our philologists." Back in America there was a similar mixture, although the majority were very much in favor.

A rival grammarian, Lyman Cobb, who had already taken it upon himself to savage the *Speller,* now turned his attentions to the *Dictionary* in a series of articles written for the *Albany Argus.* Predictably he was especially exercised by Webster's spelling system which, he felt, failed in what should be the primary aim of such systems: orthographic uniformity. But Cobb, while impassioned, was hardly disinterested. He had his own spelling book to peddle and Webster, as the market leader, was the man to beat. Far more representative of Webster's reception was the all-out encomium. Chancellor James Kent, giving the anniversary address of the Phi Beta Kappa Society, was typically unrestrained in his enthusiasms. The *Dictionary* was "a work of profound investigation and does infinite honor to the philological learning and general literature of this country." Such edifices as the Pyramids, the Parthenon, "obelisks, arches and triumphant monuments" would all, in time perish. The *Dictionary* would outlive them all. Only two men might rival Webster's fame: Columbus and Washington. Heady, hyperbolic stuff, but it is unlikely that Webster, after so many rebuffs and so many problems, did not relish every syllable.

Noah Webster died on May 28, 1843. A second edition of his *American Dictionary* had appeared in 1841, somewhat more orthodox in many respects than its first edition, and including 5,000 words omitted from that earlier work. Webster was still not rich—he had had to mortgage his house to finance the publication which was not particularly successful—but he remained celebrated as the great guardian and teacher of the "American tongue." His 1828 edition had succeeded both in America and in England, where, other than Johnson, it had so far only one main rival, Charles Richardson's *New Dictionary of the English Language,* a work which like his own drew on Horne Tooke's philological theories for its etymologies, and which also vilified Johnson as the supposed root of all lexicographical evil. In America, however, Webster also faced a rival, and one far more threatening than Richardson.

Joseph Emerson Worcester was a schoolteacher and the author of a number of textbooks on geography and history. He was born in Bedford, New Hampshire on August 24, 1784 and like Webster could trace his ancestry back to an early immigrant from England. Like Webster too, he had been reared in the strict traditions of Calvinist fundamentalism and brought up on a farm, which neither he nor his fourteen brothers and sisters were permitted to leave until they turned twenty-one. His father, Jesse, also taught school and contributed occasionally to the press. Such intellectual leanings must have passed on to his children: all but one became teachers. At twenty-one Joseph Worcester duly left home, and registered at Phillipps' Academy, where his classmates, who had not had to work away their childhoods in farm laboring, were aged nine. He left after four years and in 1809 entered Yale. He graduated, after a successful academic career, in 1811. He was twenty-seven. For the next five years he taught at a private academy in Salem, where one of his pupils was the future writer Nathaniel Hawthorne.

In 1817 Worcester published his first work: *A Geographical Dictionary or General Gazeteer,* which was followed a year later by *A Gazeteer of the United States.* His lexicographical work began in 1827 when he edited a new edition of a popular dictionary: *Johnson's English Dictionary as improved by Todd and abridged by Chalmers, with Walker's Pronouncing Dictionary combined.* This was, as has been seen, one of the staples of the American dictionary market and Worcester's edition was particularly highly regarded, described in the *North American Review* as "the most complete manual of the kind that has yet appeared."[49] Armed with such expertise Worcester took on a new project: in 1829 he abridged Webster himself. This was presumably an amicable arrangement; certainly Worcester had nothing but praise for the book on which he worked, calling it "a work of vast learning and research, containing the most complete vocabulary of the language that has yet appeared, and comprising numerous and great improvements upon all works of the kind . . ."[50] The job, according to Friend,[51] was not an especially welcome one: Worcester was more interested in working on his own dictionary, but he took it for the experience and presumably the money, a fee of $2,000. It runs to 940 pages and is slightly larger than Webster's original, using terms that Worcester had discovered while working on Todd's "Johnson," and from other sources. As he would in his own work of 1830, he gave great precedence to rules of pronunciation. Webster's definitions were cut down, and all but the "most important" etymologies and the vast bulk of citations ignored. It would be five years before open warfare broke out between the two men, but Webster, through his son-in-law Chauncey Goodrich, who had been deputed to supervise any such editions, made it clear that he disliked Worcester's work. He accused Worcester of tampering with the text he had been given and, despite being the older man, deplored the innate conservatism of his approach. The aims that underpinned his original text, which revealed as much a profession of deeply felt personal convictions as it did a list of words and definitions, had been traduced. Goodrich, however, who after Webster's death would help the Merriam Brothers in their gradual elimination of his idiosyncrasies from their editions of the *Dictionary,* was more than satisfied. Writing on July 27, 1828, to acknowledge Worcester's taking on of the job, he told him, "There is no man in the United States . . . who would be equally acceptable."

In 1830, by now an experienced lexicographer, Worcester produced the first of his own dictionaries: the *Comprehensive, Pronouncing and Explanatory Dictionary,* which he had begun preparing while he was working on his edition of Todd's "Johnson." It aimed to appeal to all classes, not just the mass market, but the literate and scholarly too, and thus proclaimed itself to be taking a middle course between Johnson and Webster. He added a number of new words, although perhaps somewhat fewer than he claimed, aimed for a spelling system somewhere between Johnson's traditionalism and Webster's advances, and avoided etymology altogether—a move that while it restricted the usefulness of his work, at least ensured there were no embarrassing howlers. His particular specialty was pronunciation, the rules for which he based on no less than twenty-six varied authorities. In general, notes Krapp, Worcester "showed greater common sense and better judgment than Webster."[52]

The book appeared to no great furor until on November 26, 1834 in *The Palladium,* published in Worcester, Massachusetts, there appeared a piece that, in retrospect, would be seen as the first shot in a "dictionary war" that would make the Blount-Phillips encounters of two centuries earlier seem no more than a harmless spat.

A gross plagiarism has been committed by Mr. J. E. Worcester on the literary property of Noah Webster, Esq. It is well known that Mr. Webster has spent a life, which is now somewhat advanced, in writing a dictionary of the English language, which he published in 1828 in two quarto volumes. Three abridgements have since been made; one in octavo form and two still smaller, for families and primary schools. To aid in the drudgery of providing these abridgements, Mr. Webster employed Mr. Worcester, who after becoming acquainted with Mr. Webster's plan, immediately set about appropriating to his own benefit the valuable labors, acquisitions, and productions of Mr. Webster. He has since published a dictionary, which is a very close imitation of Webster's; and which, we regret to learn, has since been introduced into many of the primary schools of the country. We regret this, because the public, inadvertently, do an act of great injustice to a man who has rendered the country an invaluable service, and ought to receive the full benefit of his labors. If we had a statute which could fix its grasp on those who pilfer the products of the mind, as readily as our laws embrace the common thief, Mr. Worcester would hardly escape with a light mulct. At all events before people buy his wares, they would do well to inquire how he came by them.

Worcester replied in *The Palladium* on December 10. He noted that he had started work on his *Dictionary* long before he began his abridgment of Webster and that in any case there were many differences between the two books. His response was temperate and reasonable but on December 17 the *Palladium* published a letter from Webster himself, claiming that Worcester had indeed purloined, and worse still not acknowledged, a number of his definitions. There were, according to his follow-up letter of January 28, 1835, some 121 of these. On February 11 came Worcester's rebuttal: he gave a detailed list of his sources for the 121 definitions. The vast majority (ninety) were already available in other dictionaries and others were not even in Webster's first edition. The correspondence continued through spring 1835 and, according to Friend, "Worcester's defense [was] a good deal more impressive than Webster's accusations, which tend to grow querulous . . . and reveal clearly that the older man felt his livelihood endangered by the popular acceptance of the Comprehensive."[53] Webster's response, on February 18, underlines his frustration: "My Quarto Dictionary [the 1828 edition] cost me about *twenty years of labor and 20,000 dollars.* For this labor and such an expense I could never receive remuneration had the market been left open . . . How unkind then was it, for *you,* who had been intrusted with the task of making an abridgement, and had been well rewarded for it, to sit down and introduce some of my improvements into a book of your own compilation . . . Now, Sir, rather than treat *you* in this manner, I would rather beg my bread." And, one might feel, were Worcester's success to continue, that was just what poor Webster envisaged. Presumably he was further disconcerted by the adoption of Worcester's work by the literati and academics of Harvard and Boston, and by conservatively minded dictionary buyers across the country. It was a statement of scholarly support for his rival that would continue throughout the next twenty-five years and in some diehard cases beyond. He responded, in 1841, by publishing a new edition, *Webster's Unabridged.* It bore all the marks of a hasty piece of work, aimed at sales rather than at a proper revision, and was not especially successful.

The first salvos of the dictionary war had long since faded away when in 1846 Worcester produced *A Universal and Critical Dictionary of the English Language,* a much expanded version of his previous effort. Working on the basis of Todd's version of Johnson, he had hugely expanded the word list, adding around 27,000 new words and bringing the total to around 83,000. He had ranged widely in search of material, looking at the works of Ash, Richardson, Smart (*Walker Remodelled,* 1836), many technical and scientific dictionaries, general encyclopedias, and numerous other works. The one predecessor he had sedulously ignored was Webster: mindful of their previous encounter, he declared that he had not, to the best of his knowledge, "taken a single word, or the definition of a word"[54] from his former employer. He rejected citations, but provided authorities for any word (marked by an asterisk) not already included in "Todd." The majority of these authorities, he explained, were English and not American. It was typical of his conservative approach, and that of his potential readers, that he still equated "authority" with English, rather than American writers. He also went out of his way to congratulate his rivals, including the shade of the cantankerous Webster. "With his usual modesty and sober good sense," say Sledd and Kolb,[55] "Worcester pointed out that although Johnson's Dictionary had won most general acceptance as a standard, the 'most considerable' of his British successors, Richardson, had done much for anyone who wanted to study the history of the language, while Webster had produced 'the greatest and most important work on English lexicography'[56] since 1755. 'It is a work of great learning and research, comprising a much more full vocabulary of the language than Johnson's Dictionary, and containing many and great improvements with respect both to the etymology and definitions of words; but the taste and judgement of the author are not generally esteemed equal to his industry and erudition.' "[57]

"Perhaps," add Sledd and Kolb, "the last remark might have been spared." Indeed, but it was not and the peace that had seemed to have curbed the dictionary war a decade earlier quickly turned out to be no more than an extended, impermanent truce. Worcester's dictionary might have been characterized by its "scholarly good sense, moderation and absence of stridency,"[58] but the response its appearance elicited was quite another matter. The situation, of course, had changed a good deal since the two lexicographers had swapped letters via *The Palladium.* Webster was dead, and the rights to his dictionaries had been snapped up by two businessmen from Springfield, Massachusetts—the brothers Charles and George Merriam, who were already established as publishers of Bibles, text- and law books. They employed Chauncey Goodrich to prepare a new revision of the original edition—that of 1841 had pleased no one. This, the first of what continue to be a long line of *Merriam-Webster* dictionaries, appeared a year after Worcester. Geared for maximum sales, it was priced at $6, a substantial reduction on the 1828 price of $20.

What followed was nearly twenty-five years of intermittent hostilities in which the books themselves came to symbolize not simply opposed systems of lexicography but a whole range of social, cultural, and above all commercial rivalries. "Worcester *vs.* Webster came to mean not only linguistic conservatives and moderates *vs.* radicals and liberals, but, with some inevitable extremist distortion and oversimplification, Anglophiles *vs.* Americanizers, Boston-Cambridge–Harvard *vs.* New Haven–Yale, upperclass elegance *vs.* underbred Yankee uncouthness."[59] There were, undoubtedly, true believers on either side, whose emotions were stirred not by commerce but by culture, but had the commercial battle not been engaged, it is unlikely that the cultural one would have been so ferocious. Above all it was the commercial struggle that was the most energizing to its protagonists. Immigrants flooded into America throughout the nineteenth century in ever-increasing numbers. Far more than in any other country the dictionary was viewed as a sign of social and cultural attainment. It was also vital, to its mass-market purchasers, as the ultimate linguistic authority. Thus, there was serious money to be made, and the dictionary war showed a cutthroat ruthlessness that rarely reflected the products over which it was being fought. It was a verbal war, as was fitting, but it was still remarkably vicious.

Typical were the barely concealed blackmail tactics engaged in by Mason Bros. of New York, who had been leased the rights to publish a number of Webster's school pamphlets. Writing to Messrs. Cowperthwait & Co. of Philadelphia, their correspondent stated:

> If you are interested in Worcester's Dictionaries or are using influence for them we, and the other publishers of Webster, would be glad to know it. We have often heard that such was the case, but have paid no attention to it . . . We of course do not question your right to work for these books or any others, but would like a clear understanding in the matter, as we are disposed to reciprocate favors in these book matters. Please to show your flag.[60]

They also asked whether Cowperthwait's had "joined hands with the Worcester interest." To this note was attached a list of publishers with whom Masons dealt, whom they wished to inform as to the Cowperthwait position, "as their agents are able to do something in geography matters without much trouble." That "something" was to ensure that Warren's geography textbook, which Cowperthwait published and distributed, would be pushed out of Boston's schools. Cowperthwait's responded that "We should have great pleasure in defining our position with reference to Worcester's Dictionaries, were it not for the implied threat which accompanies your letter. As it is, a decent self-respect prevents our replying to it." Nor was the threat merely implied. Pieces

attacking Warren began appearing in the Boston press and the book was discussed adversely in school committee meetings. Finally Cowperthwait's
revealed the correspondence in a pamphlet, complaining that "The grossest
misrepresentations were put forth through the press . . . while their traveling
agents have unscrupulously done little else but to vilify, traduce, and slander
both Dr. Worcester and ourselves." It was quickly established that the most
active slanderers were the firm of W. B. Smither & Co. and that of G. and C.
Merriam—holder of the main Webster rights. Commenting on the row, the
Boston *Daily Advertiser* doubted "if the history of mercantile morality contains
a blacker page than is here disclosed."[61]

A sidebar to the controversy came when the British publisher Henry G.
Bohn issued an edition of Worcester's *Universal and Critical Dictionary of the
English Language* in 1853. The dictionary itself appeared as written, but Bohn,
who had bought the plates from Worcester's publishers, changed the title page
and the introduction in ways that were guaranteed to cause trouble. The new
title included the phrase "compiled from the materials of Noah Webster,
LL.D." and while "Worcester" appeared on one line, "Webster," in much larger
type, was on the one above him. Worcester's careful negation of any debts to
Webster, which had been featured in the preface of the American edition, was
simply dropped from the text and to conclude the distortions, the back of the
book announced "Webster's and Worcester's Dictionary." The inevitable
charges and countercharges ensued; all that can reasonably be stated is that
Worcester, who attempted to deal with the matter in his pamphlet *Gross Literary Fraud Exposed: Relating to the Publication of Worcester's Dictionary in London,*
had no part in the depiction, and that Bohn (1796–1884), whose fortune was
made from the sale of "remainder copies" and cheap reprints, was obviously not
the most reputable operator. As Worcester remarked, were he able to lay out
the details of Bohn's business practice, "I think it would appear to be . . . as
commercially dishonorable, as this literary enterprise is fraudulent and dis-
graceful."

The arguments sputtered on through the 1850s. Typical was the controversy
in 1853 between Merriams and the writer Washington Irving (1783–1859).
Two years earlier Merriams had sent Irving a copy of Webster's *Dictionary* and
he duly replied to thank them. In his letter he stated that Webster's spelling
was not to his taste and that he could not therefore "make it my standard."
Nonetheless, Irving agreed that there was much merit in the dictionary "as a
whole and that in many respects, I find it an invaluable *vade mecum.*" On July
29, 1853 the Boston *Daily Advertiser,* never a Webster enthusiast, ran a piece
explaining that the paper had been sent a 48-page advertising manual, issued

by Merriams and puffing Webster's *Dictionary*. They noted that among the reams of congratulatory quotations was one from Washington Irving, in which he apparently recommended the entire work. However, on consulting Irving himself, it appeared that his praise had been taken out of context. A letter in which he set out his complaint was included in the article. The piece went on to warn readers that, among those who had been quoted, Irving was not the only one who had resisted actually using Webster as an authority, whatever Merriams' puff might imply. Merriams hit back, quoting Irving's original letter of thanks, plus passages from his works which, they claimed, comprehensively proved that Webster was indeed his authority, on spelling and everything else. The Merriam letter also notes one further aspect of the "war." "We must confess that [Dr. Webster] committed one unpardonable sin—*he did not graduate at Cambridge University* [now Harvard] . . . we should hope this might not be deemed a perpetual *casus belli* upon him, in his memory and his literary progeny." It did not require this sarcastic "apology" to reveal that there was a good deal more going on than a simple clash of lexicographies.

As this controversy shows, the ins and outs of the dictionary war were often tedious: it was a struggle of attritional trench warfare rather than one of dashing cavalry operations. It soon descended to a level of minutiae that none but the most dedicated of enthusiasts could entertain. Only the constant presence of potentially lost profits gives one an understanding of the lengths to which those involved were willing to go. The clash over the Bohn affair, in which Worcester appears as the defendant, and Merriams as the affronted prosecutor, is a classic example. Not only did Worcester issue his pamphlet, but Merriams countered with theirs, Worcester was forced to fight back, Merriams rejoined, and so on.[62]

A new edition of Webster, the *Pictorial Quarto Unabridged,* appeared in 1859; and in 1860, unbowed by nearly fifteen years of constant feuding, Joseph Worcester published his last and best work: *A Dictionary of the English Language.* It was, in the words of Sledd and Kolb, his "masterpiece."[63] The arrival of the two books inevitably fanned into flame ashes that should by any standard have gone cold long before. As ever, the supporters of both works pitched in at the other's expense. The New York *World* of June 15, 1860 offered a review of both works by George P. Marsh, who awarded the palm to Worcester. In the end Webster was "unscholarly and unsound" whereas Worcester, whose advice on spelling and punctuation—taking the English rather than the American viewpoint—provided a safer standard, offered "the completest repertory of the English tongue." To keep the pot boiling, the *World* included a review of this review. Here the author, signing himself "Equal Justice," stated that while the two ranked pretty equally as far as spelling, pronunciation, and the word list were concerned, in etymology Webster, despite possessing the errors of his time, "is still instructive and inspiring, often sagacious and always full. Worcester is meager, unscholarlike and of little worth . . . in definitions Webster maintains his unquestioned supremacy." But, he added, in the end the two works complemented each other "and every literary man who can, will choose to have the two."

Neither reviewer showed himself especially outspoken, but when the second piece was published as a pamphlet by Merriam—*The Two Dictionaries, or the Reviewer Reviewed*—the old combativeness was back, as absurd as ever. *Their* man, they announced, was far and away superior, and such matters as content or accuracy didn't come into it:

> The vocabulary proper of Webster contains 99,780 words, the appendices 40,276, making a total of 140,056; that of Worcester 103,855, the appendices 28,551, total 132,406, making 7,650 more in Webster than in Worcester. The number of ems [a printer's measure] in Webster is 14,747,352; in Worcester 13,273,532, leaving a balance of 1,473,820 ems of printed matter in favor of Webster.

When the Boston *Congregationalist,* a religious newspaper, published an editorial warning its readers off Worcester, Merriams bought up large quantities of the paper and circulated them as widely as possible; they also reprinted the leader as an advertisement. As ever, Worcester's partisans launched a counterattack. In their pamphlet *A Comparison of Worcester's and Webster's Quarto Dictionaries,* they printed a list of eminent writers who "would not sully their pages with Websterian spellings"[64] (they included Longfellow, Hawthorne, Worcester's old pupil, and Daniel Webster, Webster's distant kinsman, among many others) and, offering their own version of the numbers game, "sixty-seven recommendations from presidents and professors of universities and colleges, forty-two from other distinguished scholars and literary men, nine from representatives of government publications, eleven foreign testimonials and thirty from leading periodicals." These luminaries included Oliver Wendell Holmes, Horace Mann, Thomas Carlyle, Napoleon, and Dickens—who might, had he not already long finished his book, have seen the excesses of the warring lexicographers as suitable material for the "American chapters" of *Martin Chuzzlewit.* Finally the editors threw in a couple of negative reviews of Webster, from the *Atlantic Monthly,* which declared that Worcester's was "the most complete and accurate [work] of any hitherto published" and stated that he had "unquestionably come off victorious." It further referred to Webster's illustrations as "primer pictures . . . more fitted for a child's scrapbook than for a volume intended to go into a student's library." The second review, from the *Christian Advocate,* similarly deplored the Webster woodcuts.

Yet, for all these learned recommendations, pamphlets, praises, and puffs, it was Worcester, not Webster, who would go to the wall. A clue to Worcester's demise can be seen, perhaps, in his particular success in England. *A Dictionary of the English Language* is, says Wheatley "the work upon which his fame will rest . . . [a] most admirable dictionary";[65] the London *Athenaeum* pronounced it "the best existing English lexicon." The *Quarterly Review,* published in Edinburgh, acclaimed it as Britain's dictionary of choice. But America was far from unanimously Anglophile, least of all among its new immigrants, and praise from England might rebound badly across the Atlantic. Webster, or the dictionary produced under his name, had always been touted as a byword for patriotism and nationalist enthusiasm. In the end Worcester stood for the élite and Webster for the populist viewpoint. Outside the academic groves of Harvard, the niceties were unimportant and the more that Worcester's defenders stressed them, the less appealing he seemed. The mass market wished to be told what to do: and they preferred the way that Webster, "their" lexicographer, told it.

The book that sealed Webster's triumph was published in 1864: the revision of Webster by the German scholar C. F. Mahn that is known as the Webster-Mahn. It is ironic, of course, that the edition of Webster that would confirm his work's success should be almost completely denuded of everything that he had once made central to his labors. Very little of the "nu speling" remained; his guidelines to pronunciation were much altered and, most important of all, the embarrassing, misdirected etymologies were completely cast aside. This edition, Webster without Websterisms as it were, trounced all opposition. Not only was Worcester vanquished, but Merriams would dominate the dictionary market for another twenty-five years, at which point the six-volume *Century Dictionary* (1889–91) and the single-volume Funk and Wagnalls *Standard Dictionary* (1894) arrived to eat, if only a little, into its share. After the appearance of the Webster-Mahn it was only a matter of time before Worcester vanished. There was one last edition in 1886, but its appearance was more gesture than sales opportunity. By 1870 the battle was over: the nationalist Americans had triumphed, on their own turf at least. The war of the dictionaries was over. In retrospect, it seemed very much a commercial battle, but the refinements and reissues that its struggles demanded also helped move American lexicography forward, perhaps more urgently than it might otherwise have progressed. "It is possible," wrote Allen Walker Read, "to downgrade the War of the Dictionaries as merely a matter of commercial rivalries, and in part it was. But much evidence indicates that the dictionary was regarded as a civilizing influence, and people took sides out of crusading zeal."[66]

Nor was "Webster" the only winner. By allowing the Merriam brothers to purchase the unsold rights in his work, and to convert the name of a man into that of a product, Noah Webster had defined the role of American dictionaries: unlike England, where the next great dictionary would be produced, often reluctantly, and always parsimoniously, by a university, Webster and his future rivals would always be linked to a publisher. It would make such publishers, whether Merriam, Random House, Funk and Wagnall, or their peers, the great authorities of language. The old academic gurus had been displaced and the masters of commerce, rather than of language, would continue to dominate. The alluring fantasy of populism, as filtered through the harsh realities of commercial interest, had, neither for the first nor final time, won the day. Not for nothing was it claimed that George Merriam was wont to remark, "Thank God for Worcester!" The history of "Webster," once the Merriams had taken up his work, was that of the company and not of the man. And if "Webster" became the most influential synonym for "dictionary," then its success would also elevate Webster the man into a new role as "the father of American lexicography." Criticism no longer mattered. Noah Webster, for all his faults, had been transmuted from fallible flesh and blood into a national institution, as much a part of American mythology, as Allen Walker Read has described him, as town meetings, the fostering of public libraries, or "bundling."[67]

12

The New Philology

On February 2, 1786, with Johnson two years in his grave and Webster musing on his *Dissertations* and preparing his *Spelling Book* for its reissue, Sir William Jones, then a judge of the supreme court of judicature at Fort William, Calcutta, and a widely respected orientalist, delivered his fourth anniversary discourse to the Asiatick Society of Bengal. The society, founded on January 15, 1784, was very much his creation, and its intent was to promote on a public level the study of the orient. These discourses were essentially progress reports on the state of his own researches into oriental cultures. Between 1785 and 1792 they covered variously the Arabs, the Tartars, the Persians, and other Asian races. That of 1786 was "On the Hindus" and in it he delivered an opinion which, while greatly developed and refined in the hands of those who took it up, would change the whole direction of nineteenth-century philology and thus of the dictionary making in which it played so vital a part.

> The Sanscrit language, whatever be its antiquity, is of a wonderful structure; more perfect than the Greek, more copious than the Latin, and more exquisitely refined than either, yet bearing to both of them a stronger affinity, both in the roots of verbs and in the forms of grammar, than could possibly have been produced by accident; so strong indeed, that no philologer could examine them all three, without believing them to have sprung from some common source, which, perhaps, no longer exists:

there is a similar reason, though not quite so forcible, for supposing that both the Gothick and the Celtick, though blended with a very different idiom, had the same origin with the Sanscrit; and the old Persian might be added to the same family, if this were the place for discussing any question concerning the antiquities of Persia.[1]

What Jones was saying, in short, was that if indeed there was any sort of ur-language, such as the "Chaldee" conjured up by Noah Webster, then for the bulk of European tongues that language appeared to be Sanskrit, "the dominant classical and scholarly language of the Indian sub-continent, the sacred language of Hinduism (with Pali), a scriptural language of Buddhism, and the oldest known member of the Indo-European language family."[2] The literal meaning of Sanskrit, in its own vocabulary, is "well-formed."

Sir William's theory would not be accepted at once—Noah Webster, for instance, derided his supposed inadequacies—and as will be seen below, the school of Horne Tooke, followed to an extent by Webster and more slavishly by Charles Richardson, would not be defeated overnight. But with hindsight one can see that Jones' presidential address paved the way for what has been christened by Hans Aarsleff "The New Philology"[3] and more generally "comparative philology": language studies based not on the old philosophical bases that dominated eighteenth-century philology, but on a new historical method, that would in turn dominate the nineteenth century, classically in the example of the methodology that underpinned the *New [Oxford] English Dictionary*. With this new system there developed a set of fixed principles through which languages could be systematically compared one with another, looking at their sound systems, their grammar, and their vocabulary. From now on, as far as possible, philological assumptions would be based on proper historical research rather than abstract assumptions. The days of searching for some desired "universal grammar," which had underpinned much previous language theory were over; as posited by Sir William Jones and his successors, future studies would require the backing of historical fact.

William Jones was born in Westminster on September 18, 1746. His father died when he was only three and his mother, a formidably intellectual woman, superintended his education until he departed for Harrow School in 1753. "Read, and you will know" was her primary maternal dictum, and her son duly took that advice. At Harrow he showed himself an exceptional scholar, learning the usual classics and teaching himself Hebrew, Arabic, French, and Italian in his spare time. His preferred amusement was chess, but for lighter moments he apparently recreated Harrow and its surroundings as parts of ancient Greece and with his friends reenacted the great moments of mythology. A suggestion that he should bypass university and go straight into law was quashed; young Jones deplored the bad Latin in which the laws were written. Instead in 1764 he went, as a scholar, to University College, Oxford to read oriental languages, picking up German, Spanish, and Portuguese on the side. Too poor, even with his award, to pay the fees, he gained a job tutoring seven-year-old Earl Spencer, son of Lord Althorp and as such an ancestor of the recent Princess of Wales. As well as teaching the boy he joined him in his riding, fencing, and dancing lessons. He stayed a tutor for five years, working toward his degree at the same time. He graduated M.A. in 1773.

Jones' first book, a translation from a Persian life of Nadir Shah, a volume brought to England by King Christian VII of Denmark, was published in 1770. Other translations followed, until in 1771 there appeared his *Grammar of the Persian Language.* By 1772, when he was elected a fellow of the Royal Society, he was acclaimed as the country's leading orientalist. A year later he was asked, at the same time as David Garrick, to join the intellectual élite of the Literary Club, where Johnson, Edmund Burke, and others could be found. He continued to make important translations, often of oriental poetry. Among his major publications was *The Moallakat, or, the Seven Arabian Poems which were suspended on the Temple at Mecca* (1783). Joshua Reynolds, a fellow Club man, painted the portrait which appeared as the frontispiece. If orientalism brought acclaim, it did not bring a decent income, and in 1774 Jones was called to the bar at the Middle Temple. He then proceeded to establish himself as a leading theoretical lawyer, if not as a great advocate. His "Essay on Bailments" (goods delivered in trust for the fulfillment of an agreement) was especially respected, notably in America. Jones also took a stab at politics, presenting himself as a possible candidate for the old seat of Oxford University. His unabashed liberalism—he deplored Britain's opposition to American independence, and attacked her enthusiastic espousal of the slave trade—was seen as too unnerving for the essentially conservative public. His membership of the Constitutional Society, where fellow members included Thomas Paine, whose pamphleteering fueled two revolutions, and John Horne Tooke, whose dedicated radicalism would lead him to prison, can only have reinforced such fears. He dropped out of the election rather than face the embarrassment of what would have been an overwhelming defeat. In 1783, despite the Establishment's delaying tactics—punishment no doubt for his outspoken liberalism—Jones was both knighted and appointed to what must surely have been his dream job: working for the legal system in India. The decade from his arrival there in December 1783 to his death in April 1794, would be the most important of what by modern standards was a tragically short life.

There had been Englishmen in India for many years, and many of them had become imbued with the culture they found there. Typical was the controversial Governor-General Warren Hastings (1732–1818), to whom Jones had sent a copy of his *Grammar* and who had been offered—but rejected—the first presidency of the Asiatick Society. But few had the natural leanings toward scholarship that Jones did. He studied Hindu chronology, music, and chess; he planned an exhaustive botanical study and researched widely in both flora and fauna; the asoka tree, famed in Indian mythology, was named *Jonesia asoka* in his honor by Dr. William Roxburgh (1751–1815), superintendent of the Calcutta Botanic Garden and a fellow member of the Asiatick Society. But his primary interests were the law and linguistics. According to Henry Morse Stephens, writing in the *DNB,* Jones had an almost missionary belief in the need to spread his scholarly findings among a wider audience.[4] As far as language was concerned, there were the anniversary discourses, plus a continuing succession of translations of the oriental classics. In the legal sphere he saw himself as the "Justinian of India,"[5] whose main task was to establish a solidly based legal system upon which in turn the edifice of British rule could rest assured. To push this project ahead Jones determined to master all the intricacies of Indian law and surrounded himself with a team of Indian experts, both Hindu and Muslim. He would never finish his study, but he did publish the first part, *Institutes of Hindu Law,* in 1794. In 1793 his wife, Anna Maria, whom he had married in 1783, left India for England in the hopes of improving her failing health. She survived, but Jones did not. Very depressed at her departure, he seems to have fallen into a decline and died on April 27 the following year. The directors of the East India Company erected a monument to his memory in St. Paul's Cathedral.

Jones was "the greatest Indian scholar the world had yet seen."[6] He knew thirteen languages thoroughly and another twenty-eight reasonably well. Even in his lifetime he had a reputation as a modest and delightful man, and the politician John Courtenay, writing in his *Morals and Literary Character of Dr Johnson* (1786), characterized him as "Harmonious Jones." Despite his obvious intellectual attainments, he was neither arrogant nor pedantic. In an age when Britain's contempt for those she ruled was as poisonously wholehearted as ever it would be, Jones' refusal to subscribe to the general racism made him an admirable exception. It was a two-way street. Jones knew that he could glean more from one-to-one relationships with Indians than ever he could from mere secondhand reading. He was good to them, they responded in kind. His Indian friends and informants were as devastated by his death as any Englishman.

The most immediate effect of Jones' new philology came in the area of etymology, an area of study that, for all the many and varied efforts lexicographers and philologists had put into it, was still at best an inexact science: one in which, as Voltaire put it, "the consonants are of very little importance, and the vowels of none at all."[7] Jones' discoveries, especially as amplified by his successors, would change all that. The theory of radicals or roots, as used by Webster, simply didn't hold water anymore. The fact that two or more words sounded alike, and seemed to have the same root consonants, could no longer be put forward as proof of any real relationship. Polite but firm, Jones made the point:

> I beg leave, as a philologer, to enter my protest against conjectural etymology in historical researches, and principally against the licentiousness of etymologists in transposing and inserting letters, in substituting at pleasure any consonant for another of the same order, and in totally disregarding the vowels: for such permutations few radical words would be more convenient than *cus* or *cush,* since, dentals being exchanged for dentals, and palatals for palatals, it instantly becomes *coot, goose,* and, by transposition, *duck,* all water-birds, and evidently symbolical; it next is the *goat* worshipped in *Egypt,* and, by a metathesis, the *dog* adored as an emblem of *Sirius,* or, more obviously, a *cat,* not the domestick animal, but a sort of ship, and, the *Catos,* or great sea-fish, of the *Dorians.*[8]

Such a position was the antithesis of Webster. Loath to cause offense, Jones went on to say that he wasn't trying to ridicule the advocates of the old system, but when judged by his strictly historical researches, that system no longer worked.

It is impossible to trace the details of Jones' hypothesis here, nor the way in which it gradually came to influence the most forward-thinking of his philological contemporaries and successors. Although profound, his influence was infinitely greater in Europe, especially Germany, than it would be in England for a good half century. A number of his fellow members of the Asiatick Society duly profited from his breakthrough, and went on to develop his theories in their own scholarly researches. But in the wider world of language studies, he remained an outsider. In at least one dimension this can be traced to the paradoxes of Empire. The East had a role, but it did not involve challenging the beliefs of homegrown scholarship. It has been suggested that the lexicography of the second half of the century, culminating in the *New English Dictionary,* can be seen as an imperial project: certainly its harnessing of the inventiveness and energy of nineteenth-century Britain is an extension of the energies more usually found in the context of empire-building and trade. But the initial rejection of the "New Philology" shows the downside of that same imperialism: use the East for trade by all means, but do not respect its learning as a rival to Western knowledge. Thus it was in France and Germany, where such imperial conceits did not apparently impede scholarly advancement, that Jones' ideas first caught on. Alexander Hamilton, a member of the Asiatick Society and later Professor of Persian and Sanskrit at the Collège de France in Paris, was sought out as a teacher by such nascent philologists as Schlegel, de Chézy, and Fauriel. He returned to England in 1808 and began teaching at the empire-dominated public school, Haileybury. His Parisian pupils, rather than the English schoolboys being groomed to keep the imperial masses in their place, carried on his and Jones' ideas.

However, imperialism was not the only barrier to the "New Philology." The bulk of England's cultural authorities were united in their scorn for all things Indian. Jeremy Bentham, the great proponent of Utilitarianism, despised Eastern learning; the historian Macaulay saw only stereotypes—"What the horns are to the buffalo, what the paw is to the tiger, what the sting is to the bee . . . deceit is to the Bengalee."[9] At least one linguist, Dugald Stuart, dismissed Sanskrit as no more than a form of "kitchen Greek," a patois concocted by the Brahmins as a secret jargon, designed to protect their religion in the wake of Alexander's conquest of India.[10] The most formidable opponent was James Mill (1773–1836), one of the theoreticians of Utilitarianism and the author of the *History of British India* (1818). To Mill, Hindu India represented everything he hated. As such its supposed "culture" could not be considered in the same breath as that of England. Sanskrit was as culpable as any other aspect of the country. That Mill had no knowledge of the language, nor any firsthand experience of the country, did not, of course, deter him in the slightest from his pronouncements. If anything he saw his ignorance as a bonus—the facts he might have gleaned in India itself would have perverted the purity of his theorizing. As Aarsleff notes, "Nothing could be more directly opposed to Jones' 'unremitting application . . . to a vast and interesting study, a *knowledge of India,* which I can only attain in the country itself.' "[11] It was hardly surprising that Mill, who through the fame he had won with his *History* also held an influential post in the home office of the East India Company, was a major impediment to the spread of Jones' discoveries.

The Continent was less pigheaded. The Berlin Academy had first expressed its interest in questions of language during the 1750s. Its prize essays specialized in asking such questions, and the wealth of replies they elicited showed just how much the topic appealed to the country's intellectuals. Among the most important of these essays was Johann David Michaelis' *A Dissertation on the Influence of Opinions on Language and of Language on Opinions* (1759). A scholar of Göttingen University, he pointed out the overriding importance of vernacular, rather than literary language, noting that "language is a democracy where use or custom is decided by the majority."[12] He rejected the claims of the learned since they had only "a narrow genius." Even more important was his suggestion that "etymology is the voice of the people" and that while language may well be seen as a historical record, that did not mean, whatever other eighteenth-century philologists might wish, that it automatically conformed to a philosophical truth.[13] It was vital, therefore, that etymologies be worked out correctly, because the burden of incorrect assumptions could lead to far greater errors. The extension of Michaelis' theories was then taken up by the German philosopher Johann Gottfried von Herder (1744–1803) and expounded in his prize essay of 1771. Herder, one of the great opponents of the Enlightenment and a founder of German Romanticism, believed, as far as his language theories went, that in language one sees the very essence of a people, its common experiences and its historical and national identity. It was this concept that would be taken up by a number of nineteenth-century nationalist movements which saw language as a way of setting the true boundaries of a nation, rather than the artificial physical boundaries which had been imposed by the political demands of imperial powers. The "Aryan" strain of the "New Philology" is inescapable. Its theories ran a direct line from classical Greece to the modern day; any possible influences from Semitic or African roots were neatly excised. "Aryan" equaled "civilized," in language as much as blood. Even the much-revered Max Müller, Oxford's professor of philology and as such an indirect but important influence on the *NED,* was not above such beliefs. He deplored the racist inferences that were drawn from his work, and publicly disassociated himself from them, but as a proponent of the Aryan-based German philology he was, willy-nilly, their advocate. Nor was the idea alien to the larger world. The belief that the Aryan language should dominate the "lesser breeds" fitted all too well with the prevailing imperialist ideology.

Later still, as expounded by Josef Goebbels, it would form the basis for what might be termed "Nazi linguistics," the purging of the national word store of "alien," typically French and "Jewish," strains. If one agrees with George Steiner, the "academicism and ponderousness" that accompanied such nineteenth-century philological rule making was far from socially positive, however advantageous it might have been to the advance of dictionary making. It not only "produced that fearful composite of grammatical ingenuity and humourlessness which made the word 'Germanic' an equivalent for dead weight" but also

stands as the very first step on the road to the brutalized jargon that Victor
Klemperer, hinting grimly at the plethora of acronyms that so entranced the
Nazis, has termed *LTI: Lingua Tertii Imperii* (Language of the Third Reich).
"Philology," in Steiner's words, "places words in a context of older or related
words. It gives the language formality, not form. It cannot be a mere accident
that the essentially philological structure of German education yielded such
loyal servants to . . . the Nazi Reich."[14]

Like Herder, Friedrich von Schlegel (1772–1829) is numbered among the
founding fathers of German Romanticism, and like him he saw the importance
of language. After a spell as *Privatdozentur* at Jena University he left Germany
for Paris in 1802, accompanied by the writer and emancipist Dorothea Veit.
There he studied Sanskrit under William Jones' colleague Alexander Hamilton
who in turn lived with Schlegel and Veit, although he apparently preferred not
to eat with them. They were married in 1804. Hamilton passed on his own
mentor's theories and Schlegel was duly impressed. The fruits of this education
came in 1808, with the publication of his book *Über die Sprache und Weisheit der
Indier* ("On the Speech and Wisdom of India"). Schlegel has since been credited
with the near-singlehanded advocacy of the importance of Sanskrit but he is
substantially indebted to Jones. Unlike Jones, whose findings were those of a
lawyer, schooled in a basis of provable fact, Schlegel interlarded his philology
with mystical musings, which may have suited the emergent Romanticism,
but tended to bury Jones' simpler statements. Aarsleff goes so far as to dismiss
Schlegel's importance altogether. "It is very interesting, at times beautiful and
certainly romantic, but it can hardly be called an empirical program for the
study of language. Jones was the source for the parts that were of value, and it
is a good question whether language studies would not have taken the same
course without [Schlegel's essay]. The discourses were widely read, Schlegel's
book caused excitement, but no person who took all of it seriously would ever
have arrived at what came to be called comparative philology."[15]

The next major figure to advance that new form of philology, Franz Bopp
(1791–1867), came to Sanskrit as a disciple of both Jones and Schlegel. Aged
just twenty-one, he set out in late 1812 to walk from his home in Aschaffen-
burg, Germany to Paris where like Schlegel he began studying Sanskrit. Four
years later he published his first book, *Über das Conjugationssystem das Sanskrit-
sprache . . .* ("On the System of Conjugation in Sanskrit . . ."). Bopp embarked
on a task as yet unachieved: tracing the links between Sanskrit, Persian, Greek,
Latin, and German. He was appointed professor of oriental literature at Berlin
University in 1821 and as well as composing a Sanskrit grammar and a Latin
and Sanskrit glossary he worked between 1833 and 1852 on his magnum opus:

the *Comparative Grammar of Sanskrit, Zend, Greek, Latin, Lithuanian, Old Slavic, Gothic and German.* This was by far the most important advance in the discipline to date and in his preface, Bopp's English translator, Edward Eastwick, said that Bopp had "created a new epoch in the science of Comparative Philology . . . corresponding to that of Newton's Principia in Mathematics, [or] Bacon's Novum Organum in Mental Science . . ."[16]

Two other European figures should be added to this pantheon of early comparative philology. Rasmus Kristian Rask (1787–1832) was born in Copenhagen, Denmark. He began his long association with Copenhagen University in 1808 as an assistant keeper of the library and went on to become librarian and professor of oriental languages. In 1818 he produced his major work: *Investigation of the Origin of the Old Norse or Icelandic Language.* This was primarily a comparison of the Scandinavian languages with Latin and Greek; Rask was the first philologist to make the connection between the Celtic languages—Breton, Irish, Welsh, etc.—and the Indo-European family. He also pointed out that Basque and Finno-Ugric, still the subject of much debate, are not part of the same family.

The last member of these founding fathers is Jakob Grimm (1785–1863), who with his brother Wilhelm (1786–1859) is best known for their collection of fairy tales, but who was a notable grammarian and philologist in his own right. The brothers also initiated the production of one of the most important dictionaries of the nineteenth century—the *Deutsches Wörterbuch*—although neither would live to witness its completion. The boys were still young when in 1796 their father, Phillipp Wilhelm, a lawyer and the town clerk of the town of Hanau in the state of Hesse, died. The problems this caused were compounded when in 1808 their mother died too and 23-year-old Jakob was left at the head of a family of four brothers and one sister. Despite their difficulties, Jakob and Wilhelm moved from high school to the University of Marburg where they were influenced by the works of Clemens Brentano, a devotee of German folk poetry, and of Friedrich von Savigny, whose pioneering work in historical jurisprudence gave them the basis for all their subsequent research methods, and of Herder, whose romanticism naturally led him toward folk poetry.

By 1816 the brothers were working together in the library of the elector of Hessen-Kassel. Wilhelm had been jobless until 1814 through ill health, but that year he took the library post. Jakob had worked as secretary to the War Office in Kassel since 1806, and had, among other tasks, attended the Congress of Vienna, which between 1814 and 1815 settled the peace of Europe for the next century. Once united, they would work together for the rest of their lives.

Fascinated by the political and social changes of their times and the challenges they promoted, the brothers looked for the reasons behind them. These they found in the distant past, which they saw as the basis of everything that would follow, both in German and other societies. The aspect of that past on which they concentrated was that of folk poetry: the songs and tales of the people. Between 1812 and 1815 they published *Kinder- und Hausmärchen,* some 200 tales collected mainly from oral sources. Other collections would follow, establishing the "Brothers Grimm" as the first, and most influential collectors of what were generally known as "fairy tales." Of the two, Wilhelm was definitely the leading spirit in this area. His elder brother, while doing his share, had his own agenda, notably in the world of linguistics. His *Deutsche Grammatik* appeared between 1819 and 1837. In this context *deutsch* does not mean German as a single nation, but German as in a range of related languages. Aside from tracing the development and relationships between these languages, which no one had yet achieved, the book postulated what came to be known as "Grimm's law," a linguistic constant that governs the correspondence among consonants in genetically related languages. Grimm was the first philologist to create a properly scientific system of etymology.

This world of peaceful, progressive study was shattered in 1829 when the elector failed, possibly for political reasons, to offer the brothers the advancement they had expected on the death of a professional colleague. They promptly quit his employ, moving to the University of Göttingen. Here Jakob wrote the *Deutsche Mythologie,* a groundbreaking work in which he outlined the pre-Christian traditions and beliefs of German society. But once again the Establishment turned against the Grimms. When Ernest-Augustus, the new king of Hanover, repealed the state constitution, which he felt was overliberal, the brothers, with five other Göttingen professors, sent him a note of complaint. They were all dismissed and three of them, including Jakob although not Wilhelm, were ordered to leave the kingdom. A variety of other states, both in Germany and in the wider European world, offered them employment, but they chose Berlin, to which they had been invited by Frederick Wilhelm IV, king of Prussia. Here they began their most ambitious project: the *Deutsches Wörterbuch.* It was intended to become the ultimate German dictionary, a guide for the user of both spoken and written language and, with its basis in the complete spread of German literature from Luther to Goethe, a scholarly reference work of the highest order. In a system that presaged the *New English Dictionary* they offered for each word its historical variants, its etymology, and its semantic development. Citations from idioms and proverbs supported the varieties of usage. The work was begun as a source of income: it would take both their lives, and those of several generations of lexicographers before it was finished. They had reached the letter D at Wilhelm's death; Jakob was only able to push on to F. The dictionary was finally finished in 1960, and by then it had inspired imitators in Britain, France, the Netherlands, Sweden, and Switzerland.

It was not only the *Wörterbuch* that advanced both their reputation and that of the new philology. In March 1830 the *Foreign Review* published a notice of Jakob Grimm's *Deutsche Grammatik,* written by Rasmus Rask. Among those who must have read it were two British scholars of Anglo-Saxon, Benjamin Thorpe (1782–1870) and John Mitchell Kemble (1807–57), a son of the actor Charles Kemble and nephew of Sarah Siddons. Both men appreciated the importance of European philology: Thorpe went in 1826 to study with Rask; Kemble in 1831 to visit Grimm, who soon proclaimed him one of his most talented pupils. The pair did more than any other English scholars to bring home the German developments, especially in Thorpe's translation of Rask's *Grammar of the Anglo-Saxon Tongue,* and of another Danish philologist, N. F. S. Grundtvig's prospectus for the publication of texts to be included in a proposed *Bibliotheca Anglo-Saxonica.* This new interest in the Anglo-Saxon world, of which its language was just a part, had been growing through the period. Both Thorpe and Kemble were among those who published histories of the era. That said, while popular interest was expanding, the universities remained aloof. The country's first ever professor of English language and literature was only appointed (and not at Oxford or Cambridge, but at the new University of London) in 1828. He was not a devotee of German philology. Not until the 1830s, under the impulsion of Thorpe and Kemble, did the situation change. They too required a push. It came from Professor Grundtvig, acknowledged as the greatest contemporary Anglo-Saxon expert, who, unlike any British scholar, had for some time been taking serious notice of England's original Anglo-Saxon texts. Touring the country's great libraries, whether in the universities or in private houses, he had unearthed so many such texts that native scholars gradually began to realize that they might have some value. It was Grundtvig who first suggested the publication of the texts but it was Thorpe, after seeing a prepublication copy of his *Prospectus,* who preempted his plan and launched his own scheme for bringing such materials to a wider public. Between 1832 and 1850 Thorpe and Kemble, backed by the Antiquarian Society, published a large number of Anglo-Saxon manuscripts. It was their editions, most importantly Thorpe's *Analecta Anglo-Saxonica* (1834) that would ensure the triumph of the new philology in England. There was much scholarly controversy, some of it remarkably embittered, but by the 1840s, the struggle was effectively over: henceforth the scientific, rather than the philosophical method, would reign supreme. As Kemble put it, "The laws of a language, ascertained by wide and careful examination . . . are like the laws of the Medes and Persia and alter not."[17]

The most impressive, if indirect result of their efforts would be the *New English Dictionary:* Kemble's premature death, in February 1857, came but nine months before Richard Chenevix Trench, dean of Westminster, delivered his address "On Some Deficiencies in Our English Dictionaries" to the Philological Society and set the creation of the *NED* in motion. Trench had known Kemble for many years: they had been founding members of the Cambridge Conversazione Society, latterly known as the Apostles. In years to come the society would be linked with the Cambridge "homintern" of the 1930s; in Trench's day, they discussed poetry and religion. Another member, F. D. Maurice, would found the movement known as Christian Socialism, and nicknamed "muscular Christianity"; among his youthful acolytes was another man who would have a profound influence on the *NED:* Frederick Furnivall. But all this was in the future. The Philological Society would not be founded until 1842, the influential *Deutsches Wörterbuch* did not begin appearing until 1854, and Dean Trench's recommendations for the production of a British equivalent would not crystallize into lexicographical action until 1858. All that would be the result of the "New Philology," but before that could take its place in British linguistics, the "old philology" and its vociferous supporters would still have a good deal to say.

Whether one backed or opposed the developments in Germany, scholarly philology was bound by certain rules, and whatever his idiosyncrasies and however abstruse his theory, the scholar accepted them. But scholars by no means had the field to themselves. As George Sampson put it, writing his introduction to the Everyman edition of Chenevix Trench's *On the Study of Words* (1927): "When education was restricted to a few, and consisted largely in a cultivation of verbal niceties, those who used words used them well. Etymology was a recreation of English country gentlemen. They enjoyed the life of a word as they enjoyed the death of a fox." Typical is the Rev. George William Lemon (1726–97), a retired Norfolk schoolmaster whose *English Etymology* (in which he defied reality to trace every English word back to a Greek root) was just one of a series of works with which he whiled away his years; others include a Greek grammar, an unpublished translation of Virgil, a history of the Wars of the Roses, and a new edition of Dugdale's *History of Imbanking and Draining the Fens and Marshes.*

Nor did one have to be a gentleman as such. One of the least likely etymologists was John Cleland, whose *Way to Things by Words, and to Words by Things* appeared in 1766. Cleland (1709–89) is generally recalled for his salacious novel *Memoirs of a Woman of Pleasure* (1748), known popularly as *Fanny Hill* and perhaps the only piece of best-selling pornography to achieve its effects without the inclusion of a single obscenity. His interest in philology seems out of character, but like Sir William Jones he served for a while in the East India Company, first as a soldier, then as an administrator in Bombay. It was at this time, *c.* 1740, that he wrote the draft of the *Memoirs* but it would also appear that while in India he developed, as would Jones, an interest in Sanskrit—at which point the two men differ. Cleland's philological abilities can be seen in the subtitle of his book: "A Sketch of an Attempt at the Retrieval of the Antient Celtic, or, Primitive Language of Europe. To which is added, A succinct Account of the Sanscort [*sic*], or Learned Language of the Bramins. Also Two Essays, the one On the Origin of the Musical Waits at Christmas. The other On the Real Secret of the Free Masons." His inadequacy is underlined in another title, that of a pamphlet issued in 1787: "Specimen of an Etimological Vocabulary or Essay by means of the Anilitic Method to retrieve the ancient Celtic." The spelling alone betrays him. In any case, for Cleland philology was simply one more vain attempt to keep the wolf from his door. *Fanny Hill* was his only success. Medical treatises, journalism, and a play called *Timbo-Chiqui* "or, the American Savage" (1758) were equally unsuccessful. As he aged he grew increasingly depressed, embittered by his experiences and offensive to his once wide and successful circle of friends, who included David Garrick, Lawrence Sterne, and James Boswell. He lived alone in a chaotic book-filled household, hovering on the fringes of smart society. Rumors as to his possible homosexuality abounded. He died in 1789, solitary and wretched, abandoned by his friends and utterly disappointed in his life.

However, Cleland, Lemon, and others were merely footnotes. The main players offered a substantially higher profile. If 1786 was an important year for philological and thus lexicographical progress, then it was also a landmark for the diehards of an older tradition. In Calcutta Sir William Jones was laying down the bases of a new world; in London, with the publication of his major work *The Diversions of Purley,* John Horne Tooke was giving the most authoritative version of the old.

Tooke was born plain John Horne in Westminster on June 25, 1736, the son of John Horne, poulterer to, among others, Frederick Prince of Wales, who died owing thousands in unpaid egg and chicken bills. His son was educated at Westminster, Eton, the Soho Square Academy, and with a private tutor and, thanks to a fellow pupil's injudicious knife-play, lost an eye while still young. After Cambridge he joined the Inner Temple, but his father, determined that he become a clergyman, forced him to take Holy Orders. From there on, says the *DNB,* Horne's life was dominated by "the hard fate which forced into holy orders a man eminently qualified for a career at the bar."[18] He was ordained in 1760 and was apparently an adequate preacher who also studied medicine and established a dispensary for his parishioners. In 1763 he became traveling tutor to the son of John Elwes (1714–89), a notorious miser who ate only partridge and, despite heavy gambling and a number of ill-advised investments, still left £250,000 at his death. The pair traveled abroad, although it is unlikely that Horne earned much from this experience: Elwes' doctrine vis-à-vis education was to avoid it: "Putting things in people's heads," he declared, "is the best way to take money out of their pockets." Back in England in 1765 Horne plunged immediately into what would be the first of many controversies: his campaign against the prosecution of the radical MP John Wilkes for alleged sedition. Horne wrote an anonymous pamphlet defending Wilkes, and promised to reveal himself were there a prosecution. He escaped arrest since the authorities were worried that his hints at an illicit relationship between the earl of Bute and the king's mother, conveyed by printing the plans of their adjoining houses at Kew, might be revealed in court. Judiciously he left once more for Europe where, among others, he met the lexicographer and elocutionist Thomas Sheridan (who would be commissioned to write his dictionary by the same earl of Bute), temporarily escaping his creditors. He also met Voltaire, Sterne, and, in Paris, Wilkes himself. Back in London in 1768 he entered a new Wilkes controversy, that of the forthcoming Middlesex election, and speechified in his hero's favor, promising, among other things, to "dye his [clerical] black coat red." His involvement in the campaign brought him to court, where he was sued for slander following an especially inflammatory speech. Fined £400, he had the conviction overturned on appeal. He was also a founding member of the "Society for Supporting the Bill of Rights," a pro-Wilkes movement which met at the London Tavern and attracted a wide selection of metropolitan firebrands. But Horne grew disenchanted with Wilkes, whom he saw as subverting the society to his own needs, rather than promoting those of a wider political program. The pair split and indulged in a long and acrimonious dispute, which descended quickly to personal abuse; typical was Horne's claim that after he had left some smart suits with Wilkes for safekeeping, the MP promptly pawned them. Horne backed Wilkes' rival in the next sheriff's election in London, only to see his candidate trounced and himself burned in effigy.

In 1775 he entered a new controversy: over American independence. He joined those who wished to raise a subscription for "our beloved American fellow subjects [who] preferred death to slavery [and] were for that reason only inhumanly murdered by the king's troops" at the battle of Lexington. Horne was deputed to hand the cash over to Benjamin Franklin. The authorities took no notice at the time, but a year later some of the printers of the appeal were fined and in 1777 Horne himself was tried for his impudence, fined £200, and jailed for a year. Within the King's Bench prison he was allowed to occupy his own small house, entertain his friends, and go out once a week for dinner at the Dog and Duck, a Lambeth tavern selling not just liquor but a variety of medicinal spring waters that were recommended by Dr. Johnson. Horne preferred claret, drinking a good deal during his sentence, and later claiming it had given him gout. But prison had a more positive aspect: it was at this time that he turned to what would become a lifelong obsession: philology. This interest followed his writing of a pamphlet—"A Letter to Mr Dunning on the English Particle," published on April 21, 1778—in which he discussed the use of prepositions and conjunctions arising from a sentence that had come up during his trial. It was on this small pamphlet that his major work, *The Diversions of Purley* (1786), would be based. Indeed, according to Coleridge, there was nothing in the larger work that could not, in essence, be found in its predecessor.

In 1782 John Horne became John Horne Tooke, adding to his surname that of his friend William Tooke, a gentleman of Purley, then a village south of London. Out of prison, he took rooms in Dean Street, Soho, where he lived with his two illegitimate daughters, Mary and Charlotte Hart. He continued to indulge in a variety of political agitations, corresponding with French and American revolutionaries and, in 1794, posing as a French spy in an attempt to trap the government into conducting a prosecution that could only leave them looking foolish. His offense in 1777 had been "seditious libel"; this was treason. Tooke was duly arrested, tried, and acquitted. In his defense it was claimed that he was actually a peace-loving man who, to use a coaching metaphor, might start a journey with such hotheads as Tom Paine on their way to Windsor, but would always get out at Hounslow (a few stops earlier). In 1801 he was elected MP for Old Sarum, one of the pre-1832 Reform Bill "rotten boroughs," but lost his seat in the next election, in 1802. For the remainder of his life he lived, as quietly as such a man could, at his house in Wimbledon. Here he gave lavish dinners for his celebrity friends, among them Godwin, Bentham, and Coleridge. Rather than bloody mayhem, he opted for a new means of settling disputes: drinking matches in which large amounts of Madeira, port, and brandy would be consumed. Typical opponents were Richard Porson, the great Oxford classicist, and Boswell, Johnson's biographer. Tooke invariably won. Porson, indeed, was a regular sparring partner. A serious drinker and smoker, he was quite capable of sitting alone all night, consuming much liquor and many pipes, and

would be found in the morning, seemingly immobile, by the servants. His preferred method of ending an argument was to belabor his opponent with a poker.
In their arguments there was never any actual violence, but Porson ran Tooke
very close. On one occasion, as recounted by Edith Sitwell,

> Mr Tooke won a victory over the professor . . . when the latter had threat-
> ened to "kick and cuff Mr Tooke", and to bring in the poker as umpire.
> Mr Tooke said that the duel must be fought not with pokers but with
> brandy, and quarts of brandy at that. When the second quart was half-
> finished, the Professor sank into unconsciousness beneath the table, and
> the triumphant Mr Tooke . . . drank the health of the vanquished in
> another glass of brandy and, after instructing the servants to "take great
> care of the Professor", joined the ladies, weaving his way, without osten-
> sible difficulty, into the drawing room, where tea was being served.[19]

Tooke had other eccentricities. Among his preoccupations was his own death
and burial: he wished to be buried in his own garden in a massive black marble
tomb. In the event his death, on March 18, 1812, was followed by interment in
Ealing cemetery.

His real memorial, however, was the philological treatise published in 1786
and somewhat expanded in 1798: ΕΠΕΑ ΠΤΕΡΟΕΝΤΑ or "The Diversions of
Purley." Far from the guide to rural jollity that some disappointed reviewers
claimed they had expected, this was a revolutionary treatise on language that
aimed to overturn linguistic *données* and institute a new philology of its own. In
the event this "dangerous book"[20] has come to be seen as the last great repository of "the old philology." Its effects can be seen in Webster's *American Dictionary* of 1828 and Richardson's *New Dictionary of the English Language* of 1837.
It was also the last example of etymology pursued as a gentlemanly pastime.

Tooke's linguistics depended on one central theory: every single word was in
itself a separate thing. All words, in his view, could be reduced back to an original noun, or perhaps a verb. The verb, he explained, was what we say, the noun
was the thing that we say it about. There were no other parts of speech. As to
the influence of the mind on language: "The business of the mind as far as it
concerns Language . . . extends no further than to receive impressions, that is,
to have Sensations or feelings. What are called its operations, are merely the
operations of Language."[21] Words existed to communicate thought and to do so
"with dispatch." Thus prepositions, pronouns, and adjectives were simply
abbreviations of the primary forms; they had entered language as refinements,
which had developed as it progressed from its "rude and tedious" origins. They

were necessary simply to speed things up. If this were true, then there was no need for any further theorizing. Like any devotee of his own beliefs, however farfetched others might declare them, Tooke sailed blithely on. For such enthusiasms, say Sledd and Kolb, Tooke "may be safely described as one of the most systematically frantic etymologists who ever lived. By pure reasoning a priori he reached certain conclusions about language, which he then attempted to support—naturally with complete success—by the appeal to etymology."[22] All this demands a complex and in the eyes of more scientific philologists, gloriously specious system of etymology.

"If 'the original Mother tongue' had no abbreviations, but only necessary words, nouns and verbs must be etymologically discoverable in all other word-classes and even in prefixes, suffixes, and inflectional endings."[23] To sustain such a belief was hugely demanding, but Tooke was quite capable of keeping all manner of contradictory balls in the air. As ever, facts were suborned to fantasy. If one had to find links, then links would be found, come what may. The sound of individual letters, for instance, was utterly mutable. "The difference between a T and a D is so very small, that an Etymologist knows by the *practice* of languages, and an Anatomist by the reason of that practice, that in the derivation of words it is scarce worth regarding."[24] And if something really held out against the theory, then it was obvious that somewhere along the line there must exist some form of linguistic "missing link," which devotees would simply have to take as read. This concept was christened "subaudition," defined as "the act of mentally supplying something that is not expressed." It is not too harsh to suggest that such a concept, by no means unknown in traditional grammar where it is used to make otherwise irregular phrases conform to normal grammatical standards, came as a godsend to a theorist as arcane as Tooke.

What Sledd and Kolb term his "midsummer madness"[25] fills the pages of the *Diversions.* A classic example is his treatment of the word *bar* and all its derivations. The links he makes are specious yet magnificent: "A bar in all its uses, is a defence: that by which any thing is fortified, strengthened, or defended. A barn (bar-en, bar'n) is a covered inclosure, in which the grain &c. is protected or defended from the weather, from depredations &c. A baron is an armed, defenceful, or powerful man. A barge is a strong boat. A bargain is a confirmed, strengthened agreement . . . A bark is a stout vessel. The bark of a tree is its defence: that by which the tree is defended from the weather &c. . . . The bark of a dog is that by which we are defended by that animal."[26] As Aarsleff adds sardonically, "In the midst of these etymologies, it is comforting to be told that 'there is nothing strictly arbitrary in language.' " Nor was Tooke satisfied with setting out his own theories; he savaged those who had not

enjoyed their blessing, notably Samuel Johnson, who had through his ignorance offered etymologies that deceived his readers with "fraud, and cant, and
folly." Foolish Johnson, who had not known that the word *from* descends
directly from the Anglo-Saxon and Gothic noun *frum,* meaning 'BEGINNING'
and nothing else." Working without this fundamental fact he had "numbered
up twenty different meanings of this Preposition" and even gone so far as to
offer a variety of citations. Yet he had simply refused to acknowledge that
"FROM continues to retain invariably one and the same single meaning"
throughout.[27] It was comments of this sort, presumably, along with allied marginalia, that ensured that when Tooke's library was sold, his annotated copy of
Johnson's *Dictionary* fetched £200, almost one sixth of the total proceeds.

Tooke's philology seems untenable in the face of what would follow. But there
was political method amid his etymological madness. Linguistic studies, so
important to the late eighteenth and early nineteenth century, were dominated
by class. Johnson's *Dictionary,* Bishop Lowth's *Grammar* (1762) and James Harris' *Hermes* (1751, a universal grammar), the most influential books of the period,
all took as their readers the privileged classes. As Olivia Smith points out,

> To speak the vulgar language demonstrated that one belonged to the vul-
> gar class; that is, that one was morally and intellectually unfit to partici-
> pate in the culture. Only the refined language was capable of expressing
> intellectual ideas, while the vulgar language was limited to the expres-
> sion of the sensations and the passions. Such a concept required making
> the refined as different from the vulgar language as possible while also
> requiring that certain types of thought and emotions be advocated to the
> detriment of others.[28]

Describing Johnson's preface as "yet another text which disparages the language while it teaches it,"[29] she notes that to Johnson "illiterate" meant unable
to speak Latin or Greek. Such élitism excluded the vast bulk of the population.
Only John Wesley, who deliberately aimed his work at this culturally silent
majority, and those such as John Ash, whose *Grammatical Institutes* (1760) was
specifically aimed at "young Gentlemen designed merely for Trade," allowed
the "unlearned" an opportunity to improve themselves. Aside from its purely
linguistic and lexicographical achievements, the importance of Johnson's
devotedly conservative work was that, in its long-lasting position as "*the* Dictionary," it helped perpetuate the conservative point of view.

For a writer like Tooke, who might have been to Cambridge but whose
background and beliefs were far from those of the Establishment, this conserv-

ative attitude to language was anathema. In his eyes it conspired against the
mass, however articulate, negating their attempted criticisms of society by stating flatly that their vulgar "illiteracy" rendered such criticism de facto irrelevant. Thus, as he stated in the *Diversions* "he had political reasons for wanting
to disprove previous theories, and that language, as it was generally understood, was a source of distortion which interfered with political life. [His] theory was an exceptionally retaliatory one, which was aimed at previous theories
and at ideas about language both philosophically and as they impinged upon
social life."[30] The literal meaning, the etymology of *etymology* is the "true," i.e.,
original word. To Tooke Johnson's version of that "truth" was politically biased,
élitist, and ultimately wrong. His own theories, equally politicized, were
designed to make the necessary correction. The problem, however, is that no
matter how principled his theories, they proved erroneous. Tooke should have
heeded his old Constitutional Society colleague, William Jones. It is easy to
suggest that ideology, especially when pursued as assiduously as was Tooke's,
tends to blur intellectual rigor. But Johnson was, in his way, an equally dedicated ideologue—yet he is seen as the greater man, and his theories, while as
ignorant as were Tooke's of linguistic advances, survived, in the form of the
continuing authority of his *Dictionary,* almost until the end of the nineteenth
century. In the end one must look to public taste. Tooke, as Olivia Smith says,
was a protester when few protested. He had backed Wilkes, been jailed for his
pro-American activities, had befriended that great bugaboo Tom Paine. He had
his supporters, some of them influential, but to many he seemed a jeremiah.
People wanted linguistic reassurance, not revolution, and for that, uncaring of
the niceties of particles or proper nouns, they preferred Dr. Johnson.

Hindsight makes for wonderful vision. Politics aside, however absurd his
purely lexicographical beliefs appear today, at the time Tooke's theories were
widely respected, at least among the more radical thinkers. His was seen as the
epitome of scientific method. Thus William Hazlitt, writing in 1825 on "The
Late Mr. Horne Tooke": "Mr. Tooke . . . treated words as the chemists do sub-
stances; he separated those which are compounded from those which are not
decompoundable. He did not explain the obscure by the more obscure, but the
difficult by the plain, the complex by the simple. This alone is proceeding upon
the true principles of science: the rest is pedantry and petitmaîtreship." There
were critics: John Mitchell Kemble declared that "with all his swaggering upon
the subject even he was barbarously ignorant of all the Teutonic tongues; and
owes what reputation he has enjoyed solely to a happy knack of outbullying his
opponents upon subjects with which he and they were alike conversant"[31] but
he was an exception. Tooke, unsurprisingly, had no doubts, stating confidently

that "all future etymologists, and perhaps some philosophers, will acknowledge their obligation to me."[32]

Not all, perhaps, but there were certainly some. Tooke's disciples, often less intellectual, but utterly devoted to the Master, produced works that were even more bizarre than his own. Typical is Walter Whiter's *Etymologicon Universale or Universal Etymological Dictionary* (1822–5), which paraded a range of ludicrous fancies, all based on Hookian reductions: he linked, for example, *Earth, heart, hurt, hart* (the animal), *harsh,* and even *hearse.* A friend of the Gypsy expert George Borrow (author of *Lavengro* and *Romany Rye*) and, like Tooke, of Porson, Whiter was admired (perhaps to excess) for his learning but censured for his character. "I pity Whiter," remarked Baron Merian. "A great etymologist, perhaps the greatest that ever lived. A genius, certainly, but it seems, like most eminent artists, dissolute."[33] This "dissolution," it would appear, took the form of Whiter's annual celebration of April 23, St. George's Day, when he invited his friends to a picnic and demanded that each compose and recite a poem, either in Latin or English. But one cannot trust the Baron: his assessment of Whiter's *Etymologicon* was that it was "splendid, a very fine book indeed." Among Whiter's other works is a *Dissertation on the Disorder of Death, or that State called Suspended Animation* (1819), in which he offered his suggestions on the possible resuscitation of those otherwise assumed to be dead.

Alexander Murray, an autodidact linguist who won a place at the University of Edinburgh in 1804, rose to become professor of oriental languages there in 1812 but died of consumption within a year. His *History of the European languages, "or, Researches into the Affinities of the Teutonic, Greek, Celtic, Sclavonic and Indian Nations,"* appeared in 1823. Its premise was that since all speech was based on action—"a few short interjectional syllables"—there were just nine "words" (in fact syllables) at the root of all language. These were *ag, bag, dwag, gwag, lag, mag, nag, rag,* and *swag.* These worked as both nouns and verbs and each represented some form of violent action. As time passed both actions and "words" had been gradually softened into compounds and thence modernity's multiplicity of tongues. Somewhat more respectable was David Booth, whose *Introduction to an Analytical Dictionary of the English Language* appeared in 1806. The dictionary for which this was the equivalent of Johnson's plan appeared in 1830. Booth's aim was to explain words "in the order of their natural affinity, . . . the signification of each is traced from its etymology." The dictionary, compiled "independent of alphabetical arrangement," was a thematic hodge-podge, based on Booth's reading of Tooke. It left little mark.

The most important of Tooke's disciples, however, is Charles Richardson (1775–1865), whose *New Dictionary of the English Language* (1837) was based on

Tooke's theorizing and popularized Tooke to an extent the old controversialist's own works could never have managed. The dictionary was originally designed to form part of the *Encyclopedia Metropolitana,* which began appearing in 1818. That project, which was to have included a "Philosophical and Etymological Lexicon" written by its editor Samuel Taylor Coleridge, foundered, but the dictionary still appeared, nineteen years later. It was by no means a wholly bad book, and its citations, which are the first to reach back to such fourteenth-century authors as Chaucer, Piers Plowman, and Gower, surpass those of Johnson, whose earliest selections are from the late sixteenth century. Indeed, Richardson based the whole weight of his book on citations: there were no detailed definitions as such, just a mass of quotations from which the meaning and usage of a given word was to be inferred. It was by opting to follow Tooke on etymology that Richardson moved beyond this worthwhile endeavor and entered a highly dubious arena.

Richardson, a schoolmaster at Clapham Common, south London, entered the fray in 1815, when he published *Illustrations to English Philology,* which combined an attack on Johnson with a defense of Tooke. He acknowledged Johnson's importance, both in his word list, from which he would openly borrow, and from his plan, although Richardson felt that Johnson himself had failed to follow it through adequately. Like that transatlantic Johnson baiter and fellow advocate of Tooke's theories, Noah Webster, Richardson saw his own work as improving on the Doctor's efforts. However, vilifying Johnson was as nothing to glorifying Tooke. No man, he wrote in the preface to his *Dictionary,* "can possibly succeed in compiling a truly valuable Dictionary of the English Language, unless he entirely desert the steps of Johnson, and pursue the path which Tooke has pointed out."[34] Johnson's etymologies, limited to his starting period of the sixteenth century, were useless; they were "loose, vague, and various"; his citations were laughable.[35] Tooke, on the other hand, was the lexicographer's true role model.

Due, perhaps, to his extension of the citation base, Richardson gained a positive response that fails fully to reflect his slavish acceptance of Tooke. James Murray, for instance, who had no time at all for Webster's erroneous etymologizing, ignores Richardson's fantasies and sees him purely as a quote collector, noting that his work "still continues to be a valuable repertory of illustration";[36] Wheatley agrees and refers to Richardson's "great" dictionary without further critical analysis.[37] The *Gentleman's Magazine,* once a bastion of Johnson's coterie, approved, as did the *Quarterly Review,* which would so deplore the Tookian Webster and laud the Johnsonian Worcester; the *Spectator* called it "the most complete dictionary ever published, as regards the etymology and primitive meaning of words, the successive growth of their secondary significations, the gradual advance and changes of the language, the vast body of quotations from all our authors, both ancient and modern, and in consequence, the skeleton history of the English language which it indirectly presents"[38] and Richard Chenevix Trench characterizes the work as "the only English dictionary in which etymology assumes the dignity of a science." Given that it would be Trench whose comments on the "deficiencies" of English dictionaries would lead directly to the *New English Dictionary,* and who was certainly no follower of Tooke, it was a comment that, as Sledd and Kolb note, "should have caused the Dean acute embarrassment."[39] In fairness, that citation is out of context: Trench's comment appears in the overview of English dictionaries that Worcester appended to his own work of 1860. In any case, Trench never dissembled as far his attitude to Tooke was concerned. He understood him well enough, but paid him his dues. As he put it in *On the Study of Words* (1851), "Whatever may be Horne Tooke's shortcomings, whether in occasional details of etymology, or in the philosophy of grammar, or in matters more serious still, yet, with all this, what an epoch in many a student's intellectual life has been his first acquaintance with the *Diversions of Purley.*"[40] Sledd and Kolb are less charitable. Richardson's etymologies, they add, "too often insult the simplest principles of historical linguistics" and his debt to Tooke has rendered "his borrowed method . . . so perverse that the possibility of calling it historical becomes dubious."[41] In short, they note, Richardson's tortured attempts to justify Tooke's and his own theories come down finally to "necromancy."[42] Allen Walker Read has dismissed Richardson's mentor as "benighted" and Richardson's own work as "a monument of misguided industry."[43] Nonetheless, it is necessary to separate the two strands of Richardson's work, the etymologies on the one hand and the quotations on the other. Richardson's broader range of sources has to be acknowledged as a real step forward, and if his etymologies are specious, the method that underpins his collection of citations, and his appreciation of their immense importance in the definition of terms and usage, where they suggest far subtler nuances of meaning than are possible with a simple definition, can be seen as a precedent for the *New English Dictionary.*

13

The New English Dictionary

The Philological Society "for the investigation of the Structure, the Affinities, and the History of Languages; and the Philological Illustration of the Classical Writers of Greece and Rome" was established at a meeting held in London on May 18, 1842. The Society was not wholly new: it had existed as a student body at University College, London for some years, but its adult incarnation was an important step forward, reflecting the increasingly influential part philology had come to play in English scholarship. Its creation had been suggested by the linguistic historian, historical geographer, and Anglo-Saxon expert Edwin Guest (1800–80), who nine days earlier had issued a printed announcement of its inception. For the next six months the fledgling Society gathered members, some 203 of whom had signed up by the time of the inaugural meeting, held on November 25. As secretary Guest read out the list of members: they were mainly clergymen and often academics, among whom were such figures as the philologist Hensleigh Wedgwood, grandson of the potter Josiah, Dr. Thomas Arnold of Rugby School, and Professor Thomas Key of University College. (Of these Wedgwood was perhaps the most important in terms of the future *New English Dictionary.* Cousin of Charles Darwin, Wedgwood would prove himself one of the country's leading etymologists, a rival to Walter Skeat, generally acknowledged as the best of his era. His own etymological lexicon was judged to be "a work far in advance of all its predecessors, displaying an extraordinary command of linguistic material,"[1] although his achievement was slightly marred by his refusal to accept wholeheartedly the latest in etymological theory. However great his reputation would become, Wedgwood did not start off well. His last place in the Cambridge classical tripos of 1824 created an alternative to the traditional "wooden spoon": the "wooden wedge" was metaphorically awarded to similarly inept undergraduates for the next sixty years.) Other members were veterans of another linguistic group, the Etymological Society of Cambridge, which had met through the 1830s. The members then heard the society's first ever paper. Delivered by Professor R. G. Latham, professor of English language and literature at University College, it discussed "the dialects of the Papuan or Negrito race, scattered through the Australian and other Asiatic islands."

Early meetings of the society were held in a room rented from the London Library, itself still a relatively recent foundation (it had opened in 1841, the inspiration of Thomas Carlyle who had despaired of the book delivery at the British Museum Reading Room). The society and the library, unsurprisingly, shared a number of members. There they remained, helping meet the rates bills, until the 1870s, when the society was forced out by the ever-increasing numbers of the library's books. Although the battles over the importance of Anglo-Saxon had been won, and linguistic academe had taken on board the importance of the new philology, the Philological Society, where one might have expected such topics to gain pride of place, was oddly reticent in its inclusion of them in its Friday-night discussions. Instead its concerns were those of classical philology, the dialects and etymologies of English and ethnological philology, dealing with languages that fell outside the Indo-European family, and were thus extraneous to the Sanskrit studies that lay at the root of German philological advance. However, if the members ignored state-of-the-art philology, their studies of English as such were consistently strong. Among the fruits of this learning was the belief that in time the English language would become the most widely disseminated on earth, a situation the members believed would have a twofold benefit—to literature and, reflecting the profession of so many members, to the Church. It was hoped, among other things, that such a development might even reunite the divided Christian faiths, split between Rome and Canterbury since 1536.

Among those who held this position was the individual to whom, more than to any other, should be credited the initial inspiration for the undertaking that would become the *New English Dictionary*.[2] Richard Chenevix Trench was born on September 5, 1807 in Dublin. He was brought up in England, educated at Harrow and then Trinity College, Cambridge, where he was elected a member of the Apostles and befriended, among others, John Mitchell Kemble, F. D. Maurice, Alfred Tennyson, and Richard Monckton Milnes. He read Spanish, and even wrote a play, *Bernardo del Caprio,* which Macready, the great tragedian, was considering putting on stage; Trench destroyed the manuscript some years later. After Cambridge he appears to have suffered from depression and attempted to cure his miseries by visiting Spain and flirting briefly with the more romantic aspects of the political situation there, although his interest was sustained more by his affection for Spanish literature than by any deep knowledge of Spanish politics. On his return to England he joined the Church and proceeded to take on a series of livings. Although his biographer Bromley suggested that he was in many ways the paradigm of the gentleman parson, best fitted for life in a country parish, blending his theological duties with his literary pursuits, Trench pursued a more active career. It advanced steadily: in October 1856 he became dean of Westminster and in November 1863 archbishop of Dublin. He died on March 28, 1886, aged seventy-nine. He is buried in Westminster Abbey.

Trench's clerical career is important—especially in terms of his opposition to Prime Minister Gladstone's campaign to disestablish the Irish Church, and in his administration of that Church in the wake of Gladstone's victory—but it is as a scholar that he is most valuable here. He began writing shortly after leaving Cambridge, dealing first with theological concerns, but gradually moving toward linguistics. He was no great comparative philologist, but his knowledge of the English language since 1500 was outstanding, possibly unrivaled. He was dean of Westminster when he joined the Philological Society and in February 1845 announced his intention of delivering a lecture to the students of the Diocesan Training School in Winchester. Its topic was to be "Language as an Instrument of Knowledge." In the event he gave not one but five lectures and had them published in 1851, slightly rewritten, as a book, *On the Study of Words.* In 1854 he delivered four more lectures, on much the same topics, to the pupils of King's College School, Taunton. These too appeared in a book: *English Past and Present* (1855). The books were enormously popular: *On the Study of Words* had reached its nineteenth edition by 1886, while its successor was in its fourteenth in 1889. Trench's clerical peers appreciated his work, which they saw as expounding the philosophy of religious language; lay readers were equally impressed. As Hans Aarsleff remarks, "Both books did far more than any previous publication to make language study popular, and without that popularity it seems unlikely that the *New English Dictionary* would have been able both to get the readers it needed and to arouse the general interest that sustained it."[3] Trench's lectures, while influential, concentrate on the philosophy and the history of language, rather than on lexicography. His aim was to demonstrate the moral role of language; philology was, as it were, an afterthought. But simply by virtue of making himself into one of the country's foremost linguistic experts, he had amassed, virtually as a by-product, a substantial knowledge of the state of the nation's dictionaries. Thus, two years after the lectures to King's College, in his role as a leading light of the Philological Society, he turned his intellect firmly in that direction. Talking now to his intellectual peers, rather than to young students, he delivered on November 5 and 19, 1857 two papers "On Some Deficiencies in our English Dictionaries." The papers, which were published in 1858 (and republished in 1860), cover what Trench delineates as the seven "deficiencies" in the currently available dictionaries, by which he meant essentially those of Johnson and Richardson. Trench did not declare himself to be the architect of a new dictionary, but the detail of his analysis, and the remedies that devolve from his suggestions, make his talks into the most detailed plan for a lexicographical work since that published by Johnson more than a century earlier. The *New English Dictionary* may not have sprung fully formed from Trench's head, but its genesis can be traced to his remarks, and it is easy, looking at the finished work, to see the extent to which all those who worked on the realized *Dictionary* were indebted to the dean. As John Simpson, coeditor of the second edition of the *OED,* has remarked, "If this was not a lexicographical Bill of Rights, it was at least a manifesto for dictionary-makers."[4]

Trench divides his criticisms into seven points, the essentials of a dictionary. These deal with obsolete words, the status of "word families," the need to find first uses as far as possible, the need to include every alternative meaning of a word, the listing of a wide range of synonyms, the use of literary citations to establish usage, dating, and etymology, and the need to exclude certain categories of "nonstandard" English. To these he adds some prefatory remarks concerning the role of the lexicographer and a summing up. The dictionary, he declares, is quite simply "an inventory of the language."[5] Like the language it represents, the word list it lays out is neither static and fixed, nor is it "good" or "bad." "It is no task of the maker of it to select the 'good' words of a language. If he fancies that it is so, and begins to pick and choose, to have this and to take that, he will at once go astray . . . He is an historian . . . not a critic."[6] He has little time for what he terms the "pretensions" of the Académie, and while he stands back from making a direct criticism of the *Dictionnaire,* he makes clear his view of those who seek to "fix" a language: "Those who desire, are welcome to such a book; but for myself I will only say that I cannot understand how any writer with the smallest confidence in himself, the least measure of vigour and vitality which would justify himself in addressing his countrymen in written or spoken discourse at all, should consent in this matter to let one self-made dictator, or forty, determine for him what words he should use and what he should forbear from using."[7] Such a work, he adds, is not worthy of the name "dictionary." And he concludes this opening salvo by stating that the student of language may learn as much from the so-called errors of a language as from its "proper" uses. A dictionary is not an arbiter of taste, it "is an historical monument, the history of a nation contemplated from one point of view." To offer that history in its fullness, the dictionary must, subject to certain limits, be as comprehensive as reasonably possible.

He then makes his way through his seven "deficiencies." Starting with "obsolete terms" he notes the way in which some lexicographers have attempted to exclude or restrict such terms. But what exactly is meant by obsolete? Surely, he suggests, any word that the reader is likely to encounter ought to be included. What point is there in having a work of reference, in this case of the English language, to which one cannot properly refer. Nor can one allow some "obsolete" words and exclude others, as both Johnson and Richardson have attempted. The rule should be all or none, and Trench opts firmly for all. That said, he would exclude dialects and provincialisms. The dictionary is to be a collection of *standard* English; such terms do not qualify. Yet if these words have entered general use, however localized their origins, they must then gain admittance. As to point two, word families, Trench calls for as wide as possible a consideration of such groups. In many cases this means simply the acknowledging of the various suffixes— *-en, -er, -ly, -ness, -y*—that accrue to the basic term and create in this way different parts of speech. Likewise there should be room for negative forms, diminutives, and those that denote a female version of a male original. Equally important is point three, the dating of words, and their lifespan in the language. Some, he notes, appeared early and are set to last; others appear, have their moment, and die away. But all should be included. Only slang, which is what one must assume he means by the products of "that rabble of scribblers who hang onto the skirts of literature, doing their worst to profane and degrade it and language," is held to be beyond the pale. Above all, he notes, the lexicographer must search out "the *first* authority for a word's use in the language . . . the register of its birth."[8] Obviously that means a written citation; prior spoken use cannot be dated. A cited first usage may not, of course, always be the actual first usage, and the lexicographer must accept that later generations, or even more dedicated contemporaries, will inevitably amend his dates, but try he must. (For the truth of this assertion one need look no further than the work of the late Jürgen Schäfer, whose listing of usages that predate the *OED* was cut off only by his premature death.[9] Indeed Schäfer, who offered around 5,000 examples himself, estimated that in all some 29,000 of the first edition's 240,000 entries, more than 12 percent, could be antedated by at least fifty years.) And like a human biographer, the biographer of words must give the moment of linguistic death as well as of birth.

Given that "it is one of the primary demands that we make upon a Dictionary, that it should . . . present us with the history of words,"[10] it is vital that the development of each word should be traced via suitable citations. By this means the usage can be illustrated, as well as the nuances of meanings as the word proceeds from year to year. Johnson "is very faulty here," letting himself give only the latest meaning and ignoring, on all too many occasions, the alternatives. Richardson is better, but he too lacks consistency. Nuance is also central to Trench's sixth heading: the listing of synonyms. Latin and Greek lexicons do this as a matter of course, so too should those of English. The main classical dictionary to which Trench referred was the joint work of Henry Liddell (to whose daughter Alice Charles Dodgson first recounted the tale that became *Alice in Wonderland*) and of Robert Scott—*A Greek-English Lexicon*—which had appeared in 1843, the product of nine years' work. Generally seen as an exemplary piece of lexicography, the *Lexicon* was based, as its subtitle explained, "on the German Work of Francis [Franz] Passow." Passow (1786–1833) was a classical scholar and lexicographer who in 1812 had produced a critique of Johann Gottlieb Schneider's *Greek-German Dictionary* (1797–98). In this critique, *Über Zweck, Anlage und Ergänzung Griechischer Wörterbücher,* Passow laid down his own principles for dictionary making, and subsequently displayed them in his own *Handwörterbuch der Griechischen Sprache* (1819–23). He stated that no word should ever be included in a dictionary without a proper authority and added, in his most far-reaching dictum, that citations must always be listed in chronological order. Whether the earliest was the "best" was totally irrelevant. The point of the citations was to illustrate historical development: this could only be done by tracing the changes from earliest to latest. It was a rule that would be adopted wholeheartedly by the editors of the *NED.* Passow was not the only German to whom Trench turns. The Grimms, in their *Deutsches Wörterbuch,* have also succeeded in offering a "large and instructive collection of materials"[11] in this area. Trench avoids any discussion of the philological theories behind etymology, but he does record, as point six, the potentially beneficial use of citations, once again, to help in assessing the origins of headwords. In many cases such citations actually explain such an origin, serving as a tiny essay on the topic. To include these would serve two purposes; the citation works simply as an indicator of usage, while its intrinsic information helps illustrate the linguistic background. Finally, in his seventh heading, Trench deals with materials that, despite his strictures as to the desirability of all-inclusiveness, can safely be rejected. These words were typically jargon (or professional and occupational slang) and technical and scientific terms, and he upbraids both Johnson and Webster for their admission of such material, usually bloated out by a lengthy definition. Other terms that should be avoided are the sort of compounds—cloud-capt, flower-enwoven—that bespatter certain types of literature. Although, as ever, he is willing to accept the finer sort, such as those created by John Milton.

His points made, Trench sums up. The main difficulty, he suggests, in attempting to make a new dictionary that would take proper note of his suggestions is the sheer volume of research. To create the sort of history of the language that he envisages would necessitate the absorption and analysis of every word of that language. In other words, to create one great book, researchers would be duty-bound to read all the rest. That cannot be. But it is feasible that a new team of readers could, were there enough of them, and had they been given a proper reading list, far surpass such predecessors as Johnson, restricted inevitably to random, serendipitous forays into the vast mass of available literature. The Grimms were employing no less than eighty-three readers; a similar team should be assembled for an English dictionary. Members of the Philological Society itself, he hoped, would see themselves as suitable readers. They would be substantially helped, he says, were the editors of old English texts to add a glossary to their publications. Editions of the great classical texts offer such a glossary as a matter of course; why should English language works be exempted.

The idea of creating an English dictionary that could stand alongside the Grimms' work-in-progress did not originate with Trench, although his paper gave such ideas an unprecedented impetus. The Philological Society could hardly have ignored the Grimms' progress—indeed both men were honorary members. And although the members had been wary of allowing the new philology to take up too much of their time, the fact that Johnson's work was more than a century old and Richardson's, while much newer, was deficient in many respects, could not have escaped them. The nature of their concerns had to mean that they appreciated, however tangentially, the need for some form of new English dictionary. Nor was the idea that such a dictionary should be created not by an individual but by a team completely new. The orientalist and numismatist William Marsden (1754–1836), who had authored his own *Dictionary of the Malayan Language* (1812), had offered his *Thoughts on the Composition of an English Dictionary* in 1834. He suggested that since the task was obviously beyond a single author, a society be formed to create the dictionary. He proposed a Royal Society of Literature that could undertake the task. In the event Marsden was right, although how much, if at all the Philological Society was aware of his *Thoughts* is not known. Wheatley, in his *Chronological Notes,* does give Marsden a brief acknowledgment.

As far as the society was concerned moves, however gradual, had begun on June 18, 1857, when three members, Trench, Herbert Coleridge, and Frederick Furnivall, were appointed as an "Unregistered Words Committee." The brief of this committee was to amass "words and idioms formerly unregistered in any dictionary." The assumption was that these, once properly codified, would be published as a form of supplement to existing works. This, as Aarsleff says, was truly "one of the major events in the history of language study."[12] The committee promised to report on their preliminary findings at the society's next meeting, on November 5. Its first move, in July, was to issue a circular which suggested that, since Johnson and Richardson fell equally short of representing a *Lexicon totius Anglicitatis* ("a dictionary of all Anglicisms"), it had been suggested that the collection of materials that could form the basis of a national dictionary might well be undertaken. In case the dictionary had to be put off, any materials so collected would be deposited in the British Museum, where they could be used by some future lexicographer.

Come November, the Committee, however important, did not in the event report as scheduled. Instead members heard the first half of Trench's paper on the "deficiencies" of English dictionaries. Two weeks later he delivered part two. The report of the Unregistered Words Committee was shelved, and members' interests focused on Trench's paper. After noting, at the meeting of December 3, that the Committee's report be "received and laid on the table," rather than read and debated, a resolution that a "scheme, for a completely new English Dictionary, might shortly be submitted to the Society" was passed. The scheme was then introduced at the first meeting of the new year, on January 7, 1858. Trench's paper was then edited for publication later that year and in August the plan for the new dictionary's creation was published.

What exactly changed the society's mind and transferred their attention from the production of a supplement to one of an entirely new national dictionary is debatable. The clarity and force of Trench's essay was obviously one factor. One has only to read it to see that here is a man who knows and loves his language and wishes, in what is in effect a plan for a new dictionary, to place that knowledge and affection at its service. Like Johnson, Trench could have said with no taint of immodesty, "I knew very well what I was undertaking— and very well how to do it—and have done it very well." But Trench was not the only inspiration. There was a purely practical side: Coleridge, as the committee's secretary, reported that some seventy-six volunteers had begun work on the supplement; they had assessed some 121 works. This was sterling progress, but it had some notable drawbacks: in the first place every single one of the words the readers were unearthing had to be checked against three current dictionaries (Johnson, Richardson, and Webster) to see whether it had already been registered. This took time. On top of that it soon became dauntingly clear that the supplement, if carried to its logical end, would be larger than all those works to which it was intended to form only an adjunct. Logically, and logistically, the creation, from scratch, of a brand new work, taking in Trench's plan, Passow's methodology, and the advances developed by the new philology, would be the best way forward.

Of the three members of the committee, Trench, while undoubtedly the project's "founding father," would soon return to his clerical pursuits. The practical work of pushing the new dictionary ahead devolved onto the committee's secretary Herbert Coleridge (1830–61), the grandson of the poet Samuel Taylor Coleridge. After Eton and a double-first at Oxford he had qualified at the bar, but was freed, thanks to a small private income, to pursue his first love: philology. It was this interest, especially as regarded Sanskrit and Icelandic, that brought him into the Philological Society and thence to his post on the Unregistered Words Committee. His *Glossarial Index to the Printed Literature of the Thirteenth Century* (1859) provided an invaluable reading list for the first team of readers. In time Coleridge would, as a natural development of his secretaryship, become the first editor of what was still best known as the "Philological Society's Dictionary." Tragically, he died in 1861, aged only thirty-one. He would have no further influence on the dictionary, but it is worth considering, as has John Willinsky,[13] just what sort of dictionary would have been produced had he lived. Judging by the *Canones Lexicographici, or the Rules To Be Observed in Editing the New English Dictionary . . .* Coleridge saw a tripartite work that was far broader than that actually produced and which in some ways recalled an older tradition. There would be a section devoted to mainstream language, which would include provincialisms, dialect, slang, Americanisms, and colonialisms. A second part concentrated on technical and scientific terms, as well as the proper names of people and places, while the third offered an "Etymological Appendix." Coleridge also called for the inclusion of "every word in the language, for which sufficient authority, whether printed or oral, can be adduced."[14] The concept of including oral evidence, and thus treating English as the living and changing language that it undoubtedly was, did not survive Coleridge's death. It might not ever have been achieved even had he survived: the pinning down of oral sources is always hard—dictionaries still opt for print—and the methodology, seen in the extensive questionnaires that underpin a work such as today's *Dictionary of American Regional English,* did not yet exist. But there was a more pressing influence working against the acceptance of oral usage. The debt to German philology, which drew so heavily on the study of classical tongues, proved too great. English was hardly a "dead" language, but as Willinsky suggests, its treatment in the *NED,* especially where the citations are concerned, sometimes resembles that of Greek or Latin.

But Coleridge did not live and the nature of "his" dictionary remains pure supposition. His role as the moving force behind the *Dictionary* was taken up by two men in turn. One of these was James Murray, whose involvement would not begin fully until 1879, when he signed the contract to become its editor. No individual has ever been, nor ever will nor should be, so closely identified with the *Dictionary.* But Murray's importance comes later. The other, whose name is vital to the project, but whose life encompassed such a range of other undertakings that his lexicography seems at times just one more diversion amid so many, was Frederick Furnivall, the third member of the Unregistered Words Committee. And if anyone can be seen as transforming the researches that would become the *New English Dictionary* from nascent supplement to full-blown lexicographical undertaking, then he is the man.

To take a suitably linguistic metaphor, Furnivall is slang where Murray is standard English. No one could have been more different from Murray, the self-effacing, auto-didact Scottish dominie, than was Furnivall, an ebullient, outgoing, often embarrassing but seemingly unembarrassable figure. Frederick James Furnivall was born on February 4, 1825 in Egham, Surrey. His father George was a devotedly pious doctor who had fancied a military career but turned to medicine at his mother's request. His main claim to fame was to have attended Mary Shelley in her confinement eight years prior to his son's birth. His practice flourished and he set up a lunatic asylum, Great Foster House, which was sold for £200,000 at his death. Furnivall was educated at a variety of private schools before, in 1841, entering University College, London, founded in 1826 as a low church alternative to Oxbridge and thus known by its detractors as that "godless college in Gower Street." Here he led, in miniature, the life that he would follow for the remainder of his years: a wide interest in matters academic, reading that covered the whole spectrum of available literature, personal involvement in any religious or political controversy worth an argument, a growing interest in social history and an appreciation of sports (especially boxing and rowing), entertainments, and parties. It was busy, energetic, improving, and seemingly unending. In October 1842 he went up to Trinity Hall, Cambridge. There he showed himself very pious, took up what would become twenty-five years of vegetarianism, and beseeched his father to back him in a partnership with Daniel Macmillan, the bookseller and publisher. His father, who may have enjoyed Frederick's ecclesiastical enthusiasms, had less time for his commercial ones: the plea was turned down. A nondrinker and nonsmoker at Cambridge, he remained so all his life.

He graduated B.A. in 1846 (he took his M.A. in 1849) and moved back to London where he joined the chambers of Bellenden Ker, a conveyancer, at Lincoln's Inn. He was called to the bar in 1849. He made new friends, notably the influential socialist John Malcolm Ludlow (1821–1911), whose opinions began gradually to influence his own. It was at this time that Furnivall adopted what would become his sartorial trademarks: a beard and a tie of pink ribbon. Unexceptional now, a definite statement then. His cultural interests were unabated: he saw Wordsworth read ("Unpleasant manner, but poetry good stuff") and Jenny Lind sing. He joined the radical Whittington Club, an institution whereby members of the middle classes attempted to offer some of the advantages of West End club life to their less privileged brethren of the East. Here he met real-life radicals and fostered what was becoming a lifetime's commitment to social problems and their possible solution. Paradoxically, for all his "leftie" acquaintance, his involvement in the Chartist uprisings of 1848 was as a special constable, sworn in to quell the much-feared but nonexistent "revolution."

Shortly after the collapse of Chartism Furnivall joined a new group: the Christian Socialists. This group had been founded by F. D. Maurice, professor of English literature, history, and theology at King's College, London and once, alongside Chenevix Trench, a member of the Cambridge "Apostles." Furnivall was one of Maurice's foremost supporters, as were Ludlow, the chemist Charles Mansfield, and the young writer Charles Kingsley. They formed Bible classes and working men's cooperative societies. All very earnest, no doubt, and deeply felt, but not particularly successful. Like any such coterie of high-minded do-gooders, the Christian Socialists blithely assumed that their program of religiosity and good works would be welcomed by the hapless proletariat who would thus be freed from their burden of bestial self-indulgence. The cooperative societies duly failed, but rather than acknowledge the essential shortcomings of their schemes, Maurice and his young men promptly recreated them in a new guise: the London Working Man's College, which opened in 1854. It was at this stage that the inner group was joined by a new member, Thomas Hughes, the hagiographer of Thomas Arnold, the "Doctor" of Rugby School, and like his hero a member of the Philological Society. It was in his devotion to the college that Furnivall showed himself to be somewhat removed from Maurice. They clashed constantly: over the admission of women to the college (Furnivall, ever appreciative of a pretty face, was all for it), over the possibility of excursions on the Sabbath (Furnivall, once more, was addicted to Sunday exercise), and similar issues. It was at this time that Furnivall, as the college bear-leader, began taking his students on botanical and geological expeditions, on lengthy walking trips, on rowing parties, cricket matches, and picnics. Alongside this he taught them English literature and grammar. As well as teaching the basics to those less fortunate, Furnivall was intensifying his own involvement in the more sophisticated aspects of the English language. University College was a center of such studies and he undoubtedly benefited from his immersion there. He joined the Philological Society in 1847 and became, with the founder member T. H. Key, its joint secretary in 1853.

Before looking fully at Furnivall's involvement with the *Dictionary* it is worth glancing at some other aspects of the life of this tempestuous, eccentric Victorian. Above all Furnivall was an indefatigable founder of societies, one of the great motive forces of contemporary scholarship. There would be seven in all, founded between 1864 and 1886: the Early English Text Society, the Chaucer Society, the Ballad Society, the New Shakspere [*sic*] Society, the Wyclif Society, the Browning Society, and the Shelley Society. Of these, it is the Early English Text Society (henceforth EETS) that is of primary lexicographical concern. It was thanks to the EETS that the new German philology gained an even more secure grasp on English letters; at the same time, as noted by H. R. Steeves in his history of such societies, the EETS and similar institutions became "indispensable as an agency for the effective realization of the rapidly expanding aims of contemporary scholarship."[15] In his list of "deficiencies" Trench had called for editors of old English texts to provide proper glossaries for the benefit of scholars, whether lexicographers or others. Furnivall's founding of the EETS in 1864 was a direct response, albeit somewhat belated, to that call for help. Among its publications, which are still appearing, was Furnivall's own edition of Harman's *Caveat,* Wheatley's edition of Levins' *Manipulus,* and the three-volume *Promptorium parvulorum* by Thomas Way, an antiquarian based in Cannes whose only other claim to fame was in the reputation of his father, Lewis, a wealthy barrister whose life was devoted to a somewhat different society, that for promoting Christianity among the Jews. To quote the writer John Michelle, Lewis Way's interest occurred "when he was riding near Exmouth in Devon. He happened to remark on a fine stand of oak trees, and was told that their name was the 'Oaks of à la Ronde' and that their late owner, Jane Parminter, had left a will forbidding anyone to cut them down until the Jews had been brought back into Palestine. Mr Way was so struck by the idea that he began reading his Bible, learnt from it of the British mission to convert the Jews and became a full-time benefactor of the Society founded for that purpose."[16] It was unfortunate for the Society that sometime later its chief accountant discovered that no such reference existed, thus removing much of its raison d'être.

At the same time the EETS fed on the popular Victorian interest in medieval England as well as in the formation of societies such as this, which, as Benzie puts it, promoted the practice of "bringing people together in the spirit of cooperation to form committees and societies."[17] There had been earlier societies, typically the Roxburghe Club (for which Furnivall had edited a number of works), but they had been élitist institutions, a hangover from a period when the gentleman of private means could indulge his literary pretensions alone in a book-lined study. Furnivall's societies were far more open. The man who held court in an ABC teashop at 66, New Oxford Street—where he indulged his appetite for sweet, sugary cakes—and organized a rowing club at Hammersmith for the waitresses who worked there—for whom he designed a new kind of scull—was hardly likely to promote an intellectual closed shop. To him there was no difference between the EETS, with its membership of scholars and clergymen and its links to what might be termed the country's foremost site of literary endeavor, and his weekly expeditions on the river with his girls, or his involvement in a cricket club for "working lads." He must have been especially pleased when in 1867 a group of Sunderland workers formed a club, their specific ambition being to raise a joint subscription to the EETS. His personality undoubtedly endeared him to his lower-middle- and working-class friends, who must have found his openness delightful. Still, it could not be, however hard both sides tried, the perfect union of like minds. He was, inevitably, dealing with them *de haut en bas:* Christian socialism did not mean egalitarianism, and his choice of allegiance when faced with Chartism has been noticed. As the many anecdotes of his relations with his less privileged friends make clear, Furnivall was always in charge. Yet he offered an infinitely more appealing role model than the alternatives: Utilitarianism or the evangelical church, both of whom meddled gleefully in "improving" the working classes, each peddling an agenda a good deal less palatable than Furnivall's. If nothing else, Furnivall had a sense of humor. Nor would his pet project, the *Dictionary,* in all its ten massy volumes, exactly recommend itself for everyday use, however bent on self-improvement a man or woman might be. Cost alone militated against its availability. Furnivall may have seen himself as offering the kind of people's dictionary as did John Wesley a century earlier, but Wesley really did provide a lexicon for the mass market; like it or not, Furnivall's contribution was to a self-evidently élitist work.

Compared with the traditional image of the Victorian scholar, let alone that of the lexicographer of any age, Furnivall's is of a distinctly flesh-and-blood human being. His private life was conducted with as much energy as his public undertakings. In 1862 he had appalled his middle-class peers by marrying Eleanor Dalziel, better known as Missy or Lizzy, the sister of W. A. Dalziel, a student teacher at the Working Men's College. Dismissed by Furnivall's contemporaries as a "pretty lady's maid," she combined wifely duties with those of a dictionary maker's amanuensis. One visitor to their home watched her clear away the supper dishes (roast potatoes, asparagus, and coffee) only to replace them with piles of research papers, sorting, transcribing, and arranging the resulting material for use in the dictionary. In fact Lizzy was no maid—her father was a market gardener—and the real scandal was the discrepancy between her and Furnivall's age. It had also been noticed that Lizzy and Furnivall had been, as Benzie discreetly puts it, "inseparable" long before they were married. None of which would have caused Furnivall a moment's concern. A determined proponent of women's rights, he would have been incapable of accepting any constraints on Lizzy's freedom of action; as an equally dedicated social rebel he would have been singularly unimpressed by the pieties of his peers. The couple had two children. Ena died aged only four; Percy, brought up in his father's liberal, agnostic principles, went on to success as a surgeon and as a cycling champion. In 1882 Furnivall faced a new scandal. He had left Lizzy, who had turned out to be somewhat lazy, with a penchant for sitting dully in a chair, and begun an affair with a new young woman. This time his inamorata really had been a lady's maid: she was the strikingly pretty sister of one of his students and now his own secretary—Teena Rochfort-Smith. Furnivall was fifty-seven, she was just twenty-one. Poor James Murray was so shocked at this news that when he received a letter informing him of Furnivall's affair he carefully stuck stamp paper over the signature of the correspondent who had delivered the news. Furnivall, of course, was unmoved by any such worries. In 1883 he moved Teena into his house in St. George's Square, off Primrose Hill. The continuing presence there of his wife did not, apparently, worry him. She left a few months later, moving to adjacent Hampstead with their son. Sadly for Furnivall, his new affair was to be tragically short-lived. Visiting a relation in Yorkshire, Teena was burnt to death when on August 28 a lighted match flared up, ignited her dress and she was unable to douse the flames. It was noted that the match was of the type known as "Domestics." It took her eight days to die and Furnivall composed a memoir of her life which he presented to the British Museum.

A friend of Kenneth Grahame, who became secretary of the New Shakspere Society, Furnivall took him sculling on the river and was, it appears, the first person to encourage Grahame to add to his work at the Bank of England an attempt to become a creative writer. Among the results was *The Wind in the Willows,* in which Furnivall is seen in the character of the Water Rat, a figure, like himself, with a passion for boats and the river. Furnivall never missed a chance to scull every Sunday—he was still putting in 15–20 miles at the age of eighty-two. Grahame also imbued his character with a little of Furnivall's literary appetites. As Mole, Badger, Rat, and Toad prepare to drive the stoats and weasels from Toad Hall and an emotional Toad declares that "We learned 'em!", Rat is quick to correct him: "We taught 'em," he explains, is the proper phrase. Indeed, Humphrey Carpenter, in his study *Secret Gardens* (1985), has suggested that Rat stands for the "outdoor, gently muscular world of Christian socialism" into which fussy, houseproud, "slightly effeminate" Mole is being initiated.[18] But Rat, stickler for grammar and muscular Christian though he may be, is no great controversialist. Furnivall certainly was. George Bernard Shaw, whose own celebrity was beginning as Furnivall's started to fade, and knew a fellow scrapper when he saw one, suggested that the pugnacious philologist had only become an agnostic because he could never forgive Christ for failing to put up a fight in Gethsemane. A typical exploit was his review, in the January 12, 1867 issue of the literary journal *The Reader,* of a new edition of Johnson, edited by the philologist R. G. Latham. In it Furnivall set about Latham's introduction, suggesting that Latham had surpassed even Johnson in his egocentricity and arrogance: this was Johnson's dictionary, yet, unbelievably, Latham made no mention whatsoever of its author. As the *Pall Mall Gazette* of January 18 pointed out in a piece teasingly headlined "Shocking Suicide of a Reviewer," this was hardly surprising. The introduction in question had not been penned by Latham: it was Johnson's own.

More serious, and certainly longer lasting, was Furnivall's feud with the poet Algernon Charles Swinburne. Swinburne, whose other brush with lexicography comes, as will be seen, in his relations with the slang collector John Camden Hotten, for whose dubious publishing company the poet wrote such works of flagellant pornography as *The Romance of the Rod,* took exception to Furnivall's role as doyen of the New Shakspere Society. In 1876 he clashed with Furnivall over a piece dealing with various technicalities in the meter of *Henry VIII,* a play attributed in part to Shakespeare, but not included in the First Folio. The pair swapped letters and the matter seemed to die, but so loathsome did the poet find the philologist's society that he composed two parodies of "The Newest Shakespeare Society" and published them in *The Examiner* in April 1876. In 1877 Furnivall hit back, questioning Swinburne's knowledge of Chaucer. Replying in a letter to the *Athenaeum* in February 1877, Swinburne characterized the New Shaksperians as "dunces" and "churls" and singled out their leader as "the most bellicose bantam cock that ever defied creation."[19] By 1879 the combatants were in full cry. Swinburne mocked those "dunces [who] accept and circulate as gold the current brass of German pedants" and attacked the "indecorous nakedness of their undraped absurdity." Furnivall, sorely tried, abandoned all restraint. Writing in the *Spectator* he told Swinburne "to teach his grandmother to suck eggs" and added that his ear was "a poetaster's, hairy, thick and dull." He sent Swinburne's friends a succession of libelous postcards and went back to the roots of his enemy's name to call him "Pigsbrook." Where Furnivall looked to Anglo-Saxon, Swinburne preferred Latin. Furnivall was promptly transformed into "Brothel-dyke" (from the Latin *fornix* and *vallum*). He wrote scatological anti-Furnivall verses in which he attacked "Fartiwell and Co." and the "Shitspeare Society." A denunciation of Furnivall as "tipsy" misfired: Furnivall had been a teetotaler for forty years; Swinburne's excessive drinking was well known. The row lumbered on into the 1880s, dragging in such luminaries as Edmund Gosse and Edward Dowden. In the end it faded, but it was the death knell of the New Shakspere Society. Its members, embarrassed by the controversy, quietly moved elsewhere. Its last publication appeared in 1882 and that was that. The protagonists, presumably, were exhausted, although Edmund Gosse, for one, wondered how seriously Furnivall had ever taken it in the first place. Undoubtedly he had acted, Gosse said, "like a man demented," what one had to wonder was how genuine his act had ever been. Certainly, as his devoted biographer John Munro pointed out, "He never understood or attempted to understand the quality of tact. It was a species of dishonesty. What he held to be true, was to be upheld in the face of all opposition, with unfaltering directness and clarity; what he held to be false was denounced with Athanasian intensity and resolution."[20] But Furnivall was a born controversialist, who reveled in trouble for its own sake. It is quite likely that some of his squibs and rejoinders were simply a means of prolonging the fun. It was not a lifestyle, however, that held universal appeal and his language and his tastes offended many. He also had the unfortunate habit of passing on letters that had been considered confidential. Confidentiality may have smacked of hypocrisy to a man who seemed to hide so little; others were less open-minded. The historian Professor Edward Freeman cannot have been alone in turning down membership of the EETS because of its founder. "Put Furnivall in an asylum," he declared, "and I will join . . . at once."

Furnivall died on July 2, 1910. He was eighty-five and still embroiled in the majority of his lifelong passions; the mourners at his funeral represented men and women from every side of his life. Members of his various societies turned up, as did those who supported his rowing club, the Working Men's College or his campaigns to ban Thames-side publicans or to overturn the grim pleasure–denying Sabbatarianism of Victorian Britain. He would be widely mourned, but his greatest monument remains the *New English Dictionary*.

As a former member of University College, Furnivall had been imbued as a young man with the new philology. Kemble and Thorpe, who had sat respectively at the feet of Grimm and Rask, both taught there; T. H. Key, a future secretary, with Furnivall, of the Philological Society, and from 1842 England's first professor of comparative philology, had in turn learned the new scholarship from Friedrich Rosen, who had studied in Germany before joining the College faculty. Furnivall's Greek professor, Henry Malden, was a devotee. There are no records of the day-by-day progress of Furnivall's growing expertise in philology, but in 1847 he joined the Philological Society. If he was a novice at first, he soon became one of its leading members; less scholarly no doubt than some of his academic fellows, but, as one may expect from Furnivall, dedicated, keen to learn, and above all enthusiastic. He read a number of papers, including "On an Unregistered Sense of the Word *Thing* and Its Base *the*" (May 26, 1859) and "An Account of Some Early English Poems" (March 27, 1862). He was not the only young man to join at the this period: among what might be called the "second generation" of members were Henry Benjamin Wheatley, whose *Chronological Notices of the Dictionaries of the English Language*[21] remains one of the best critical assessments available to those studying in this field; Henry Sweet, an editor of the *Epinal Glossary* and a man who would become one of Murray's most valuable cohorts; Alexander Ellis, a mathematician and FRS, among whose achievements was the introducing of James Murray to Melville Bell, and his son, Alexander Graham Bell, inventor of the telephone and a pupil of Murray's; and finally Richard Morris, a schoolmaster and later editor for the EETS, as well as being a pioneer in scholarly dialect studies. Another important lexicographer, Walter Skeat, editor of Oxford's great *Etymological Dictionary*, joined a few years later.

In 1857 Furnivall was one of those deputed to the Unregistered Words Committee; very soon the drive that launched this committee transferred itself to a bigger project still: the assembly of materials for a completely new national dictionary. Furnivall's own account of the *Dictionary*'s inception was published in the London *Morning Post* on February 22, 1910:

In November 1858 [*sic*] Trench wrote us a paper on the duty of making a supplement to the dictionaries of Johnson and Richardson. Herbert Coleridge, a grandson of the poet, came forward and said "I should like to take part in this." The question was who should work with him. I refused absolutely, on which [Thomas] Watts, who was head of the Book Department in the British Museum, reminded me that I was secretary of the Society, and that if I was asked to do a thing it was my duty to do it; so we began. We went on for about a year and a half, and then I said, "People who want a word will first look at Johnson and then at Richardson, and then at ours. Why not amalgamate it and have one dictionary?" I communicated my idea to Trench. He said, "It is a very fine idea if you can carry it out, but I do not think you can." So we went on collecting words. At its meeting on January 7, 1858, the society resolved that, instead of a supplement, a new dictionary of the English language should be prepared under the authority of the Philological Society . . .[22]

Furnivall's dates—he was an old man when he gave the speech from which this story was taken—were somewhat shaky, but it would seem that he was indeed the motive force behind the shift from supplement to dictionary proper. Trench undoubtedly kicked off the idea with his discussion of lexicographical "deficiencies," but it was Furnivall who picked up the ball, as it were, and started running with it. Some scholars have suggested that he can even be credited with developing the idea from scratch, but that is surely to give him excess due. The Unregistered Words Committee may have predated Trench's lectures, but the enthusiasm with which the society transferred its attention from the initial scheme to its successor, leaves no doubt as to Trench's importance.

The meeting of January 7, 1858, at which "the Philological Society's dictionary" was proposed, set up two committees: Trench, Coleridge, and Furnivall, the old collectors of unregistered words, were now reconstituted as the Literary and Historical Committee; Hensleigh Wedgwood (whose *Dictionary of English Etymology* would appear a year later) and Professor Malden would deal with etymology. It was further laid down that in any "questions of doubt as to the form which any article shall assume, the decision of the Literary and Historical Committee shall be final."[23] There were six resolutions in all: other than the decision to make the Supplement into a full-scale dictionary, and the establishment of the two committees, the Society thanked those who had already worked collecting unregistered words and hoped they would transfer their efforts to the new project; deputed Furnivall and Coleridge to start looking for a suitable printer; and announced that "the Philological Society will afford every assistance in its power to enable its Committees to make a Dictionary worthy of the English Language." A fortnight later Furnivall issued a circular calling for more volunteer readers. It was all highly exciting, for no one more than Furnivall and Coleridge who, as C. T. Onions put it in the *OED*'s own historical introduction, "were still in early manhood, had not only all the optimism of youth, but were embarking on an uncharted sea, quite unwitting of the long course which had to be sailed before the farther shore could even come into sight."[24] For all the excitement, the early months show a certain reticence by those involved to make their endeavors public. The plan was announced in August 1858 and, as requested, Furnivall and Coleridge began sounding out potential printers; in November Messrs. Trübner & Co. contracted to take on the job. In 1859 the Literary and Historical Committee published a "Proposal for the Publication of the New English Dictionary by the Philological Society." It laid down a number of rules, notably that the dictionary was to contain "every word" of English literature and that it was to be subject at all times to the "historical principle." It also set out the "rules and directions for collectors" and listed three groups of books, those appearing from 1250 to 1526, from 1526 to 1674, and 1674 to 1858. The year 1526 was that of the first printed English New Testament, that of 1674 was Milton's death. But they also, perhaps coincidentally, represented certain shifts in the formulation of the language. In lexicographical terms the first slightly predates Sir Thomas Elyot's dictionary, the second comes after the major "hard-word" dictionaries, those of Blount and Phillips, had appeared, and the move toward the general works of the eighteenth century was beginning to accelerate.

By the end of 1859 Coleridge had been officially appointed editor, and submitted a brief progress report. He also helped draw up a draft set of rules for what would in 1860 be published as "Canones Lexicographici, or rules to be observed in editing the New English Dictionary . . ." On May 30, 1860 he wrote a letter to Trench, the second edition of whose essays was about to appear, informing him about the latest developments. He says that volunteers, guided by the "Canones," are hard at work, and that Passow's historical principles remain their guiding light. He also adds that the title of an *English* dictionary is "no longer strictly applicable" and announces the involvement of the Hon. G. P. Marsh, of Burlington, Vermont who has offered his services as the society's American secretary. Marsh would enlist his own team, although no details were yet available. Coleridge ran down the current researchers, 147 in total, of whom 89 were actually working as required. The others, whose enthusiasm had not been sustained, were dismissed as "hopeless." Even the 89 were further divided into Class I, some 30 "first-rate" individuals, Class II, 15 "of inferior merit," and Class III who, since they had yet to submit specimens of their work, could not be judged. He regretted the lack of material—"British Museums and Bodleians are not dotted over the land like circulating libraries"—but reckoned that the Society's volunteers were as good as any employed by the Grimms, who had admitted that of their team of 83 readers, only 6 came up to their "beau ideal."[25] He went on to detail progress on the three literary periods and concluded with what would turn out to be a sadly overoptimistic assessment. Coleridge had arranged for a small block of pigeonholes to be built, fifty-four in all, which would hold perhaps 100,000 quotation slips, prepared by readers and ready for sorting as the basis of the dictionary's historical citations. The pigeonholes were half full already, and, said Coleridge, "I confidently expect, unless any unforeseen accident should occur to paralyze our efforts, that in about two years we shall be able to give our first number to the world."

There was just such an accident: Coleridge's own death. Fresh from a drenching rainstorm, he had attended a Philological Society meeting, sitting damply as the hours passed. The chill he caught turned into consumption and he died on April 23, 1861. He was only thirty-one. Hard at work to the very end, his bed was strewn with books and slips; his last words, supposedly, were, "I must begin Sanskrit tomorrow." His final piece of work had been to compile a "basis of comparison," drawn from the specimen material he had already been sent, and covering the letters A–D. The word list he amassed was to serve as a guide to further collecting. Poor Coleridge, he was as little able to calculate the real conclusion of the work he had set in motion as he was capable of foreseeing his own death. Talking in 1911, Sir James Murray noted that the citations gathered for the dictionary now numbered between five and six million—some 1.25 million were incorporated in the finished work; the pigeonholes required totaled 2,500. And like Coleridge, Murray would not live to see the final volume published.

Furnivall announced Coleridge's death to the society on April 25. When the second part of the "basis of comparison" (covering E–L) appeared in September, Furnivall's preface included this tribute: "Since the publication of the First part of this Basis, our proposed Dictionary has received a severe blow by the death of its first Editor, the able and accomplished Herbert Coleridge. In its service he caught the cold that resulted in his death. All through his illness he worked for it whenever leisure and strength allowed; and his last attempt at work . . . was to arrange some of its papers."[26]

With Coleridge dead, the editorship passed to Furnivall. Trench was still nominally part of the Literary Committee, but it was not his primary concern and he was forced to abandon his active involvement when in 1863 he took up his post as archbishop of Dublin. He continued to offer citations, gleaned from his own reading, to the dictionary makers but his influence, while substantial, was effectively over. It was doubtless satisfying for him to see the publication of the *Dictionary*'s first installment, properly known as a fascicle, in 1884, shortly before his death. In any case, it had been one of Coleridge's last wishes that Furnivall, now aged thirty-six, should take up the work and see it through to its conclusion. It was a popular choice: Coleridge's sudden death had indeed been a serious blow, and it required the sort of energy Furnivall found second nature to drive the project forward. As Hensleigh Wedgwood wrote to the new editor, "I am very glad you are able to undertake the dictionary, which must otherwise have gone to pot."[27] On May 23 Furnivall addressed the society for the first time as editor. It was clear that he, unlike his predecessor, appreciated all too well the full challenge of the project before him. More volunteers must be recruited, more reading lists assembled, more books gutted for citations, more materials pigeonholed for subsequent use. Above all a new rank of employee, the subeditor, was to be engaged. These men were to take on the daily grind, the lexicographical donkey work, placing themselves between the readers and the editor. They would deal with the minutiae while their editor, to steal a phrase from P. G. Wodehouse's Stanley Featherstonehough Ukridge, a figure whom in his more positive aspects Furnivall might be said to resemble, concerned himself with "the big, broad, flexible outlook." Yet for all his vision, even Furnivall had no real understanding of the full enormity of what he had undertaken. That it was a big job was never in doubt; just how big was something that neither Furnivall nor any other of the dictionary's pioneers really grasped. Coleridge's fantasy of publication in two years was obviously out of the question, but Furnivall believed that five years' work should certainly bring some results. In the hope of helping the larger scheme, he proposed in March 1862 that a concise version of the dictionary be prepared. This, he was sure, could be finished by 1865 and promised its putative publisher, John Murray, that this would be so. It was, alas, another illusion. One could not create a "concise" edition unless there was a larger one from which to work. The plan was abandoned, and the first *Concise Oxford Dictionary* would not appear until 1911.

It would not be overstating the case to suggest that without Furnivall the *Dictionary* would indeed have "gone to pot." He had too many external interests to act as a fully engaged, day-to-day editor—nor was he especially desirous of acting as one—but it was his energy and dedication which kept others working. He also understood that editors could always be obtained: his task was to amass the material on which they could work. What in other areas of life might have been the negative aspects of his personality—the bullish determination, the refusal to act tactfully, the absolute self-belief that helped persuade waverers of their own duty to join in the great scheme—were invaluable in this crisis. In 1862 he called for new volunteers. It is a characteristically forthright appeal:

> We have set ourselves to form a National Portrait Gallery, not only of the worthies, but of all the members, of the race of English words which is to form the dominant speech of the world. No winged messenger who bears to us the thoughts and aspirations, the weakness and the littleness, of our forefathers; who is to carry ours to our descendants: is to be absent,—
>
> Fling our doors wide! all, all, not one, but all, must enter: for their service let them be honoured; and though the search for them may sometimes seem wearisome, and the labour of the ingathering more irksome still, yet the work is worthy and the aim unselfish. Let us, then, persevere.

Furnivall, as might be imagined, was a constant source of energy and encouragement. He issued lists of books to be read and to be cut up—such volumes were supposed to be secondhand copies, or the worn-out rejects of the circulating libraries, but it was not always so, and more than one reader cheerfully vandalized sixteenth-century black-letter rarities. He encouraged the readers and issued instructions to his subeditors. They were to coddle the reader, to become friends with him, and thus keep him happily at work:

> Lastly, having finished the strict business of an Article, I exhort you . . . to indulge in a little chat with your Reader, noting for him the chief points of interest in the history you have set before him, moralizing shortly on them if you will, and giving any additional facts . . . in short, telling him all you wish him to hear. Being good sense and well put, as of course it will be, Editor and Publisher will be only too glad to find room for it.[28]

For the ten years during which he was in charge, Furnivall issued annual progress reports. They start well enough, but as the decade passes activity gradually runs down until in 1872 the editor is forced to admit that "the progress in the Dictionary has been so slight that no fresh report in detail is needed." Furnivall's energies had not slacked—his foundation in 1864 of the EETS and four years later of the Chaucer Society were both aimed directly at feeding the *Dictionary* with vital texts, and he of course was still assiduously reading and collecting—but those of the readers had evidently diminished. The *Athenaeum*, scenting problems, opined that "the general belief is, that the project will not be carried out."[29] Even more important, it appeared that the Philological Society was no longer fully behind its dictionary. In his presidential address of 1868, Alexander Ellis had implied that "a Society is less fitted to compile a dictionary than to get the materials collected."[30] He also suggested that in the Society's view, Henry Sweet, rather than Furnivall, was their editor of choice. In some ways they were right, but they were also ungrateful. Furnivall lacked the patience and the perfectionism to make the ideal editor of what he termed "the Society's Big Dictionary," but no one could have rivaled his perseverance.

The 1870s saw an even more precipitate decline, with many readers and subeditors simply sending their materials back to Furnivall. In 1879, the worst year of all, some two tons of material were returned. But by then Furnivall was no longer in charge. In October 1871 he had advertised for a new editor. Henry Sweet, the society's choice, turned down the opportunity; Furnivall turned to Henry Nicol, who agreed, but he was too ill and too busy on other projects to take up the task. The problem was unresolved, but it festered on and in 1875 the Reverend George Wheelwright, a subeditor for ten years, demanded that Furnivall act and thus end what he called "the intolerable suspense under which we now groan."[31] Furnivall accepted the urgency of the situation and now focused on a new candidate: James Murray, a teacher at Mill Hill School in north London and a member of the Council of the Philological Society. Murray, it appeared, had unguardedly mentioned to Furnivall that, all things being equal, he might like to have a go at editing the dictionary. That was all that Furnivall required. He began lobbying for Murray's appointment, a campaign that was furthered shortly afterward by a completely chance development. In 1876 the American publishers Harper and Brothers, who wanted to succeed where Worcester had failed, and oust Merriam's editions of Webster from their near-unassailable position as America's best-selling dictionaries, called upon the London publisher Alexander Macmillan to find them a suitable editor. Macmillan's first choice was Henry Sweet: again he rejected the offer of editorial power. But Furnivall had his own plans. Once he heard of the request, he began working "like a busy spider"[32] to enlist James Murray. At the same time he pushed forward another scheme. Macmillan may have envisaged a new dictionary, far shorter than the one the society had been preparing. Furnivall saw their interest as heaven sent. He would offer them his materials, for the right price of course, and they would publish the Philological Society's dictionary. It was so magnificent a project, how could they resist—no publisher could possibly opt for a lesser work when they had Furnivall's brainchild on offer.

Furnivall was in his element, scheming, plotting, reassuring Murray (whom he had taken to addressing as "Mr. Editor"), Macmillan, the society. Inevitably negotiations broke down. Money, the size of the dictionary, the simple presence of Furnivall himself proved too many sticking points. Macmillan backed out. Confident as ever, Furnivall instructed "Mr. Editor" to start preparing specimens of the work to show to new publishers; Walter Skeat, an Anglo-Saxon expert and the secretary of the newly formed English Dialect Society, was sent to Cambridge to sound out the university press while Henry Sweet approached Oxford. When Oxford hesitated Furnivall arrived to address the delegates of the OUP, promising Murray as editor, a team of nearly 400 readers and a guaranteed financial windfall. Would Macmillan have even considered the dictionary, he asked, had the firm not been sure that it would have made money? It was their mistake to drop out, and now Oxford could benefit. In 1878 Murray was officially appointed editor, for an initial payment of £175, and on February 7, 1879, the Philological Society and the Oxford University Press signed a contract to produce the *Dictionary*. Furnivall had one last task: to reclaim all the materials he had sent out for research. By May 1879 that too was complete, although many letters had been taken out of England.

With that job done Furnivall relinquished his role as titular editor. He had held the *Dictionary* together for eighteen years, and while he would never have equaled Murray as an editor, there were few who doubted that his importance to the work was enormous. Emotional energies aside, he contributed some 30,000 quotations to the finished work, making him one of the leading collectors. Nor did he ever stop. Only months before his death he was still scanning the press for new words, cutting and annotating and forwarding his discoveries to Murray. His last concerns were to gather the new terminology of the airplane and the automobile. Not that his interference was always welcome. Murray must have found him a burden at times and on one occasion his frustration burst out when he said of his predecessor, "He speaks of himself as a former 'Editor;' he never edited one word—only supervised the Reading."[33] Elisabeth Murray sums up the contradictions: "No one worked harder than Furnivall to get publication [of the *NED*] started, no one did more to cause difficulties. His impetuosity, tactlessness, and frequent downright rudeness, time and again imperilled the whole project, and yet it was his persistence which saved it."[34] It is the story of his life. Murray's irritation, it should be added, was balanced by the affection that he also felt toward Furnivall. In 1910 Furnivall warned him of his impending death from cancer, noting in a letter that began by discussing Murray's entry for "tallow ketch" that "our Dict. men go gradually, & I am to disappear in 6 months . . . It's a great disappointment, as I wanted to see the Dict. finished before I die. However the completion of work is certain. So that's all right." Murray was deeply shocked, and confided in his daughter Hilda that it made him wonder as to whether he too might not see the great work finished.

His reply to Furnivall, however, lacked any doubts or sentimentality. He must surely have delighted to receive Murray's note: "Would it give you any satisfaction to see the gigantic TAKE in final? Before it is too late?"[35]

Furnivall cannot have been an easy man, nor apparently did he wish to be. But the *NED* owes an enormous debt to his efforts, and it is best to leave the author of the historical introduction that prefaces the edition of 1933, to pass final judgment:

> Although he took no part in the actual editing of the Dictionary in its ultimate form, he never ceased to contribute liberally to its stores, both from the publications of [his] societies and from other sources including his daily morning and evening paper. If the Dictionary at one period quotes the Daily News and at another the Daily Chronicle, it is because Furnivall had changed his paper meanwhile. Through his early organization of the collecting and sub-editing, and his lifelong contributions, the work of Furnivall pervades every page of the Dictionary, and has helped in a great degree to make it what it is. He was fortunate in living long enough to see assured the completion of the work to which he had given so much of his busy life.[36]

James Augustus Henry Murray,[37] the single individual most associated, and rightly so, with the *Dictionary* was the antithesis of the editor he succeeded. He was born near Hawick, Roxburghshire, on February 7, 1837, the son of Thomas Murray, a clothier. A precocious learner, Murray stood out from the farmers' and small tradesmen's sons among whom he was educated. "James Murray will never make a farmer," was the opinion, "he always has a book in his pocket."[38] Aged seventeen he became a master at Hawick Grammar School and three years later head of the town's Subscription Academy. At the same time, as an enthusiastic member of the Hawick Archaeological Society, he developed his interests in antiquities and natural science, as well as in languages, notably the local dialects. He married in 1862, but his wife died two years later, despite the family having left Hawick for the supposedly warmer climate of London, where Murray held a job with the Chartered Bank of India. In 1867 he married again, and with his wife Ada would have six sons (Wilfrid, Oswyn, Ethelwyn, Harold, Ethelbert, Aelfric) and five daughters (Hilda, Elsie, Rosfrith, Gretchen, Gwyneth). In 1870 he joined Mill Hill School as a master and in 1873 graduated B.A. from London University. In 1878 he was appointed editor of the *Dictionary,* a job that soon took over so much of his life that in 1885 he was forced, reluctantly, to abandon his teaching, leaving behind what he saw as a "golden age" at Mill Hill, and move to Oxford. He would spent the remainder of his life totally immersed in his great project.

Although Murray was in so many ways the opposite of Furnivall—devoutly religious (in his Congregationalist creed) where Furnivall rejected God, shy and formal where Furnivall rushed bull-like into any situation—the one characteristic that they share, common to so many of these Victorian scholars, is energy. Aside from his work on the *Dictionary* Murray spent fifteen years as a deacon of his chapel in Oxford; he involved himself in the liberal politics of which he was a supporter; he gardened and collected stamps, he cycled—cutting a wonderful figure with his white beard and Canterbury cap, mounted on his Humber tandem tricycle, sometimes with a child, sometimes with a fellow lexicographer; he took his large family, known toward the end of his life as "the Dic and the Little Dics," on three-week-long seaside holidays to North Wales, Torquay, and elsewhere, where they walked and built elaborate sandcastles. As paterfamilias of "Sunnyside," the family house at 78 Banbury Road in north Oxford, he governed his family as might be expected from a man so imbued with the strict traditions of his faith, but, like some Dickensian cliché—stern but fair, an eye that could pierce and sparkle too—he also seems to have enjoyed a sense of romping fun. He usually rose at five in the morning, family prayers for all followed at eight, and at lunch, the day's main meal, all would assemble for an occasion at which no fidgeting or chattering was allowed. Older children had to grip the table's edge to prevent any deviation. Sundays were as severe as might be imagined: evening prayers, Sunday school, where the elder children taught. They were all made to follow their abstemious father in taking the pledge. Nor was smoking permitted in the house. Yet equally he threw himself wholeheartedly into annual festivals of Easter, Halloween, Christmas. His telling of ghost stories was especially notable.

Religion permeates Murray's life, as in different ways it does that of Johnson and Webster before him. But if Johnson's religion seems, for all his Anglican protestations, as much an expected by-product of his high Toryism as any real devotion, and Webster's faith presents itself as a convenient vehicle for his crabbed fundamentalism, Murray, "a god-fearing teetotal non-smoking family-begetting bizarrely learned teacher,"[39] found in his religion the justification for a life of dedicated work. To learn and to spread that learning was to serve God. And God repaid the favor: Murray seems to have had a working knowledge of virtually every language, whether living or dead, and to learn them he repaired spontaneously to the Bible. There were few languages into which Holy Writ had not been translated, and Murray took advantage of any edition on offer. His granddaughter recounts the story of a visit to Hawick in 1856 by the Hungarian nationalist Louis Kossuth. Among the thirty-eight welcoming banners that bestrode the high street was one that declared in impeccable Magyar *Jöjjö-el a' te orszagod! ("Thy Kingdom come").*[40] For Murray his dictionary was the supreme statement of that devotion, his own cathedral of words, as it were, although unlike those great monuments of faith his work was and never will be concluded. Writing in 1903 to Lord Bryce, Murray declared of his far-from-complete lexicographical labors:

> I think it was God's will. In times of faith, I am sure of it. I look back & see that every step of my life has been as it were imposed upon me—not a thing of choice; and that the whole training of my life with its multifarious & irregular incursions into nearly every science & many arts, seems to have had the express purpose of fitting me to do this Dictionary . . . So I work on with a firm belief (at most times) that I am doing what God has fitted me for, & so made my duty; & a hope that He will strengthen me to see the end of it . . . But I am only an instrument, only the means that He has provided, & there is no credit due to me, except that of trying to do my duty; Deo soli gloria.[41]

As far as philology was concerned Murray was an autodidact. He had not attended university—and in any case only University College would have been much use even had he done so—but his fascination with the dialects of lowland Scotland set him on a path from which he never deviated. Murray perceived that language, unlike the nations that used it, was not tied to physical, political boundaries. The people of Hawick, just north of the border, spoke in the same way as did those to the south of that linguistically arbitrary line. Language was a whole thing, a continuum, and should be studied as such. He became an amateur of phonetics, in which guise he attended Melville Bell's lectures on "Visible Speech," a system "that uses stylised depictions of tongue and lip positions and looks very fearsome . . . but, being rational and consistent, it works."[42] He taught Bell's son, Alexander Graham, the rudiments of electricity, and Bell would one day call him "the grandfather of the telephone."

Murray came to philology very much as a disciple of Henry Sweet, widely regarded as the leading comparative philologist of his generation. Sweet, who would come to be the model for Shaw's Henry Higgins, of *Pygmalion* and latterly *My Fair Lady* fame, was born in London, the son of a barrister, on September 15, 1845. His early childhood was bedeviled with fits and shortsightedness, although both disappeared. After attending King's College, London he went, in 1864, to Heidelberg University in Germany, where he came face-to-face with the new philology, acquainting himself particularly with the works of Rasmus Rask. He entered Balliol College, Oxford in 1869, and while his linguistic abilities impressed Professor Max Müller, who in time would come to be one of the *Dictionary*'s greatest allies, his fourth-class degree in classics did not. There would be no academic job. By 1871 he was a member of the Philological Society, and like Murray had become interested in Bell's Visible Speech. The immediate result of this was Sweet's *Handbook of Phonetics* (1877). A year earlier he had published his *Anglo-Saxon Reader,* a landmark in Anglo-Saxon studies; after this came the *Elementarbuch des gesprochenes Englisch* (Germany 1885, England 1890) which, as the *DNB* says, "taught phonetics to Europe."[43]

In an age when every outstanding scholar seemed to be "the father" of something, Sweet's metaphorical paternity is that of phonetics. As a sad reflection, no doubt, of the respect (or lack of it) accorded to this still relatively nascent subject, Sweet, for all his impressive learning, held no official academic position until 1901 when Oxford created a readership in phonetics for him to occupy. He had applied for a variety of chairs, but only one, at Liverpool, had been offered, and circumstances forced him to reject the position. The greatest blow fell when he was rejected, although backed by nearly all of his European peers, in his application to succeed Max Müller as doyen of comparative philology. This plunged Sweet, never a happy man, into a state of self-destructive bitterness. Furnivall was argumentative, but for him rows were as much a pleasure as a pain. For Sweet his feuding and estrangements amounted to what in retrospect looks like a severe case of paranoia. As C. T. Onions kindly puts it, "Sweet was prone to magnify chance sayings and doings out of all proportion to their significance."[44] But he was not wholly to blame. "A more general spirit of magnanimity towards a great worker and thinker would have made his position easier." This was not to be. As Elisabeth Murray notes, quoting a correspondent's plaint to Murray, "He was often, it was said, 'splendidly right, but nobody could be more deplorably and pigheadedly wrong' and his rudeness was at times colossal."[45] Murray himself, while sympathizing, and hoping that some form of academic recognition would perhaps rid Sweet of his delusions, accepted that many people would prefer that such a job not be found in Oxford, where people "fear troublesome collisions may occur, through his faculty of running his head against stone walls."[46] The readership was, at best, a sort of consolation prize, and Sweet knew it. He died on April 30, 1912. He left no children.

Ironically, in rejecting one of the few offers he did receive, Sweet had turned down what could have been the greatest prize of all: the editorship of the *Dictionary.* It was his refusal, followed by the physical weakness of Furnivall's candidate Henry Nicol, that brought James Murray into the frame. When he signed a contract to undertake the work in 1879, Murray's first task was to gather in all the material that had been spread about Britain and indeed the world during the eighteen years of Furnivall's stewardship. The papers, books, and slips poured back, and it seems that many readers and subeditors were delighted to be rid of what, however keenly they had undertaken it, had now become an appalling burden. It was not the easiest of tasks—the work had been dispersed far and wide and it took Furnivall, who supervised it as his last job as editor, a good deal of research. H, for instance, was in Florence; one sack of quotations came back with a dead rat entombed amid the slips, another carried a live mouse; a broken hamper, abandoned in a Harrow vicarage, came back with I; fragments of "Pa" turned up in an Irish stable, although most of the material had been used for lighting fires; one subeditor wrote in apologetically, promising "to search for the rest [of his letter], which had been disposed by his wife in a lumber-room."[47]

Murray looked at what he had accumulated and sensibly and swiftly cut his losses. For the project to succeed it needed to be started afresh. Once again there was an appeal for readers, once again materials were sent out to those who volunteered. As a base from which to operate Murray had built a shed in the back garden of his house in Mill Hill. It was jokingly named the "Scriptorium," a place fittingly defined in Murray's own dictionary as "a writing-room; spec. the room in a religious house set apart for the copying of manuscripts." The family knew it as "the Scrippy." The inspiration for this shed was, like much else, Furnivall's, and like much else it was adopted less to emulate him than in the hope of avoiding his errors. Just as Furnivall's keen but slapdash system had in the end led to the restarting of the whole project, the chaos that Murray had seen at Furnivall's home, where every room seemed to be sinking beneath the weight of ever-accumulating dictionary material, made it clear that his own house, destined to play host to a far larger project, must not be similarly swamped. Thus the advent of the Scriptorium, a corrugated iron shed, measuring some thirty feet by fifteen, that with its gray walls and brown roof looked vaguely like a nonconformist chapel, although one visitor compared it to "a tool house, a washhouse or a stable."[48] Whatever the resemblance, it is unlikely that those readers who noted Murray's signing of each fascicle's introduction "The Scriptorium, Oxford" realized that for all its image of a medieval, monkish retreat, the actual Scriptorium was an ugly, damp outhouse, carefully dug into a deep trench, so as not to disturb the aesthetic sensibilities of Murray's next-door neighbor.

Aesthetics aside, it was here that Murray sat with his subeditors, just as had Johnson with his amanuenses in Gough Square. Surrounded by 1,029 pigeonholes, far more than Coleridge's original 54, all stuffed with citations, the sub-editors sorted, while Murray, seated on a stool that set him a foot higher than his fellow workers (Johnson before him had surveyed the work from on high), made his own invaluable contributions to the work. His was the responsibility for defining, indicating pronunciation (based on his own system, although this would be replaced in the second edition by the International Phonetic Alphabet), and using the millions of citations to prepare the historical illustrations of usage that are still the dictionary's greatest achievement. Soon, like so many aspects of the project, the volume of slips outgrew Murray's anticipated needs, and the pigeonholes were rebuilt as shelves. They surround the editor in many of the photographs that illustrate Elisabeth Murray's biography, a womb of intellectual effort, cradling the embryonic dictionary in row after row of tightly packed literary references. As year followed year, the *Dictionary* became, as one correspondent suggested to its editor, "the largest single engine of research working anywhere in the world."[49]

Anyone who has used the *Dictionary,* and then looks at the suggestions that form the basis of Dean Trench's inspirational essay, can see that its makers were generally loyal to his vision. Murray seems to have accepted above all the necessity for comprehensiveness. There is no doubt that the language he used at home, and would have expected from his family and friends, was free of what might be seen as coarseness. But as a professional, and as the creator-in-chief of what was intended to be the world's finest dictionary of the English language, he resisted, unlike Webster, the temptation to impose on others the standards emanating from his own beliefs. Alongside the classics of literature one can find citations from some of the earliest "slang dictionaries"—Copland, Awdeley, Harman—as well as much of the bawdy terminology that occurs in such playwrights as Dekker and Middleton. Certain words, many of which still possess sufficient magic to frighten those who confuse an assemblage of vowels and consonants with the objects or acts that they describe, are nonetheless absent. Murray was a pragmatist as well as a professional, and the middle-class taboos of Victorian (and later) England were observed. Fortunately his successors have been less constrained and, as Anthony Burgess remarks, "One can imagine Murray in heaven nodding his beard in approval at the scholarly treatment of 'fuck' and 'cunt.' "[50] That said, Murray's successor Robert Burchfield recalls finding "against all expectations, that a few members of staff had no stomach for the crudities of sexual and scatological vocabulary. I had assumed from the beginning that *Homo lexicographicus* was a chalcenterous species of mankind, that is, a person with bowels of brass . . . But when the time came for the verification in the Bodleian Library of some of the richer uses of the words *cunt* and *fuck* I was told by the library research assistant . . . that she had had 'quite enough of the kind of filth found in Partridge and other dictionaries of slang.' "[51] Burchfield ended up finding the references himself.

Taboo terms aside, and notwithstanding Trench's strictures, Murray also chose to include a far more extensive technical and scientific vocabulary than had any previous compiler—even if he chose to abandon Coleridge's plan for a separate technical section. Burgess also points out the extent to which Murray's attention to the way the dictionary looks—its basic typography, which helps render sometimes complex information satisfyingly clear, hugely enhances the ease of its use. While the second edition, set on and destined for access by computer, reset the basic material (although it maintains Murray's overall style), one can still use the original edition, and certainly that which appeared in 1933, without any difficulty. It is unlikely that many people consult the *OED* for the simple purpose of looking up a word's meaning, there are smaller dictionaries for that, but were they to do so, they would find, irrespective of edition, that Murray's original design is as easy to use as ever.

Murray's readers were a far cry from Johnson's impoverished band of Grub Street irregulars. They came from a wide circle of enthusiasts, among whom must be numbered the editor's own children, who were initially paid 6d a week for half an hour's work a day sorting slips. The payment gradually increased with age and experience. The dictionary provided their pocket money; it also gave them remarkably precocious vocabularies. It was tedious work, and the children were always happiest when one of Furnivall's parcels, crammed with press clippings, arrived. Reading the stories, however truncated, that surrounded the citations was much more fun than wading through drier realms of literature. Other readers and assistants are better known. The young J. R. R. Tolkien, whose own expertise in Anglo-Saxon stands firmly behind his great creation "Middle Earth," was one; Leslie Stephen, future editor of the *DNB* and father of the arch-Bloomsberries Virginia and Vanessa Stephen was another, as were the novelist Charlotte M. Yonge, who also worked as a subeditor and, somewhat later, the aphorist Logan Pearsall Smith who read proofs. Other well-known figures included Flinders Petrie, W. M. Rosetti, and Owen Seaman. G. L. Apperson, whose magnum opus is his collection of *English Proverbs* (1929), was an important contributor, as he was to a simultaneous project, Farmer and Henley's seven-volume *Dictionary of Slang*. Among the most prolific, other than Furnivall, were the otherwise unsung William Douglas, who provided an astounding 136,000 citations, Dr. T. N. Brushfield (50,000), T. Henderson (48,000) and Rev. J. Pierson (of America) (46,000). Only Marghanita

Laski, who provided an unrivaled 250,000 citations for the *Supplements* of 1972–86, surpassed them.

Reading the list printed in Volume One of the finished dictionary, one must assume that most were dedicated but unexceptionable figures. Like the society from which their work drew its original impetus, there are many clergymen; unlike the society's membership list, there are also many women. Miss Jennet Humphreys of Cricklewood supplied 18,700 quotes, Miss E. F. Burton of Carlisle 11,400, and the Misses Edith and E. Peronnnet Thompson 15,000 between them. There are many more. Some, however, were far from ordinary, however bland their listing. One of the most assiduous readers was James Platt, Jr. who died on February 10, 1910, aged forty-nine. He had first come to Murray's attention in 1882, when he read a paper to the Philological Society in which he attacked Professor Toller's revision of Joseph Bosworth's *Anglo-Saxon Dictionary* for the OUP. Murray backed young Platt, he too had disliked the work, and had advised the Press against publication, but many members saw the critique as brash and unseemly; a motion was passed deploring his lèse-majesté and his failure to observe the rules of literary good manners. Platt was shattered. He abandoned his studies in Anglo-Saxon and retreated from view.

Then, in 1899, he reemerged, writing in the *Athenaeum* his opinion on the etymology of a word due to be included in the *NED*. Murray was impressed and urged Platt, who was more than happy to do so, to involve himself fully in the *Dictionary*. He was especially good when it came to etymologies that required a knowledge of the lesser known, more obscure languages of Asia, Africa, or the Americas. But this invaluable resource was painfully shy. A linguistic polymath he was far happier with words on paper, of whatever origin, than the simplest English sentence in his mouth. He was described as a man who "had learnt a hundred languages and forgotten his own." Shyness notwithstanding, Platt was a hands-on researcher who trawled London's rookeries and flashhouses for evidence of linguistic exotica, picking up foreigners on the street and swapping his services as a guide or interpreter for a smattering of their own linguistic expertise. When Platt died, still a relatively young man, in 1910, Murray, many years his senior, bemoaned that "I know no one, and cannot hope ever to find any one . . . to whom I can send any strange alien word and say 'What language can this belong to' with a very sure and well-founded expectation that in a day or two there will come an illuminating answer."[52]

Less charming, but equally competent, was another reader, one Dr. W. C. Minor, a man on whose services the nascent *Dictionary* was hugely dependent. Bad health forced him to quit the project in 1902, but he had already amassed tens of thousands of quotations. In 1897, when the great "Dictionary Dinner" was held to honor Murray and his senior coworkers, Minor was duly invited: bad health, he explained, kept him from attending. Similarly, when Murray invited him to spend a few days as his guest in Banbury Road, Minor pleaded his ailments. Instead, he invited Murray to visit him, at an address in Berkshire. This Murray did, alighting at Crowthorne Station, where he found a liveried servant and a smart brougham awaiting him.

> At the end of a two-mile drive through the country the horses turned into the courtyard of a large brick building of forbidding appearance. A little puzzled, James followed a servant up a gloomy staircase and along corridors to a well-furnished office in which an official looking man was seated at the desk. James advanced to greet Dr Minor, but the official hastened to say that he was not Dr Minor, but the Governor of Broadmoor Criminal Lunatic Asylum. Dr Minor, he explained, was an inmate.[53]

Minor, it turned out, was a rich American, who had fought for the North in the Civil War as an army surgeon. During his service he had been ordered to brand a deserter, a task that had deeply upset him. His mental state was further assailed after an attack of sunstroke and he began believing, exhibiting a degree of paranoia that Henry Sweet might have admired, that a band of otherwise anonymous Irishmen were pursuing him, seeking revenge for the branding. He entered an asylum, from which he was discharged, ostensibly cured. He left America for London, where he took up introductions to various figures, including the art critic John Ruskin. Unfortunately it soon became tragically clear that Minor was far from cured. His fantasies had begun to return and, sensibly, he reported his fears to a police station. But his manner there, and the way he described his problem, did not impress the desk sergeant. He was sent on his way. His dismissal would prove a mistake. Minor was returning to his lodgings in Lambeth, on the night of February 17, 1872, when he became convinced that he was being followed. He turned round, saw a man close behind and promptly shot him dead. Far from being some Irish hitman, hell-bent on revenge, his victim was an otherwise blameless night stoker at the nearby Lion Brewery. There had been no witnesses, but Minor returned to the police, this time to give himself up. He was committed to Broadmoor for life, and as a rich man enjoyed the relative comforts of a private room and the facility to maintain an expanding collection of books for which he was allowed to send out.

Some years later he opened one of these books and discovered in it a copy of Murray's leaflet calling for volunteer readers. Without revealing his circumstances Minor contacted Murray and began work, mainly offering obscure words that he had culled from his own library. It was thus that Murray visited him. More visits followed, although the meetings were never easy. Murray explained to his colleague William Craigie, who would in time become the *Dictionary*'s third editor, that "In his lonely and sad position he requires a great deal of nursing, encouraging and coaxing and I have had to go from time to time to see him . . . it has been no light part of my unknown & unrecognized duties to keep him interested."[54] The relationship did continue and in 1905 Minor helped Murray out with some extra expenses that arose on a trip to South Africa. When in 1910 an American visitor to the Scriptorium was told Minor's story, a campaign was begun to obtain his release. This was eventually granted by the Home Secretary, Winston Churchill, and Murray and his wife, Ada, went to Broadmoor to say good-bye. Minor was able to return to America, albeit to another asylum. There he died in 1921.

"The study of language may beget madness," declared Anthony Burgess,[55] and while he was referring to Murray's own sometimes monomaniacal preoccupation with his *Dictionary,* the phrase could as well be enlisted when considering another reader whose reliability as a scholar was balanced by his instability as a human being. Dr. Fitzedward Hall, whose name even sounds like an Oxford College, was born in Troy, New York on March 21, 1825. He was educated as a civil engineer and was poised to enter Harvard in 1846 when he was sent by his family to track down one of his four brothers, who had run off to Calcutta, India. His ship arrived off the coast in September, and was promptly wrecked at the mouth of the Ganges. Hall survived the wreck and to pass the time before he could return to America began taking lessons in Sanskrit and Hindi. So fascinated did he become that he decided to remain, and spent the next three years on his studies. By 1853 he was sufficiently competent to be appointed professor of Sanskrit at the Government College, Benares. Further teaching jobs followed before in 1857 he joined the British side against the Indian Mutineers and fought for nine months as a rifleman. He visited Europe in 1860, being awarded a D.C.L. from Oxford, and finally quit India for good two years later. He returned to London to take up the posts of professor of Sanskrit at King's College, London and librarian of the India Office. By now he was a widely acknowledged expert not merely in Sanskrit and Hindi, but in English language and literature, in which he had been interested from his earliest years in America. He edited a number of texts for the EETS before leaving London in 1869 and moving to Marlesford, Suffolk.

The circumstances that occasioned this sudden move are still mysterious. It appears that in 1869 Hall had fallen out badly with Professor Theodor Goldstücker (1821–72), a fellow specialist in Sanskrit and Hindi and, like Hall, a member of the Philological Society. Coincidentally Goldstücker was also the one-time teacher of A. C. Burnell, who with Colonel, later Sir Henry Yule, cowrote *Hobson-Jobson* (1886), the unsurpassed lexicon of Anglo-Indian colloquialisms. Quite what abstruse controversy set the two at each other's throat is unknown, but the result was that Hall was suspended from the society, lost his job at the India Office, where Goldstücker was also employed, and took a form of voluntary exile in the countryside. At the same time it was rumored that not only was he a hopeless drunkard but he also worked as a foreign spy. Another man might have laughed, Hall did not. The hothouse atmosphere of nineteenth-century philology was all too prone to such arguments, although Hall seems, as his subsequent behavior bears out, to have taken such slights more personally than most. Burgess describes the philologists as a "gang" (as, coincidentally, did the royalist writer John Rowland [1606–60] in 1658), and for whatever reason, they turned on the hapless Fitzedward Hall. Nor was he much happier in his rural fastness. Driven further and further into his delusions, he announced that his marriage had failed, thanks to the machinations of a local clergyman. He grew increasingly antagonistic toward his neighbors, and indeed to Britons as a race, claiming that all his problems stemmed from the "fiendish hatred" that they had toward America. The locals were no more amicable than had been the London academics, and in 1906 Murray received a lengthy missive from the former rector of Hall's local parish, denouncing the latter as an immoral man and a spurious academic. The first may or may not have been true, as far as Murray was concerned, the second was simply nonsense. The two men communicated daily for twenty years and on his preface to volume I of the *Dictionary* Murray wrote gratefully of Hall's contribution, calling it "the most generous literary assistance which the annals of literature can show."[56] Hall also contributed 2,200 words and phrases to Joseph Wright's *English Dialect Dictionary* and prepared so much material for the *NED* that following his death on February 1, 1901, Murray sent a team of 100 volunteers to comb his library and transcribe all the quotations he had left marked ready for those letters still to be completed. The depth of Murray's regard for Hall is perhaps best seen in a letter he sent when Hall was ill: rather than sign it, as was normal, "yours truly," he wrote "yours very affectionately." For a man who could hardly bear to pronounce a name without its full and formal title, this was indeed an emotional unburdening.

Whether pursued by eccentrics, paranoids, or just plain loyal readers and subeditors, the work of preparing the *Dictionary* continued from year to year. Burdened by the seemingly unending task, Murray was persuaded to take on a number of assistant editors: Henry Bradley joined in 1888, William Craigie in

1901, and Charles Onions, who had joined the staff in 1895, became the third assistant editor in 1914. Murray never especially liked the new situation, but he appreciated, however reluctantly, that it was necessary. Even with the four men working independently (Bradley took over L, M, S–Sh, St, and W–We and was in the end responsible for 4,590 of the *NED*'s 15,487 pages—his 23-page treatment of *set* remains his lexicographical *chef d'oeuvre;* Craigie was responsible for N, Q, R–Re, Re–Ry, Si–Sq, U, V, Wo–Wy, and Onions for Su–Sz, Wh–Wo, X, Y, Z), it would still take many years before the final volume appeared.

Henry Bradley (1845–1923) was born in Manchester, the son of a farmer turned textile maker. After an education at Chesterfield Grammar School Bradley began work as a clerk for a cutlery firm in Sheffield, and in his spare time pursued a variety of hobbies, among which was the study of languages. He remained a clerk for the next twenty years, during which time he mastered a number of languages—European, classical, and even Hebrew. Just as Murray had done twenty years earlier, Bradley moved to London, in 1884, in the hope of finding a climate better suited to his wife Eleanor's poor health. Here he began working as a freelance writer, and it was a piece in the *Athenaeum* on the first volume of the *NED* that alerted Murray to his capabilities. He was recruited in 1889 as a coeditor and succeeded Murray as editor-in-chief on the latter's death in 1915. He moved to Oxford, which awarded him an honorary degree, and although he continued to write when requested, his life became as inextricably dedicated to the *Dictionary* as had that of his predecessor. Outside the *Dictionary* he is best known for his work on English place names. For all his expertise, Bradley's appointment was not something that James Murray particularly welcomed. Apart from anything else, he was bedeviled by the constant presence of Furnivall, urging that any coeditor be paid £400 a year, a sum far greater than the dictionary's endlessly stretched budget could easily support. But the real problem was one of ego. Even so saintly a figure as Murray is painted found the diminution of absolute control hard to take. This was his project, he wanted to keep it that way. But, as Murray well knew, were some help not recruited the odds were that it would soon be nobody's project. The university would simply withdraw such support as it offered if production did not accelerate. Fortunately Bradley appreciated Murray's feelings. He stressed that whatever his title, there should be no idea of equality: Murray was *the* editor, and that was how it should be. Bradley died, suddenly, in May 1923, but by then two more coeditors had been taken on, the first of which appointments, it transpired, had been presented to Murray as a virtual *fait accompli.* It cannot have improved his *amour-propre* to find that this new man, William Craigie, who had been asked to join the project by the university (whose delegates had failed to inform Murray until the deal was sealed), was, unlike himself, yet another Oxford man. Fortunately he had other charms: his origins and his undoubted brilliance as a lexicographer.

Like his employer, Craigie (1867–1957) was a lowlander, the son of a jobbing gardener from Dundee. Even as a schoolboy he began learning phonetics, and after a successful career at St. Andrews University went, as a scholar, to Oxford, where he was enrolled first at Balliol and latterly at Oriel College. He took a first in classics and traveled to Copenhagen, where he studied Icelandic. Back home, he began working as assistant to the professor of Latin at St. Andrews, and published a number of books, including a study of Robert Burns and translations from Icelandic folktales which were used by Andrew Lang in his *Fairy Books*. His fascination with the northern languages never abated, and he and his wife invariably traveled in Scandinavia for their holidays, augmenting his linguistic knowledge as they went. He was especially revered in Iceland, where his work was seen as more than equal to that of any local scholar. In 1897 he was invited to join the *Dictionary* staff and began work as a coeditor four years later. He remained in Oxford until 1925, and worked on both the *Dictionary* and the supplement, of which he wrote some 50 percent. He was knighted for these labors in 1925. At the same time he was appointed to a number of academic posts, notably that of professor of Anglo-Saxon in 1916. Although he remained one of the *Dictionary's* editors, Craigie moved in 1925 to Chicago, where he had been appointed professor of English, and began work on what would become the *Oxford Dictionary of American English*. He stayed until 1936, then returned to England. For the rest of his life he concentrated on preparing his own *Dictionary of the Older Scottish Tongue*. He had reached the letter I in 1955, at which time age (he was eighty-seven) forced him to abdicate the task. Craigie was generally recognized as the outstanding dictionary maker of his era, with an especial interest in Old Norse and Anglo-Saxon studies on both sides of the Atlantic. He desired, as he put it, to "complete the record of English" by creating a number of "period dictionaries" (a term coined by L. C. Wharton, then secretary of the Philological Society), of which his own works were but a part. Addressing the Philological Society he noted that "each definite period of the language has its own characteristics, which can only be appreciated when it is studied by itself, and which are necessarily obscured when it merely comes in as one link in the long chain of the language as a whole."[57] He suggested three such dictionaries: Old English, Middle English (1175–1500), and Tudor and Stuart English (1500–1675).

The last of the coeditors, and in time the fourth editor of the *NED* was Charles Onions (1873–1965). Born and educated in Birmingham, he had obtained an external degree from University College, London, supplier of so much inspiration to the *Dictionary* already. He joined the staff in 1895, and in 1914 was made a coeditor. This elevation presumably halted the Murray children's teasing chants of "Charlie is my darling" which had hitherto accompanied their meetings. He worked on various letters and helped Craigie with the supplement. At the same time as assisting Murray, he wrote widely on grammar, whether English or French. His major work is the *Oxford Dictionary of English Etymology,* which appeared posthumously in 1966 and replaced Walter Skeat's earlier etymological work. He was also director of the EETS from 1945 to 1957 and edited the first edition of the *Shorter Oxford English Dictionary* (1933). The EETS/*OED* link was maintained when in 1956 Robert Burchfield, soon to be appointed editor of the four *Supplements* (1972–86), became the journal's editorial and subscriptions secretary.

Murray seems to have tolerated rather than welcomed his assistants, and Elisabeth Murray quotes a number of notes and letters which make it clear that he often forgot that they were, if only nominally, equals, and he was not a stern teacher faced with errant pupils. His character made intimacy impossible, although Bradley and Craigie both spent many evenings with their chief, mulling over the whys and wherefores of some abstruse piece of etymology. The situation was not helped by Furnivall, who took a certain impish delight in causing trouble between Murray and his senior employees. He was particularly keen on setting Bradley against Murray by alleging that the latter failed to treat him with sufficient respect and gave him insufficient credit for his work. Fortunately Bradley refused to take this bait. Nor was Murray always at one with Craigie, whose scholarship was at times less rigorous and who, in his chief's opinions, tended to squander the *Dictionary's* precious space on unnecessary material. Murray's rebukes could be surprisingly embittered: one ten-page missive virtually accuses Craigie of treachery, adding that "no part of my work [is] so onerous and unpleasant to me as that of looking through your copy."[58] Yet in the end these were internal matters: few observers outside the closed world of the Scriptorium, or the Old Ashmolean building (where Bradley ran his team), had any illusions as to who was the personification of the *Dictionary.* Murray *was* the *NED,* and as volume followed volume, both his place of work and his own self became objects of scholarly pilgrimage.

If the sheer internal logistics of preparing the *Dictionary* offered their own problems, then the main external factor, that of ensuring a steady flow of finances, was equally problematic. The history of earlier dictionary makers had traditionally included a degree of penuriousness, Johnson scrimping along on his fifteen hundred guineas, Noah Webster making his vain appeals to the worthies of New England, but the financing of the *NED* takes one into a new world. It was the first English dictionary to be produced, for all Murray's preeminence, by a professional team, and for the first time the business side of things had to be taken properly into account. Elisabeth Murray charts the ups and (mainly) downs as her grandfather struggled to find the finances that would keep the *Dictionary* in production. Reporting on the great "Dictionary Dinner" of 1897, a *Times* leader characterized the whole enterprise as "the greatest effort probably which any university, it may be any printing press, has taken in hand since the invention of printing . . . It will not be the least of the glories of the University of Oxford to have completed this gigantic task." Glory it might be, and the vice chancellor's dinner duly honored Murray and his team, but it had taken Oxford some time to appreciate the fact. In fairness, neither its editor nor its publishers really appreciated the extent of the task before them when they signed their contract in 1879. Neither party knew how long the book would be, nor how many years it would be in the making. Proper planning was rendered even more nebulous by Oxford's difficulties in deciding quite how the work should be seen: like many publishers then and now the OUP had a dual-track policy: there were scholarly works and there were commercial ones. The question was, which exactly was the *NED?* The problem was never really solved. Taken day by day, that attitude fluctuated: when the university saw it as business, its delegates fought to keep costs down; when it saw it as a scholarly work its members sought to interfere in the creative process, notably in 1883 when the Master of Balliol, Benjamin Jowett, seemed keen to replace Murray and edit the work himself.

Murray's own interest was in the work and only the work—contractual details could be worked out later. For a writer this was idealism, for a publisher naïveté to be exploited. As the years went by Murray found himself tied to an agreement that worked very much in the university's favor. The situation was not helped by Murray's sense of intellectual and social inferiority in the face of the Oxonians. A self-educated provincial, he deferred to them as authority figures; the university men seem to have found this a perfectly satisfactory state of affairs. His total fee was to be £9,000, of which an initial £2,100 was paid in advance. Murray envisaged around thirteen to fourteen more years working on nothing but the *NED:* he was supposed to do this, and keep himself and his family, on the remaining £6,900. In the event neither he nor his family ever gained a single penny from the work, over and above the salary he received. As for the Philological Society, its members agreed on a percentage of the profits; this was given up in 1900 when, rather shortsightedly, they relinquished all rights in the work in return for an annual fee of £50, which would help in the publication of their annual *Transactions*. For the everyday details, readers are once more commended to Ms. Murray; suffice it to say that the attitude of the university and its press, which for many years varied between apparent indifference and obsessively penny-pinching scrutiny, cannot have lightened the fearsome burden of compilation. The difficulties affected Murray's health—both mental and physical—and the situation was not helped by Furnivall, who managed to combine a proclaimed reverence for the delegates of the OUP with a posture that, if only for Murray's benefit, cast them as grasping and hostile. As Murray wrote to the aristocratic businessman Henry Hucks Gibbs, Baron Aldenham,

> I have really, in my anxiety to press on & complete the preliminary work, spent far more than I ought upon it: partly also goaded to it by Mr Furnivall, who has continually said "You must get this, & you must do that, & you must pay somebody to do the other thing," and whose possessing idea seemed to be the fear that I should make money out of the work! I am not a capitalist, but a poor man, and have only saved a few hundred pounds in anticipation of the time when I should have to spend some on the further education & starting in life of my boys, by annual savings to which the Dictionary put a stop . . . I have had to say rather bitterly: "I took up the Dictionary as a student, asking only to be repaid the income I sacrificed in its behalf, and to be furnished with the necessary assistance, and I find myself . . . with an incessant struggle to make ends meet, & failing in the struggle" . . . it is certain that we have all underestimated the cost to somebody . . . and that it is I on whom the consequences fall, & whom they threaten to crush.[59]

Hucks Gibbs sympathized with Murray, and whoever takes the credit for inspiring the *Dictionary* as a piece of scholarship, it is he who should receive it for maintaining the book as a business proposition. He saw Murray's contract, with its limits as to the size both of the *Dictionary* and of his fee, as quite unfair. He lent Murray money, which was used to pay the staff and for other running costs. Later, after Murray moved to Oxford, there was launched the Murray Indemnity Appeal, which brought in some extra funds, and Walter Skeat lent Murray £1,500. Thus the *Dictionary*'s funding limped along. Not until the late 1890s, thanks to a combination of circumstances—a regular flow of production, a new and much more sympathetic vice chancellor, the appointment of Bradley and Craigie as assistant editors—did things improve. Then, at last, it seemed to both parties that this was a project which for all its problems, had finally appeared and, having been seen to be as good as its editor had always promised, would continue to do so.

The first installment or fascicle of the *New English Dictionary* was published on February 1, 1884. It covered the words from A to "Ant." It had been just under five years in the making. The research was much further advanced, but obviously production had to be stepped up. Murray did his sums and announced that with the right quantity and quality of assistants, he should be looking at the last volume in eleven years. In the event it would take another forty-four. The completed work ran to ten volumes, incorporating 15,487 pages, of which 7,207, marginally less than half, had been edited by Murray himself: the letters A–D, H–K, O, P, and T. The first completed copies were sent to King George V and President Coolidge of America. The sixth volume had been funded by the Worshipful Company of Goldsmiths and on June 6, 1928 the company held a gala dinner at Goldsmith's Hall, at which the prime minister, Stanley Baldwin, spoke in glowing terms of the achievement. By then, unsurprisingly, the language had, as ever, moved on and expanded. A new edition was published in 1933. It included a supplement, which aimed to make good the inevitable gaps in the word list that had developed over the long period of editing. Its patchy construction reflected its role as what might be termed an "afterthought." Robert Burchfield, editor of the four subsequent supplements, dismisses it as "a riffraff assemblage of casual terms, in no way worthy of the magnificent monument to which it formed an extension."[60] But if professionals might carp, the monument was what mattered. Now retitled the *Oxford English Dictionary,* it was repaginated in twelve volumes, plus the supplement.

James Murray died in his Oxford home on July 26, 1915. His dictionary would not be completed for another thirteen years, but he must have felt satisfied. He had earned his share, however belatedly, of temporal honors—a knighthood in 1908, many honorary degrees, including those from Oxford and Cambridge, a membership of the British Academy—but above all, he could rest assured that he had carried out his earliest desire: to worship his God through the excellence of his work.

As for the *Dictionary,* it was already an institution. It was not the first dictionary "on historical principles" to be proposed, but it was the first to emerge from the presses. Unlike Johnson or Webster, "Murray," as it was occasionally known, was less reviewed than respected. Opening his Romanes Lecture of 1900, Murray had joked how the term "dictionary" had for many years been generally synonymous with Johnson's *Dictionary.* Now, thanks to his own efforts, there was a new synonym. Cited in Parliament and in court, referred to respectfully in the press, purchased by an increasingly enthusiastic public (albeit in smaller numbers than might have been hoped) *The Dictionary* had another editor: James Murray.

Eighty years on, with a second edition in both print and on CD-ROM, and with a third already in preparation, the *OED* remains the world's greatest repository of the English language. It is not perfect: the work of Jürgen Schäfer in finding earlier "first use" dates is being continually emulated. Nor would some scholars agree that its methodology or its content represent the ideal in dictionary making. Some areas, notably the eighteenth century, are underresearched, and the whole tone is overwhelmingly Anglocentric, hardly surprising in a work that is, in its own way, one more triumph of Britain's imperial moment. It is also, as many have opined, an unashamedly élitist document, an incredibly sophisticated guide for those who wish to read the great body of English literature, from the early twelfth century onward. However, as John Simpson, its current coeditor, has said, "Nowadays we have the Dictionary itself against which to make comparisons. The original readers were working in a vacuum, and the editors could only rely . . . on the materials presented to them by their readers."[61] Hindsight is as efficacious in assessing this dictionary as it is any other. In the end, however, it remains the great climax of lexicographical effort, setting a pattern for virtually any subsequent historical dictionary. The computerized dictionaries that lie in the future will doubtless cover wider ground, calling upon the resources of their huge corpuses to pluck ad hoc materials for each and every type and size of work proposed from the electronic pigeonholes of their gigabyte-sized scriptoria. They will also offer a range of cross-referencing, in its most literal sense, that has never before been available. But the efforts of what Philip Howard has termed the "great word factory" remain unrivaled.

When the completed *Dictionary* appeared in 1928, the *Periodical* described it as follows:

> The superiority of the Dictionary to all other English Dictionaries, in accuracy and completeness, is everywhere admitted. The Oxford Dictionary is the supreme authority, and without a rival. It is perhaps less generally appreciated that what makes the Dictionary unique is its historical method; it is a Dictionary not of our English, but of all English: the English of Chaucer, of the Bible, and of Shakespeare is unfolded in it with the same wealth of illustration as is devoted to the most modern authors. When considered in this light, the fact that the first part of the Dictio-

nary was published in 1884 is seen to be relatively unimportant; forty-four years is a small period in the life of a language.[62]

As to its editor, the delegates of the Clarendon Press, whose attitude to Murray's work had so long and so frequently left so much to be desired, finally paid him the respect he was undoubtedly due. Minutes for their meeting on October 22, 1915 record that, "At the beginning Sir JAMES MURRAY laid the lines and drew the plan of the Dictionary, and when it is completed half the printed pages will be his; the Delegates acknowledge the debt which they, and with them the University and the world of scholarship, owe to the unremitting labour and the distinguished skill of the original editor of the Dictionary."

One of the purposes of this book has been to show that Johnson's ironies notwithstanding, the lexicographer is no drudge, harmless or otherwise. The triumph to which James Murray dedicated his life surely proves that to be the case. Let him then have the last word. Concluding his Romanes Lecture, he gave his feelings thus:

The structure now reared will have to be added to, continued, and extended with time, but it will remain, it is believed, the great body of fact upon which all future work will be built. It is never possible to forecast the needs and notions of those who shall come after us, but with our present knowledge it is not easy to conceive what new feature can now be added to English lexicography.

14

Slang: Part II

If the progress of mainstream English lexicography between the eighteenth and nineteenth centuries can be seen in one aspect as representing the gradual enfranchisement of "vulgar" English as a language worthy of literary and scholarly attention, then the collection of slang during the same period shows the way the term "slang" moves from representing, as an inaccurate synonym, the jargon of criminals and beggars, properly known as cant, to embracing the wider slang of "mainstream" users. In terms of the linguistic authorities, who still isolated most working-class usage as beyond the cultural pale, slang remained an onlooker at the lexicographical feast, gazing like some Dickensian waif through brightly lit windows as standard English welcomed more and more words to its party. Johnson, after all, had apostrophized all working-class usage as "cant," by which he meant simply vulgar, nonclassical speech, although the subconscious identification of the vast majority of the population with criminality undoubtedly reflects Johnson's staunchly élitist Toryism. Slang would not get through the door until the late twentieth century, when the *OED*'s *Supplements* (1972–86), followed by its Second Edition (1989), at last admitted the former poor relation.

A number of slang dictionaries appeared between the eighteenth century and the start of the twentieth. Most important among them are Francis Grose's *Classical Dictionary of the Vulgar Tongue* (1785), John Camden Hotten's *Slang Dictionary* (1859), and John Farmer and W. E. Henley's *Slang and Its Analogues* (1890–1904, 7 vols.). One of the first compilers actually predates the eighteenth century, albeit briefly. *A New Dictionary of the Terms ancient and modern of the Canting Crew, in its several Tribes of* Gypsies, Beggars, Thieves, Cheats, *etc.* by the otherwise anonymous "B.E., Gent." appeared sometime between 1690 and 1700. Its nearest "standard" equivalent was John Kersey's revision of Edward Phillips' *New World of Words,* and where Kersey had expanded the older "hard-word" dictionary by including many examples of the everyday vocabulary, so did B.E. expand the old cant glossary by including more general slang and col- loquialism. His title may have implied a continuation of the cant tradition, but his word list was far more adventurous. Like Elisha Coles, eighty years later, he suggested that his book was worth reading since by understanding its vocabu- lary, readers might "secure their *Money* and preserve their *Lives.*" He added that the book was "wholly New." This may have been a slight exaggeration, but so much more extensive is his work that, as Starnes and Noyes declare, "its debt to any predecessor is negligible."[1] More debatable is their assertion that B.E.'s move into the wider world of general slang came because he found "the actual canting material too slight to fill a book and resorted to padding in the form of the inclusion of many slang and specialized terms." A purist might object to his inclusion of a variety of mainly military or naval jargon terms, but B.E., as a slang collector, was very much following the example of his mainstream peers. The slang vocabulary had long expanded beyond the confines of cant; if the mainstream "hard words" might be seen as scholars' cant, then the gradual inclusion in "straight" lexicography of everyday vocabulary is logically paral- leled by the inclusion of everyday slang.

Like Robert Copland before him, B.E. set off a whole chain of slang dictio- naries. His inclusion of "civilian" slang brought to an end the Copland- Awdeley-Harman progression and initiated a new one. As Eric Partridge makes clear,[2] both Grose and Hotten are hugely indebted to B.E.; so too are Farmer and Henley, and so too, though he had yet to embark on his own work, which takes as its base Farmer and Henley, was Partridge himself. Farmer even reprinted B.E. in his *Choice Reprints of Scarce Books and Unique MSS* (1899). That said, B.E.'s content far outweighs his form. There is no attempt at etymology (nor would there be until Hotten, and his etymologies were by no means uni- versal nor consistent); the headwords often differentiate insufficiently the vari- ous meanings; nor is the same part of speech always chosen for the headword (today one would expect the nominative noun or first-person singular verb) and there is a good deal of material that is strictly ephemeral—a problem that every slang lexicographer has to face, so inevitably transient is a proportion of what, properly, is a spoken rather than written tongue. There were no citations, but there weren't in standard lexicography either: Johnson was still sixty years ahead; Farmer and Henley would pioneer the style for slang dictionaries. Indeed, even Partridge falls down here: he cites at best by title, rather than by full quotation; not until Jonathan Lighter's *Historical Dictionary of American Slang* (1994 *et seq.*) would readers find the level of citations that would be expected in the *OED* or any other historical dictionary, although Gary Simes' *Dictionary of Australian Underworld Slang* (1993), a relatively tiny work, does attain the Oxford standard.

B.E. and his immediate successors may not have offered citations, preferring it seems to draw on firsthand knowledge or, after B.E., on the dictionaries of their predecessors, but they were available. It was not without foundation that Jonathan Swift, calling in 1711 for the "Correcting, Improving and Ascertaining [of] the English Tongue" issued a proposal which, if boiled down to its very essence, demanded the outlawing of slang. As in the seventeenth century, the use of slang, alongside its collection, was widespread. Playwrights such as William Congreve (1670–1729) and George Farquhar (1678–1707), among the last representatives of Restoration drama, have their slang passages in plays such as Congreve's *The Way of the World* (1700) and Farquhar's *The Beaux Stratagem* (1707). Swift was presumably more than normally exercised by the writings of one Ned Ward, a pamphleteering publican of whose many works the most celebrated are *The London Spy* (1698), a guide to metropolitan high and low life that Londoners, as Roy Porter puts it, "lapped up,"[3] and his play *Durgen: a Plain Satyr upon a Pompous Satirist* (1729), an attack on Alexander Pope. Ward, known to the *DNB,* if to no one else, as Edward, is dismissed there as "a humourist of 'low extraction' and little education."[4] Born in Oxfordshire, he lived briefly in the West Indies before returning to London and setting up as a publican in Moorfields. In 1699 he moved to Fulwood's Rents, near Gray's Inn, and opened up a punch-house and tavern (possibly named the King's Head). Here he dispensed liquor and held court, regaling his customers with tales of the poets and authors he had met. In 1705 he published *Hudibras Redivivus,* an antigovernment attack that saw him fined and placed in the pillory. Here he was given a hard time by the mob, so much so that Pope coined the term "as thick as eggs at Ward in the pillory."[5] Pope, the "Pompous Satirist" of *Durgen,* was never a fan. The *Dunciad*[6] also suggests that Ward's appalling verses were sent to the colonies, where they were traded for second-rate tobacco. He died in 1731 and is buried in St. Pancras churchyard. A dedicated High Tory, Ward is an important source for social historians: "Though vulgar and often grossly coarse," sniffs the *DNB,* "his writings throw considerable light on the social life at the time of Queen Anne, and especially on the habits of various classes in London." These writings, while not invariably so, are regularly repositories of slang, and while the eighteenth-century lexicographers might ignore them, their successors were more appreciative. These few titles might suggest a taste of what he offered, and there was much: *The Poet's Ramble after Riches* (1691), *Female Policy detected, or the Arts of a designing Woman laid open* (1695), *A Step to Stir-Bitch Fair, with Remarks upon the University of Cambridge* (1700), *Adam and Eve stripped of their Furbelows, or the Fashionable Virtues and Vices of both Sexes exposed to Public View* (1710), and *The Delights of the Bottle, or the Compleat Vintner* (1720).

Shortly before Ward's death there appeared another anonymous general slang dictionary: *A New Canting Dictionary* (1725). As Partridge has summed it up its editor "listed a fair number of terms not in B.E., wrote a useful introduction, and appended a collection of nineteen 'canting songs.' " If anything he reversed B.E.'s advances. Many of the colloquialisms were excluded and cant once more gains primacy. As was the custom, the author promoted his work as a prophylactic against theft: with this vocabulary "an Honest Man, who is obliged to travel . . . may secure himself from Danger; which is the principle design of compiling this Vocabulary."[7] But the greatest importance of the *New Canting Dictionary* is in its adoption by Nathan Bailey, who used it as the foundation of the 36-page slang appendix that he included in the later editions of his *Universal Etymological English Dictionary* (1727). But Bailey's acknowledgment of the language of the streets remained an exception. Samuel Johnson may have based his own word list on Bailey, but as a disdainful critic of the "illiterate" masses, the slang addendum was one section he carefully overlooked. B.E. and the *New Canting Dictionary* between them provided sufficient material for a variety of plagiarists, usually using one or both of their works as the basis of a cant glossary. Thus *The Regulator* (1718), written by Charles Hitchin, offered "An Account of all the Flash Words now in vogue . . ." At least half were plucked from the 1725 work. Hitchin was a corrupt City Marshal who doubled as a receiver of stolen goods. His pamphlet was written as an express attack on his rival Jonathan Wild, who combined *his* receiving with a position as a "taker" of the very thieves with whom he cheerfully traded. B.E. was the source of the self-promoted "Captain" Alexander Smith, the fifth edition of whose *Compleat History of the Lives and Robberies of the Most Notorious Highwaymen, Footpads, Shoplifts, & Cheats of Both Sexes* (1719) has a 200-word glossary, all lifted verbatim. The book also offers the *Thieves' Exercise,* a list of thirty cant commands, which are supposed to be practiced by "Young Beginners" under the tutelage of their criminal "Superiors." *The History and Curious Adventures of Bamfylde Moore Carew, King of The Mendicants* (1745), a picaresque autobiography by Bampfylde Moore-Carew, has a 300-word glossary. It is drawn mainly from the *New Canting Dictionary,* although some editions offer a "Vocabulary of the Words Used by the Scottish Gypsies," which enters new territory.

Slang pops up in a variety of eighteenth-century literary productions. Smollett offers some, as do the playwrights Oliver Goldsmith and Richard Brinsley Sheridan, whose father Thomas had made his own contribution to mainstream lexicography in his *General Dictionary of the English Language* (1780). In 1781 there appeared George Parker's *View of Society in High and Low Life.* Parker, who obviously knew the worlds of which he wrote, seems sadly to have eluded the biographical dictionaries, and his self-description, "Librarian to the College of Wit, Mirth and Humour," as appended to the title page of his *Life's Painter of Variegated Characters in Public and Private Life* (1789) hardly helps. However, the *View of Society . . .* has a biographical section, before it turns to an analysis of the world, and language, of a wide range of professional thieves. Parker was an eccentric figure, a friend of such celebrities as Johnson, Reynolds, and Goldsmith. He was by turns a soldier, actor, and lecturer, and the *View of Society . . .* tells the story of his adventures as a traveler. Joining a group of beggars in Dunkirk, he travels with them and notes no less than 74 discrete varieties of villain, plus their special techniques. Like Greene and Dekker long before, he gives a detailed rundown of their activities, although there is no cant dictionary as such. *Life's Painter . . .* makes up for this gap in its fifteenth chapter, where a list of some 125 terms is included, along with illustrative anecdotes. Typically one starts off by explaining the nature of *hot* or *flannel* (a mixture of beer and gin, flavored with nutmeg, egg, and sugar) then moves on to a tale of "that darling of his age, Dr. Goldsmith," his entering one night into a "ken" (a rough public house), his meeting there with Ned Shuter, a "crap-merchant" (a hangman), their subsequent conversation, and Goldsmith's horror at Shuter's grim reminiscences.[8] Parker shows especial delicacy in his introduction to this section, which starts in Chapter 14. He enters into it, he explains, "with a fearful foot, and I do beseech my fair readers to shun it, lest, in this primrose path, they meet a snake in the grass," and a few paragraphs later urges again that "the fair reader will pass over the following pages; for the man who could be capable of instilling poison into the chaste recesses of female breast, deserves not the name of man, nor the happiness a virtuous and fond female can bestow."[9] He then proceeds, as had the sixteenth-century glossarists, to create a dialogue, brimming with cant, and some slang. This is the material which the next chapter's glossary explains.

Among Parker's "variegated characters" is one group particularly worthy of note: "*Slang Boys.* Boys of the slang: fellows who speak the *slang* language, which is the same as *flash* and *cant,* but the word *slang* is applied differently: when one asks the other to shake hands, that is *slang us your mauley.* To exhibit anything in a fair or market, such as tall man or a cow with two heads, that's called *slanging,* and the exhibitor is called the *slang cull.*"[10]

One of the few mainstream lexicographers of the period willing to admit slang to his word list was John Ash, whose *New and Complete Dictionary of the English Language* appeared in 1775. It was Ash, conveniently dead, who took the blame when New England's Puritan critics took exception to the efforts of the early American lexicographers Samuel Johnson, Jr. and the Reverend Elliott when it was discovered that despite their protestations of self-censorship, the word *foutra* ("fuck") had managed to slip through their earnest defenses.

The fanciful thesis that an individual's character is determined by his or her surname is doubtless just that—fantasy—but for those who cling to the concept, few individuals give better hope of its possibility than Captain Francis Grose, writer of *The Classical Dictionary of the Vulgar Tongue* (1785 *et seq.*).[11] Grose was indeed gross—and he apparently appreciated the pun, although he preferred others to resist it—an outsize figure in every way. A veritable Falstaff of lexicographers, Grose was a hugely fat man whose servant allegedly strapped him into bed to prevent the covers slipping from his vast belly; he was well known for his consumption of porter and his telling of stories. He was born in late 1730 or early 1731 in Greenford, Middlesex. His father Francis, a Swiss from Berne and probably himself born Grosse, was a jeweler who fitted up the coronation crown either of George II, as suggested in the *Gentleman's Magazine,* or George III as the *DNB* has it. His collection of prints and shells was sold in 1770 and the British Library holds the catalog of his prints, books, and drawings.

Grose, Jr. was classically educated, as was the contemporary custom, but preferred enrollment at Shipley's drawing school to entering a university. In 1766 he was elected a member of the Incorporated Society of Artists; from 1755 to 1763 he was Richmond Herald; in 1757 he became a member of the Society of Antiquaries and between 1763 and 1769 he was paymaster of the Hampshire Militia. Here, he declared, he needed only two account books: his left and right hip pockets. Receipts went into the right one, and disbursements appeared from the left. It was a characteristically unfussy attitude, but perhaps not wholly prudent. "The unscrupulous," says Partridge, "imposed upon him."[12] Such problems were temporarily solved by his father's death, in 1769, but the fortune that devolved upon the heir was soon spent. He had quit the Hampshire Militia on receiving his legacy, but in 1778, relatively impoverished once more, he joined its Surrey counterpart, in which he served as captain and adjutant until his death. He was also court-martialed in 1778, although the precise reason—presumably "some boyish prank"[13]—remains unknown. Whether or not as a result of this, he found himself, as he wrote to a fellow antiquary, the solicitor William Hutchinson, "tied by the leg to the drudgery of the Drill, endeavouring to teach a parcel of awkward and vicious boobies their right hands from their left, without being able to steal one hour for the pencil."[14] By the early 1780s these "onerous" military duties had become increasingly nominal.

Parade-ground tedium notwithstanding, Grose had in fact always managed to find some time "for the pencil." The first part of his *Views of the Antiquities of England and Wales* appeared in 1773; the complete work was finished fifteen years later. He was responsible for many of the illustrations, although the text was created by a number of other hands. Two studies of military antiquities, of which he was especially knowledgeable, appeared between 1785 and 1789. A trip to Scotland resulted in *The Antiquities of Scotland* (1789–91) and in 1791, after making a brief visit the previous year, he began what would have been *The Antiquities of Ireland*. It did not appear: on May 12, while dining in Dublin with Horace Hone, a miniaturist and the son of his old friend the portrait painter Nathaniel Hone, he suffered a fatal apoplectic fit. He is buried in the graveyard of Drumcondra Church, near Dublin. Noting his series of "Antiquities," the *St James Evening Chronicle* suggested these lines as his epitaph: "Here lies Francis Grose, | On Thursday, May 12, 1791, | Death put an end to his | VIEWS AND PROSPECTS." Grose left a wife, Catherine, and five daughters and two sons. Of these latter, Daniel, after several campaigns in America, became the first deputy governor of the newly established penal settlement in Botany Bay, New South Wales.

As attested from all quarters, Grose was excellent company, a *bon viveur* and one celebrated for his "good humour, conviviality and friendship," qualities which, as considered by the *Gentleman's Magazine,* were judged even more acceptable than his undoubted literary abilities. His obituarist's comments, while fulsome, are echoed without reservation in many contemporary memoirs.

> He had the earliest habits of adapting himself to all tempers; and, being a man of general knowledge, perpetually drew out some conversation that was either useful to himself or agreeable to the party. He could observe upon most things with precision and judgement; but his natural tendency was to humour, in which he excelled, both by the selection of anecdotes and his manner of telling them. It may be said, too, that his figure

rather assisted him, which was in fact the very *title page to a joke*. He had neither pride nor malignity of authorship; he felt the independency of his own talents, and was satisfied with them, without degrading others. His friendships were of the same cast, constant and sincere, overlooking little faults, and seeking out greater virtues, he had a good heart, and, abating those little indiscretions natural to most men, could do no wrong.[15]

Like Johnson, Grose established his own coterie, which met in a specially reserved private room on the premises of Hooper's bookshop in High Holborn. A variety of literary figures joined him there to enjoy his wit and anecdotes. He was also a patron of a Holborn tavern, the King's Arms, a popular haunt of literary men, journalists, actors, and similar figures. Unlike Johnson, however, Grose was especially happy in Scotland. His antiquarian researches had taken him north in 1789 and soon, while meeting a variety of fellow devotees, he was introduced to the poet Robert Burns. The two men hit it off at once, and Burns capped their acquaintance with a poem: "On Captain Grose's Peregrinations Through Scotland," a tribute that includes the oft-quoted couplet "A chiel's among ye, takin notes | And, faith, he'll prent it." In this same poem he describes the Falstaffian Captain as "a fine, fat fodgel [squat and plump] wight | of stature short, but genius bright." Burns' affection for this friend who displayed such a "sterling independence of mind"[16] is displayed once more in the later "Ken Ye ought o' Captain Grose?":

> *The Devil got notice that Grose was a-dying*
> *So whip! at the summons old Satan came flying:*
> *But when he approach'd where poor FRANCIS lay moaning,*
> *And saw each bed-post with its burden a-groaning,*
> *Astonish'd, confounded, cry'd Satan: 'By God,*
> *I'll want him, ere I take such a damnable load!'*

It was also in honor of his friend's powers as a storyteller that Burns wrote the ghostly narrative poem *Tam O'Shanter*, his last major work, in 1791.

As the quintessential "jolly fat man with a heart of gold" Grose, weighed down by his bulk, and tired out by his pursuit of pleasures, especially convivial and liquorous ones, needed a good deal of sleep. Indeed, his legend stresses his partiality to such relaxation. Grose himself once declared that he was "the idlest fellow living, even before I had acquired the load of adventitious matter which at present stuffs my doublet."[17] When one member of the Antiquarian Society drew Grose's portrait, he appended these lines: "Now ****, like bright Phoebus, is sunk into rest, | Society droops for the loss of his jest; | Antiquarian debates, unoccasion'd with mirth, | To genius and learning will never give birth. | Then wake, brother member, our friend from his sleep, | lest Apollo should frown, and Bacchus should weep." He was, naturally, also a trencherman of renown. In the "Biographical Sketch" attached to his edition of the *Classical Dictionary,* Pierce Egan describes Grose's meeting, in Dublin, with a butcher, who was requesting him to make some kind of purchase. Grose refused to buy, saying that he "wanted nothing" but "at last a butcher starts from his stall and, eyeing Grose's figure from top to bottom . . . exclaimed, 'Well, sir, though you don't want anything at present, only say you buy your meat of me; and by G— you'll make my fortune.' "[18]

In its notice of his death, the *Gentleman's Magazine* praised Grose's antiquarianism, and delighted in his good nature, but turned fastidiously from his slang lexicography, allowing only that "in 1785 he published 'A Classical Dictionary of the Vulgar Tongue' which it would have been to his credit to have suppressed."[19] It passes without even a denunciation over his *Provincial Glossary* (1788). Yet at two centuries' remove, it is as a lexicographer, rather than an antiquary, that he matters. Building on B.E., but appealing to a much wider audience, and providing them with a substantially larger word list, Grose's work made it clear that there was more to slang than the professional cant of thieves and beggars. The usual suspects are duly rounded up—*abram-cove, autem bawler, bawdy basket, bene darkmans,* and their roguish like—all culled from the sixteenth-century glossaries, but like B.E. he has taken on board the larger world of general slang. In Grose the reader has moved beyond the surreptitious whispering of sixteenth- and seventeenth-century villainy and into the wider arena, where "civilians" as well as crooks use the "parallel" vocabulary of slang. It is in Grose that readers first discover *birthday suit* (although Smollett appears to have been the actual coiner), *chop and change, gam* (a leg, long since exported to America), *shag* (to copulate), *slag* (a pejorative common to the twentieth-century works of both Frank Norman and Robin Cook) and much, much more. His book went into several editions: that of 1785 was followed by another in 1788 and a third in 1796, by which time the original 3,000 headwords had been increased to 4,000. This third edition was republished, only marginally expanded, in 1811, when its title page declared it to be "a Dictionary of Buckish Slang, University Wit, and Pickpocket Eloquence." Retitled as the *Lexicon Balatronicum* ("the jesters' dictionary"), it acknowledged Grose's original efforts, but cited this edition as being "considerably altered and enlarged, with the modern changes and improvements, by a Member of the Whip Club." The *Lexicon* also claims to be targeting a classier audience than did Grose, whose "circulation was confined almost exclusively to the lower orders of society. [Captain Grose] was not aware . . . that our young men of fashion would at no very distant period be as distinguished for the vulgarity of their jargon as the inhabitants of Newgate . . ." Not that the target was *that* classy: it is the uninitiated, "the cits of Fish-Street [and] the boors of Brentford . . . the whole tribe of second rate Bang ups" who were to be "initiated into all the peculiarities of language by which the man of spirit is distinguished from the man of worth. They may now talk bawdy before their papas, without the fear of detection, and abuse their less spirited companions, who prefer a good dinner at home to a glorious *up-shot* in the highway, without the hazard of a cudgelling."[20]

Grose may have taken slang out of the "padding-ken" and placed it more firmly in the public eye, but in one aspect of his lexicography he was linked most definitely to his predecessors. Modern slang collection tends, like its mainstream equivalents, to rely on the printed text for its researches. Such twentieth-century specialists as the late David Maurer have indeed pursued hands-on fieldwork, eliciting slang, or more properly cant, from a wide variety of criminal or quasicriminal sources, but they remain the exception. The nature of historical dictionaries, slang or otherwise, is to depend on print and eschew oral evidence. Grose would have had none of that. He picked up much of his research firsthand during his nightly wanderings through London's criminal slums, accompanied only by his man Batch and later by his companion, "a funny fellow" properly named Tom Cocking, whom he christened "The Guinea Pig." He wandered the low-life streets of London, or indeed whatever town in which he might temporarily find himself, in search of the *echt* vocabulary of the street. It was these wanderings that inspired his *Dictionary.* Pierce Egan ran down his adventures in the introduction to his edition of Grose:

Batch and his master used frequently to start at midnight from the King's Arms, in search of adventures. The Back Slums of St Giles's were explored again and again; and the Captain and Batch made themselves as affable and jolly as the rest of the motley crew among the beggars, cadgers, thieves, etc., who at that time infested the "Holy Land" [the "rookery" of St Giles's]. The "Scout-Kens" [watch-houses], too, were often visited by them, on the "look-out" for a bit of fun; and the dirty "smokepipes" in Turnmill Street did not spoil the Captain's taste in his search after character. Neither were the rough squad at St Kitts, and "the sailor-boys cap'ring a-shore" at Saltpetre Bank, forgotten in their nightly strolls . . . In short, wherever a "bit of life" could be seen to advantage, or the "knowledge-box" of the Captain obtain anything like a "new light" respecting mankind, he felt himself happy, and did not think his time misapplied.[21]

It was these "nocturnal sallies" and the language that "continually assailed his ears" that, as Egan notes, inspired Grose to compile his dictionary. His book would go on to dominate nineteenth-century slang lexicography, providing a core vocabulary for his first major successor, Hotten, before being finally displaced, in form but by no means wholly in content, by the historical method that underpins the efforts of Farmer and Henley.

Grose saw but two editions of his book through the press. The third and that retitled as the *Lexicon Balatronicum* (1811, effectively the fourth), appeared posthumously. In 1823 came another, also called the "third" edition, but in fact the fifth. This was authored by Pierce Egan, a Regency clubman and a leading light of boxing's "Fancy." Egan (1772–1849) was born in the London suburbs, where he spent his life. By 1812 he had established himself as the country's leading "reporter of sporting events," which at the time meant mainly prizefights and horse races. The result of these reports, which won him a countrywide reputation for wit and sporting knowledge, appeared in the four volumes of *Boxiana, or, Sketches of Modern Pugilism,* which appeared, lavishly illustrated, between 1818 and 1824. So successful was *Boxiana* that Egan turned to his other interest, the world of London clubmen, themselves devotees of the Turf and the Ring. In 1821 he announced the publication of a regular journal: *Life in London,* appearing monthly at a shilling a time. It was to be illustrated by George Cruikshank (1792–1878), who had succeeded Hogarth and Rowlandson as London's leading satirist of urban life. The journal was dedicated to the King, George IV, who at one time had received Egan at court. The first edition of *Life in London* "or, the Day and Night Scenes of Jerry Hawthorn, esq., and his elegant friend, Corinthian Tom, accompanied by Bob Logic, the Oxonian, in their rambles and Sprees through the Metropolis" appeared on July 15, 1821. Egan's creation was an enormous, instant success, with its circulation mounting every month. Pirate versions appeared, featuring such figures as "Bob Tallyho," "Dick Wildfire," and the like. Printmakers speedily knocked off cuts featuring the various "stars" and the real-life public flocked to the "sporting" addresses that Egan had his heroes frequent. There was a translation into French. At least six plays were based on Egan's characters, contributing to yet more sales. One of these was exported to America, launching the "Tom and Jerry" craze there. The version created by William Moncrieff—whose knowledge of London and of its slang equaled Egan's—was cited, not without justification, as "The Beggar's Opera of its day." Moncrieff (1794–1857) was one of contemporary London's most successful dramatists and theatrical managers. His production of *Tom and Jerry, or, Life in London* ran continuously at the Adelphi Theatre for two seasons; it was Moncrieff as much as Egan who, as the *DNB* has it, "introduced slang into the drawing room."[22] This was his big hit, as it was Egan's, but Moncrieff wrote widely (some 170 plays in all) and at various times was manager of Astley's Music Hall (famous for its equestrian expertise) and the pleasure dome of Vauxhall Gardens. Like Cruikshank he would move from Egan to Dickens, producing *Sam Weller, or the Pickwickians* in 1837.

Life in London appeared until 1828, when Egan closed it down. John Camden Hotten brought out a collected edition in 1871, but the work had a greater influence prior to that—the rip-roaring world it portrayed undoubtedly prefigures that of Dickens' *Pickwick Papers* (published just eight years later); Cruikshank's illustrations, of course, helped both men with their success. Nor did "Tom and Jerry" vanish with Egan: the celebrated duo have been perpetuated in Warner Brothers' cartoon cat and mouse and as the male protagonists of BBC television's sitcom *The Good Life.* Such international triumphs by no means stilled Egan's pen. He published his report of the trial of John Thurtell and Joseph Hunt, whose murder of William Weare provided Regency England with one of its juiciest courtroom melodramas; sales, not to mention the author's ego, were boosted when Thurtell allegedly mentioned, just seven hours before his execution, that among his final wishes was a desire to read Egan's coverage of a recent prizefight. He provided regular reportage of the major capital trials, as well as such satirical legal pieces as "The Fancy Tog's Man *versus* Young Sadboy, the Milling Quaker." He launched a new journal, *Pierce Egan's Life in London and Sporting Guide,* a weekly newspaper priced at eightpence-halfpenny, in 1824. Other works included sporting anecdotes, theatrical autobiographies, guidebooks, and "fancy ditties." Among his later efforts, in 1838, was a series of pieces on the delights to be found on and immediately adjacent to the Thames. It was dedicated, with permission, to the young Queen Victoria and featured the illustrative work of his son, also Pierce Egan (1814–80), a good artist but a lesser writer, whose blood-and-thunder romances included *The Snake in the Grass* (1858), *Love Me, Leave Me Not* (1859), and *My Love Kate, or the Dreadful Secret* (1869).

In addition, states the *DNB,* Egan "furnished the 'slang phrases' to Francis Grose's Dictionary of the Vulgar Tongue." This is patently incorrect. "Egan's Grose," as it is generally known, is by no means an original work, although it does embellish its predecessor with the inclusion of a variety of mainly sporting Regency slang. He also cuts the "*coarse* and *broad* expressions"[23] which Grose had allowed and notes the way that some slang terminology, typically *rum*—once a positive term, but by 1820 generally the reverse—had altered. Such alterations cannot have caused Egan excessive trouble. His had always been a slangy style. As Don Atyeo has explained, *Boxiana* is riddled with "Fancy slang": " 'Ogles' were blackened, 'peepers' plunged into darkness, 'tripe-shops' received 'staggerers', 'ivories' were cracked, 'domino boxes' shattered, and 'claret' flowed in a steady stream."[24] And as his own character Corinthian Tom explains in *Life in London,* "A kind of *cant* phraseology is current from one end of the Metropolis to the other, and you will scarcely be able to move a single step, my dear JERRY, without consulting a *Slang* Dictionary, or having some friend at your elbow to explain the strange expressions which, at every turn, will assail your ear." Such a dictionary is what Egan offers, hoping in sum that his efforts work "to improve, and not to degrade mankind; to remove *ignorance,* and put the UNWARY on their guard; to rouse the *sleepy,* and to keep them AWAKE; to render those persons who are a *little* UP, more FLY: and to cause every one to be *down* to those tricks, manoeuvres and impositions practised in life, which daily cross the paths of both young and old."[25]

Egan's was not the only slang dictionary to appear in 1823. Almost simultaneously there was published *Slang,* "a Dictionary of the Turf, the Ring, the Chase, the Pit, of Bon Ton and the Varieties of Life . . ." It formed, claimed the title page, "the completest and most authentic Lexicon Balatronicum hitherto offered to the notice of the Sporting World" but this latter comparison was pure commercial flummery: the genuine *Lexicon Balatronicum,* itself largely purloined from Francis Grose, had appeared a dozen years earlier. If any volume might be seen as its true successor, it was Egan's revision of Grose; it was not this dictionary, compiled by one "John Bee, Esq." No doubt its author, properly named John Badcock (*fl.* 1813–30), and like Egan a sporting journalist, did take the *Lexicon* as his sourcebook, but a comparison of any pages drawn from the two volumes shows how far Badcock's attempt to improve upon the original has only diluted its quality. Merely to take the respective opening pages: the *Lexicon* starts by listing "abbess, abel-wackets, abigail, abram, and abram cove"; Bee has "Abatures, abbess, Abbott's Priory, ABC-darian, abigail, abrac, and abrahamers" before reaching "abram." Of these the first is staghunting jargon, the fourth standard English and the sixth and seventh, which appear in no previous slang dictionary, are not considered worthy of inclusion by either Hotten or Farmer and Henley, although Partridge, generous to a fault, does revive them, more than a century later. As for "Abbott's Priory," which refers to Sir Charles Abbott (1762–1832), Lord Chief Justice from 1818 to 1832 and as such the administrator of the King's Bench Prison, for which this is a synonym, Grose had died before the term entered use. The pattern persists throughout the dictionary. Badcock himself regularly wrote on boxing and racing, either as "Jon Bee" or "John Hinds." As he states on the title page of his slang dictionary, he edited variously *The Fancy, or true Sportsman's Guide,* a monthly partwork offering "authentic Memoirs of Pugilists," *The Annals of Sporting and Fancy Gazette* (1822–8, 13 vols.), and *The Living Picture of London* (1818). He also produced, under the pseudonym "Oloff Napea, ex-officer of cavalry," the *Letters from London* (1816), which purported to be the "Observations of a Russian during a residence . . . of ten months." He also wrote various works on the horse. His last effort, a study of the works of the dramatist Samuel Foote, appeared in 1830. Since nothing else followed it is assumed that he died then or soon after.

For a man whose work falls markedly beneath that of his peers, or perhaps for that very reason, Badcock is insufferably pleased with himself. Running down his near contemporaries, and explaining the rationale behind his own work, he remarks that "Captain Grose was much too gross, even for his day, besides which, his work is become antiquated, stale, and out of date; the *Count's*[26] . . . were indeed *vaut-rien,* as that *life* had been; and our friend Dr [Hewson] Clarke's augmentations [of Grose for the *Lexicon Balatronicum*] . . . added to the structure lead, rather than beauty or strength. Nat Bailey should be forgotten: he is even older than Grose, and twice as nasty."[27] Badcock goes on to savage Egan, whose edition of Grose he sets in December 1822, "undertaken in great haste, the printer thereof learning that the materials for the present dictionary were in train . . . How it has failed a comparison will show."[28] Aside from correcting these inadequates, Badcock explains that while every other profession has gained a dictionary, laying out what he terms its "slangery," or more accurately its jargon, the occupations of the sporting gentry have been overlooked. It is his intention to remedy the omission. The comparison he requests has been made above: it is not to Badcock's credit.

Space does not permit a proper study of the various nineteenth-century writers who provided slang glossaries or incorporated a greater or less amount of slang in their works. Eric Partridge[29] offers a far more extensive overview of such material, and the interested reader is directed to his *Slang: Today and Yesterday,* a genuinely groundbreaking study, and the foundation for his own slang lexicography. Byron's friend Thomas Moore, Walter Scott, Bulwer Lytton, Disraeli, Ainsworth, Dickens, Douglas Jerrold, Henry Mayhew, and many others not principally associated with this side of language added to slang's popularity. Two figures do stand out, and sadly one of them remains anonymous. In 1857 "Ducange Anglicanus" published *The Vulgar Tongue,* "A Glossary of Slang, Cant and Flash Words and Phrases Used in London from

1839 to 1859." There were just 250 copies printed and it was intended to assist Literary Men, the Officers of the Law and Philanthropists, in their intercourse with Classes of English Society who use a different Phraseology, only understood by their own fraternity.[30] *The Vulgar Tongue* offers in fact a pair of glossaries, the first collected by the author, the second from a report presented to the government in 1839. In addition there is "The Leary Man," a flash song, and a tailor's handbill written in slang, with a translation into standard English on the reverse. Ducange's pseudonym is presumably a nod to the French polymath Charles Dufresne, Sieur Du Cange (1610–88), whose *Glossarium ad scriptores mediae et infimae Latinitatis* had appeared in 1678, and had been reprinted between 1840 and 1850. The volume is notably slim, there are around only 500 words, but it appears to be accurate, although one critic, who had his own work to promote, was less than complimentary, declaring the work to be "a silly, childish performance, full of blunders and contradictions."[31] Its most important contribution is that for the first time rhyming slang, which rather than a genuine slang should perhaps be equally well described as an often ephemeral dialect of London's cockneys, is included in a printed work. Ducange Anglicanus, who quotes a number of critics, includes lines from Charles Astor Bristed, who in his essay "The English Language in America" (Cambridge Essays, 1855) sets down a definition of this alternative, parallel language that makes him, according to Partridge, the first scholar to do so. His definition is twofold: its first half refers to the slang of specialist or closed interest groups, the professional slang that provides what a modern classification would term jargon; the second half deals with "mainstream slang," "expressions consecrated, as it were, to Momus from their birth, devoted to comic or would-be comic literature and conversation, always used with a certain amount of ludicrous intent, and which no person, except from slip of the tongue or pen, or unfortunate habit, would employ in serious writing or discourse."[32]

The second individual worth plucking from the larger mass is James Hardy Vaux (1782–?), cited above as "The Count" (one of his various pseudonyms) and, by default, the first compiler of a slang, or indeed of any other type of dictionary in Australia. Vaux was a swindler and pickpocket, of no particular individuality, whose criminal career led him, like many peers, to a sentence of transportation to the then penal colony of New South Wales, Australia, where he arrived in 1801. Indeed Vaux, who managed to escape twice, was transported on three separate occasions before succumbing to respectability and, subsequent to completing yet another jail sentence in August 1841, effectively vanishing from history. Prior to this, however, he published in 1819 his *Mem-*

oirs, a volume that covered the first thirty-two years of his life and misadventures. As an appendix to the memoirs he included *A Vocabulary of the Flash Language,* explaining that this glossary, which runs to around 750 headwords, was a necessary guide to the cant words and phrases that he had included in his text. This may have been so, but the original publication of the *Vocabulary* had in fact predated the *Memoirs* by seven years. At the time Vaux was confined in Newcastle, known as the Hell of New South Wales, after being condemned for a theft from Judge Advocate Ellis Bent at Sydney. Published a year after the *Lexicon Balatronicum,* the vocabulary inevitably replicates much of Grose's research, although with its emphasis on *flash* or criminal terminology it reverts to the older type of cant collection. There are relatively few purely "civilian" terms. And for all its historical importance to Australian lexicography its attachment to Australia is purely geographical. Just as the bulk of American slang was still essentially that of London, so too was that of the convicts who had, as they put it, been *bellowsed* or *marinated* to the Antipodes. Homegrown Australian slang had not yet evolved.

If the first half of the nineteenth century was dominated by extensions, revisions, or plagiarisms of the work of Francis Grose, then the thirty years from 1859 remain the province of a slang lexicographer of equal importance: John Camden Hotten (1832–73). Hotten, christened John William Hotten, was born in St. John's Square, Clerkenwell, on September 12, 1832. His father, William, had moved to London from the West Country, and worked as a master carpenter and undertaker. At the age of fourteen young John was apprenticed to John Petheram, a Chancery Lane bookseller, in whose employ he gained a precocious interest in rare and curious books. It was during this apprenticeship that Hotten was supposedly hit, for some long-lost reason, by the historian Thomas Babington Macaulay. Some twenty-five years later Hotten's last work would be on *Macaulay the Historian* (1873). In 1848 he and his brother sailed for America, where Hotten remained until in 1856 he reemerged in London. Here he capitalized on his teenage interests to open a small bookshop at 151b Piccadilly (now the site of the Ritz Hotel). This was replaced, once Hotten had established himself as a success, by larger premises on the opposite side of the street at 74–75 Piccadilly. Hotten seems to have been considered somewhat "fast" and definitely modern by his contemporaries. Today he would be termed a workaholic. Writing to the *Bookseller* shortly after his death, the correspondent "R.H.S." laid out a day that lasted, with only the briefest of lunch breaks, from ten in the morning to nine at night. After that the work in hand, or even an aspirant author, would be taken home for further consideration (although he was less forthcoming when they demanded money). There was, he suggested, "something heroic in all this, even if of a degenerate modern kind." Hotten, in the writer's eyes was "essentially 'a man of the time' [who] felt he must keep pace with the railroad speed of the age, or leave others to outstrip him in the race."[33]

While across the Atlantic he had made himself into something of an expert in American literature and among his earliest publishing ventures were editions of such contemporary Americans as Bret Harte, Oliver Wendell Holmes, James Russell Lowell, and Artemus Ward. That these were generally pirated editions—no contracts were signed nor royalties paid—had no effect on their sales, although one such author, Mark Twain, wrote to the *Spectator* (on September 20, 1872) complaining that not only was Hotten paying him nothing for his work, but that the publisher had taken it upon himself to add extra chapters, from his own pen, to the original manuscript. "I feel," wrote Twain, "as if I wanted to take a broomstick and knock that man's brains out. Not in anger, for I feel none. Oh! not in anger! but only to see, that is all. Mere idle curiosity." For all that, Hotten was not without honor across the Atlantic. In 1901 it was announced that an Indianapolis literary society was to place a tablet to the publisher in their library, as an acknowledgment of his "introducing certain famous American authors to the British reading public." No irony, one must assume, was intended.

Other, more legitimate publications included C. G. Leland's celebrated poem "Hans Breitmann's Party"; in 1889 Leland himself would help compile a slang dictionary in his turn. Hotten also wrote biographies of William Thackeray—creator of the fictional Becky Sharp, that dedicated anti-Johnsonian—and of Charles Dickens, who for all the slang that can be found in his works, on September 24, 1853 had penned an outspoken antislang piece in issue 183 of his journal *Household Words*. He believed, like many before and after him, that slang was ruining the language, substituting cheap verbal shortcuts for genuine wit. Hotten also edited collections of Christmas carols, translated the popular historical novels of the French duo writing as Erckmann-Chatrian, wrote a record of the life of the explorer H. M. Stanley, published one of the first ever guides to philately—Bellars and Davie's *Guide to Postage Stamp Collecting* (1864)—and much besides. He also wrote under a variety of pseudonyms, typically as "Titus Brick," author of *Awful Crammers, a New American Joke-Book* (1873). All in all Hotten wrote or contributed to some twenty-five traceable works.

Hotten was a "near-scholar"[34] whose fame was balanced by his notoriety. Alongside his own writing, his skillfully worked out general publishing, which R.H.S. praises as "gauging the public taste, and supplying it with exactly the sort of literary pabulum it required"[35] and the slang lexicography which qualifies him for this book, his success, or at least a good deal of his income, rested on his exploitation of what Partridge called "the by-ways"[36] of Victorian life. One byway that he explored enthusiastically was that of pornography. Compared with less savory publishers, whose shops clustered along the notorious Holywell Street (formerly running off the Strand, long subsumed beneath the Australian High Commission in what is now the Aldwych), Hotten was a relatively admirable figure. Henry Spencer Ashbee, the bibliographer of pornography, praised him as "industrious, clever but not always reliable." Hotten had a special affection for this side of the business, calling it his "flower garden," in which bloomed such titles as *The History of the Rod,* the illustrator Thomas Rowlandson's *Pretty Little Games* (a series of ten erotic plates), and *The Romance of Chastisement.* He also published A. C. Swinburne's *Poems and Ballads* (1866) which, while hardly obscene, had been withdrawn from the bookshops by Bertrand Payne, a director of the poet's earlier, more timid publisher Moxon. Hotten paid Moxon's, which was appalled by Swinburne's growing, if undeserved reputation as a pervert, £200 for their stocks of the *Poems,* plus sheets of an unpublished work on Blake. It was a wise move—the *Poems* proved a bestseller—although the poet never really got on with his publisher. That said, Swinburne, who appreciated flagellant pornography himself, helped Hotten with another piece of titillation: *The Romance of the Rod.*

Hotten died on June 14, 1873, at his house on Haverstock Hill near Hampstead, either of "brain fever" or, as some claimed, of a surfeit of pork chops. His final works were *The Golden Treasury of Thought* and a comprehensive list of those who emigrated to America in the seventeenth century. His business was sold for £25,000 to form the basis of another publisher, Chatto and Windus.

The other "byway" along which Hotten traveled was that of slang. His edition of the sixteenth-century German "beggar book" the *Liber Vagatorum* (the *Book of Vagabonds*) with its foreword by Martin Luther, appeared in 1860. But he had already published his own equally valuable contribution to the genre. The *Dictionary of Modern Slang, Cant and Vulgar Words* appeared in 1859, the work, said the title page, of "a London Antiquary." It sold out quickly, was rapidly reprinted and ran to several editions. It remained the authoritative work for nearly forty years and still holds an important place in slang lexicography. Aside from the word list itself, which expanded from the 4,500-odd entries of the first edition to around 6,000 by the 1867 version, Hotten made substantial advances in every aspect of his task. For the first time ever, a slang dictionary offered an overview of its subject. Hotten prefaced his work with a "History of Cant, or the Secret Language of Vagabonds" and a "Short History of

Slang, or the Vulgar Language of Fast Life." B.E. and Grose both made the distinction between cant and slang, but neither had specified exactly what the distinction was. Hotten explains it in some detail, although he notes in his preface that "although in the Introduction I have divided Cant from Slang, and treated the subjects separately, yet in the Dictionary I have only, in a few instances, pointed out which are Slang, and which are Cant terms." As he says, "Many words which were once Cant are Slang now" and gives *prig* and *cove* as typical examples. His histories of both speech varieties are extensive, if not always conclusive. A glance at the running heads gives a flavor: "Vulgar Words from the Gypsy," "The Inventor of Canting Not Hanged," "Our Old Authors Very Vulgar Persons," "The Poor Foreigners Perplexity." He includes, as a bonus, the entire cant glossary listed in Richard Head's *The English Rogue* (1665), which itself drew, of course, on such predecessors as Harman and Dekker. He has lists of rhyming slang and of backslang, both prefaced by a brief history and discussion. There is, again for the first time ever, a "Bibliography of Slang and Cant," listing some 120 titles, plus his own critical comments on each. This bibliography, aside from any other aspects of the *Dictionary,* has proved invaluable to researchers. Hotten stresses that above all this is a dictionary of "*modern* Slang— a list of colloquial words and phrases in *present* use—whether of ancient or modern formation."[37] Thus he has omitted obsolete terms. He has also, unlike Grose, opted to exclude "filthy and obscene words"[38] although he acknowledges their prevalence in street talk. He touches on jargon, without describing it as such, and thus deals, both in his introduction and in the *Dictionary,* with the terminology of the beau monde, politics, the army and navy, the church, the law, literature, and the theater. He has a list of slang terms for money, one of oaths, one for drunkenness (still the greatest of sources for slang terminology) and deals with the language of shopkeepers and workmen. It is, for a relatively condensed work, a little over 300 pages in all, a great achievement.

In Hotten one sees the bridge between Grose, who for all his own advances was still using only the most basic of lexicographical disciplines, and Farmer and Henley's historically based lexicography, including citations, numbered homonyms, and an attempt to include all the available vocabulary. In many ways Hotten's most important contribution is that for the first time ever one finds an effort, by no means consistent, nor invariably accurate, to trace the etymology of the slang vocabulary. As his title page promises, Hotten's words came "many with their etymology, and a few with their history traced," but as he makes clear at the very head of the dictionary itself, "Slang derivations are generally indirect, turning upon metaphor and fanciful allusions, and other than direct etymological connexion. Such allusions and fancies are essentially temporary or local; they rapidly pass out of the public mind; the word remains, while the key to its origin is lost."[39] That problem continues to assail slang lexicographers; the underlying ephemerality of an essentially spoken language (although the late twentieth century has seen a vast increase in printed, filmed, televised, or even sung sources) will always hinder attempts to chase down the origins of slang. Hotten, however, did his best. Taking an average spread, he manages some form of etymology for about 50 percent of the entries. The more rigorous constraints of modern lexicography, extending even to slang collection, would frown on such prosing, but Hotten's definitions and etymologies make for an enjoyable as well as an informative read.

CODDAM,   a low public-house game, much affected by medical students and cabmen, three on each side. The game is "simplicity itself," but requires a great amount of low cunning, and peculiar mental ingenuity.

GOD BLESS THE DUKE OF ARGYLL!   a Scottish insinuation made when one shrugs his shoulders, of its being caused by parasites or cutaneous affections.—*See* SCOTCH FIDDLE, SCOTCH GREYS. It is said to have been originally the thankful exclamation of the Glasgow folks, at finding a certain row of iron posts, erected by his grace in that city to mark the division of his property, "very convenient to rub against."

PIN,   "to put in the PIN" to refrain from drinking. From the ancient peg tankard, which was furnished with a row of PINS, or pegs, to regulate the amount which each person was to drink. A correspondent gives a different explanation. "When an Irishman makes a vow or promise to abstain from drinking, for a time, he puts a PIN in the righthand cuff of his coat. So that, in case he should ever forget his promise, he will see the pin, like an accusing angel, when lifting the glass to his mouth." A MERRY PIN, a roisterer.—*See* PEG.

The best-selling *Slang Dictionary* remains Hotten's only foray into lexicography, other than the reprinted *Liber Vagatorum*. In the endpapers of the 1867 edition he announced "A Dictionary of Colloquial English": it did not materialize.

Exactly contemporaneous with Hotten there appeared America's first essay into slang lexicography, George Washington Matsell's *Vocabulum* (1859). It was the first such volume to appear in the United States, and would remain pretty much unique for some time to come. Its only possible predecessor is a short glossary appended by Edward Judson to his moralizing series *The Mysteries and Miseries of*

New York (1848), itself cribbed from Eugène Sue's *Les Mystères de Paris* (1842–43). Despite modern America's wonderful profligacy as regards slang, the progress of such vocabulary during the nineteenth century seems to have been generally restrained. Indeed, American slang was a relatively late arrival in its own country. Dialect, a linguistic development that can be generalized as a primarily rural phenomenon, grew up much faster. A glance at the *Dictionary of American Regional English* (1985, 1991) shows many local usages that go back to the late eighteenth and early nineteenth century. The citations in *DARE*'s slang equivalent, the *Historical Dictionary of American Slang* (1994) tend to start somewhat later. There are earlier terms, of course, but on the whole these are imports, usually from England. There are few early to mid-nineteenth-century terms that cannot be found in Grose or Hotten. Slang, however widely it may spread, is very much a creature of the city. If dialect is the language of the field and farmyard, then slang is that of the street and tavern, and in nineteenth-century America, certainly prior to the Civil War, the cities that provided such spawning grounds were relatively rare. There would be an explosion of slang in the last half of the century, as cities grew and communications between them expanded to match, but in 1859 Matsell's effort was very much that of a pioneer. Nor are these the only factors that might have inhibited the study and indeed the spread of slang. As far as language was concerned, the citizens of republican America were more "Victorian" than those Victorians who lived much closer to the eponymous monarch herself. If such standard English words as "leg" and "shirt" were found beyond the pale (the newspaper editor James Gordon Bennett caused a certain frisson when his *New York Herald* refused to print the former as "limb" and the latter as "linen") then the full-blooded expressions of genuine slang presumably caused even greater outrage. And as Jonathan Lighter, editor of the *HDAS* has pointed out, the very idea of an intellectual, let alone academic, consideration of the language of the streets was de facto suspicious. In the first place, the linguistic conservatism of contemporary British lexicography, epitomized by Samuel Johnson and his epigones, had dismissed slang, if it even bothered to notice it, as the language of the unlettered and thus the unimportant. It was too coarse, too rough, in modern terms, too *street*. And even with Johnson long dead, for the British academics of the mid-nineteenth century, the members of the Philological Society or the contributors and subscribers to the publications of the EETS, there were "more serious scholarly tasks at hand, such as the editing of medieval manuscripts and the reconstruction of lost languages."[40] Even that most democratic of lexicographers, Frederick Furnivall, seems to have eschewed the language that he must have encountered among his shopgirls and self-improving working men. Thus in nineteenth-century Britain, where slang had been established for centuries, one can count the slang collectors on very few fingers. To study the vocabulary in America, where Britain's intellectual standards still counted, and where there was precious little slang to work with anyway, one requires fewer still.

Insofar as he issued a slang dictionary in mid-nineteenth-century America, Matsell is therefore a pioneer. The vocabulary he offered, and the motivation behind his work, however, are less original. Chronology militates against Matsell's having been able see Hotten's work, but he presumably had a copy of Grose, probably in Egan's edition, since much of his word list apes that which he would have found there. This is not to belittle Matsell: if American slang was still primarily an import, such similarities were inevitable. His motivation is similarly secondhand. Matsell terms himself a lexicographer, albeit much to his own surprise. "To become a lexicographer, certainly never entered into my calculation, or even found a place in the castle building of my younger days; and if a kind friend had suggested [it] to me . . . I would have simply regarded him as a fit subject for the care of the authorities."[41] And in the strictest sense, his demurrer is right. The *Vocabulum* is not a "dictionary" as such; it harks back to the work of Thomas Harman, another law officer who attempted to offer his professional peers, and by extension the law-abiding public, a key to the language of those whom they wished to see controlled. It is a tradition that has yet to die: *The Signs of Crime,* "a Field Manual for Police" (1976), in essence a crammer for ambitious British bobbies by the then Deputy Assistant Commissioner David Powis, includes a 36-page "glossary of words commonly used by thieves, cheats and ponces." Like these men, Matsell was working primarily to educate his own employees. "Experience has taught me that any man engaged in police business cannot excel without understanding the rogues' language"[42] and he intended to remedy that want.

Matsell was undoubtedly the most colorful of such policemen-turned-lexicographers. When he edited his glossary he had recently retired after a dozen years as New York City's first ever chief of police. He would return in 1874 under a new title, commissioner, but it would be a brief tenure. A former Tammany Hall politician, Matsell was a notorious character. As a politician he had been a keen supporter of a properly organized police force, replacing the random collection of municipal functionaries who had hitherto struggled to maintain law and order in the ever-expanding metropolis. When in 1845 such a body, the New York Police Department, was established, Matsell got the job. It was a generally popular appointment, although one critic apostrophized the gargantuan chief, who weighed more than 300 pounds (around 22 stone), as "a Beastly Bloated Bobby."[43] Matsell proved nothing if not accommodating in his enforcement of the city statutes. His was a very passive regime, bending cheerfully to the current political wind. Political connections far outweighed the demands of the law. If a given ward chose to enforce drinking or gambling laws, then Matsell's men would jump to close down saloons or raid illicit casinos; if such enthusiasm was not forthcoming, the police were certainly not in the business of encouraging it. In outward show, however, Matsell was exemplary. He put the police into uniforms, on the lines of their British contemporaries, and instituted proper training. He established a rudimentary system of communication between his office and the various precincts. But in the end Matsell was perceived to be at least as sinful as those whom his men pursued. His enforcement of the Fugitive Slave Law of 1850 had him branded a "slave catcher" by Horace Greeley's *Tribune;* his financial affairs were seen as dubious at best; he skimmed the profits of the city's gambling dens; his dealings with the restoration of stolen property echoed those of London's Jonathan Wild, the eighteenth-century "thief taker" who personally fenced the stolen goods he had confiscated from the original robbers; he ran a lucrative "referral" trade, passing on arrested people to a coterie of lawyers who paid him a kickback for every new client. It was even claimed that he extorted money from clients of the well-known, and much vilified, abortionist and specialist in contraception, Madame Restell, also known as Ann Lohmann and actually an Englishwoman born Caroline Ann Trow. It was further suggested that Matsell worked as her partner. Whatever their relationship, Restell gained a renewed notoriety in 1874 when, by now an old woman, she was driven to suicide by the repellent and ridiculous "vice crusader" Anthony Comstock, who greeted the news that she had cut her throat rather than face prison with the comment that, to his great satisfaction, she was the fifteenth individual who had chosen such a course after falling beneath his scourge. Matsell responded to all such attacks with an outraged innocence, inviting "the most searching investigation" and blaming "evil disposed persons, seeking the advancement of their own ends,"[44] but his tenure does seem to have brought him many material rewards. His basic salary can hardly have funded the twenty-room house in Viola, Iowa, where he and his family spent their summers. It boasted a 3,000-acre estate and a brimming wine cellar. Their parties were legendary.

What brought Matsell down, ironically in a town where the police have long been associated affectionately with the Irish community (not for nothing do the slang terms *shamus, shamrock,* and *muldoon* all mean policeman), was the accusation that he allowed too many Irish immigrants to enter the force. Matsell claimed that their representation echoed that of the population at large (some 28 percent of the citizens, 27 percent of the force) but his accusers had found a lever to topple him, and they used it. Even Matsell's own origins were investigated. He claimed to have been born in America; his attackers alleged that he had emigrated from England. He was then tried for "alienage"—no alien could be chief of police—but after a trial that was described by the *New York Times* as "a kind of judicial saturnalia," he was acquitted. It did not hinder his cause that both the judges were Democrats, as was he, and that one, Mayor Fernando Wood, had presided over his original appointment. He survived this time, but the pressure remained. In 1857, when the NYPD was reorganized as the Metropolitan Police Department, he lost his job. He turned his attentions to the *National Police Gazette,* "the only authentic record of Crime and Criminal Jurisprudence in the United States." It aimed, declared the advertisement Matsell included in the endpapers of *Vocabulum,* at "the enforcement of justice, honesty and truth," but its "chaste and forceful" articles tended toward a tabloid celebration of lurid excess, mixing lowlife, sex, and sport, all areas of interest very dear to its editor's heart. Matsell returned, amid much controversy, as one of New York's police commissioners, in 1874. This time, however, he lasted but two years. Ironically once more, it was Tammany Hall, his original backer, that saw him off. His alleged failing was in keeping the streets clean; in fact the politicians resented his attitude to the liquor laws. The laxity of thirty years past was no longer acceptable. Illegal drinking had to go, and with it went George Matsell's job.

Back in Europe two slang collections appeared in the 1880s. Heinrich Baumann's *Londonismen* (*Slang und Cant*) appeared in Berlin in 1887. It expanded Hotten's word list and effectively replaced him, but as a German publication never really impinged on the English-speaking market. Among its idiosyncrasies was the use of a tiny gallows symbol to denote the cant, rather than general slang vocabulary. The second such work, that of Albert Barrère and C. G. Leland, which appeared in the booksellers under the title *A Dictionary of Slang, Jargon and Cant* in 1889–90 (there had already been a slightly earlier, privately circulated edition), has always suffered by comparison with that of their successors, Farmer and Henley. Their work was smaller, two volumes to their successors' magisterial seven, and they were unfortunate in having barely twelve months' pause between their first volume and that of the new collection, but they are far from devoid of merit. Like Nathan Bailey, whose efforts were swamped in Johnson's wake, Barrère and Leland suffer less from their scholarly failings than from their timing.

As well as themselves, the compilers enlisted the aid of a variety of experts. As Barrère boasted in his preface, "The present is the first Slang Dictionary ever written which has the benefit of contributors who thoroughly understood Celtic dialects, Dutch, German and French slang . . . [and] Pidgin-English, Gypsy and Shelta . . ." Their dictionary is the first to include American slang and "the rich and racy slang of the fifth continent—the mighty Australian commonwealth."[45] Among the consultants are Sir Patrick Colquhoun (1815–91), a diplomat, author, and oarsman, whose extensive attainments included speaking "most of the tongues and many of the dialects of Europe";[46] Major Arthur Griffiths (1838–1908), a former inspector of prisons (and deputy governor of both Millbank and Wormwood Scrubs jails) who turned his experiences into such nonfiction best-sellers as *Secrets of the Prison House* (1893) and *The Brand of the Broad Arrow* (1900); the bohemian, journalist, and theatrical manager John Hollingshead (1827–1904), who wrote for *Household Words, Punch,* and other prominent weeklies (he campaigned to permit theatrical performances before 5 P.M., thus instituting the matinée, and as manager of the Gaiety Theatre brought works by W. S. Gilbert—including Gilbert's first collaboration with Arthur Sullivan—Charles Reade and Dion Boucicault to the stage); the pro-temperance, antigambling campaigner the Rev. J. W. Horsley (1845–1921), a botanist, Alpinist, freemason, and prison chaplain, and Charles Mackay, LL.D. (1814–89) the poet and journalist, who mixed such posts as that of the *Times'* special correspondent during the American Civil War with the writing of song lyrics and of a wide variety of books, many on London or the English countryside. His own contribution to lexicography was *A Dictionary of Lowland Scotch* (1888).

As an introduction Leland wrote "A Brief History of English Slang." Partridge[47] is especially condemnatory of this, describing one of its broader generalizations as "childish," but in his attribution of much early cant to Gypsy origins, his acknowledgment of the role of Celtic words in slang etymologies, especially as regards Shelta (the tinkers' jargon), as well as that of such European inputs as those from Dutch and Italian, Leland seems not so far from the opinions offered by Partridge himself. He also notes the late-eighteenth-century arrival of Yiddish, the importing by veterans of the Indian army of the Anglo-Indian pidgin known from the title of the dictionary of such language that had appeared three years earlier as "Hobson-Jobson" and "the last and not least important element . . . Americanisms."[48] None of which should have led Partridge, usually so generous, to so curt a dismissal. But he was *parti pris:* his own work would be based on Farmer and Henley. Understandably, if not wholly fairly, he seems to have stuck with the home team. And indeed, *Slang, Jargon and Cant* is by no means perfect: if nothing else, as indicated by its size, it lacks a number of the words that Farmer and Henley chose to include, and in their decision to allow what would elsewhere be excluded as "jargon," Barrère and Leland extend, perhaps overkindly, the definition of what is properly "slang"; their illustrative citations, while plentiful, are undated, which seems to defeat the point of their being included in the first place; their differentiation of senses, and the general arrangement of entries, is distinctly inferior to their rivals—the material, while often copious and accurately defined, is too jumbled for easy access; they are often overly discursive and not a little moralistic. They occupy then, as suggested, the same position as did Bailey: almost as good as Johnson, but not quite. And it is that "not quite" which leaves them vulnerable to the contemporary excellence of their successors.

In 1890, just as the *NED* was getting properly into its stride, there was published the first of the seven volumes of what could reasonably be called its slang equivalent: *Slang and Its Analogues,* by John S. Farmer and his unlikely coauthor, the far-right-wing poet W. E. Henley. They were to Grose and Hotten as Murray and his team were to Johnson and their work displays a similar degree of scholarship, replete with quotations from slang's equivalent of the "classics," sometimes lengthy etymologies, and synonyms from various European languages. John Farmer, the lexicographer of the pair, had already produced a book of "Americanisms," which updated that produced around midcentury by John Bartlett, he of *Familiar Quotations* fame. Farmer's work proves him an accomplished scholar, but there seems to be little biographical record other than in the fact of his books. As well as the two mentioned already, he edited *Musa Pedestris,* a collection of canting songs and allied verses, and, like some of the Oxford lexicographers, had edited reprints of a number of long-unprinted works, in his case drawn from Tudor sources. His *Tudor Facsimile Texts* appeared in 1907. As "Dr Farmer" he was to be found as a regular contributor to *Notes and Queries.* One slight deviation from the norm came with his appearance in court, in 1890, charged with obscenity. The complainant was his own printer and the book in question, although no further information seems to exist, was presumably volume one of the slang dictionary, dealing with the letters A and B. As well as language, Farmer appears to have had an interest in spiritualism. His book *A New Basis of Belief in Immortality* appeared in 1881; an earlier edition had appeared the previous year under a slightly different title. It is a thoroughly sympathetic treatment of a quasireligious movement which, as he admitted, still faced "vehement opposition [from] a large section of the cultivated classes." Farmer was optimistic: he saw it as a liberalizing movement, well attuned to the modern world, and he envisaged that very soon it would be "widely felt, not only in the social, but also . . . in the religious life our our times."[49] Other spiritually inclined works included *Ex Oriente Lux* and *Twixt*

Two Worlds. (Spiritualism, for whatever reasons, seems to have appealed to the lexicographers. The etymologist Hensleigh Wedgwood, an important influence on the *OED,* was a devotee and wrote regularly for the spiritualist periodical *Light.*)

Farmer's coauthor, William Ernest Henley, "the most belligerent Tory man of letters of their generation,"[50] presents a far more substantial figure. He had his blind spots too, notably a benightedly xenophobic patriotism, but one cannot imagine him giving much truck to spectral messengers and wafting ectoplasm. Like Albert Barrère, who enlisted C. G. Leland to help with his earlier labors, Farmer must have felt it necessary to take on a proven literary figure; Henley's name appears as joint author on all but the first volume of the dictionary. Henley was a major figure in late Victorian letters, although his ultrapatriotic versifying has long since been considered a subject fitter for humor than the homage it was paid at the time. Henley was born in 1849, the son of a Gloucester bookseller. His childhood was marked by two influences, one the teacher and Manx poet T. E. Brown (1830–97), who suggested to Henley "such possibilities in life and character" as he had never dreamed.[51] The other, less immediately positive, was a bout of tubercular arthritis that cost him a foot. In 1873, fearing the loss of its pair, he went to the Edinburgh Infirmary, where he was tended by Joseph Lister, the pioneer of antisepsis. While in hospital he began writing poems—"Invictus," a stoic account of life on the ward, won him particular fame—and, through Leslie Stephen (editor of the *DNB* and Virginia Woolf's father), met a fellow invalid, Robert Louis Stevenson. The pair became close friends, but their literary collaborations, notably on a dramatized version of Stevenson's tale *Deacon Brodie,* came to nothing. Henley would provide Stevenson with a far more important inspiration: he is the model for "Long John Silver" in *Treasure Island* (1883). He can also be found, as "Burly," in Stevenson's essay "Talk and Talkers," where his "boisterous and piratic" persona comes to the fore. Henley repaid the compliment in his poem "Apparition," which describes the wraith-like Stevenson. Henley left the Infirmary in 1875 and began contributing to the *Encyclopaedia Britannica.* These labors, mainly on French biography, proved dull and Henley moved to London where he edited a weekly journal, *London.* This folded and Henley turned freelance, contributing to most of the major weeklies of the time. From 1882 to 1886 he edited the *Magazine of Art,* in which he championed the French sculptor Rodin and promoted Stevenson's cousin R. A. M. Stevenson as an up-and-coming art critic.

In 1889, back in Edinburgh, he began editing the *Scots Observer,* set up by a group of wealthy Tories to challenge the Liberal *Saturday Review.* By 1891 the paper, renamed the *National Observer,* had moved with its editor to London. For

a figure whose politics were uncompromisingly far to the right, Henley's journalism was surprisingly nonpartisan. The overall agenda was patriotic imperialism, but Henley saw himself as much an aesthete as he did a jingo. Thus he
courted a variety of contributors, mixing J. M. Barrie (who used Henley's wife
Anna in his character "Reddy" in *Sentimental Tommy* [1896]), Rudyard Kipling,
Thomas Hardy, Andrew Lang, Arthur Morrison (in whose short stories of East
End wretchedness can be found a good deal of slang), H. G. Wells, W. B. Yeats
(a nationalist of his own hue, who "admired him beyond words"), and of course
his friend Stevenson. These young men, the stars of the future, christened by
Max Beerbohm "The Henley Regatta," helped create what John Gross has
called "easily the most bracing and unconventional review of the day."[52] But in
commercial terms the *Observer* had little clout. It rarely sold more than 2,000
copies of an issue and, as Gross puts it, "was too Conservative for most intellectuals, and too intellectual for most Conservatives."[53] In 1894, when the paper
changed ownership, Henley was forced to resign. He moved to another weekly,
the *New Review,* where he remained until 1897.

The *New Review* offered its readers some of the best of current literature:
Joseph Conrad's *The Nigger of the Narcissus,* Henry James' *What Maisie Knew,* and
H. G. Wells' *The Time Machine* were all serialized there. It also ran Kipling's
"Barrack Room Ballads," and as Gross has noted, it was as its editor that Henley himself became the "Bard of Empire."[54] Hospital memoirs aside, his early
poems might have been generally lightweight stuff, but in 1892 he found a
new voice when he published "The Song of the Sword," which celebrated the
weapon as "Clear singing, clean slicing; | Sweet spoken, soft finishing; | Mak-
ing death beautiful . . . | Arch-anarch, chief builder, | Prince and evangelist, | I
am the Will of God; | I am the Sword." One reviewer, at least, was unimpressed,
responding to Henley's warlike alter ego: "No you're not; you're only an
Ancient Pistol." But Henley persisted in his bloodthirsty versifying, especially
when the hysterical patriotism of the Boer war gave him and his less discriminating contributors the chance to throw off some truly hyperbolic propaganda.

Yet for all this arch-conservatism Henley remained a contradictory figure,
typically when it came to his treatment of sex. His criticisms, collected and
well received in the 1890 volume *Views and Reviews*—"a mosaic of scraps and
shreds recovered from the shot rubbish of some fourteen years of journalism"—
were in the end unremarkable, but there were few Victorians who would have
described a character as "a kind of Walking Phallus" or have dealt with Robert
Burns, lewd verses and all, without the slightest qualm. He was even, briefly, a
friend of Oscar Wilde, although his savaging of Wilde's novella *The Picture of
Dorian Gray* put paid to that relationship; thereafter they loathed each other.

When Wilde faced disgrace in 1895 his erstwhile friend gloated in print at the "pleasant sight" of "Oscar at bay" and jeered that "Holloway and Bow Street have taken his hair out of curl in more senses than one."[55] Wilde did not respond, but in a letter of 1897 remarked that Henley "has had to face every difficulty except popularity."[56] Wilde died in 1900; Henley did not survive him for very long. He had been forced to abandon hands-on editing in 1899, when the *New Review* collapsed, and thereafter worked on his verses and on the occasional literary piece for the *Pall Mall Magazine.* In 1903 he suffered an accident when trying to get out of a still-moving train at Woking Station. He never recovered and died on June 11. Whatever his subsequent image in English letters, his lengthy entry in the *DNB* is wholly respectful.

It was presumably in yet another role, that of organizer of the series of "Tudor Translations"—John Florio's translation of Montaigne was the first—each adorned by an introductory essay by a leading scholar of the day, that he met John Farmer, who was also working on the resuscitation of sixteenth-century literature. Their joint work laid down new standards for slang lexicography and, if one remembers that their great successor Eric Partridge was actually handed Farmer and Henley's seven volumes as the basis on which to assemble his own efforts, remains the source of much that has followed. Nor had Farmer any illusions as to the importance of what he (Henley had yet to be recruited) had done. Writing in his "Prefatory Note" to volume one he begins by citing Samuel Johnson, noting that the Great Lexicographer's problems had been his too, and then quotes his contemporary James Murray as regards the difficulties inherent in attempting to quarantine one variety of language, in this case slang, from all the others. He explains how he has made his own decision as to the borderline, basing it on the standards of literary and nonliterary English laid out in Annadale's edition of Ogilvie's *Imperial English Dictionary* (which took as its source Webster, rather than Johnson). That done, Farmer set off into what he terms the " 'Dark Continent' of the World of Words."[57]

As even the briefest glance at his work will show, Farmer (and in due course Henley) has taken slang lexicography into a new dimension. Quite simply he has adopted the same historical method that the *NED,* not to mention its European peers, had done. All but a few headwords come with a number of citations, set out just as in a standard English dictionary, to illustrate usage and nuance. These quotes take in "the whole period of English literature from the earliest down to the present time"[58] and are arranged as far as possible from "first use" to current use. The entire work offers around 100,000 of these citations, mainly harvested by Farmer himself, although 12,000 came from G. L. Apperson, who also contributed 11,000 quotations to the *NED,* for which he subedited portions of the letters B and C, and whose own major work is *English Proverbs*. As well as citations Farmer included wherever possible foreign synonyms for his slang terminology. These were predominantly French (Albert Barrère, himself author of a dictionary of *Argot and Slang* [1902] as well as his English slang work, is credited as a major source) and German, although the occasional foray further afield can be found. The extent to which, even in their imagery, French and German slangs parallel English is remarkable. Finally, as well as listing and defining the individual terms, Farmer offers substantial lists of synonyms— that for the *monosyllable* (the vagina), for instance, runs to thirteen columns, while *greens* (sexual intercourse) runs to seven. No other slang dictionary, until Richard Spears' *Slang and Euphemism* (1981), would offer similar lists. There are errors, typically in the citations, where dates and even the quotes themselves may have fallen foul of the sheer volume of the undertaking, but the overall achievement of Farmer and Henley far outweighs such slips. As Eric Partridge put it in his encomium of John Farmer, "Slang and Its Analogues . . . is one of the three or four most remarkable one-handed achievements in the whole record of dictionary making. His definitions are sound, his distinguishing of shades of meaning is careful and delicate, his comments are shrewd and scholarly, his essayettes on important or interesting or puzzling words are entertaining, and his understanding of the nature and tendencies of slang is remarkable. His psychology is as penetrating as his research is astounding."[59] He would also provide the groundwork for the successor whose own researches would dominate slang lexicography for most of the twentieth century: Eric Partridge himself.

While George Matsell was something of a lone voice in nineteenth-century America, the twentieth century saw great leaps forward in the country's development of slang lexicography. As any reader of popular American fiction will be aware, American slang, typically as found in the "hard-boiled" novels of Dashiell Hammett, Raymond Chandler, and their peers among the pulp magazine authors of the 1920s and 1930s, and their postwar successors such as George V. Higgins, Elmore Leonard, and Carl Hiaasen, to mention just the cream of a substantial crop, has become central to the nation's literary culture. Add to that film, television and, most recently, the slang-drenched lyrics of the "gangsta rappers" of the country's black ghettoes, and one has an enormous and ever-expanding slang vocabulary. That its glossarists and collectors have been legion is hardly surprising. The pages of such journals as *American Speech* (founded by H. L. Mencken in 1925) are full of cant and slang, while the flow of slang dictionaries continues unabated. Nor can the old distinction between "English" and "American" slang be maintained any longer. Eric Partridge could claim that his slang dictionary dealt with English and Commonwealth English only, and in 1937 (its first edition) such a claim could just about be accepted, but as World War II gave way to the 1950s and 1960s, and the great tide of American culture broke over Europe, and in particular over Britain, the line, if drawn, appeared increasingly artificial. By the editions of the 1960s Partridge had given way, although the surrender was tacit: suffice it to say that the volume of "Canadian slang" that was appearing in his dictionary might have surprised many Canadians.

Various titles stand out amid the flow of twentieth-century American slang dictionaries. In 1950 there appeared *The Dictionary of American Underworld Lingo,* edited by Hyman E. Goldin, a prison chaplain, and two assistants, Frank O'Leary and Morris Lipsius, both serving lengthy terms. They in turn had the consulting skills of such hands-on experts as "Bad Bill," "Bubbles," "Chop-Chop," "Dippo," "Iggy," "Slim," "Stubs," and "The Colonel," all of whom list their modus operandi and the jails to which it has led them. Setting aside the theatricality of their nicknames, the villains and their three editors assembled an impressive lexicon of underworld jargon. The role of such "lingo" as a truly "foreign" language is emphasized by the division of the book into Underworld-English and English-Underworld sections. The problems with any such work is that "Bad Bill," "Butch," and the boys may have told "the sky pilot" what they felt he wanted to hear, but such skepticism is probably unfair. This in-depth research was not new; it forms the basis of the many glossaries compiled by David W. Maurer, who gained admission to the Ohio State Pentitentiary where he spent nine months collecting the material that would become "The Lingo of the Jug-Heavy" and "The Lingo of the Good People." Maurer was as much a sociolinguist as a lexicographer, and never published an actual dictionary. His influence on any compiler of underworld jargon, Partridge included, was nonetheless substantial. Another compiler who based his work on his own experiences was Godfrey Irwin, whose *American Tramp and Underworld Slang* derived from his twenty years tramping the roads and railways of America. The book was published in 1931, by Eric Partridge. All these, however, are essentially collections of cant. General slang dictionaries, as opposed to a regular flow of articles in journals both learned and popular, were rarer. While both criminals and policemen might collect cant as a legitimate part of their professional activity, American lexicography looked somewhat askance at plain old slang collection.

The first American lexicon to be named a *Dictionary of Slang,* edited by Maurice Harley Westeen, appeared in 1934; it was little more than an expanded version of Matsell. Eight years later came Lester V. Berrey and Melvin Van Den

Bark's *American Thesaurus of Slang.* Based on Roget's tried-and-tested system, this was predominantly devoted to mainstream slang, although there were sections dealing with various jargons. The catholicity of its selections brought in a wide vocabulary, even if negative critics were less than charitable, suggesting that the editors had admitted far too many terms, expanding the concept of "slang" beyond reasonable limits and far into what could best be termed colloquialisms. It remains an impressive compendium, but must often be taken with care. The book that dominated American slang dictionaries for more than thirty years appeared in 1960. *The Dictionary of American Slang* was the product of two men, Harold Wentworth, editor of the *American Dialect Dictionary* and on the staff of *Webster's Second International Dictionary* (1934), and Stuart Berg Flexner, a senior lexicographer at Random House and a teacher, like Wentworth, at Cornell University. Given the fields of his research, Wentworth's "slang" dealt very much in regionalisms and colloquialisms; Flexner covered the language of the cities, including that of the underworld, show business, crime, teenagers, and allied phenomena. He also dealt widely with the coinages of the armed forces. Their book was revised in 1967 and 1975 before a new edition, *The New Dictionary of American Slang,* edited by Robert L. Chapman, appeared in 1986. Like the work of Eric Partridge in Britain that of Wentworth and Flexner lacks one important ingredient of modern lexicography: the citation. Both the Americans and the Briton (or more properly New Zealander) make an attempt to offer citations, but neither achieves the level of consistency and comprehensiveness that might be found in, say, the *OED.* This has been wholly remedied in what will undoubtedly prove to be the best American slang dictionary of this century: Jonathan Lighter's *Historical Dictionary of American Slang* (1994 *et seq.*). He benefits, as an American, from the need to research only two centuries of vocabulary (the earliest British slang terms go back to the fifteenth century) and unlike Partridge he had a number of assistants, as well as an academic post to give the economic security denied to his English predecessor, but all that is in the end tangential. With only one volume (covering A–G) of the four as yet published, there is no doubt that Dr. Lighter's work provides for American slang a depth of lexical comprehensiveness and historical research, typically in its mass of citations, that springs straight from Sir James Murray.

There remains, for the purposes of this chapter and this book, but one lexicographer: the slang collector Eric Partridge. Like many people who devoted their lives to a single, overriding pursuit, his is a relatively simple biography. Eric Honeywood Partridge was born on February 6, 1894 on a farm in the Waimata

Valley, near Gisborne, North Island, New Zealand, the same outpost of what was then the British Empire that would in 1923 see the birth of the *OED*'s Robert Burchfield. He was the first white child to be born in the area. He moved with his family to Brisbane, Australia, in 1907 and there attended grammar school. His love of literature showed itself early: aged thirteen he had already written a novel (an English public school story) and a number of short stories. His translations from French poetry began appearing in 1914. He was also, thanks to a literary father, able to use dictionaries—"those . . . sources of sober, never-disillusioning entertainment"—from the age of seven. He left school at sixteen and began working as a trainee teacher in Queensland and New South Wales. He won a scholarship to the University of Queensland and began reading classics, before switching to French and English. As it did for so many of his contemporaries, the First World War interrupted his studies, and in April 1915 he joined the Australian infantry. He served successively in Egypt, at Gallipolli, and on the Western Front where he fought in that bloody subsection of the battle of the Somme known as "the second Pozières." More than 15,000 ANZACs died fighting for this single ridge; Partridge was wounded but he survived. Looking back, he saw the war, while "in its general aspects a curse and a disaster," in the end to be "a blessing" in the experiences, both communal and personal, that it brought. For Partridge, as he admitted, it, and its successor, would be a professional and thus commercial boon too: there are few coiners of slang more profuse than the armed services.

Back in Australia he returned to university, took his B.A., and departed for Oxford University where he read for his M.A. in eighteenth-century English romantic poetry and for a B.A. in comparative literature. After Oxford he taught briefly at a Lancashire grammar school, and then at the universities of Manchester (1925–6) and London (1926–7). In 1927 came the great turning point in his life. Never a happy public speaker—despite what must have been the natural allure of his expertise for the talks producers of the BBC he would rarely allow them to place him in front of a microphone—he abandoned teaching and turned to a new career: that of "man of letters."

To back this he founded the Scholartis Press (a blend of "*schol*arly" and "*artis*tic"), which started with capital of £100 (later increased to £300) and survived until 1931 when, like so many small businesses, it foundered in the Depression, leaving its proprietor bankrupt. His first office had been at 1b, New Oxford Street, not that far from the ABC where Frederick Furnivall had "held court" thirty-odd years before. Later the firm moved to number five, then round the corner to 30 Museum Street, a stone's throw from the British Museum, where for fifty years he would become as permanent a feature as the

Reading Room itself in which, at his regular seat K1, he worked. He was joined later by two directors—Captain Bertram Radcliffe, MC and Wilson Benington (who struggled on with the Press even after the bankruptcy)—plus a secretary and errand boy, but Scholartis was always a hand-to-mouth operation. Nonetheless, as Partridge reminded his public, writing a somewhat premature "history" of the press in 1930, "We have made our way almost on our own; without acquaintances among reviewers, without friends among journalists, without taking another publisher's authors with us, and without previous experience."[60] There were nearly 100 titles in all, announced in annual catalogs which appeared under Ambrose Bierce's line: "At best a book is not too beautiful, at worst it is hideous." Twenty-two came from Partridge himself, either as author or editor. Partridge and Radcliffe also issued a journal, *The Window.* Most, including three novels by "Corrie Denison" (Partridge's pseudonym), made no real mark on the literary world but three of them indicated an important new interest for the editor-in-chief. *Songs and Slang of the British Soldier,* edited by Partridge with John Brophy, appeared in 1930; Partridge's edition of Francis Grose's *Classical Dictionary of the Vulgar Tongue* in 1931, and between them, in 1930, came the British edition of Godfrey Irwin's *American Tramp and Underworld Slang.*

In 1932 Partridge began working as a freelance and a year later came his first attempt at lexicology: *Words, Words, Words!* This was swiftly succeeded by his first look at the topic that would dominate his professional life: slang. Commissioned by Routledge, where the publisher Cecil Franklin had noticed his language-related Scholartis publications, *Slang Today and Yesterday* appeared in 1933; the book that sprang from these relatively tentative explorations into the topic, *A Dictionary of Slang and Unconventional English,* was published in 1937. Seven expanded and amended editions would appear in his lifetime. An eighth, posthumous edition (edited by Paul Beale) appeared in 1984. *A Dictionary of the Underworld,* dealing with English and American cant, was published in 1949; revised editions appeared in 1961 and 1968. *Origins,* his etymological dictionary, appeared in 1958 (revised 1961 and 1966). Partridge was a wide-ranging, prolific author, driven both by his desire, almost literally, to "preach the word," and by the need for cash. His bibliography, excluding juvenilia and the Scholartis publications, runs to some thirty-five titles, a good many of them running to more than a single edition. Aside from the dictionaries as such, the majority were lexicological: writing about words in one form or another. Among them were *Shakespeare's Bawdy* (1947), *Chamber of Horrors,* "a Glossary of Official Jargon" by "Vigilans" (1952), and *Comic Alphabets* (1961). He also wrote on punctuation: *You Have a Point There* (1953) and, in an attempt to topple Fowler's

English Usage from its dominance of the field, *Usage and Abusage* (1942). Partridge joined the Army Education Corps in World War II, later moving to the correspondence department of the RAF. Demobbed in 1945, he returned to work and continued in a career that left him unassailably as Britain's leading solo lexicographer. As well as the wordbooks he was a regular book reviewer, especially in the *Daily Telegraph,* and peppered literary editors with postcards declaring: "I am the right person to review this book." A good cricketer and tennis player in his earlier years he was a regular at Lords, the Oval, and Wimbledon, and wrote professionally on tennis. He died on June 1, 1979, a resident of a West Country nursing home, but still working on the revision of his *Dictionary of Catch Phrases,* the original of which had appeared in 1977. His wife, Agnes Vye-Parminter, whom he had married in 1925, had predeceased him, and he was survived by a single daughter.

Partridge appears here, singled out at the very end of these histories, for what may seem to be one overriding qualification. It is not that he is the sole unmentioned modern maker of dictionaries, nor are his works, which in the end concentrate on the margins of language, the best or most influential. But in an age of teams, of academic sinecures, of publishing house reference departments and substantial advances, Partridge remains in many ways the classic lexicographer of his time. After all, like "Webster" and "Johnson," "Partridge" stands among the dictionary's eponyms. Even Murray, other than for a brief period when a few Oxonians talked of "Murray's dictionary," cannot claim that honor. The great teams of editors, researchers, readers, checkers, and the rest whose labors go to make up a modern dictionary, and who stand, mainly mute but for a line's acknowledgment, behind today's works of language reference, have their place, but it lacks the individual's cachet. The world of macrolexicography, which dominates the marketplace, and is dominated by that market's demands in its turn, lacks what for want of a better word one must call the romance of the profession as carried out by a dedicated individual. Sidney Landau, in his treatise on lexicography, includes a grim page of potential costings: so many subeditors, so many readers, so many this and that at so many dollars and cents for so many hours—the backbone, no doubt, of contemporary lexicography, especially as carried out behind the imprints of publishing houses, or the colophons of university departments. All very important, but all sadly devoid of the human element.

Partridge, above all, offers a human dimension. He has, in a world where wit is at a premium, a sense of humor. As Anthony Burgess put it, he was not a linguist but a philologist, quite literally a "lover" of words.[61] And on his amorous passage he trips, he stumbles, he falls. Cheerfully refusing to admit linguistics into his lexicographical work, he always wants to make some kind of statement. Today's *OED,* especially when it comes to slang, is filled with the hard-nosed, factual, but ultimately frustrating admission: "Etymology unknown." Such an admission was wholly alien to Partridge. For him something was always better than nothing—even if that something often erred dangerously on the side of guesswork. Indeed, Partridge's refusal to acknowledge defeat could lead to terrible howlers—his original etymology for *nafka,* meaning a prostitute and quite simply the London adoption of a synonymous Yiddish word, suggested the possible elision of the English "naughty girl"—but he could be inspired. His etymological dictionary, *Origins,* was for many readers even more important than his studies of slang and cant. It is unlikely that without his efforts, flawed though they may be, there would have been anything like the breadth of slang lexicography that has characterized the twentieth century.

He was, says a source at his publishers Routledge and Kegan Paul, the original nutty professor: the big overcoat, the cigarette, the long white hair adrift, and the egg stains on the tie fresh only on the good days. This may be unfair, but the image is not wholly unpleasant. The encomia gathered in the posthumous tribute *Eric Partridge in His Own Words* do not completely disabuse one of the same feeling. What recurs is this element of basic humanity. One cannot, it seems, be much farther away from the corpus-based productions (and producers) of today's dictionaries. Living, as he did, on advances and royalties alone, unblessed by any academic stipend, unwilling and unable (thanks to weak vocal cords) to capitalize on his knowledge by way of broadcasting, let alone television, it is not surprising that on occasion he bent rules that were more easily honored by better-off writers. Sir Randolph Quirk has noted one such slip:[62] his study of jargon, published in 1952, followed his attempt to oust Fowler's hegemony as the country's usage maven. Since the jargon booklet was supposedly authored by the anonymous "Vigilans" it gave Partridge the opportunity for page after page of unashamed logrolling. Aside from the regular references to Partridge's own *Usage and Abusage,* as well as to other of his works, "Vigilans" writes in his preface of his "special debt" to Mr. Eric Partridge.[63] Seven pages on, Partridge, as editor of the Language Library, the list on which the book appeared, is commending (without explanation) the efforts of his alter ego. This is lexicographical plagiarism taken into a new dimension; it is also all too human. Partridge may have attempted to pass this off as a "literary jest"[64] but it looks more like the effort of a man who quite literally could not afford to pass up the opportunity of a little self-advertisement. Nor was this the sole example. His edition of Grose carries an epigraph (writ equally hugely on the back jacket) from "Corrie Denison": "There is far more of imagination and enthusiasm in the making of a good dictionary than in the average novel." In the composition of its forematter too, it would appear—Corrie Denison, after all, was yet another *nom de plume.* Yet if he took a little under what some might denounce as false pretenses, he more than made up for it with his endless availability as an arbiter of linguistic queries. His correspondence was voluminous, and for all those who offered him material, there were dozens more to whom he provided much-sought answers.

All of which is acceptable in its way. But what of his lexicography? Partridge is virtually unique this century in his "solo artistry" not simply because few other dictionary makers have had the perseverance, the knowledge, the dedication, or even the financial impetus to work in this way. Does *anyone,* the questioner asks, still write dictionaries by themselves? He did, and there is no doubt that viewed from 1996, his work suffered accordingly. If one takes *Webster* or the *OED* as a touchstone, then Jonathan Lighter's ongoing *Historical Dictionary of American Slang* will, when its final volume appears sometime around the turn of the millennium, prove to be a "better" work. Its inclusion of citations alone gives it a substantial advantage. But Partridge's work, read around the English-speaking world, America included, is a one-volume dictionary. Dealing with a demotic tongue, it appears in a reasonably demotic format. The *Historical Dictionary of American Slang* will run to four volumes. The author of the *DSUE* may lack, as Randolph Quirk has pointed out, "the magisterial scholarship, meticulous authentication and consistency of presentation"[65] that make the *OED* so monumental a work, but without Partridge there could never have been the same level of modern slang lexicography. The *OED* cites him more than 770 times. Nor does the *DSUE* offer a guide to pronunciation, which is in some ways a greater omission. The very nature of slang is in its orality. Perhaps for more than any other dictionary maker the problem for the slang lexicographer is that once a word or phrase has been written down, it has probably lost its bloom, and may even have been abandoned by those who coined it. Yet that same orality demands, it might be said, a guide to pronunciation, the way the word sounds. But it is perhaps an impossible task. Partridge himself pointed out that one would never know, for instance, how Victorian Londoners actually pronounced the slang they used, any more than a classicist will learn how Latin actually sounded in the mouths of its users.

What he did do, however, was amass a lexicon of English slang that will be overtaken—such is the nature of language—but never surpassed. Like any modern slang lexicographer, he was essentially a linguistic voyeur—kneeling at the keyhole to scribble down the vocabularies of worlds in which he could never take an active part—but his eyesight surpassed that of most contemporary rivals in its clarity and its breadth of vision. If only by gathering together the whole range of his predecessors, from Copland onward, he unified a vocabulary that might otherwise have vanished. His own first efforts were based on Farmer and Henley's seven-volume work of the 1890s, passed on to him for revision by his publishers, but he moved far beyond their admittedly impressive efforts. He had, of course, the *OED* against which to assay his discoveries and theories (they were forced to use the vastly inferior *Century Dictionary*), but as his many appearances in the second edition make clear: the debts were mutual.

It is perhaps sentimental to say so, but in the context of this book at least, Partridge comes over as the Platonic lexicographer: outside mainstream academe, fighting a constant battle for funds, prolific, dedicated, above all an *enthusiast*. Partridge was the least godlike of men, and work gave him an authority that he may not have sought, but which remains associated with his name. It is not too much to suggest that he will have few successors. The symbolism is easy but irresistible: Partridge's seat K1 hosts a computer terminal now, and very soon the whole Reading Room will be gone, at least as he knew it, to be replaced, apparently, by a cafeteria for visiting tourists.

To sum up Partridge and in so doing to offer a tribute to the many lexicographers who preceded him and worked, like him, very much on their own, one can do worse than borrow from the detective writer Raymond Chandler, one of Partridge's many correspondents. Describing his own efforts in a letter of 1957, Chandler suggested that "To accept a mediocre form and make something like literature out of it is in itself rather an accomplishment." In the hierarchy of language, slang is that "mediocre form"; what Partridge did was make, if not literature, then something profoundly literate out of his spurned lexicon.

15

The Modern World

⌒⟋

The twentieth century has seen lexicography expand as never before. Mass literacy and mass communications have guaranteed that the demand for dictionaries has continued to grow. Whatever the fate of the printed page, the English language, or rather the American version of that language, stands preeminent around the globe. If the men who called for an English academy, and for the codification of the English language at the start of the eighteenth century, were partially impelled by their fears of the rise of a francophone world, they could rest easy today. English is the language of scientific discourse, of airline pilots, of popular culture, of the Internet, of international communication, and of business. There are, as mapped by the *Oxford Companion to the English Language,* some 104 countries in which English is a "significant language." With all this expansion there have, unsurprisingly, been certain changes in dictionary making over the period.

Concluding his Romanes Lecture in June 1900, Sir James Murray suggested that with the creation of the *New English Dictionary* "lexicography has for the present reached its supreme development."[1] It was a magnificently confident, even arrogant, statement for a man whose own work, however splendid, had barely reached the letter J, and for a project which not that long ago had been struggling to gain the full support of its supposed backers, but viewed from nearly a century on, Murray must be given at least the benefit of the doubt. The substance of academic English-language dictionary making has indeed remained very much within the shadow of Murray's achievement. Looking at the two major ongoing projects in American lexicography, the *Dictionary of American Regional English* and the *Historical Dictionary of American Slang,* one can see Murray's legacy on every page. Such works have refined the original system, but it underpins every entry. The historical method, worked out in the Scriptorium and brought to fruition over forty years of publication, has yet to be effectively challenged. Nor need it be: the clarity, the intelligence, the sheer user-friendliness—at least to the academic or scholarly user—of Murray's method is a worthy model. Only in one area can a major change be seen: in the arrival of the computer into the world of word gathering. The increasing availability of the corpus, a vast assemblage of material among which the lexicographer can browse at will, is making for far wider word lists and offering a far easier access to all the nuances and gradations of usage that must be set out. The corpus itself is less of a novelty. Once the lexicographers began including illustrative citations, it was necessary first to establish a plan of reading. Johnson, for all his biases, did just that; the Oxford lexicographers had such a list, established by Herbert Coleridge at the very outset of the Philological Society's deliberations. Where the computer scores is in the potential all-inclusiveness of the corpora it holds. The *omnium scibile* of the Scholastics may have returned via the multigigabyte hard disk.

But if the form of the dictionary has remained relatively constant, its role has definitely altered. Above all, as Geoffrey Hughes has pointed out, the dictionary and its makers have experienced a gradual demystification.[2] Like those of religion itself, the old myths have proved harder to peddle. The audience has wanted to see behind the scenes, although, paradoxically, once taken around it has not always been that enthusiastic. Sometimes, it appears, the old magic is best left alone. The majority of the lexicographers considered above, and the dictionaries that they produced, were rooted in what might be termed an élitist tradition. They were scholars, whether professionally or as a a sideline to their mainstream work, and they wrote for those whose background or aspirations were similar. And on the whole those who used these great dictionaries were satisfied with the status quo. If the lexicographer was, if not actually God, then at least one of his ministers, their congregation remained passive and accepting. Nor did Wesley change that image. Indeed while he might have been writing for a new audience, Wesley was the most theocratic of dictionary makers: he was, after all, the real thing. The founder of Methodism had no need to hide behind a metaphorical ministry: if any lexicographer truly set out to lay open the mysteries of the language to the unlearned, it was him. However, Wesley did write for a hitherto untapped audience and in so doing was very much a lone voice. Over the last century and more that voice has been hugely amplified as such mass-market dictionaries as Funk and Wagnalls', Chambers', Longman's, Collins', and the like have appeared, and with them the subsets of "Webster" and the *OED*.

The greatest change of all, for the purposes of this book, is that of the lexicographer's own role. On the one hand he, and now she, have retained their priestly role, especially in America, and especially in the world of what America terms "college" and Britain "concise" dictionaries, but like real-life religion, the linguistic variety cannot pontificate with quite such infallibility. Nor are individual lexicographers as important any longer. In the main such individuals have been relegated to the margins. In a century when dictionaries tend more and more to be known by the name of their publisher rather than that of the author, the best-known eponymous work is probably "Partridge," i.e., the *Dictionary of Slang and Unconventional English* by Eric Partridge. "Webster" has certainly survived as a synonym for "dictionary," but Noah Webster had become a brand name rather than a person within years of his death.

Paradoxically, while few dictionary users could name a lexicographer— Robert Burchfield, editor of the *OED*'s *Supplements* and Frederick Cassidy, editor of *DARE* are as important as anyone to the world of language, but neither is likely to appear on a Trivial Pursuit card; such specialists as Noel Osselton or Gabriele Stein are for fellow practitioners only—they still expect the compilers to take responsibility for their work. The controversy over the third edition of *Webster's New International* has been branded the "second dictionary war"; more recently the imperatives of the Political Correctness lobby have been pushing their way forward.

The growth of the popular dictionary, from Wesley's nineteenth-century heirs onward, represents the most obvious area of demystification. The popular dictionary, less scholarly than its great academic peers, and aimed at a far wider audience, typically the general public or the college student, has boomed during the twentieth century. Of the thousands of English-language dictionaries that exist today a large proportion target this lucrative market. It is these dictionaries that provide the commercial impetus for such major dictionary publishers as Random House, Houghton Mifflin, Merriam-Webster, Longman, Collins, Chambers, and the rest. Oxford, somewhat tardily, entered the popular marketplace with its *Concise Oxford Dictionary* (1911), but the flow of Oxford dictionaries of many sizes, all culled ultimately from the major work, has long since made up for that. But such dictionaries are not simply a modern phenomenon, and it is necessary to glance briefly backward, to see from where emerge the roots of what most people mean when they talk of "the dictionary" today.

While John Wesley's *Complete English Dictionary* (1753) might have been seen as filling an increasing need, that of extending to the lower classes the information that his contemporary Samuel Johnson made so impressively available to their literate superiors, his work stood in isolation for nearly a century. However, when the popular dictionary did begin to emerge in Britain, it was aimed not simply at a specific group, Wesley's Methodist followers, but at anyone who needed such information. When the Chambers brothers began producing their reference works they described themselves as "publishers for the people." The Grimms in Germany and Pierre Larousse in France targeted the same public: the lower-middle and working classes. The rationale remained the same—the education, and thus emancipation of those who lacked the privileges of the élite—but the constituency was far greater. Inspired by the French and American revolutions, mass education was seen as a panacea for inequality. There was often a sense of evangelism behind their publication, and many mass-market dictionary publishers were also publishers of Bibles and religious tracts. The same "muscular Christianity" that appealed to Frederick Furnivall can be seen in the background of this drive toward popular education. As Tom McArthur has written,

> These popular dictionaries were the lineal descendants not only of the monastery copyists of the so-called Dark Ages, but also of the printers and reformers who sought in the sixteenth century to give everyman's conscience into his own keeping. Such publishing houses . . . have offered their customers a kind of secular salvation through literacy and an awareness of the power of words and organised information. They were not as radical and incendiary as Karl Marx and Friedrich Engels, but they played a comparable role in the transformation of society. Where Marx and Engels preached historical determinism and the last great revolution, these puritanical capitalists put in every bookstore better works of reference than had been available in the past to princes and prelates—and at manageable prices. They were to the mind what piped water, cheap soap and good public transport were to the body.[3]

They were not, however, agents of revolution. The dictionary helped unlock the gates, it made no effort to blast them down. If anything they have served as a form of social regulation. As Béjoint says,

> Those dictionaries did not propose radical changes in social values; they merely tried to give a large number of people access to the cultural her-

itage of their societies . . . Together with grammar-books, obligatory schooling, language academies, and more recently the mass media, they have been part of an arsenal of regulating instruments used by modern societies to ensure the smooth functioning of the linguistic code, to prevent it from becoming a myriad of subcodes, in spite of the division of the population into numerous subgroups, and eventually to maintain a sort of social cohesion.[4]

Regulatory subtext aside, the new generation of mass-market dictionaries were still ostensibly populist. And given this intrinsic ethos it was fitting that the model for the first of such works came from the republican Noah Webster. It was equally apt that its author, John Boag (1775–1863), was like Wesley an evangelist, preaching Scottish Congregationalism, often at large open-air meetings. Never a rich man (his greatest annual income was £30), Boag finally settled in the small living of Blackburn, Linlithgow, where he kept a day school. Here he compiled his dictionaries, setting out on the task when he was already seventy. Boag produced two dictionaries: the *Popular and Complete English Dictionary* (1848) and the *Imperial Lexicon of the English Language* (1852). Boag, according to the *IEL,* was, as a "lexicographical beachcomber,"[5] aware of what was worth scavenging from among his peers and predecessors, but lacking the personal ability that would make his findings into something new and worthwhile. His use of Webster's word list meant that he created as far as possible an up-to-the-minute lexicon, but by reverting to Walker's eighteenth-century standards of pronunciation, he undermined his pretensions to modernity. Nonetheless Boag had some popularity, and in the absence of any major rival, the *Popular Dictionary* sold well enough until the publication of Ogilvie's *Imperial Dictionary* in 1850. John Ogilvie (1797–1867), like Boag a Scot, worked as a plow-man before, in 1818, an accident led to the amputation of one of his legs. He turned to schoolteaching and simultaneously pursued his own studies, graduating M.A. at Mirischal College, Aberdeen, at the age of thirty-one. In 1836 the publishers Blackie recruited him to annotate an earlier Biblical history then, in 1838, asked him to prepare a revised edition of "Webster." The *Imperial Dictionary, English, Technical and Scientific,* began appearing in 1847; when finished two years later it was issued in two large volumes. Basing his efforts on Webster's word list, Ogilvie included as many English neologisms as he could find, adding some 15,000 words to Webster, plus another 20,000 in the supplement which appeared with the revised edition of 1863. Many, however, were combinations rather than genuine additions and, as Wheatley remarked, serve only to "encumber" the original.[6] Ogilvie's real enthusiasms lay in the technical and scientific vocabulary. In pursuing this area, which was generally excluded from the *NED*—science being somewhat alien to the scholarly interests of the Oxford élite—Ogilvie backed his definitions with many illustrations. It was another aspect that, like the word list, reflected American lexicography, where the encyclopedic dictionary, replete with nonlexical material, has always maintained its popularity.

Ogilvie's dictionary was taken over after his death by the third of these Scottish lexicographers, Charles Annandale, whose edition appeared in 1882. His own *Concise Dictionary of the English Language* followed in 1886. Annandale's revision of Ogilvie maintained the encyclopedic content but improved the purely lexicographic. Obsolete words were cut, pronunciation guides improved, and the layout made for far easier reference. Like its predecessors, Annandale's work sold well: the mass-market dictionary was undoubtedly an established point in the lexicographical landscape. There remained one drawback: what all such dictionaries required was a single authority upon which they could draw. Webster was American, the English market required something homegrown. The *NED,* of which the first fascicle appeared in 1884, would provide just what was needed. One last popular dictionary deserves mention. Not all of these compilers turned to America for inspiration. Hyde Clarke, whose *New and Comprehensive Dictionary of the English Language* appeared in 1855, remained within the English tradition. His work, long since overtaken, stands as a direct link between the old and new styles of dictionary. His word list is limited to just 100,000 words, and, in what was then a revolutionary move, he noted the importance of colloquial, nonliterary English. Scholarly dictionaries had invariably looked to tried-and-tested classics; the mid-nineteenth century, with its flourishing newspaper press, ought to look at the English people spoke, as well as what they read and, if capable, wrote. In his method and his appreciation of the spoken word, Clarke prefigured twentieth-century thinking; in the way of such prophets he was ignored in his own time. Even the popular dictionary required heft; many words and plenty of encyclopedic content. Clarke eschewed excess and the public sadly eschewed his work.

Boag, Ogilvie, Annandale, and Clarke were all individual lexicographers. The dictionaries issued by the Chambers brothers, William and Robert, were simply one more aspect of a firm that had been established in 1819 as a general publishers. The sons of a bankrupt Peebles draper, the Chamberses bought themselves a hand-operated press, the first product of which was the *Songs of Robert Burns.* In 1832 they launched a magazine—*Chambers Journal*—which climbed to a circulation of 80,000 a week. In 1834 they launched their "part-work," *Chambers's Information for the People,* a series of broadsheets dealing with science, mathematics, history, geography, and literature. This sold an astounding 2 million copies. After the 100-title *Education Course* they began issuing *Chambers's Encyclopedia,* another educational blockbuster which appeared in 520 weekly parts from 1859 to 1868. It was still appearing, in new editions, a century later. It was logical that they should sooner or later add a dictionary to their list. It appeared in 1861 when A. J. Cooley edited a *Dictionary of the English Language; Chambers's English Dictionary* appeared in 1872. Its most recent edition was published in 1988.

As far as America was concerned, it was hardly surprising that the populist approach that satisfied Webster would prove just as appealing to his successors. Some of the major dictionaries of the late nineteenth century, typically the *Century Dictionary* (1889–95), might well have been compared to the emerging *NED* in terms of size and scholarship, but they came to the topic with very different aims in mind. The unashamed élitism of the *NED* simply didn't wash in America, even in the most scholarly of works.

The *Century Dictionary and Cyclopedia,* edited by the philologist William Dwight Whitney, began appearing in 1889. Whitney (1827–94) combined orientalism and the writing of grammars with his lexicography. Like many of England's dictionary makers, Whitney had studied at the feet of the German philologists, notably Franz Bopp. When he returned to Yale his Sanskrit professor, Edward Salisbury, resigned in his favor and paid for his successor's salary out of his own pocket. Among his many works was a Sanskrit grammar that is still used today. The series of lectures he gave on language in 1867 and 1875 were widely reported. Among those they influenced was the French philologist Ferdinand de Saussure and through him Whitney can be seen as a very early founder of structuralism. Within his lifetime Whitney was best known for his *Essentials of English Grammar,* which ran to eighteen editions between 1877 and 1903. Whitney's dictionary encompassed three parts—the Dictionary proper, a Cyclopedia of Names, and an Atlas. By the time publication was complete it ran to eight large volumes and 7,000 pages. A wide-ranging reference work, its "Encyclopedic Lexicon of the English Language" formed the most important part. While it was a primarily American work, it had begun in 1882 as an adaptation of Ogilvie's *Imperial Dictionary,* thus completing a neat circle, since the *Imperial* had itself first looked to America. However, that same circle brought with it certain problems and the *Century* included a disclaimer, referring to "certain owners of American copyrights" who had "claimed that undue use of matter so protected has been made in the compilation . . ." These owners were, of course, G. & C. Merriam, who had initially permitted the *Imperial Dic-*

tionary to use material taken from their editions of "Webster." As well as this disclaimer, the *Century* agreed with Merriam that there would be no spinoffs from their large work. Merriam was thus left free to exploit the school market, for which they had not that long ago fought and won the "dictionary war." Despite this stricture, which kept the *Century* from establishing the same sort of lexicographical dynasty as have "Webster" and the *OED*, the *Century* published a supplement in 1909 and a revised edition, the *New Century Dictionary,* in 1927. It then vanished, although not before a number of small dictionaries had taken it for their basis and thus, the Merriams notwithstanding, incorporated it, however invisibly, into the American lexicographical tradition. It also won a place in Britain. When the *Century* appeared the *NED* had barely begun publishing and its editors both noted and quickly began replicating the American prototype's infinitely superior coverage of technical and scientific material.

That the evangelical role in dictionary making proved equally strong on both sides of the Atlantic is hardly surprising. Mainstream lexicography in America had always involved a strong clerical presence—it was hardly likely that the popular version would be any different. America's first determinedly popular dictionary, Isaac Kauffman Funk's *Standard Dictionary of the English Language,* appeared in 1893. Isaac Funk (1839–1912) was trained as a Lutheran minister in Springfield, Ohio, and spent the twelve years from 1861 to 1872 as a pastor in Ohio and New York before being appointed editor of the *Christian Radical,* based in Philadelphia, Pennsylvania. In 1876 he returned to New York, where he set up a printing house; his old school friend, Adam Willis Wagnalls, joined the enterprise a year later. The decision to market a dictionary was taken in 1890 and in three years it was ready for publication. Funk was very much a team player. He employed more than 740 editors, specialists, and readers and aimed "to produce a dictionary that would provide essential information thoroughly and simply."[7] The dictionary they created was geared very much to contemporary life. Unlike the historical dictionaries, Funk and Wagnalls placed current meanings first, obsolete and archaic ones second, and etymologies last. Such innovations would become the norm in popular dictionary publishing. Appreciating the need of his readers for linguistic guidance, he gave two pronunciations for each entry: one representing the popular pronunciation, the other showing the precise one. For all that American popular dictionaries are particularly important to their readers for their pre- and proscriptivism—if a word is not "in the dictionary" it isn't a legitimate word—Funk, creator of one of the most popular of all, resisted laying down the law. Like the beleaguered editors of *Webster's Third International* seventy years later he declared that the dictionary could only describe language, not dictate its rights and wrongs; in 1893 this comment, which itself only echoed the views of Chauncey Goodrich, Noah Webster's own chosen successor, passed without furor. Like Webster, Funk advocated spelling reform and was a member of the Simplified Spelling Board. After his death his brother Benjamin Franklin Funk and Benjamin's son Charles Earle Funk took over the business, vastly expanding the production of every type of dictionary. Like "Webster," "Funk and Wagnalls" became a synonym for dictionary—there is no other so prevalent— and even starred briefly as a popular catchphrase: "Look that up in your Funk and Wagnalls!" a regular exclamation on the late sixties' television comedy show *Rowan and Martin's Laugh-In.* Other than Johnson's cameo in *Vanity Fair* it may be one of the few such "fictional" appearances.

The enormous popularity of the Funk and Wagnalls dictionaries was especially helped by one of their editors, the British-born Francis Horace Vizetelly, generally known as Frank. Frank Vizetelly (1864–1938) was the son of Henry Vizetelly (1820–94), publisher, journalist, engraver, and editor, a figure whose defiance of the strictures of late-Victorian taste, as prescribed by the circulating libraries and the demands of the three-decker novel, would eventually lead him to jail. Vizetelly specialized in cheap, single-volume editions of literary works, and, in association with the much-vilified sex educator Henry Havelock Ellis (1859–1939), the Mermaid series of unexpurgated reprints of "The Best Plays of the Old Dramatists." He also published translations of Flaubert, Gogol, Tolstoy, the Brothers Goncourt, and early detective fiction from Gaboriau and du Boisgobey. By 1888 he had published, with some deletions, seventeen novels by Émile Zola, an author whose fame in his native France was balanced only by his lurid reputation in England where such an authority as Tennyson condemned his books as "the drainage of your sewer." The authorities had not hitherto bothered with Vizetelly, but his publication of Zola's *La Terre* in 1888 excited the interest of the National Vigilance Association, a contemporary antivice society particularly exercised by the French novel, and simultaneously provided the Establishment, which had become increasingly agitated by the growth of French "naturalist" writing, with an excuse to attack this bugbear. Vizetelly was charged with "uttering" and "publishing certain obscene libels," notably Zola's novel and books by de Maupassant, Daudet, Flaubert, and Gautier. After a trial in which one juryman objected to passages from the novel being read out in court, Vizetelly was fined and *The Times* condemned the book as "mere and sheer obscenity, naked shameless and unutterably vile" and stated "We cannot but rejoice, therefore, that Mr. Vizetelly has acknowledged his offence and been punished for it." That the major "erotic" incident in *La Terre* was the mating of a cow and a bull was not specified. In 1889 Vizetelly repeated the offense, publishing works by Zola, de Maupassant, and Paul Bourget. Despite a petition for his release, signed by many eminent figures, and his patently obvious ill health, he was sentenced to three months in prison. The NVA journal remarked sanctimoniously, "We trust that his imprisonment may not unduly affect his health." His company was bankrupted and he died in 1894. His son Frank proved less controversial, becoming one of America's leading lexicographical gurus. His column "The Lexicographer's Easy Chair," published in the *Literary Digest* (another Funk and Wagnalls publication) made him the nation's leading authority on the meanings and usage of words; it also helped spread the sales of his company's books.

In 1913, when the company published its *New Standard Dictionary of the English Language,* edited by Frank Vizetelly and offering readers some 450,000 headwords, it seemed that Funk and Wagnalls would never relinquish their importance in American lexicography. In the event this was not so. Isaac Funk's determination to promote spelling reform, which had been sustained in all the company's dictionaries, proved their undoing. These reforms, which remained integral to the dictionaries until the 1940s, gradually alienated readers. The company also blundered badly in failing to revise the *New Standard.* When Merriam-Webster published the 1934 second edition of the *New International,* there was no response from their major competitor. Funk and Wagnalls remained a dictionary name into the 1960s, but their great days were long gone.

The flow of popular dictionaries on both sides of the Atlantic, and indeed in such lexicographically enthusiastic countries as Germany and France, where Pierre Larousse and Emile Littré laid down the basis of a flourishing modern marketplace, shows no sign of diminishing. Whether their quality matches their quantity is another matter. A number of commentators have noted that all too often what is loudly touted as a "new" work is no more than an old one under new covers. Whether, however, such criticisms extend beyond the professional lexicographical community is debatable.

If the subject of the public's involvement in lexicography, of what the dictionary user requires, desires, and what he or she is offered by the dictionary maker, has been left to this final chapter, it is because the whole idea of genuinely public involvement comes so late to lexicography itself. If one looks at the introductions offered by early lexicographers, at Johnson's "Plan" and his subsequent "Preface," even at Dean Trench's exegesis on the ideal dictionary, the mass user is notable only by his or her absence. The user is considered, of course, but that user is almost invariably an intellectual, a fellow scholar, an aspirant, if not an actual "priest." Even in America the role of the user in the process was secondary. And on the whole, as has been noted, the user has been reasonably happy to accept what was placed on offer. In Britain, where the role of the dictionary is primarily seen as that of a description of the national language, a dictionary passed muster if it offered exactly that, and as substantially as possible. In America, where readers wished to be told, via the dictionary, which words they could use and how best to use them, the dictionary was perfectly acceptable so long as it laid down those laws. However, once one moves beyond the practical, dictionaries take on certain abstract properties, and it is when these are perceived as being tampered with or worse still discarded, that the public, usually so acquiescent, starts to kick up a fuss. These properties fall roughly into four main categories: the dictionary as a guardian of linguistic purity; the dictionary as a repository of society's collective knowledge; the dictionary as a guardian of absolute and eternal truth; and of the moral and ideological values of society. Once again, in all of these, one sees the lexicographer in priestly mode. It has been suggested that none of these concepts truly holds water, any more than do the credulous myths that underpin religion. The "real" dictionary cannot come up to the standards that its users wish to impart to it. But in the end that hardly matters: if a dictionary on these lines is more fantasy than fact, it is still the fantasy that attracts the buyers.

It has also been suggested that the days of lexicographical authority are dead, that like society itself there is no longer an overriding standard to which one can appeal, and which in turn may be imposed and accepted. Yet if this is so, it seems that the majority of dictionary buyers, rather than rejoice in this freedom of intellectual choice, appear to resent it, or at least find it a little too unrestrained. The swing to the right, which has supposedly overtaken the larger society, has touched lexicography too. The congregation still desires its priest, however much the priest may offer to lay aside his or her vestments. Thus it is when the priest is seen as abrogating his function, as tossing away the centuries of prescriptivism, that the "congregation" starts, most vociferously, to complain. Nor is this the petty censorship of a few localized bigots, forcing their own fears onto the larger community. The clashes over the publication of *Webster's Third International Dictionary,* popularly abbreviated as *W3,* have been termed the second "dictionary war." That indeed it was, but on this occasion the battle was joined not so much between rival publishers, although some would jump enthusiastically forward to capitalize on "Webster's" perceived weaknesses, as between the lexicographers and the public for whom they worked. Asked to use their own brains, to make their own decisions, the dictionary buyers and the critics, journalists, and scholars who interceded for them, rebeled.

W3, a revision of its predecessor of 1934, which in turn had been based on *Webster's New International Dictionary* (1909), was effectively the eighth edition of Noah Webster's original work of 1828. Its main advances, under its editor Philip Babcock Gove (1902–1972), were the inclusion of a greater range of technical and specialized material, more precise etymologies and a general move away from America's traditional prescriptive lexicography, toward a more descriptive, British style. Many archaisms had been dropped—the dictionary now "began" in 1755—proper names had largely been abandoned and the usual encyclopedic material, so essential to decades of American dictionary making, had been left aside. Most of its predecessor *W2*'s illustrations had been omitted. If anything, the work was more scholarly than *W2:* a wide range of minutely detailed pronunciation variations were included; symbols had been included to take the place of repeated headwords; only "God" and trademarks were printed with an upper-case initial letter. All these things might have been open to criticism, but these were mere practicalities. In what was a cultural and ideological struggle facts were of secondary import; it was theories that would excite so much complaint.

It might be suggested that for a large, "unabridged" dictionary such as "Webster," with its 450,000 headwords, there should in any case be no place for a pre- or proscriptive word list. The role of such a dictionary is to display the language to as great an extent as possible. That, in essence, was the argument put forward by Gove and his supporters, typically such linguists and lexicographers as Raven I. McDavid, Allen Walker Read, I. Willis Russell, and Robert L. Chapman. It was not, however, what many commentators—typically the amateur, but hugely respected "word men" of the press, some teachers, and certain rival lexicographers—wished to hear. If Webster, the very cornerstone of American lexicography, and thus the repository of every aspect of linguistic yeas and nays, was casting aside its responsibilities, what hope remained? For its critics *W3* represented a gross abnegation of responsibility. It was not a dereliction of duty they intended to let go by. The attacks on *W3* began in a piece in the *New York Times* of October 12, 1961. Using a term that would become increasingly widely heard in the decade to come, the writer accused Merriam-Webster of surrendering to the "permissive school"; eight days later the *Chicago Times* used the term again, and wondered how a writer could possibly write decent English if "Webster" itself refused to say what exactly was "good English." The idea that the writer might be able to make up his or her own mind was not, of course, entertained. The concept of Gove as a harbinger of permissiveness was especially ironic: as his biographer Herbert Morton has said, Gove was "conservative in his political and social views . . . difficult to approach and autocratic, indifferent to the opinions and concerns of others."[8] This was a man whose first words to his wife-to-be had been to suggest she dress more modestly (a dress revealed her ankles as she bent forward) and who enforced a near-Trappist silence upon his editors. None of which made him any less of a lexicographer, but it hardly set him among the radicals.

As the attacks gathered force and the controversy swept on into a new year the dictionary was accused of dealing "a serious blow" to the English language, of willfully abandoning its role as the guardian of linguistic purity and of betraying the legacy of Noah Webster himself. Not everyone was so exercised against *W3*. Its defenders rejoiced in the expansion of American English and praised *W3* for opening its pages to the actual, rather than the idealized, vocabulary. British reviewers saw it quite simply as a major contribution to lexicography. Robert Burchfield, only four years into the creation of the *OED*'s *Supplements,* realized that he would need to take as much notice of *W3* as had James Murray of the *Century.* But Gove's supporters were drawn mainly from his peers and they looked at the dictionary from an essentially professional viewpoint. Theirs might not be unequivocal praise, but the criticisms were those that Gove could understand. The attacks that hurt were those from the self-appointed arbiters of language. Rarely professional dictionary makers, they trumpeted their pontifications with the glib assurance of the ignorant. The mass public, seduced by form over content, found them infinitely plausible.

To turn from the general to the specific, the area in which *W3* appeared to terrify its critics most was in its dropping of such labels as "colloquial" and "informal" and replacing them by such as "nonstandard," "substandard," and, occasionally, "slang." What was especially upsetting was the inclusion of the word *ain't,* which was noted as being "used orally in most parts of the U.S. by many cultivated speakers" even though its definition included the demurrer "though disapproved by many and more common in less educated speech." *W2* had hitherto prescribed it as simply "illiterate" or at best "dialect." The Toronto *Globe & Mail* spoke for many when, after perusing the advance publicity material, it fulminated on September 8, 1961 that the dictionary's embrace of *ain't* "will comfort the ignorant, confer approval upon the mediocre and subtly imply that proper English is the tool only of the snob . . ." At the height of the Cold War such laxity might, it implied, even bring about the nuclear apocalypse: "In the caves, no doubt, a grunt will do."[9] Nor was literary usage any more satisfactory. Critics balked at the justification of terms through their use in such writers as Henry Miller, Mickey Spillane, or Polly Adler, a brothel keeper turned best-selling memoiriste; the literary standing of past and future presidents—Harry S Truman and Richard Nixon—was less than popular too.

That there were perfectly good reasons for many of the changes between *W2* and *W3* was irrelevant. *W2,* at 600,000 entries, was simply as large as a single-volume work could be. The old days of simply adding more pages to each successive dictionary were over. For every new entry that came in—and there had been many coinages over the past twenty-six years—one must be excised. Cuts had to be made, and Gove prepared a 17-point list of material that would either be cut outright (the gazetteer, the bulk of foreign terms, virtually all the traditional encyclopedic material such as names of fictional characters, mottoes, and proverbs, names of organizations, and the like) or substantially shortened (slang and dialect, illustrations, etc.). To Gove it was all perfectly logical. To his critics it was certainly not.

As far as the language issues were concerned, it was the old clash between the pragmatists and the ideologues, between those who set down as far as possible what really was happening and those who wished only to perpetrate some utopian fantasy. At the same time it could be seen as epitomizing the continual divergence of opinion between those who *make* dictionaries (who quite naturally wish their work to reflect the current advances in their profession) and those who *use* them (who prefer that what they have set up as this most authoritative of books, should remain, other than perhaps in the inclusion of a certain number of acceptable neologisms, absolutely the same). Philip Gove and his assistants had no doubts: "For us to attempt to prescribe the language would be like *Life* reporting the news as its editors would prefer it to happen,"[10] he remarked in answer to the *New York Times* attack, and later, writing in 1967, he added, "Lexicography should have no traffic with guesswork, prejudice, or bias or with artificial notions of correctness and superiority. It must be descriptive and not prescriptive."[11] But the idea that a lexicographer should be an objective figure, simply laying out the linguistic stall, responsible for its arrangement but not for the quality of the goods displayed, held no sway with the anti-Webster ideologues. Ambrose Bierce may facetiously have defined a dictionary as "a malevolent literary device for cramping the growth of a language and making it hard and inelastic"[12] but it appeared that what he threw off as a jibe was for many a utopia.

One of the most splenetic of *W3*'s critics, Wilson Follett, whose attack was entitled "Sabotage in Springfield" (Springfield, Massachusetts is the home of Merriam-Webster), saw "what will rank as the great event of American linguistic history in this decade . . . [as] a very great calamity." *W3* had "thrust upon us a dismaying assortment of the questionable, the perverse, the unworthy and the downright outrageous."[13] Readers were destined for "disappointment and shock"[14] and the piece is studded with denunciatory epithets: "snap judg-

ments . . . a scandal and a disaster . . . crude neologisms, shabby diction . . ."
and so on. Even greater venom emerges when faced with *W3*'s dogged refusal to
tell him what is or is not "correct" usage. This, it appears, is insupportable.
Worst of all, there is, he implies darkly, some form of "predetermined rhetorical
pattern, may be [*sic*] products of a theory"[15] underpinning the whole enterprise.
As one does when reading the criticisms of the somewhat more cautious Jacques
Barzun, another conservative scholar who saw *W3*'s populism as a dangerously
"political" document, one senses a cold warrior of lexicography speaking. Finally
Follett refuses to free the dictionary makers of their responsibilities. If they
stumble, the whole edifice may fall. He cited as "the rock-bottom practical
truth" his view that "the lexicographer cannot abrogate his authority if he wants
to. He may think of himself as a detached scientist reporting the facts of language, declining to recommend use of anything or abstention from anything;
but the myriad consultants of his work are not going to see him so . . . The fact
that the compilers disclaim authority and piously refrain from judgements is
meaningless; the work itself, by virtue of its inclusions and exclusions, its mere
existence, is a whole universe of judgements received by millions as the Word
from on high." If the lexicographer will not acknowledge his priestly role, the
congregation will fall into sin. If the definer will not take his duties seriously,
what is he encouraging but "subversion and decay? To the swallower of the definition it never occurs that he can have drunk corruption from a well that he has
every reason to trust as the ultimate in purity."[16] For the more hysterical of the
complainants, the "shamans," as Dwight Bolinger termed them[17] of knee-jerk
prescriptivism, it was a veritable betrayal of their faith. They had set "the dictionary" on high, now the lexicographers, their priests, appeared to have abandoned them. The more anguished of the criticisms seemed at times like the cries
of lovers betrayed. Yet in many ways the lexicographers, of whatever persuasion,
should have been delighted that their "drudgery" was capable of generating such
heat. As Raven McDavid pointed out somewhat later,

> In 1961 there was far more newspaper concern, editorial and otherwise,
> with the Merriam-Webster's Third New International Dictionary than
> with American policy toward Southeast Asia, and the good grey *New York
> Times* objected far more strenuously to the real or imagined defects of the
> Third than it did to Mr. Kennedy's taking what turned out to be irre-
> trievable commitments to South Viet Nam.[18]

But there was another, wider dimension to the furor: in the nonlexicographical world the clashes over *W3* denoted a very definite cultural gulf, one that

would be seen throughout the sixties. Webster was an institution, and like so many institutions, it was perceived as weakening, as kowtowing to popularism, as running with the mob instead—as the traditionalists wished—of curbing its distasteful excesses. As the linguistic authority Mario Pei put it in the *Saturday Review*, "[The] battle was not merely over language. It was over a whole philosophy of life. Should there be a directing class, qualified as such by reason of intellect, education and general culture, or should there be unbridled democracy with a nose counting process to determine what was good and what was bad?"[19] It was a question that would be posed time and time again through the sixties and beyond. The jury remains out, but prosecution and defense each continues to plead its case. Follett's intemperate, ultimately fearful, attack was one of many. Under the headline "New Dictionary Cheap, Corrupt" the *Detroit News* trembled as it wondered what might happen when the "sentry forsakes his post . . . [the] guardian ceases to guard . . ."[20] Samuel Johnson would have approved of the sentiment, but he had discovered long since that these attempts to "fix" a language were futile. Another linguistic panjandrum, the very antithesis of Johnson, would have enjoyed the squabbles. No one, suggested H. L. Mencken, ever lost money underestimating the intelligence of the public; the mistake in this case was to overestimate it.

Ironically, for all the accusations of excessive populism, there was and continues to be no group more keen on maintaining the lexicographical status quo than the public itself. Survey after survey records that dictionary users, in America at any rate, want their dictionaries to lay down the lexical law. The last thing, apparently, they desire is to use their own judgment. Not only that, they yearn for the full compass of encylopedic material to be included too. The immediate response to *W3* as far its rivals were concerned was to jump on the traditionalist bandwagon and assert, as loudly and profitably as possible, their conservative beliefs. The American Heritage Company went so far as to make a bid to buy out G. & C. Merriam, their avowed intention being to "save" a great institution. The company's chairman, James Parton, promised that "We'd take the Third out of print! We'd go back to the Second International and speed ahead on the Fourth. It'll take two or three years . . ."[21] This bid was foiled and instead the company began preparing its own dictionary, published in 1969 as the *American Heritage Dictionary*. It is ironic, although perhaps predictable, that this self-proclaimedly traditionalist dictionary should have been the first mainstream American dictionary to include the word *fuck*. Its editor, William Morris, however, made his larger policy absolutely clear: the *AHD* would "faithfully record our language, the duty of any lexicographer, but it would not, like so many others in these permissive times, rest there. On the contrary, it would add the essential dimension of guidance, that sensible guidance towards grace and precision which intelligent people seek in a dictionary . . ."[22] Such views have been challenged by Sidney Landau, who suggests that it is prescriptivism, not descriptivism, that actually invalidates a dictionary's claims to real authority: "Even if a dictionary is supposed to be prescriptive, as we were told the *American Heritage Dictionary* was to be, it cannot be prescriptive and be an honest work . . . defining is not a process of value judgement. If one started to make value judgements, one would find oneself contradicting or ignoring the evidence one hundred times a day, and one might as well discard all citations of actual usage and fabricate a metaphysical universe of correct speech forms that would be of interest only to oneself."[23] After all, one of the underpinnings of "the dictionary" is a presumption of neutrality, of lexicographical objectivity: abandon that and the myth of authority is de facto weakened. Time, Inc. and CBS also looked at the company: neither made a bid. In the end Merriam-Webster did fall to a new owner: Encylopaedia Britannica, Inc. Since 1964, when the takeover was achieved, there has been no further major revision, although addenda to *W3* have appeared and the wide range of Webster's "college" dictionaries continue to appear.

The prescriptivism/descriptivism debate is of course not quite so simple. The responsible prescriptive lexicographer does not simply lay down the law at the prompting of his or her own whim, motivated by no more than a desire to impose their solipsistic credo on the wider world. Chapter and verse is duly cited, although what an older era termed "the best writers" is nothing if not a subjective assessment. For liberals the hysterical response to *W3* of a Wilson Follett smacks of mossy-backed censorship. But in one respect he is right: the lexicographer *is* responsible (practically, however, rather than morally) for the word list. Given that the genuinely "unabridged" dictionary is out of the question, the omission of a single word that might qualify, through whatever use, as "English" means that a prescriptive decision has been taken. Nor can the descriptivists, by the very nature of their devotion to describing, omit some form of acknowledgment of the way language has been used as time has passed. The difference, however, between stating, as do the prescriptivists, this is right, that is wrong, and simply laying out the varieties of usage, just as the dictionary offers varieties of definition, is what draws the line between one form of lexicography and another. The most obvious example of such use is the treatment of taboo or "insulting" language. The descriptivist will include the term and note it as "derogatory" or "offensive" or "taboo." The prescriptivist will merely omit it. It should also be acknowledged that outside the major general-purpose dictionaries, and sometimes within them, there has been a slight trend toward greater prescriptivism. The *Concise Oxford* (seventh edition, 1982) appends a symbol—D—to warn that a given term is one which "although widely found, is still the subject of much adverse comment by a significant number of educated writers." Oxford's transatlantic publication, the *Oxford American Dictionary* (1980) has some 600 specific guidelines as to usage. As for "ain't," the inclusion of which in *W3* caused so much heartache, the *OAD* declares unblushingly that the word "is avoided in standard speech." A 1973 Random House dictionary offered a mealier mouth, but left no one who worries about these things in the slightest doubt as to its own position: "Ain't is so traditionally and widely regarded as nonstandard that it should be shunned by all who prefer not to be considered illiterate." Emily Post must be smiling.

In the end the argument remains as unresolved as does the ever-expanding language defy efforts to "fix" it. One can only warn against an excess of smugness by either side. The mistake, suggests Rosamund Moon, is to believe in any myth of authority in the first place. "The real subversiveness of dictionaries does not lie in their condoning or even encouraging nonstandard uses, as the critics of *WNID3* [*W3*] claimed, but rather in their practice of covertly promoting the personal views of the lexicographers responsible while overtly setting out those views as if fact. Dictionaries' claims to 'authority' are hollow: the UAD [Unidentified Authorizing Dictionary] is a myth."[24]

Reviewing the *Random House Webster's College Dictionary* (1991), *Time* magazine assailed its editors for their inclusion of such words as *chairpersonship, herstory, humankind,* and *womyn,* suggesting, in terms reminiscent of the *W3* arguments, that such catholicity failed to "protect English from the mindless assaults of the trendy." For "trendy," read Politically Correct or PC, the current sticking point in linguistic usage, which affects the writing of dictionaries as much as any other form of text.

It is all too easy to mock the excesses of PC. Many deserve such mockery. However much the defenders may argue the need for such changes in terminology, the very term "political correctness" smacks of cant—the hypocritically pietistic variety, rather than honest criminal slang. The true believer, however secular the "religion," requires the apostate to justify that belief. The urge to save humanity, said Mencken, is almost always a false front for the urge to rule.[25] Neither irony, humor, nor self-knowledge penetrate that carapace of self-satisfaction. The dictionary, with its mythical "authority" already in place, is a particularly susceptible target. Attacking that authority is at the heart of much PC criticism, but it can also be exploited. As Geoffrey Hughes has noted, "awareness that a dictionary has an authoritative format and status has led to

works being put out under the title of 'dictionary' which turn out to be glossaries with a clear ideological or 'consciousness-raising' content."[26] *The Dictionary of Cautionary Words and Phrases* (1991), compiled, according to its
foreword, by Multicultural Management Program Fellows, a group of journalists from a range of big-city American newspapers, aims to facilitate PC journalism. Thus it defines as follows:

> *Articulate:* Can be considered offensive when referring to a minority, par-
> ticularly a black person, and his or her ability to handle the English lan-
> guage. The usage suggests that "those people" are not considered well
> educated, articulate, and the like. *Burly:* An adjective too often associated
> with large black men, implying ignorance, and considered offensive in
> this context. *Community:* Implies a monolithic culture in which people
> act, think, and vote in the same way. Do not use, as in Asian, Hispanic,
> black, or gay community. Be more specific as to what the group is: e.g.,
> black residents in a northside neighborhood. *The Myth:* Avoid any word,
> description, or phrase that contributes to the stereotype of black males as
> strictly athletic, well proportioned, or having high sexual drives and
> exaggerated sex organs. *Woman:* The preferred term for a female adult.
> Girl is appropriate only for those 17 years old and under. Avoid gal and
> lady. Also avoid derogatory terms for women, such as skirt, broad, chick,
> bimbo, bumbo, babe, ball and chain, and little woman. Also avoid adjec-
> tives describing female physical attributes or mannerisms such as pert,
> petite, foxy, buxom, fragile, feminine, stunning, gorgeous, statuesque, or
> full-figured.

It is, to reiterate, easy to mock. And censorship, even of this superliberal,
ultrapatronizing variety, is invariably dangerous. Yet to stay, for a moment, in
the lower case, it is possible to argue that every dictionary, including supposedly general-purpose dictionaries with ostensibly nary an ax to grind, has, in
some way, been "politically correct." None more so than that of Samuel Johnson, whose High Tory subtext was dedicated unequivocally to maintaining the
governmental status quo. Although Follett had enlisted his arguments in a
misguided cause—*Webster's Third* has long since become as respected an arbiter
of linguistic mores as any of its peers or predecessors, proving, as *Business Week*
had suggested back in 1961, that Merriams' only real mistake had been to
publish "twenty years ahead of its market"[27]—in refusing to allow the lexicographer to shuck off all responsibility for the prejudices endemic to his or her
work, he is reflecting the views of many critics, professional and otherwise, in

this poststructuralist world. If such authorities as George Lukács are right, and the nature of any piece of writing is determined by the social background and ideological standpoint of the writer, why should the lexicographer be different? Whether creating a descriptive or prescriptive dictionary, the lexicographer is in some way *parti pris.* If, as has been the thesis of this book, one accepts that the lexicographer is more priest than drudge, however wearisome his living may often be, it would seem obvious that the task, however ostensibly disinterested, brings with it an inescapable burden of personal bias. There are so many points of possible contention: the sources from which a word list is compiled—strictly literary or general and colloquial, written or oral—the inclusion or exclusion of certain words—"standard" language only or examples of slang, dialect, jargon, and other "marginal" vocabularies—the definitions of those words, their accenting, and pronunciation, the stance that is taken on a given etymology, the text that is used to produce a citation. To an extent some of these questions can answered by the nature of the dictionary—a learners' dictionary works on certain assumptions, as does one prepared for schoolchildren or college students, while specialist dictionaries tend to dictate their own word lists—but even here, there is room for individual prescriptivism, however well obscured. It does not need the out-and-out partiality of a Johnson or a Webster, whose definitions of key words leave one in no doubt as to their standpoint, to see the dictionary as a code for current cultural and ideological assumptions. The French writer H. Meschonnic has suggested that the dictionary is exactly the sort of text "that one should read between the lines, where the conflicts, the hidden and ignored oppositions, the clichés that make up the family album of a culture can be detected more easily than anywhere else."[28] Dictionaries, adds the feminist Deborah Cameron, "speak only for some people, and their authority is political, not grammatical." As such, they may not be valueless, especially for those who "aspire to educated middle-class usage . . . [but] they are not the objective and exhaustive record they claim to be."[29] Nor are definitions, whatever their biases, as static as they may appear. The reader takes that which is required. The novelist and linguistic gamester Georges Perec showed, in a project entitled Automatic Production of French Literature (PALF), how by choosing a series of dictionary definitions any one line may be worked through to reveal itself as any other. Thus Mallarmé's celebrated line "The presbytery has lost none of its charm nor the garden its splendour" can, if one follows the line from definition to definition, always choosing the most suitable branch (since many single words are open to a number of definitions, any one of which can be chosen), reveal itself as Karl Marx's "Workers of the world, unite!"

Such biases also spring from chronology: the period in which a particular lexicographer was working. To criticize the *OED*, as a recent book has done,[30] as overly middle-class, masculinist, chauvinist, imperialist, and insulting to minority groups, is to batter down an open door. Judged by the narrow standards of contemporary political correctness, of course the *OED*, and any other dictionary of its time (as well as many that have followed), fell into these errors. Its citations, while more broadly based than those of Samuel Johnson, betray the biases and inclinations of its makers—although Sir James Murray and his fellows were less obvious about, and indeed less conscious of, what they were doing. What one cannot do, however much the advocates of PC would wish to, is rewrite century-old history from today's viewpoint. That way lies the thought police and the one dictionary that presumably such revisionists could enthusiastically accept: the eleventh, perfected edition of the *Newspeak Dictionary* of George Orwell's *1984,* endlessly rewritten, endlessly slimmed down, endlessly revising history to maintain its own ideological conceits. "The purpose of Newspeak," wrote Orwell, "was not only to provide a medium of expression for the world-view and mental habits proper to the devotees of Ingsoc, but to make all other modes of thought impossible."[31] The assumed role of the dictionary as a proscriptive tract is central to every critique, no matter what its ideological origin. The conservative voices that assailed *W3* and the ultraliberal ones that pursue today's dictionaries may preach a different gospel, but their impetus remains the same. Only the texts of the theology have altered. The process is endlessly recycled and no doubt in a century's time the strictures of the politically correct will seem as absurd and as tied to their time as do today the imperialist certainties of a century past.

None of which is to dismiss the very real problems to be found in dictionary after dictionary. These fall into a number of groups. The position of the obscenities, the taboo terms for sexual and excretory activities, has been dealt with at the start of this book. For better or worse, such terms, once standard English, will continue to affront, for whatever reason, a certain section of the population. They will be excluded from some general-purpose dictionaries, included in others. It may be, as Allen Walker Read suggested in his celebrated discussion of "an obscenity symbol" (i.e., the word *fuck*), that humanity needs linguistic taboo. Alternatively, it may be, as the comedian Lenny Bruce pointed out, that the censorship of the words is all that gives them power. Turn on the lights and the scuttling horror in the corner is only a terrified mouse. Dictionary users will continue to make their own choices, but as far as descriptive inclusiveness is concerned, those lexicographers who choose to brave the wrath of the censors will undoubtedly be producing more honest works than those who prefer to bend the knee.

Obscenities, on the whole, have not exercised the advocates of political correctness as much as have terms of racist and "gender" abuse. Some usages bracket the two: the word *cunt,* either as an anatomical term or an abusive one, is generally disliked. Terms such as *dago, wop, kike, nigger, chink,* and the rest have been given regular houseroom within a variety of dictionaries for many years. The *OED* has *dago* in 1723, *nigger* in 1786, *kike* in 1904, *chink* in 1901, and *wop* in 1912. All these, in the second edition, are marked as "offensive" or "derogatory" with the exception of *dago,* granted a reprieve perhaps on account of its assumed "period" flavor. Compound words dependent on racial stereotypes have been equally frequent, especially when one looks at slang, where xenophobic Britain, for instance, has offered a whole series of national enemies: the Spanish ("old Spanish practices"), the Dutch ("Dutch courage") and the French ("French leave"), although the Germans, against whom two world wars were fought in twenty-five years, have for some reason virtually escaped all condemnation, other than in the propaganda of the wars themselves and, latterly, in the headlines of the tabloid press. The French, Britain's ostensible allies in both those wars, remain the number-one linguistic stereotype: their crime, no doubt, being a failure to parade the necessary hypocrisy as regards sexuality. In America Hungarians, Turks, Greeks, Poles, and Mexicans, to name a few, all join the unfortunates.

However the most celebrated "affair" to be focused on such language relates to the word *Jew,* especially when used as a verb: "to Jew" or "to Jew down." Writing as both a Jew and a lexicographer (of slang, that repository of so many racist, xenophobic terms) this author finds it all very simple: include the word, opprobrious though it undoubtedly is, and mark it as derogatory, offensive, or whatever. But do not on any account exclude it. It may not change anyone's attitudes—those most in need of PC correction are least likely to acknowledge it—but the point will have been made. This is what one finds in the *Supplements* and second edition of the *OED,* but not, it would seem, without a struggle. Robert Burchfield, editor of the *Supplements,* has described at length his crossing of swords with a Salford businessman who, in 1969, "came on the scene and complained that the definitions of *Jew* were 'abusive and insulting and reflected a deplorable attitude toward Jewry.' "[32] Nor was this the first such complaint. As early as 1924, four years before the *Dictionary* had been completed, the *Jewish Chronicle,* reviewing the *Pocket Oxford Dictionary,* had suggested that defining a Jew as an "unscrupulous usurer or bargainer" and "to Jew" as "to cheat, over-reach" implied a "sinister meaning." This criticism was rebuffed by Robert W. Chapman of the OUP, who pleaded the descriptive lexicographer's neutrality. He further suggested that the negative stereotyping of Jews was neither better nor worse than that of the French, the Dutch, and so on. The OUP, however, took note of the complaint and began labeling the "sinister" term as "derogatory" or "opprobrious." Nonetheless, forty-five years later, the press was facing the same complaints once more. This time the controversy reached the High Court where, in 1973, an action claiming for the words to be struck from the dictionary on the grounds of their being "derogatory, defamatory and deplorable" was rejected. The definitions, with their demurrers, stood. A similar policy can be seen in *W3* although the demurrers appear to have been something of an afterthought. While the verb is marked as "usu. taken to be offensive," the noun has no such addendum. The random nature of such annotations is seen even more blatantly in Eric Partridge's *Usage and Abusage*. First published in 1947, it appeared well into the 1980s with this entry: "*nigger* belongs only, and then in contempt or fun, to the dark-skinned African races and their descendants in America and the West Indies. Its application to the native people of India is ignorant and offensive."[33]

One can argue that "Jew" in these "sinister" contexts is an especially emotive term—an example not simply of racism or xenophobia, but a stereotype that has formed the justification for a good deal of Christian theology, not to mention its logical conclusion, the Holocaust. But other terms are equally emotive. Dictionary definitions of "Palestine" and even more so "Palestinian," "Arab," and "Pakistan" have all caused much fury. Copies of one dictionary, considered in Pakistan to have misdefined the etymology of the nation's name, were withdrawn from bookshops and libraries, called in from buyers and ceremonially burnt. In 1995 a member of India's Janata Party sought to have the word "pariah" removed from the *Shorter Oxford* on the grounds that the caste system, in which "pariah" referred to a specific and lowly grouping, was no longer part of Indian society. The dictionary's editor defended the inclusion, stressing the frequent use of the word in a nonspecific context.

The bottom line is that all these words, like *Jew* and the rest, have to be included, albeit with a maximum of sensitivity. The *OED*, for instance, defines "Palestine" as "The name of a territory on the eastern shore of the Mediterranean," and prior to defining "Palestinian" offers 150 words explaining the current political situation. *W3*, on the other hand, is less circumspect. A "Palestinian" is simply "a native or inhabitant of Palestine" and is cross-referred to "Israeli." To what extent these definitions, neutral though they are doubtless proclaimed as being, are influenced by the lobbying of Israeli or Palestinian groups can only be debated. Interested parties may not like some of the definitions, but the descriptive dictionary has its own interest: setting out the language as it is, rather than as one pressure group or another feels it ought to be.

The problems with such loaded terms as "Zionist" or "fundamentalist" lead on to politics. Here one can see "Newspeak" at its most virulent. It would be naïve to underestimate the covert politicization of generations of British and American dictionaries but on the whole the sledgehammer tactics to be found in those produced by the Soviet and Chinese Communist systems are more worthy of note. Value-laden terms such as *democracy, patriotism, capitalism, imperialism,* and *communism* all appear in a substantially different version to that which might be expected in a Western dictionary. The OUP arranged with their Russian counterparts for the production of their *Advanced Learner's Dictionary* (1974) in a "special" version. Thus where a Western reader might find Communism defined as "ideology that proclaims the abolition of class oppression and exploitation, and the foundation of society based on the common possession of the means of production and the equal distribution of goods," their Soviet peers saw "a theory revealing the historical necessity for the revolutionary replacement of capitalism by Communism." Chinese censorship is even less subtle. Thus in *A Dictionary of Contemporary Chinese* (1979): "*Democracy, democratic rights:* refers to the rights enjoyed by the people to freely express their political opinions and participate in the government. Democracy has a class nature. Under a capitalist system, there are only bourgeois class democratic rights, there are no proletariat class democratic rights. In China people enjoy extensive and real democracy." This dictionary continues to propagandize even on "internal," ostensibly nonpolitical terms. Contexts for certain words reflect the overriding theories: "*Anzang* (meaning dirty, filthy): Eliminate the filthy thoughts of bourgeois individualism"; "*andan* (meaning dismal, gloomy): The prospects for capitalist countries are gloomy."[34]

However, the West can be equally culpable. Noah Webster's none-too-subtle incorporation of theological precepts into his dictionary can be found more recently in the *Thorndike-Barnhart Beginning Dictionary* (1964). In this work, aimed at U.S. primary schools, dozens of otherwise neutral terms are defined through religion. Thus "The Star in the East was the *sign* of Christ's coming"; "Christ came to *save* the world"; "Christ is called the *Rock* of Ages"; "Jesus died on the *cross*";[35] and so on. (In all cases the italicized word is that which is being defined.) It is an eternal problem. Roger Scruton's *Dictionary of Political Thought* was published in Britain by Macmillan in 1982. Although the author warns readers, in the introduction, that his claimed "impartiality is itself a kind of partiality,"[36] nowhere does the publisher explain Scruton's own credentials as one of Thatcherism's leading intellectuals. But author's credits are rarely subtitled "keeper of the flame" or "rabid right-winger." In dictionaries as elsewhere, *caveat emptor.*

The debate over gender is a more recent phenomenon, a product of the emergent feminism of the late 1960s and early 1970s. And while minorities may have complained that dictionaries have traditionally traduced them through vilification and/or stereotyping, feminists saw themselves as facing even deeper prejudice. For all the breadth and complexity of lexicography, no matter what the given project,

> For women . . . the ultimate outcome is the same: whether descriptive or prescriptive, authoritarian or democratic, massive or minimal, systematic or quixotic . . . dictionaries have systematically excluded any notion of women as speakers, as linguistic innovators, or as definers of words. Women in their pages have been rendered invisible, reduced to stereotypes, ridiculed, trivialised or demeaned. Whatever their intentions, then, dictionaries have functioned as linguistic legislators which perpetrate the stereotypes and prejudices of their writers and editors, who are almost exclusively male.[37]

Cheris Kramerae, whose plaint this is, is coauthor with Paula A. Treichler of the *The Feminist Dictionary*, "a dictionary of feminist thinking and word-making; a conceptual guide to that subset of the lexicon concerned with feminism; a documentation of feminist perspectives, interpretations of words, and contributions to linguistic creativity and scholarship; and a dictionary itself made by feminists."[38] As such it falls, as its editors note, into the area occupied by such quasi-"dictionaries" as Flaubert's *Dictionary of Received Ideas* and Bierce's *Devil's Dictionary*—although it lacks the irony of the one and the cynicism of the other. It is not a dictionary in which one looks up words in the expected way. For instance those who search for a definition of "ability" find only this: "ability 'Is sexless' (Christabel Pankhurst CALLING ALL WOMEN February 2, 1957)." Nor would the traditional dictionary offer "abominable snowmen of androcratic academia: Scholars dominated by male-centered traditions." Headwords are very much drawn from an alternative lexicon; definitions are consciously oppositional to what is dismissed as the "male" norm, they are also more encyclopedic, even discursive, than would usually be expected; the tone is hortatory and to the jaundiced reader somewhat martyred as regards its consideration of traditional lexicography: those who are not positively with me, runs the subtext, must be aggressively against me. By the standards that inform the majority of works mentioned in these pages, the dictionary fails as a lexicographical work, but those standards are indisputably "male standards," restricting lexicography to the world of "patriarchal authoritarianism." Thus, as its editors point out, using "a flexible format is a conscious effort to honor the words and arguments of women, to liberate our thinking about what can be said about language and to guard against lexicographical ownership of words and definitions."[39] They want quite specifically to produce something that is not the traditional "dicktionary." Whether this justifies such obeisance to PC as this paragraph must be left to the dictionary's user: "We are also aware of the need to pay close attention to the words of disabled women, some of whom call others *TABS*—'temporarily able-bodied.' One question is whether we make an effort to expunge phrases from our language like 'stand up for what you believe' or 'blind as a bat' . . ."[40] The user must also make her or his decision as to the need for justifying the use of alphabetical order (which of course puts men before women, although housework before war) as not being "a value judgment."

Jibes against PC aside, there is much in the feminist viewpoint. The male bias in dictionary making has been noted earlier in this book, and for all the recruitment of women by dictionary publishers, and even the still-rare essays in feminist-specific lexicography, it has not altered. It is perhaps in self-defense that women seem to have corralled for their own intellectual discussions a substantial chunk of the metalexicographical world. However, one does not have to agree with Anthony Burgess' dismissive remark, "One thing that men have done better than women, despite feminist dictionaries, is lexicography,"[41] to feel that once again there is an attempt to rewrite history (itself, of course, a predominantly male construct for many years) for the sake of ideological utopia. Jane Mills, whose *Womanwords* (1989) is more an explanatory thesaurus of antifemale stereotyping than a dictionary as such, has suggested that, "Lexicographers deserve much of the criticism leveled against them. But not all of it . . . the basic source material of a lexicographer has been the written word, and most books have been, and still are, written and published by men. Dictionaries which chronicle usage are not necessarily prescriptive. If in the past a dictionary failed to refer to a young woman as a 'girl' the lexicographer would have been failing in his job had he not used the term which the rest of society used and understood."[42] That said, there has been a gradual shift in emphasis. This is particularly common in works aimed at children, where short contextual sentences are used to back up the primary definition. Comparing such sentences in two editions of the same dictionary, published respectively in 1968 and 1983 Sidney Landau offered these examples. *"Cherish:* A mother cherishes her baby" (1968) becomes "Parents cherish their children" (1983), while *"Seize:* In fright she seized his arm" (1968) becomes "In fright I seized her arm" (1983). How much this influences the young reader is debatable. The larger world must conspire with the dictionary, however rigorously nonsexist, to effect that level of social revolution. Once again, one is forced to assess the current "priestliness" of the lexicographer and his or her "sacred book." All of this cultural prejudice, conscious or otherwise, may well be reprehensible; likewise a perfect world might well have been a very different place—experience, unfortunately, indicates a harsher reality. The problem for the advocates of PC, in lexicography as elsewhere, is that they demand "what should be" in a world where there is only "what is." Such fantasies failed to work for the prescriptivist critics of *W3;* it is unlikely that they will gain any greater advances for those who would impose what is seen as a far more alien ideology on the dictionary. The grim truth that underlies dictionary reform, as much as any other, is that so much preaches only to the converted.

There is insufficient space here, alas, to look fully into the complex question that can be boiled down to a single phrase: "Whose English?" Nor has this book intended to take on board such topics. At no point does there seem to have been an adequate answer. English English was established by the eighteenth century, but as the failure of John Ray to gain sufficient status for dialect has shown, it was already a language as much determined by what was left out as by what was acknowledged as "right." If as far as gender is concerned the language seems resolutely masculine, then as regards class "English" meant, and continues to mean, middle-class English, even if, as Deborah Cameron suggests,[43] that too is no more than a given dialect in itself. The citation gatherers of the *NED* virtually ignored the language of the vast industrial working class, based mainly in the north of England. To look only at the press, the inclusion of which in itself was only tolerated after James Murray demanded it, while the readers acknowledged *The Times* and the *Daily Mirror,* such publications as *The Black Dwarf* (circulation in 1819 12,000) or the *Northern Star* (circulation *c.* 1838 of 60,000) are all but invisible. *Blackwood's Magazine,* a solidly middle-class, southeastern publication may have reached only 10,000 readers, but it is cited more than 5,700 times. William Cobbett's left-of-center *Political Register* reached as many as 50,000, it is cited but 154 times. Circulation is not a be-all or end-all of inclusion, but the bias is inescapable. In this light the *NED* appears as a parlor pink among dictionaries: unassailably democratic in its treatment of the words it allowed in, but markedly less unbending in its distribution of invitations.

American English, pioneered by Webster, lauded by Mencken, began emerging alongside the newly independent nation itself. Despite initial mockery from the "mother country" and a degree of snobbish embarrassment at home, it survived, prospered, and is today the dominant mode of the language, but for some it remains aberrant. There are, after all, a number of books of

"Americanisms" but none, although there have been plans to fill this gap, of "Briticisms." Talking in 1988 the fiercely nationalistic MP Enoch Powell pronounced, "Others may speak and read English—more or less—but it is our language, not theirs. It was made in England by the English, and it remains our distinctive property, however widely it is learnt or used."[44] In the end it seems that might is right. Powell's xenophobic fantasy might have rung true in 1896, but not in 1996. American has been the imperial language of the twentieth century, just as English was of the nineteenth. Yet even in democratic America there seems only to be room for a single "privileged form." Just as the non-middle-class British dialects were pushed back to the linguistic margins, so has the language of another group that is perceived as marginal to mainstream society: a subset of American English, Black English, continues to fight for its position, but remains outside the standard. Nor, while there are several dictionaries and glossaries of Black slang, are there dictionaries of Black English as such. The irony that Professor Hugh Jones, calling for a "fix'd" language as far ago as 1721, included in his list of *true English* speakers "the Native Negroes" has made little difference.[45]

As far as dictionary makers were concerned, the "standard English" that their works embodied (and which emerged as a phrase in 1836) is "the consensus . . . of what educated speakers accepted as correct."[46] That goes for "standard American" too. As R. O. Williams, writing of *Our Dictionaries* in 1890, put it: "If pressed to say definitely what good American English is, I should say, it is the English of those who are believed by the greater number of Americans to know what good English is." The root, of course, was class, and the philologist Henry Sweet, who taught Murray and was himself once considered as a possible editor of the *OED,* summed it up in his *History of English Sounds* (1908): "Standard English, like Standard French, is now a class dialect more than a local dialect: it is the language of the educated all over Great Britain." It is thus the "prestige variety of the language"[47] and, as is seen by those who demand prescriptive rather than descriptive dictionaries, the prestige variety is the variety of choice. There is perhaps a parallel in this privileged vs. populist division with the social attitudes of those *bien-pensant* liberals who yearn, from the comfort of their own late-twentieth-century lives, for the "charming" deprivations of a fantasy past. Those whose lives are still impoverished are less sentimental. Similarly in language; those whose language variety has cut them off from the "prestige" environment would prefer to sacrifice the picturesque for the socially profitable.

In all of these debates, the lexicographer is in an invidious position. Damned if he (or she) does, and damned if he (or she) doesn't. The role of the dictionary maker is to reflect the language, which in turn is a reflection of the culture in which it exists. If the culture in part is racist, sexist, and in other ways politically incorrect, then so too in part must the dictionaries be. The best they can offer is some parenthetical declaration that a given word or phrase, in a given definition or usage, is so. Otherwise, if they start censoring out such material, of what real worth can they be considered? As Richard Chenevix Trench stressed in 1857, the lexicographer is a historian, not a law giver. The problem is the extent to which dictionary users still opt for the latter role. The lexicographer has traditionally been asked to take on the role of God, or at least that of a priestly interpreter. In the end such a request, however enthusiastic, cannot be granted. The lexicographer is part of the culture too; the language in which he deals is his as well. To ask that he absent himself from that culture is to ask too much. To abandon the subjectivity of a Johnson or Webster is feasible, even desirable. To abandon all humanity, to achieve some Platonic perfection of an entirely disinterested dictionary is impossible. Even the great computerized corpora must be refined by human agents. Georg Lukács is right: the dictionary maker is part and parcel of the dictionary that is made. The intrusion may be limited, but to ask otherwise is to not merely to chase the sun, but to suppose one can catch it too.

NOTES

1 INTRODUCTION

1 Starnes and Noyes, p. 47
2 Mengham, p. 112
3 Ibid.
4 Hobbes, p. 105
5 Ibid.
6 Quoted in Mengham, p. 112
7 Mengham, p. 112
8 Moon, p. 59
9 Ibid.
10 Starnes and Noyes, pp. 195–6
11 Wheatley [2], pp. iii–iv
12 Zgusta, p. 15
13 Hartmann [1], p. 99
14 Cowper, *Retirement* (1782)
15 Hulbert, p. 42
16 Béjoint, pp. 105–6
17 Quoted in Béjoint, p. 106
18 *A Defence of Poetry* (1821)
19 *OED*
20 McArthur [1], p. 79
21 Béjoint, p. 37
22 *OED*
23 *Webster's Third New International*
24 *Collins Concise Dictionary,* London, 1989
25 Johnson, *Dictionary of the English Language*
26 Trench [2], p. 4
27 Zgusta, p. 197
28 Béjoint, p. 8
29 Metalexicographer: one (generally an academic) who writes about dictionaries but does not actually compile them. Coined by the French writers A. Rey and S. Delasalle in 1979 as *metalexicographie;* the term has yet to surface in the *OED*.
30 Rey-Debove, pp. 20–7
31 Rey, *Littré: l'humaniste et les mots* (1970)
32 Cocteau, *Le Potomak* (1913)
33 Béjoint, p. 18
34 Rey (1977), p. 88
35 Aitchison, p. 11
36 Ibid., p. 12
37 Béjoint, p. 24
38 Wilde, *The Canterville Ghost* (1891)
39 Béjoint, p. 116
40 See Landau, p. 65
41 Ibid.
42 Béjoint, p. 55
43 Quoted in *IEL,* p. 29
44 *IEL,* p. 29
45 Raven I. McDavid, quoted in *IEL,* p. 29
46 Moon, p. 63
47 Landau, p. 35

48 "f. Latin *plagiarius* one who abducts the child or slave of another, a kidnapper; a seducer; Also . . . a literary thief," *OED*.
49 Starnes and Noyes, p. 183
50 *IEL,* p. 2,006
51 Ibid.
52 Landau, p. 36
53 Hartmann [1], p. 47
54 Ibid., p. 47
55 Partridge [1] (1st ed. 1937), p. vi
56 Stein, p. 69
57 Green, p. 277
58 Drabble, p. 837
59 Quoted in Read 1934, p. 270
60 Webster: Letter to the Hon. John Pickering; quoted in Read 1934, p. 274
61 Quoted in Read 1934, p. 273
62 Read 1934, p. 274
63 Landau, p. 184

1   THE FIRST LEXICOGRAPHERS

1 Murray, pp. 6–7
2 Hartmann [1], p. 211
3 Ibid., p. 213
4 Worcester, p. xiii
5 While it is generally assumed that "Homer" represents a collection of writers rather than an individual, the singular, representing the work rather than its authors, will be used here.
6 Lemprière, n.p.
7 Wilson, pp. 4–5
8 Ibid.
9 Ibid. p. 57
10 Pope, *Dunciad* 4, pp. 227–8
11 *IEL,* p. 1,788
12 Ibid., p. 1,789
13 Starnes, pp. 50ff.
14 Ibid., p. 69
15 Stein, p. 183

2   THE MIDDLE AGES

1 Murray, pp. 8–9
2 McArthur [1], p. 52

3 Drabble, p. 34
4 McArthur [1], pp. 76–7
5 Quoted in James, p. 166
6 Stein, pp. 32–43
7 Bacon, *Opera Inedita,* p. 457
8 *DNB,* p. 1,468
9 Wright, p. x
10 Wright [2], p. viii
11 Starnes, p. 15
12 Ibid., p. 16
13 Wright [2], p. xvi
14 Wright, *Volume of Vocabularies,* p. 142
15 Wright [2], pp. 244ff.
16 Starnes, pp. 5–6
17 Stein, pp. 74ff.
18 Starnes, p. 9
19 Herrtage, p. ix
20 EETS 1932, pp. xvi–xx
21 Chandos, *Boys Together* (1984), p. 230
22 Wood, vol. 1, col. 39

3   THE MOVE FROM LATIN

1 Burke & Porter, pp. 23–50
2 Schäfer [1], p. 1
3 Ibid.
4 See McCrum, p. 93
5 Stein, p. 121
6 McArthur, p. 82
7 Philemon Holland, Camden's *Britannia* (1610)
8 Major, p. 13
9 Jones
10 Crofts, pp. lxx–lxxiv
11 Schäfer [1], p. 1
12 Rev. H. Waller, *Doctrinal Treaties,* ed. Park. Soc.
13 Elyot, *Castell of Helth*
14 Crofts, pp. cxlv–clxiv
15 Murray, p. 17
16 Starnes, p. 67
17 Quoted in Starnes and Noyes, p. 7
18 See Stein, p. 174
19 Starnes, p. 149
20 Fuller, p. 55
21 *DNB,* p. 2,307
22 Ibid.

23 Withals, Prologue (1602 ed.)
24 Ibid.
25 Aubrey, ii, p. 290
26 *DNB,* p. 434
27 Marprelate: Epistle, ed. Peteram, p. 59
28 Ibid., p. 43
29 Have You Any Work, p. 47
30 Ibid., p. 60
31 Ibid., p. 10
32 Ibid., p. 43
33 Stein, pp. 207–10
34 Starnes, pp. 103–4
35 Wood, *Athenae Oxoniensis,* i, col. 548
36 Levins, p. 2
37 Wheatley, p. 226
38 Levins, Dedication, *passim*
39 Wheatley, p. 227
40 Fuller, p. 591
41 Stein, p. 336
42 *DNB,* p. 994
43 Fuller, p. 591
44 Starnes, p. 232

4   VULGAR TONGUES

1 Bough & Cable, p. 187
2 *DNB,* p. 1,582
3 Wheatley, p. 223
4 *DNB,* p. 1,582
5 Wheatley, p. 223
6 Stein, pp. 128–9
7 Wheatley, p. 223
8 Stein, p. 256
9 R. C. Simoni, *Italian Scholarship in Renaissance England* (1952), pp. 55–6; 58; quoted in Stein, p. 378
10 Wood, vol. 2, col. 380
11 Yates, p. 228
12 Starnes, p. 134
13 Wood, vol. 1, col. 359
14 Jones, *The Triumph of the English Language* (1953), p. 283, quoted in Bennett, p. 128
15 Bullokar, *Booke at Large,* n.p.
16 Ibid.
17 Wood, vol. 1, col. 150
18 *Gentleman's Magazine,* May 1800, p. 420
19 Fuller, *Worthies,* p. 599
20 Ibid.
21 Mulcaster, *The First Part of the Elementarie,* p. 274 (1925)
22 Ibid., p. 187

5   SLANG: PART I

1 Schäfer [1], pp. 1–10
2 Hotten, p. 45
3 Partridge [1], pp. 37ff.
4 Burke, p. 193
5 Hotten, p. 44
6 Mencken [1], p. 575
7 Quoted in *Liber Vagatorum,* trans. Hotten
8 Judges, p. 491
9 *DNB,* p. 436
10 Barrère and Leland, p. x
11 Partridge [3], pp. 13–14
12 Partridge [1], p. 45
13 "This young tramping girl can spin a good yarn, and fucks well for a penny; and steals and cheats so smartly, all over the countryside."
14 Quoted in Starnes and Noyes, p. 219
15 *DNB,* p. 929
16 Ibid.
17 Quoted in Storojenko, p. 6
18 Dyce, p. 2
19 Quoted in Storojenko, p. 11
20 Quoted in ibid., p. 12
21 Storojenko, p. 31
22 Quoted in ibid., p. 19
23 Jordan, p. 5
24 Greene [2], pp. 5–10
25 Ibid., p. 89
26 Ibid., p. 96
27 Quoted in Judges, p. 67
28 Judges, p. 492
29 Harman, p. 27
30 In Grosart, *Complete Works,* X, p. 71
31 Storojenko, pp. 41–2
32 Greene [1], p. 14
33 Ibid.
34 Storojenko, p. 62
35 *Harvey's Works,* ed. Grosart, vol. I, pp. 168–71

6   **THE SEVENTEENTH CENTURY:**
    HARD WORDS

1   Murray, p. 27
2   Osselton, p. 175
3   Ibid., p. 183
4   Ibid., p. 182
5   Illson, p. 27
6   Schäfer [1], p. 4
7   Ibid.
8   Ibid., p. 9
9   Fuller, p. 687
10 Wood, vol. 1, col. 497
11 *DNB*, p. 897
12 Fuller, p. 500
13 Ibid., p. 587
14 Pope, *Dunciad*, i
15 Fuller, p. 587
16 Starnes and Noyes, p. 128
17 Wheatley, pp. 229ff.
18 Baugh & Cable, p. 232
19 Murray, p. 28
20 Ibid, p. 32
21 Wood, vol. 4, col. 53
22 Starnes and Noyes, pp. 42–4
23 Ibid., pp. 37ff.
24 Druid, f. Gaelic *draoi:* a magician
25 Starnes and Noyes, p. 46
26 Winwood, *Memorials,* iii
27 Fuller, pp. 134–5
28 Godwin, p. 140
29 *DNB*, p. 1,658
30 Ibid.
31 Godwin, p. 52
32 Wood, vol. 4, col. 53
33 Ibid.
34 Wheatley, p. 236
35 Coles, quoted in Wheatley, p. 238
36 Starnes and Noyes, p. 63
37 Ibid., pp. 190ff.

7   **THE SEVENTEENTH CENTURY:**
    VARIATIONS AND THEMES

1   Wood, vol. 2, col. 146
2   Burke & Porter, p. 117
3   Ibid., p. 121
4   Burke, p. 121

5   Starnes and Noyes, p. 210
6   *DNB*, p. 994
7   Collier, *Great Historical, Geographical, Genealogical and Poetical Dictionary* (1705)
8   Starnes, p. 311
9   *Reliquiae Hearniae,* August 30, 1734
10 *DNB*, p. 17
11 Ibid, p. 1,608
12 Ibid, p. 1,384
13 Wheatley, p. 231
14 Ibid., p. 230
15 Worcester, p. lv.
16 Green, *Cassells Dictionary of Slang:* f. 14C SE *cockney:* a mother's darling, a spoilt child, thus a weak, effeminate adult; this was adopted in rural dialect to describe the supposedly "soft" inhabitants of cities and large towns, who compounded their unpopularity by their ignorance of country ways and words. The link to "Bow-bells" is first cited in 1600 and appears for the first time as a dictionary definition in Minsheu's *Ductor in Linguas* (1617). The SE itself seems to be rooted in *cocken ay:* a cock's egg, or a small or malformed egg; Partridge also suggests, on the basis of a rhyme attributed to Hugh Bigot, earl of Norfolk (d. *c.* 1177) that a parallel root of *cockney* lies in the fabulous land of *Cock-aigne,* and as such a synonym for London; the *OED,* however, notes that the reference is probably to the traditional "King of Cockneys," a kind of Master of the Revels chosen by the students at Lincoln's Inn on Childermas Day (Dec. 28).
17 *DNB*, p. 445
18 Pepys, p. 121
19 Wheatley, p. 237
20 Johnson, p. 9
21 Wheatley, p. 248
22 Ibid., p. 239
23 *OED:* OE. hselhnutu = Du. hazelnoot, LG. haselnot, hasselnt, OHG. hasalnuz, mod.G. haselnusz. The nut of the hazel, a well-known fruit.
24 *OED:* OE. hassuc, of uncertain etymology. Some have conjectured derivation from Welsh hesg: sedges.
25 Wheatley, p. 239

8   THE EARLY EIGHTEENTH
CENTURY

1   Osselton in Hartmann, ed. *Lexicography: Principles and Practice* (1983), p. 17
2   McArthur [1], p. 96
3   Wheatley, p. 240
4   Starnes and Noyes, p. 69
5   Ibid., p. 70
6   Long, p. 30
7   Starnes and Noyes, p. 73
8   Ibid., p. 110
9   Murray, p. 36
10 Starnes and Noyes, p. 123
11 Humphreys, *Correspondence of Doddridge,* iii, pp. 424ff.
12 *DNB,* p. 1,872
13 Gove, p. 314
14 Ibid., p. 311
15 Ibid., p. 314
16 Starnes and Noyes, pp. 184–5
17 Riddick, p. 26
18 Johnson, Preface, p. 12
19 Altick, p. 35
20 *South Atlantic Quarterly,* vol. 29, p. 281 (1930)
21 Quoted in Altick, p. 36
22 Altick, p. 36
23 Wheatley [1], p. 250
24 In *The Bookworm: An Illustrated Treasury of Old-Time Literature* (1888)
25 Wheatley [3], p. 45
26 *Gentleman's Magazine,* 1809, p. 1,058
27 Boswell, ii, p. 226
28 Ibid., iii, p. 364
29 *Gentleman's Magazine,* 1809, p. 1,063
30 Ibid.
31 *DNB,* p. 633
32 Boswell ii, p. 171
33 *Gentleman's Magazine,* 1809, p. 1,057
34 Wheatley [3], pp. 45–6
35 *DNB,* p. 902
36 Starnes and Noyes, p. 76
37 Wheatley, p. 242
38 *DNB,* p. 399
39 Pepys, p. 414
40 Ibid., p. 431
41 Starnes and Noyes, p. 78
42 Ibid., p. 83
43 Ibid., pp. 82–3
44 Ibid., p. 126

9   SAMUEL JOHNSON:
THE PIVOTAL MOMENT

1   *IEL,* p. 1,798
2   Harvey and Heseltine, p. 206
3   McArthur [1], p. 95
4   *DNB,* p. 1,329
5   Wheatley [1], p. 249
6   Starnes and Noyes, p. 152
7   Martin, *Physico-Grammatical Essay*
8   Starnes and Noyes, p. 151
9   Ibid., p. 152
10 De Maria, p. 111
11 Reddick, pp. 28ff.
12 Clifford, p. 48
13 PMLA LI (1937), pp. 785–802
14 De Maria, *passim*
15 Mengham, p. 113
16 Ibid., pp. 113–14
17 De Maria, p. 122
18 Johnson, Preface, p. 24
19 Ibid., p. 27
20 *Edinburgh Review,* June 1, 1755
21 *Public Advertiser,* October 10, 1755
22 This version of the story is dated 1795, and quoted by Allen Walker Read, who owned Croft's copy of Johnson, in which Croft had written the tale; a later version, 1829, extends the one lady to two and gives Johnson the teasing response, "What, my dears! then you have been looking for them."
23 Mencken supp. 1, p. 156
24 Sledd, p. 101
25 Boswell, p. 161
26 Murray, p. 42
27 Greene, *Samuel Johnson* (1970)
28 *OED:* "Of, belonging to, or characteristic of Dr. Samuel Johnson . . . applied esp. to a style of English abounding in words derived or made up from Latin."
29 Baugh and Cable, p. 270
30 Tooke, pp. 211–12
31 Sledd, p. 19
32 Chambers, p. 4

33 Clifford, p. 146

34 Johnson, p. 13

35 Chambers, p. xvii

36 Sledd, p. 31

37 Tooke, p. 119

38 Sledd, p. 39

39 Ibid.

40 Martin, "Physico-Grammatical Essay,"
    p. 11

41 Sledd, p. 9

42 Burchfield [2], p. xi

43 Conrad, p. 373

44 Mengham, p. 117

45 Burgess, p. 273

10   AMERICA: THE YEARS BEFORE WEBSTER

1 Hartmann [1], pp. 221ff.

2 Cooper, *Notions of the Americans* (1828)
   Quoted in Baugh and Cable, pp. 348–9

3 Webster [1], i, p. 22

4 Ibid., pp. 20–3

5 Wheatley [1], p. 257

6 Krapp, p. 354

7 Ibid.

8 Wheatley [1], p. 263

9 Krapp, p. 356

10 *Collections of the Massachusetts Historical
    Society* II, June 1832, quoted in Hart-
    mann [1], p. 200.

11 *Gentleman's Magazine,* xlvi, 1796

12 Krapp, p. 356

13 *Connecticut Magazine,* 1899, quoted in
    Burkett, p. 11

14 Ibid., p. 12

15 Ibid., p. 13

16 Johnson

17 Friend

18 Steger, p. 23

19 Burkett, p. 21

20 John Todd, *The Story of His Life* (1877),
    quoted in Burkett, p. 23

21 *American Review* I (April–June 1801) pp.
    215–16

22 Burkett, p. 21

23 Sprague, *Annals of the American Pulpit*
    (1866), quoted in Burkett, pp. 30–1

24 Ibid., p. 29

25 Alexander, p. 23

26 Krapp, p. 359

27 *Monthly Magazine,* quoted in Mencken
    [1], p. 127

28 Krapp, pp. 358–9

29 Ibid., p. 351

30 *DNB,* p. 1,820

31 Buck, pp. 974–5

32 Ibid., p. 1,146

33 Rowson intro.

11   AMERICA: NOAH WEBSTER AND JOSEPH WORCESTER

1 Quoted in Read [2], p. 1,145

2 Ibid., p. 1,154

3 Ibid., pp. 1,162–63

4 Ibid., p. 1,170

5 Read [2], p. 1,179

6 Bryson, p. 116

7 Jefferson, letter to James Madison,
   August 12, 1801

8 Burkett, p. 117

9 Mencken [1], p. 385

10 Hartmann [1], p. 198

11 Ibid., p. 197

12 Mencken [1], p. 380: "The six new char-
    acters were a modified *a* for the long *a* in
    ball, an *h* upside down for the *u* in *unto,* a
    combination of long *s* and *i* for the *sh* in
    wish, a y with a curled tail for *ng,* an *h*
    with a curled tail for the *th* in *think,* and
    a somewhat similar *h,* but with a wavy
    appendage at the top, for the *th* of *thy.*
    Franklin expunged *c, w, y* and *j* . . . as
    unnecessary."

13 Webster: letter to Timothy Pickering
    1817, Quoted in Baugh and Cable, p. 361

14 Webster [1]

15 *The American Magazine,* 1788, quoted in
    American Speech IX (1934), p. 131

16 Webster [2], Preface, p. xxiii

17 Mencken [1], p. 9

18 Webster [2], p. ix

19 Friend

20 Ibid.

21 Mencken [4], p. 16

22 Krapp, p. 361

23 Webster, letter to Jonas Platt, 1807, quoted in Friend, p. 23

24 Webster, letter of 1839

25 Quoted in Snyder, p. 322

26 Webster [3], Preface

27 Ibid.

28 Murray, p. 43

29 Krapp, p. 367

30 Friend, p. 45

31 Webster [3], Preface

32 Murray, p. 43

33 Webster [3]

34 Franklin Edgerton, *Notes on Early American Works in Linguistics,* American Philosophical Society LXXXVII (1944); quoted in Sledd, p. 197

35 Webster [3]

36 Sledd, pp. 197–8

37 Webster [3]

38 Friend, p. 79

39 Mencken [2], p. 26

40 Rollins, chapter 8, *passim*

41 Webster [3]

42 Rollins, p. 125

43 Krapp, p. 365

44 Ibid.

45 Rollins, p. 130

46 Ibid., p. 137

47 Ibid., pp. 137–8

48 *Quarterly Review*

49 Quoted in Sledd, p. 203

50 Webster [3], *Abridged* intro, p. vii

51 Friend, p. 88

52 Krapp, p. 371

53 Friend, pp. 83–4

54 Worcester [2], p. lxiv

55 Sledd, p. 203

56 Worcester [2], p. lxiv

57 Ibid., p. lxv

58 Friend, p. 92

59 Ibid., p. 85

60 Quoted in Burkett, pp. 226–7

61 Quoted in Friend, p. 86

62 For those who wish to follow the blow-by-blow progression of this and other arguments, a study of Eva Mae Burkett's work, pp. 199–255, is highly recommended.

63 Sledd, p. 203

64 Friend, p. 87

65 Wheatley, p. 280

66 *IEL,* p. 1,991

67 Ibid., p. 1,990

12 THE NEW PHILOLOGY

1 Jones, *Works III* (1807), pp. 34–5

2 McArthur [2], p. 885

3 Aarsleff, p. 6

4 *DNB,* p. 1,100

5 Teignmouth, *Memoirs . . . of Sir William Jones* (1807), p. 88

6 Aarsleff, p. 115

7 Crystal, p. 85

8 Jones, *Works,* pp. 199–200

9 Macaulay, *Essay on Warren Hastings,* quoted in Aarsleff, p. 139

10 Aarsleff, p. 139

11 Ibid., p. 142

12 Michaelis, *Dissertation,* quoted in Aarsleff, p. 145

13 Aarsleff, p. 146

14 Steiner, pp. 119–20

15 Aarsleff, p. 159

16 Quoted in Aarsleff, p. 161

17 Aarsleff, p. 201

18 *DNB,* p. 2,097

19 Sitwell, p. 180

20 Burgess, p. 273

21 Tooke, p. 25

22 Sledd, p. 183

23 Ibid., p. 184

24 Tooke, p. 193

25 Sledd, p. 185

26 Tooke, p. 84, quoted in Aarsleff, p. 63

27 Tooke, pp. 184–7, quoted in Sledd, p. 185

28 Smith, p. 2

29 Ibid., p. 13

30 Ibid., pp. 115–16

31 Kemble, quoted in Francisque Michael, *Bibliothèque Anglo-Saxonne* (1837)

32 Tooke, vol. 1, p. 146

33 Quoted in *DNB,* p. 2,256

34 Richardson, C., p. 17

35 Ibid., p. 248

36 Murray, p. 44

37 Wheatley, p. 276

38 *Spectator,* July 29, 1837
39 Sledd, p. 187
40 Trench, p. 4
41 Sledd, p. 188
42 Ibid., p. 189
43 *Britannica Macropedia,* vol. 5, p. 717

13 **THE** *NEW ENGLISH*
    DICTIONARY

1 *DNB,* p. 2,219
2 Although the *New* and *Oxford English Dictionaries* are of course synonymous, and
   the latter name has been the accepted one
   for the last sixty years, I shall continue,
   for purposes of chronological accuracy, to
   use the title "New" as far as this early
   period is concerned. The change of title
   did not emerge until 1933. It was also, for
   a brief preliminary period, known as the
   "Philological Society's Dictionary"; this
   title will be used where relevant.
3 Aarsleff, pp. 234–5
4 *IEL,* p. 1,961
5 Trench [2], p. 4
6 Ibid., pp. 4–5
7 Ibid., p. 5
8 Ibid., p. 29
9 See Schäfer, vol. 2, *passim*
10 Trench [2], p. 44
11 Ibid., p. 48
12 Aarsleff, p. 258
13 Willinsky, pp. 30–2
14 *Transactions of the Philological Society*
    (1857), p. 3
15 Steeves, quoted in Banzie, p. 73
16 Michelle, *Eccentric Lives and Peculiar
    Notions* (1984), p. 167
17 Benzie, p. 26
18 Carpenter, p. 156
19 Quoted in Benzie, p. 200
20 Munro, p. lxxxii
21 *Transactions of the Philological Society*
    (1865), pp. 218–93
22 Quoted in Benzie, p. 87
23 *OED,* Historical Intro., p. viii
24 Ibid.
25 Trench, pp. 72–4

26 *OED,* Historical Intro., p. x
27 Quoted in Benzie, p. 93
28 Murray, K., p. 138
29 Quoted in Murray, K., p. 139
30 *OED,* Historical Intro., p. xi
31 Quoted in Murray, K., p. 140
32 Murray, K., p. 140
33 Ibid., p. 142
34 Ibid., p. 148
35 Quoted in Murray, K., p. 304
36 *OED,* Historical Intro., p. xii
37 For a full discussion of Murray's life, both
    domestic and professional, readers should
    turn to the absolute authority, *Caught in
    the Web of Words* by K. M. Elisabeth Mur-
    ray (1977). It is to this book that all Mur-
    ray studies are indebted.
38 *DNB,* p. 2,807
39 Burgess [2], p. 274
40 Murray, K., p. 33
41 Quoted in Murray, K., p. 341
42 Burgess [2], p. 275
43 *DNB,* p. 2,915
44 Ibid.
45 Murray, K., p. 77
46 Quoted in ibid.
47 *OED,* Historical Intro., p. xii
48 Murray, K., p. 242
49 Letter from Charles Cannan, quoted in
    Burchfield [2], p. 197
50 Burgess [2], p. 278
51 Burchfield [2], p. 16
52 Quoted in Murray, K., p. 307
53 Murray, K., p. 306
54 Quoted in Murray, K., p. 307
55 Burgess [2], p. 279
56 *NED,* Preface (1888), p. xiii
57 Quoted in *IEL,* p. 1,437
58 Quoted in Burchfield [2], p. 195
59 Quoted in Murray, K., p. 211
60 Burchfield [2], p. 191
61 *IEL,* p. 1,963
62 Quoted in Murray, K., p. 313

14 **SLANG: PART II**

1 Starnes and Noyes, p. 222
2 Partridge [1], p. 62

3   Porter, p. 184

4   *DNB,* pp. 2,195–96

5   Pope, *Dunciad,* iii, 34

6   Ibid., i, 234

7   Quoted in Starnes and Noyes, p. 222

8   Parker, pp. 152–5

9   Ibid., pp. 129, 131

10 Ibid., p. 152

11 The biographical material that follows is indebted to the brief, but definitive essay appended by Eric Partridge to his edition (Scholartis Press, 1931) of the *Classical Dictionary,* which itself was largely based on the *DNB,* Egan, and the cross-references that Grose's biographer there, the numismatist Warwick Wroth, provided.

12 Partridge [5], p. 381

13 Ibid.

14 Quoted in Partridge [5], p. 382

15 *Gentleman's Magazine,* June 1791, 1:581

16 Quoted in Partridge [5], p. 384

17 Ibid., p. 387

18 Egan, p. xxxix

19 *Gentleman's Magazine,* June 1791, 1:493

20 *Lexicon Balatronicum* (1811), p. vi

21 Egan, pp. xxvi–xxvii

22 *DNB,* p. 1,395

23 Egan, p. xxi

24 Atyeo, p. 146

25 Egan, p. xxviii

26 James Hardy Vaux, the self-styled Comte de Vaux, see below

27 Bee, p. iii

28 Ibid., p. ix, note

29 Partridge [1], pp. 80–108

30 MacLachlan, p. 221

31 Hotten, p. 281

32 Quoted in Partridge [1], pp. 94–5

33 The *Bookseller,* July 2, 1873, p. 549

34 Partridge [1], p. 95

35 The *Bookseller,* July 2, 1873, p. 548

36 Partridge [1], p. 95

37 Hotten (1867 ed.), p. viii

38 Ibid., p. xv

39 Ibid., p. 65

40 Lighter, p. xxvii

41 Matsell, p. iii

42 Ibid., p. v

43 Quoted in Richardson, J, p. 56

44 Ibid., p. 69

45 Barrère and Leland, p. vii

46 *DNB,* p. 2,398

47 Partridge [1], p 105

48 Barrère and Leland, p. xviii

49 Farmer and Henley, p. v

50 Gross

51 *DNB,* p. 2,690

52 Gross

53 Ibid.

54 Ibid.

55 Quoted in Gross

56 Quoted in Richard Ellman, *Oscar Wilde* (1987), p. 502

57 Farmer and Henley, p. viii

58 Ibid., p. x

59 Partridge [1], p. 106

60 Quoted in Crystal, p. 237

61 Crystal, p. 26

62 Ibid., p. 21

63 Partridge [6], p. 7

64 Quoted in Crystal, p. 21

65 Crystal, p. 24

15   THE MODERN WORLD

1   Murray, p. 49

2   Hughes, p. 244

3   McArthur [1], p. 135

4   Béjoint, p. 104

5   *IEL,* p. 1959

6   Wheatley [1], p. 285

7   McArthur [1], p. 423

8   Morton, pp. 2–3

9   Quoted in Sledd and Ebbitt, p. 54

10 Ibid., p. 92

11 Gove, *The Role of the Dictionary,* p. 7

12 Bierce, *The Devil's Dictionary* (1911)

13 Follett, p. 73

14 Ibid., p. 74

15 Ibid., p. 76

16 Ibid., p. 77

17 Bolinger, *Language, the Loaded Weapon* (1980)

18 In Congleton et al., *Papers on Lexicography* (1979), pp. 17–28

19 *Saturday Review,* November 14, 1964, pp. 82–4

20 Sledd and Ebbitt, p. 127
21 Quoted in Morton, p. 224
22 *American Heritage Dictionary,* p. vi
23 Landau, p. 32
24 Moon, p. 68
25 Mencken, *Minority Report* (1956)
26 Hughes, pp. 243–4
27 Sledd and Ebbitt, p. 57
28 Quoted in Béjoint, p. 122
29 Cameron, p. 84
30 Willinsky
31 Orwell, *1984* (1948), p. 299
32 Burchfield [2], p. 113
33 Partridge, *Usage and Abusage* (1963), p. 203

34 Quoted in Moon, pp. 78–9
35 Quoted in Landau, p. 308
36 Scruton, n.p.
37 Kramerae, p. 8
38 Ibid., p. 12
39 Ibid., p. 17
40 Ibid., p. 18
41 Burgess [2], p. 255
42 Mills, p. ix
43 Cameron, p. 83
44 Quoted in *The Independent,* April 23, 1988
45 Jones, *Accidence to the English Tongue,* p. 15
46 Sidney Greenbaum in Ricks and Michaels [2], p. 18
47 Ibid., p. 17

BIBLIOGRAPHY

Aarsleff, Hans. *The Study of Language in England 1780–1860.* Princeton, N.J., 1967.

Aitchison, Jean. *Words in the Mind.* Oxford, 1987.

Altick, Richard D. [1] *The English Common Reader.* Chicago, 1957.

————. [2] *The Scholar Adventurers.* London, 1973.

Ames, Herbert and Dibdin, Thomas, eds. *Typographical Antiquities of Great Britain.* London, 1810–19.

Atyeo, Don. *Blood and Guts: Violence in Sports.* London, 1979.

Aubrey, John. *Brief Lives.* London, 1693.

Barrère, Albert and Leland, C. G. *A Dictionary of Slang, Jargon and Cant.* London, 1889.

Baugh, Albert C. and Cable, Thomas. *A History of the English Language.* London, 3rd ed., 1980.

B. E., Gent. *A New Dictionary of the Terms ancient and modern of the Canting Crew . . .* (c. 1690.)

"Bee, Jon." [John Badcock] *Slang, a Dictionary of the Turf, the Ring, the Chase, the Pit, of Bon Ton and the Varieties of Life . . .* London, 1823.

Béjoint, Henri. *Tradition and Innovation in Modern Dictionaries.* Oxford, 1994.

Bennett, H. S. *English Books and Readers 1603–40.* Cambridge, 1970.

Benzie, William. *Dr. F. J. Furnivall: Victorian Scholar Adventurer.* Norman, Okla., 1983.

Boissier, Gaston. *Etude sur la vie et les ouvrages de M. T. Varron.* Paris, 1861.

Bolton, W. P. and Crystal, David, eds. [1] *The English Language: Essays by English and American Men of Letters,* vol. 1, 1490–1839. Cambridge, 1966.

————. [2] *The English Language: Essays by English and American Men of Letters,* vol. 2, 1858–1964. Cambridge, 1969.

Brown, J. M. "An Early Rival of Shakespeare" in *New Zealand Magazine,* no. 6. 1877.

Bryson, Bill. *The Mother Tongue.* London, 1990.

Buck, Claire, ed. *Bloomsbury Guide to Women's Literature.* London, 1992.

Burchfield, Robert. [1] *Studies in Lexicography.* Oxford, 1987.

————. [2] *Unlocking the English Language.* London, 1989.

Burchfield, Robert et al., eds. *Supplements to the Oxford English Dictionary.* Oxford, 1972–86.

Burgess, Anthony. [1] *Homage to Qwerty Uiop.* London, 1986.

———. [2] *A Mouthful of Air.* London, 1992.

Burke, Peter. *"Heu dominae, adsunt Turcae:* A Sketch for a Social History of post-Medieval Latin" in Burke & Porter, eds.

Burke, Peter and Porter, Roy, eds. *Language, Self and Society: A Social History of Language.* London, 1991.

Burkett, Eva Mae. *American Dictionaries of the English Language before 1861.* New York, 1939.

Calepino, Ambrogio. *Dictionarium ex optimis quibusquam authoribus studiose collectum. . . .* Reggio, 1502.

Cameron, Deborah. *Feminism and Linguistic Theory.* London, 1985.

Carpenter, Humphrey. *Secret Gardens: A Study of the Golden Age of Children's Literature.* London, 1985.

Cassidy, Frederick, ed. *Dictionary of American Regional English,* vol. 1. Cambridge, Mass., 1985.

Cassidy, F. and Hall, J., eds. *Dictionary of American Regional English,* vol. 2. Cambridge, Mass., 1991.

Chenevix Trench, Richard. [1] *On the Study of Words & English Past and Present.* London, 1851, 1855.

———. [2] "On Some Deficiencies in our English Dictionaries" in *Transactions of the Philological Society.* London, 1857.

Claiborne, Robert. *The Life and Times of the English Language.* London, 1990.

Clifford, J. L. *Dictionary Johnson: Samuel Johnson's Middle Years.* London, 1980.

Cockeram, Henry (H.C., Gent.). *The English Dictionarie or, an Interpreter of Hard English Words.* London, 1623.

Congleton, J. E. and Elizabeth. *Johnson's Dictionary: A Bibliographical Survey 1746–1984.* Terre Haute, Ind., 1984.

Conrad, Peter. *The Everyman Guide to English Literature.* London, 1985.

Cressy, David. *Literacy and the Social Order: Reading & Writing in Tudor and Stuart England.* Cambridge, 1980.

Crofts, H. H. S., ed. *The Book called the Governor.* London, 1883.

Crystal, David, ed. *Eric Partridge in His Own Words.* London, 1980.

De Maria, Robert, Jr. *The Life of Samuel Johnson.* Oxford, 1993.

Denecke. Brothers Grimm entry, in *Encyclopaedia Britannica* 15th ed., Macropedia 8:427–9.

Dictionary of National Biography (compact ed., Oxford, 1975).

Drabble, Margaret, ed. *The Oxford Companion to English Literature.* 5th rev. ed. Oxford, 1995.

Dyce, Alexander. [1] *Dramatic and Poetical Works of Robert Greene and George Peele.* 1858.

———. [2] *Collected Plays and Poems of Robert Greene.* 1831.

Elyot, Thomas. *The DICTIONARY of Syr Thomas Eliot knight.* London, 1538.

Encyclopaedia Britannica (15th ed).

Farmer, John S. *A New Basis of Belief in Immortality.* 1881.

Farmer, John S. and Henley, W. E. *Slang and its Analogues.* London, 7 vols., 1890–1904.

Florio, John. *Queen Anna's New Worlde of Wordes.* London, 1611.

Follett, Wilson. "Sabotage in Springfield" in *The Atlantic Magazine,* January 1962, pp. 73–7.

Franklyn, Julian. *Rhyming Slang.* London, 1960.

Friend, J. H. *The Development of American Lexicography.* 1798–1864.

Fuller, Thomas. *The Worthies of England.* (3 vols., 1662) John Freeman, ed. London, 1952.

Gibbon, Edward. *The Decline and Fall of the Roman Empire.* London, 1776–88.

Gladstone, Jo. "New World of English Words" in Burke and Porter, eds.

Godwin, William. *The Lives of Edward and John Phillips.* London, 1815.

Gove, Philip, ed. *Webster's Third New International Dictionary of the English Language.* Springfield, Mass., 1961.

Gove, Philip. "Notes on Serialization and Competitive Publishing: Johnson's and Bailey's Dictionaries (1755)," Oxford Bibliographical Society, 1940.

Green, Jonathon. *The Encyclopedia of Censorship.* New York, 1990.

Greene, Robert. [1] *Repentence.* London, 1592.

———. [2] *The Second part of Conny-Catching.* London, 1592.

Grosart, Alexander. *Complete Works of Robert Greene 1881–3.* Huth Library Series, vol. 1.

Gross, John. *The Rise and Fall of the Man of Letters.* London, 1969.

Harman, Thomas. *Caveat for Common Cursetours.* Viles and Furnivall, eds. EETS, London, 1869.

Hartmann, R. K. K. [1] *History of Lexicography.* London, 1987.

———. [2] *Dictionaries and Their Users.* Exeter, 1979.

Harvey, Sir Paul, and Heseltine, J. E., eds. *The Oxford Companion to French Literature.* 1959.

Hausmann, F. J., O. Reichman, H. E. Wiegand, and L. Zgusta, eds. *Dictionaries: An International Encyclopedia of Lexicography,* 3 vols. 1989–91.

Hayashi, Tetsuro. *The Theory of English Lexicography.* Amsterdam, 1978.

Head, Richard. *The Canting Academy.* London, 1673.

Herrtage, Sidney J. H., ed. *Catholicon Anglicum.* (1483) EETS 75, London, 1881.

Hibbert, Christopher. *The Personal History of Samuel Johnson.* London, 1971.

Hobbes, Thomas. *Leviathan.* C. B. Macpherson, ed. London [1651] 1968.

Hotten, John Camden. *The Slang Dictionary.* London, 1859 et seq.

Howatson, M., ed. *Oxford Companion to Classical Literature,* 2nd ed., Oxford, 1989.

Hughes, Geoffrey. *Words in Time.* London, 1988.

Hulbert, J. R. *Dictionaries British and American.* London, 1968.

James, Gregory. *Lexicographers and their Works.* London, 1989.

Jordan, John Clark, Ph.D. *Robert Greene.* Columbia. New York, 1915.

Judges, A. V. *The Elizabethan Underworld.* London, 1930.

Knights, L. C. *Drama and Society in the Age of Jonson.* London, 1937.

Kramerae, Cheris and Treichler, Paula A. *The Feminist Dictionary.* New York, 1985.

Krapp, G. F. *English Language in America.* New York, 1925.

Landau, Sidney I. *Dictionaries: The Art and Craft of Lexicography.* New York, 1985.

Leavitt, Robert Keith. *Noah's Ark: New England Yankees and the Endless Quest.* Springfield, Mass., 1947.

Lemprière, J. *Bibliotheca Classica.* London, 1792.

Lexicon Balatronicum "by a Member of the Whip Club." London, 1811; Papermac, 1981.

Liber Vagatorum: The Book of Vagabonds. ed. John Camden Hotten. London [1528] 1860.

Lighter, Jonathan. *The Historical Dictionary of American Slang,* vol. 1, A–G. New York, 1994.

Long, P. W. "English Dictionaries before Webster" in *Bibliographical Society of America Papers IV.* 1909.

MacLachlan, Noel, ed. *The Memoirs of James Hardy Vaux.* London, 1964.

Major, John M. *Sir Thomas Elyot and Renaissance Humanism.* Lincoln, Neb., 1964.

Matsell, George Washington. *Vocabulum.* New York, 1859.

Matthews, M. M. *Survey of English Dictionaries.* New York, 1933, 1966.

Mayhew, A. L., ed. *The Promptorium Parvulorum.* EETS Extra Series CII. London, 1908.

Mayor, J. E. B. "Latin-English Lexicography" in *The Journal of Classical and Sacred Philology,* vol. 2. 1855.

———. "Latin-English Lexicography" in *The Journal of Classical and Sacred Philology,* vol. 4. March 1857.

McArthur, Tom. [1] *Worlds of Reference.* Cambridge, 1986.

McArthur, Tom, ed. [2] *The Oxford Companion to the English Language.* Oxford, 1992.

McCrum, Robert, William Cran, and Robert MacNeil. *The Story of English.* London, 1986.

Mencken, H. L. [1] *The American Language.* 4th ed., New York, 1936.

———. [2] *The American Language Supplement 1.* New York, 1945.

———. [3] *The American Language Supplement 2.* New York, 1948.

———. [4] *The American Language.* Abridged and edited by Raven I. McDavid and David W. Maurer. New York, 1980.

Mengham, Rod. *The Descent of Language: Writing in Praise of Babel.* London, 1993.

Middleton, Thomas and Thomas Dekker. *The Roaring Girle, or Moll Cut-Purse.* London, 1611.

Mills, Jane. *Womanwords.* London, 1989.

Moon, Rosamund. "Objective or Objectionable: Ideological Aspects of Dictionaries" in *English Language Research 3.* Birmingham, Eng., 1989.

Moore-Carew, Bampfylde. *The Life and Adventures of Bampfylde Moore-Carew.* London, 1745.

Morton, Herbert C. *The Story of Webster's Third.* Cambridge, 1994.

Munro, John, ed. *Frederick James Furnivall: A Volume of Personal Record.* Oxford, 1911.

Murray, J. A. H. "The Evolution of English Lexicography," Oxford Romanes Lecture. Oxford, 1900.

Murray, J. A. H. et al., eds. *The New English Dictionary/The Oxford English Dictionary.* Oxford, 1928, 1933.

Murray, K. M. E. *Caught in the Web of Words.* London, 1977.

Osselton, Noel. In Hartmann [1].

Parker, George *Life's Painter of Variegated Characters in Public and Private Life.* London, 1789.

Partridge, Eric. [1] *Slang Yesterday and Today.* 4th ed., London, 1970.

———. [2] *A Dictionary of Slang & Unconventional English.* 2 vols., 8th ed., London, 1970.

———. [3] *A Dictionary of the Underworld.* 3rd ed., London, 1968.

———. [4] *A Dictionary of Catch Phrases.* London, 1979.

Partridge, Eric, ed. [5] *A Classical Dictionary of the Vulgar Tongue* by Francis Grose. 3rd ed., 1931. London, 1963.

———. [6] "Vigilans" *Chamber of Horrors: A Glossary of Official Jargon.* London, 1952.

Pepys, Samuel. *The Shorter Pepys.* Ed. Robert Latham. London, 1985.

Pinker, Steven. *The Language Instinct.* New York, 1994.

Porter, Roy. *A Social History of London.* London, 1994.

R., S. (Samuel Rid/Samuel Rowlands). *Martin Mark-All, Beadle of Bridewell.* London, 1610.

Read, Allen Walker. [1] "An Obscenity Symbol" in *American Speech* 9:4 Baltimore, Md., 1934.

———. [2] "Projects for an Academy to Regulate Speech" in *PMLA* 51, 1936.

Reddick, Allen. *The Making of Johnson's Dictionary 1746–1773.* Cambridge, 1990.

Reynolds, Leighton D. and N. G. Wilson. *Scribes & Scholars—A Guide to the Transmission of Greek and Latin Literature.* Oxford, 1968.

Richardson, Charles. *Illustrations to English Philology.* London, 1815.

Richardson, J. F. *The New York Police.* New York, 1970.

Ricks, Christopher and Michaels, Leonard, eds. [1] *The State of the Language.* Berkeley, Calif., 1980.

———. [2] *The State of the Language.* London, 1990.

Rollins, R. W. *The Long Journey of Noah Webster.* Philadelphia, Pa., 1980.

Schäfer, Jürgen. *Early Modern English Lexicography,* 2 vols. Oxford, 1989.

Seger, Stewart A. *American Dictionaries.* New York, 1913.

Shoemaker, Ervin C. *Noah Webster: Pioneer of Learning.* New York, 1936.

Simes, Gary. *A Dictionary of Australian Underworld Slang.* Melbourne, 1993.

Simpson, David. *The Politics of American English 1776–1850.* Oxford, 1986.

Sitwell, Edith. *English Eccentrics.* London, 1933.

Sledd, James H. and Ebbitt, Wilma R. *Dictionaries and* THAT *Dictionary.* Chicago, 1962.

Sledd, James H. and Kolb, Gwin J. *Dr. Johnson's Dictionary.* Chicago, 1955.

Smalley, Vera E. *The Sources of* A Dictionarie of the French and English Tongues, *by Randle Cotgrave.* [London, 1611] Baltimore, Md., 1948.

Smith, Olivia. *The Politics of Language 1791–1819.* London, 1984.

Snell-Hornby, Mary. "The Bilingual Dictionary—Victim of its own tradition?" In Hartmann [1].

Snyder, K. Allen. *Defining Noah Webster: Mind and Morals in the Early Republic.* Univ. Press of America, 1990.

Stanbridge, John. *Vocabula.* EETS 1932: xvi–xx; Introduction by Beatrice White; London, 1932.

Starnes, DeWitt T. *Renaissance Dictionaries.* Austin, Tex., 1954.

Starnes, DeWitt T. and Noyes, Gertrude E. *The English Dictionary from Cawdrey to Johnson.* Chapel Hill, N.C., 1946.

Stein, Gabriele. *The English Dictionary before Cawdrey.* Tübingen, 1985.

Steiner, George. *Language and Silence.* Oxford, 1967.

Storojenko, N. *Life of Greene.* In Dyce [2].

Thomas, Thomas. *Dictionarum Linguae Latinae et Anglicanae.* London, 1587.

Tooke, Horne. *The Diversions of Purley.* London, 1786–1805.

Warner, Oliver. *Chatto & Windus: A Brief Account of the Firm's Origin, History and Development.* London, 1973.

Way, A., ed. *Promptorium Parvulorum sive Clericorum . . .* Camden Society, London, 1843–65.

Webster, Noah. [1] *Dissertations on the English Language.* Boston, 1789.

———. [2] *The Compendious Dictionary.* Boston, 1807.

———. [3] *American Dictionary of the English Language.* Boston, 1828.

Weinreb, Ben and Hibbert, Christopher, eds. *The London Encyclopedia.* London, 1983.

Wells, John. *Rude Words: A Discursive History of the London Library.* London, 1991.

Wells, Ronald A. *Dictionaries and the Authoritarian Tradition.* The Hague, 1973.

Wheatley, H. B. [1] "Chronological. Notices of Dictionaries of the English Language" in *Proceedings of the Philological Society,* 1865.

———. ed. [2] Levins: *Manipulus Vocabulorum.* Camden Society, London, 1867.

———. [3] "Notes on Some English Heterographers" in *Transactions of the Philological Society.* 1865.

Willinsky, John. *Empire of Words: The Reign of the OED.* London, 1994.

Wilson, Nigel G. *Scholars of Byzantium.* London, 1983.

Withals, John. *A Shorte Dictionarie English and Latin for Yonge Beginners.* London, 1553.

Wood, Anthony à. *Athenae Oxonienses.* Oxford, 1691–2.

Worcester, Joseph. [1] *A Dictionary of the English Language.* Boston, Mass., 1863.

———. [2] *A Universal and Critical Dictionary of the English Language.* Boston, Mass., 1864.

Wright, Thomas. [1] *A Volume of Vocabularies.* London, 1857.

———, ed. [2] Johannis de Garlandia: *De Triumphis Ecclesia.* London, 1856.

———. [3] *Biographia Britannica Literaria.* London, 1842.

———. [4] *Dictionary of Obscure and Provincial English.* London, 1857.

———. [5] and Wülcker, R. P. *Anglo-Saxon & Old English Vocabularies.* London, 1884.

Wynne-Davis, Marion, ed. *Bloomsbury Guide to English Literature.* London, 1989.

Yates, Francis A. *John Florio: The Life of an Italian in Shakespeare's England.* Cambridge, 1934.

Yule, Henry, and A. C. Burnell. *Hobson-Jobson: A Glossary of Colloquial Indian Words and Phrases . . .* Calcutta, 1886.

Zgusta, Ladislav. *The Manual of Lexicography.* London, 1971.

American Speech

Gentleman's Magazine

Linguistics: an International Review

Notes & Queries

Proceedings of the Modern Language Association

INDEX